Springer Proceedings in Business and Economics

Springer Proceedings in Business and Economics brings the most current research presented at conferences and workshops to a global readership. The series features volumes (in electronic and print formats) of selected contributions from conferences in all areas of economics, business, management, and finance. In addition to an overall evaluation by the publisher of the topical interest, scientific quality, and timeliness of each volume, each contribution is refereed to standards comparable to those of leading journals, resulting in authoritative contributions to the respective fields. Springer's production and distribution infrastructure ensures rapid publication and wide circulation of the latest developments in the most compelling and promising areas of research today.

The editorial development of volumes may be managed using Springer Nature's innovative EquinOCS, a proven online conference proceedings submission, management and review system. This system is designed to ensure an efficient timeline for your publication, making Springer Proceedings in Business and Economics the premier series to publish your workshop or conference volume.

This book series is indexed in SCOPUS.

Richard C. Geibel · Shalva Machavariani
Editors

Digital Management and Artificial Intelligence

Proceedings of the Fourth International Scientific-Practical Conference (ISPC 2024), Hybrid, October 10–11, 2024

Springer

Editors
Richard C. Geibel
IU International University and E-Commerce Institute
Cologne, Germany

Shalva Machavariani
East European University
Tbilisi, Georgia

ISSN 2198-7246 ISSN 2198-7254 (electronic)
Springer Proceedings in Business and Economics
ISBN 978-3-031-88051-3 ISBN 978-3-031-88052-0 (eBook)
https://doi.org/10.1007/978-3-031-88052-0

This Springer imprint is published by the registered company Springer Nature Switzerland AG
The registered company address is: Gewerbestrasse 11, 6330 Cham, Switzerland

Preface

Four successful annual international conferences have already been held with a focus on digital management. The latest "**International Scientific-Practical Conference (ISPC 2024)**" dealt with the current topic "**Digital Management and Artificial Intelligence**" and took place on *10 and 11 October 2024* as a hybrid conference in Cologne, Germany.

The **IU International University** organized the ISPC 2024 together with the partner institutions **East European University** from Georgia, **Adelphi University** from USA and **E-Commerce Institute** from Germany.

The conference provided a forum for **77 presentations** by **130 scientists** from **11 countries** and **4 continents**, in which relevant aspects of digitization and AI were discussed. This conference was held at the largest university in Germany, IU International University, with more than 130,000 students in a **hybrid** format, i.e., participants attended both at the conference venue in Cologne and online via Zoom video conferencing.

The upcoming **ISPC 2025** will focus on current topics of **Digital Management**, and it will take place end of *September 2025.* We are looking forward to a lively participation at the **5th ISPC** and a further growth of the conference series with an increasing internationalization.

MaryAnne M. Hyland
Shalva Machavariani
Richard C. Geibel

Acknowledgements

On behalf of the organizing team of the International Scientific-Practical Conference (ISPC) 2024, we extend our heartfelt thanks to everyone who contributed to making this event a resounding success. We are deeply grateful to our partner institutions—**East European University** (Georgia), **Adelphi University** (USA), **IU International University** (Germany), and the **E-Commerce Institute** (Germany)—for their invaluable collaboration, as well as to our supporters: **AOK Rheinland/Hamburg, gkv informatik, STARTPLATZ**, and the **Alliance for AI & Humanity (AAIH)** from Singapore. Their support and commitment were instrumental in making this conference possible.

We also wish to express special appreciation to our keynote speakers Dr. **Sven Schütt**, Prof. Dr. **George Lazarashvili**, Prof. Dr. **MaryAnne Hyland**, Prof. Dr. **Louisa Specht-Riemenschneider,** Dr. **Ulrich Arnold**, Dr. med. **Dennis Witt**, Dr. **Lorenz Gräf**, Dr. **Anton Ravindran** and whose inspiring contributions set the stage for productive discussions on digital transformation and artificial intelligence. Their insights and expertise provided a profound foundation for the exchange of ideas throughout the event. A warm thank you goes out to the students and all supporters who attended and engaged with enthusiasm and curiosity, adding fresh perspectives and a dynamic energy that enriched the experience for all participants.

Our gratitude also extends to the dedicated presenters and moderators who ensured the smooth progression of each session, facilitating in-depth discussions and a rich exchange of ideas. Special thanks go to **Tatia Gherkenashvili, Teona Shugliashvili, Kelly Schütz, Irakli Gazdeliani & Tea Munjishvili, Ulrich Arnold & Alina Holle, Ia Natsvlishvili & Tamta Lekishvili, Nia Todua & Giorgi Tavadze, Christian Lucas** & **Sebastian Arend, Katja Grupp & Sameer Joshi** for their remarkable efforts and professionalism.

To everyone who played a role in ISPC 2024, we extend our sincerest thanks. Your dedication and active participation made this conference an exceptional platform for innovation, collaboration, and knowledge-sharing in the realms of AI and digital transformation.

Conference Program

Conference Booklet
ISPC 2024
4th annual International Scientific-Practical Conference
"Digital Management and Artificial Intelligence"
10 and 11 October 2024

ISPC 2024 is the 4th international annual conference organized by **East European University** (Georgia) together with its partners **Adelphi University** (USA), **IU International University** (Germany), and **E-Commerce Institute** (Germany). It is supported by **AOK** Rheinland/Hamburg, gkv informatik, STARTPLATZ, Friedrich-Ebert-Foundation, Web de Cologne, and the German Entrepreneurship Organization FGF.

Conference Venue and format
It is aiming to provide a forum for presenting and discussing relevant aspects of Digitalization and AI. This conference will be held at the largest university in Germany, **IU International University**, with more than 130,000 students in a **hybrid** format, i.e. participants can attend both at the conference venue in Cologne or online via Zoom video conferencing.

IU International University
Campus Gerling Quartier
Hildeboldplatz 20
50672 Cologne, Gemany
https://www.iu.de/en/campus/cologne/

Registration and Fee
Prospective participants are kindly requested to register until **9. October 2024.**
Registration via http://bit.ly/ISPC2024 or via QR code for ISPC 2024 is **free of charge**.

Eligibility and Language

Researchers, practitioners, master and doctoral students from the conference organizing universities and other higher education institutions. The Conference language is **English.**

Richard C. Geibel
Chairman ISPC 2024
Professor IU International University
Professor h.c. EEU, Tiblisi, Georgia
ISPC 2024 will take place over two days, with **welcome speeches, announcements and keynote speeches** on the first day and **scientific presentations** on the second day.

Conference opening on Thursday, 10. Oktober 2024
(big hall ground floor or Zoom – https://us02web.zoom.us/j/85697617773?pwd=rjbSMI I8NbweMK29oVGJ0Zp1bdMQp1.1)

14:00–15:00	*Arrival of participants*
15:00–16:30	**Conference Opening** Prof. Dr. **Richard C. Geibel**, Chairman ISPC 2024 Dr. **Sven Schütt**, CEO, IU International University Prof. Dr. **Kakhaber George Lazarashvili**, Rector, East European University, Georgia Prof. Dr. **MaryAnne Hyland**, Dean of Business School, Adelphi University, USA
16:30–16:45	*Break*
16:45–17:45	**Keynote speeches and presentations** Prof. Dr. **Louisa Specht-Riemenschneider**, Federal Data Protection Commissioner Dr. **Ulrich Arnold**, Managing Director, gkvi informatik, Germany Dr. med. **Dennis Witt**, Specialist in Human Genetics, IU Alumnus Dr. **Lorenz Gräf**, Founder and CEO, STARTPLATZ, Incubator & Accelerator
17:45–18:00	**Acknowledgment** **Organizing team and supporters**
18:00–18:30	*Break*
18:30–21:30	*Dinner* (self-pay) Restaurant and brewery "**Päffgen**", 3-min walk to Friesenstrasse 64-66

Conference presentations on Friday, 11. Oktober 2024
(big hall ground floor and 3rd floor or Zoom – https://us02web.zoom.us/j/85697617773?pwd=rjbSMII8NbweMK29oVGJ0Zp1bdMQp1.1)

08:30–09:00	*Arrival of participants*
09:00–09:15	Dr. **Anton Ravindran**, President, Alliance for AI & Humanity, Singapore
09:15–09:30	**Explanation of the 7 sessions**
09:30–09:45	*Break*
09:45–12:30	**Scientific presentations** in **7 parallel sessions, Slots 1 to 5**
12:30–13:15	*Lunch*
13:15–16:00	**Scientific presentations** in **7 parallel sessions, Slots 6 to 10**
16:00–16:20	*Break*
16:20–17:00	**Ceremonial presentation of certificates, Announcement of ISPC 2025 and closing**
17:00–18:00	*Drinks and finger food*
18:00–21:30	*Dinner* (self-pay) Restaurant and bistro "H&A **Tagesbar**", 2-min walk to Friesenstrasse 72

Friday Session 1:	Digital Management	
Hybrid:	Big hall ground floor or Zoom	
Moderators:	Richard C. Geibel & Kelly Schütz, IU & Fontys University	
Zoom Link:	https://us02web.zoom.us/j/85697617773?pwd=rjbSMII8NbweMK29oVGJ0Zp1bdMQp1.1	
	Zoom Entrance Code: 725615	
Time	Slot	Speaker
09:45–10:10	1	**Kelly Schütz, Sebastian Arend, Richard C. Geibel**, Fontys University Nether-lands, Media University, IU International University *Opportunities and challenges of Social Commerce - An analysis of different strategies of selected companies*
10:20–10:45	2	**Finn Geffken**, IU International University *The TikTok Effect: Changing the Landscape of Online Shopping*
10:55–11:20	3	**Darius Zumstein, Grzegorz Chodak**, FHNW Northwestern Switzerland *AI in E-Commerce: Overview of Applications, Benefits and Challenges*
11:30–11:55	4	**Tan Kaitlynn Poa, Lukman Alfakihuddin**, Arizona University, Sampoerna University Jakarta, Indonesia *Imperative of AI-Generated Personalized Algorithm Influencing Consumer Experience in Tokopedia*
12:05–12:30	5	**Christian Tuschner, Hella Hörsch, Nina Lorenz, Harald von Korflesch**, University of Koblenz, Germany *Leading Virtual Temas in the Context of e-Leadership: Insights into Challenges from a Leader´s Perspective*
12:30–13:15 Lunch		
13:15–13:40	6	**Diana Murtagh-Böhm, Tamara Wehrstein**, IU International University *Digital Business Management: A fresh perspective on digital business models*
13:50–14:15	7	**Larissa Pfeiffer, Carolin Egger, Mirko Bendig, Irina Tiemann,** IU International University *The use of AI in energy utility companies: A case study on potential fields of application and impact on innovation*
14:25–14:50	8	**Leon Casper, Richard Geibel**, E-Commerce Institute Cologne, Germany *AI as an enabler for customers acquisition through Embedded Finance Solutions in E-Commerce*

(*continued*)

(*continued*)

15:00–15:25	9	**Rachel John Robinson, Victor Ndubuisi Mbogu**, IU International University *Analysing Network Threats using a Cybersecurty tool*
15:35–16:00	10	**Brigitte Huber, Julia Levasier, Stephanie Wittemann**, IU International University *Did it really change everything? Exploring media coverage of artificial intelligence before and after the launch of ChatGPT*

Friday Session 2:	AI and Digital Transformation Across Sectors	
Hybrid:	3rd floor, room 3.11 or Zoom (Entrance Code: 1234)	
Moderators:	Irakli Gazdeliani & Tea Munjishvili, Ivane Javakhishvili Tbilisi State University	
Zoom Link:	https://iubh.zoom.us/my/ispc2024.session.2?pwd=C5Zr0mHfLFDirkZfacLJE6Sw2ZijF0.1&omn=62405594113	
	Zoom Entrance Code: 1234	
Time	Slot	Speaker
09:45–10:10	1	**Otar Japaridze, Marina Metreveli,** East European University *Modern trends and prospects of mountain tourism business development and assistance*
10:20–10:45	2	**Giorgi Katamadze,** Batumi Shota Rustaveli State University *The role of digital management and artificial intelligence for Georgian business entities in post-pandemic period*
10:55–11:20	3	**Giorgi Shaburishvili,** International Black Sea University *Digital transformation in construction: AI leadership styles and project success*
11:30–11:55	4	**Tatia Gherkenashvili,** East European University *Way to Implementing Innovation driven Personnel-Fit OE at Georgian Universities*
12:05–12:30	5	**Marina Shioshvili, Lili Bibilashvili,**East European University *Skills needed for digital transformation using AI (based on healthcare field in Georgia)*

(*continued*)

(*continued*)

12:30–13:15 Lunch		
13:15–13:40	6	**Nodar Silagadze, Levan Silagadze,**Tbilisi Free Academy *Digital economy challenges in Georgia at the modern stage of globalization*
13:50–14:15	7	**Irakli Gazdeliani,** Ivane Javakhishvili Tbilisi State University *Artificial intelligence and economic policy*
14:25–14:50	8	**Lela Aduashvili,** Ivane Javakhishvili Tbilisi State University *Artificial intelligence and digitalization: changing the rules ofthe gamein vegetable isndustry*
15:00–15:25	9	**Mariam Tvaradze,** East European University *Digital transformation in Georgian winemaking: empowering SMEs through innovation*
15:35–16:00	10	**Discussion and Session Sum Up**

Friday Session 3:	Digital Health	
Hybrid:	3rd floor, room 3.12 or Zoom	
Moderators:	Ulrich Arnold & Alina Holle, gkv informatik	
Zoom Link:	https://iubh.zoom.us/my/ispc2024.session.3?omn=67139712536	
	Zoom Entrance Code: 1234	
Time	Slot	Speaker
09:45–10:10	1	**Markus Schlobohm**, Digital Health Expert *Potentials of Digital Health*
10:20–10:45	2	**Sami Gaber**, Medical Doctor and Co-Founder docport GmbH *Digital health for better patient care*
10:55–11:20	3	**Stefanie Kemp,** Sana Clinics, **Rüdiger Hochscheidt**, Consultant for Digitalization in Healthcare *Digital systems in hospitals*
11:30–11:55	4	**Markus Leyck Dieken**, Medical Doctor and Digital Health Expert *The telematics infrastructure as the basis of a digital structure for the German healthcare system*
12:05–12:30	5	**Markus Leyck Dieken**, Medical Doctor and Digital Health Expert *The electronic identities as player licenses for users in Germany and the EU*

(*continued*)

(*continued*)

12:30–13:15 Lunch		
13:15–13:40	6	**Christopher Grieben, Anna Martin-Niedecken, Niels Nagel,** Hochschule für angewandtes Management *Digitalization in prevention and rehabilitation*
13:50–14:15	7	**Susanna Zsoter**, Cancer Warrior *Promoting patient-centeredness through digital healthcare*
14:25–14:50	8	**Alina Holle, Vanessa Hering, Markus vom Scheidt**, gkv informatik *Stakeholders in digital health*
15:00–15:25	9	**Aylin Güler, Susan Pellegrini**, gkv informatik *Cloud computing in digital healthcare*
15:35–16:00	10	**Vanessa Pedulla, Vanessa Hering, Markus vom Scheidt,** gkv informatik *Artificial intelligence in healthcare*

Friday Session 4:	AI and Sustainability in Business and Education	
Hybrid:	3rd floor, room 3.13 left side or Zoom (Entrance Code: 1234)	
Moderators:	Ia Natsvlishvili & Tamta Lekishvili, Ivane Javakhishvili Tbilisi State University & East European University	
Zoom-Link:	https://iubh.zoom.us/my/ispc2024.session.4?pwd=5CbLh4ovn99VvvdPZNJiD2DK7a33e5.1&omn=61580903729	
	Zoom Entrance Code:1234	
Time	Slot	Speaker
09:45–10:10	1	**Ia Natsvlishvili,** Ivane Javakhishvili Tbilisi State University *Supporting factors and barriers to circular business model innovation in the era of digital transformation*
10:20–10:45	2	**Vasil Kikutadze, Tamta Lekishvili**, East European University *AI and the evolution of learning outcomes in higher education: a strategic approach*
10:55–11:20	3	**David Sikharulidze, Kakhaber Lazarashvili, Natia Gegelashvili, Tamar Tkhelidze,** East European University *The impact of social media on consumers' decision-making process in hotel industry*

(*continued*)

(*continued*)

11:30–11:55	4	**George Abuselidze, Gia Zoidze,** Batumi Shota Rustaveli State University, Georgia *Sustainable economic development, international security and technology transfer in the age of artificial intelligence*
12:05–12:30	5	**Gulnaz Erkomaishvili**, Ivane Javakhishvili Tbilisi State University *Digital economic policy in Georgia*
12:30–13:15 Lunch		
13:15–13:40	6	**Eter Kharaishvili, Ia Natsvlishvili, Tamar Lazariashvili,** Ivane Javakhishvili Tbilisi State University *Digitalization of Georgia's agro-food industry: challenges and opportunities for sustainable development*
13:50–14:15	7	**Teona Shugliashvili, Tea Munjishvili,** East European University, Ludwig Maximilian University Munich, Ivane Javakhishvili Tbilisi State University *Advancing machine comprehension of the Georgian language*
14:25–14:50	8	**Manana Lobzhanidze,** Ivane Javakhishvili Tbilisi State University *Digital transformation of higher education in Georgia: challenges and opportunities*
15:00–15:25	9	**Elene Dundua,** International Black Sea University *Corporate ethics in the AI era: balancing technological advancement with social responsibility*
15:35–16:00	10	**Discussion and Session Sum Up**

Friday Session 5:	Digital Transformation and AI Projects Across Industries	
Online:	3rd floor, room 3.13 right side or Zoom (Entrance Code: 1234)	
Moderators:	Nia Todua & Giorgi Tavadze, Ivane Javakhishvili Tbilisi State University & East European University	
Zoom-Link:	https://iubh.zoom.us/my/ispc2024.session.5?pwd=m4ePcMTQTBaqNoq8bIYQaNQ9Bxbqsb.1&omn=68044623278	
	Zoom Entrance Code: 1234	
Time	Slot	Speaker
09:45–10:00	1	**Nugzar Todua, Nia Todua**, Ivane Javakhishvili Tbilisi State University *The impact of social media on consumers' online information behaviour*

(*continued*)

(*continued*)

10:05–10:15	2	**Shalva Machavariani, Temur Maisuradze**, East European University *Utilizing an interactive web-portal focused on integrating university learning-research process and SME requirements*
10:20–10:35	3	**Roya Anvari,** University of Georgia *Enhancing team performance through emotional intelligence leadership: a digital management and artificial intelligence perspective in Qatar airways*
10:35–10:50	4	**Roya Anvari,** University of Georgia *Artificial intelligence adoption in recruitment, positive organizational shock, and career development in higher education institutions in Nigeria*
10:55–11:10	5	**Givi Duchidze, Vazha Zeikidze,** East European University, National Defense Academy of Georgia *Development of immersive technologies in military education*
11:10–11:25	6	**Lia Kvirchishvili,** East European University *Safeguarding job security: nurturing employee resilience in the age of artificial intelligence*
11:30–11:45	7	**Maia Aghaia,** Sokhumi State University *An impact of digitalization in English Language teaching process*
11:45–12:00	8	**Levan Imnaishvili, Maguli Bedineishvili, Tea Todua, Archil Chovelidze,** Georgian Technical University *Development of a remote laboratory experiment model in the hyflex format of teaching*
12:05–12:30	9	**Sophio Ugrekhelidze,** Business and Technology University *The role of digitalization and artificial intelligence in education administration (case of accreditation procedure)*
12:30–13:15 Lunch		
13:15–13:30	10	**Mariam Burmistrova,** East European University *Strategies for perfecting delegation in digital era*
13:30–13:45	11	**Tamar Matcharashvili, Ioseb Mamukelashvili,** East European University *Cross-country analyses of the challenges in online higher education and the need to implement the ARCS model*

(*continued*)

(*continued*)

13:50–14:15	12	**Roya Anvari,** University of Georgia *Digital leadership and artificial intelligence: a literature review*
14:25–14:40	13	**Natia Tsiklauri, Marina Endeladze,** Georgian Technical University, East European University *International Challenges with digital transformation to manage pandemics and viral infections*
14:40–14:55	14	**Levan Tholikidze, Qetevan Kveselava, Irakli Bochorishvili,** National defense Academy of Georgia *Impact of neural networks on artificial intelligence*
15:00–15:15	15	**Tamar Khutsishvili,** East European University *Challenges of e-commerce in Georgia*
15:20–15:35	16	**Tinatin Rodonaia,** East European University *Challenges of telecommuting: insights into Georgian employee experience*
15:40–16:00	17	**David Jalagonia, Marine Khubua, Eliso Chokhonelidze,** Sokhumi State University *Contemporary aspects of digitalization of corporate sustainability reporting*

Friday Session 6:	Applications of AI	
Online:	3rd floor, room 3.07 or Zoom	
Moderators:	Christian Lucas, IU & Sebastian Arend, E-Commerce Institute	
Zoom Link:	https://iubh.zoom.us/my/ispc2024.session.6?omn=62281663977	
	Zoom Entrance Code:1234	
Time	Slot	Speaker
09:45–10:10	1	**Jonas Polfuß**, IU International University *Navigating the Hype: Evaluating the Impact of AI in SME Marketing*
10:20–10:45	2	**Laura-Maria Altendorfer**, **Nele Hansen, Josef Arweck, Carla Aschendorf,** IU International University *AI for a Good Cause: Challenges, Criticism, Wishes and Opportunities of NPOs in Public Relations Work*
10:55–11:20	3	**Muslum Ibrahimov, Ganira Ibrahimova**, IU International University *Developing Digital Entrepreneurial Ecosystems: Diversity and Integration in Networked Business Environments*

(*continued*)

(*continued*)

11:30–11:55	4	**Michele Dilenge**, IU International University *Digital foundation of start-ups: Challenges and current developments*
12:05–12:30	5	**Anne-Selina Adamek**, Metzler Vater live GmbH *Integrating Artificial Intelligence in Corporate Event Planning Processes – A Current Assessment of German Event Agencies*
12:30–13:15 Lunch		
13:15–13:40	6	**Ann-Cathrin Nordhoff**, Do it + Garden, Migros-Genossenschafts-Bund, **Darius Zumstein**, FHNW School of Business, Switzerland *Use and Influence of LLMs for Optimizing Product Texts in E-Commerce*
13:50–14:15	7	**André de Almeida**, Do it + Garden, Migros-Genossenschafts-Bund, **Darius Zumstein**, FHNW School of Business, Switzerland *Influence of AI in the generation of product texts on the conversion rate: Practical experiment in e-commerce using the example of doitgarden.ch*
14:25–14:50	8	**Jonathan Black-Branch**, IU International University *Revolutionizing and Transforming Business Operations: The Impact and Potential of Intelligent Automation*
15:00–15:25	9	**Johannes Nuenning**, Strategy Consultant for Innovators *How established companies can foster Innovation at "Zero" cost and why Digitalization requires them to act accordingly*
15:35–16:00	10	**Carmen Birkle, Claudia Hess**, IU International University *Integrating Data Ethics in Smart Cities: Insights from Leading European Cities*

Friday Session 7:	Benefits of AI	
Online:	3rd floor, room 3.15 or Zoom	
Moderators:	Katja Grupp & Sameer Joshi, IU International University	
Zoom Link:	https://iubh.zoom.us/my/ispc2024.session.7?omn=66247963350	
	Zoom Entrance Code:1234	
Time	Slot	Speaker
09:45–10:10	1	**Manuel Etzkorn, Yvonne Römer, Masoumeh Tavakoligargari, Nihal Lamdaghri, Mariya Avdzhieva, Harald v. Korflesch**, University Koblenz *The interface between Technology Transfer and Artificial Intelligence:A Systematic Literature Review*

(*continued*)

(*continued*)

10:20–10:45	2	**Georg Herzwurm, Wolfram Pietsch**, University of Stuttgart, FH Aachen *Digitalisation and AI as Moving Targets*
10:55–11:20	3	**Phineas Speicher, Lutz Becker**, Kode GmbH, Germany *LLMs as your "second brain" – How AI will affect the way we solve Problems*
11:30–11:55	4	**Julian Antonio Walter**, University of Ludwigshafen *The influence of artificial intelligence in e-commerce on consumer behaviour*
12:05–12:30	5	**Lukman Alfakihuddin, Angelina Priscilla Tan**, Sampoerna University Jakarta, Indonesia *Ai-Driven Features, Brand Experience and Their Impacts on Purchase Intention: Samsung S24 Case Study in A Developing Country*
12:30–13:15 Lunch		
13:15–13:40	6	**Sameer Joshi, Ranjani Ramnath**, IU International University *Harnessing Artificial Intelligence to Transform Primary Education: Applications, Challenges, and Future Directions*
13:50–14:15	7	**Katja Grupp, Clare Hindley,** IU International University *Enhancing creative and analytical thinking through the use of AI in management education: a student perspective*
14:25–14:50	8	**Susanna Minder, Amelie Schweiger**, IU International University *Artificial Intelligence and its possible advantages in skin cancer diagnostics*
15:00–15:25	9	**Mohammadsadegh Solouki, Gissel Velarde**, Universidad Privada Boliviana, IU International University *AI-Powered Fashion: Integrating CNN Architectures for Classification and Recommendation*
15:35–16:00	10	**Mateo Lopez-Ledezma, Gissel Velarde**, IU International University *Cyber Security Data Science: Machine Learning Methods and their Performance on Impbalanced Datasets*

Best Presentation Certificates

Once again, "**Best Presentation Certificates**" will be awarded during the ISPC to recognize the special achievements of the speakers.

Young Scientist Certificates

For young scientists who do not have a PhD yet, we would like to sponsor special "**Young Scientist Certificates**" to motivate them to continue with their scientific career. In addition, **Springer Nature** offers special and free support for a possible publication of their complete thesis in a standalone book.

Conference Organization Committee

Prof. Dr. **Shalva Machavariani**
Vice Rector in Scientific Affairs
East European University, Georgia

Prof. Dr. **MaryAnne Hyland**
Dean of Business School
Adelphi University, USA

Prof. Dr. **Richard C. Geibel**
IU International University
Institute Director ECI, Germany

Advisory Committee to support the 4th ISPC

- Dr. Ulrich Arnold, Managing Director, gkv informatik, Wuppertal
- Dr. Jörn Block, Professor at University Trier
- Dr. Wolfram Pietsch, Professor at Fachhochschule Aachen
- Dr. Ludwig Theuvsen, Professor at University Göttingen
- Dr. Harald von Korflesch, Professor at University Koblenz
- Dr. Peter Witt, Professor at University Wuppertal

Scientific Committee for double blind peer review procedure

- Dr. Charles R. Baker - Professor for Accounting and Law Department, Robert B. Willumstad School of Business, Adelphi University, Garden City, New York, USA
- Dr. Lutz Becker - Professor for Management and Leadership, Dean of Studies of the Master's program Sustainability Management & Leadership, Areas of research: Digital and societal transformation, strategy and leadership, sustainable business development
- Dr. Zviad Gabisonia - Lawyer, General Director of the Shota Rustaveli National Science Foundation of Georgia (2018–2021), Professor of the Faculty of Law and International Relations of the Technical University of Georgia and Tbilisi Open University, Director of the Commercial and Private Law Research Institute
- Dr. Christian Lucas - Professor for Business Administration and Marketing at IU International University, Dean of Studies of the Bachelor's program Marketing Management

- Dr. Vladimir Papava - Georgian economist, Doctor of Economic Sciences (1989), Professor (1995), Academician of the National Academy of Sciences of Georgia (2013), Minister of Economy of Georgia (1993–2000), Rector of Tbilisi State University (2013–2016)
- Dr. Jonas Polfuss - Professor for Marketing at IU International University, areas of research: International Marketing, Digital Branding and Online Marketing, Hiphop, China

Coordination Team to support the organization

- Tatia Gherkenashvili, Dep. of Scientific Research and Development, EEU, t.gherkenashvili@eeu.edu.ge
- Teona Shugliashvili, Ph.D. Candidate, Ludwig Maximilian University, t.shugliashvili@campus.lmu.de
- Sebastian Arend and Kelly Schütz, Project Manager, E-Commerce Institute, info@ecommerceinstitut.de
- Leona Trautner, Project Manager, IU International University, leona.trautner@iu.org
- Alina Holle, Project Manager, gkv informatik, alina.holle@gkvi.de
- Assoc. Prof. Dr. Tea Munjishvili, Ivane Javakhishvili Tbilisi State University, tea.munjishvili@tsu.ge

Publication
Proceedings of the 4th annual International Scientific-Practical Conference (ISPC 2024) titled "**Digital Management and Artificial Intelligence**" is in the publication process and will be soon after the conference published in the book series "**Springer Proceedings in Business and Economics (SPBE)**" which is *indexed by Scopus.*

Recommended Conference Hotels
Motel One Mediapark
Am Kümpchenshof 2
50670 Cologne, Germany
+49 221 270 751 0
koeln-mediapark@motel-one.com

OR

25 hours Hotel
Im Klapperhof 22-24
50672 Cologne, Germany
+49 221 162 53 0
thecircle@25hours-hotels.com
https://www.motel-one.com/en/hotels/cologne/hotel-cologne-mediapark/
https://www.25hours-hotels.com/hotels/koeln/the-circle
All hotels are 1–3 min (200–500 m) away from the conference venue.

Travel Advise
If you arrive by **train**, you should arrive at Cologne Central Station. From there, you can easily transfer to the subway and travel to Friesenplatz. From there the International University is a 4-min walk.

If you plan your visit by **car** our suggestion is to leave the car at "Contipark" garage, Kaiser-Wilhelm-Ring (https://bit.ly/ISPC-Parking). From there it is a 3-min walk to the event.

Venue and history
The Gerling complex, originally designed by a well-known sculptor and architect, features a conservative, authoritative architectural style. Key buildings include the Friedrich-Wilhelm building and the "Torhaus", with a plaza that is now fully pedestrianized. The complex underwent a significant renovation, preserving the historic facade while updating it to meet modern standards of energy efficiency, safety, and technology. The area includes a mix of historic and contemporary architecture, with high-quality residential and office spaces spread across 130,000 square meters in a prime city-center location.

The complex houses the IU, where the ISPC 2024 conference will take place:

IU International University
Campus Gerling Quartier
Hildeboldplatz 20
50672 Cologne, Gemany
https://www.iu.de/en/campus/cologne/

The facilities

Conference Publications

Three annual international conferences with a focus on digital management have already taken place. The latest **"International Scientific Practical Conference (ISPC) 2023" focused on the topic of "Digital Management to Shape the Future"** and took place on *24. and 25. November 2023* as a hybrid event in Tbilisi, Georgia.

The East European University (EEU) organized together with the E-Commerce Institute (ECI) a very successful conference with great effort, at which 27 presentations were given in three parallel streams by 41 authors from the four continents of Africa, America, Asia, and Europe.

https://link.springer.com/book/10.1007/978-3-031-45601-5
https://link.springer.com/book/10.1007/978-3-031-20148-6
https://link.springer.com/book/9783031665165

Partner Organisations

ADELPHI UNIVERSITY NEW YORK	Adelphi is a modern metropolitan university with a uniquely personalized approach to learning. It is dedicated to transforming students' lives through world-class academics, a focus on student success, and a warm and inclusive community. => https://www.adelphi.edu
EAST EUROPEAN UNIVERSITY	East European University is a private university accredited in Georgia that strives to ensure implementation international educational standards in teaching and research and to build notable educational center oriented on the ideals of democracy and humanism. => https://eeu.edu.ge
iu INTERNATIONAL UNIVERSITY OF APPLIED SCIENCES	IU International University of Applied Sciences (IU) is a university with 130.000 students, 250 study programs, and 4.000 employees. We are also our students, alumni and all the staff who work behind the scenes to make sure you have a great time at university. => https://www.iu.de/en/university/
eCommerce Institut Köln	The E-Commerce Institute Cologne develops business concepts for companies and institutions based on scientific research. The mission of the E-Commerce Institute is to help develop and implement future-oriented and sustainable e-commerce projects based on empirical research and application-related studies with and for companies. => https://ecommerceinstitut.de/en/
ALLIANCE FOR AI&HUMANITY	Alliance for AI & Humanity (AAIH, Singapore) is working to advance responsible development and use of AI by addressing the most important pressing ethical, privacy and legal challenges related to the use of these technologies and helping guide efforts in the development and deployment of AI to enhance the quality of peoples' lives. => https://www.aaih.sg
FGF e.V. Entrepreneurship • Innovation • Mittelstand	The FGF is the leading and most important scientific association for entrepreneurship, innovation and SMEs in the German-speaking world. => https://www.fgf-ev.de/en/
FRIEDRICH EBERT STIFTUNG	The Friedrich Ebert Foundation was founded in 1925. As a non-profit political foundation, we are united with social democracy and the trade union movement in the pursuit of freedom, justice, solidarity and the preservation of peace. => https://www.fes.de/stiftung/ueber-die-fes
LIBF	LIBF Limited is an accredited and awarding body, providing professional qualifications, undergraduate and postgraduate degrees, and qualifications at Levels 1, 2 and 3. => https://www.libf.ac.uk

(*continued*)

(*continued*)

AOK	The health insurance company AOK Rheinland/Hamburg. The online portal 'Meine AOK' offers many advantageous functions relating to your AOK insurance. Many of these can be used both in the app and on PC. => https://www.aok.de/pk/rh/
gkv informatik unternehmen synergien	gkvi is one of the leading IT service providers in the statutory health insurance market and has implemented the centralised collection of contributions for over 17 million insured persons on behalf of its customers. => https://www.gkvi.de
STARTPLATZ	We transform small ideas into great innovations. In our vibrant network, we bring entrepreneurs, founders and corporates together to shape small ideas and empower great minds. => https://www.startplatz.de/en/
WEB DE COLOGNE	Web de Cologne is the large network of the digital economy in the Rhineland and an initiative of Cologne-based companies from the digital economy that is a relevant economic factor. => https://webdecologne.de
	Ivane Javakhishvili Tbilisi State University (TSU) according to the 2024 edition of the Center for World University Rankings (http://cwur.org/2024.php), is among the top 5% of the universities globally, placing1,047th out of 20,966 universities. TSU also stands as the top-ranked university in Georgia according to the same rankings. => https://www.tsu.ge/en

Contents

Artificial Intelligence in E-Commerce – Overview of Applications, Benefits and Challenges

Darius Zumstein[1(✉)] and Grzegorz Chodak[2]

[1] Digital Marketing, Institute for Competitiveness and Communication, FHNW School of Business, Riggenbachstrasse 16, CH-4600 Olten, Switzerland
darius.zumstein@fhnw.ch

[2] Department of Artificial Intelligence, Wroclaw University of Science and Technology, Wybrzeze Wyspiańskiego 27, 50-370 Wroclaw, Poland
grzegorz.chodak@pwr.edu.pl

Abstract. Since 2018, trends, developments and challenges in e-commerce have been systematically researched conducting a representative long-term study among 624 online retailers in the DACH region (Germany, Austria and Switzerland). The latest study in 2024 reveals surprising results: 54% of all e-commerce companies are already using artificial intelligence (AI) to create and translate texts, primarily with ChatGPT. In nine out of ten cases, this leads to time savings, more content, reduced personnel costs, and to faster text creation and translations.

42% of the online retailers create product information, such as product texts in the web shop, with the help of AI. Thanks to search engine-optimized product texts using generative AI, this leads to a higher reach on Google in the discipline of search engine optimization (SEO), and thus to more product page visits, sales and to higher conversion rates. One in four online retailers create images and videos with the help of AI. 20% of the retailers use AI in digital marketing, for example for targeting or managing advertising campaigns. Large language models (LMMs) are also implemented in online shop searches, such as product search, filters and product finders. Three quarters of online retailers believe that AI-based searches will become standard in two to five years.

However, only one in six retailers uses AI in analytics for data analyses. Furthermore, AI has high potential for sales and customer service: Nine percent of the online retailers offers an AI-based service chatbot or customer support. Additionally, 20% of the retailers are in the process of planning and implementing such chatbot services. Moreover, six percent have already implemented an AI-based sales chatbot and 17% plan to implement one.

A detailed analysis of AI applications in online shops is a valuable contribution to e-commerce theory and allows future trends for the business to be identified.

Keywords: Artificial intelligence · e-commerce · online retail · AI-generated product texts · chatbots

R. C. Geibel and S. Machavariani (Eds.): ISPC 2024, SPBE, pp. 1–15, 2025.
https://doi.org/10.1007/978-3-031-88052-0_1

1 Introduction

In electronic commerce, the past year was turbulent. The emergence of generative AI models based on the transformer architecture, such as ChatGPT, DALL-E, Gemini and Stable Diffusion, has also had a significant impact on e-commerce. Thanks to its digital nature, e-commerce offers numerous use cases for generative AI (GenAI), from creating product descriptions to customer support and software development. Swiss online retailers have also recognized this trend and are taking advantage of the opportunities offered by GenAI. In the fall of 2023, for example, the Swiss Coop Group's DIY (do it yourself) store format JUMBO introduced the first AI-based chatbot "JUMBot" (Scherrer, 2023; JUMBot, 2024). Shortly thereafter, BRACK.CH followed with its own AI sales chatbot (BRACK.CH, 2023). In the summer of 2024, Migros Group's DIY store Do it + Garden followed with its AI chatbot "Digi" (Do it + Garden, 2024).

The explosion of online sales in 2020 to 2021 in the wake of the coronavirus crisis was followed by a correction in 2022 with a slight decline in sales. The e-commerce market recovered somewhat in 2023, with sales returning to 2021 levels (Zumstein et al., 2023, p. 10, HANDELSVERBAND.swiss, 2023). The first author estimate that Swiss online retail will grow by between four and five percent to around 15 billion Swiss francs in 2024 (Zumstein & Oehninger, 2024, p. 10).

2 Theoretical Foundation and Previous Research

2.1 E-Commerce

E-commerce has become a key component of global retail, changing traditional business models by enabling goods and services to be bought and sold through digital platforms. The growth of global e-commerce has been driven by technological advances, including but not limited to the proliferation of smartphones and their increasingly rich functionality, enabling, for example, augmented reality shopping (Baltierra, 2023), and the rapid development of artificial intelligence (Pallathadka et al., 2023). These innovations have enabled consumers from all over the world to enjoy a wider range of products. According to Verhoef et al. (2021), the rapid digitisation of the retail sector has led to the creation of omni-channel strategies that integrate both online and offline customer experiences and driving sales growth. The development of e-commerce has also introduced significant challenges in logistics, customer service and data management (Iglesias-Pradas & Acquila-Natale, 2023). Akter & Wamba (2016) highlight that data-driven decision-making in e-commerce is critical to achieving operational efficiencies, as it allows companies to analyse consumer preferences and optimise their offerings in real time. What's more, with increasing competition in the digital marketplace, companies need to continuously innovate their business models, which can be achieved using advanced technologies such as machine learning (Sharma et al., 2022).

2.2 Artificial Intelligence

In recent years, the growth of interest in artificial intelligence (AI) has reached unprecedented levels, largely driven by the development of large language models such as ChatGPT (Deng & Lin, 2022, Subramanian, 2024). This growing enthusiasm is reflected in academic circles, where the impact of AI in e-commerce is increasingly being studied. For example, Bawack et al. (2022) analyzed bibliometric data from 4,335 publications related to AI in e-commerce, highlighting the rapid proliferation of research in this field. Boukrouh & Azmani (2024) indicated 8,372 papers published from 1995 to 2023 concerning AI in e-commerce. Song (2009) and Singh (2021), proposed classification of AI application in e-commerce and selected the following areas: automated purchase handling systems, automated product recommendation systems, artificial assistant, high degree of personalization, effective visual immersiveness. Chodak & Chawla (2022) distinguished three primary areas of AI appliance in e-commerce: logistics, facilitation for the customer and marketing. Different Authors researched on the effect AI-generated product texts in Marketing (Theobald et al., 2021; Wecke, 2024). Chodak (2024) detailed the areas of AI applications in e-commerce distinguishing automated picking processes, picture analysis in barcode identification, demand forecasting, autonomous delivery robots and drones, chatbots, AI personalization and recommendations, automated order systems, AI-driven ads and search engine optimization (SEO). Wang et al. (2023) have conducted an empirical evaluation of technology acceptance model (TAM) for AI in e-commerce.

3 Research Method

3.1 Sample

The growth in e-commerce in recent years (Hofacker et al., 2023; Heinick, 2023; Lone & Weltevreden, 2023; Rudolph et al. 2024; Wölfle & Leimstoll 2022), and the online boom during the coronavirus crisis are important reasons for conducting this study for the seventh time (Zumstein & Oswald, 2020; Zumstein et al., 2021, 2022, 2023). The aim of this research is to find out more about current developments in online retail. The Institute of Marketing Management (IMM) at the Zurich University of Applied Sciences (ZHAW) and the Institute for Competitiveness and Communication (ICC) at the University of Applied Sciences and Arts Northwestern Switzerland (FHNW) jointly investigated the question of how e-commerce in general and AI applications in particular are currently developing. From a management research perspective, the objects of the research project are all online retailers in Switzerland and Austria with a.com,.ch or.at domain that are registered and sell in Switzerland or Austria. The focus is not only on large, well-known online shops, but also on small and medium-sized online shops and companies (SMEs). The study data was collected from March 27, 2024 to July 31, 2024 as part of an online survey using Qualtrics software. Of over 4,800 online retailers contacted, 624 participants completed the majority of the questionnaire. Unless otherwise stated, the sample size (n) is 624.

3.2 Study Participants

516 Swiss (83%) and 85 Austrian online shop operators (13%) took part in the online retailer survey 2024. Two percent of respondents stated Germany and two percent another country as their country of origin.

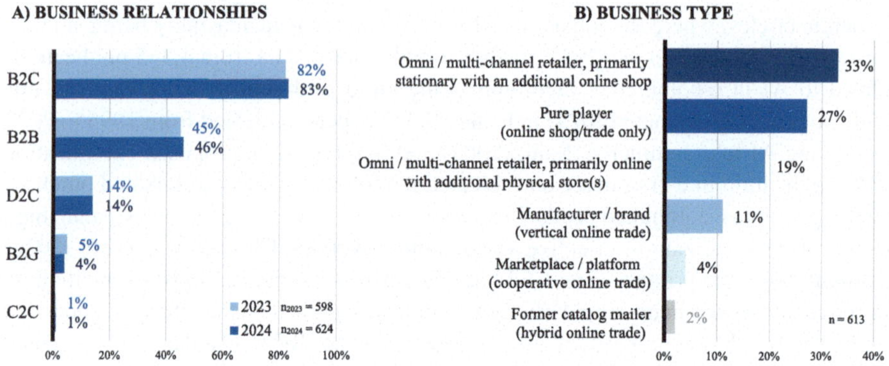

Fig. 1. A) What kind of business relationships does your online shop support; B) Which business type (sales model) is your online shop most likely to be assigned to?

83% of participants operate an online shop in the *business-to-consumer* sector (B2C in Fig. 1A). At 46%, almost half of respondents sell in the *business-to-business* (B2B) segment. 14% operate a manufacturer online shop (D2C; direct-to-consumer) and one percent only are *consumer-to-consumer* (C2C) platforms like eBay.

The online retailers were surveyed with regard to their sales model or business type according to Heinemann (2023, p. 213). The results are summarized in Fig. 1B: One third of the study participants are primarily *brick-and-mortar retailers* with a supplementary online shop. 27% of the respondents classify themselves as *pure players*, which have no physical stores and, according to Heinemann's definition (2023, p. 213), generate 70% of their sales online. On the other hand, 19% of the omni-/multi-channel retailers categorized themselves as "*primarily online with additional retail stores*". Figure 1B shows that more than 11% of study participants are manufacturers or brands that sells its products directly to end customers (D2C). Around four percent of the study participants describe themselves as a *digital marketplace* or a digital platform. The former catalog mail order companies, so-called hybrid online retailers, are rarely to be found in the sample with two percent of mentions.

3.3 Turnover and Employees of the Online Shops

Exactly a quarter of the online retailers surveyed operate a very small online shop with revenues of less than 100,000 Swiss francs or euros in 2023 (see Fig. 2A).

A fifth have revenues between 100,000 and 500,000 Swiss francs or euros and are therefore (rather) small online shops. One fifth of the retailers had revenues between one and five million Swiss francs or euros, while five percent had revenues between five and ten million Swiss francs or euros. Seven percent have revenues between ten and 25 million Swiss francs or euros and are therefore rather large. 12% of the online shops surveyed generate sales of more than 25 million Swiss francs or euros and can therefore be counted among the 50 largest online shops in Switzerland. Figure 2B shows that 54% of the online shop operators surveyed have o*nly one to four employees* (including marketing, logistics and IT; Measured in full-time equivalents, shortly FTE). Six percent large online shop operators have 51 to 100 or over 100 employees.

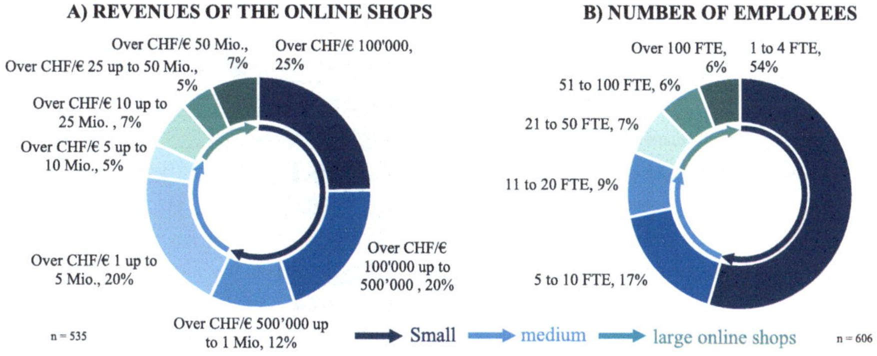

Fig. 2. A) What was the revenue of your online shop in 2023? B) How many employees (in full-time equivalent; FTE) work for your online shop (incl. Marketing, logistics, IT)?

4 Analysis and Results of the Online Retailer Survey 2024

4.1 Overview on AI Applications in E-Commerce

AI can be used in companies along the value chain for various purposes. This can be in marketing, online shop operations and customer service, but also in logistics, strategic planning or offer planning. This study focuses on *AI applications in marketing* (such as content creation, personalization and analysis), in *online shop operations* (such as AI sales advisor, AI search, product recommendations and AI-generated product texts) and in *customer service* (such as intelligent call centers, personalization, e.g. for support or AI customer advisor).

4.2 Generative AI and Translation

Following exploratory research into possible AI applications in e-commerce in the Online Retailer Survey 2023 (Zumstein et al., 2023), the topic was systematically explored in greater depth in this current study. The first and most important question is *in which area of digital commerce and marketing AI is used in the company* (see Fig. 3). This revealed that 54% of online retailers use *AI to translate texts into foreign languages* (such as German, French, Italian and English). Large online shops with more than 21 employees (64%) use AI to translate texts more frequently than small online shops with four or fewer employees (49%).

A similar number, 53% of retailers, use generative AI such as ChatGPT for *text creation* (in second place in Fig. 3). The data shows that large online shop operators (with 63% of responses) use AI to create texts more frequently than small ones (with 46%).

4.3 Generating Product Texts and Search Engine Optimization with AI

Surprisingly, already 42% of retailers use AI to *create product information in their online shop*. A further 17% plan to generate their product texts by AI in the future. Larger online

Fig. 3. In which area of Digital Commerce & Marketing do you use AI in your company?

shop operators create product texts with AI more frequently than small ones. A third of online retailers are already using *AI for search engine optimization* (SEO), for example by optimizing product texts and keywords with the help of AI. In B2C, among large and pure players, AI is used more frequently for SEO than in B2B, among small and Omni channel players. Thanks to AI, further 18% of the participants also hope to achieve higher reach and visibility on Google in the future.

One in four retailers use AI to *create images and videos for their online shop*, and one in five plan to do so in the future. Other 20% use *AI in marketing campaigns*, for example when targeting the target group on Instagram, Facebook, LinkedIn and Google, or directly when analyzing and managing campaigns.

4.4 Further Applications of AI in E-Commerce

The algorithms and models of search functions are currently undergoing rapid development. In Fig. 3, 16% of online retailers confirm that they already use *AI-based product searches, filters or finders* in their online shop.

Surprisingly few, just 16% of respondents, use *AI in analytics*, for instance for data analyses. Moreover, 12% are *programming with AI tools like Co-Pilot*. At nine percent, AI is also still *rarely used in customer service*, for example in a service chatbot for customer support. Nevertheless, at 20%, a large number are planning to use AI to relieve the burden on customer service in the future. A similar number of nine percent applies

AI to the *personalization of content or offers.* Algorithms process various data in the background in *debt collection,* such as credit checks when purchasing on account, as well as in *fraud prevention and detection.* In 32 online shops (six percent in Fig. 3), AI is used *for sales and customer advice.* Here, users can ask questions (about a product, problem, solution, etc.) in a chatbot, which generative AI (usually integrated LLMs such as ChatGPT) answers. In rare cases, *AI is used in pricing* (e.g. for calculating offers or pricing) and *in forecasting* (e.g. sales or revenue forecasts). With four percent mentions, the AI use case of *procurement,* in which an auto-buying system automatically orders products, ranks at the bottom of Fig. 3.

4.5 Benefits of AI in E-Commerce

As shown in Sect. 4.2, text creation with generative AI such as ChatGPT is by far the most widely used AI application in e-commerce. All 472 online retailers who create texts with AI or are currently testing it were asked what the *benefits of AI are in content creation* (see Fig. 4). With 89% of mentions, the *time saving* associated with AI content creation was clearly the most frequently mentioned benefit. AI tools such as ChatGPT deliver the desired texts or articles within seconds, saving users a lot of time. This time saving frees up time and capacity in (content) marketing for other employee activities. All types of companies and industries benefit equally from the time saved by AI. Large companies with more than 21 employees in e-commerce save slightly more time (with 93% of responses) than small ones (with 85%).

Translating texts into other languages is also quick and easy with AI-based translation tools such as DeepL or Google Translate. In Switzerland in particular, with its four national languages, content such as product texts in most online shops is translated into German, French, Italian and often also into English. Large online shops with many product pages must translate texts into other languages more frequently (70%) than small shops (62%).

With 46% of responses in Fig. 4, *more content* can be created in marketing thanks to AI. This is a major advantage, especially for SMEs with limited human and financial resources. 42% of online retailers also stated that they have *lower personnel costs* thanks to the use of AI. Further 35% of the 472 AI-using online retailers confirm that AI leads to *higher content quality* because GPT may create more comprehensible texts than humans. All companies and sectors benefit equally from the high content and language quality of LLMs, regardless of whether they are B2C or B2B, large or small, pure players or omnichannel retailers.

A major advantage of creating texts with prompting is that this *leads to higher findability and a better ranking in search engines such as Google.* This is confirmed by one in three online retailers. Online retailers in B2B appear to be somewhat less active in SEO (with 29% of responses) than those in B2C (with 36%). The following Sect. 4.6 takes a closer look at the SEO effects of AI on product texts.

The benefit of AI appears to be less significant in terms of content actuality and relevance: only 18% and 15% respectively confirm that AI content is *more up-to-date and more relevant for the target group.* For large online shops with automated publication processes, content is more often up to date than for the smaller shops. At 23%, large providers also tend to offer more relevant content more often, e.g. thanks to personalization.

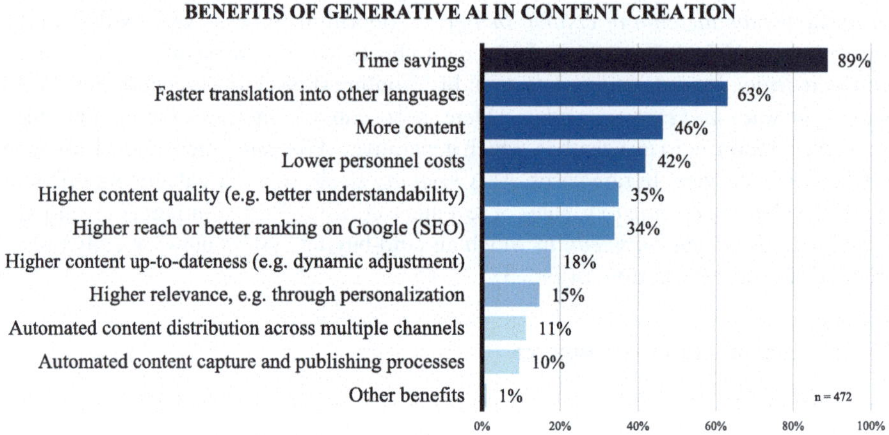

Fig. 4. What is the benefit of AI in content creation? (Multiple answers are possible)

Modern, often AI-based software solutions enable companies to *capture and publish content automatically and to play it out automatically via multiple channels* such as websites, newsletters and social media (Peter et al., 2024). This is already the case for ten or eleven percent of the companies surveyed in the online retailer study.

In an open-ended question, the survey also asked where online retailers generally see the *greatest benefits and opportunities* in the specific application of AI in e-commerce. Of these, 299 out of 604 (50%) retailers wrote freehand texts, which the first author evaluated and summarized in Table 1. By far the most frequently mentioned benefit, with 63 mentions (#1 in Table 1), was again the *time saving* associated with the use of AI.

All benefits mentioned by participants are described in detail in the study results (Zumstein & Oehninger 2024).

4.6 AI-Generated Product Texts

Online retailers who had product texts generated with AI were asked in the study what improvements they had noticed as a result. Out of 281 respondents, 169 (60% in Fig. 5) stated that *AI-generated product texts had a higher quality of information* than those written by humans. High information quality is characterized here by meaningful and useful product information for online shop users. Thanks to AI, small retailers can increase the quality of information (with 62% of responses) more often than large retailers (with 48%).

A good half state that they have *higher product data quality* thanks to the use of AI tools, for example due to complete and up-to-date product data. Large online shop operators are significantly more likely to improve product data quality (wit 61% of mentions) than small ones (with 39%). This could be explained by the fact that the large providers have often more data to gather, store, clean, use and maintain than the small ones. For 44% of respondents, the publication of *AI-generated product texts led to a higher reach or a better ranking in search engines* such as Google. Small

Table 1. Where do you see the greatest benefits or opportunities in using AI in e-commerce? (n = 299)

#	AI Benefits in E-Commerce	Mentions	#	AI Benefits in E-Commerce (continued)	Mentions
1	Time saving	63	31	Simplification / Flexibility	5
2	Content / text creation	46	32	Creation of advertising texts & images	4
3	Increase process efficiency / productivity	31	33	Appropriate choice of words	4
4	Personalized offers / recommendations	30	34	Increasing the data-driven nature	4
5	Personalized content	22	35	Fraud detection	4
6	Optimization in customer service	19	36	Quality inspection / quality assurance	3
7	Cost reduction	17	37	More efficient planning	3
8	Support for SEM (SEO & SEA)	16	38	Improving the user experience	3
9	Creation of product texts	15	39	Creation & optimization of newsletters	2
10	Customer advice / sales	15	40	Improvement in requirements planning / purchasing	2
11	Increase in marketing efficiency	14	41	Improvement in customer acquisition	2
12	Automation in marketing & sales	14	42	Additional information on product use	2
13	Simple / fast translations	13	43	Improvement in communication	2
14	Analytics (data analysis & forecasting)	13	44	Reduction in chat / telephone support	2
15	Better product recommendations	11	45	Faster response to requirements	2
16	Product data maintenance / categorization	11	46	Interception of incorrect orders	1
17	Improvement of the search / filter	10	47	Increasing expertise	1
18	Savings in personnel	10	48	Automation of processing	1
19	Better / more relevant content	9	49	Scaling of measures	1
20	Cost / resource savings	8	50	More up-to-date information	1
21	Idea generation & research	8	51	Extended navigation options	1
22	Increase in sales / turnover	8	52	Faster decision-making	1
23	Multilingualism (website, service center)	7	53	Faster time-to-market	1
24	Cross-selling & guided selling	7	54	Relief for employees	1
25	Better targeting in advertising	7	55	Credit check	1
26	Support with programming	6	56	Greater focus on solutions	1
27	Better images / product presentation	6	57	Improvement in advertising placement	2
28	Automation of routine activities	5	58	Little benefit	3
29	Increase in quality	5	59	No benefit	27
30	Pattern recognition / segmentation	5	60	I don't know	15

online retailers (with 47%) benefit more frequently from AI-supported SEO than large ones (with 38%). A quarter of online retailers also stated that AI-based solutions led to *better product classification or product categorization* in the online shop system or PIM (product information management).

One in five online retailers were able to *increase the number of visits to product (detail) pages*, increase the *conversion rate and achieve more revenues and sales* thanks to AI-based product texts. Omnichannel retailers (with 24% mentions) can increase the conversion rate much more often than pure players (nine percent) thanks to AI-generated product texts. For few respondents (four percent in Fig. 5), AI product texts increased the *basket value*. Therefore, product texts have no significant influence on the size of the shopping cart in terms of units or basket value, in contrast to recommendations for alternative and additional products.

4.7 AI in Search and Chatbots

With the intensive and increasing use of ChatGPT and chatbots, internet users are becoming used to asking entire questions or formulating orders (prompts) in search fields (more research results on AI-based chatbots see Adam et al., 2020; Crowder, 2024; McTear & Ashurkina, 2024). Due to these expectations, providers of search engines and search functions on websites and online shops are increasingly forced to adapt their search algorithms and models and expand them with LLMs. As stated in Sect. 4.4 and mentioned by study participants, AI will fundamentally *change the search function in online shop and product searches*. Therefore, 272 AI-using online retailers were whether they believe that an AI-based search function (such as that of ChatGPT or Google's Generative

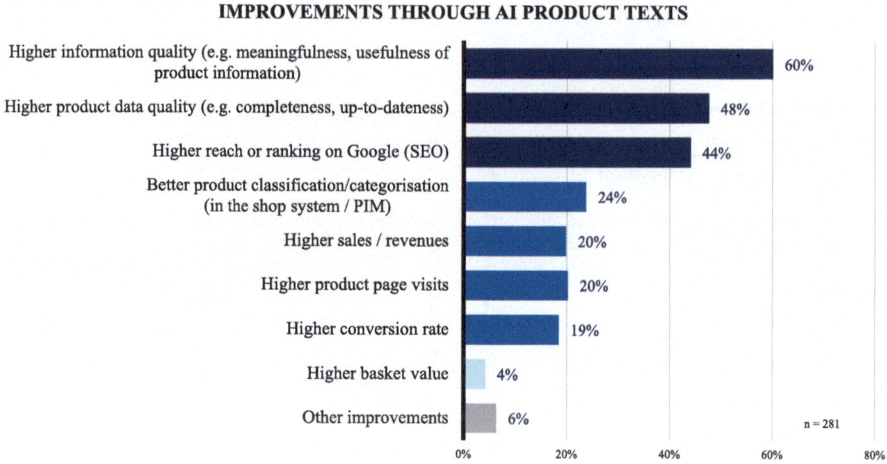

Fig. 5. What improvements have you noticed thanks to AI-based product texts? (Multiple answers are possible)

AI Search) or AI chatbots will become standard in online shops. 98.2% of respondents agreed with this question. A minority of 7.4% believe that AI-based search functions and chatbots will only become standard in the long term, in six to ten years. A *large majority of 73% believe that AI-based search and chatbots will become standard in the medium term*, i.e. within two to five years. Almost one in twenty online retailers even think that this will become standard in the short term, i.e. this year or next year.

4.8 AI Challenges in E-Commerce

Those online retailers for whom the AI application represents a medium or major challenge were asked in an open-ended question about where they currently see the *biggest challenges for AI in e-commerce.* 90 of the 244 (37%) study participants responded in a text field. One of the biggest challenges is that the *missing know-how and expertise regarding AI* (with 15 mentions in Table 2). The second most frequently mentioned challenge for online retailers when using AI in e-commerce is the *implementation or integration of AI* into the company's IT (information technology) landscape (#2 in Table 2). Online retailers are challenged to *maintain their focus.* All challenges mentioned by participants are described in detail in the study results (Zumstein & Oehninger 2024).

5 Discussion and Recommendations

5.1 AI in E-Commerce

AI developments are influencing many areas of the digital value chain. Section 4 showed that AI is most frequently used in (product) text creation and translations. This saves a lot of time, personnel and money. AI also provides inspiration and ideas, supports marketing campaigns, product searches and data analysis. Only a few (mostly large)

Table 2. Where do you currently see the biggest challenges in applying AI in e-commerce? (n = 90).

#	AI Challenge	Mentions	#	AI challenges (continued)	Mentions
1	Lack of know-how / expertise on AI	15	31	Costs of the models / tools	1
2	Implementation / integration	14	32	Derivation of the ROI	1
3	Tool / software / system selection	7	33	Missing starting point	1
4	Missing use cases (application cases)	7	34	Expectations of the users	1
5	Missing use cases with business impact	6	35	Loss of reality	1
6	Lack of quality (results, answers)	6	36	Lack of quality control	1
7	Data protection	6	37	False information / fake news	1
8	Data security	6	38	Immature AI images	1
9	Lack of overview	5	39	Overregulation in the EU	1
10	Lack of budget / financing	5	40	Source reference	1
11	Dynamics, speed, fast pace	4	41	Lack of understanding	1
12	Correct application / implementation of AI	4	42	Lack of credibility	1
13	Lack of correctness of AI	4	43	Correct timing	1
14	Lack of focus / focus	3	44	Ethical / responsible behavior	1
15	Costs (IT, development, integration)	3	45	Technology choice	1
16	Selection of suitable implementation partners	3	46	Technical challenges	1
17	Lack of time	3	47	Interface problems	1
18	Lack of personnel	3	48	Data quality	1
19	Lack of customer benefit	3	49	Fear of missing out on a development	1
20	Lack of trust (doubt)	2	50	Difficulty keeping up with the big players	1
21	Lack of acceptance (by customers)	2	51	Management / company by in	1
22	Lack of relevance	2	52	Personnel management	1
23	Lack of meaningfulness	2	53	Motivation of employees	1
24	Prioritization	2	54	Needs-oriented advice	1
25	Dependence through competition	2	55	Testing & learning	1
26	Effectiveness of use	2	56	Loss of control	1
27	Buzzword / Hype	2	57	Overload	1
28	Legal situation / legal certainty	2	58	Definition of AI	1
29	Lack of experience	1	59	Not in use	1
30	Lack of accuracy	1	60	Don't know	2

retailers are already using AI for sales or service chatbots. One remarkable finding of this study is that between nine and 21% of online retailers are currently planning and testing different AI applications. This means that many companies are currently investing in AI. Enterprises are actively exploring and testing the various possibilities of AI. It is therefore recommended that all other retailers who are not yet experimenting with AI and are taking a wait-and-see approach should tackle the issue. For every retailer, regardless of business model, strategy, size or sector, it is important to identify *potential AI use cases with business impact*. Although there are many AI challenges to overcome, the benefits and opportunities clearly outweigh them.

5.2 Recommendations for Online Retailers

Various options for action can be derived for online shop operators from the findings of the Online Retailer Survey 2024. In conclusion, following list shows *14 recommendations* for action in various areas. They can help online operators to position themselves optimally in e-commerce for the dawn of the AI age. The list of recommendation is not exhaustive and serves as inspiration.

1. Analyze all business processes where AI can save the most time
2. Create and maintain high-quality product, web, sales and customer data with the help of AI
3. Use AI to classify and categorize products, and for recommendation systems
4. Use and promote (generative) AI for inspiration and idea generation throughout the company
5. Create texts with AI and ensure quality control in the process

6. Improve, document and possibly standardize prompting when writing (product) texts
7. Translate all texts and offer a multilingual online shop with AI tools such as DeepL
8. Create product images with AI, test their effect and analyze click and conversion rates
9. Create product texts with AI and compare performance (e.g. conversion rate, online revenues)
10. Optimize product texts with AI tools for search engines (SEO)
11. Automate and thus scale the product copywriting, editing and publication process
12. Use AI to automatically answer customer e-mails, calls or messages and in service (chat and/voice) chatbots to stem the growing flood of e-mails and rising customer service costs
13. Examine the potential savings and benefits of sales and consulting chatbots
14. Offer fast and expert advice in customer service thanks to AI

6 Conclusions, Limitations and Further Research

The study provides an in-depth analysis of the adoption and use of artificial intelligence (AI) in the Swiss and Austrian e-commerce sector. The results of the study show that a majority of online retailers are already using AI tools to create and translate texts. In addition, this study looks at different applications of AI in e-commerce, including generating product descriptions and SEO optimization. 34% of retailers are using AI to optimize keywords and content for higher search engine reach and rankings. This *study confirms empirically …*

1. that AI is broadly used in e-commerce practice
2. many different e-commerce use cases with business impact
3. the extent, depth and diversity of the potential benefits and value of AI in e-commerce
4. the numerous challenges that online retailers face in business practice
5. that developments and trends in AI are very fast and
6. that companies invest and test much in AI.

The survey was conducted on a large, representative sample of companies, which allows to conclude that there is a high probability of high market representativeness. However, it should be borne in mind that, with such a rapidly changing e-commerce environment and the extraordinary pace of development of AI, it will be necessary to repeat this type of survey on a regular basis and in international markets, considering innovations that are emerging all the time.

Further research could focus on …

1. international studies and benchmarks on AI in digital marketing and sales
2. representative samples of
3. different sectors (industries)
4. specific AI use cases
5. specific AI benefits
6. specific AI challenges
7. further practical insights and strategic/operational recommendations to
8. small-/medium-sized enterprises (SME), e-commerce start-ups and
9. large corporations.

References

Adam, M., Wessel, M., Benlian, A.: AI-based chatbots in customer service and their effects on user compliance. Electron. Mark. **31**(2), 427–445 (2020). https://doi.org/10.1007/s12525-020-00414-7

Akter, S., Wamba, S.F.: Big data analytics in E-commerce: a systematic review and agenda for future research. Electron. Mark. **26**, 173–194 (2016). https://doi.org/10.1007/s12525-016-0219-0

Morales, J., Silva-Aravena, F., Valdés, Y., Baltierra, S.: Virtual reality and augmented reality applied to e-commerce: a literature review. In: Agredo-Delgado, V., Ruiz, P.H., Correa-Madrigal, O. (eds.) Human-Computer Interaction. HCI-COLLAB 2022. Communications in Computer and Information Science, vol. 1707, pp. 201-213. Springer, Cham (2023). https://doi.org/10.1007/978-3-031-24709-5_15

Bawack, R.E., Wamba, S.F., Carillo, K.D.A., Akter, S.: Artificial intelligence in E-Commerce: a bibliometric study and literature review. Electron. Mark. **32**(1), 297–338 (2022). https://doi.org/10.1007/s12525-022-00537-z

Boukrouh, I., Azmani, A.: Artificial intelligence applications in e-commerce: a bibliometric study from 1995 to 2023 using merged data sources. Int. J. Prof. Bus. Rev. **9**(4), e4537 (2024). https://doi.org/10.26668/businessreview/2024.v9i4.4537

BRACK.CH (2023, October 24). BRACK.CH launches new AI product consultancy. https://www.brack.ch/news/2023/10/24/brack-ch-lanciert-neue-ki-produktberatung

Chodak, G., Chawla, Y.: Artificial intelligence in online stores' processes. In: Garg, D., Jagannathan, S., Gupta, A., Garg, L., Gupta, S. (eds.) Advanced Computing: 11th International Conference, IACC 2021, Msida, Malta, December 18–19, 2021, Revised Selected Papers, pp. 214–228. Springer International Publishing, Cham (2022). https://doi.org/10.1007/978-3-030-95502-1_17

Chodak, G.: The Future of E-commerce. Innovations and Developments. Palgrave Macmillan, Cham (2024). https://doi.org/10.1007/978-3-031-55225-0

Crowder, J.: AI Chatbots. Springer, Colorado Springs (2024)

Deng, J., Lin, Y.: The benefits and challenges of ChatGPT: an overview. Front. Comput. Intell. Syst. **2**(2), 81–83 (2023). https://doi.org/10.54097/fcis.v2i2.4465

Do it + Garden. DigiChat (2024). https://www.tgarden.ch/de/cp/ki-chat?srsltid=AfmBOoqPJb0AJZHmzccCYOD1GNw32jnlpjweFtNTgxjEWtx6p46pngnN

HANDELSVERBAND.swiss (2024). Online Retail Market Switzerland 2023 (in German). https://handelsverband.swiss/wp-content/uploads/2024/03/Onlinehandelsmarkt-Schweiz-2023-Medien-Stand-13.3.2024.pdf

Heinemann, G.: Der neue Online-Handel: Geschäftsmodelle, Geschäftssysteme und Benchmarks im E-Commerce (14th edition). Springer Fachmedien, Berlin (2023). https://doi.org/10.1007/978-3-658-41653-9

Heinick, H.: Industry Report Online Retail 2023. IFH COLOGNE (2023). https://www.ifhkoeln.de/produkt/branchenreport-onlinehandel-2023

Hofacker, L., Höbner, P., Niemeier, D., Peters, L.: E-Commerce Market Germany 2023. EHI Retail Institute e.V. and ecommerceDB GmbH (2023). https://www.ehi.org/produkt/studie-e-commerce-markt-deutschland-2023

Iglesias-Pradas, S., Acquila-Natale, E.: The future of e-commerce: overview and prospects of multichannel and Omni channel retail. J. Theor. Appl. Electron. Commer. Res. **18**(1), 656–667 (2023). https://doi.org/10.3390/jtaer18010033

JUMBot (2024). JUMBot: dein cleverer Berater (in German). https://www.jumbo.ch/de/service/jumbot.html

Kreutzer, R.T.: Practice-Oriented Marketing: Basics – Instruments – Case Studies. Springer, Berlin (2023). https://doi.org/10.1007/978-3-658-31990-8

Lone, S., Weltevreden, J.: European E-Commerce Report 2023. Amsterdam University of Applied Sciences & Ecommerce Europe (2023). https://www.eurocommerce.eu/app/uploads/2023/11/2023-european-e-commerce-report-light-version-nov-update-v2.pdf

McTear, M., Ashurkina, M.: Transforming Conversational AI. Apress, Berkeley (2024)

Pallathadka, H., Ramirez-Asis, E.H., Loli-Poma, T.P., Kaliyaperumal, K., Ventayen, R.J.M., Naved, M.: Applications of artificial intelligence in business management, e-commerce and finance. Mater. Today Proc. **80**, 2610–2613 (2023). https://doi.org/10.1016/j.matpr.2021.06.419

Peter, M.K., et al.: E-Commerce Automation Report 2024 (2024). FHNW. https://doi.org/10.13140/RG.2.2.32130.29123

Rudolph, T., Kralle, N., Schraml, C.: Omni-Channel Management in Germany, Austria and Switzerland 2024. Research Center for Retail Management (2024). https://shop.irm.unisg.ch/products/omni-channel-management-in-deutschland-osterreich-und-der-schweiz-2024

Scherrer, A.: Feature Friday: AI consulting with JUMBot. Carpathia Digital Business Blog. Carpathia: E-Business, E-Commerce, Cross-/Omni-Channel, Digital Transformation Blog (2023). https://blog.carpathia.ch/2023/09/01/feature-friday-ki-beratung-mit-jumbot/

Sharma, M., Sharma, V., Kapoor, R.: Study of E-commerce and impact of machine learning in e-commerce. In: Bilgaiyan, S., Singh, J., Das, H. (eds.) Empirical Research for Futuristic E-Commerce Systems: Foundations and Applications, pp. 1–22. IGI Global (2022). https://doi.org/10.4018/978-1-6684-4969-1.ch001

Singh, R.: A study of artificial intelligence and E-commerce ecosystem - a customer's perspective. Int. J. Res. Eng. Sci. Manage. **4**(2), 78–87 (2021)

Song, X.: The application of artificial intelligence in electronic commerce. J. Phys. Conf. Ser. **1302**, 032030 (2009). https://doi.org/10.1088/1742-6596/1302/3/032030

Subramanian, S.: Large Language Model-Based Solutions: How to Deliver Value with Cost-Effective Generative AI Applications. John Wiley & Sons, Incorporated, Boston (2024)

Theobald, E., Malthaner, M., Föhl, U.: AI schlägt Mensch?! (in German). HMD **58**, 922–936 (2021). https://doi.org/10.1365/s40702-020-00658-z

Verhoef, P.C., et al.: Digital transformation: a multidisciplinary reflection and research agenda. J. Bus. Res. **122**, 889–901 (2021). https://doi.org/10.1016/j.jbusres.2019.09.022

Wang, C., et al.: An empirical evaluation of technology acceptance model for artificial intelligence in e-commerce. Heliyon **9**(8), e18349 (2023). https://doi.org/10.1016/j.heliyon.2023.e18349

Wecke, B.: Wachstum durch den Einsatz von Generativer KI: Funktionsweise und Anwendungsgebiete im Marketing. Springer Fachmedien Wiesbaden, Wiesbaden (2024).https://doi.org/10.1007/978-3-658-44041-1

Wölfle, R., Leimstoll, U.: Commerce Report Switzerland 2022: Values and services in the focus of commerce (2022). https://www.fhnw.ch/de/die-fhnw/hochschulen/hsw/iwi/e-business/e-commerce-report-schweiz/media/commerce-report-schweiz-2022.pdf

Zumstein, D., Oswald, C.: Online Retailer Survey 2020: Sustainable Growth of E-commerce and Challenges in Times of Crisis. ZHAW Zurich University of Applied Sciences (2020). https://doi.org/10.21256/zhaw-2389

Zumstein, D., Oswald, C., Brauer, C.: Online Retailer Survey 2021: Insights into the E-commerce Boom in Switzerland and Austria. ZHAW Zurich University of Applied Sciences (2021). https://doi.org/10.21256/zhaw-2413

Zumstein, D., Oswald, C., Brauer, C.: Online Retailer Survey 2022: Success Factors and Omnichannel Services in Digital Commerce. ZHAW Zurich University of Applied Sciences (2022). https://doi.org/10.21256/zhaw-2432

Zumstein, D., Oswald, C., Brauer, C.: Online Retailer Rurvey 2023: E-commerce after Corona: Skills Shortage, Overdistribution and Artificial Intelligence. ZHAW Zurich University of Applied Sciences (2023). https://doi.org/10.21256/zhaw-2469

Zumstein, D. Oehninger, F.: Onlinehändlerbefragung 2024 – Anwendungen, Vorteile und Herausforderungen der künstlichen Intelligenz im E-Commerce, ZHAW Zurich University of Applied Sciences (2024). https://doi.org/10.21256/zhaw-2503

Digital Business Management: A Fresh Perspective on Digital Business Models

Diana Murtagh-Boehm(✉) and Tamara Wehrstein

IU University of Applied Sciences, Bad Honnef, Germany
{diana.murtagh-boehm,tamara.wehrstein}@iu.org

Abstract. This paper explores the concept of digital business models in the context of digital transformation and their distinction from traditional business models. Digital transformation is reshaping businesses globally, altering how value is created and delivered through the strategic use of technology and data. While the term "digital business model" has gained widespread usage, its definition remains ambiguous. This paper clarifies the concept by examining existing theories and proposing a theoretical framework for digital business management. It argues that digital business models do not represent a fundamentally new type of business model but rather reflect a shift in how data and technology are leveraged to meet business objectives. The framework presented provides insights into how organizations can effectively navigate the digital landscape by integrating digital technologies into traditional business practices. The paper concludes by emphasizing the need for precise definitions and terminology to advance research and practice in digital business management.

Keywords: Digital business model · business model · digital technologies · digital age · digital transformation · digital business · digital business management

1 Introduction

Digital transformation involves the integration of digital technology into all aspects of an organization (Ismail et al., 2017; Kraus et al., 2022), leading to infrastructural changes and potentially creating new business models. Companies that fail to adapt to the digital era risk becoming obsolete, while those that can adapt thrive (Schwartz, 2002). Thus, in today's digital age, businesses are increasingly turning to technology to transform their operations and create new value propositions. The term "digital business model" has become ubiquitous in discussions about this transformation, but its precise meaning and implications for companies remain somewhat elusive. This article seeks to clarify the concept of digital business models and explore how they differ from traditional business models.

The paper is organized as follows: Section 2 reviews the theoretical foundation, with a focus on digital technologies, the value of data in the digital age and the concept of

R. C. Geibel and S. Machavariani (Eds.): ISPC 2024, SPBE, pp. 16–30, 2025.
https://doi.org/10.1007/978-3-031-88052-0_2

business models. In Sect. 3, the digital business model concept is revisited, and a theoretical framework for business management in the digital age is proposed. The discussion section argues that a business model serves as a conceptual framework illustrating how an organization creates and delivers value to its customers. It is suggested that digital business models are not fundamentally different from traditional ones, but instead represent a shift in how businesses leverage data and technology to achieve their objectives. The paper emphasizes the need for clear definitions and boundaries in the terminology surrounding digital business models and highlights the interaction between technology and traditional business practices.

2 Digital Technologies and the Value of Data in the Digital Age

The founder and executive chairman of the world economic forum wrote 2016 in his book the Fourth Industrial Revolution "[w]e are at the beginning of a revolution that is fundamentally changing the way we live, work and relate to one another" (Schwab, 2017, p. 1). The concept of the Fourth Industrial Revolution emphasizes the significant impact of technological change on various aspects and facets of societies and economies. Eight and a half years later we are, arguably, amid the fourth industrial revolution, defined by the rapid flow of information due to data centralization and the rise of digital technologies (Philbeck & Davis, 2019). This revolution fits within the broader context of the 21st century, a period marked by the shift from the industrial era to the digital age. The advent of the computer has been pivotal in this transition, leading to the emergence of the information-driven digital age. Spanning from the 1960s to the present, this era is distinguished by the growing importance of information, where the management, electronic processing, and sharing of data play a fundamental role (Menz et al., 2021).

"Digitalization calls for new ways of workplace communication and collaboration and can be understood as the use of digital technologies and data (digitized and natively digital) to create revenue, improve business, and replace/transform business processes (not simply digitizing them). [...] it also creates an environment for digital business." (Kraus et al., 2022, p. 2) Digitalization is reshaping technology, which serves as the primary catalyst for societal and economic change (see Fig. 1). Within society, this is evident through the altered methods of communication between individuals. For business, it encompasses shifts in value creation, business models and the nature of work. Consequently, technology plays a pivotal role in driving these societal and economic changes (Kollmann & Schmidt, 2020). Digitalization has brought disruptive changes to societal, industrial, economical and individual levels (Ismail et al., 2017).

While digitalization focuses on the adoption of digital tools to optimize existing processes, digital transformation involves a broader, strategic overhaul of business operations. One way to describe digital transformation is the incorporation of digital technologies and business processes within a digital economy (Ismail et al., 2017). A narrower definition is "the integration of digital technology into all aspects and operations of an organization, which in turn leads to infrastructural changes in how the organization is operated and delivers value to its customers" (Kraus et al., 2022, p. 2). The latter definition shows that digital transformation is more complex and involves various aspects of an organization. Kraus et al. (2022) further postulate that digital transformation has a more extreme impact and can lead to the creation of entirely new business models as a result of changing the organizational processes, products and/or operations. This is in line with the argumentation of Verhoef et al. (2021) who state that "digital transformation is a company-wide phenomenon with broad organizational implications in which (…) the core business model of the firm is subject to change through the use of digital technology." (Verhoef et al., 2021, p. 892).

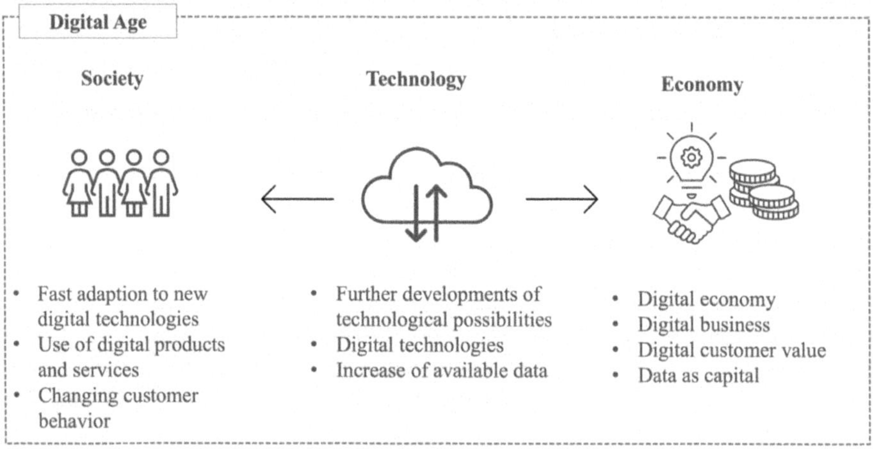

Fig. 1. Technology as the core driver for changes in society and the economy. Source: Murtagh-Boehm & Wehrstein (2024), based on Kollmann & Schmidt (2020).

Factors that contribute to the digital transformation of businesses and to the development of the digital economy can be categorized into internal drivers and external triggers (Ismail et al., 2017). Internally, companies are motivated by declining sales, operational needs for efficiency, employee desires for improved interaction, and corporate social responsibility requirements (Horváth & Szabó, 2019). Ismail et al. (2017) argue that digital transformation is mainly externally driven by innovative startups challenging incumbent firms and tech-savvy customers. Kraus et al. (2022), albeit acknowledging internal and external drivers, also point out the value creation aspect of digital transformation for both B2B as well as B2C sectors and industries. The value adding aspect in the digital world can also be observed as some connected industry actors become complementors as their products or services are adding value or creating demand for those products or services of other actors, changing market structures and engaging in both cooperation and competition, known as coopetition (Menz et al., 2021). Another interesting value creation aspect in the digital age is that digitalization presents a paradox in corporate strategy: while there is significant potential for value creation, the new industry participants often struggle to capture a substantial portion of that value. Menz et al. (2021) give the example of WhatsApp, which despite having over two billion users and creating significant communication value, has not monetized its business yet. All authors agree that our economy is driven by innovative technologies. Today, there are several relevant technologies that have had a significant impact on various aspects of our private and professional lives. These technologies have significantly shaped the digital age and continue to drive innovation and transformation across various industries.

These technologies and the accompanying technological innovations have fundamentally transformed the behavior and interaction among individuals. Simultaneously, these technologies have drastically reduced the costs associated with searching, analysing, storing, and distributing information (Menz et al., 2021). The internet, for example, with its ability to provide information that is accessible anytime, anywhere, and with precise accuracy, illustrates how information in the digital age has become both more abundant and concentrated (Chaffey et al., 2019). Digital technologies enable the collection of vast amounts of data, which needs to be transformed into meaningful information (Bächle et al., 2021; Dillerup & Stoi, 2016) as the value of this information is determined by how individuals perceive it and the significance they assign to it. Information can generate various types of value, such as entertainment or business value, depending on what people are willing to pay for it (Shapiro & Varian, 1999).

The digital age offers businesses new opportunities to outperform competitors and meet customer needs through the intelligent use of data. These opportunities extend beyond merely transmitting, storing, and processing large volumes of data (Philbeck & Davis, 2019). According to Birkinshaw (2018), the growing availability of meaningful data is driving changes in organizational structures and processes. Menz et al. (2021) further argue that digital technologies are not only reshaping organizations but also redefining the rules of competition and revolutionizing entire industries. As a result, digital transformation is profoundly impacting management practices and how business models deliver value.

In conclusion, digital transformation is a crucial issue for companies all over the world. If corporations are not able to adapt to the digital age they risk becoming victims of digital Darwinism[1], a scenario where only the most flexible, tech-savvy businesses survive, while others may become obsolete (Schwartz, 2002). The most adaptable, technologically progressive companies will prosper, while those resistant to digitalization potentially face obsolescence. Those who thrive in the digital age will outlast those who do not, underscoring the importance of staying current and flexible in the face of technological advancements. The ability to leverage data and information for decision-making and delivering value is crucial. As Zeng (2017) noted, data is the oil of the 21st century, and technological progress will determine survival in this new era of digital competition (Zeng, 2017).

2.1 Defining Digital Business and Digital Business Management

Digital business refers to organizations that leverage digital technologies not only for operational processes but also for customer engagement and strategic decision-making through data analysis. As highlighted by Verhoef et al. (2021), these businesses utilize

[1] **Digital Darwinism.** The term refers to the phenomenon where businesses or organizations that fail to adapt and embrace digital technologies are at risk of becoming obsolete and being outcompeted by those that do. It's a concept that highlights the importance of staying relevant in the digital age to survive and thrive in the ever-evolving landscape of technology and consumer behavior.

digital tools for internal and external communication, sales, and data-driven insights, making the effective use of customer data central to their operations. The origins of digital business can be traced back to the rise of digital technologies, particularly the internet and computer systems. E-commerce, one of the earliest forms of digital business, allowed companies to transact online, removing geographical barriers and expanding market opportunities (Wirtz, 2019). While e-commerce focuses on online transactions, digital business encompasses a broader range of activities, integrating aspects such as e-communication, e-collaboration, and e-education, as noted by Chaffey et al. (2019).

Establishing a clear definition of digital business is complex due to varied interpretations and overlapping terminologies like e-business and e-commerce (see Table 1). The specific term "digital business" has only recently been introduced. While many definitions emphasize the use of internet and mobile technologies, others adopt a technology-neutral perspective. However, all acknowledge the transactional nature of digital business (Lynn et al., 2022).

Overall, the lack of consensus on a standardized definition and the inherent complexities of digital transformation pose challenges for understanding the impact of digital business on socio-economic and managerial realms in the digital age (Lynn et al., 2022).

When considering the definitions it's clear that digital business is a subset of the digital economy. Wirtz (2019) extends this idea, suggesting that the digital economy is a result of the information society. As digital technologies made information more accessible, they transformed how economies operate, allowing for increased access to data, remote collaboration, and online transactions (see Fig. 2).

What exactly constitutes a digital business, however, is not yet clearly defined and the question arises as to how developments in the digital age are impacting businesses. In essence, digital business is a broad concept that covers a wide range of activities, far beyond just online sales. It includes any business that uses digital technologies and the internet to transform its operations, processes, and interactions. The goal of digital business is to enhance efficiency, improve customer experiences, and develop new business models through technology. Based on the explanations above, the following definition is proposed:

A digital business operates within the digital age and (1) utilizes digital technologies for value creation, transforming data into relevant information within its specific business context. Additionally, (2) it employs digital technologies for internal and external communication and collaboration, with the overarching goal of enhancing customer value. As digital technologies increasingly shape consumer behavior, (3) a digital business is both influenced by and influences the needs of the information society. Moreover, (4) it can navigate the complexities of the digital age, demonstrating the capability to (5) rethink and transform its underlying business model by leveraging data generated through digital technologies.

The discussion of digital business inevitably leads to the role of management in this context. According to Drnevich et al. (2020), management is centered on the efficient and effective practices within organizations and the ability to address challenges arising from a constantly evolving environment. The complex and multidisciplinary nature of digital transformation, which affects strategy, organization, marketing, supply chain, and information technology, challenges traditional management approaches. Managers

Table 1. Definitions of digital business

Authors	Definition
IBM (1997)	A secure, flexible and integrated approach to delivering differentiated business value by combining the systems and processes that run core business operations with the simplicity and reach made possible by Internet technology
Wirtz (2000)	[...] is defined as the initiation, negotiation and/or transaction of a business between economic subjects which is electronically realized through communication networks
Chen (2005)	Business that is conducted using electronic networks or electronic media. Sometimes used synonymously with e-commerce and sometimes used more widely to include other business activities in addition to buying and selling
Papazoglou & Ribbers (2006)	E-business can be defined as the conduct of automated business transactions by means of electronic communications networks (e.g., via the Internet and/or possibly private networks) end-to-end
Chaffey (2009)	All electronically mediated information exchanges, both within an organization and with external stakeholders supporting the range of business processes
Laudon & Traver (2014)	[...] is the use of Internet, the World Wide Web (Web) and mobile apps to transact business
Schneider (2017)	The term electronic commerce or (e-commerce) [...] includes all business activities that use Internet technologies. Internet technologies include the Internet, the World Wide Web and other technologies such as wireless transmissions on mobile telephone networks
Chaffey et al. (2019)	How businesses apply digital technology and media to improve the competitiveness of their organisation through optimising internal processes with online and traditional channels to market and supply
Kollmann (2022)	*Theoretical perspective:* Digital Business is the utilization of information technologies for the preparation (information phase), negotiation (communication phase), and execution (transaction phase) of business processes between economic partners through innovative communication networks *Practice-oriented perspective*: Digital Business is the use of innovative information technologies to sell something, offer or exchange information through virtual contact, provide comprehensive customer support, and enable individual contact with market participants

Source: Murtagh-Boehm & Wehrstein (2024), as cited in Kollmann, 2022; Lynn et al., 2022; Wirtz, 2019.

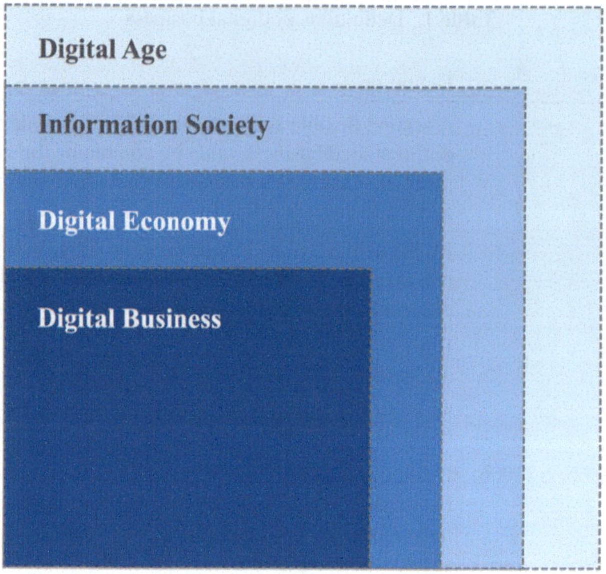

Fig. 2. Digital business at the center of today's complex transformation. Source: Murtagh-Boehm & Wehrstein (2024), based on Wirtz (2019).

today must contend with the rapid emergence of new digital technologies, as businesses are inextricably linked to societal and economic developments (Verhoef et al., 2021). Hence, it is not without reason that Verhoef et al. (2021) emphasize the multidisciplinary aspect of digital transformation stating that digital transformation is "a change in how a firm employs digital technologies, to develop a new digital business model that helps to create and appropriate more value for the firm" (Verhoef et al., 2021, p. 889). As a result, management is inherently digital in the current era, meaning that modern management practices must incorporate digital developments and cannot be separated from them (see Fig. 3).

2.2 Business Models in the Digital Age

A business model outlines how a company creates, delivers, and captures value by "deliver[ing] value to customers, entic[ing] customers to pay for value, and convert[ing] those payments to profit" (Teece, 2010, p. 172). According to Joan Magretta (2002), business modelling is "the managerial equivalent of the scientific method – you start with a hypothesis, which you then test in action and revise when necessary" (Magretta, 2002, p. 90). This perspective aligns with Teece (2010), who views the business model as a reflection of management's hypothesis about customer preferences and the organizational and operational requirements to meet those needs while generating profit (Teece, 2010). As the concept of the business model has gained popularity among scholars, managers, and consultants since its origins in 1957, its definition and meaning have evolved over time (Perelygina et al., 2022) (see Table 2).

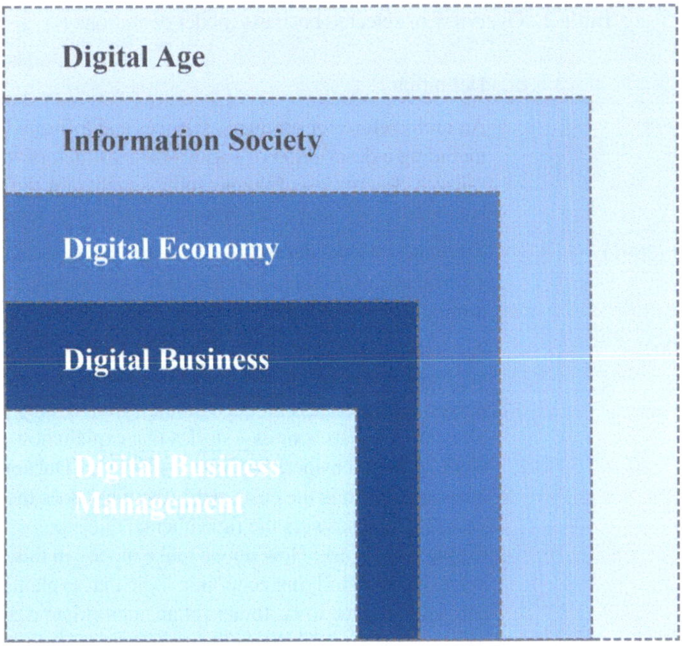

Fig. 3. Digital business management as response to the requirements of the digital age. Source: Murtagh-Boehm & Wehrstein (2024).

In addition to the definitions surrounding the concept of business models and the various archetypes or patterns, there is also ongoing discussion about the term "digital business models." However, there is no universally accepted definition of what constitutes a digital business model. Perelygina et al. (2022) stated, "the concept of digital business models is also interpreted differently by different academics" (Perelygina et al., 2022, p. 2). Only a few definitions of digital business models offer a more explicit explanation of the term. Some scholars view a business model as digital if it is driven by a single technology or define it from a specific perspective, such as Industry 4.0 (Perelygina et al., 2022). Others equate digital business models with e-business or interpret them as models based on the Internet of Things (Perelygina et al., 2022). Alternatively, some link the term to internal IT resources, focusing on "important activities such as digitizing an existing business or crafting new digital business models" (Teece, 2018a, p. 46).

Some scholars overemphasize descriptions of the internet's influence on a business model in the context of innovation (Böttcher et al., 2022; Teece, 2018b), labelling this as a digital business model. Veit et al. (2014) argue that a "business model is digital if changes in digital technologies trigger fundamental changes in the way business is carried out and revenues are generated" (Veit et al., 2014, p. 48). Similarly, Weill & Woerner (2013) state that digital business models refer to "how [companies] engage their customers digitally to create value, via mechanisms such as websites and mobile devices" (Weill & Woerner, 2013, p. 71). Additionally, Caputo et al. (2021) highlight that new forms of business models developed in the digital age are characterized by a "decreased

Table 2. Overview of selected business model definitions

Authors	Definition
Timmers (1998)	An architecture for products, services and information flows, including a description of various business actors and their roles; A description of the potential benefits for the various business actors; and a description of sources of revenues
Amit & Zott (2001)	A business model depicts the content, structure, and governance of transactions designed so as to create value through the exploitation of business opportunities
Magretta (2002)	A good business model remains essential to every successful organization, whether it's a new venture or an established player. […] Business models, though, are anything but arcane. They are, at heart, stories – stories that explain how enterprises work. A good business model answers Peter Ducker's age-old questions: Who is the customer? And what does the customer value? It also answers the fundamental questions every manager must ask: How do we make money in this business? What is the underlying economic logic that explains how we can deliver value to customers at an appropriate cost?
Johnson et al. (2008)	A business model, from our point of view, consists of four interlocking elements that, taken together, create and deliver value. The most important to get right, by far, is the first. Customer value proposition, profit formula, key resources and key processes
Teece (2010)	A business model articulates the logic and provides data and other evidence that demonstrates how a business creates and delivers value to customers. It also outlines the architecture of revenues, costs, and profits associated with the business enterprise delivering the value. […] In essence, a business model embodies nothing less than the organizational and financial 'architecture' of a business
Osterwalder & Pigneur (2010)	A business model describes the rationale of how an organization creates, delivers, and captures value
Ritter & Lettl (2018)	Archetypes describe generic logics of how firms do business, i.e. business-model archetypes are general, well-known business model logics. Business-model archetypes are typical models of value creation (…)
Gassmann, O. et al. (2020)	(…) repeating patterns build the core of many new business models

Source: Murtagh-Boehm & Wehrstein (2024), based on Wirtz, 2019.

reliance on physical elements" (Caputo et al., 2021, p. 490; Erevelles et al., 2016). Bican and Brem (2020) define a digital business model as "enhanced resource optimization, characterised by intangibility, businesses' uniqueness, and core values, centring around experience, platform, and content" (Bican & Brem, 2020, p. 10). What these definitions and explanations have in common is the emphasis on digital technologies as a force that impacts established business models. The term "digital" within the context of digital business models can be interpreted as an elevated level of resource optimization achieved through the use of digital technologies (Bican & Brem, 2020). See Table 3 for a selection of definitions for digital business model.

Table 3. Overview of selected digital business model definitions

Authors	Definition
Veit et al. (2014)	A business model is digital if changes in digital technologies trigger fundamental changes in the way business is carried out and revenues are generated
Weill & Woerner (2013)	Digital business models refer to "how [companies] engage their customers digitally to create value, via mechanisms such as websites and mobile devices"
Gassmann, O. et al. (2020)	(…) the digitalisation business model consists of transforming an existing product or service into a digital variant. (…) within the E-commerce business model, traditional products or services are delivered via online channels, this removing overheads associated with running physical branch infrastructure
Bican & Brem (2020)	A digital business model is an enhanced resource optimization, characterised by intangibility, businesses' uniqueness, and core values, centering around experience, platform, and content

Source: Murtagh-Boehm & Wehrstein (2024).

It is important to recognize that a business model, whether labelled as digital or not, and a strategy are distinct concepts. Although they are often used interchangeably, they serve different purposes in contributing to a company's success. While they are not the same, they rely on each other. A business model describes how different parts of a business fit together and create value, but it doesn't address competition directly. Conversely, a strategy deals with competition by outlining how a business will outperform rivals through uniqueness and offering something that others cannot duplicate (Magretta, 2002; Veit et al., 2014; Zott et al., 2011). In essence, a strategy is about differentiation. If all companies offer the same products or services to the same customers, none will thrive. That's where the competitive strategy comes in, enabling a company to stand out and gain a competitive edge (Magretta, 2002). Business models act as a bridge connecting a company's strategy and its processes. While the strategy's primary goal is to surpass competitors, the business model articulates the rationale behind creating value and efficiently managing a company's resources. Changes in the business model can directly impact business processes and required resources (Veit et al., 2014) (see Fig. 4).

The terms "business models," "business model patterns," "archetypes," and "digital business models" are frequently discussed in the context of digital transformation, a clear distinction between these concepts is, however, is often missing. Due to the complex

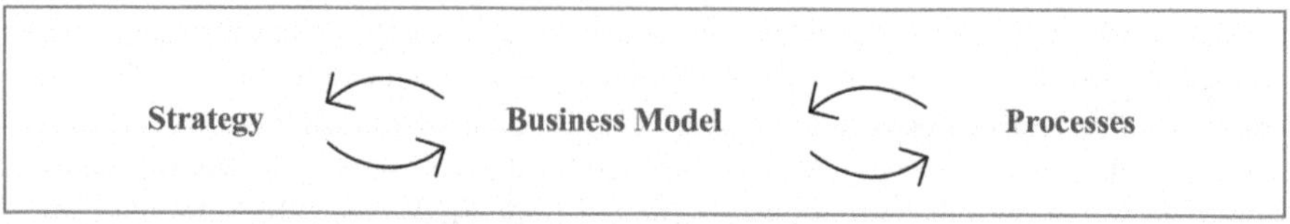

Fig. 4. Business model as intermediary between strategy and business processes. Source: Murtagh-Boehm & Wehrstein (2024), based on Veit et al. (2014).

and multidisciplinary nature of digital transformation, an imprecise definition of the conceptual framework that outlines how a business creates and delivers value to its customers (Teece, 2010) can lead to competitive disadvantages if a business fails to understand and then implement this framework effectively in the digital age. In this context, returning to the discussion of what constitutes a digital business model, the question arises: in the digital age, characterized by digital technologies and the abundance of available data, what distinguishes a business model from a digital business model when data is the foundation for constructing that model?

3 Reconsidering Digital Business Models

The term "digital business model" is commonly used by academics, students, consultants, and managers to describe any approach to conducting business that leverages information and communication technologies, including the internet, to deliver value to customers. However, it is important to recognize that a business model is a conceptual framework that outlines how a business creates and delivers value to its customers (Teece, 2010). Teece defines as a model that "articulates the logic and provides data (…) that demonstrates how a business creates and delivers value" (Teece, 2010, p. 173). Additionally, as Magretta (2002) notes, "business modelling is the managerial equivalent of the scientific method" (Magretta, 2002, p. 90), involving the formulation of hypotheses, data collection, analysis, learning from the results, and adapting the business model as needed based on these insights.

The digital age compels companies to undergo digital transformation, which entails comprehensive changes driven by digitization and digitalization. This transformation focuses on how digital technologies can be strategically leveraged to meet customer needs and secure competitive advantages (Caputo et al., 2021; Verhoef et al., 2021). As organizations increasingly utilize digital technologies, they gain access to more data than ever before (Erevelles et al., 2016), which can enhance decision-making processes. Data utilization has always been a fundamental component of business modelling, and the digital age amplifies this aspect through the generation and application of digital data. Thus, the classification and usage of the term "digital business model" needs to be reconsidered as there is no need to differentiate between business models and digital business models; the managerial task remains the same: effectively using data for business modelling.

A business model serves to explain the rationale behind a company's value proposition and substantiate its ability to create and deliver value to customers. The advent of digital technologies has augmented the availability of data, thereby enhancing the precision and depth of business modelling. This shift brings a new perspective to business models and highlights the managerial responsibility of data utilization.

In summary, there is no such thing as a digital business model; rather, there are business models whose foundations are rooted in a data-centric perspective and management are responsible to foster this perspective and include it in their management practices. Building on the previous discussion, the following theoretical framework (see Fig. 5) is proposed for managing business models in the digital age.

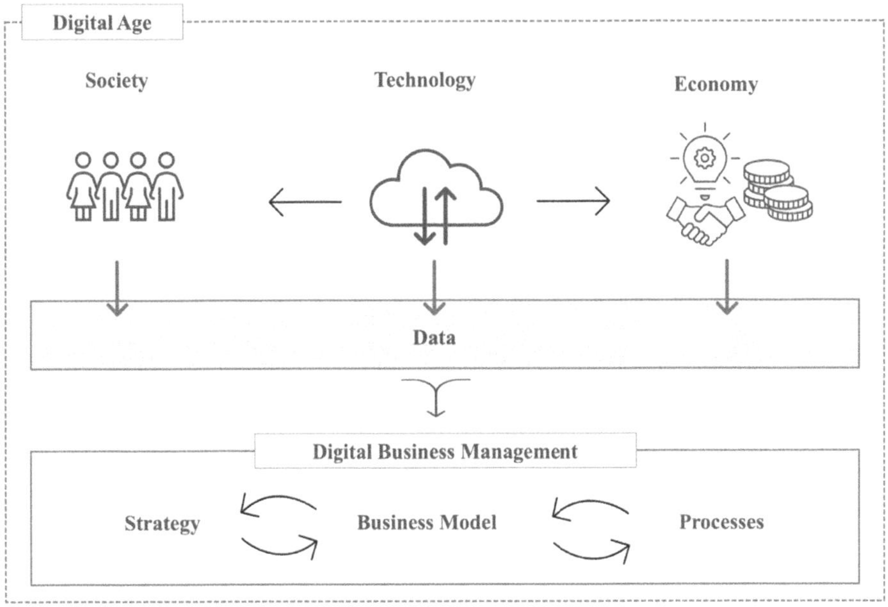

Fig. 5. Theoretical framework for business management in the digital age. Source: Murtagh-Boehm & Wehrstein (2024).

4 Discussion and Conclusion

In the current conversation surrounding digital business models, it is evident that the term has become increasingly vague. This ambiguity can lead to misunderstandings and may obstruct the digital transformation efforts that companies aim to achieve. To effectively promote digital transformation, it is vital to establish clear definitions and precise boundaries for the terminology used.

The term "digital" has been adopted to reflect the zeitgeist of our time; however, it does not necessarily mean that a business operates exclusively in the digital world. Traditionally, business models have always relied on data, even when that data was manually collected and analysed. It is important to recognize that any business model making decisions based on data can be classified as data-driven. In today's increasingly digital world, this data is frequently in digital form. Even businesses that primarily operate offline, such as brick of mortar stores, depend on digital data, like sales information. This leads to the question: Does a business model operating in a digital context differ fundamentally simply because it employs digital technologies? Or is the distinction more about how the data is utilized?

The question of whether a business model in a digital context differs fundamentally due to the use of digital technologies or primarily through data utilization highlights a critical debate in modern business practices. On one hand, digital technologies can fundamentally alter a business model by enabling new ways of delivering products and services, enhancing customer interactions, and streamlining operations. For example, online platforms allow for direct sales to consumers, while automation can improve efficiency and reduce costs. On the other hand, the distinction might be more about how businesses leverage data. In a digital context, companies can collect and analyse vast amounts of data, providing insights into customer behaviour and market trends that were previously inaccessible. This data-driven approach can significantly enhance decision-making and personalized marketing efforts, even if the overarching business model remains similar to traditional counterparts. Ultimately, the discussion centres on whether digital transformation reshapes the very nature of business models or primarily enriches them through improved data use and analysis. The line between technology-based and digital business models is often indistinct. In the digital age, nearly every business model—be it traditional or digital—has some data-driven aspect. The management of these models also occurs within the framework of the digital landscape, blurring the distinctions between traditional and digital strategies. Companies should prioritize customer satisfaction, regardless of whether their operations are online or offline.

A crucial element of any business model is its data foundation. In discussions regarding digital business models, we must remember the insights from experts like Magretta (2002) and Teece (2010) on the importance of data in business frameworks. The concept of digital isn't novel; rather, we leverage digital technologies to enhance the efficiency and effectiveness of our businesses. In conclusion, it is essential to establish clear definitions and distinct terminology in discussions about digital business models. Only then can we effectively advance digital transformation and fully leverage the benefits of digitization.

Hence, one could argue that digital business models are all business models that utilize technologies and digital data to create value, optimize processes, and enhance customer interactions, regardless of whether they take place on digital platforms or use traditional distribution channels.

References

Bächle, M., Dauer, S., Kolb, A.: Einführung in die Wirtschaftsinformatik. De Gruyter (2021)

Bican, P.M., Brem, A.: Digital business model, digital transformation, digital entrepreneurship: is there a sustainable "digital"? Sustainability **12**(13) (2020). Article 13. https://doi.org/10.3390/su12135239

Böttcher, T.P., Weking, J., Hein, A., Böhm, M., Krcmar, H.: Pathways to digital business models: the connection of sensing and seizing in business model innovation. J. Strateg. Inf. Syst. **31**(4), 101742 (2022). https://doi.org/10.1016/j.jsis.2022.101742

Caputo, A., Pizzi, S., Pellegrini, M.M., Dabić, M.: Digitalization and business models: where are we going? A science map of the field. J. Bus. Res. **123**, 489–501 (2021). https://doi.org/10.1016/j.jbusres.2020.09.053

Chaffey, D., Edmundson-Bird, D., Hemphill, T.: Digital Business. 7th edn. Pearson (2019). https://elibrary.pearson.de/book/99.150005/9781292193359

Dillerup, R., Stoi, R.: Unternehmensführung: management & leadership. Strategien, Werkzeuge, Praxis, vol. 5. Franz Vahlen (2016)

Drnevich, P.L., Mahoney, J.T., Schendel, D.: Has strategic management research lost its way? **1**, 35–73 (2020). https://doi.org/10.1561/111.00000004

Erevelles, S., Fukawa, N., Swayne, L.: Big data consumer analytics and the transformation of marketing. J. Bus. Res. **69**(2), 897–904 (2016). https://doi.org/10.1016/j.jbusres.2015.07.001

Horváth, D., Szabó, R.Z.: Driving forces and barriers of Industry 4.0: do multinational and small and medium-sized companies have equal opportunities? Technol. Forecast. Soc. Chang. **146**, 119–132 (2019). https://doi.org/10.1016/j.techfore.2019.05.021

Ismail, M.H., Khater, M., Zaki, M.: Digital business transformation and strategy: What do we know so far. Cambridge Serv. Alliance **10**(1), 1–35 (2017)

Kollmann, T.: Digital Business: Grundlagen von Geschäftsmodellen und -prozessen in der Digitalen Wirtschaft. Springer Fachmedien (2022). https://doi.org/10.1007/978-3-658-37069-5

Kollmann, T., Schmidt, H.: Einführung in die digitale transformation. In: Kollmann, T. (ed.) Handbuch Digitale Wirtschaft, pp. 961–984. Springer Fachmedien (2020). https://doi.org/10.1007/978-3-658-17291-6_67

Kraus, S., Durst, S., Ferreira, J.J., Veiga, P., Kailer, N., Weinmann, A.: Digital transformation in business and management research: an overview of the current status quo. Int. J. Inf. Manage. **63**, 102466 (2022). https://doi.org/10.1016/j.ijinfomgt.2021.102466

Lynn, T., Rosati, P., Conway, E., Curran, D., Fox, G., O'Gorman, C.: Digital Towns: Accelerating and Measuring the Digital Transformation of Rural Societies and Economies. Springer International Publishing (2022). https://doi.org/10.1007/978-3-030-91247-5

Magretta, J.: Why Business Models Matter. Harvard Bus. Rev. (2002). https://hbr.org/2002/05/why-business-models-matter

Menz, M., et al.: Corporate strategy and the theory of the firm in the digital age. J. Manage. Stud. **58**(7), 1695–1720 (2021). https://doi.org/10.1111/joms.12760

Perelygina, M., Kucukusta, D., Law, R.: Digital business model configurations in the travel industry. Tour. Manage. **88**, 104408 (2022). https://doi.org/10.1016/j.tourman.2021.104408

Philbeck, T., Davis, N.: The fourth industrial revolution: shaping a new era. J. Int. Aff. **72**(1), 17–22 (2019). Business Source Ultimate. https://search.ebscohost.com/login.aspx?direct=true&AuthType=sso&db=bsu&AN=134748789&site=eds-live&scope=site&custid=s6068579

Schwab, K.: The Fourth Industrial Revolution. Crown (2017). https://books.google.de/books?id=GVekDQAAQBAJ

Schwartz, E.I.: Digital Darwinism: 7 Breakthrough Business Strategies for Surviving in the Cutthroat Web Economy. Crown (2002). https://books.google.de/books?id=S4r5INmK6gkC

Shapiro, C., Varian, H.R.: Information Rules. Harvard Business School Press, A strategic guide to the network economy (1999)

Teece, D.J.: Business models, business strategy and innovation. Long Range Plan. **43**(2–3), 172–194 (2010)

Teece, D.J.: Business models and dynamic capabilities. Long Range Plan. **51**(1), 40–49 (2018). https://doi.org/10.1016/j.lrp.2017.06.007

Teece, D.J.: Profiting from innovation in the digital economy: enabling technologies, standards, and licensing models in the wireless world. Res. Policy **47**(8), 1367–1387 (2018). https://doi.org/10.1016/j.respol.2017.01.015

Veit, D., et al.: Business models. Bus. Inf. Syst. Eng. **6**(1), 45–53 (2014). https://doi.org/10.1007/s12599-013-0308-y

Verhoef, P.C., et al.: Digital transformation: a multidisciplinary reflection and research agenda. J. Bus. Res. **122**, 889–901 (2021)

Weill, P., Woerner, S.L.: Optimizing your digital business model. MIT Sloan Manag. Rev. (2013)

Wirtz, B.W.: Digital Business Models: Concepts, Models, and the Alphabet Case Study. Springer (2019)

Zeng, M.L.: Smart data for digital humanities. J. Data Inf. Sci. **2**, 1–12 (2017). https://api.semanticscholar.org/CorpusID:63569460

Zott, C., Amit, R., Massa, L.: The business model: recent developments and future research. J. Manag. **37**(4), 1019–1042) (2011)

The Use of AI in Energy Utility Companies: A Case Study on Potential Fields of Application and Impact on Innovation

Larissa Pfeifer[1(✉)], Carolin Egger[2], Mirko Bendig[3], and Irina Tiemann[1]

[1] IU Internationale Hochschule GmbH, Bremen, Germany
larissa.pfeifer1@iubh-fernstudium.de, irina.tiemann@iu.org
[2] IU Internationale Hochschule GmbH, Bad Reichenhall, Germany
carolin.egger@iu.org
[3] IU Internationale Hochschule GmbH, Hamburg, Germany
mirko.bendig@iu.org

Abstract. Innovation management is crucial for the competitiveness and success of companies across various sectors. Incorporating sustainability into innovation is increasingly essential as stakeholders demand more sustainable solutions. This integration requires a comprehensive approach, considering the complexities of sustainability and the innovation process. Artificial intelligence (AI) offers promising tools to enhance sustainability in innovation management, improving efficiency, and facilitating decision-making. However, AI also presents challenges such as ethical, environmental, and legal implications, necessitating responsible and transparent use.

The energy industry exemplifies the intersection of innovation, sustainability, and AI. Driven by Germany's energy transition initiative ("Energiewende"), which began in 2011, the industry is transitioning from traditional to renewable energy sources like wind, solar, and biomass. This transition requires utility companies to adopt innovative approaches, moving from centralized to decentralized energy generation.

This study explores AI applications within one of Germany's top five utility companies, with a significant share of renewable energy. The company's activities span various sectors including energy networks, telecommunications, IT, mobility, and hydrogen, presenting multiple AI application fields. The research investigates how AI can drive innovation, and the capabilities required for leveraging AI in innovation. The methodology includes a literature review and a case study, involving semi-structured interviews with experts from different departments of a utility company. Eight interviews were conducted and analyzed using qualitative content analysis.

The results show that AI can play a significant role in fostering innovation throughout the innovation process, if it is combined with the application of specialized AI skills, as well as domain-specific knowledge and process understanding. Effective use of AI could drive not only process and product innovations but also the transformation of entire business models. Practical recommendations include providing employees with hands-on experimentation opportunities, implementing AI toolkits to reduce concerns, and launching pilot projects to identify use cases. Furthermore, organizations must build digital competencies and maintain

R. C. Geibel and S. Machavariani (Eds.): ISPC 2024, SPBE, pp. 31–47, 2025.
https://doi.org/10.1007/978-3-031-88052-0_3

a realistic understanding of AI's capabilities to leverage its long-term benefits effectively. To address limitations and test the generalizability of findings, future research could involve quantitative studies across a larger sample of energy utility companies and expand to other industries for a broader understanding of AI's role in supporting innovation processes.

Keywords: Digitalization · Artificial Intelligence · Utility Companies · Innovation · Sustainability

1 Introduction

Innovation has long been a critical driver of competitiveness and success for companies across diverse industries. Today, innovation plays a key role in managing the massive transformation due to the challenges of the global climate crisis. This is true even and especially for the energy industry. An illustrative example is the German energy industry, influenced by the energy transition initiative ("Energiewende") launched in 2011, which is undergoing a fundamental transformation from traditional fossil fuel-based energy sources to renewable ones such as wind, solar, and biomass (Krebs & Hagenweiler, 2021, p. 2–3; Parthie, 2022, p. 15; Pittel, 2012, p. 22). This transition demands not only the adoption of renewable energy technologies but also the rethinking of how energy is generated, distributed, and consumed. Energy utility companies (utility companies) play a central role in this shift, and their ability to innovate is crucial for advancing the energy transition. As these companies move from centralized energy production models to decentralized, renewable-based systems, they face both technical and operational challenges that require customer-centric and innovative solutions (Doleski, 2020, p. 33, 35).

Due to the challenges through its transformation, the German energy sector provides a compelling case study for examining the intersection of AI, innovation, and sustainability. The utility companies face increasingly complex challenges, the ability to innovate effectively has become even more vital. Within this landscape, integrating sustainability into the innovation process has emerged as a key focus, largely driven by growing stakeholder demands for environmentally and socially responsible solutions (Elkington 1998, Preuss 2007, Roth 2009). This shift necessitates a holistic approach to innovation, one that accounts for both the technological advancements and the environmental and societal impacts of new developments. Among the various tools that are reshaping innovation, artificial intelligence (AI) has gained prominence due to its potential to enhance efficiency, improve decision-making, and enable more sustainable solutions (Füller et al. 2022, Tekic & Füller 2023, Holmström & Carroll 2024).

In the context of sustainability-focused innovation, AI offers a range of promising applications. By processing vast amounts of data, identifying patterns, and optimizing complex systems, AI can facilitate innovation management processes, enabling companies to make more informed, data-driven decisions. However, the integration of AI into innovation is not without challenges. As the use of AI grows, ethical, environmental, and legal considerations must be addressed to ensure responsible and transparent deployment (Kar et al. 2022, Vaio et al. 2020, van Wynsberghe 2021). These concerns are particularly relevant in the energy sector, where sustainability is paramount.

AI offers significant potential for addressing these challenges in the energy industry, particularly in supporting the innovation processes of utility companies. By leveraging AI technologies, energy companies can improve the efficiency of their operations, optimize resource management, and accelerate the development of new sustainable energy solutions. Furthermore, AI can enhance key stages of the innovation process, from idea generation to prototyping and beyond, by offering predictive insights and streamlining complex decision-making (Bouschery et al. 2023, Bilgram & Laarmann 2023, Bilgram et al. 2023, Bendig et al. 2024).

This paper investigates how AI can drive sustainable innovation, the associated opportunities and risks, and the capabilities required for leveraging AI in innovation. Hereby, it explores the use of AI within one of Germany's top five utility companies, with a specific focus on its potential applications and impact on innovation and sustainability. The company in question has a substantial portfolio of renewable energy activities and operates across various sectors, including energy networks, telecommunications, IT, mobility, and hydrogen. This diversity presents multiple fields where AI can be applied to drive innovation and support the company's broader sustainability goals. To sum up, the paper aims to answer the following research questions:

(1) Which phases of the innovation process benefit the most from AI, and how can utility companies use this to create innovative business models and innovations? (2) How does AI help to promote different types of innovation in utility companies? (3) What new capabilities are needed to create innovations with AI in the context of innovation in the energy sector?

The structure of this paper is as follows: First, a literature review outlines the current state of research on AI, innovation, and sustainability, focusing especially on the linkages between them: AI applications in the energy sector and its role in innovation management. This is followed by a description of the research methodology, particularly the expert interviews conducted within the selected utility company. The findings from these interviews are then analyzed to identify key areas where AI can drive innovation in this context. Finally, the paper concludes with actionable recommendations for effectively deploying AI technologies in utility companies, ensuring that these innovations support the broader energy transition and contribute to a sustainable future.

2 Theoretical Foundation

The theoretical framework of this paper focuses on three aspects: AI, innovation, and sustainability. Therefore, the following sections show the basic concepts and theories and form the basis for their interaction.

2.1 Artificial Intelligence

The foundations of today's artificial intelligence (AI) technology date back to antiquity, with Aristotle first establishing rules for rational thought and formal logic (Russell & Norvig, 2022, p. 24). Alan Turing advanced these ideas, proposing the concept of machine intelligence in his 1950 work "Computing Machinery and Intelligence," introducing what is now known as the Turing Test (Turing 1950). The term "artificial intelligence" was coined in 1956 by John McCarthy and colleagues during the Dartmouth Summer Research Project on AI (McCarthy et al. 1955).

AI technology includes key sub-areas such as weak AI, strong AI, and superintelligence, each with different levels of complexity and autonomy (Häfner & Morf 2019; Neu et al. 2022). Machine learning (ML) and deep learning (DL) are central components, where ML allows machines to learn from data, and DL uses multi-layered neural networks for complex data pattern recognition (BDEW 2020; Häfner & Morf 2019). AI applications have numerous capabilities, including computer vision, natural language processing, and system control (BDEW 2020). However, integrating AI poses challenges such as data quality, cybersecurity, and the need for technical expertise (Danish 2023). The European Union's AI Act aims to regulate AI technology by categorizing risk levels and ensuring legal certainty (European Commission 2023).

The energy sector offers various AI applications in generation, trading, storage, transport, and sales. For instance, AI predicts production from renewable energy sources and optimizes energy trading strategies (Hamid & Ganne 2023; epilot 2023). Predictive maintenance and grid stability are also improved using AI (Hamid & Ganne 2023; Kreutzer & Sirrenberg 2019). Despite recognizing AI's potential, energy companies often face integration challenges due to insufficient data management and technical infrastructure (Aichele 2021; Danish 2023). Addressing these challenges can help leverage AI for improved efficiency and innovation while navigating accompanying risks (Wang 2023; Russell & Norvig, 2022).

2.2 Innovation

Innovation consists of two parts: the development of an idea or invention and its realisation in a business project or useful application (Roberts, 2007, p. 36). Disselkamp (2017, pp. 17–18) emphasises the applicability and perceived novelty of an innovation, listing features such as benefit advantage, originality, and the type of innovation. He differentiates between product and process innovation. Product innovations involve newly developed or improved products, services, or concepts that customers value and purchase (Disselkamp, 2017, p. 21; Hauschildt et al., 2016, p. 6). They aim at external markets to achieve effectiveness (Hauschildt et al., 2016, p. 6). Process innovations focus on internal improvements in production, core, or support processes, enhancing efficiency, customer satisfaction, safety, and environmental protection (Hauschildt et al., 2016, p. 6; Vahs et al., 2023, pp. 73–91; Disselkamp, 2017, p. 24). They utilize new resource combinations for cost, quality, reliability, or speed benefits (Hauschildt et al., 2016, p. 6). Another distinction is usually seen in incremental innovations which refine existing markets and technologies, while disruptive or radical innovations create market breakthroughs (Dodgson et al., 2014, p. 6; Salter & Alexy, 2014, p. 31).

Ideas transition to innovations through a structured process comprising various phases. Rogers (2003, Chapter 4 outlines a six-phase innovation process encompassing need recognition, R&D, marketing, dissemination, user acceptance, and consequences.

Hauschildt et al. (2016, pp. 21–22) propose a seven-phase model: ideation, discoveries, theoretical research, invention definition, prototype development, market introduction, and ongoing commercialisation. Osterwalder and Pigneur (2011, p. 253) present a five-phase business model approach: Mobilise, Understanding, Design, Implement, and Monitoring. Tidd and Bessant (2011, p. 72) detail a four-phase process: searching for opportunities or risks, decision-making, transformation through implementation, and value maintenance. Despite differing phase delineations, a consensus exists among different authors and scientists that the innovation process generally includes the four phases of idea generation, concept development, testing/prototyping, and implementation (Hauschildt et al., 2016, p. 22, Tidd and Bessant, 2011, p. 72), Osterwalder and Pigneur 2011, p. 253, Vahs et al., 2023, p. 291).

AI can enhance the innovation process by identifying relevant needs and efficient solutions early on (Füller et al., 2022, p. 3; Haefner et al., 2021, pp. 2–4). It can also help in idea evaluation and selection without bias (Brem et al., 2023, p. 774). In concept development, AI accelerates prototype creation and testing (Bilgram & Laarmann, 2023, p. 19). AI's influence necessitates reorganising innovation teams to collaborate closely with data scientists (Füller et al., 2022, p. 5; Kakatkar et al., 2020, p. 181). The use of AI in innovation management holds high disruptive potential (Füller et al., 2022, p. 5) and may evolve through stages from supporting human decision-makers to partially replacing them in generating innovative ideas (Haefner et al., 2021, p. 6). However, the technology's maturity for fully autonomous integration remains a future prospect.

2.3 Sustainable Business Models

Over the past decade, the innovation management discourse has shifted its focus from products, services, corporate resources and capabilities, and revenue models to a more strategic and comprehensive view of business models. (Baden-Fuller & Morgan, 2010, Wirtz et al., 2016). There are numerous definitions of the term business model in the literature, generally agreeing that a business model outlines how an organisation creates value for itself and its customers (Gassmann et al., 2013, pp. 176–177; Osterwalder & Pigneur, 2011, p. 18; Schallmo, 2018, p. 18; Vahs et al., 2023, pp. 73–91). Simultaneously, the limitations of purely profit-driven business models have become apparent, while the potential and promise of sustainability-oriented business models (SBMs) have been increasingly identified and discussed (e.g., Kiron et al., 2013, Schaltegger et al., 2016, Breuer et. al. 2018, Lang-Koetz et al., 2023). The idea of doing good as a company is not entirely new. In their groundbreaking article "Creating Shared Value", published in the Harvard Business Review in 2011, Porter and Kramer (2011) present the concept of a value-based organisation of economic activities. The basic idea is that companies should not only generate profits while minimising the social and environmental impact of their actions, but rather actively work to create shared value for society and the company. Porter and Kramer (2011, p. 17) argue that instead of a mutual balancing of corporate goals and social needs, a synergy should be created in which economic success and social good are promoted simultaneously.

Technologies are critical drivers for business model innovations (Kreutzer, 2017, p. 45), including data analytics, cloud computing, social media, Internet of Things, and blockchain (Pflaum & Schulz, 2019, p. 5; Sauer et al., 2019, p. 24). AI is anticipated to dominate future market offerings via intelligent products and services (Kett et al., 2021, p. 58; Pflaum & Schulz, 2019, p. 17). Integration of AI enhances services through personalisation, automation, flexibility, and convenience (Kett et al., 2021, p. 64), necessitating companies to adapt their business models to evolving customer needs (Kett et al., 2021, p. 66).

In the energy sector, traditional offerings like electricity and gas lack differentiation, compelling companies to innovate (Aichele, 2021, p. 153). One promising direction is the integration of decentralized energy assets, such as solar, wind, batteries, heat pumps and e-mobility, as well as the creation of new business models such as regional energy communities (Ibarra et al. 2023). These business models promote localized, sustainable energy generation and distribution, enabling both individual households and communities to produce, store, and trade energy. The complexity of managing such decentralized systems makes AI a crucial enabler. AI can support new product development (Aichele, 2021, p. 154), and enable energy production and consumption data analysis for internal and external use (Aichele, 2021, pp. 156–157). Digital technologies have already begun transforming the energy sector (Bertoli, 2022), and AI's role is key in handling the intricacies of decentralized energy solutions, empowering utility companies to make sustainability a core part of their strategies.

2.4 Research Gap and Deriving Research Questions and Assumptions

Despite significant advancements in AI and its applications, a comprehensive understanding of how AI fosters innovation within energy utility companies remains underexplored. The literature underscores AI's potential to enhance various stages of the innovation process, yet specific insights into its practical implementations and the resulting effects on both product and process innovations are sparse. This gap necessitates a detailed examination of AI's role in innovation management, which in turn forms the basis for the authors' research inquiries.

Therefore, the first research question mentioned in the introduction aims to elucidate the extent to which AI facilitates innovation in companies, probing whether AI indeed creates added value across all phases of the innovation process, as posited in Assumption 1: AI can be used to create added value in all phases of the innovation process and provide the necessary capabilities.

The second question seeks to identify the specific domains where AI can spawn innovative business models and innovations, aligning with Assumption 2: AI can be used in both product and process innovations.

Further, the third question investigates the emergent competencies required to leverage AI for innovation, thereby reflecting Assumption 3: New capabilities are needed to create innovations with AI.

These research questions and assumptions collectively aim to bridge the existing theoretical gap by offering a structured analysis of AI's transformative potential in the energy sector, particularly in the context of fostering innovation and developing sustainable business models.

3 Research Method

This research adopts a qualitative case study approach, using expert interviews to gather in-depth insights into the use of artificial intelligence (AI) in utility companies. The case study is used to explore specific characteristics of an individual company rather than aiming for generalizable results across all cases (Kaiser, 2021, p. 7). This approach allows for a detailed understanding of AI applications within a particular context, which can lead to the development or adjustment of relevant theories based on the findings.

The research questions are addressed using a case study of one of the five largest utility companies in Germany. The company is selected because its size, sectoral diversity, and emphasis on renewable energy make it a valuable subject for exploring AI potential for sustainable business. Located in northwestern Germany, the company integrates a large amount of renewable energy into its electricity grid and operates across various business sectors, including energy networks, telecommunications, IT, mobility, and hydrogen. These diverse business areas provide multiple potential applications for AI, making the case study particularly relevant for this research.

After establishing the theoretical foundations, expert interviews are initiated, which are well-suited for gathering expert knowledge on specific topics (Gläser & Laudel, 2006, p. 38; Meuser & Nagel, 2009, p. 465). The selection of experts plays a crucial role in determining the quality of the information gathered (Gläser & Laudel, 2006, p. 113; Jäger & Reinecke, 2009, p. 47). The experts are chosen based on their professional roles and experience with digital technologies, particularly AI, within their respective business areas.

To capture a comprehensive view of the utility company, experts from various departments and business areas, including both technical and commercial sectors, as well as different hierarchical levels, are interviewed. This diversity of perspectives helps to ensure a well-rounded analysis of AI potential within the company, despite not covering all areas of the business. In total, seven internal interviews are conducted, along with one interview with an expert from another major German utility company, to gain an external perspective (see Table 1).

Table 1. Overview of the expert interviews conducted

Interview partner	Interview role and business area	Date
IP1	Head of the Business Innovation Group	13.02.2024
IP2	Employee in the IT department	14.02.2024
IP3	Head of the storage business	14.02.2024
IP4	Sales employee	16.02.2024
IP5	Head of grid business	19.02.2024
IP6	External IP: Project manager in data strategy	26.02.2024
IP7	Member of the Executive Board	28.02.2024
IP8	Employee in Human Resource	07.03.2024

Source: Own illustration

The interviews are conducted between February 13 and March 7, 2024, via Microsoft Teams. On average, each interview last 36 min. Audio recordings are transcribed immediately after the interviews using the transcription feature in Microsoft Word, which provide full transcripts with timestamps. The transcription process follows the guidelines set by Gläser and Laudel (2006, pp. 188–189). Following the transcription, all texts are reviewed, and any errors generated during the automated transcription process are corrected. In the final step, the transcriptions are anonymized, ensuring that the identity of the interview participants could no longer be determined (Gläser & Laudel, 2006, p. 189).

The gathered data is analyzed using qualitative content analysis (Kuckartz & Rädiker, 2022, p. 39). The analysis follows a content-structuring qualitative approach, which involves categorizing and coding the information using a predefined coding system. This method allows for a systematic evaluation of the data while ensuring transparency and adherence to scientific standards (Gläser & Laudel, 2006, pp. 43–44). By applying a deductive-inductive approach, both theory-driven and data-driven insights are integrated into the analysis process, providing a comprehensive understanding of the AI potential in the case study (Kuckartz & Rädiker, 2022, p. 132). The categorization system is hierarchical, consisting of main and subcategories, and is refined through continuous verification against the research questions (Kuckartz & Rädiker, 2022, pp. 62, 102). The coding process is carried out using MAXQDA software.

4 Analysis and Results

To answer the first research question, the interview partners are asked to assess the potential of AI in different phases of the four-phase innovation process. To structure the analysis, the following categories are deductively derived from the theory: the main category of AI use in the innovation process, with the corresponding subcategories of idea generation, concept development, prototyping & testing, and implementation.

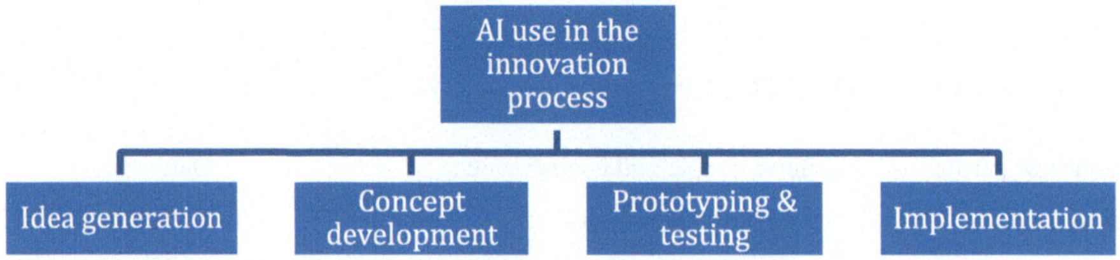

Fig. 1. Coding categories research question 1. Source: Own illustration.

Most experts confirm that AI could be used in all phases and provide examples for each.

- Idea generation: AI is seen as particularly useful in the generation and collection of ideas, acting as a "sparring partner" for idea research and helping to identify trends and relevant data (IP1-3, 5, 6, 8). However, some experts indicate that AI tends to combine existing concepts rather than generate entirely new ideas (IP3, 5).

- Concept development: Experts find it harder to envision AI's role here. AI could support pre-structuring ideas or recommending methods for further development (IP1, 5), but human judgment remains critical in this phase (IP5, 6, 8).
- Prototyping and testing: AI is seen as useful for quickly visualizing ideas through image generation, creating program code for prototypes, and generating AI-based personas to test prototypes (IP2–6). AI helps to reduce errors and iteration loops (IP3, 5).
- Implementation: Similar to the concept development, AI's role is seen as more limited by the importance of human decisions. However, experts predict future advancements in AI for marketing and product launch strategies (IP5).

When asked to select the phase with the highest potential for AI use, most of the experts chooses idea generation (IP1, 3, 7, 8), followed by prototyping and testing (IP2, 5, 6), with a few also emphasizing the potential in the concept development and implementation phase (IP4, 5).

To answer the second research question, the interview partners are asked to evaluate whether AI has greater potential for driving product innovations or process innovations within the energy supply company. To structure the analysis, the following categories are deductively derived from theory: the main category of type of innovation, with the corresponding subcategories process innovation and product innovation.

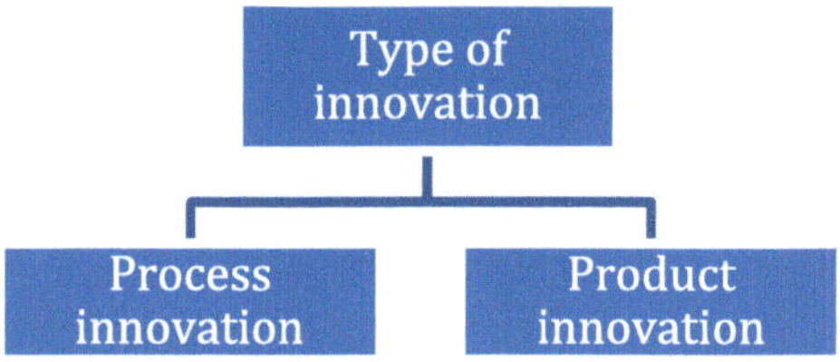

Fig. 2. Coding categories research question 2. Source: Own illustration.

Process innovations: All experts emphasize the significant potential of AI to optimize internal processes. They mention various advantages, including increased efficiency, cost savings, and improved customer service. AI's role in streamlining operations is seen as crucial, as smoother processes provide the foundation for the development of innovative products. For instance, IP1 and IP6 highlighted that internal process improvements should come first, allowing the company to operate more effectively and enabling quicker market introduction of new products. Other experts (IP2, IP3, IP5) also stress that AI could lead to better resource allocation, allowing the company to handle higher process loads expected in the future.

Product innovations: While potential of AI to optimize product innovations are not seen as main focus by the experts for the utility company under study, a few experts (IP1, IP3, IP7) acknowledge AI's potential in this area, especially for hardware-based products like solar systems or AI-enhanced services such as dynamic electricity tariffs. However, experts like IP3 are sceptical about the company's ability to compete with existing market solutions in these product fields, suggesting that external partnerships or acquisitions may be more effective. IP2 also states that AI's primary contribution to product innovation might lie in creating unique selling points to enhance customer loyalty.

In conclusion, although experts recognize AI's potential to contribute to both product and process innovations, all agree that the greatest potential lies in process innovations, though some acknowledged AI's value for both innovation types. Optimizing internal operations with AI is seen as critical for boosting efficiency, reducing costs, and ultimately enabling the energy supply company to remain competitive in a rapidly evolving market.

To address the third research question, the interviewees are asked to identify the skills and resources required to fully leverage AI's potential. The responses regarding competence requirements for AI implementation are derived inductively from the interviews and organized into three key subcategories: basic digital skills, specialized AI skills, and process and contextual understanding.

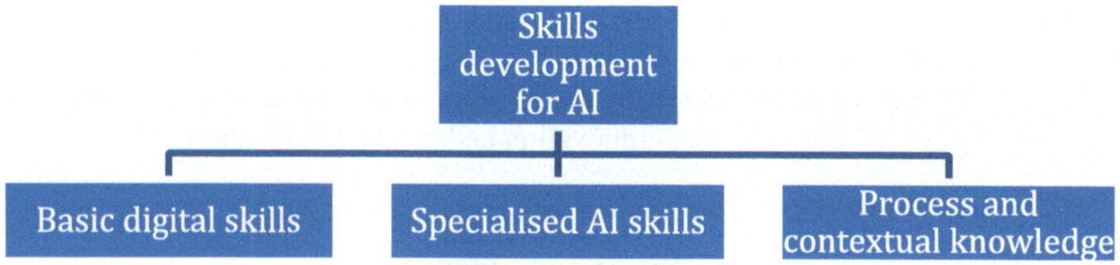

Fig. 3. Coding categories research question 3 Source: Own illustration.

Basic Digital Skills: Experts emphasize the need for basic digital literacy across the entire organization, ensuring that all employees have a fundamental understanding of data and its effects. While not everyone needs to become a data scientist, a general openness to digital topics and data literacy is essential (IP1, IP5, IP6). Additionally, developing AI literacy is noted as critical to assess AI's opportunities and risks (IP2), with data protection also needing attention (IP4).

Specialized AI Skills: For employees directly involved in AI initiatives, more advanced training is required. This includes expertise in cloud-based AI, machine learning (ML), and IT architecture (IP2, IP5, IP7). Specific roles like Cloud AI Engineers are highlighted, who must be skilled in evaluating AI models, identifying use cases, and managing AI systems (IP2, IP7). There is also a need for developing AI models tailored to the energy sector (IP7). Data science skills, already being developed in the company, are seen as vital to fully realize AI's potential (IP1-4).

Understanding Processes and Context: Some experts stress that in addition to technical skills, employees must have a deep understanding of internal processes to effectively identify where AI can provide solutions, such as optimizing inefficient processes (IP3, IP4).

Experts also highlight the importance of leadership development in AI skills, noting that upskilling must occur at all levels, including management (IP6). Skills development can happen through internal training or recruitment, depending on the company's needs

(IP8). However, the HR department did not confirm the existence of a formal skills catalog for AI-specific roles (IP8).

In conclusion, a mix of basic digital literacy, advanced AI skills, and process understanding is crucial for the successful integration of AI into the company's operations.

5 Discussion and Recommendations

To examine the first research assumption findings from the literature and expert interviews are used to analyze the use of AI across the four phases of the innovation process. The literature and expert interviews agree that AI can be applied in all phases of the innovation process, with the greatest potential seen in idea generation phase. Studies by Füller et al. (2022) and Haefner et al. (2021) highlight AI's ability to process vast amounts of data, identify problems, and find solutions efficiently. This view is echoed by the experts (IP1-3), who noted that AI can generate ideas that humans may overlook, serving as a "sparring partner" in research (IP1-3; IP5; IP6; IP8). Mülroth and Grottke (2022) also argue that AI can recognize trends earlier than traditional tools like the Gartner Hype Cycle, a statement supported by IP5 and IP8. However, Bilgram and Laarmann (2023) caution that AI-generated ideas can be superficial, a concern shared by experts (IP3; IP5), as AI often recombines existing concepts rather than creating novel ideas.

In the concept development phase, both the literature and experts see fewer AI applications. However, AI can assist in unbiased idea selection, as decisions can be based on data (Brem et al., 2023; Füller et al., 2022; Haefner et al., 2021). Experts identify AI's potential for pre-structuring ideas (IP1) and recommending methods to assess feasibility (IP5). Despite these benefits, the role of AI in this phase is seen as limited, as human judgment remains crucial in decision-making (IP5; IP6; IP8). A balance between AI insights and human expertise is still necessary for a successful concept development.

In the prototyping and testing phase, there is a broad agreement that AI can significantly accelerate and enhance the process (Bilgram & Laarmann, 2023; IP2–6). Both literature and experts emphasize AI's role in rapid prototype development and testing, such as using AI for image generation or coding (Brem et al., 2023; Füller et al., 2022; IP5). AI can also evaluate prototypes through AI-generated personas or tools like ChatGPT (Bilgram & Laarmann, 2023; IP2; IP6).

The implementation phase offers so far fewer examples in both the literature and expert interviews. Brynjolfsson and McAfee (2017) and Kreutzer and Sirrenberg (2019) highlight AI's potential in targeted marketing strategies, a use case confirmed by IP5. Experts indicate that AI's role in implementation is similar to the concept development, where human input remains critical (IP4; IP6). However, IP5 suggests that future advancements in AI could expand its role in this phase by combining AI's analytical abilities with human creativity.

Using the evolutionary stages of AI elaborated by Haefner et al. (2021) the findings here indicate that the integration and usage of AI in the innovation management shows a collaborative approach between AI and the persons involved, especially in the steps of idea generation and prototyping. This implies that the evolutionary stage of "Expanding" is already achieved in this case (Haefner et al., 2021).

To evaluate the second research assumption, expert interviews are analyzed concerning AI's potential for innovation in the energy supply company. All experts (IP1-8) confirm that the greatest potential for AI innovations lies in process innovations, which is critical for enabling product innovation later. Functional, efficient processes are necessary to introduce innovative products quickly and successfully (IP1), with particular focus on enhancing customer satisfaction through streamlined processes (IP2, IP4). While AI's use for product innovation is not dismissed by the experts, they see emphasized a greater need for process improvements beforehand.

These ambiguous results may be attributed to several factors. Firstly, the results may be case-specific to the company in question or to the energy sector as a whole. This is due to factors such as the presence of complex processes, a lack of progress in optimising and digitalising processes, and the high level of requirements in the industry, including those related to security, documentation and certification requirements. Secondly, the ambiguous results may be attributed to the fact that AI-driven innovations can fundamentally reshape entire business models. This makes the distinction between product and process innovation more complex. This is particularly relevant for sustainable business models, which are inherently more intricate and often require a systemic approach (Bocken et al., 2019). In the context of sustainable innovations, a more holistic consideration of business models is essential, encompassing sustainability orientation, extended value creation, systemic thinking, and the integration of stakeholders (Breuer et. al., 2018). These factors blur the lines between discrete innovation types and necessitate a broader understanding of how AI impacts not just individual components but the entire business model.

The third research assumption, addressing skills required for AI-driven innovation, draws on both the literature and expert interviews. There is consensus that basic digital skills are foundational for handling data effectively and setting the stage for AI adoption (Büchel et al., 2023; Demary & Mertens, 2023; IP1, IP5, IP6). These skills include understanding data structures, interpreting statistics, and data analysis (Davenport, 2019). In addition to digital literacy, IP2 stresses the importance of basic AI skills to ensure that employees use AI safely and effectively.

Moreover, the need for specialized AI skills is highlighted (IP6, IP7), such as developing energy sector-specific AI models and operating AI systems (IP2, IP7). However, both the literature and experts agree that not every employee needs to be an AI specialist (Kirschner & Thompson, 2024; IP5). AI competence should be distributed strategically across the company, with focused expertise in critical areas.

In addition to technical skills, process and contextual knowledge are necessary for successfully applying AI in industry (IP3, IP4). According to Davenport (2019), this expertise enables companies to target AI applications effectively. However, while AI can enhance some skills, it may also disrupt or eliminate existing roles (Paschen et al., 2020), highlighting the need for companies to adapt proactively (Morandini et al., 2023).

The experts under study here (IP8) and academic scholars suggest the development of a skills catalogue that outlines the competencies required for working with AI. If such a catalogue does not exist, it should be developed, and skill gaps should be addressed through training and development programs (Morandini et al., 2023). In conclusion, AI has significant potential to drive innovation in business models and processes, but its successful implementation depends on equipping employees with the right blend of basic and specialized skills, along with industry-specific process knowledge.

6 Conclusions, Limitations and Further Research

In summary, AI can play a significant role in fostering innovation throughout the innovation process, if it is combined with the application of specialized AI skills, as well as domain-specific knowledge and process understanding. The effective utilisation of AI has the potential to drive process and product innovations, as well as the transformation of entire business models. In the energy industry, the current focus is on process innovation, which can be attributed to factors such as the complexity of processes, the lack of progress in digitalisation, and the high level of requirements in the industry. The current state of AI in supporting innovation within companies suggests that AI has evolved to play a collaborative role. The findings suggest that some organizations have already reached the "Expanding" stage of AI evolution, where human-AI collaboration enhances creativity and efficiency in innovation processes. However, critical perspectives highlight concerns over the current capabilities of the AI, the risk of diminishing human agency, and challenges in decision-making based solely on AI. Looking forward, future advancements may see AI taking a more autonomous role in innovation management, yet careful consideration must be given to balancing automation with human oversight, ensuring that AI continues to complement rather than replace human creativity, particularly in the context of sustainable innovations.

The findings of this research are intended to provide utility companies with practical guidance on harnessing the potential of AI, enabling them to successfully navigate an increasingly digital and competitive landscape. The results height that employees should be given sufficient time to familiarize themselves with the technology through hands-on experimentation in a controlled environment. Providing an AI toolkit can help reduce fears and reservations by encouraging experimentation. Pilot projects with diverse user groups should be initiated to identify practical use cases. It is also essential to equip the organization with the necessary digital competencies and establish a realistic understanding of AI's capabilities to avoid overestimating short-term benefits while recognizing the long-term potential.

Despite the valuable insights, several limitations of the work could be acknowledged. First, the focus on a single utility company limits the generalizability of the findings to the whole energy utility sector in Germany or beyond. While the case study offers a deep exploration of AI applications in the specific context under study, the results may not fully reflect the dynamics of other companies or sectors. Additionally, the use of qualitative expert interviews might contain a degree of subjectivity, particularly as the selected experts displayed a strong enthusiasm for AI.

Therefore, one approach for future research is to validate the assumptions and findings of the exploratory approach here. One option would be to address the limitations by conducting quantitative studies across a larger sample of energy utility companies to test the generalizability of the findings. Expanding the scope to include other industries or companies would also provide a more comprehensive understanding of how AI can support innovation processes in different contexts. Furthermore, it is of interest to survey the awareness, the degree of utilisation, and the current and future relevance of the respective AI tools in corporate innovation management beyond a sector focus. Also, investigating the role of AI in different types of innovation, such as product innovation, could reveal varying levels of importance and applicability depending on the sector. Future research should explicitly focus on business models as the primary unit of analysis, particularly in the context of AI-driven innovations. A deeper exploration of how AI can support sustainable business models is essential to better understand the role of AI in fostering sustainability-oriented innovations. This includes examining how AI can facilitate extended value creation, stakeholder integration, and systemic thinking within these models.

References

Aichele, C.: KI-Technologien für Utility-Unternehmen. In Betriebswirtschaftliche KI-Anwendungen: Digitale Geschäftsmodelle auf Basis Künstlicher Intelligenz (S. 153–165). Springer Fachmedien Wiesbaden (2021). https://doi.org/10.1007/978-3-658-33532-8

Baden-Fuller, C., Morgan, M.: Business models as models. Long Range Plan. **43**(2/3), 156–171 (2010)

BDEW: Künstliche Intelligenz für die Energiewirtschaft (2020). https://www.bdew.de/energie/digitalisierung/kuenstliche-intelligenz-fuer-die-energiewirtschaft/

Bendig, M., Tiemann, I., Egger, C., Koloska, K.: Nachhaltigkeit als notwendiges Kriterium im Innovationsmanagement: Wie KI-Tools neue Wege eröffnen und Nachhaltigkeitsorientierung im Entwicklungsprozess erleichtern. In: Just, V., Bodemann, M., Paul, A., Weber, J. (Editors). Innovative Nachhaltigkeit, Springer (2024). (in publication)

Bertoli, E. (07. Januar 2022). The potential of digital business models in the new energy economy. IEA. https://www.iea.org/articles/the-potential-of-digital-business-models-in-the-new-energy-economy

Bilgram, V., Laarmann, F.: Accelerating innovation with generative AI: AI-augmented digital prototyping and innovation methods. IEEE Eng. Manage. Rev. **51**(2), 18–25 (2023). https://doi.org/10.1109/EMR.2023.3272799

Bilgram, V., Link, D., Lang-Koetz, C.: Generative KIs in Kreativprozessen: Praxiserfahrungen aus den ersten Monaten mit ChatGPT & Co. Ideen- und Innovationsmanagement (2023)

Bilgram, V., Laarmann, F.: Accelerating innovation with generative AI: AI-augmented digital prototyping and innovation methods. IEEE Eng. Manage. Rev. **51**, 18–25 (2023)

Bocken, N.M., Boons, F., Baldassarre, B.: Sustainable business model experimentation by understanding ecologies of business models. J. Cleaner Prod. (2019)

Bouschery, S.G., Blazevic, V., Piller, F.T.: Augmenting human innovation teams with artificial intelligence: exploring transformer-based language models. J. Prod. Innov. Manag. (2023)

Breuer, H., Fichter, K., Lüdecke-Freund, F., Tiemann, I.: Sustainability-oriented business model development: principles, criteria and tools. Int. J. Entrepreneurial Vent. **10**(5), 256–286 (2018)

Brem, A., Giones, F., Werle, M.: The AI digital revolution in innovation: a conceptual framework of artificial intelligence technologies for the management of innovation. IEEE Trans. Eng. Manage. **70**(2), 770–776 (2023). https://doi.org/10.1109/TEM.2021.3109983

Brynjolfsson, E., McAfee, A.: The business of artificial intelligence. Harvard Bus. Rev. 18 Juli 2017. https://hbr.org/2017/07/the-business-of-artificial-intelligence

Büchel, J., Engler, J., Mertens, A.: The demand for data skills in German companies: evidence from online job advertisements. EconPolForum **24**(2), 56–61 (2023)

Danish, M.S.S.: AI in energy: overcoming unforeseen obstacles. AI 4(2), 406–425 (2023). https://doi.org/10.3390/ai4020022

Davenport, T.H.: The AI Advantage: How to put the Artificial Intelligence Revolution to Work (First MIT Press paperback edition). The MIT Press (2019)

Demary, V., Mertens, A.: Zwischen Chance und Herausforderung: KI in Unternehmen. ifo Schnelldienst 76(8), 9–12 (2023)

Disselkamp, M.: Innovationen und Veränderungen, 1st edn. Verlag W, Kohlhammer (2017)

Dodgson, M., Gann, D., Phillips, N.: Perspectives on innovation management. In: The Oxford Handbook of Innovation Management, S. 3–25. Oxford University Press (2014)

Doleski, O.D. (Hrsg.): Realisierung Utility 4.0 Band 1: Praxis der digitalen Energiewirtschaft von den Grundlagen bis zur Verteilung im Smart Grid. Springer Fachmedien Wiesbaden (2020). https://doi.org/10.1007/978-3-658-25332-5

Elkington, J.B.: Partnerships from cannibals with forks: the triple bottom line of 21st-century business. Environ. Qual. Manage. **8**, 37–51 (1998)

epilot: Künstliche Intelligenz in der Energiebranche. epilot, 05. Dezember 2023. https://epilot.cloud/blog/epilot/kuenstliche-intelligenz-in-der-energiebranche/

European Commission: Commission welcomes political agreement on AI Act, 09 Dezember 2023. https://ec.europa.eu/commission/presscorner/detail/en/ip_23_6473

Füller, J., Hutter, K., Wahl, J., Bilgram, V., Tekic, Z.: How AI revolutionizes innovation management – Perceptions and implementation preferences of AI-based innovators. Technol. Forecast. Soc. Chang. (2022). https://doi.org/10.1016/j.techfore.2022.121598

Gassmann, O., Frankenberger, K., Csik, M.: Geschäftsmodelle: Branchenlogik durchbrechen. In: Praxiswissen Innovationsmanagement: Von der Idee zum Markterfolg (3., überarbeitet und erweiterte Auflage, Hanser, S. 175–193 (2013)

Gläser, J., Laudel, G.: xperteninterviews und qualitative Inhaltsanalyse als Instrumente rekonstruierender Untersuchungen (2., durchges. Aufl). VS Verlag für Sozialwissenschaften (2006)

Haefner, N., Wincent, J., Parida, V., Gassmann, O.: Artificial intelligence and innovation management: a review, framework, and research agenda☆. Technol. Forecast. Soc. Chang. **162**, 120392 (2021). https://doi.org/10.1016/j.techfore.2020.120392

Häfner, N., Morf, P.: Management von AI-initiativen in unternehmen. In: Digitale Transformation gestalten: Geschäftsmodelle, Erfolgsfaktoren, Checklisten (2., überarbeitete und erweiterte Auflage, S. 43–57), Hanser (2019)

Hamid, M., Ganne, A.: Artificial Intelligence in energy markets and power systems. Int. Res. J. Modern. Eng. Technol. Sci. (2023). https://doi.org/10.56726/IRJMETS35943

Hauschildt, J., Salomo, S., Schultz, C., Kock, A.: Innovationsmanagement (6., vollständig aktualisierte und überarbeitete Auflage), Verlag Franz Vahlen (2016)

Holmström, J., Carroll, N.: How Organizations Can Innovate with Generative AI. Business Horizons (2024)

Ibarra, D., Igartua, J.I., Mendoza, J.M.F.: Sustainable business models for renewable energy communities and their ecosystem. In: New Business Models Conference Proceedings 2023. Maastricht University Press (2023). https://doi.org/10.26481/mup.2302.09

Jäger, U., Reinecke, S.: Expertengespräch. In: Empirische Mastertechniken: Eine anwendungsorientierte Einführung für die Marketing - und Managementforschung, Gabler, (1. Aufl, S. 29–76) (2009)

Kaiser, R.: Qualitative Experteninterviews: Konzeptionelle Grundlagen und praktische Durchführung. Springer Fachmedien Wiesbaden (2021). https://doi.org/10.1007/978-3-658-30255-9

Kakatkar, C., Bilgram, V., Füller, J.: Innovation analytics: leveraging artificial intelligence in the innovation process. Bus. Horiz. **63**(2), 171–181 (2020). https://doi.org/10.1016/j.bushor.2019.10.006

Kar, A.K., Choudhary, S.K., Singh, V.: How can artificial intelligence impact sustainability: a systematic literature review. J. Cleaner Prod. (2022)

Kett, H., Evcenko, D., Falkner, J., Frings, S., Neuhüttler, J.: Künstliche Intelligenz als Veränderungstreiber für Geschäftsmodelle. In Künstliche Intelligenz im Dienstleistungsmanagement: Band 1: Geschäftsmodelle – Serviceinnovationen – Implementierung, S. 54–78. Springer Fachmedien Wiesbaden (2021). https://doi.org/10.1007/978-3-658-34324-8

Kirschner, K., Thompson, C.: These are the skills employers are looking for as AI use expands, according to leaders in Davos. Business Insider, 17. Januar 2024. https://www.businessinsider.com/generative-ai-era-important-skills-jobs-leaders-davos-2024-1

Kiron, D., Kruschwitz, N., Haanaes, K., Reeves, M., Goh, E.: The Innovation Bottom Line, MIT Sloan Management Review Research Report Winter 2013, Cambridge (2013)

Krebs, H.-A., Hagenweiler, P.: Innovationen und künstliche Intelligenz entlang der energiewirtschaftlichen Wertschöpfungskette unter Berücksichtigung der Datensicherheit und des Datenschutzes. Kassel University Press (2021). https://kobra.uni-kassel.de/handle/123456789/12727

Kreutzer, R.T.: Treiber und Hintergründe der digitalen Transformation. In Digitale Transformation von Geschäftsmodellen: Grundlagen, Instrumente und Best Practices, S. 33–58. Springer Fachmedien Wiesbaden (2017). https://doi.org/10.1007/978-3-658-12388-8

Kreutzer, R.T., Sirrenberg, M.: Künstliche Intelligenz verstehen: Grundlagen – Use-Cases – unternehmenseigene KI-Journey. Springer Fachmedien Wiesbaden (2019). https://doi.org/10.1007/978-3-658-25561-9

Kuckartz, U., Rädiker, S.: Qualitative Inhaltsanalyse: Methoden, Praxis, Computerunterstützung: Grundlagentexte Methoden (5. Auflage). Beltz Juventa (2022). https://content-select-com.pxz.iubh.de:8443/media/moz_viewer/5e623532-20b8-4f33-b19e-4a1db0dd2d03/language:de

Lang-Koetz, C., Reischl, A., Fischer, S., Weber, S., Kusch, A.: Zukunft des Innovations managements: Nachhaltigkeit. In: Ambidextres Innovations management in KMU. Springer Gabler, Heidelberg (2023). https://doi.org/10.1007/978-3-662-66458-2_7

McCarthy, J., Minsky, M.L., Rochester, N., Shannon, C.E.: A proposal for the Dartmouth summer research project on artificial intelligence (1955). http://jmc.stanford.edu/articles/dartmouth/dartmouth.pdf

Meuser, M., Nagel, U.: Das Experteninterview—Konzeptionelle Grundlagen und methodische Anlage. In Methoden der vergleichenden Politik - und Sozialwissenschaft: Neue Entwicklungen und Anwendungen (S. 465–479). VS Verlag für Sozialwissenschaften (2009). https://doi.org/10.1007/978-3-531-91826-6

Mühlroth, C., Grottke, M.: Artificial intelligence in innovation: how to spot emerging trends and technologies. IEEE Trans. Eng. Manage. **69**(2), 493–510 (2022). https://doi.org/10.1109/TEM.2020.2989214

Morandini, S., Fraboni, F., De Angelis, M., Puzzo, G., Giusino, D., Pietrantoni, L.: The impact of artificial intelligence on workers' skills: upskilling and reskilling in organisations. Inform. Sci. Int. J. Emerg. Transdiscip. 26, 39–68 (2023). https://doi.org/10.28945/5078

Neu, M., Müller, M., Pothen, B., Zingel, M.: Anwendungsfelder und Herausforderungen der Künstlichen Intelligenz: Wie KI die Gesellschaft und Marketing beeinflusst. Springer Fachmedien Wiesbaden (2022). https://doi.org/10.1007/978-3-658-38891-1

Osterwalder, A., Pigneur, Y., Verfasser: Business Model Generation: Ein Handbuch für Visionäre, Spielveränderer und Herausforderer (edsbvb.BV039856576). Campus Verlag, Bibliotheksverbund Bayern (2011). http://www.content-select.com/index.php?id=bib_view&ean=9783593411538

Paschen, U., Pitt, C., Kietzmann, J.: Artificial intelligence: building blocks and an innovation typology. Bus. Horiz. **63**(2), 147–155 (2020). https://doi.org/10.1016/j.bushor.2019.10.004

Parthie, S.: Europas Energiemarkt im Umbruch? ifo Schnelldienst, 75. Jahrgang (12/2022), 15–17 (2022)

Pflaum, A., Schulz, E.: Auf dem Weg zum digitalen Geschäftsmodell: „Tour de Force“ von der Vision des digitalisierten Unternehmens zum disruptiven Potenzial digitaler Plattformen. In Digitale Geschäftsmodelle – Band 1: Geschäftsmodell-Innovationen, digitale Transformation, digitale Plattformen, Internet der Dinge und Industrie 4.0 (S. 3–21). Springer Fachmedien Wiesbaden (2019). https://doi.org/10.1007/978-3-658-26314-0

Pittel, K.: Das energiepolitische Zieldreieck und die Energiewende. ifo Schnelldienst, 65. Jahrgang (12/2012), 22–26 (2012)

Porter, M.E., Kramer, M.R.: Creating shared value. Harv. Bus. Rev. **89**, 62–77 (2011)

Preuss, L.: Contribution of purchasing and supply management to ecological innovation. Int. J. Innov. Manag. **11**, 515–537 (2007)

Roberts, E.R.: Managing invention and innovation. Res. Technol. Manag. **50**(1), 35–54 (2007)

Rogers, E.M.: Diffusion of Innovations, 5th ed). Free Press (2003)

Roth, S.: Non-Technological and Non-Economic Innovations. Contributions to a Theory of Robust Innovation, 2nd Edition. Sociology of Innovation eJournal (2009)

Russell, S.J., Norvig, P.: Artificial intelligence: A modern approach (Fourth edition, global edition). Pearson (2022). https://elibrary-pearson-de.pxz.iubh.de:8443/book/view/99.150005/9781292401171?

Salter, A., Alexy, O.: The Nature of Innovation. In: The Oxford Handbook of Innovation Management, S. 26–49. Oxford University Press (2014)

Sauer, R., Dopfer, M., Schmeiss, J., Gassmann, O.: Das Geschäftsmodell: Gral der Digitalisierung. In: Digitale Transformation gestalten: Geschäftsmodelle, Erfolgsfaktoren, Checklisten (2., überarbeitete und erweiterte Auflage, S. 19–32). Hanser (2019)

Schallmo, D.R.A.: Geschäftsmodelle erfolgreich entwickeln und implementieren: Mit Aufgaben, Kontrollfragen und Templates. Springer Berlin Heidelberg (2018). https://doi.org/10.1007/978-3-662-57605-2

Schaltegger, S., Hansen, E., Lüdeke-Freund, F.: Business models for sustainability: origins, present research, and future avenues. Organ. Environ. **29**(1), 3–10 (2016)

Tekic, Z., Füller, J.: Managing innovation in the era of AI. Technology in Society (2023)

Tidd, J., Bessant, J.R.: Managing Innovation: Integrating Technological, Market and Organizational Change, (4. ed., reprinted). Wiley (2011)

Turing, A.M.: Computing machinery and intelligence. Mind **59**(236), 433–460 (1950). https://doi.org/10.1093/mind/LIX.236.433

Vaio, A.D., Palladino, R., Hassan, R., Escobar, O.: Artificial intelligence and business models in the sustainable development goals perspective: a systematic literature review. J. Bus. Res. **121**, 283–314 (2020)

van Wynsberghe, A.: Sustainable AI: AI for sustainability and the sustainability of AI. AI Ethics **1**, 213–218 (2021)

Vahs, D., Brem, A., Oswald, C.: Innovationsmanagement: Von der Idee zur erfolgreichen Vermarktung (6. Schäffer-Poeschel Verlag, Auflage) (2023)

Wang, R.: The 12 Major Risks of AI: opportunities abound and optimism is warranted, but so is a degree of caution. CRM Magazine, 27(8), 13. Gale Business: Insights (2023)

Wirtz, B., Pistoia, A., Ullrich, S., Göttel, V.: Business models: origin, development and future research perspectives. Long Range Plan. **49**(1), 36–54 (2016)

Analyzing Network Threats Using a Cybersecurity Tool

Victor Mbogu[1] and Rachel John Robinson[2(✉)]

[1] Arden University, Berlin, Germany
[2] IU International University of Applied Science, Berlin, Germany
rachel.john-robinson@iu.org, info@rachel-johnrobinson.com

Abstract. Due to the ongoing development of network threats, preventing threats has become a top priority for all sectors within the industry. The text examines network threats using a cybersecurity tool that incorporates network forensic models to enhance the mitigation of network threats. Moreover, it explores various facets of network forensics and tackles distinct categories of network vulnerabilities by proficiently analyzing a specific threat with the assistance of the cybersecurity tool. The study examines the methods by which network threats can infiltrate the system and how network forensics models integrate appropriate tools for analyzing these threats. It aims to guide the user in choosing the most suitable tool for analyzing threats using the network forensics model. The study aims to systematically review and evaluate network forensics principles, methods, and cybersecurity applications. Also it aims to find and analyze network threats from different researchers, focusing on discovering new attack patterns, standard methods, and implications for network security. With this it would be easy to identify and investigate network threats using a network forensic tool and to recommend solutions to prevent future threats. Additionally, the suggested study improves cybersecurity, reduces network-based threats, and boosts resilience. It provides insights into network forensics, investigates emerging threats, analyses threats with forensic tools, and suggests proactive measures to improve cybersecurity. It aids organizations in securing their digital assets and navigates cyber threats. By analyzing network risks with network forensic tools, researchers can find novel attack pathways, evaluate detection methods, and develop cyber defenses. With this study's expertise, people and organizations can establish and implement more robust security protocols and network designs, enhancing cybersecurity. This study illuminates the shifting threat landscape and develops forensic methods to increase cyber defenses and reduce cyberattacks on our digital infrastructure.

Keywords: Cybersecurity · Network threats · Emerging threats · Attack patterns · Forensic tool

1 Introduction

The digitalization of data worldwide has increased the rate of cybercrime globally, and the need for digital forensics has become increasingly demandable in information technology. Hence, implementing digital forensics in the computing world will aid in fighting cybercrime by detecting underlying culprits.

R. C. Geibel and S. Machavariani (Eds.): ISPC 2024, SPBE, pp. 48–68, 2025.
https://doi.org/10.1007/978-3-031-88052-0_4

The increase in cybercrime has made the need for cyber and digital forensics crucial today. A report by the National Crime Records Bureau (NCRB) shows that cybercrime doubled from 2016 to 2018 and is predicted to increase as much as four times today [1]. Internet crimes are rising, challenging network forensics analysis tools, researchers, and investigators. To combat network and digital crimes, credible, advanced research is essential. Network threats are malicious software, phishing schemes, or denial of service attacks (DDoS) that disrupt network activities to steal data [1]. Also it states digital forensics uses scientific methods to evaluate electronically stored data and discover the events that lead to an occurrence [2]. Computer and digital forensics are essential fields that include people of all professions. Deepening into digital forensics will reveal network, database, mobile, memory, and data or disc forensics [3]. This project focuses on the Network forensics domain, a science centered on discovering and retrieving data surrounding a cybercrime within a networked environment. One subfield of computer forensics, known as "network forensics," looks into internal and external networks in search of clues about where a cyberattack originated [3]. As we all know, most attacks move through a network before hitting the target, leaving some traces. "Every contact leaves a trace," says Locard's exchange principle, and the internet is no different.

With cybercrime and attacks increasing daily, digital network forensics is crucial, particularly in network leakage, suspicious network traffic, or data theft. Digital network forensics mainly involves investigating and analyzing network traffic suspected to be compromised by cybercriminals using cyber exploitation or DDoS attacks, also known as network threats. This research aims to provide a comprehensive overview of network forensics and investigate and analyses network threats using a digital network forensics tool.

1.1 Project Objectives

i. To systematically review and evaluate network forensics principles, methods, and cybersecurity applications.
ii. To find and analyze network threats from different researchers, focusing on discovering new patterns, standard attack methods, and implications for network security.
iii. To identify and investigate network threats using a network forensic tool.
iv. To recommend solutions to prevent future threats or attacks on a network.

1.2 Research Questions

The research questions align with the project objectives and aim to explore the various aspects of network forensics, network threats, and the function of forensic tools in threat identification and mitigation.

i. What are the core ideas and techniques of network forensics, and how do they support the examination and study of threats originating from networks?
ii. What kinds of network threats have cybersecurity experts found, and what conclusions can be drawn from their research?
iii. What are network forensic tools' main features and functions, and how can they identify, evaluate, and counteract various network threats?

iv. What are the typical obstacles and constraints related to network forensic analysis, and what steps can be taken to overcome them to increase threat detection and response efficacy and efficiency?
v. What suggestions and remedies can be made based on the results of a network forensic study to improve overall cybersecurity resilience and thwart potential threats or attacks on a network?

1.3 Significance of the Study

The proposed study is highly significant in tackling major difficulties and increasing knowledge in cybersecurity, specifically in network forensics. The study attempts to accomplish the following by aligning with the project objectives:

i. Presenting an Overview of Network Forensics: Grasping the basic principles of network forensics is crucial to effectively detecting and responding to threats. This study thoroughly examines network forensics principles and procedures, equipping cybersecurity experts and forensic analysts with the necessary knowledge and skills to investigate and analyze threats within a network [4].
ii. Examining Network Threats by Various Researchers: Due to constant changes in cyber dangers, researchers must engage in ongoing study and analysis of emerging risks and attack strategies. This study enhances the overall knowledge of cybersecurity threats, vulnerabilities, and attack vectors by examining network threats from various researchers. As a result, organizations can improve their ability to anticipate, identify, and mitigate potential hazards [5].
iii. Identification and Analysis of Network Threats using Network Forensic Tools: Such as Wireshark, tcpdump, etc., are essential for identifying, examining, and reducing network-related risks by offering features for recording, monitoring, and analyzing network traffic. This study improves the effectiveness and efficiency of threat detection and response by using these tools to identify and explore network threats. As a result, it promotes network security and resilience [5].
iv. Suggestions for Mitigating Future Threats or Attacks: Network forensic analysis assists organizations in identifying and fixing network infrastructure gaps, reducing security risks, and preventing future attacks. This study provides network forensic investigation-based remedies to assist organizations in improving their cybersecurity and avoiding intrusions [5].

The suggested study improves cybersecurity, reduces network-based threats, and boosts resilience. It provides insights into network forensics, investigates emerging threats, analyses threats with forensic tools, and suggests proactive measures to improve cybersecurity. It aids organizations in securing their digital assets and navigates cyber threats.

2 Theoretical Foundation

Following a thorough review of the literature on network forensics frameworks and threats, it is crucial to formulate well-defined questions that may be addressed to gain a comprehensive comprehension of the subject. How do current research findings in network forensic analysis contribute to our understanding of emerging threats and attack vectors in cybersecurity, and how can this knowledge be utilized to enhance threat detection and mitigation strategies? What is the impact of recent research in network forensic analysis on our comprehension of emerging cybersecurity threats and attack methods? How can we apply this knowledge to improve our ability to detect and mitigate these attacks? What are the most common hurdles and constraints in network forensic analysis, particularly when investigating complex network threats?

2.1 How Network Forensics and Network Security Differ

Network forensics and security differ. Data from firewalls and intrusion detection systems is collected for network security forensics, a lengthy procedure. The attacks are investigated using this data analysis. However, not all crimes compromise network security regulations and are subject to prosecution. Only network forensics can solve these crimes [6]. To make networks more secure, "General Network Forensics" is used, and "Strict Network Forensics" is used to collect proof that complies with rules and laws [7].

Computers are safeguarded by network security, while attack data is preserved by network forensics. Network security solutions identify and prevent unwanted activity. Monitoring occurs continuously throughout the day. After receiving a crime notification, network forensics examines the attack retrospectively. Due to time limits and the uniqueness of each crime, each case is specific [8].

Two critical applications of network forensics are examined. Network surveillance is the initial security step in detecting anomalous data flow and unauthorized breaches. A hacked system may delete all log files by a hostile user, and Network proof may be the only forensic evidence. In law enforcement, network forensics is used to reconstruct transmitted data, perform keyword searches, and analyze human discourse in emails and other communication channels [9].

Detailing the difference between these two, emphasizing that Network Forensics grows to investigate, detect, and apprehend the rapid rise in cybercrimes. Despite this growth, network forensics needs clarification. Studying attacker behavior helps detect

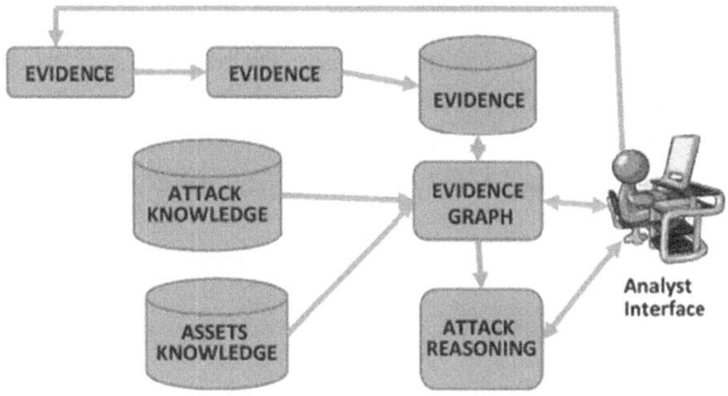

Fig. 1. Network Forensic Analysis Design [10]

patterns and prevent future assaults. Using incoming and outgoing traffic patterns, network forensics evaluates numerous assaults [10]. Many explanations exist for network forensics. Figure 1 shows its designs.

Network security protects information transmission by preventing, detecting, and fixing security breaches [10]. The NIST defines cybersecurity as securing an automated information system and ensuring its integrity, availability, and confidentiality. Network security protects confidentiality, integrity, and availability. An illustration of how network security breaches are being compromised is below (Fig. 2):

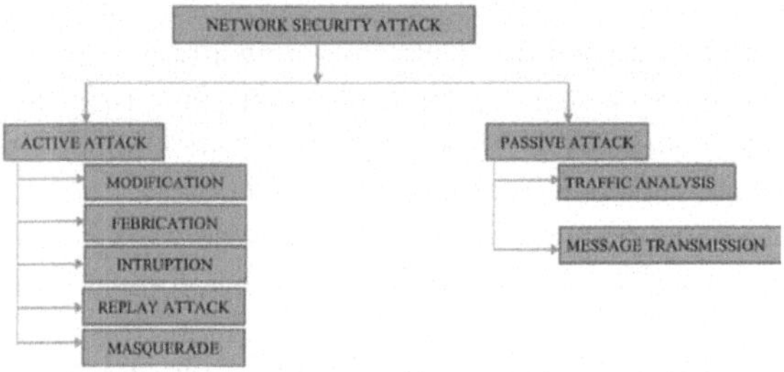

Fig. 2. Shows Network Security Attacks [10].

Network forensics traces attacks to their root source and assigns them to hosts, people, or networks. It can anticipate future assaults by using penetration data to create attack patterns. Attack data analysis and source identification are crucial to network forensics. Parsing and studying complex protocols to classify and cluster network events and understand attacks requires large volumes of data.

Further research is required to categorize attack patterns and recreate attack methodologies to comprehend better attackers' goals and strategies [11]. Network forensics data must be analyzed to establish if an inquiry is needed. Investigators must first attribute an attack to a network or host to analyze a network. The result must be court-acceptable. For log and network analysis, traces must lead to attack sources. IP spoofing can be overcome to track the perpetrator's origin [12].

Chains can significantly succeed in detecting and profiling TCP connections and launching attacks. The only problem is creating an architecture database and IP location mapping to locate an attacker by location. These protocol events must be resolved as IPv6 becomes more popular and operational [8].

In [13] it states that one of the biggest obstacles in network forensics is active and passive network monitoring, mainly when dealing with wireless networks and live investigations.

2.2 Network Forensic Frameworks

Many frameworks for network forensics have been suggested, and they all have advantages and disadvantages [14]. DFRWS initially proposed digital forensics in networked systems. The purpose of these frameworks is to direct and examine data from networks and investigate intrusions [15].

Nevertheless, substantial knowledge gaps exist in using these frameworks, creating process models, and developing analytical tools. An example of a suggested framework is an integrated generic process model for digital forensics [15]. Another unique method is the concept of distributed network forensics, which leverages distributed approaches for automated evidence collection and attack attribution [16].

According to [17], the Network Forensic Investigation Framework (NFIF) is an all-inclusive method for conducting network forensic investigations, including data reduction, analysis, reporting, and acquisition. It stresses the significance of forensically good network traffic capture, preservation, analysis, and interpretation. Several scenarios have used this paradigm, including expanding it to include network routers in investigations.

2.3 Network Forensic Analysis Tools

Network forensics specializes in data packet and network traffic collection, monitoring, recording, and analysis. It uses network technologies for these tasks. Network forensics helps identify and track malicious transmissions [18]. Many systems monitor traffic in real-time. This monitoring requires a lot of human and technological resources and is unsuitable for networks more extensive than a workgroup. Generally, archiving all traffic and studying subsets is more practical. This method is called reconstructive traffic analysis or network forensics [19].

In [20] asserts that network forensics analyses network communication events. To fully understand the scenario, examine low-level network protocols. Tools are essential to reduce complexity. Tools aid investigators by summarizing key points, grouping similar data into clusters, and drawing attention to relevant details [21]. e.g., Retrieving the details of transferred files, extracting users' credentials, and analyzing and presenting the data in a clear and understandable format. Traditional forensics toolkits like EnCase, The Sleuth Kit (TSK), and Autopsy have features, capacities, and usability incompatible with the many network forensic analysis tools available [22].

2.4 Types of Network Threats

A wide variety of malicious activities can be classified as network threats. These activities aim to exploit weaknesses in computer networks and put security at risk. Many well-established types of network dangers have been detailed in academic journals:

The objective of DoS and DDoS attacks is to overload the network access of legitimate users with excessive traffic, impeding their regular functioning. DDoS attacks are designed to overwhelm a server or network with harmful traffic to restrict user access [24]. Messages, connection requests, and malformed packets slow down or crash the target system, denying service to legitimate users or systems. Recently, DDoS assaults have become one of the most significant Internet vulnerabilities [25].

MitM attacks involve an attacker secretly collecting, intercepting, and perhaps altering data or eavesdropping on private communication. Unauthorized users, known as protocols, can view and modify system data without affecting current users [26]. ARP spoofing and SSL stripping are used to hijack Wi-Fi networks. SSL headers and HTTP packets from a computer's application layer (Layer 7 on the OSI model) encrypt data. The URL would change to HTTPS and turn green on secure sites. This study shows a MitM attack can turn off security to redirect traffic from a victim's machine to an attacker's [27].

A combination of malicious software is malware, a collection of programs created to infiltrate or harm a computer system without the owner's consent [28]. Malware frequently targets unsuspecting users through anonymous email messages and conceals its harmful payloads within attachments to popular file formats like Adobe Acrobat and Microsoft Office documents [29]. To point out that social engineering attacks can be classified into four distinct phases: (i) gathering target information, (ii) establishing a bond with the intended client, (iii) using the data at hand to initiate the attack, and (iv) vanishing without a trace. The attacker uses emotional manipulation to get the victim to divulge important information or make security-related blunders during the exploitation phase. During the exit phase, the perpetrator disappears [30].

Malicious insiders are employees, contractors, or partners authorized to access data from a business's system or network. These individuals deliberately abuse their access privileges to compromise the organization's data or computer systems [31]. The relatively new discipline of social cybersecurity includes insider threat research among its many components [31].

Ransomware is an increasingly severe problem in cyber security. It locks or encrypts data and then demands payment to unlock it [32]. Due to its quick evolution, multiple families and malware variations have emerged [33].

There are typically three distinct types of ransomware attacks [29]. First, a crypto worm is an independent ransomware that replicates. Second, anyone with money can buy a shadow market Ransomware-as-a-Service (RaaS) distribution kit. RaaS programs make attacks easy for non-technical people. They are usually distributed semi-manually via exploit kits as drive-by downloads or hazardous spam emails by uncontrolled intruders. The third ransomware attack is an automated active adversary. These attackers search the internet for vulnerable IT systems with tools. After finding such systems, criminals carefully plan the ransomware attack to wreak the most harm.

2.5 Impact of Network Threats

The impact of network threats is a global concern, with wireless network systems and cybersecurity threats identified as top dangers [30]. These threats have significant implications for defense and security, targeting physical, social, economic, and cyber domains [34]. The rapid evolution of these threats challenges sustaining adequate security levels.

The complexity of current networks and services significantly increases the dangers to individuals and organizations. To mitigate these dangers, researchers have proposed many anomaly detection systems. Unfortunately, existing tools often can't adjust to new architectures, threats, or zero-day attacks [34].

2.6 Research Challenges and Internet User Anonymity

The main objective of network forensics is to detect and analyse any potential security breaches and risks and then incorporate these patterns into Intrusion Detection and Prevention Systems (IDPS) to mitigate future damages [35]. Several options allow forensic investigators or network administrators to monitor network traffic actively. Networks larger than a single workgroup cannot support real-time monitoring due to the high human and hardware resources cost. Archiving all gathered traffic and analyzing it based on specific requirements is typically a more pragmatic approach.

It is essential to highlight that the level of detail in the dataset is a significant obstacle. [36] identified the challenge of obtaining a suitable and sufficient dataset for examination as a substantial obstacle in network forensics.

Network forensic frameworks guide forensic investigations but have limits. Network forensic analysis begins with network traces and assault detection. The traces include IDS and firewall logs, network service and application logs, and sniffer and NFAT packet grabs [36]. The task is to recognize valuable network occurrences and document essential characteristics for each occurrence to save the smallest amount of information with the greatest likelihood of reliability. This leads to a decrease in the amount of data storage needed. Data digest is adequate for detecting malicious behavior, whereas a complete capture is necessary for reconstructing the details of an attack.

Network forensics analysis has many challenges, just like other forensic investigations. The initial challenge is traffic data interception. Network design and security may limit data capture by sniffer tool traffic. The network admin can use scan ports on network devices to fix this. Data correlation is challenging in network forensics. Correlation might be causal or temporal. Timestamps are crucial in the latter case. An attacker can encrypt data using an SSL VPN. Network investigators can see the address and port but not the data stream. Additional logging and investigation are needed to determine tainted data. Attackers can use zombie machines, intermediary hosts, or remote proxy servers to identify the source of an attack. The attackers' original addresses are difficult for network investigators to trace. Given these factors, network forensics investigators focus on PCAP files or network packet capture. Examining data packets sent over a network for things like protocols, IP addresses, ports, timestamps, malicious code, user agents, application servers, and OS versions is essential. Various traffic sources provide this information [36].

In this "blind" virtual world that the Internet generates, computers play the role of submissive servants and humans the role of savvy masters. Promoting open knowledge exchange relies on privacy communication. Therefore, the individual using the computer and communicating over the Internet is anonymous [37].

3 Research Methodology

This chapter offers an extensive overview of the research methodology, focusing on how secondary qualitative data processing approaches were employed. Qualitative methods are essential for revealing Subtle, detailed observations and perspectives, considering the study's reliance on secondary data.

3.1 Methods of Qualitative Data Analysis Selection

Due to the wide variety of qualitative information found in secondary sources, thematic analysis was developed to examine and make sense of it all. Thematic analysis, which finds, evaluates, and reports data patterns or themes, is well-suited to exploratory research. The research's commitment to ensuring secondary data sources are accurately and thoroughly analyzed using theme analysis as the significant method for qualitative data analysis is evident. Interpretive research embraces this fact since people's experiences and interpretations are inherently subjective. With this philosophy, thematic analysis works. Its use permits the examination of secondary facts from multiple angles, consistent with the ontological principle that subjective realities exist. The exploratory study is well-suited to the inductive thematic analysis method, which permits topics to arise organically from data.

3.2 Rationale for Conducting Thematic Analysis

This research uses thematic analysis because of its adaptability, ease of use, and ability to be applied to a wide range of research issues and concepts. Researchers can uncover patterns and meanings in qualitative data by breaking complicated issues into simpler ones. Also, the research is methodologically sound because theme analysis has been validated to evaluate qualitative data.

Due to its simplicity and capacity to handle vast volumes of heterogeneous data, thematic analysis was selected over grounded theory or narrative analysis. Given the limitations of this study, iterative and time-consuming data collection and analysis may be necessary to use grounded theory. Narrative analysis fosters data storytelling, while thematic analysis identifies and analysis's themes.

3.3 Data Collection and Selection Criteria

A comprehensive review of pertinent literature, reports, and qualitative investigations is made possible by smoothly integrating theme and secondary data analysis. Thematic analysis solves research problems by identifying essential themes and insights through meticulous data classification and analysis. Forensic investigation of networks begins with collecting network traces and identifying attacks. These traces consist of IDS and firewall logs, packets captured by sniffers and NFATs, and records created by applications and services on a network [38]. Detecting network activities and entering minimum qualities for each event to retain data with the most evidence might be difficult, but this will reduce storage needs. Breaking data into bits will reveal malicious behavior and rebuild attack behavior.

As stated above, this project will employ a qualitative research method to help us understand the context of the problem it will address. As previously stated, this project will not include physical data. Instead, it will rely on research conducted by many authors to enhance our understanding of evaluating network hazards using a network forensic tool in Cybersecurity. In addition, underneath each study question is a summary of the steps used to gather data, including the terms and phrases that were looked up. Further, academic publications such as books, journals, and conference papers are the primary means of collecting data for network forensics, threat analysis, and vulnerability assessment. These sources are the backbone of the research, offering a wide array of viewpoints and ideas from recognized authorities on the subject. Research on network forensics and data security is essential to the selected secondary data. Field professionals reviewed this study's sources, ensuring data reliability. We can only include sources with articles within the last 1–5 years to keep our data current due to technology's dynamic nature. This category contains network forensics reports from respectable organizations, conference papers, and journal articles. However, knowledge of network forensics materials from prior years is necessary.

3.4 The Approach to Data Analysis

The analysis will be done by investigating different research works on network threats from other authors and suggesting an improved method to detect and prevent network threats using a particular network forensic tool. Multiple essential steps make up data analysis:

i. Approaches to Classification: Various network risks, vulnerabilities, and attack vectors are identified and categorized by analyzing the gathered literature. This entails sorting and classifying the data according to shared features, traits, and trends.
ii. The Framework for Network Forensics: This framework investigates network forensics' central concepts and approaches to comprehend the theoretical underpinnings and practical uses of forensic analysis in cybersecurity.
iii. Network Tool Analysis: The widely used network forensics tool Wireshark analyses recorded network traffic in search of suspicious patterns, potential security incidents, and indicators of compromise (IOCs). Discovering and evaluating these threats requires gathering and analyzing data from packets in a network. Based on the analysis done by other researchers, the tool-in approach will be evaluated.
iv. Threat and Vulnerability Analysis: The research delves deeply into network vulnerabilities and threats, investigating their origins, effects on network security, and possible ways to lessen their severity. This process includes finding typical attack entry points, ranking their seriousness and probability, and analyzing current defenses and solutions [39].

3.5 Limitations

One possible issue with using published material is publication bias, which occurs when studies with positive or meaningful results are overrepresented. The inclusion of pertinent literature in the study may be hindered owing to barriers to entry or institutional restrictions that restrict access to specific credible sources.

Due to data privacy and protection rules, the project may be restricted in actively observing and analyzing network packets and traffic. Using network forensics tools without explicit permission must comply with the legislation of a particular country. To operate with real-time active network traffic data, individuals must obtain authorization and a warrant from the Computer Security Incident Response Team (CSIRT).

4 Results and Discussions

This section elaborates on utilizing network forensics alongside network forensic models and frameworks. It examines network characteristics and the objectives of these concepts and frameworks to illustrate how they collectively influence various aspects of mitigating network threats.

4.1 Understanding How Network Forensics Paradigms Prevent Threat

This section discusses how network forensics models detect and mitigate cybersecurity threats. Network forensics collects, analyses, and interprets network traffic data to detect and resolve security problems. Our practical grasp of network forensics makes this valuable research for real-world cybersecurity strategies.

The suggested Network Forensic Tools theme taxonomy is shown in Fig. 3. This context contains framework type, technique, example, intended dataset, forensic analysis, investigation duration, execution parameters, and purpose function. Traceback, converged networks, attack graphs, and distributive and intrusion detection systems are framework-based NFT implementation methodologies [40]. In forensic analysis, NFT uses logging, packet tagging, and heuristics. NFT analyses target dataset data, VoIP, and network models. The target instance chooses which traffic to study: complete packets, packet headers, or network nodes. Forensics determine centralization or decentralization. Static and dynamic forensic analysis differ in investigation time. By execution definition, NFT techniques are proactive or reactive, and the objective function parameter defines their goal.

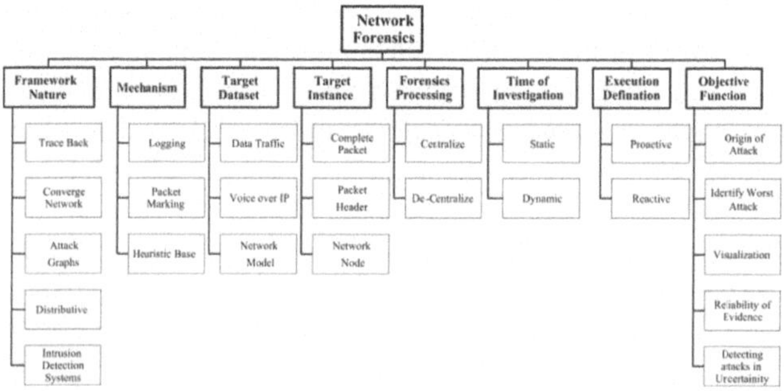

Fig. 3. Thematic Taxonomy of Network Forensics [40]

It is proposed that to prevent internal and external assaults; network security must incorporate proactive digital forensic models. This strategy aims to enhance intrusion detection by collecting real-time data and analyzing it through centralized traffic monitoring. In highlighting the importance of network security's specialized investigative capabilities in identifying and preventing harmful activities [40]. In discussions how converging systems rely on network forensic models to facilitate organized investigations and quicker responses. It is stated that one of the goals of the first DFRWS was to present a framework for applying digital forensic science to networked contexts; this was the first of several models that have been proposed [41]. A digital forensic analysis follows the procedures described by the DFRWS paradigm. Figure 4 illustrates these procedures.

Figure 4 demonstrates how network forensics concepts and techniques help prevent network threats. As stated previously [41], network forensic examinations provide a

Fig. 4. DFRWS Digital Investigative Framework (Author).

thorough method. Figure 5 shows the nine elements that comprise the proposed framework, all based on the digital forensic model and including new steps specific to network forensics.

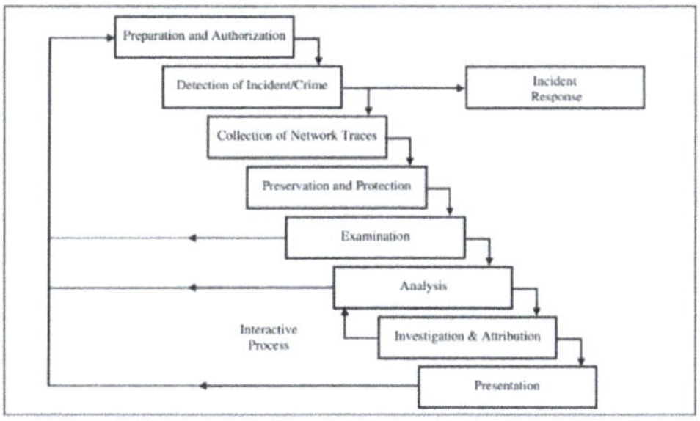

Fig. 5. Generic process model for network forensics [41].

The above network forensics framework demonstrates investigators' need to adopt a systematic and meticulous strategy to get valuable, legally admissible, and scientifically rigorous evidence for presentation [38].

Figures 4 and 5 depict network forensics risk assessment methodologies and the following list shows how they improved threat prevention. Addressing security issues, complying with laws, and preventing repeats helps each stage.

Network forensics models improve proactive threat intelligence, early detection, incident response, forensic analysis, and identification, reducing cybersecurity risks. With these models' complicated algorithms and analytical methods, organizations may respond to security threats in real time, gather forensic evidence, and proactively identify future dangers. Businesses can better respond to incidents, strengthen cybersecurity, and mitigate cyber risks. Network forensics models improve cybersecurity resilience, threat visibility, and decision-making.

4.2 Investigating Network Threats and Cybersecurity Findings

Cybercrime is quickly rising to the ranks of the world's most pressing problems. Numerous unsuccessful attempts have been made to combat its ever-increasing prevalence by eliminating known and potential dangers like Trojan horses and viruses. In [42] Both stress the need for cutting-edge technology and approaches to identify and stop network threats.

Figure 6 shows the different numbers of data risks. Systems must generally be safeguarded from active and passive threats like eavesdropping, spoofing, impersonating, phishing, misuse, and illegal access. Security technologies and strategies must be integrated to thwart these attacks [43].

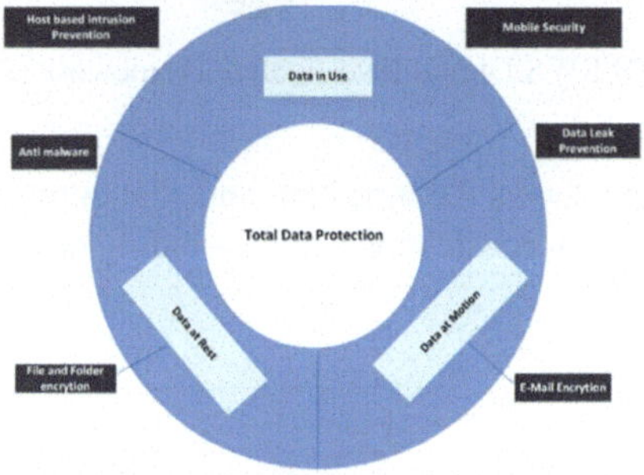

Fig. 6. Various Threats (Author).

More complex attacks often consist of multiple stages utilizing different approaches. Malware and DDoS attacks were employed in over 50% of the assaults, and social engineering was used in one out of three attacks. The report below concludes with the following statistics in Fig. 7. Biggest Cyber Security Threats Identified by Security Leaders in APAC-based Organizations:

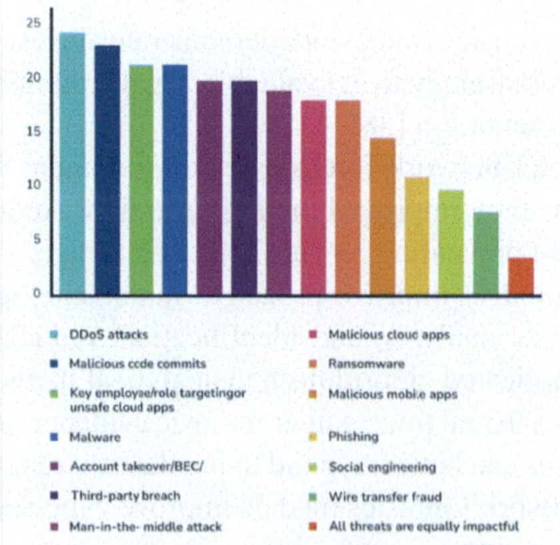

Fig. 7. Cyber Security Breach Statistics [43].

4.3 General Categories and Characteristics of Security/Network Attacks

Understanding data security involves four key concepts: interruption, interception, modification, and fabrication [44]. Interruption occurs when data availability is compromised, often due to system crashes or denial-of-service attacks. Measures such as backup and restoration are crucial for mitigating these risks. Interception focuses on maintaining data confidentiality, needing robust authentication and access restrictions to ensure that only authorized individuals can access critical information. Modification safeguards data integrity against intentional or unintentional alterations, utilizing robust validation algorithms and multi-layered security measures. Fabrication attacks aim to deceive recipients about the data source, emphasizing the importance of authentication methods like usernames, passwords, and digital certificates. These concepts are vital for maintaining the trustworthiness and reliability of data across different contexts.

The literature study shows that security attacks can be passive or active based on their characteristics. Interception is a passive attack that monitors data without changing it to retrieve sent data. Due to their non-modifying nature, disclosure of message content and traffic analysis are hard to detect. Active attacks involve falsifying information. Assaults use masquerade, replay, data modification, and denial of service. These assaults impersonate and impair network functions. Network forensics analysts must understand these attack types to address network security issues effectively as in Fig. 8.

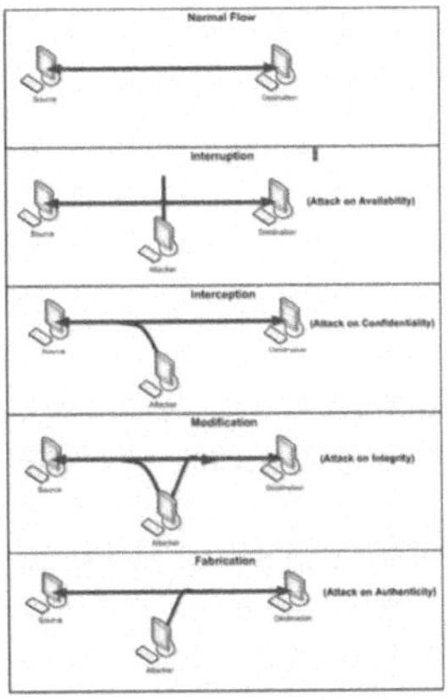

Fig. 8. Shows Basic Types of Security Attacks [44].

Historically, malware assaults occurred at specific points of vulnerability within hardware devices, software components, or network infrastructure, taking advantage of inherent weaknesses in the design and implementation of each layer. Give a thorough rundown of the most common security holes in an existing information system's hardware, software, and network components as in Fig. 9 [45].

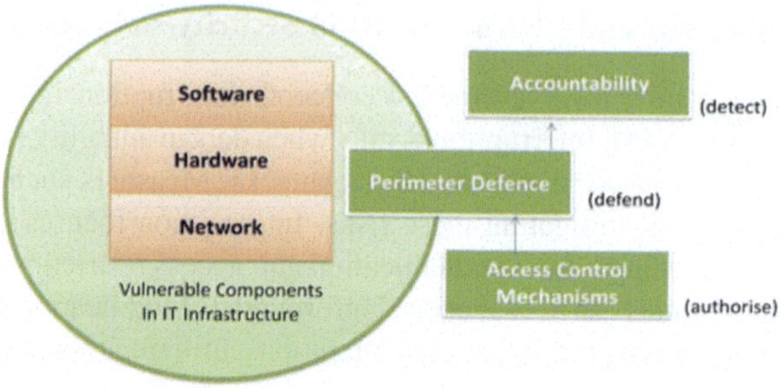

Fig. 9. Vulnerabilities and Defense Strategies in Existing Systems [45]

4.4 Analysis of Network Forensics Tools

Cybersecurity professionals and forensic analysts commonly leverage multiple network forensic analysis technologies to examine and assess security occurrences. It is stated that with the help of Network Forensic Analysis Tools (NFATs), administrators can keep tabs on networks, record any unusual activity, aid in investigating network crimes, and develop an appropriate response to incidents. In addition to assisting with intellectual property protection, NFATs can aid in evaluating network performance, analyzing risks, forecasting future attack targets, and analyzing insider fraud and resource usage. Forensic tools continued to be developed in response to specific threats and not due to coordinated efforts [46].

According to [47], several general-purpose tools exist, including protocol analyzers, network forensic analyzers, and packet collectors (sniffers). These tools can be further categorized into subgroups:

- Packet sniffers such as dumpcap, pcapdump, and netsniff-ng can capture and store network packets to files.
- Some well-known protocol analyzers are Tcpdump, Tshark, Tstat, and Wireshark. Based on how they analyse recorded traffic, you can classify these tools as packet-centric or session-centric.
- The NFAT toolset includes Xplico and NetworkMiner. These tools can analyse traffic content since they are data-centric.

Regardless, two of the most popular Network Security Monitoring (NSM) tools are tcpdump and Wireshark tools for detecting network security occurrences and problems.

The description of network forensic analysis tools (NFATs) and network security and monitoring (NSM) tools is presented in Fig. 10 below:

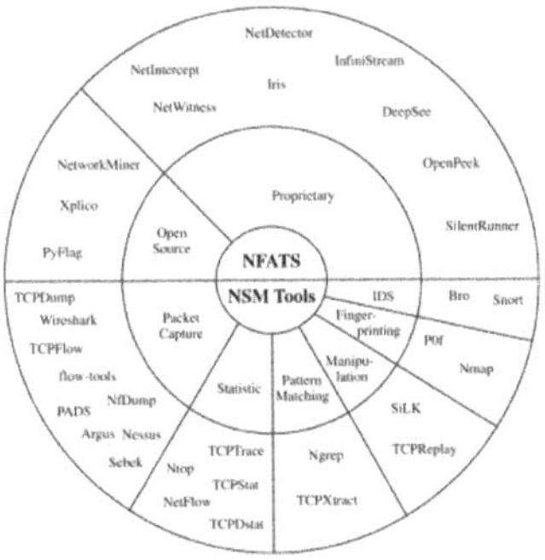

Fig. 10. Network security and monitoring (NSM) tools [47].

4.4.1 Evaluation of Features and Capabilities of Network Forensic Tools

See (Table 1).

Table 1. Features and Capabilities (Author).

Evaluation Features	Description
Protocol Decoding and Reconstruction	Understanding packet contents through precise decoding of network protocols. Allowing for the reconstruction of broken communication and data streams through session reconstruction
Timestamping and Metadata Analysis	Timely investigations based on precise timestamps of network activities. The ability to collect and analyse packet metadata, such as addresses, ports, and headers, through metadata analysis
File Extraction and Analysis	Support with extracting and analysing files of different kinds that have been transmitted over a network. Analysis of file contents to detect indicators of malicious activity
Packet Capture and Filtering	Capable of collecting data in real-time or using packet capture algorithms (PCAP) and Efficient packet filtering using IP addresses, protocols, ports, and packet contents as a criterion
Cross-Platform Integration	Integration with SIEM systems, network monitoring solutions, and forensic tools allows for smooth data exchange
Visualization and Reporting	Tools for data visualization, including graphs, timelines, and charts, for showing network traffic. Possibility to generate detailed reports outlining the outcomes of analyses
Ease of Use and User Interface	User-friendly, intuitive design components create easy-to-navigate and interact-with interfaces. Functionalities for improved workflow, such as search capabilities and customizable dashboards, are also included

4.4.2 Comparison of Open-Source and Commercial Forensic Tools

See (Table 2).

Table 2. Open-source and Commercial (Author).

Feature	Open-Source Forensic Tools	Commercial Forensic Tools
Value	Without cost	Payment for licensing or subscription
Qualities and Operational Capabilities	Comprehensive set of features and capabilities	Enhanced capabilities and tailored components
Community Support	Community involvement and joint development initiatives	Staffed vendor groups offering expert assistance
Personalization and adaptability	Adaptability and personalization choices	There are personalization options compared to free and open-source alternatives
Cooperation and Integration	Compatible with other programs, both open-source and commercial	Competence with industry standards and the ability to integrate proprietary systems
Practicality and User-Friendliness	Differences in usability and design of user interfaces	Smooth navigation and user-friendly interfaces
Training and Support	Dependence on customer-driven discussion boards and digital manuals	Programs for training and certification, as well as dedicated technical support

Network forensic models and tools can counter many types of network threats. According to the rules provided by the network models, this can be accomplished, as shown in Fig. 11.

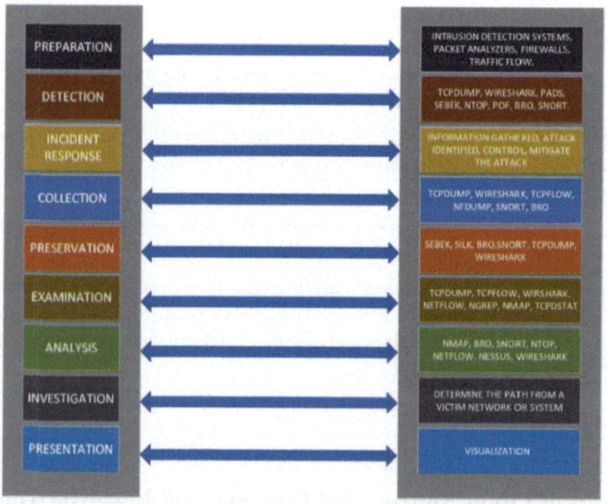

Fig. 11. Network Models and Tools for Countering Threat (Author).

People employ various attack methods to cause network disruptions for multiple reasons. Websites, databases, and corporate networks are common targets for attackers who seek to exploit their vulnerabilities [48]. Attackers typically employ tools specific to the attack they intend to carry out. Network security research professionals and private security experts have also made various defensive measures available. All these tools serve unique functions and have unique user interfaces.

The first step is to sort the available tools into two broad groups: those designed for attackers and those for network defenders. Network security tools are organized in a taxonomy in Fig. 12. They inevitably display subcategories for each fundamental category based on their shared traits.

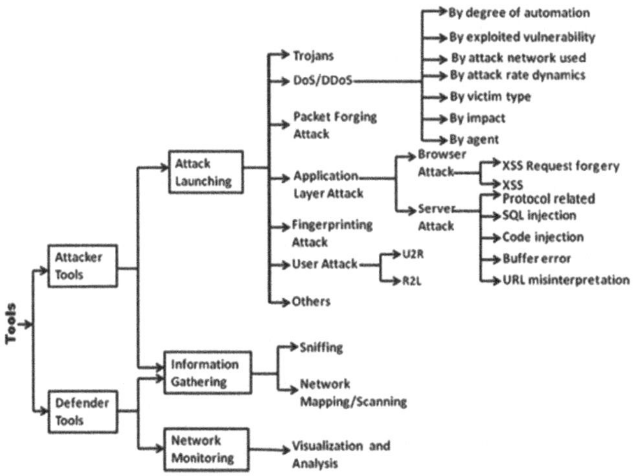

Fig. 12. Taxonomy of network security tools [48].

Thus far, this study has presented various threat models, analyzed and evaluated their merits, presented network forensics, and examined the significance of network forensics. In addition, it has looked at the results for each study topic, which throws light on different parts of cybersecurity resilience, network analysis, and threats to networks.

5 Discussion and Recommendations

An organization can strengthen cybersecurity by identifying and responding to threats in real time using threat intelligence and continuous monitoring. To implement a defense-in-depth strategy, many tires of security controls must be used, and they must be updated and patched frequently. This strategy also involves implementing responsibility and raising awareness among workers by providing cybersecurity education.

Network threats are among the most critical attacks in cyber technology today, evolving in every sector. Several recommendations arise from the conclusions derived from the research questions, closely coinciding with the study's main objectives. Firstly, the study highlights the importance of investigating sophisticated forensic techniques and procedures to understand network forensics comprehensively. This involves exploring new forensic models that can be adjusted to keep up with changing cyber threats and technologies. The goal is to enhance the ability to detect and analyze network risks.

Furthermore, one can manage who has access to what assets and lessen the effect of breaches by segmenting your network. This requires regularly finding and fixing security holes through penetration tests and assessments. Prepare for potential incidents by creating a plan and practicing it. These safeguards will make you more resistant to cyberattacks and less likely to suffer a security breach.

6 Conclusions, Limitations and Further Research

The overview of network threats in cybersecurity has illuminated modern networks' vast challenges, from malware infections to DDoS attacks and data breaches. Grasping the nature and characteristics of these threats is a cornerstone in developing robust defense strategies. By scrutinizing the features and capabilities of both open-source and commercial forensic tools, organizations can fortify their incident response capabilities and mitigate the impact of security breaches. Moreover, examining research challenges in network forensic analysis has underscored several pressing obstacles and constraints, including data acquisition issues, resource limitations, and skills shortages. The urgency of addressing these challenges cannot be overstated, as it is crucial for improving the effectiveness and efficiency of forensic investigations.

This research underscores the importance of robust network forensic practices in safeguarding network infrastructure and data assets from cyber threats. The study relied solely on secondary sources due to limited financial resources and a specific research scope. Nevertheless, attempts were undertaken to thoroughly analyze and interpret the diverse discoveries to deduce possible resolutions. It is crucial to recognize the existence of specific constraints and potential sources of inaccuracy that could have influenced the study results.

Furthermore, future research should prioritize thorough investigations into specific network threats, such as malware and DDoS attacks, from many angles. Comparative studies can provide insights into the effectiveness of cybersecurity strategies in reducing different network threats, enhancing our overall understanding of threat landscapes. The study recommends examining the performance of forensic tools, such as snort, in real-world scenarios while detecting and analyzing network threats. In addition, integrating machine learning and artificial intelligence tools can automate and improve the processes of identifying and addressing threats, enhancing incident response capabilities.

References

1. Ozkaya, E., Islam, R.: Inside the Dark Web. CRC Press (2019)
2. Ezenwoye, O., Liu, Y., Patten, W.: Classifying Common Security Vulnerabilities by Software Type. consensus.app, pp. 61–64 (2020)
3. Douzet, F.: Cyber-Security Challenges (2018). https://doi.org/10.1093/oso/9780198790501.003.0031
4. Oz, H., Aris, A., Levi, A., Uluagac, A.S.: A survey on ransomware: evolution, taxonomy, and defense solutions. ACM Comput. Surv. (CSUR) **54**(11s), 1–37 (2022)
5. Kolodenker, E., Koch, W., Stringhini, G., Egele, M. Paybreak: defense against cryptographic ransomware. In: Proceedings of the 2017 ACM on Asia Conference on Computer and Communications Security, pp. 599–611 (2017)

6. Gupta, S., Sharma, L.: Exploitation of Cross-Site Scripting (XSS) vulnerability on real world web applications and its defense. Int. J. Comput. Appl. **60**(14), 28–33 (2022)
7. Alharahsheh, H.H., Pius, A.: A review of key paradigms: Positivism VS interpretivism. Global Acad. J. Humanities Soc. Sci. **2**(3), 39–43 (2020)
8. Snoke, T.D., Shimeall, T.J.: An updated framework of defenses against ransomware. Technical report, Carnegie-Mellon Univ Pittsburgh, PA (2020)
9. Falco, G.J., Rosenbach, E.: Confronting Cyber Risk: An Embedded Endurance Strategy for Cybersecurity. Oxford University Press (2022)
10. Helmbrecht, U., Plaga, R.: New Challenges For It-Security Research In Ict (2019)
11. Elbardan, H., Kholeif, A.O., Elbardan, H., Kholeif, A.O.R.: An interpretive approach for data collection and analysis. In: Enterprise Resource Planning, Corporate Governance and Internal Auditing: An Institutional Perspective, pp. 111–165 (2017)
12. Hindy, H., et al.: A taxonomy of network threats and the effect of current datasets on intrusion detection systems. IEEE Access **8**, 104650–104675 (2020)
13. Robinson, R.J.: Insights on cloud security management. Cloud Comput. Data Sci. 212–222 (2023). https://doi.org/10.37256/ccds.4220233292
14. Jang-Jaccard, J., Nepal, S.: A survey of emerging threats in cybersecurity. J. Comput. Syst. Sci. **80**(5), 973–993 (2019)
15. Agba, M.S., Rijami, J.: Data integrity in research: a fundamental prerequisite for credible research output across disciplines and professions. Int. J. Democracy Dev. Stud. **5**(2), 31–45 (2022)
16. Yaqoob, I., et al.: The rise of ransomware and emerging security challenges in the Internet of Things. Comput. Netw. **129**, 444–458 (2017)
17. Kettani, H., Wainwright, P.: On the top threats to cyber systems. In: 2019 IEEE 2nd International Conference on Information and Computer Technologies (ICICT) (2019). (978-1-7281-3323-2)
18. Paquet-Clouston, M., Haslhofer, B., Dupont, B.: Ransomware payments in the bitcoin ecosystem. J. Cybersecur. **5**(1), tyz003 (2019)
19. Gibson, C.P., Banik, S.M.: Analyzing the effect of ransomware attacks on different industries. In: 2017 International Conference on Computational Science and Computational Intelligence (CSCI), pp. 121–126. IEEE (2017)
20. McIntosh, T., Kayes, A.S.M., Chen, Y.P.P., Ng, A., Watters, P.: Ransomware mitigation in the modern era: a comprehensive review, research challenges, and future directions. ACM Comput. Surv. (CSUR) **54**(9), 1–36 (2021)
21. Beaman, C., Barkworth, A., Akande, T.D., Hakak, S., Khan, M.K.: Ransomware: recent advances, analysis, challenges and future research directions. Comput. Secur. **111**, 102490 (2021)
22. Botacin, M., Ceschin, F., Sun, R., Oliveira, D., Grégio, A.: Challenges and pitfalls in malware research. Comput. Secur. **106**, 102287 (2021)
23. Blythe, J.M.: Using behavioural insights to improve the public's use of cyber security best practices (2014)
24. Robinson, R.J.: IoT Solutions for Smart Parking - Sigfox Technology. Comput. Sci. Eng. Int. J. (CSEIJ), **v14**(2), 1–13 (2024). https://www.cseij.org/papers/v14n2/14224cseij01.pdf. https://doi.org/10.5121/cseij.2024.14201
25. Sabillon, R., Serra-Ruiz, J., Cavaller, V., Cano, J.: A comprehensive cybersecurity audit model to improve cybersecurity assurance: the cybersecurity audit model (CSAM). In: 2017 International Conference on Information Systems and Computer Science (INCISCOS), pp. 253–259. IEEE (2017)
26. More, R., Rane, D.: Comprehensive study of network forensic. Int. J. Multidisciplin. Res. **5**(5), (2023)

27. Mouton, F., Leenen, L., Venter, H.S.: Social engineering attack examples, templates and scenarios. Comput. Secur. **59**, 186–209 (2016)
28. Paul Joseph, D., Norman, J.: An analysis of digital forensics in cyber security. In: Advances in Intelligent Systems and Computing, pp. 701–708 (2018)
29. Shah, A.: Evaluating network forensics applying advanced tools. Int. J. Adv. Eng. Manag. Sci. **9**(4), 01–09 (2023)
30. Sharma, S., Singh, T.: Ransomware: a severe cyber security threat in the digital era. Int. J. Sci. Res. Sci. Technol. **6**(1), 211–218 (2019)
31. Sachowski, J.: Digital Forensics and Investigations. CRC Press (2018)
32. Rahamathullah, U., Karthikeyan, E.: Distributed denial of service attacks prevention, detection and mitigation – a review. SSRN Elec. J. (2021)
33. Rao, U.: Overview of cyber security. Int. J. Adv. Res. Sci. Commun. Technol. 47–51 (2023)
34. Yadav, C.S., Gupta, S.: A review on malware analysis for IoT and android system. SN Comput. Sci. **4**(2) (2022)
35. Yassir, A., Ismaeel, A.A.K.: Current computer network security issues/threats. Int. J. Comput. Appl. **155**(1), 1–5 (2016)
36. Yeo, S., Birch, A., Bengtsson, H.I.J.: The role of state actors in cybersecurity: can state actors find their role in cyberspace? typeset.io, pp. 217–246 (2016)
37. Zaher, M.A., Eldakhly, N.M.: Cyber attack detection in wireless adhoc network using artificial intelligence. Int. J. Wirel. Ad Hoc Commun. **6**(2), 18–33 (2023)
38. Mansfield-Devine, S.: Ransomware: the most popular form of attack. Comput. Fraud Secur. **2017**(10), 15–20 (2017)
39. Locard, E.: La police et les méthodes scientifiques. Les Éditions Rieder (1934)
40. Mirkovic, J.: Distributed Denial-of-Service Attack. In: The SAGE Encyclopedia of the Internet (2018)
41. Miner-Romanoff, K.: Interpretive and Critical Phenomenological Crime Studies: A Model Design. The Qualitative Report (2015)
42. Mendyk-Krajewska, T., Mazur, Z.: Problem of network security threats. IEEE Xplore (2020)
43. Morariu, C., Stiller, B.: DiCAP: distributed Packet Capturing architecture for high-speed network links. IEEE Xplore (2022)
44. Gebhardt, T., Reiser, H.: Network Forensics for Cloud Computing. hal.inria.fr (2023)
45. Deri, L.: nCap: wire-speed packet capture and transmission. IEEE Xplore (2015)
46. Cusack, B., Lutui, R.: Including Network Routers In Forensic Investigation. In: Australian Digital Forensics Conference (2023)
47. Darijević, V.: Cyber crime as a security risk on the internet. Megatrend revija **18**(2), 257–266 (2021)
48. Davenport, D.: Anonymity on the Internet: why the price may be too high. Commun. ACM **45**(4), 33 (2022)

Modern Trends and Prospects of Mountain Tourism Business Development and Assistance

Otar Japaridze[1(✉)] and Marina Metreveli[2]

[1] East Europian University, Tbilisi, Georgia
Otar.jafaridze@eeu.edu.ge
[2] Georgian Technical University GTU, Tbilisi, Georgia
metrevelimarina11@gtu.ge

Abstract. Based on the relevancy of general development of the tourism business, the presented work set a goal of identifying the needs and problems of separate directions of mountain tourism.

I stage: Qualitative study - was intended for identification of weighty opinions of official or unofficial parties interested in mountain tourism in regard to mountain tourism problems and possible prospects of development.

II stage: Quantitative study - was aimed to quantitative assessment of opinions of travelers and local mountain guides and their reflection in percentage terms, in regard to challenges facing mountain tourism and prospects of this direction.

The conducted studies main findings are:

- uncontrolled building activity initiated in the developed touristic regions - as a hazardous factor, which poses danger to authenticity of the local environment and, as a consequence, its sustainable development;
- transformation of tourism into the leading sector of economy in the developed touristic regions increased the dependence on this branch. At the very first crisis, this reliance had an adverse effect on the economic conditions of the local population due to sharp decline of touristic flow and loss of the sole source of income under crisis conditions;
- among positive factors caused by tourism development - remigration of local population of the region, which vivified and newly populated-developed the abandoned and emptied villages;
- tourism development has led to awareness raising of Georgia as a country having a development potential of mountain tourism that in its turn promotes attraction of financially reliable tourism segment;
- study has revealed those specific strengths or challenges, which encounter in regard to mountain tourism according to the regions, as well as traveler's behavior preferences in the light of local or international tourists;

Recommendations elaborated based on the research outcomes, which will promote travel business development, are represented in the work, as well.

Keywords: Tourism · mountain tourism · sustainable development · ecotourism

R. C. Geibel and S. Machavariani (Eds.): ISPC 2024, SPBE, pp. 69–86, 2025.
https://doi.org/10.1007/978-3-031-88052-0_5

1 Introduction

The natural, geographical and cultural possibilities of our country are maximally mobilized to meet the interests of tourists. Accordingly, there are different types of tours from among the tourist trips - which serve to meet the most varied interests of tourists.

The share of our country's tourism potential can be said to comes largely from the promotion and popularization of the high mountain tourism business, because the types of mountain tourism are interesting and attractive not only for those who are fond of adventure tours, but it can meet the needs of tourists with almost all types of interests. (Diasamidze M. 2015) But due to the lack of detailed studies and statistics tailored directly to mountain tourism and the interests of people who are fond of travelling in the mountains - it is natural that specific problems cannot be considered - taking into account the views and interests of both external and internal tourists in the planning of measures to promote mountain tourism (UNWTO 2018).

Identifying the challenges and requirements facing tourism and then solving them - first of all, is a priority of the country, and then of the tourism business - without jeopardizing the authenticity of the cultural heritage of the country, thus - the sustainable development of tourism (UNWTO 2023).

That is why the purpose of this work is to promote the development of mountain tourism business in Georgia - based on the combination of the latest scientific literature of the field and empirically obtained data - specially selected and processed, which will give us the opportunity to identify and plan the necessary measures for the development of mountain tourism, how to develop and use the tourism potential of the mountain and, hereby, the business, without jeopardizing the concept of sustainable development of tourism.

2 Theoretical Foundation

Positive factors and threats of mountain tourism development.

More than 65% of Georgia's relief is mountainous, which in turn makes it one of the attractive countries in the world tourism market. According to the statistics of the World Tourism Organization, mountain tourism has about 20% of global tourism and plays a major role in the development of the tourism industry. (Khakhishvili, T. 2021) The mountain is one of the great assets for the tourism industry all over the world. Its natural resources attract a wide variety of visitors. Which in turn makes it one of the best tourist destinations. It plays a major role in GDP growth and job creation. (Liyun, Z., Rita Yi, M., Jotikasthira, N., Jinkun, S., & Yunyi, M. 2022).

At the same time, it often becomes vulnerable to such factors as environmental impact, socio-economic and cultural factors (M. Metreveli, 2012). The mountain environment is very sensitive to such interventions and often contains threats. That is why the development of tourism in the mountains should take place by taking care of the existing one and taking into account the economic vision of the country in the overall strategy. (Nepal, S. 2002) This ensures the development of tourism not only at the expense of tourists, but also through the development of specific tourist infrastructure. Which in turn will be related to the minimization of harmful ecological and socio- cultural impact. (Liyun, Z., Rita Yi, M., Jotikasthira, N., Jinkun, S., & Yunyi, M. 2022).

The religious, gastronomic and cultural traditions in the mountain, its authentic relief diversity and peculiarities attract tourists with different interests and preferences, and only in this way, the mountain tourism is highly sustainable and profitable (WTO 2004).

However, it should be taken into account that the increase in the popularity of mountain tourism can harm the natural environment, because tourism companies, depending on the increase of their income, overload specific destinations, and the competitive market itself cannot distribute resources. In order to reduce these negative factors, it is necessary to coordinate the state and the private sector, it will contribute to the sustainable development of the mountain tourism. (UNICEF Georgia.)

The modernisation of mountain tourism has become more relevant in view of the pandemic and post-pandemic - because the post-pandemic period has radically changed the existing requirements for the tourism business and has put this field to face new, contemporary challenges. This applies to the tourism business in the mountainous regions as well, because the pandemic has become a hindrance for mountain regions on the one hand, and a great opportunity on the other hand, as post-pandemic tourism has become more focused on distancing, fresh air, travelling in nature, etc. (Naciye, G. U., & Akbiyik, A. 2020) That is why the search for mountain tourism is relevant and that is why mountain tourism had begun to recover much earlier than other destinations.

3 Research Method

The research methodology planned to achieve the aim of the work was defined as follows:

Main hypothesis: Unlike other tourist destinations, the greater "sustainability" of mountain tourism is due to the natural/authentic environment of mountain regions and the naturally existing variety of resting/leisure activities - not the infrastructural development of mountain regions according to modern standards.

Sub-hypothesis: Accordingly, the main obstacle to maintaining the sustainability of the business potential of mountain tourism is the chaotic development in the mountainous regions developed for tourism - which threatens the main motivators for tourists to rest in the mountains - the authenticity of the regions, cultural-historical- gastronomic heritage, traditional mountain tourist attractions - which will gradually reduce the tourist interests of the mountainous regions.

Purpose of the Study

The purpose of the study is to determine the business potential of the mountainous regions of Georgia, to identify its development trends and perspectives.

Study Tasks

1. Analysing the world experience and determining the possibility of its implementation/adaptation in the reality of Georgia;
2. Determining the current crises in the world and identifying ways to avoid them or mitigate their negative effects;

3. In the direction of sustainable development, study of the existing situation in mountainous regions and evaluation of the effectiveness of the processes;
4. Evaluation and determination of the effectiveness of the measures taken at both the regional and centralized governance levels;
5. Identification of factors facilitating and hindering the development of mountain tourism - identification of the challenges and opportunities that mountain tourism has in modern reality and the subjects participating therein (comparison of regions).
6. Identification of specific needs and problems of individual mountain tourism destinations - according to specific regions and different tourist profiles. Also taking into account the post-crisis needs;
7. Determination of profiles of mountain tourists and identification of their behavioural characteristics - visualization of motivators and demotivators of walking in the mountains.

4 Methodology

Qualitative study: Department of Tourism, travel companies, tourism experts, local mountain guides and hotel representatives, international and local travellers; (A total of 30 people were interviewed).

Quantitative research: International and local travellers, local mountain guides; (A total of 700 people were interviewed: 500 Georgians; 200 Foreigners).

5 Analysis and Results

When analysing the world's best practices, the respondents emphasize such factors that are already well implemented in the world tourism standards - the presence of certified mountain guides, construction of mountain huts, constant updating of hiking and trekking trails and marking with modern standards, the existence of modern safety systems and rescue equipment - which we see in Georgia as a true ideal, although it does not have a systematic and organized character - which hinders the development of Georgian mountain tourism using modern standards, because the safety of tourists depends on it, as well as the provision of high-quality services to them and the preservation of the authenticity of the environment.

Speaking about the international experience of mountain tourism, the respondents participating in the study put special emphasis on the model of such countries as Switzerland, France, Austria, Italy- whose resort arrangement is focused on the principles of regional management and with this structure can be well adapted to the possibilities of tourism development in the regions of Georgia. The examples of Bhutan and Andorra were also emphasized. To the respondent's opinion, against the background of various crises in the world today - such as the post-pandemic period, war in the region, economic instability - one of the main challenges in Georgia is that there is no mountain tourism development strategy in the state - therefore, there is no effective regulation from the state, which would contribute to the smooth development of mountain tourism in Georgia in the context of global crises. Also, the low qualification of the people working in the sector and the malfunctioning of the mining and rescue services, are called important challenges, ignoring the principles of sustainable development, breaking the authenticity of the environment. The necessity of market diversification was highlighted, in order to attract high- budget tourists.

With regard to the sustainable development of the country, the respondents emphasized the economic benefits that are currently obtained from tourism in the regions and in which the participation of the local population is significantly high. It should be noted that in those regions of Georgia, where tourism is more or less developed (Svaneti and Kazbegi regions), there is a remigration of young people and local employment - many abandoned villages have been settled again and we are facing a fairly high rate of return migration. However, we have such problems as low of population awareness, enforcement of laws, high development in tourist centers.

The respondents conversed about the efficiency of measures carried out by the government and noted that for the development of mountain resorts both the planning of development of resort areas and the search for investors are in progress. Marking and development of the construction design of walking/hiking trails is in an active phase. The inclusion of the local population in the development of mountain tourism and the raising of their awareness in this regard through various trainings are mentioned to be an event that has great importance.

When speaking about the hindering and facilitating factors of tourism, first of all, the respondents pointed out the lack of monitoring of the implementation of legal requirements and also the absence of statistics on the correct loading of tourist regions.

The reason for underdevelopment of tourism in a specific region is primarily the smallness of the local population, which is accompanied/or caused by infrastructural deficiencies: Roads, schools, outpatient clinics, electricity and other engineering communications - which in itself is an obstacle for tourism and, therefore, for the development of the region. Solving of the mentioned problems will also solve the issue of easy access to these regions.

Among the factors necessary for the development of mountain tourism in the regions, the respondents of the study mention the need to develop those attractions that have the potential of a given region and are demanded by tourists. Among the necessary needs for the development of tourist attractions, the appropriate tourist infrastructure, service personnel/guides with the necessary qualifications and, of course, the inventory specific to the attraction - to ensure security, are mentioned first.

The respondents also consider the possibility of developing eco and ethno tourism as having potential. The results of the quantitative research conducted to determine the tourist profiles, their attitudes, requirements, reasons for satisfaction-dissatisfaction and behavioural preferences are as follows:

On the question **"What does mountain tourism mean to you"**, the answers are interestingly different according to Georgian and foreign tourists: (Fig. 1).

As we can see, unlike Georgians, foreign tourists in mountain tourism include cultural tourism and gastro tourism in addition to traditional mountain tourism fields.

We find interesting answers to the question: **"What are the main problems you face when dealing with mountain tourism"?** (Fig. 2).

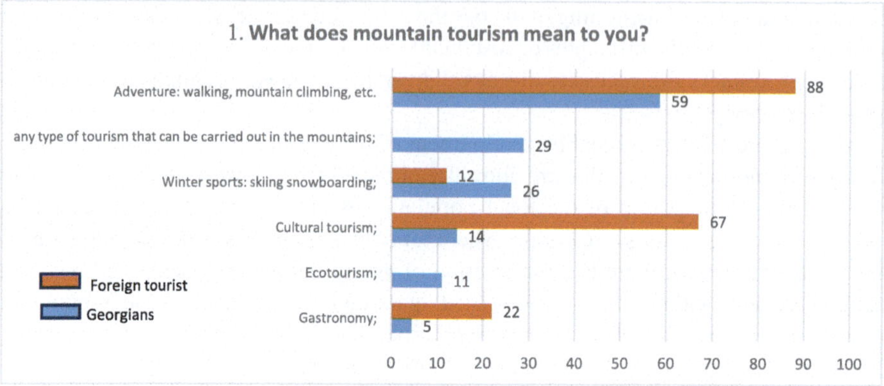

Fig. 1. Question 1

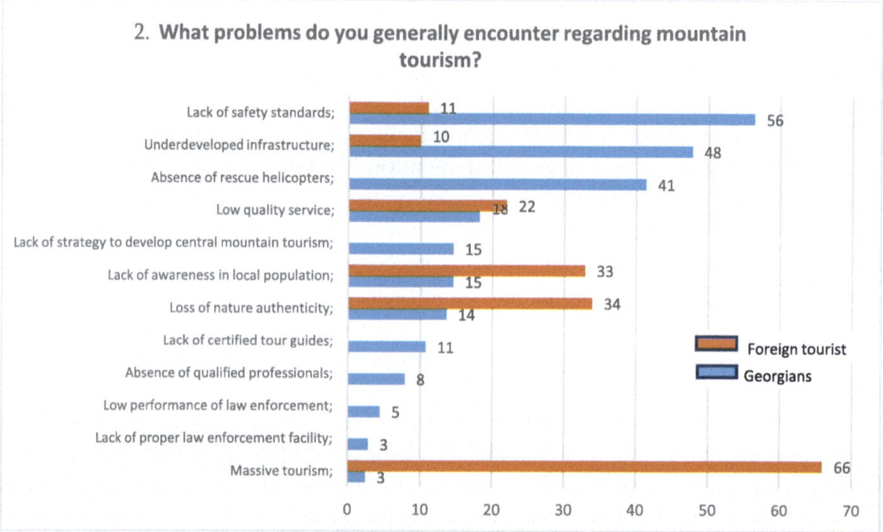

Fig. 2. Question 2

As we can see, while the main problems of mountain tourism for Georgian tourists are the non-compliance with safety standards and underdeveloped infrastructure, foreign travellers emphasize mass tourism, the loss of authenticity of the environment and the ignorance of the local population in the principles of tourism.

The respondents were also asked, **what threats they saw in mass tourism** (Fig. 3).

As we can see in the Fig. 3, Georgian and foreign travellers have very different perceptions here - 32% + 17% of Georgians perceive mass tourism as a positive factor and do not expect any threat from it, only 20% of them associate mass tourism with uncontrolled constructions. Contrary to this, foreign tourists (69%) see serious threats

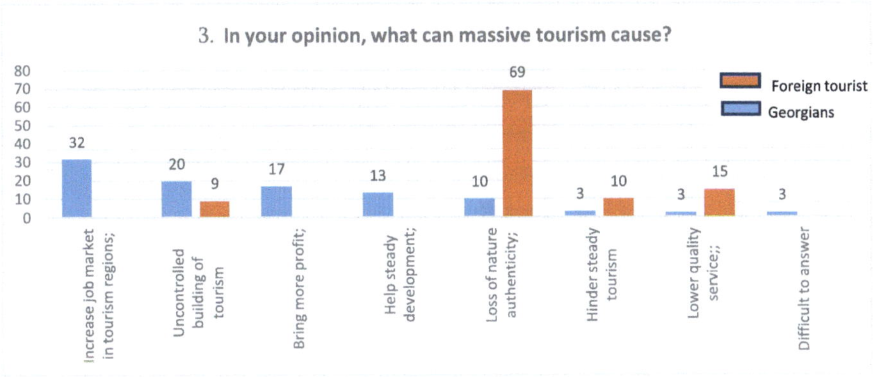

Fig. 3. Question 3.

of destroying the authenticity of nature in mass tourism and also note that it will inevitably lead to a drop in the quality of services.

The study also identified the most popular tourist places for Georgian and foreign tourists (Fig. 4).

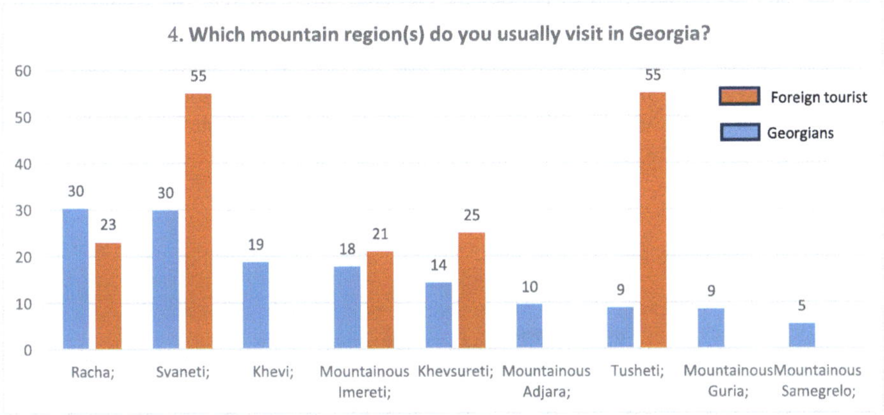

Fig. 4. Question 4

It is noteworthy that Racha, Svaneti, Khevi and mountainous Imereti are leading among the most popular regions for Georgian travellers. And for foreign tourists - Tusheti, Svaneti and Khevsureti.

The answers to the following question identify the reasons for such choice (Fig. 5),

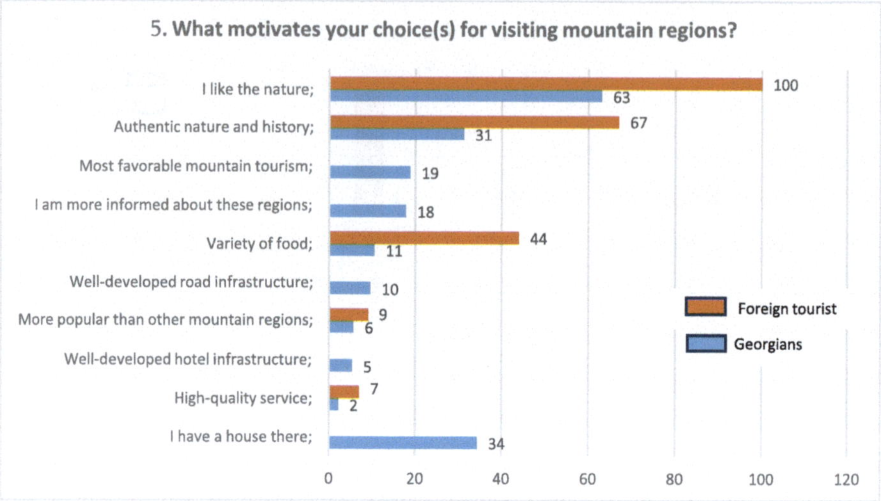

Fig. 5. Question 5

Both foreign and Georgian tourists are motivated to visit the region by its natural and at the same time authentic environment. However, there are also different answers - according to which foreign tourists are particularly attracted by the gastronomic features of the chosen region, while the choice of Georgian travellers is largely determined by having their own home in a specific region (which, of course, was not unexpected). The following question of the study was about popular mountain destinations for Georgian and foreign tourists (Fig. 6).

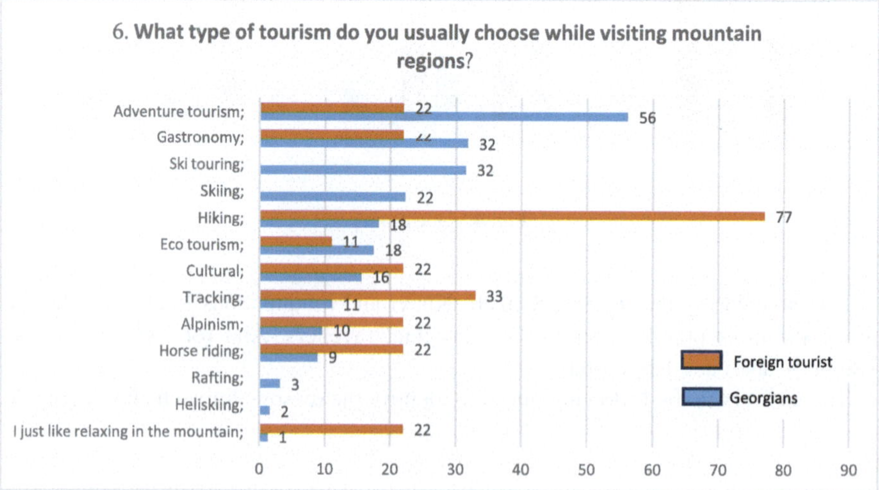

Fig. 6. Question 6

As we can see, here too we have a different picture from the point of view of Georgians and foreigners: 56% of Georgian travellers prefer adventure tourism, while 32% prefer skiing and ski tourism. And 77% of foreigners are engaged in hiking and 33% in trekking. It is worth noting the special interest of foreign travellers in mountaineering and horse-riding tourism, which significantly differs from those of Georgian travellers. (See Fig. 6).

Here we find tourist attractions desirable for both types of tourists, such as: Gastro tourism 32% and 22%, cultural tourism - 22% and 16%, eco-tourism - 18% and 11%.

The respondents of the quantitative survey - both Georgians and foreigners - also talked about the positive and negative factors they faced while travelling in the mountains.

Among the positive factors, both Georgians and foreigners name the culture of the region, the cleanliness of the environment and the local cuisine which have equal importance (Fig. 7). It is worth noting that foreign travellers single out the feeling of security among the positive factors.

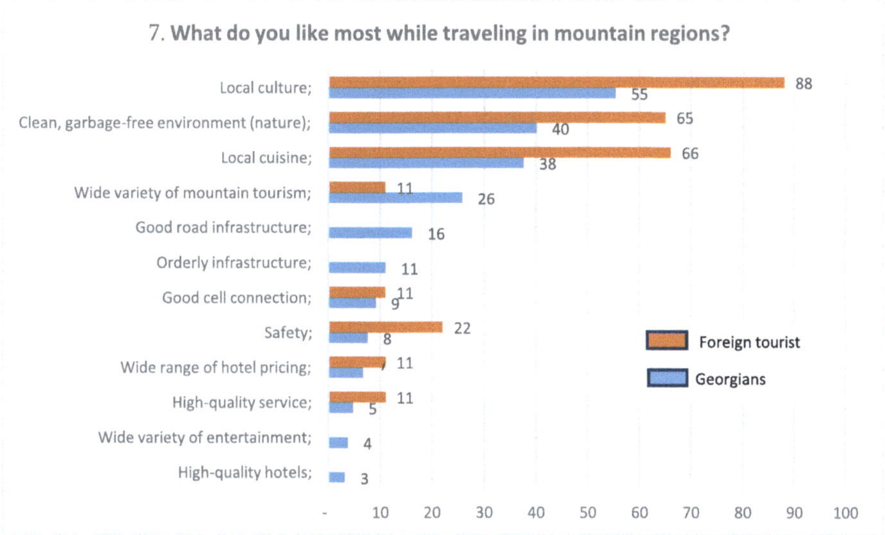

Fig. 7. Question 7

However, it should be noted that, in addition to the positive aspects, the survey respondents also focus on the negative aspects and say that the most negative perceptions of mountain travelling are related to the presence of the fact of littering of the environmental in a number of cases (47%/33%), bad road infrastructure (48%/33%), poor mobile internet (44%) and non-organized tourist infrastructure (33%) are particularly painful for foreigners, and low-quality services and the absence of high-class hotels are also noticeable to them (Fig. 8).

We also asked the respondents which region in their experience was the least developed for tourism in Georgia and what was the reason for that (Figs. 9 and 10).

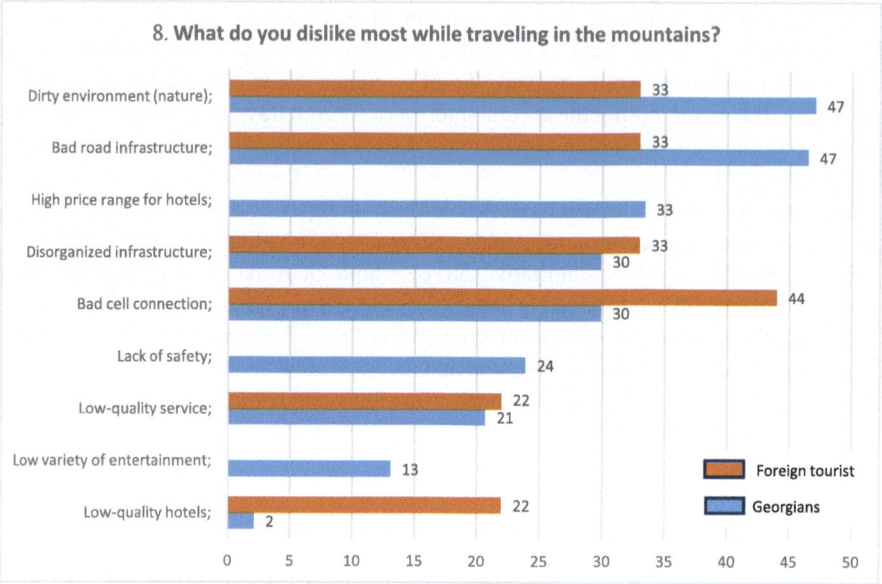

Fig. 8. Question 8

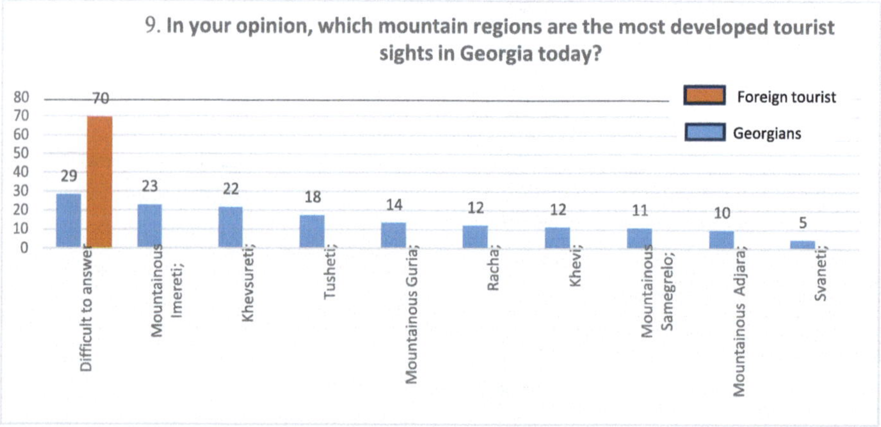

Fig. 9. Question 9

As it can be seen in the figure, the least developed tourist regions (both for Georgians and foreigners) were named mountainous Adjara, mountainous Guria, mountainous Imereti, followed by Tusheti and Khevsureti. And among the reasons for the poor development of tourism field in these regions, as expected, the following were highlighted with the highest percentage of significance (Fig. 10):

Among foreigners - poor information about the region (33%), non-organized mountain trails (33%), violation of the authenticity of the environment (22%) and poor quality mobile Internet (22%).

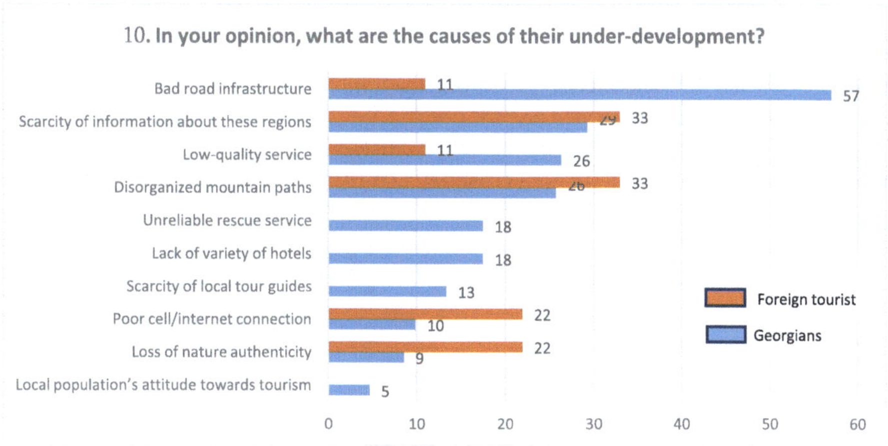

Fig. 10. Question 10

For Georgian travellers, among the reasons for the less developed regions in terms of tourism, the following is named (Fig. 10): Bad road infrastructure (57%), poor information about the region (29%), low level of service (26%), poor conditions of mountain trails (26%), poor choice of hotels (18%).

In order to complete the present information, we asked what they would like to add/improve for a more comfortable trip to the mountains (Fig. 11).

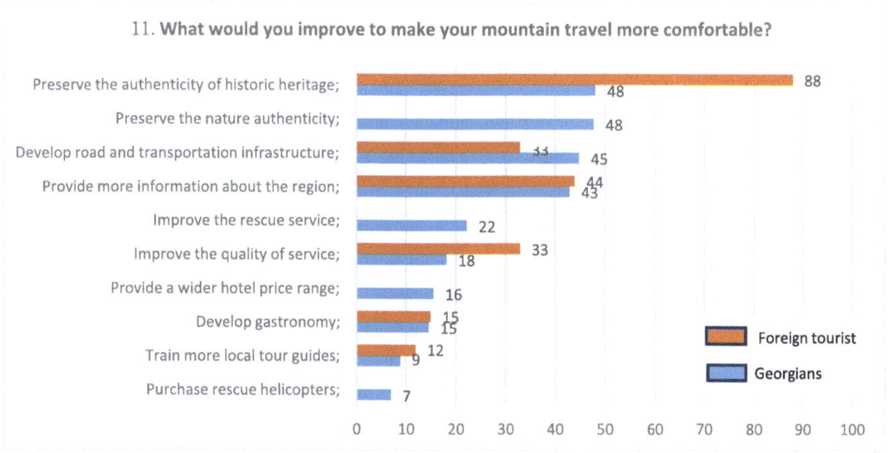

Fig. 11. Question 11

As can be seen in the figure, for both types of travellers (Georgians/foreigners), the main parameter to be improved is the need to preserve the authenticity of the environment, its cultural and natural features!

After that, it would also be a significant step forward for both segments **to increase awareness about the region** (43% and 44%), Development of transport and road infrastructure (45% and 33%), as well as promoting the improvement of service quality (33%) and facilitating the rescue service (22%).

At the end, let's see what the indicators of satisfaction with the development trends of mountain tourism are among both Georgian and foreign tourists (Figs. 12 and 13).

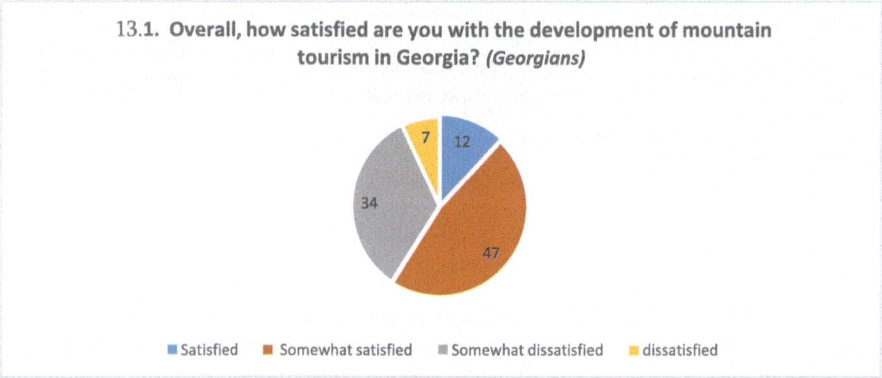

Fig. 12. Question 12

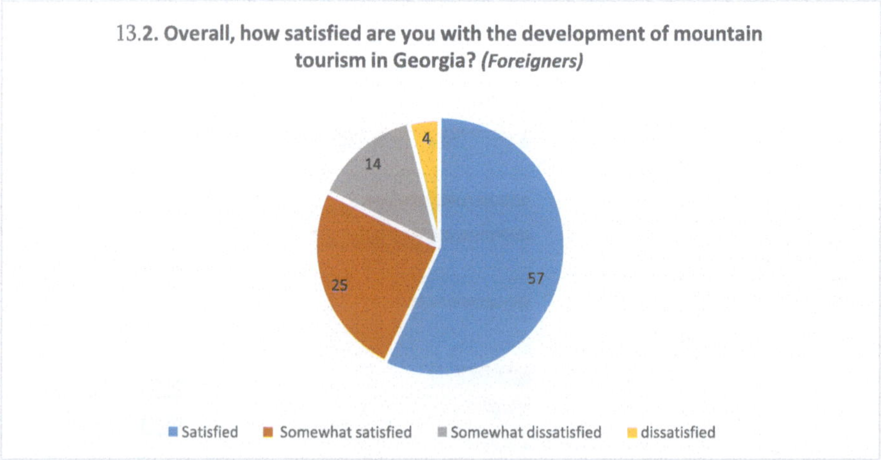

Fig. 13. Question 13

The given results indicate that foreign tourists are more satisfied with the trend of mountain tourism development in Georgia and have fewer complaints in this regard than Georgians.

6 Discussion and Recommendations

Based on the information obtained from the conducted qualitative and quantitative studies, conclusions can be made with regard to a separate research task and verify the research hypothesis.

Task 1:

Analysing the world's best practices and taking into account their experience, the main prerequisite for the development of mountain tourism in Georgia is the organization of a legal framework that will regulate the issue of certification of professional mountain guides on the one hand, and ensure the situations of purchase and use of rescue equipment, on the other hand. All of these, in turn, will bring Georgian mountain tourism closer to the world standards, provide variety of tourist attractions and safety.

Meanwhile, among the international experience, the maximum support of local tourism and the increase of the motivation of domestic travellers can be recognized as the best and most promising approach, which will insure the income of the tourism sector, if for some reason international movement of tourists is interrupted (as it happened in the conditions of the Covid-pandemic).

Taking into account the experience of the world's leading tourist countries, it is also important to create a legal framework necessary for maintaining the authenticity of the natural environment of the mountain regions, which at the same time, will be focused on solving the problems caused by excess tourism.

Task 2:

The main precondition for avoiding crises threatening the tourism sector was the diversification of tourist markets - which ensures the entry of different and highly profitable tourist flows into the country, taking into account the running of a targeted advertising policy.

The development and support of domestic tourism was considered to be the prevention of crises - it is a reinsurance mechanism for reducing international tourist flows, which usually accompanies various international crises.

As for the local crises, that is the outflow of professional personnel from the sector. Due to this, the drop in the quality of service - which will lead to the dissatisfaction of tourists. To resolve this, the process of certification of guides, as well as personnel involved in the sector, is considered important, which will solve the problem of crisis in terms of staffing.

Main problem is massive tourism, which is followed by the destruction of the authenticity of mountain regions - firstly, this is against the goals of sustainable development and it also reduces the interest of tourists in the region, because, as we have seen from the results of the research, the main motivating factor for travelling to mountain regions is the authenticity of the environment. Massive tourism causes the transformation of tourism into the main economic source occupies an equally important place - which in turn leads to the disruption of agriculture in the region and thus increases the risks of economic crises in the region, in cases where the tourism sector is endangered for any reason.

Among the crises of the tourism business is the lack of proper marketing campaigns, which will be focused on diversified, targeted markets and will strengthen the tourism image of the country in terms of achieving the desired positioning.

Task 3:

The main effect of the increase in tourist flows in the mountains is the return migration of the population, which in turn leads to the revitalization of the region and, in this respect, to the increase of its attractiveness for tourists - this factor directly involves the adherence to the principles of sustainable development and thus deserves a positive assessment.

The same cannot be said about the process of enforcement of legal regulations, which is manifested in the systematic violation of the existing legislation in terms of development in mountainous regions and thus causing irreversible damage to the environment.

Taking this into account, it is logical that the development of mountain tourism and aligning it with the plan of sustainable development should begin with improving the legislative framework and strengthening its enforcement.

Task 4:

In terms of evaluating the effectiveness of the measures taken, the communication of the measures taken in the sector to the broad society is assessed as ineffective. Unfortunately, the steps made and measures taken by the government are rarely demonstrated - which leads to low awareness of the population and the formation of the position "nothing is being done in the direction of mountain tourism" - and this, in turn, has a negative impact on the country's tourism image.

Among the necessary measures to eliminate the existing hindering factors, the necessary decentralization of the budget and strategy and the issue of integrating professional, local personnel in the sector should be emphasized. It is important to formulate tourism development strategies at the regional level and adapt them to the needs of a specific region - and then, with appropriate professional personnel, for the purpose of its implementation and monitoring.

Task 5:

When talking about the hindering and facilitating factors of tourism, the most important thing is the strict monitoring of the implementation of the legal requirements, the existence of the statistics of the correct loading of the tourist regions. The incorrect tourist load of the regions is manifested in the fact that, on the one hand, we have excessive tourist flows in the country, which leads to the unsystematic development of tourist regions and the destruction of the authenticity of the environment, and on the other hand, we have almost the same opportunities with completely untapped regions, which, due to infrastructural or other bureaucratic issues, remain literally beyond such business.

This once again convinces us that the regional strategies of tourism development, which will be adjusted directly to the tourism opportunities of a specific region, to unique attractions, will be the key to the development of the mountain and tourism in general. The given strategies should obviously take into account the existing agrarian resources of the region, solving the necessary infrastructural problems, necessary measures for the return migration of the population.

Task 6:

Among the factors necessary for the development of mountain tourism in the regions, it is important to develop those attractions that have the potential of a given region and are demanded by tourists.

The list of mountain destinations identified by the results of the quantitative survey of tourists (Fig. 6) directly determines the tourist interests and their natural segmentation. This is an ideal starting point for segmenting tourism markets, highlighting unique products, and producing targeted advertising campaigns. Which will ultimately contribute to the desired positioning of the country - to become a country offering a unique tourist product.

Among the necessary needs for the development of tourist attractions, the appropriate tourist infrastructure, service personnel/guides with basic qualifications and, of course, the inventory specific to the attraction - to ensure safety, are important.

Task 7:

It is worth noting that the quantitative survey correctly identifies the perceptions of travellers in relation to the characteristics of mountain tourism (Fig. 1). Among them, different perceptions of Georgian and foreign travellers are worth paying attention to, which is ultimately a good indication for the creation, positioning and advertising of appropriate tourist activity in both foreign and Georgian markets of mountain tourism.

The problematic aspects highlighted by the survey, which are faced by travellers when visiting the mountainous regions of Georgia (Fig. 2) - among which, the tendency to break authenticity, insecurity of.

safety standards, less developed tourist infrastructure and in many cases the low level of awareness of the local population regarding the characteristics of tourism are clearly emphasized, - indicate to the needs the mountain tourism has and which prevent the proper development of tourism.

And the different perception of the factors hindering mountain tourism for Georgian and foreign travellers is an important reference and useful information for the correct segmentation of tourist markets and the development of an adequate business model for reaching target audiences.

The danger of the perception of mass tourism by Georgian and foreign tourists is also a carrier of important information (Fig. 3), according to which it becomes clear that, compared to foreigners, Georgians generally do not see the real danger - the potential of losing the main advantage of the mountain, its authenticity - which can be threatened unconditionally unless the mass tourism is regulated. This directly points to a serious hindering factor in the development of mountain tourism in Georgia - the lack of awareness of the local population in relation to sustainable development and tourism in general.

The fact that Georgians perceive mass tourism as a positive event, while foreigners perceive it as a negative event, already indicates the dangers of tourism in Georgia and the need for measures that, on the one hand, will limit the influx of uncontrolled tourist flows into the country and, on the other hand, ensure an increase in the level of awareness of the local population.

And the fact that the main motivator for both Georgian and foreign tourists to visit the mountain is the preserved and untouched environment of the region is confirmed by the results of the survey (Fig. 5), which suggests that authenticity and gastronomic characteristics are unconditional motivators for making a choice. This, in turn, is an indication for the promotion and positioning of this or that region, for highlighting its uniqueness in the marketing strategy.

The right positioning of the country and highlighting of its uniqueness will be contributed by the positive aspects highlighted by the survey, which Georgian and foreign tourists note in their mountain travel experience (Fig. 7) and say that they are unconditionally fascinated by the untouched and different local culture, cuisine, opportunities for a variety of mountain attractions, etc. Along with the positive, it is important to pay attention to the negative aspects, such as the tendency to destroy the authenticity of the environment, the disorganized mining tourism infrastructure, the lack of professionalism in the service sector, the lack of safety standards, and what is no less noteworthy - the scarcity of information about the region/ineffective marketing activities.

The list of positive and negative factors mentioned by the respondents of the survey, which, according to their experience can be found in the characteristics of Georgian mountain tourism – compiles the tourist profiles in terms if information and creates a clear picture of the needs of current Georgian tourism.

This applies to both positive and negative parameters, as it is important for the development of the sector to eliminate negative aspects on the one hand, and to strengthen positive indicators on the other hand.

If the country is going to segment tourism markets and position itself with different/unique offers according to tourist profiles, then emphasizing the positively perceived characteristics identified by the survey, and putting the negative components into the corrective action plan - will contribute to the sustainable development of tourism.The existence of less developed tourist regions indicates that the country has sufficient potential to exploit additional tourist markets - if, of course, it resolves the infrastructural problems of the mentioned small busy regions and redistributes tourist flows in a targeted manner. On the one hand, this will solve the problem of uneven loading of regions caused by excessive tourism and, for this reason, the problem of destruction of the authenticity of the environment, and on the other hand, it will create a serious resource for additional income from tourism business in underdeveloped regions.

Despite a number of mentioned problems, which, according to tourists are found in the reality of Georgian mountain tourism, their level of satisfaction with development trends is quite high (Fig. 13) - among them, the level of foreign tourists is much higher, which is probably caused by the fact that the country's tourism.

development strategy is more focused on international travellers and their satisfaction - therefore, it takes into account their possible interests in the field of supporting the tourism business. However, knowing the interests of domestic tourists and taking them into account - and thus supporting and developing domestic tourism - is no less. Important and necessary for the stability of the country's tourism potential, which is confirmed by both the results of expert research and international experience in this field.

Verification of hypothesis

Based on the given results, we can state the correctness of the main hypotheses and sub-hypotheses and emphasize that the stability of mountainous regions is actually maintained by its natural and untouched environment, which provides a variety of opportunities to spend time in an interesting manner, because for all categories of tourists, the motivating factor for travelling to the mountains is unconditionally named as authenticity - considering that they can clearly see the negative and unresolved aspects that they encounter. Therefore, the sub-hypothesis of the research is verified, according to which everything that threatens the preserving of the mentioned natural conditions and inviolability is a factor hindering the development of mountain tourism.

Recommendations

Based on the results of the survey, the list of recommendations that should be implemented to support mountain tourism and which derive from the country's tourism needs and directly from the tourists' behavioural preferences are as follows:

Recommendation 1: The central and regional authorities, based on the experience of the world's leading countries, should regulate general safety standards and rules for using special rescue equipment; Recommendation 2: Professional training of local personnel in mountainous regions in accordance with the requirements of the tourism sector. This will promote the employment of local youth in the regions and bring the regions closer to the principles of sustainable development;

Recommendation 3: Develop a strategy for the development of mountainous regions, which will be adjusted to the specific needs of the individual region and its population;

Recommendation 4: Particular attention should be paid to the preservation of the authentic environment in the region, which in turn will be expressed in the preservation of both the nature and the architecture and existence characteristic of the region. The process should be regulated on the basis of strict monitoring of the legislative amendments and its implementation on the one hand, and on the other hand - by raising the level of awareness of the local population;

Recommendation 5: Facilitating and supporting domestic tourism. Such support can be expressed both with the right marketing campaign and with such an approach experienced in the world, such as a subscription system;

Recommendation 6: Develop appropriate marketing activities and legal regulations that ensure the proper loading of the mountainous region and avoid excessive tourism;

Recommendation 7: Introduction of marketing strategies of the country and its mountainous regions - through the segmented manner, by positioning the region and its uniqueness. Accordingly, the launch of this marketing campaign on the one hand in domestic as well as international markets - to attract more high-budget tourist flows.

7 Conclusion

To conclude, it can be said that the survey clearly showed us the real situation of mountain tourism in the perception of both experts and the main actors involved in therein - the travellers. Highlighting the uniqueness of Georgian culture, history and natural environment for travellers, which is the main motivation for their interest in Georgian mountain resorts. Emphasized the needs that, despite their admiration for the Georgian mountains, tourists see well, and the solution of which will increase the volume of mountain tourist flows and, most importantly, will make mountain tourism more important to the interests of high-budget tourists. The survey also showed the potential that the mountains of Georgia have, on the one hand, at the expense of regions that are less used for tourism, and on the other hand, at the expense of the implementation of still undeveloped - however, highly demanded and promising mountain attractions worldwide.

The present study clearly shows the role of the interested parties involved in the development of tourism business - the state, business and the local population in the development of this direction, which is spoken by both experts in the field of tourism and travellers alike.

Finally, the recommendations prepared on the basis of the survey results are a necessary prerequisite for the mountain tourism development strategy.

References

Diasamidze, M.: Formation of a Cluster in the Tourism Industry and Increasing the Competitiveness of the Regional Tourism Market. Shota Rustaveli State University of Batumi, Batumi (2015)

Khakhishvili, T.: Ecotourism cluster as an effective mechanism for increasing Georgia's competitiveness. Tbilisi: University named after Grigol Robakidze (2021)

Kostic, M., Lakićević, M., Milićević, S.: Sustainable tourism development of mountain tourism destinations in Serbia, January 2018. www.researchgate.net: https://www.researchgate.net/publication/327193211_Sustainable_tourism_development_of_mountain_tourism_destinations_in_Serbia

Liyun, Z., Rita Yi, M., Jotikasthira, N., Jinkun, S., Yunyi, M.: Economic Development and Mountain Tourism Research from 2010 to 2020: Bibliometric Analysis and Science Mapping Approach. 208 MDPI Journals Awarded Impact Factor, 27 (2022)

Metreveli, M.: Environment and Ecotourism Management. Tbilisi: Hospitality industry exam and training center (2012)

Naciye, G.U., Akbiyik, A.: Impacts of COVID-19 on global tourism industry: a cross-regional comparison. Tourism Manag. Perspect. **36** (2020)

Nepal, S.: Mountain Ecotourism and Sustainable Development, 1 May 2002. bioone.org: https://doi.org/10.1659/0276-4741(2002)022[0104:MEASD]2.0.CO;2

UNICEF Georgia. (n.d.). Sustainable Development Goals. www.unicef.org: https://www.unicef.org/georgia

UNWTO: INTERNATIONAL TOURISM AND COVID-19, 07 Mar 2023. https://www.unwto.org/: https://www.unwto.org/tourism-data/international-tourism-and-covid-19

UNWTO: TOURISM'S POTENTIAL FOR MOUNTAIN ECOSYSTEMS AND COMMUNITIES OUTLINED IN NEW REPORT, 23 April 2023. https://www.unwto.org/: https://www.unwto.org/news/tourism-s-potential-for-mountain-ecosystems-and-communities-outlined-in-new-report

World Tourism Organization (UNWTO): Sustainable Mountain Tourism-Oportunities dor Local Communities, Madrid (2018)

WTO: Indicators of Sustainable Development for Tourism Destinations A Guidebook (2004). e-unweto.org: https://www.e-unwto.org/doi/book/https://doi.org/10.18111/9789284407262

Yalcinkaya, T., Gruzel, T.: A general overview of tourism clusters. J. Tourism Theory Res. **13** (2019)

The Role of Digital Management and Artificial Intelligence in Post-pandemic Period in Georgian Business Entities

Giorgi Katamadze(✉)

Business Administration, Batumi Shota Rustaveli State University, Batumi, Georgia
Giorgi.katamadze@bsu.edu.ge

Abstract. Digital management and artificial intelligence are an integral part of the survival, maintenance and development of business processes in the pandemic and post-pandemic world. In addition, it should be noted that in the wake of the continuous processes of modern development, the Covid-19 pandemic accelerated the processes of artificial intelligence and digital management. Small and medium-sized business entities in Georgia faced a real challenge, since this segment is the most important constituents of the business sector. This paper aims at identification of the modern challenges of small and medium-sized businesses in Georgia, in particular, the role and function of digital management and artificial intelligence during the pandemic and post-pandemic periods.

The pandemic period has accelerated the integration of digital management and artificial intelligence (AI) in businesses. It triggered the digital transformation, emphasizing the significance of digital management and AI in protecting corporate stability, efficiency, and effectiveness. The post-pandemic era demonstrated the importance of digital management and AI in improving business stability and competitiveness. With these technologies businesses are able to perform more efficiently, provide much better customer service, as well as be better in decision-making, developing base for sustainability in the modern era.

The research methodology was determined based on the research objectives, using an interdisciplinary methodology, including in-depth interviews with business entities and an assessment of business entities in regards to the current research components. The objectives of the study were considered as factors for defining the research methodology.

The theoretical frame of the paper is based on basic, fundamental investigations by Georgian and international authors in the interrelated subjects. The paper contains results and recommendations based on complex research that are significant for scientific circles as well as for the business sector and society interested in this issue in general.

Keywords: Georgia · Business · Digital Management · Artificial Intelligence · Covid-19 Pandemic

G. Katamadze—Web of Science Researcher ID: AGC-4699-2022.
Scopus ID: 57225979055.

R. C. Geibel and S. Machavariani (Eds.): ISPC 2024, SPBE, pp. 87–100, 2025.
https://doi.org/10.1007/978-3-031-88052-0_6

JEL Classification: D0 · D8 · M10 · O1 · O3

1 Introduction

Artificial intelligence (AI), digital management, E-commerce and modern business processes in general went through a new, innovative, and modern transformation in the post-Covid era. The Covid -19 pandemic has significantly accelerated the development of business entities in this direction, for a variety of reasons, the most important of which include the following:

- restrictions on travel and gatherings have created the need for business to reach customers personally;
- to allow users to examine the product or service, it was necessary to deliver it remotely. This encouraged creation of websites;
- remote work necessitated the digitization of processes and document circulation;

Those were the key issues, which made business entities to consider rapid corporate transformation. The crisis turned into an opportunity for business development (Katamadze & Tsiklashvili, 2024); for some business entities, the crisis stopped their activities; however, this led the companies to reconsidering of having anti-crisis strategies, which had been on the agenda before (Katamadze 2022).

The Covid-19 pandemic has completely changed the global agenda, with a direct impact on all fields, particularly the economic one. Small and medium-sized entities are the primary job creators in Georgia, therefore they have a significant share in the country's budget. So the normal operation of this business segment was critical to the country during the general lockdown and complicated administration. The pandemic has been and remains a stress test for most business entities, and many are still struggling to overcome this challenge (Katamadze, G. 2023). A traditional way of life has been changed due to recent worldwide crises, war processes, pandemics, and innovations in technology. The increasing progression of technology and artificial intelligence are reducing the factor of humans, which is based on knowledge and expertise (Katamadze, G., Tavdgiridze, L., & Bolkvadze, M. 2024).

The current macroeconomic environment in Georgia was heavily influenced by those actions made by the Government of Georgia during the Covid-19 pandemic, which placed several sectors of the economy under close monitoring and assistance. The government tried to relieve pressure on businesses despite the strict restrictions around the world (Katamadze, G., Petrova, M., & Tsiklashvili, N. 2024). During pandemic business became more adaptable, resilient, inventive, and creative and expanded the operation in various directions (Katamadze, G., & Tsiklashvili, N. (2024).

Some researchers regard the Covid 19 pandemic as a series of failures, causing difficulties for human health, the economy, the global energy market, environmental protection, and other areas (Priya, S. S., Cuce, E., & Sudhakar, K. 2021). In fact, the list might be considered to be universal, as it includes all key areas. Shortly after the pandemic started, several scientists predicted that it would deepen socioeconomic vulnerability, widen the wealth gap, and destroy low-income countries' health-care systems (Lenzen, M., Li, M., Malik, A., Pomponi, F., Sun, Y. Y., Wiedmann, T.,... & Yousefzadeh, M. 2020). This assumption was correct, and some countries still have to deal with the post-pandemic crisis: the pandemic had dramatic impact on those countries relying heavily on imported goods. The change in global trade relations was mostly caused by logistical issues, as the supply of commodities prior to the pandemic was mainly depended on international logistics chains and markets; the reason was an insufficient, unsatisfactory level of local supply (Batty, M. 2020).

In the first year of the pandemic's spread, there was no end in sight, causing public despair and loss of confidence despite the country's size and level of development (Barua, S. 2020). However, the situation changed significantly since the end of 2021, when some sectors of economy experienced major easing of strict, restrictive regulations. The rapidly changing regulations, made it difficult and impossible to assess countries' economic activities. Some scientists believe that the fast-evolving nature of crisis caused by the Covid-19 is the major obstacle to measure global economic activity (Jackson, J. K., Weiss, M. A., Schwarzenberg, A. B., & Nelson, R. M. 2020). Despite the uncertain situation, some researchers believed that in the post-pandemic world, discretionary demand would rise as people become more cautious and global retail leverage reach new heights (Bai, H. M., Zaid, A., Catrin, S., Ahmed, K., & Ahmed, A. 2020). According to some scientists, the social-economic, political and environmental effects of the pandemic should be the subject of priority research in social and humanitarian sciences to evolve into a new knowledge that will serve as a foundation for future informed political decisions (Madeira, A., Palrão, T., & Mendes, A. S. 2020). Education's importance in the country's socioeconomic and political processes is increasing in parallel with the development of technology. The acquisition of fundamental information and strong skills is crucial for development of a country, socio-political stability, economic progress, and the development of an inclusive economy (Tavdgiridze, L., Katamadze, G., & Bolkvadze, M. 2024).

2 Theoretical Foundation

The main theoretical basis of the article is the works of Georgian and foreign researchers, which can be classified by two main criteria, particularly: works related to digitalization, online business and artificial intelligence, and the works devoted to modern technological-innovative approaches in general, among them:

- Zhang, C., & Lu, Y. (2021). Study on artificial intelligence: The state of the art and future prospects. *Journal of Industrial Information Integration*, *23*, 100224;
- Surden, H. (2019). Artificial intelligence and law: An overview. *Georgia State University Law Review*, v *35*(4);

- Loureiro, S. M. C., Guerreiro, J., & Tussyadiah, I. (2021). Artificial intelligence in business: State of the art and future research agenda. *Journal of business research, 129*, 911–926;
- Enholm, I. M., Papagiannidis, E., Mikalef, P., & Krogstie, J. (2022). Artificial intelligence and business value: A literature review. *Information Systems Frontiers, 24*(5), 1709–1734;
- Kraus, S., Durst, S., Ferreira, J. J., Veiga, P., Kailer, N., & Weinmann, A. (2022). Digital transformation in business and management research: An overview of the current status quo. International journal of information management, 63, 102466;
- Kharaishvili, E., Gechbaia, B., Tsiklashvili, N., & Katamadze, G. (2024). Digital transformation of the agricultural sector and its impact on productivity in Georgia. In BIO Web of Conferences (Vol. 114, p. 01002). EDP Sciences;
- Popova, P., Popov, V., Marinova, K., & Petrova, M. (2023, November). The Role of Digital Platforms and Big Data Analytics as a Base for Digital Service Innovation. In 2023 4th International Conference on Communications, Information, Electronic and Energy Systems (CIEES) (pp. 1–8). IEEE;

Theoretical and Practical Importance of the Article: Considering its approaches, methodology and theoretical- practical specifics, the work will be interesting for those specialists dealing with the analysis of business entities in Georgia, for researchers of innovative business processes, for scientific circles, graduate and doctoral students in general, who study the modern strategies of business entities, the implementation of technological processes and artificial intelligence in business. From a practical standpoint, the obtained results will be noteworthy for the managers of various companies, researchers, state institutions and all those interested in business activities, also for a large audience interested in technological companies and modern business software.

3 Research Method

The research was conducted combining both quantitative and qualitative methods. Along with desk analysis of official materials, an in-depth interview was conducted, the received information was evaluated according to the respective components (strategies, technologies, creation, implementation, feedback), and their correlations and deviations were identified. In addition, the information provided by each business entity was compared with the data of companies with similar characteristics, the purpose of which was to determine general trends. In order to determine the general trends, the information provided by each business entity was compared to comparable data from other business entities. To determine the theoretical framework of the research, a desk study was conducted with the final results compared with the official data and trends.

To select business entities for the interview, we based on the following criteria: (a) The date of starting the business entity's activity (at least 2 years before the Covid-19 pandemic); (b) sphere of activity of business entity (in different cities of Georgia); (c) diversity of segments of the business entity's activity; The segments of the selected business entities included the main areas of small and medium-sized businesses in Georgia.

4 Analysis and Results

Remote work and digital platforms became a way to save costs and increase efficiency. The platforms Zoom, Teams, Skype and Messenger became an integral part of business process management. The growth of technologies triggered shifting of the working environment, work schedule, workload and in general the specifics of the interaction between the employee and the task to be completed.

The widespread popularization of artificial intelligence and its practical application raises many questions, the answers to which are directly related to the quality, intensity and volume of involvement of artificial intelligence in daily life. Although "moderate use", "limited use", "use as an example" or "use for specific purposes" of artificial intelligence (AI) can be useful and have positive effects in terms of time management, it also presents certain risks and challenges, timely analysis and discussion of which is especially important in modern life. Artificial intelligence technology is becoming more developed and advanced day by day, as are the methods and tools that can be applied in the field of education and science. The ability to mechanically generate original content reduces creativity. In order to overcome plagiarism concealment algorithms, the modern world will have to work hard on the background of rapid technological advancement. Technological growth and development improves the quality of work performance; yet, in some fields the development of modern technologies creates risks depending on the specifics of the tasks, such as originality, authenticity, disregard for human factor, and so on. Up to now, companies used digital platforms, though these were specialized applications and software, used with a specific purpose such as booking, reservations systems, menu calculations programs, etc., however, the pandemic led to the expansion of programs and applications, necessitating their multifunctionality; for example, if previously these systems offered online catalogues and menus only, now they include reservation and ordering options, a variety of payment methods, and delivery tracking. This led to the need of addition of new external workforce such as delivery service employees, however, this also created the new requirements for different qualifications and skills for the employees of the companies such as modern IT fluency and sometimes even specific IT abilities.

4.1 Official, State Statistics

Prior to presenting our empirical research findings, it is interesting to have a look on information of the official state structures – the National Statistics Office of Georgia, in our case. We sought data from the following four areas:

(1) data on the use of artificial intelligence by enterprises (the purpose for such use);
(2) distribution of the application of artificial intelligence by enterprises according to their origin;
(3) share of enterprises, employing the ICT specialists;
(4) share of enterprises, engaged in online sales of goods/services;

The statistics is as follows. See Table 1.

Table 1. Data on the use of artificial intelligence by enterprises according to the purpose

Data on the use of artificial intelligence by enterprises according to the purpose				
Purpose	2020	2021	2022	2023
Marketing and Sales	34.8%	24.4%	22.9%	29.9%
Production processes	19.2%	13.8%	12.4%	16.1%
Business administration processes	11.0%	6.8%	15.1%	12.2%
Enterprise management	12.5%	15.6%	11.0%	5.4%
Logistics	3.4%	5.9%	19.0%	9.0%
ICT security	10.7%	18.0%	10.9%	12.3%
HR management or procurement	8.4%	15.4%	8.7%	15.1%
Total	**100.0%**	**100.0%**	**100.0%**	**100.0%**

Resource: https://www.geostat.ge/ka/modules/categories/106/sainformatsio-da-sakomunikatsio-teknologiebis-gamoqeneba-shinameurneobebshi

As the official data shows, in recent years artificial intelligence is used mainly for marketing and sales, as well as for production processes and HR management and recruitment. It is also noteworthy that the use of artificial intelligence in logistics has almost tripled since 2020. As well as interesting is the reduction of use of artificial intelligence in the management area from 12.5% in 2020 to 5.4% in 2023. As the statistics show, the usage of artificial intelligence in entities is multifaced, and the percentage of its use is increasing year after year. The practice of implementation of artificial intelligence is also important, particularly the way of its creation/introduction in specific companies. Here the statistics is as follows. See Table 2.

Table 2. Distribution of the application of artificial intelligence by enterprises according to their origin

Distribution of the application of artificial intelligence by enterprises according to their origin				
Origin	2020	2021	2022	2023
Created by the enterprise employees	29.0%	25.1%	16.8%	16.9%
Commercial software or systems modified by enterprise employees	13.0%	9.7%	8.4%	21.3%
Open-source software or systems modified by enterprise employees	9.2%	5.2%	9.4%	18.6%
Purchased ready-to-use commercial software or systems	27.6%	36.8%	44.2%	25.6%
An agreement signed with the company's external suppliers to develop or modify them	21.2%	23.2%	21.1%	17.5%
Total:	100%	100%	100%	100%

Resource: https://www.geostat.ge/ka/modules/categories/106/sainformatsio-da-sakomunikatsio-teknologiebis-gamoqeneba-shinameurneobebshi

As the data show, 25.6% of the enterprises acquired ready-made software, and the lowest is the number of created software by the employees of the entity with its 16.9%. The remaining percentage is filled by outsourcing or modification by the software company. However, it should be noted that the entities employing ICT specialists are mainly large companies (with their 55.9%), while the percentage of small and medium business employing the ICT specialists is 3,3% (small enterprises) and 29,4% (medium enterprises). Therefore, we believe that mainly large enterprises create artificial intelligence software or modify it.

In parallel with the analysis of AI data, it is important to consider entities that were engaged in online sales of goods or services during the pandemic and post-pandemic periods. The respective statistics is as follows (See Table 3).

Table 3. The share of enterprises that had web sales of goods / services, %

	The share of enterprises that had web sales of goods / services, %	2020	2021	2022	2023
Total	By enterprise's websites or apps (including extranets)	3.0%	2.7%	2.9%	3.1%
	By e-commerce marketplace websites or apps used by several enterprises for trading goods or services (e.g. MyMarket.ge, Wishlist.ge, Vendoo.ge, My.ge, Procurement.gov,ge, Booking.com, hotels.com, eBay, Amazon, Amazon Business, Alibaba and etc.)	1.1%	1.9%	1.9%	1.7%
	Did not have	**96.8%**	**96.0%**	**96.2%**	**96.2%**
Of which:					
Small	By enterprise's websites or apps (including extranets)	2.7%	2.4%	2.5%	2.7%
	By e-commerce marketplace websites or apps used by several enterprises for trading goods or services (e.g. MyMarket.ge, Wishlist.ge, Vendoo.ge, My.ge, Procurement.gov,ge, Booking.com, hotels.com, eBay, Amazon, Amazon Business, Alibaba and etc.)	0.9%	1.8%	1.7%	1.6%
	Did not have	**97.0%**	**96.3%**	**96.5%**	**96.6%**
Medium	By enterprise's websites or apps (including extranets)	8.8%	7.8%	12.0%	11.2%
	By e-commerce marketplace websites or apps used by several enterprises for trading goods or services (e.g. MyMarket.ge, Wishlist.ge, Vendoo.ge, My.ge, Procurement.gov,ge, Booking.com, hotels.com, eBay, Amazon, Amazon Business, Alibaba and etc.)	3.1%	3.9%	6.7%	4.9%

(*continued*)

Table 3. (*continued*)

	The share of enterprises that had web sales of goods / services, %	2020	2021	2022	2023
	Did not have	**90.6%**	**90.5%**	**86.5%**	**87.3%**
Large	By enterprise's websites or apps (including extranets)	14.9%	18.0%	22.1%	22.2%
	By e-commerce marketplace websites or apps used by several enterprises for trading goods or services (e.g. MyMarket.ge, Wishlist.ge, Vendoo.ge, My.ge, Procurement.gov,ge, Booking.com, hotels.com, eBay, Amazon, Amazon Business, Alibaba and etc.)	6.6%	8.4%	8.5%	12.1%
	Did not have	**84.0%**	**80.6%**	**76.8%**	**75.7%**

Note: The percentage is calculated only for those enterprises that had access to the Internet during the relevant period.

Resource: https://www.geostat.ge/ka/modules/categories/106/sainformatsio-da-sakomunikatsio-teknologiebis-gamoqeneba-shinameurneobebshi

As shown, a total of 13.9% of small and medium-sized enterprises sell goods and services through their **own website or application**, and 22.2% of large enterprises. In total, 36.1% of business entities sell goods and services through their own website and application. 6.5% of small and medium-sized enterprises sell goods and services through e-commerce marketplace websites or applications that is used by several enterprises to sell goods or services (ex. www.myMarket.ge; www.wishlist.ge; www.vendoo.ge; www.my.ge; www.procurement.gov.ge; www.booking.com; www.hotels.com; www.eBay.com; www.amazon.com; Amazon Business, Alibaba etc.), while the share of large businesses here is 12,1%. In total **18,6%** of enterprises use e-commerce marketplace websites.

4.2 Empirical Research with Small and Medium Business Entities

In the framework of the research conducted by us, 29 small and medium-sized companies participated that operate in various segments in Georgia; the goal of our research was to answer the following questions:

(1) Has the company changed its management strategy in recent years; which digital or online platforms has the company introduced in recent years for management?
(2) Does the company see any perspectives of AI introduction in future?

Taking into account the specificity of the research objectives, the companies' managers, their founders and finance personnel took part in it. We got valuable responses, but prior to sharing them, to get a full picture, we would like to share some responses to additional questions. The subject of general interest was whether the companies had any anti-crisis plan in place prior to the pandemic. As the survey results showed only 18,4%

of companies had an action strategy – a kind of anti-crisis strategy. 81,6% of companies, did not have any strategy for force majeure or crisis situations.

Considering the research objectives, we wanted to know which restrictions had a negative influence on business during the Covid-19 pandemic. 72.4% of the companies participating in the research name "lockdown" - prohibition of movement during the state of emergency; other companies name the individual restrictions, like transportation restrictions (6,8%); restriction on entry into the Horeca sector on the basis of vaccination (4,3%), and the remaining 16,5% of companies, name the restrictions on number of employees and the arrangement of work spaces (Fig. 1).

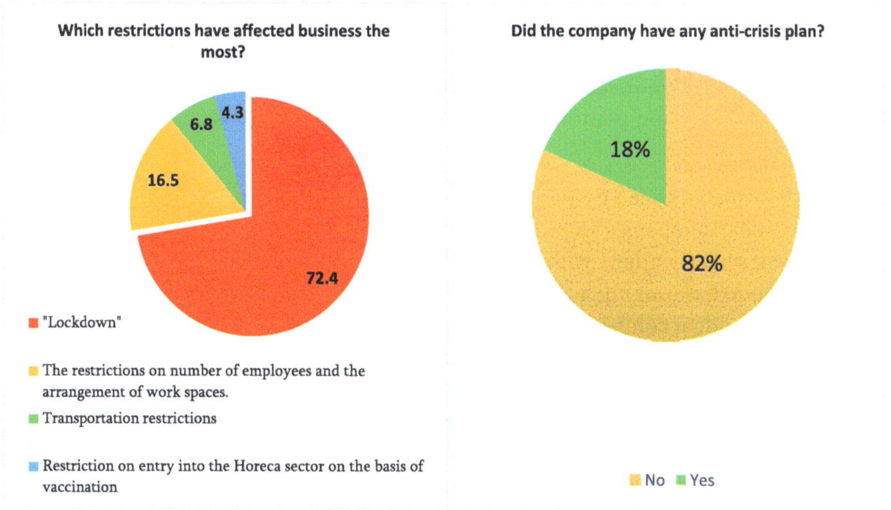

Fig. 1. Responses

As for the responses to our research questions, they are as follows:

1. Has the company changed its management strategy in recent years; which digital or online platforms has the company introduced in recent years for management?

Online Communication. The majority of companies name the addition of online tools as the most important change in their management strategy; in particular, most companies have established social network chats, where current issues are presented and discussed. According to managers and employees, online tools were mainly added during the pandemic period, however, even after the end of the pandemic, online tools are still used actively as a means of managing and monitoring of teams and individual tasks (chats - mainly messenger, Whats up, Viber, also zoom platform for video calls depending on the specifics of the business). All these led to a change in the management strategy, for example, if previously a specific day of the week was designated for a big meeting in the company, and a morning meetings were held every day for ongoing tasks, now most of the daily meetings have been replaced by online, remote communication.

Also, business plans have become long-term, in particular, posting online spreadsheets and sales plan has reduced the need for daily evaluations and task performance tracking has been simplified at the expense of simple access to online information. In addition, reduction of the number of actual, face-to-face meetings allowed to save time and decrease the current office costs (electricity, stationary, etc.).

Digitalization. It should be highlighted that most companies positively characterize digitalization, particularly menus, lists of products (balances), documentations; in general, information contained in binders is now accessible immediately and save decision-making time. The companies highlight the importance of introduction of online systems, like online booking, receiving of customer feedbacks and etc. One of the benefits of online catalogues is the saving of human resources, required for updating the products on the counters. Digital data also allows to define the best-selling product or service category across multiple categories, being crucial analytical data for determining discount categories. This helps maximum optimization of business processes, directly reflecting on the increase in the efficiency and effectiveness of the company. The integration of digitalization and online platforms have indeed transformed business operations and management strategies.

2. Does the company see any perspectives of AI introduction in future?
According to the companies' representatives, the introduction of AI in companies, first and foremost, directly aligns with the challenges of modern business and markets, represents progress, has a significant impact on company image and reputation, and has the potential to provide a competitive advantage.

The companies' representatives believe that introduction of automated, standardized, uniform processes thought AI allows to maintain quality and reduce unintentional, mechanical human errors, saving human resources, time and money. AI facilitates processing of necessary data and search for information; it makes possible to consider alternative versions and generate a ready-made SWOT analysis; it is important in terms of customer communication: the speed, uniformity of responses, level of efficiency in work, absence of an emotional factor during communication with difficult clients, etc. It also helps analyze the customers' interests and allow to offer them products, services according to their interests that has an important role in modern sales.

Indeed, AI is becoming the main component of digital management, an effective tool for the implementation of the manager's role (planning, organizing, leading and controlling) and a significant element of the sustainable development of modern business; however, there are some challenges related to the availability of finance for the appropriate infrastructure and software for small and medium-sized business entities.

In this regard, significant data is also officially provided to the National Statistics Service of Georgia on the categories of enterprises acquiring equipment and technology according to various periods, allowing to make respective conclusions. See Table 4.

Table 4. The distribution of enterprises by categories of acquired technology Acquisition of machinery, equipment or software by enterprises, %

		2020	2021	2022	2023
Total	Only based on the same or improved technology used in the enterprise before	5.6%	5.8%	5.8%	10.1%
	Only based on the new technology that was not used in your enterprise before	1.5%	1.0%	1.4%	1.9%
	Based on both of the above technologies	2.7%	2.2%	3.3%	4.5%
	Have not purchased	***90.3%***	***91.1%***	*89.6%*	*83.5%*
	Total	**100.0%**	**100.0%**	**100.0%**	**100.0%**
Of which:					
Small	Only based on the same or improved technology used in the enterprise before	5.1%	5.4%	5.4%	9.7%
	Only based on the new technology that was not used in your enterprise before	1.4%	0.9%	1.3%	*1.8%*
	Based on both of the above technologies	2.4%	1.9%	3.0%	4.1%
	Have not purchased	***91.1%***	***91.8%***	*90.4%*	*84.4%*
	Total	**100.0%**	**100.0%**	**100.0%**	**100.0%**
Medium	Only based on the same or improved technology used in the enterprise before	17.9%	15.3%	17.2%	***22.4%***
	Only based on the new technology that was not used in your enterprise before	3.0%	3.1%	4.3%	2.9%
	Based on both of the above technologies	9.1%	9.3%	12.1%	13.3%
	Have not purchased	***70.0%***	***72.4%***	*66.5%*	*61.4%*
	Total	**100.0%**	**100.0%**	**100.0%**	**100.0%**
Large	Only based on the same or improved technology used in the enterprise before	25.4%	23.4%	24.2%	*25.0%*
	Only based on the new technology that was not used in your enterprise before	…	…	…	…
	Based on both of the above technologies	…	…	…	…
	Have not purchased	***53.4%***	***54.2%***	***54.7%***	*47.3%*
	Total	**78.9%**	**77.6%**	**78.9%**	**72.3%**

… Data not available or confidential.
Source: https://www.geostat.ge/en/modules/categories/108/innovation-activity

As the data show, in recent two years, business entities of all categories (small, medium and large) have acquired new equipment and technology. Between 2020 and 2023, there was a nearly 7% growth in the procurement of equipment and technology across all business entities. It should be highlighted that the small and medium-sized business entities have positive dynamics, with their 6% (small entities) and 5.1% (medium-sized) increase in acquisition of machinery, equipment or software. It is noteworthy that in recent years, medium-sized business entities have shown a strong interest in acquiring or improving technology (2020-17.9; 2021-15.3%; 2022-17.2%; 2023-22.4%). In the light of recent developments, this dynamic is highly positive in terms of anticipating the technological transformation of Georgian business entities.

5 Discussion and Recommendations

Enterprises in Georgia, have faced similar challenges in recent years (Covid-19 pandemic, wars etc.), just like other companies around the world; the issues were particularly intensive in terms of introduction of online services and digital transformations. Our research results prove that Georgian companies are strengthening technological directions in the light of modern development, and this trend has been increasing in recent years. The volume of research in this direction has expanded, as has the state's interest. Strong business entities are the basis for state's economic stability, that is why the private and public sectors' interests in business sustainability coincide. These issues attract more researchers' attention and now we see an increasing number of publications on technological progress. The Directive 2000/31/EC of the European Parliament and the Council as of June 8, 2000 on electronic commerce can be considered an important step forward in the promotion of electronic commerce. As a result, the Georgian Law "On Electronic Commerce" was developed within the framework of USAID technical assistance and is effective as since June 13, 2023. The Law applies to entrepreneurs registered in Georgia under Georgia's Law "on Entrepreneurs", as well as to branches of international entrepreneurial societies. The Law aims to promote the proper functioning of the internal market by ensuring the free movement of information society services, to protect consumers' rights in the process of electronic commerce, to define the rights and duties of intermediate service providers, and to protect them from the imposition of general monitoring obligations (Georgian Law on Electronic Commerce, 13.06.2023). Since 2014, the project "Harmonization of Digital Markets (HDM)" is in progress with the goal of accelerating the process of harmonization of digital markets between the EU and Eastern Partnership countries, improving the functioning of the digital economy and general society by collaborative initiatives, and the harmonization and integration of legal, operational, and technological systems of national ICT policy. (https://www.economy.ge/?page=projects&s=18&lang=en).

6 Conclusions, Limitations and Further Research

Based on data for the recent years, business entities in Georgia, use artificial intelligence mainly in the direction of marketing and sales. They mostly acquire ready-made software and most of them are large enterprises; as for the small and medium-sized entities, they mainly use e-commerce sites and only 6.5% of such entities sell goods and services in this way;

Similar to other companies around the world, business entities in Georgia are actively involved in the digital processes, that makes it necessary to match their visions, strategies and plans with modern challenges; therefore, an increasing number of companies might need to change their business strategies and adapt their business model to modern trends. In this regard, it is important for business consulting companies to be equipped with the relevant skills to deal with modern challenges and be able to easily transform their strategies to adapt to the modern business processes;

It is important to support small and medium-sized business entities in acquiring the resources needed for implementation of modern technologies. Small and medium-sized business support programs are much desired, which will help them create infrastructure in line with modern challenges, it might be grant programs or low interest rate loans;

Parallel to the transformation of companies' business models and infrastructure maintenance, it is critical for business entities to focus on strengthening employees' digital skills and providing them with appropriate knowledge, as modern infrastructure and technological progress necessitate proper management and utilization.

The positive dynamics of the acquisition of technologies and equipment by business entities operating in Georgia in recent years gives us a reason to assume that all three categories of business entities (small, medium and large) are focused on addressing the challenges of the modern market and business environment and they are not lagging behind technological progress; therefore, it increases their competitiveness and creates a basis for predicting their sustainability.

Digital transformation, integration of artificial intelligence in business and improvement of online services will be the main challenge for modern business companies, and the mobilization of resources in this direction will become a growing and continuous process of business entities.

Acknowledgement. This work was supported by Shota Rustaveli National Science Foundation of Georgia, (SRNSFG) Grant number YS-22-548, Project title - "The crisis of small and medium business subjects and its prevention in the post-pandemic period in Georgia".

References

Bai, H.M., Zaid, A., Catrin, S., Ahmed, K., Ahmed, A.: The socio-economic implications of the coronavirus pandemic (COVID-19): a review. Int. J. Surg. **8**(4), 8–17 (2020)

Barua, S.: Understanding coronanomics: the economic implications of the coronavirus (COVID-19) pandemic (2020). Available at SSRN 3566477

Batty, M.: The coronavirus crisis: what will the post-pandemic city look like? Environ. Plan. B: Urban Anal. City Sci. **47**(4), 547–552 (2020)

Enholm, I.M., Papagiannidis, E., Mikalef, P., Krogstie, J.: Artificial intelligence and business value: a literature review. Inf. Syst. Front. **24**(5), 1709–1734 (2022)

Jackson, J.K., Weiss, M.A., Schwarzenberg, A.B., Nelson, R.M.: Global economic effects of Covid-19: In: Brief. Congressional Research Service (2020)

Katamadze, G.: Business entity's preventive-anti-crisis strategy model and possibilities of its implementation in Georgia. Econ. Ecol. Socium **6**(2), 38–45 (2022)

Katamadze, G.: Small and medium-sized enterprises in Georgia: classification and the legal basis for their regulation. Innov. Econ. Manag. **10**(2), 98–115 (2023)

Katamadze, G., Tavdgiridze, L., Bolkvadze, M.: Economics and children. Innov. Econ. Manag. **11**(2), 61–73 (2024)

Katamadze, G., Tsiklashvili, N.: Crisis as an opportunity of accelerated development for the business entities. USV Ann. Econ. Publ. Admin. **23**(2(38)), 87–93 (2024)

Katamadze, G., Petrova, M., Tsiklashvili, N.: Formation of the post-pandemic business environment in Georgia: challenges and predictions. In: BIO Web Conference, 2024 International Conference on Agricultural, Biodiversity and Environmental Economics (ICABEE 2024), vol. 114 (2024)

Katamadze, G.: Tourism as one of the most vulnerable sectors in terms of pandemic period in Georgia, Autonomous Republic of Ajara. Revista de turism-studii si cercetari in turism, (32) (2021)

Tavdgiridze, L., Katamadze, G., Bolkvadze, M.: Economic awareness and early childhood education. Econ. Bus. (1987–5789), **16**(1) (2024)

Kharaishvili, E., Gechbaia, B., Tsiklashvili, N., Katamadze, G.: Digital transformation of the agricultural sector and its impact on productivity in Georgia. In: BIO Web of Conferences, vol. 114, p. 01002. EDP Sciences (2024)

Kraus, S., Durst, S., Ferreira, J.J., Veiga, P., Kailer, N., Weinmann, A.: Digital transformation in business and management research: an overview of the current status quo. Int. J. Inf. Manage. **63**, 102466 (2022)

Lenzen, M., et al.: Global socio-economic losses and environmental gains from the Coronavirus pandemic. PLoS ONE **15**(7), e0235654 (2020)

Loureiro, S.M.C., Guerreiro, J., Tussyadiah, I.: Artificial intelligence in business: State of the art and future research agenda. J. Bus. Res. **129**, 911–926 (2021)

Madeira, A., Palrão, T., Mendes, A.S.: The impact of pandemic crisis on the restaurant business. Sustainability **13**(1), 40 (2020)

Popova, P., Popov, V., Marinova, K., Petrova, M.: The role of digital platforms and big data analytics as a base for digital service innovation. In: 2023 4th International Conference on Communications, Information, Electronic and Energy Systems (CIEES), pp. 1–8. IEEE, November 2023

Priya, S.S., Cuce, E., Sudhakar, K.: A perspective of COVID 19 impact on global economy, energy and environment. Int. J. Sustain. Eng. **14**(6), 1290–1305 (2021)

Surden, H.: Artificial intelligence and law: an overview. Georgia State Univ. Law Rev. **35**(4) (2019)

Zhang, C., Lu, Y.: Study on artificial intelligence: the state of the art and future prospects. J. Ind. Inf. Integr. **23**, 100224 (2021)

საქართველოს კანონი ელექტრონული კომერციის შესახებ, 13 June 2023. https://www.economy.ge/?page=projects&s=18&lang=en; https://www.geostat.ge/en/modules/categories/108/innovation-activity; https://www.geostat.ge/ka/modules/categories/106/sainformatsio-da-sakomunikatsio-teknologiebis-gamoqeneba-shinameurneobebshi

Sustainable Economic Development, International Security and Technology Transfer in the Age of Artificial Intelligence

George Abuselidze(✉) and Gia Zoidze

Batumi Shota Rustaveli State University, Ninoshvili, 35, 6010 Batumi, Georgia
george.abuselidze@bsu.edu.ge

Abstract. The purpose of the study is to assess the importance and role of artificial intelligence in terms of the sustainable development of the country and international security. Also, let us see the public's attitude towards this innovative field, the difference of opinion on what impact machine learning and artificial intelligence will have on the economic well-being of humanity, how much they know that AI is actively used in applications that we use every day, how they see the fu-ture of machine learning and artificial intelligence. The study was conducted using qualitative research methods. Also, a SWOT analysis of the use of artificial intelligence in the direction of Customer Relationship Management (CRM) has been carried out. As a result of the conducted research, we think that in the future the development of artificial intelligence will contribute to the development of separate systems and, what is noteworthy, their transformation into a single organism. The integration of systems will create the greatest opportunities to connect types of da-ta that we would not have noticed when the systems existed separately. The more extensive and diverse the set of software environments required by a business, the more data connections and linkages will be visible. The ability to solve different tasks will automatically support the self-development process of artificial intelligence. The essence of artificial intelligence - self-development and independence will be achieved when it is allowed to process more data in a unified system than in separate systems.

Keywords: Artificial intelligence (AI) · Customer Relationship Management (CRM) · Knowledge Management (KM) · Information and Communications Technology (ICT) · Sustainable Economic Development

1 Introduction

In the 21st century, IT engineers have created "smart" systems that respond to user questions instantly, automatically process huge amounts of data and help businesses make rational decisions by developing certain recommendations. Therefore, development-oriented companies need to use such technological tools as CRM systems. The main focus of the work is the revolutionary approach that serves to manage the existing information about users through artificial intelligence [1].

R. C. Geibel and S. Machavariani (Eds.): ISPC 2024, SPBE, pp. 101–113, 2025.
https://doi.org/10.1007/978-3-031-88052-0_7

The development of CRM systems is the embedding and active use of artificial intelligence elements in it. Various operations carried out in CRM through artificial intelligence will simplify and refine the existing ways to achieve the company's goals [2, 3]. The development of CRM systems is not only related to the presence of artificial intelligence. For artificial intelligence to be a powerful tool in the CRM system, it is important to develop it through machine learning methods. Accordingly, we think that the integration of the CRM systems themselves with all other systems in the company is the way to develop artificial intelligence [4, 5]. In business and economy, the collection and processing of data has a special place, because it is thanks to the processing of already existing information and results that it is possible to make future forecasts and make strategic decisions [6–8].

Over time, the use of technologies in various directions in organizations has created flexible means of data collection and analysis [9, 10]. There are three main approaches to data collection methods: (1) monitoring an organization's records, which is somewhat useful for gathering important data, (2) using action plans, which apply to many different projects and programs, and (3) documenting activities that may prove very important at the appropriate time.

Today, in all small areas of their activity in modern organizations, certain software elements are included, where a large amount of data is stored. Interdependent or separate data in different systems already creates the possibility to use them purposefully.

Collecting and storing process data is a top priority for running a business of any size [11]. Technologies can process existing data, analyze it and create certain insights based on it. Artificial intelligence is a tool for companies to collect information about customers, analyze it and take strategic steps [12, 13]. Collecting information helps businesses plan operations, make decisions, study their customers, and manage their business processes strategically [14].

Currently, data collection itself is one of the directions of business. Data brokers (companies) buy data to sell this product to other companies for a certain margin. This is a new industry that has developed and grown rapidly. For sales professionals and marketers, having this kind of information is of great value, so the demand for data is increasing and so is the industry that serves to find and sell data. This fact emphasizes the importance of data in our era.

The main findings and assumptions in the presented research are based on existing books, articles and papers on artificial intelligence and CRM technologies.

J. McCarthy, in an article [15] Explains that artificial intelligence is the branch of science and engineering required to create intelligent machines. Machine learning, which includes knowledge, knowledge representation and knowledge-based cause-and-effect algorithms [16–19].

An interesting opinion is offered by Farkas in her paper "Customer Relations" [20]. The existence of CRM systems and their development are becoming more and more important for companies. Customer relationship management is not a sub-function of marketing strategy or a separate, time-bound component of it. Nor is it a corporate information system. CRM technologies at a very fast pace have become the axis of the main business strategy, which serves constant growth. It should not be perceived as one of the functions of the business, it should be the basis of the business strategy. On the other hand, the practice of companies shows that so far CRM is used by companies as an auxiliary tool to achieve commercial goals.

According to Baran and Galka, the development of CRM and the development of the artificial intelligence element it is based on data analysis. They note that CRM software allows companies to manage large numbers of customers by analyzing all the data related to them [21]. The function of CRM is to analyze the history of customer behavior and, based on it, present the necessary means for increasing sales and improving service. The strategy of CRM systems is a long-term process of customer acquisition, retention and cooperation with them. Our research has confirmed that the data processed using CRM or other types of tools is the basis of important decisions made in companies and future plans.

Technological development has led to the formation of huge databases. Ma-chine learning development cannot be done effectively without Big Data and analytics, although analytics can exist independently without machine learning. Applications based on artificial intelligence, including customer relationship management - CRM applications without data make no sense. Also, on the contrary - the presence of an unlimited amount and different types of data does not make sense without technology.

One of the examples of connecting CRM technologies with artificial intelligence is the connection of CRM with business analytical systems - Business intelligence (BI) [22]. The BI system is one of the most tangible expressions of artificial intelligence. Integrating these two powerful systems provides more opportunities to see the company's results, which we will get as a result of connecting a lot of data in the system. In his paper, S. Ivey describes the possibilities of integrating these two systems. The above-mentioned is confirmed by the practice of the companies participating in the study, in terms of the importance of using the BI system. On the other hand, the mentioned companies rarely use these two systems in terms of integration with each other, based on which we can say that we will encounter the joint use of CRM and BI more actively in the future.

In the work "The Future of Management in a World of Electronic Brains", the author notes that "...with increasing AI capabilities, the future could also be free of human management..." [23]. With this opinion, the danger of artificial intelligence is confirmed.

2 Methodological Foundations

The study is based on qualitative research methods, which were selected de-pending on the research problem. Based on the objectives of the research, a fundamental analysis was conducted, the purpose of which is to deepen the theoretical knowledge on the issue. As part of the qualitative research, various books, articles and academic works were discussed, based on which it was determined what scientists think about the research issue. Initial presentations were received and final evaluations were formulated in the form of a conclusion.

We used the strategic planning method - SWOT analysis to assess the future development prospects of artificial intelligence. Using this method, we tried to evaluate the strengths and weaknesses, opportunities, threats and business environment of the development of artificial intelligence. As a result, we determined the level of connection between them and the main contours of its future development.

3 Results and Discussion

3.1 Artificial Intelligence and Its Practical Use

There are many different formulations of the definition of intelligence, but it would be exhaustive to say that human intelligence is the ability to understand a given situation. It is a feature of a person to adequately assess the situation and adapt to the environment and his own needs [24]. Human intelligence means the ability to reason, draw conclusions, plan processes, find the best way to solve a problem, think abstractly, learn and accumulate experience [25]. These are the main characteristics that make "Homo sapiens", as humanity calls itself, different from other creatures.

For years, humans have been trying to understand mental processes such as thinking, understanding, and making decisions [26]. They then wondered if it was possible to create a technological prototype with mental abilities similar to theirs. Right after the first computer appeared, intelligence as a definition acquired a second type - artificial.

Artificial intelligence is a computer system made of algorithms, which can take a certain action independently of a person, to decide in a specific situation, through the analysis of existing data and experience (whether it is an automated process that has already been performed many times or a completely new case). The quality of a mechanism created using artificial intelligence is measured by the complexity of the tasks it has to solve [27, 28].

Based on the prediction made by J. McCarthy in 2007 that the future perspective of artificial intelligence is its development to the level of human intelligence, we can say that the perfect model of artificial intelligence is the counter-part of natural, human intelligence [15]. Although man is by far the most intelligent creature in the world, his intelligence may be far inferior to computer intelligence. The more the capabilities of artificial intelligence develop, the more it goes beyond the maximum capabilities of the most perfect human intelligence.

We can say that the capabilities of computer intelligence are far superior to human intelligence, as it can process huge amounts of data in the shortest time with the least probability of making an error. We can disagree with J. McCarthy's opinion and say that the future model of artificial intelligence will not be like human intelligence, but a much more complete, flawless thinking model [15]. A brain that will make flawless decisions in any field and any situation.

The creation and development of artificial intelligence is closely related to all other fields of science. For computer intelligence to be like human intelligence, we need to know how our brains are organized, how we learn, develop, make decisions, and how our minds work [29]. Accordingly, artificial intelligence as a scientific discipline is based on physics, biology, chemistry, mathematics and all other sciences [30].

A person is not given intelligence at birth. It is known that it is formed by up-bringing, education, learning and development. These processes are a kind of algorithms, just as we find algorithms in computer technology. The human brain is programmed for certain things, and when faced with a new non-standard event, at best, it refers to past experiences and behaves exactly like past experiences [31, 32]. Man has already tried to create a system similar to his intelligence, based on the same principles. When he fully understands human intelligence, then he will be able to make perfect artificial intelligence as well. In the near future, sustainable economic development of society and improvement of inter-national security will be possible through the symbiotic relationship between humans and artificial intelligence (Table 1).

Table 1. Concept of Human–AI symbiosis [33]

• AI Roles	• Human Roles
Personal Intelligent Assistants • Help with information overload • Increase cognitive bandwidth • Filter, sort and navigate information resources	**Personal KM** • Train and individualize intelligent assistants • Monitor and critically assess the performance intelligent assistants
Specialized Intelligence • Provide specialized intelligence for learning in bounded environments • Present task-centered intelligence (not easily transferable across different task contexts) • Manage knowledge content	**General Intelligence** • Apply knowledge for strategic-level thinking • Translate knowledge across contexts • Discern knowledge context via self-reflection
Codification of Knowledge • Streamline low-level, high volume knowledge processes • Facilitate connecting people and generating know-how	**Collaboration of Knowledge** • Handle complex, non-routine knowledge processes • Transfer tacit knowledge through social interactions
Know-How and Know-What • Discover unnoticed patterns in (big)data • Extend know-how outside of the current knowledge resources by developing own rules	**Know-Why** • Explain inferences and justify recommendations • Train budding experts and garner organizational support • Take responsibility

Artificial intelligence makes decisions through pre-programmed algorithms. Its essence is to learn and act in a completely unknown and new situation to achieve the best result.

Thanks to natural intelligence, a person shapes his behavior and makes decisions, he also analyzes his past experiences, processes in his mind the information he possesses, analyzes all possible alternatives and tries to find the best solution to the situation.

Artificial intelligence works like human intelligence, but lacks creativity and inspiration. Its use in routine uniform processes will be quite simple and justified. Artificial intelligence algorithms are being created to perform tasks of this type, tasks that can be predicted, written in advance and guessed. It turns out that artificial intelligence can handle many of the issues that humans can handle, but there is one important differentiator. Any company's databases or software systems store millions of pieces of information, data that are beyond human capabilities to connect, analyze, or perform other actions. A person may devote a century to this seemingly simple task. There is also a great risk of error. For artificial intelligence, it does not matter the amount of information when it comes to one specific task, it acts according to a pre-written logic. Thanks to it, both time and other resources are saved, and the risk of making mistakes is reduced to zero, which is a very valuable factor for companies today [34].

Thanks to the generally accepted facts, before AI reaches the peak of its development, it is ideal for standardized processes. The logic of his behavior is well-defined in advance and acquired by experience. Artificial intelligence in today's reality is a tool that, as a result of partial participation in various fields, helps a person in the automation of general processes, the implementation of analytics and other business processes. Human intelligence has the priority to analyze a completely foreign, non-standard situation and make a decision about its action [35]. Artificial intelligence is developing in this direction, and the more experience it accumulates in routine, standard processes, the more varied the experience of artificial intelligence in the process of solving these types of tasks, the more it will be able to find a solution in non-standard situations, self-improve and teach.

For the development of artificial intelligence, there is a function that scientists call "Machine Learning". It is a method of building a data analysis model. It is based on the general idea of artificial intelligence that systems can learn and evolve from data. It can gather patterns of behavior and make decisions with minimal human intervention.

The purpose of using artificial intelligence in business is of course financial gain. By 2025, the worldwide artificial intelligence software industry is projected to generate around 118.6 billion in sales, according to market research firm Tractica [36]. Rao and Verweij in their report predict that by 2030 the financial bene-fits that artificial intelligence will bring to the global economy will be $15.7 trillion [37]. The implementation of artificial intelligence in business is not just following technological trends, but also creating services tailored to the needs of customers, implementing correct and targeted strategies by businesses, which can bring serious financial benefits to companies.

The capabilities of artificial intelligence improve and grow over time. The area of its use expands and its functional purpose develops, the system learns more, and therefore the business can use it more efficiently and effectively.

3.2 Modern Technologies of Data Collection and Analysis: SWOT Analysis of the Use of Artificial Intelligence

Various types of personal information are easily accessible today. Demographic information, contact information, a person's work experience and education, interests, activities, and the rhythm of his daily life will be searched in the social network. Businesses try to use this information to their advantage. The simplest example is online marketing. Sending a specific message to a target audience on social media is a tool used by businesses of all sizes and types today [38]. Thanks to the information available on the social network, it is possible to filter the category of users and present a specific product or service to the desired audience.

The starting point of all the above-mentioned examples of the use of artificial intelligence in practice is a set of data. All types of information about the user, his behavior or the behavior of the company are the resources thanks to which different types of systems try to make future predictions and calculate moves that will help the company achieve its goals.

Companies collect information about customers to narrowly segment customers and for each specific offer such offers that they know exactly the area of interest of their customers. Accordingly, the company efficiently spends its re-sources, sells its products or services at lower costs, and the customer receives only offers that are interesting to him. Thanks to the use of this tool, the user avoids unnecessary negotiations with companies whose products he is not interested in purchasing.

Information about customers in databases is used by companies that have re-peat customers who need a product or service periodically. Companies offer their desired products thanks to the personalization of data. By managing the information about customers, companies increase their chances of success and the level of customer satisfaction. For example, the real estate industry may use less consumer data than the food industry, home goods manufacturing, beauty, or health care industries.

Predicting customer behavior and needs is even easier with the inclusion of artificial intelligence. Below are the benefits that the combination of AI and CRM offers:

1. Efficiency of data management - all information from social networks and other sources is gathered centrally in CRM, artificial intelligence processes it and transforms it into valuable information for the company.
2. Optimal sales strategy - by predicting customer behavior, companies can make optimal decisions and avoid additional costs.
3. Increase in customer satisfaction - Artificial intelligence also improves the level of customer trust and satisfaction. One example of this is facial or voice recognition devices that are used to identify users or offer different services. In CRM, through the involvement of AI, it is possible to offer fast and quality service to customers, where the probability of errors and omissions is minimized.

Along with the advantages mentioned above, certain limitations and risks may accompany the use of artificial intelligence in customer relationship management. We have discussed this issue in more detail in the form of a SWOT analysis in Fig. 1.

As for the positive aspects of artificial intelligence. Artificial intelligence has many positive features, it can be effectively used to perform repetitive and time-consuming tasks. Intelligent robots can be programmed to reach the depths of the earth. They can be used for mining worms, for mining purposes and even for certain missions in space. They can be launched into the depths of the oceans, where humans cannot reach, and in general, through them, we can overcome the limits set for humans [39]. In systems built on smart cards, fraud is detected with the help of artificial intelligence. They are also used in financial institutions and banks. Emotion often interferes with the rational reasoning of a person, and robots do not have this obstacle, which allows them to "think" more logically and make the right decisions. The main positive feature of artificial intelligence is that it does not need to sleep or take a break, it can function non-stop. They can do the same thing tirelessly. Also, it reduces the risk to human health and safety when performing dangerous tasks.

Artificial intelligence offers so-called bots and automated processes, the main purpose of which is to free up time for human resources and to perform similar tasks faster and more efficiently [42].

Fig. 1. Generative AI in IT Services: A Comprehensive SWOT Analysis

Artificial intelligence, along with positive sides, certainly has negative sides: one of the main problems is the updating of robot programs and related costs. Also, if they are damaged, they are expensive to repair. They can store large amounts of information, but their storage, access, and expansion are not as efficient as with humans. However, they can do the same thing for a long time, many times, but with experience, the performance technique does not improve as with a human. They cannot use a different strategy from the program, even if the latter is better. They are rigid. It is dangerous for them to replace people because, in addition to the fact that a person will lose his job and his place in the world, robots lack such qualities as care, understanding, unity and others. They cannot understand the tenderness of human emotions, so no matter how intelligent they become, they will always fall short of human capabilities. If these machines fall into the wrong hands, their resources may be diverted to deviant behavior and lead to destruction [40].

One of the main limitations is related to the cost of using artificial intelligence. The acquisition and implementation of smart technologies are associated with significant financial costs. In such a case, the company, taking into account its volume and turnover, must correctly determine how rational it is to replace human resources with automated processes [41].

It is also necessary to take into account the time of implementation, which in many cases is quite long, and the time of adaptation, which is related to the assimilation of the program and the full realization of its benefits.

To explain the working principle of artificial intelligence, the system knows all possible variations of moves through algorithms. After each of our moves, it re-visits the variations and chooses which move has the best chance of winning.

Chatbots are also the most common example of using artificial intelligence in practice. A chatbot is an innovative form of communication, the functionality of which is based on interaction with artificial intelligence.

The banking field is one of those that actively uses artificial intelligence. It collects data about the user from their personal banking application, in which all the details of the user's transactions, analysis of all income and expenses are stored [14, 43]. Banks also collect information about how many times the user has used the loan calculator in the application, and after analyzing it, they offer him the appropriate product [44]. Banks also collect information about how often and mainly about what we talk about with the bank's chatbot on social networks, what type of service we use through it.

With the help of artificial intelligence, it is possible not only to consult the customer and offer a product, but also to carry out complex operations [45]. For example, Space, the first Georgian digital bank created in Georgia, has no branches, no call center and no customer service staff. Through the application, the user can independently order a card, carry out transactions, take a loan and all other banking operations [14]. The company quickly gained a place in the market and is constantly trying to develop. This is one example of how the latest, innovative technology tools help businesses grow.

By collecting customer information, companies narrowly segment their customers and target each of them with offers that they know are of particular interest to their customers. Accordingly, both parties receive interesting benefits.

The capabilities of artificial intelligence are used to manage existing information about customers and, as a result of its analysis, to plan future actions. The system that serves this purpose is called Customer Relationship Management - CRM. The Customer Relationship Management system exists as a general theoretical system as well as a technological one, represented by different types of software [46]. The use of artificial intelligence in customer relationship management systems can be used to analyze data hidden in depth that organizations cannot cover with human capabilities. Analyzing the data in CRM is not only useful within the CRM framework. This information must be analyzed with the statistical data available in the market, which may be demographic, geographic, company or industry data.

Gathering business intelligence to identify audience insights and anticipated opportunities is critical to realizing company goals. Predicting the future is a constant challenge for companies. Although predictions often fail, companies believe that given enough data, they can determine their future threats or opportunities.

4 Conclusions

The use of artificial intelligence to manage business processes such as planning, production, analysis and decision-making has a positive effect on the company's productivity and increases its efficiency and competitiveness. Risk management is an important issue for organizations, for which it is necessary to use proven methods, in which artificial intelligence can be included to analyze various issues. We think that the presence of artificial intelligence, data collection, processing and analysis through CRM or MIS should be done jointly. Connecting a Management Information System (MIS) to a Customer Relationship Management System (CRM), using artificial intelligence in both, connecting to an organization's website, accounting and reporting system, social network, or HR system will open up endless possibilities.

A detailed description of the company's internal processes, the more flexible the organizations will be internally, the more effective the processing and management of customer information will be. With the correct use of the latter, we get the following values:

1. Identification of opportunities - processing information about the company's loyal customers provides an opportunity for cross-selling. A business can analyze and offer a product to the customer that is related to the product he has bought steadily before.
2. Which customers should receive promotional offers - Companies analyze who to offer product or service promotions or other offers. To choose the right target audience, it is necessary to classify the total number of users. This will be done through databases. With the help of databases, it is possible to segment customers according to various characteristics and select a specific advertising offer for each of them.
3. Increased customer loyalty - When you love pizza, but it's inconvenient to go get it, wait in line and waste time, you can call Domino's Pizza. When a customer calls Domino's Pizza, they already know their address and the type of pizza they last ordered. This is an example of how a business can in-crease its customer loyalty level. The process should be as convenient as possible and the customer will surely return the loyalty in return. This is an example of how customer information can be managed.

4. Reactivation of customers - the customer may not necessarily be in close contact with the company all the time. The company must be under the attention of its customers. The company Intel sends a message to its passive users that they are with them. Companies strive to be constantly within the sight of their customers, because if they are out of their sight, they will soon be out of their hearts. It is to identify such a category of passive customers that companies use information about customers in their databases.
5. Avoiding errors - when there were no flexible data storage and processing systems, companies used Microsoft Excel. A large amount of confusing data was stored here, which made it difficult to show the general picture of customers and was simply a list of certain information.

For companies focused on development, it is important to use such technological tools as CRM. The idea that the integration of software used to manage business processes is a prediction of the future can be based on the rapid development of artificial intelligence as a mechanism since for the development (idealization) of artificial intelligence it is necessary to train it by solving more and more different types of tasks. Having strong, unified software will be the environment to achieve this result.

In the near future, through the integration of AI and CRM systems, we should expect:

- Complete automation of routine tasks;
- forecasting customer needs with maximum accuracy;
- Development of self-service channels (for example, Internet bots, robotic devices), etc.

Due to its content, CRM is one of the first technological areas where artificial intelligence can be used on the largest scale. It is in this direction that it is possible to create interesting products that will easily attract the attention of the user and, accordingly, increase interest in the products.

References

1. Nilsson, N.J.: Principles of Artificial Intelligence. Springer (1982)
2. Wilson, H., Daniel, E., McDonald, M.: Factors for success in customer relationship management (CRM) systems. J. Mark. Manag. **18**(1–2), 193–219 (2002)
3. Rababah, K., Mohd, H., Ibrahim, H.: Customer relationship management (CRM) processes from theory to practice: the pre-implementation plan of CRM system. Int. J. e-Education, e-Business, e-Management e-Learning **1**(1), 22–27 (2011)
4. Chatterjee, S., Nguyen, B., Ghosh, S.K., Bhattacharjee, K.K., Chaudhuri, S.: Adoption of arti-ficial intelligence integrated CRM system: an empirical study of Indian organizations. Bot-tom Line **33**(4), 359–375 (2020)
5. Ledro, C., Nosella, A., Dalla Pozza, I.: Integration of AI in CRM: Challenges and guidelines. J. Open Innov. Technol. Market Complex. **9**(4), 100151 (2023)
6. Haugeland, J.: Artificial Intelligence: The Very Idea. MIT Press, 1989
7. Veshapidze, S., Otinashvili, R., Gvarutsidze, A., Abuselidze, G., Zoidze, G.: Modern technologies to overcome the challenges of globalization. Entrepreneurship **10**(2), 22–32 (2022)
8. Chowdhary, K.R.: Fundamentals of artificial intelligence, pp. 603–649 (2020)
9. Xu, Y..: Artificial intelligence: a powerful paradigm for scientific research. Innovation **2**(4) (2021)

10. Jackson, P.C.: Introduction to Artificial Intelligence. Courier Dover Publications (2019)
11. Zoidze, G.: Strategic directions of balanced economic growth of entrepreneurial entities. J. Innov. Sustain. **7**(1), 1–22 (2023)
12. Holzinger, A., Langs, G., Denk, H., Zatloukal, K., Müller, H.: Causability and explainability of artificial intelligence in medicine. Wiley Interdisciplin. Rev. Data Min. Knowl. Discov. **9**(4), e1312 (2019)
13. Zulaikha, S., Mohamed, H., Kurniawati, M., Rusgianto, S., Rusmita, S.A.: Customer predictive analytics using artificial intelligence. Singapore Econ. Rev. 1–12 (2020)
14. Abuselidze, G., Zoidze, T.: The impact of digitalization and artificial intelligence on sustainable development and energy efficiency of the Georgian banking sector. In: E3S Web of Conferences, vol. 542, p. 01007 (2024)
15. McCarthy, J.: What is artificial intelligence? (2007)
16. Marienko, M.V., Semerikov, S.O., Markova, O.M.: Artificial intelligence literacy in secondary education: methodological approaches and challenges. CEUR Workshop Proc. **3679**, 87–97 (2024)
17. Semerikov, S., Zubov, D., Kupin, A., Kosei, M., Oliver, V.: Models and Technologies for Au-toscaling based on machine learning for microservices architecture. CEUR Workshop Proc. **3664**, 316–330 (2024)
18. Abuselidze, G., Zoidze, G.: Economic analysis of factors associated with education and em-ployment. CEUR Workshop Proc. **3364**, 24–37 (2023)
19. Abuselidze, G., Mohylevska, O., Kompanets, N., Iushchenko, L.: Modern concepts and method-ological recommendations for teaching economic disciplines: tasks of the course "Digital Man-agement of Transport Infrastructure." Transp. Res. Proc. **63**, 2759–2766 (2022)
20. Farkas, V.J.: Customer Relationships. Nova Science Publishers, New York (2011)
21. Baran, R.J., Galka, R.J.: Customer Relationship Management: The Foundation of Contemporary Marketing Strategy. Routledge (2016)
22. Ivie, S.: Building Dynamics CRM 2015 Dashboards with Power BI. Packt Publishing (2015)
23. Ferràs-Hernández, X.: The future of management in a world of electronic brains. J. Manag. Inq. **27**(2), 260–263 (2018)
24. Abuselidze, G.: Financing higher education: new challenges, incentives and opportunities. IOP Conf. Ser. Earth Environ. Sci. **1026**(1), 012066 (2022)
25. Winston, P.H.: Artificial Intelligence. Addison-Wesley Longman Publishing Co., Inc (1984)
26. Zoidze, G., Veshapidze, S.: The Modern Economy and Values. Cambridge Scholars Publishing (2022)
27. Negnevitsky, M.: Artificial Intelligence: A Guide to Intelligent Systems. Pearson Education (2005)
28. Barr, A., Feigenbaum, E.A., Cohen, P.R. (Eds.).: The Handbook of Artificial Intelligence. Heu-risTech Press (1981)
29. Nilsson, N.J.: The Quest for Artificial Intelligence. Cambridge University Press (2009)
30. Minsky, M.: Steps toward artificial intelligence. Proc. IRE **49**(1), 8–30 (1961)
31. Zoidze, G., Abuselidze, G.: Importance of healthcare economy on sustainable development of the country. Access Sci. Bus. Innov. Dig. Econ. **4**(1), 60–70 (2023)
32. Abuselidze, G.: Empirical investigation of healthcare financing and its influence on social security: peculiarities, problems and challenges. In: E3S Web of Conferences, vol. 319, p. 01030 (2021)
33. Jarrahi, M.H., Askay, D., Eshraghi, A., Smith, P.: Artificial intelligence and knowledge management: a partnership between human and AI. Bus. Horiz. **66**(1), 87–99 (2023)
34. Liu, J., et al.: Artificial intelligence in the 21st century. IEEE Access **6**, 34403–34421 (2018)
35. Garnham, A.: Artificial Intelligence: An Introduction. Routledge (2017)
36. Abuselidze, G., Mamaladze, L.: The impact of artificial intelligence on employment before and during pandemic: a comparative analysis. J. Phys. Conf. Ser. **1840**(1), 012040 (2021)

37. Rao, A.S., Verweij, G.: Sizing the prize: What's the real value of AI for your business and how can you capitalise? (2017)
38. Brynjolfsson, E., Mcafee, A.: Artificial intelligence, for real. Harv. Bus. Rev. **1**, 1–31 (2017)
39. Fetzer, J.H., Fetzer, J.H.: What Is Artificial Intelligence? pp. 3–27 (1990)
40. Copeland, J.: Artificial Intelligence: A Philosophical Introduction. Wiley (1993)
41. Datsii, N., Abuselidze, G., Zborovska, O., Zborovskyy, R., Mishchenko, D., Karpeko, N.: Public administration of de-shadowing of the economic system in the conditions of globalization. In: E3S Web of Conferences, vol. 371, p. 05013 (2023)
42. Hunt, E.B.: Artificial Intelligence. Academic Press (2014)
43. Boobier, T.: AI and the Future of Banking. Wiley (2020)
44. Abuselidze, G.: Analysis and forecasts of the impact of non-performing loans on the economy in pandemic conditions. Lect. Notes Netw. Syst. **620**, 129–143 (2023)
45. Slobodianyk, A., Maryna, A., Kosovets, H., Tsiukalo, L., Abuselidze, G.: Ensuring competitive advantages of the banking sector of ukraine in the context of global digital transformation. Stud. Manag. Finan. Account. **36**, 215–227 (2024)
46. Kumar, P., Sharma, S.K., Dutot, V.: Artificial intelligence (AI)-enabled CRM capability in healthcare: the impact on service innovation. Int. J. Inf. Manage. **69**, 102598 (2023)

Way to Implementing Innovation Driven Personnel-Fit OE at Georgian Universities

Tatia Gherkenashvili(✉)

Department of Scientific Research and Development, East European University, Tbilisi, Georgia
t.gherkenashvili@eeu.edu.ge

Abstract. Nowadays, globalization processes ongoing throughout the world, inevitability of knowledge improvement and formation of innovation driven society, as well as competitiveness existed in the market in terms of education service providing raises an issue of innovative development of higher education. Elaboration of globally competitive country requires enhancing the role of education on the way of forming a socio-economic, innovative, humanitarian, moral and ethical society.

In Georgia as in one of the post-Soviet country, higher education system weakens, which in turn prevents the innovative development of higher educational institutions, including universities. Within the causes of all problems like insufficient funding, low level of development of innovative infrastructure and culture, brain drain, lack of innovative management and etc. is considered to be non-existence of personnel-fit innovative organizational environment (Personnel-Fit OE) at knowledge producing institutions.

Due to all above mentioned, paper reviews the prerequisites of innovative development of higher education system and represents an Approach directed to implementing innovation driven personnel-fit OE at Georgian Universities developed on the bases of researches conducted with the employees (academic and administrative personnel) of Georgian private and state universities.

Keywords: Personnel-fit OE · Innovative Development · Organizational environment · Higher Education System

1 Introduction

Accelerated processes in the world as well as increased competitiveness among organizations raises the issue of multifaced improvement of educational system of the country. Due to above mentioned knowledge became the fundamental component for the development of the country.

Society's ability to produce, select, adapt, commercialize and utilize practice-based knowledge is vitally important to sustainable economic development and improved living conditions. (World Bank, 1999).

In this context, tertiary education plays a crucial role in building a strong human capital base and establishing an effective national innovation system.

R. C. Geibel and S. Machavariani (Eds.): ISPC 2024, SPBE, pp. 114–125, 2025.
https://doi.org/10.1007/978-3-031-88052-0_8

Higher education institutions (universities) contribute to countries in formation of globally competitive economies by training qualified, productive and flexible personnel and through creating, applying and disseminating new ideas and technologies.

Within the framework of the higher education system, educational institutions, especially research universities, are of critical importance for forming bright minded, creative and innovative generation of professionals, qualified specialists, scientists and researchers focused on idea generation, novelty creation and commercialization as well which will be reflected in improved national system.

Richard Florida (2002, 2006) has detailed the importance of creativity for the economic and social well-being of the country. He argues that the university plays a crucial role not only in boosting creativity itself, but also in its development.

Besides, Florida and his colleagues (2006) outline that the university must have an enormous role in economic development, they also argue that talent formation and supporting idea generation is also a central mission of the university.

In short, the university represents potential and a kind of creative hub, oriented on the regional development (p. 29) and focusing on the development of which is one of the important prerequisites for the multiple development of the country.

2 The Role of Innovative Culture on the Way of University Development

Definitions of innovation in the literature vary. In particular, some of them are general and broad, while others interpret it as the implementation of an idea for the creation of new products or services.

According to West and Farr (1990), innovation is related to novelty, it serves as a prerequisite for change.

Others indicate that" *It's the characteristic of individual and intellectual possibilities is directed on formation of new product with varied characteristics*" (Arad et al., 1997).

According to Martins and Terblanche (2003). *Innovativeness and invention ability are the key for the success of knowledge-based organization*".

Plsek (1997) names 5 factors outlining inevitability of innovativeness at organization:

1. Long term financial productivity is related to innovation;
2. Customers demand innovation;
3. Competitors become better with past innovation experience;
4. New technologies boost to innovations and in turn new technologies can't be created without innovations.

According to Schein"*To be successful and adaptable to the environment, businesses must create a culture that fosters creativity and innovation*" (Schein, 2004).

Based on Oslo Manual: *The Measurement of Scientific, Technological and Innovative Activities. GUIDELINES FOR COLLECING, REPORTING AND USING DATA ON INNOVATION,* (4th ed.) word: 'Innovation' might be defined as activity and its result.

3 Cultural Theories

Understanding the importance of culture has a significant impact on the activities of organizations. Accordingly, it is gaining more and more importance in the management of organizations. Over the years, theories of cultures have been formulated by various researchers, some of which are presented in the mentioned chapter.

The first cultural typology was developed by Geert Hofstede on 60,000 employees (employees of the multinational corporation IBM) in 70 branches of a transnational company in 50 countries as a result of a study on intercultural differences (including 116,000 questionnaires), which was published in 1980. Based on this research, Hofstede established four dimensions of national cultures: power distance, masculinity/femininity, individualism/collectivism and uncertainty avoidance. These parameters are manifested in the form of different behaviors and attitudes of individuals (Hofstede, 2010, p. 29).

Later, together with his colleague, Canadian scientist Michael Harris Bond, he conducted the "Chinese Values Survey" (CVS) in 76 countries and based on it added a fifth dimension - Long-Term versus Short-Term Orientation (LTO) (Hofstede & Minkov, 2010)., pp. 252–253).

Later in 2010 based on World Values Survey (WVS) Bulgarian scientist Michael Minkov (Hofstede & Minkov, 2010 p. 281) elaborated new sixth dimension - Indulgence versus Restraint IND).

In 2010, on the basis of the research conducted by Hofstede and his colleague Minkov on the example of 76 countries (Fig. 1), the highest index in the first dimension (power distance) was found in the countries: China, Singapore, Hong Kong, South Korea, Taiwan and Japan, where the teachings of Confucius are popular. in which five rules of human relations are distinguished (that is, established principles of interdependence apply). And the lowest rate was shown in Denmark, Israel and Austria.

The high index in the above-mentioned countries indicates that power inequality between people is an acceptable phenomenon for society members. The relationship between superior and subordinate can be polarized where there is no defense mechanism against hierarchical superiority. In society, individuals come under the influence of official authorities and adhere to hierarchical realities.

As for the second dimension (individualism-collectivism), according to the results of the research, the most individualistic countries were named: USA, Australia, Great Britain, and collectivistic: Panama, Ecuador, Guatemala. In the third dimension (masculinity-femininity), as a result of the research, it was revealed that the three most masculine countries are: Slovakia, Japan, Hungary, and the most feminine countries are: the Netherlands, Norway, Sweden. In the fourth dimension (uncertainty avoidance), the strongest index was observed in Greece, Guatemala and Portugal, and the weakest: in Denmark, Jamaica and Singapore. In the fifth dimension (long-term and short-term orientation), it was determined that the top three countries for long-term orientation are: China, Hong Kong and Taiwan, and for short-term orientation: Nigeria, the Czech Republic and Pakistan. In the last, sixth dimension (tolerance and restriction), the three most tolerant countries were found to be Venezuela, Mexico and Puerto Rico, and the most restrictive were Pakistan, Egypt and Latvia (see Table 1).

Table 1. Hofstede and Minkov Research results

#	Dimension	High indexed countries	Law indexed countries
1	Power distance	China, Singapore, Hong Kong, South Korea, Taiwan, Japan	Denmark, Israel, Austria
2	Individualism -collectivism	USA, Australia, UK	Panama, Ecuador, Guatemala
3	Masculine-Feminine	Slovakia, Japan, Hungary	Netherlands, Norway, Sweden
4	Uncertainty avoidance	Greece, Guatemala, Portugal	Denmark, Jamaica, Singapore
5	Long-Term versus Short-Term Orientation	China, Hong Kong, Taiwan	Nigeria, Czech Republic, Pakistan
6	Indulgence versus Restraint IND	Indulgent: Venezuela, Mexico, Puerto Rico	Restraint: Pakistan, Egypt, Latvia

4 Overview of Georgia in Terms of Geert Hofstede's Cultural Dimensions

4.1 Power Disdance

As already mentioned above, power distance refers to society's acceptance and expectations of power imbalance. If we consider the example of the mentioned educational institutions of Georgia, it can be said that the state universities of Georgia are characterized by a high index of power distance, which means that they have a more autocratic leadership style and centralized management. In particular, the power distance between different levels in organizations is large and decisions are made by top management without employee involvement or feedback. As for private universities, they have a low index of power distance and are characterized by a high degree of independence between upper and lower management, which means that each employed person has a more or less important status in the organization.

4.2 Trompenaar's Time Orientatioin

In Georgia's higher education institutions, there are people with a culture that has a consistent view of time, which means that they prefer to make things happen smoothly, even though it might make the result more efficient. For them, time is about money, and people can get upset if you don't keep their schedule right. In contrast, a greater proportion of the staff of organizations are carriers of a culture where time is more synchronous.

People with this culture can usually work on several projects simultaneously (albeit with schedule insecurity) and this is perceived as flexibility for them.

4.3 Individualism and Collectivism

Individualism is defined as how individuals value their own interests (Hofstede, n.d). According to countries with high individualism, the individual is the most important person and they should focus on their own achievements and be responsible for their own behaviors. Individualism reflects the relationship between the individual and the group. Also, individualistic orientation implies the belief that each person has his own value, should strive to realize his personal potential and try to cultivate personal opinions regardless of any kind of social pressure.

Collectivist orientation, on the other hand, reflects the priority of the collective over the individualistic. It is more typical of the Eastern world, where strong relationships are a priority. People integrate into groups where the interest of the group as a whole is more valuable than that of the individual. They have common goals and will protect each other throughout life (Hofstede et al., 2010, p. 91). According to sociologists, modern Russia is more individualistic than collectivistic, and it can be assumed that organizations operating in Georgia, as a member of the former Soviet Union, are more individualistic than collectivistic.

4.4 Masculinity/Femininity

Masculinity and femininity reflect the separation of the gender roles of women and men. In particular, "the degree of social differentiation of the sexes". To distinguish masculine culture from feminine culture, it is necessary to present the characteristics of masculine culture first. In particular, the primary value orientations of masculine cultures differ in the high evaluation of personal achievements, high social status is considered a confirmation of personal success; appreciates everything big and large; Avoid servants, it is considered a good tone to demonstrate success; Thinking tends towards rationality; People go to great lengths to boost their self-esteem. The primary value orientations of feminine cultures, on the contrary, promote the necessity of consensus; It is valuable to care for others, they care about other people's feelings; Humility is valued and appreciated; All of the above can be changed depending on specific socio-political circumstances. It should be noted that according to masculinity-femininity data, it is not mandatory to correspond with the country's socio-economic development or wealth, i.e. a rich and politically strong country does not mean a masculine one, and femininity is not a correlate of weakness in any way. Based on all of the above, it is possible to assume that Georgia and the organizations operating in it are more bearers of a masculine culture, although this does not a priori mean that the absolute majority is the bearer of such a culture.

The situation in Georgia is also interesting from the point of view of gender equality, which is reflected in the 2020 edition of the National Statistical Service of Georgia - Women and Men in Georgia (2020).

According to the 2006 State Concept on Gender Equality, gender equality means equal rights, responsibilities and opportunities for women and men, that is, the interests, needs and priorities of both men and women are equally taken into account. In 2015, the Government of Georgia started to nationalize Sustainable Development Goals (SDGs). The government has also identified priorities for 2030 by developing a sustainable development program, through the implementation of which by 2030 improvement in terms of gender equality is expected.

4.5 Uncertainty Avoidance

Uncertainty avoidance refers to the extent to which the bearers of this or that culture feel threatened in unknown, uncertain situations. For cultures with a high index of avoiding such situations, what is different is dangerous, and for countries with a low index, what is different is interesting. It is possible to assume that Georgia is considered to be among the countries with a high index in this direction, since people are more afraid of news and therefore avoid it in order to avoid uncertainty. However, of course, there are people in our country who, on the contrary, strive for innovations and development, therefore, for them, what is new is very interesting.

4.6 Long-Term Versus Short-Term Orientation LTO

This dimension shows how society maintains its connection with its past and at the same time how it responds to the challenges of the present and the future.

A long-term orientation looks to the future, focusing on future success values such as persistence and getting things done. He solves the problems of the present independently of the past, is flexible to adapt to the future.

Short-term orientation, on the contrary, is directed towards the values related to the past and the present, looks to the past to solve the difficulties created in the present and plans the future depending on it. It can be assumed that the Georgian nation leans more toward short-term orientation and makes certain decisions based on past experience.

4.7 Indulgence Versus Restraint - IND

A tolerant society is one that values the satisfaction of human needs and desires; It is aimed at promoting the enjoyment of life and the satisfaction of human desires. A limited society prefers the suppression of desires and restraint of pleasure. Tolerant cultures pay more attention to individual happiness and well-being. This contrasts with cultures where positive emotions are less freely expressed and happiness, freedom and leisure are not given the same importance (Maclachlan, 2013).

If we consider Georgia in terms of the mentioned dimension, we can conclude that our country is more tolerant than restrictive, since the majority of people value the satisfaction of human needs and desires;

It should be noted that the overview of Georgian citizens in terms of cultural dimensions proposed by Hofstede is based on my certain knowledge, experience and analysis of various researches around the topic.

In order to obtain more in-depth data in the mentioned direction, it is recommended to carry out a similar scale study conducted on IBM employees, which will lead to rational and real results and which will reveal the index level of Georgia in terms of the above-mentioned cultural dimensions.

5 Research

The target group of the research was the academic and administrative staff of the state and private higher educational institutions (universities) in Georgia, who were selected by a random method.

In particular, the "questionnaire" method was used in the quantitative research (an electronic Google Form self-assessment questionnaire for revealing the dominant organizational culture, which was translated from the book "Organizational Behavior, Skill-Building Approach" by American authors) (Christopher P. Neck, Jeffery D. Houghton, Emma L. Murray, 2nd ed., ISBN 978-1-5443-1754-0) and which was modified and emailed to respondents for completion.

The questionnaire consisted of 16 questions, from which the respondents had to mark their acceptable answer on a five-point scale, of which 1 = completely disagree; 2 = I do not agree; 3 = I agree more or less; 4 = I agree; 5 = I strongly agree.

5.1 Research Results

A total of 185 respondents from Georgian universities participated in the study (see Table 2), of which 73 (39.5%) respondents were representatives of private universities, and 112 (60.5%) were representatives of state universities. In particular, there were 46 women and 27 men from the universities; From private universities, 77 were women and 35 were men.

Table 2. Personnel employed at State and Private Universities

	Total	Women	Men
Private	73	46	27
State	112	77	35
Total Sum	185	123	62

As a result of the conducted research, it was revealed that private universities are more inclined towards market culture, and state universities towards adhocratic and hierarchical cultures (see Table 3).

Table 3. Dominant Organizational Culture at Georgian Universities

	HIERARCHY	MARKET	CLAN	ADHOCRACY
TOTAL SUM	41	53	39	52
PRIVATE UNIVERSITY	10	**28**	18	17
STATE UNIVERSITY	31	25	21	**35**

From the above, 14 academic staff of private universities prefer market culture; 10 adhocratic cultures, 9 clan cultures and 4 hierarchical cultures; As for administrative staff - 13 prefer clan, 13 market 8 hierarchical and 2 adhocratic culture (see Fig. 1).

Conclusion: Academic personnel in private universities are mostly inclined towards market and adhocratic organizational cultures, and administrative personnel – towards market and clan organizational cultures.

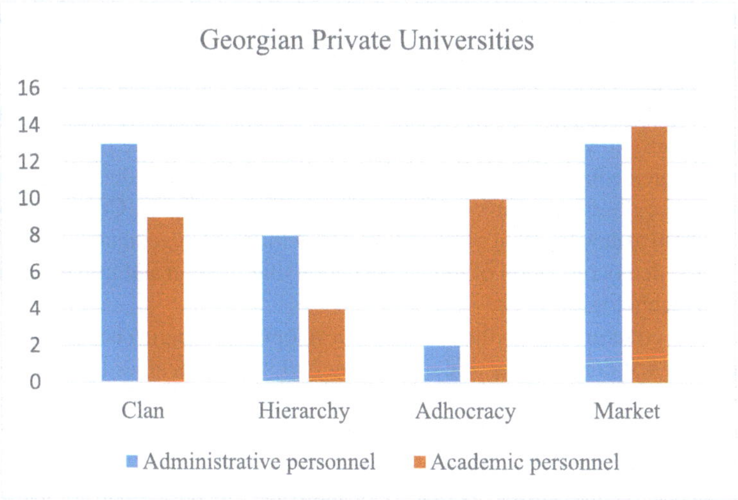

Fig. 1. Dominant Organizational Culture of academic and administrative personnel of Georgian private universities

The data of the state universities are as follows: 25 persons of the academic personnel prefer clan culture, 20 adhocratic, 11–11 hierarchical and market culture. Among the administrative staff, 20 people prefer hierarchical, 13 clan, 7 market and adhocratic culture. (See Fig. 2).

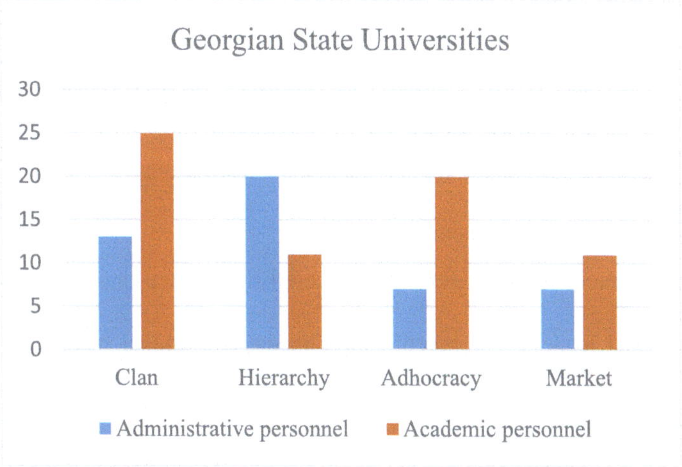

Fig. 2. Dominant Organizational Culture of academic and administrative personnel of Georgian state universities

Conclusion: Academic personnel in state universities are mostly inclined towards adhocratic organizational culture, and administrative personnel - towards hierarchical culture.

6 Way to Implementing Personnel-Fit Organizational Environment at Georgian Universities

In order for universities to develop, first of all, it is necessary that the educational system of the country in which the said educational institutions operate is well developed. Successful implementation of innovative development of higher education is possible only through the observance of systematic and cyclical principles. Common prerequisites for innovative development of educational system are management decentralization and flexibility, democratization of higher education, digitization and implementation of information technologies.

Among the prerequisites for the innovative development of higher education, it would be useful if we first consider the role of state support, which includes the establishment and implementation of an effective incentive system for universities and enterprises operating in the country. This includes the organization of joint activities by them for the implementation of innovative projects. Motivating mechanisms in this case can be tax benefits, grants, free consulting services, etc. Innovative development of the country's higher education system is possible if the country has a unified innovation strategy that is in line with the priorities of universities implementing innovative activities. Equally important areas of development of the organizational, management and economic aspects of higher education at the innovative level are the formation of a targeted financing strategy focused on the innovative development of higher education.

International projects are important in this regard, including EU, US educational programs, Fulbright program and many others. Of course, it is also important to cooperate with international institutions, to implement joint projects, to exchange employees and students to improve competencies, etc.

In the conditions of globalization, education system necessarily requires to be updated, which in turn brings to the fore the issue of the formation of world-class universities. According to J. Selmi, there are three types of strategic approaches to the formation of a world-class university:

1. Modernization of the existing higher educational institution;
2. Unification of universities;
3. Establishment of new universities.

And yet it is interesting to present the characteristics that are characteristic of world-class universities:

Unconditional leadership/competitiveness in the educational market;being in the front ranks of the world's leading universities;

- Having highly qualified personnel;
- having local and international students of high performance;
- high level of science development;
- Having highly competent researchers;
- strong material-research base;
- high level of development of fundamental and applied sciences;
- a large number of patents; high level of commercialization of innovations;
- A large number of publications of the results of the conducted research in ranked journals.

Currently, the USA, Japan, and EU countries are considered to be advanced countries, whose research universities' priority directions are nanotechnologies, information and communication technologies, biotechnologies, environment, space technologies, transport, energy, etc. In addition, research universities are involved in learning, systematization and analysis of innovative activities of the world's best research universities, which allows them to adapt to the national economy.

Ensuring a close connection between academic education, science and business is considered one of the important priorities of the modernization of the higher education system. It is also important to involve creative students in research, as they can discover unique and non-standard aspects of research.

The effectiveness of scientific activity is mainly determined by the level of commercialization of innovations of research universities. Globalization processes create real opportunities for scientists to introduce innovations in different countries. To develop the scientific activities of universities, the transfer of innovative technologies is also considered important, which includes the exchange of knowledge and achievements and making new discoveries based on them. An individual approach to each student, promotion of the implementation of their ideas, development of entrepreneurial skills and promotion of further employment is also considered important.

When talking about the innovative development of the country's national educational system, as well as the development of educational and methodological activities of universities, it is also important to focus on market requirements, creative highly qualified personnel.

It is also necessary to introduce the curriculum, programs, technologies and methodology of continuous education (especially among specialists in the direction of innovation management). It is also necessary to involve business representatives in continuous learning processes to establish business contacts.

n general, the integration of science, education and business in modern economic conditions is one of the most important prerequisites for the innovative development of higher education. One of the important issues for expanding the cooperation between the university and business is the formation of a portfolio of orders from enterprises for scientists to conduct applied research. The purpose of the cooperation between the university and the business is to ensure the commercialization of the scientific researches of university researchers, the prerequisite of which is the autonomy of the higher educational institutions, the formation of an innovative culture and the provision of the organization with an innovative infrastructure.

Autonomy helps universities to maneuver, increase flexibility and freedom to fund innovation.

7 Conclusion

The main supporting factors for the development of higher education at the national level are (see Fig. 3):

1. Development of long-term specific strategies for the development of the higher education system;
2. Establishment of innovative infrastructure;

3. Formation of innovative culture; development of a mechanism for technology transfer and commercialization of scientific research results;
4. Providing motivational and supporting initiatives of financial resources;
5. Diversification of innovative activities of universities, etc.

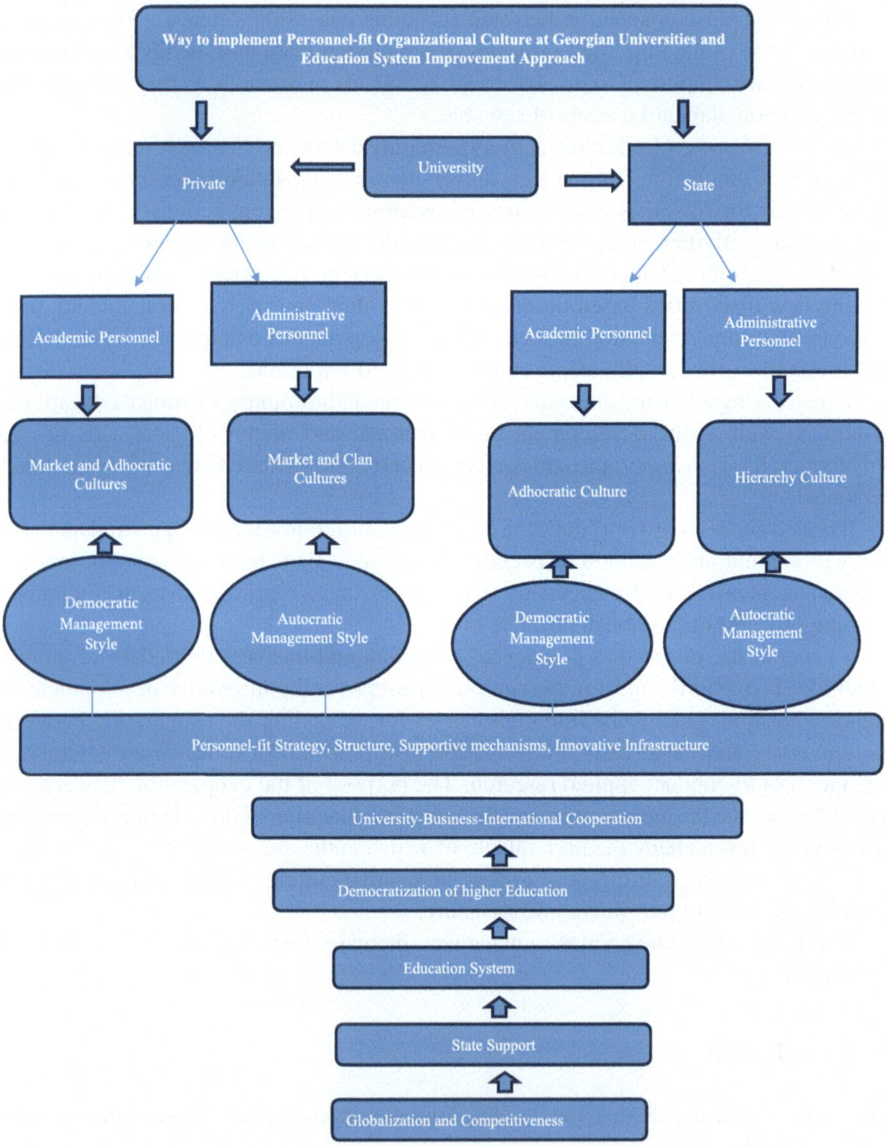

Fig. 3. Key supportive factors for higher education system development

References

Amabile T.M.: Motivating creativity in organizations: on doing what you love and loving what you do. Calif. Manage. Rev. **40**(1) (1997)

Arad, S., Hanson, M.A., Schneider, R.J.: A framework for the study of relationships between organizational characteristics and organizational innovation. J. Creative Behav. **31**(1), 42–58 (1997)

Florida, R., Gates, G., Knudsen, B., Stolarick, K.: The University and the Creative Economy (2006). http://www.creativeclass.org/rfcgdb/articles/University%20For%20City%20and%20Community%204.pdf

Florida, R.L.: The Rise of the Creative Class: And How It's Transforming Work, Leisure, Community and Everyday Life. Basic Books, New York (2002)

Hofstede, G., Hofstede, G.J., Minkov, M.: Cultures and Organizations: Software of the Mind, 3rd edn. McGraw-Hill, USA (2010)

Martins, E.C., Terblanche, F.: Building organizational culture that stipulates creativity and innovation. Eur. J. Innov. Manage. **6**(1) (2003)

OECD and Eurostat: The Measurement of Scientific, Technological and Innovative Activities. Guidelines for Collecting, Reporting and Using Data on Innovation, Oslo Manual, 4th edn., p. 20 (2018)

Schein, E.H.: Organizational Culture and Leadership. Jossey-Bass, San Francisco (2004)

West, M.A., Farr, J.L.: Innovation at work. In: West, M.A., Farr, J.L. Innovation and Creativity at Work: Psychological and Organizational Strategies, pp. 3–13. Wiley, Chichester (1990)

Georgia 2023 Report, European Comission, 8.11.2023 SWD (2023). 697 final

The World Bank Annual Report 1999 (English). World Bank Group, Washington, D.C. http://documents.worldbank.org/curated/en/282291468321230375/The-World-Bank-annual-report-1999

Skills Needed for Digital Transformation Using AI
(Based on Healthcare Field in Georgia)

Marina Shioshvili(✉) and Lili Bibilashvili

East European University, Tbilisi, Georgia
marina.shioshvili@eeu.edu.ge, lbibilashvili@cu.edu.ge

Abstract. AI fundamentally changes the labor market conjuncture. Globally, it is already known that the use of AI has changed the demands on the skills of the workforce. Employees need support from organizations in order to improve existing skills and develop new ones that will contribute to employees' mental readiness for changes.

The field in which there are steps taken in Georgia in terms of introduction of AI is the field of healthcare, therefore the research issue was studied within the scope of the mentioned field in the local labor market. The goal of the study is to demonstrate the skills that will be the driving force for the digital transformation processes through AI.

As a result of analyzing the experience in the field of healthcare in Georgia, organizations will receive information about the processes and the outcomes, which will help them to reach the digitalisation using AI. The results of the research will be no less interesting and useful for the countries whose stages of development are close to Georgian experience, as well as the frame of globalization causes similar impacts from the world mega trends like geopolitical, ecological, technological and etc., on those countries.

Keywords: Digital Transformation · Artificial Intelligence · Human Resources · Skills · Healthcare

Definition of Terms:: AI Based Digital Transformation-Using Artificial Intelligence programs · Green Skills-the knowledge abilities, values and attitudes needed to live in, develop and support a sustainable and resource-efficient society

Abbreviations

AI	Artificial Intelligence
HR	Human Resources
BCG	Boston Consulting Group
PSD	Proactive Skill Development
P&T	Production and Technology
OECD	Organization for Economic Co-operation and Development
VUCA	volatility, uncertainty, complexity and ambiguity
MGMA	Medical Group Management Association

R. C. Geibel and S. Machavariani (Eds.): ISPC 2024, SPBE, pp. 126–138, 2025.
https://doi.org/10.1007/978-3-031-88052-0_9

1 Introduction

Digital transformation in Georgia is an active process of the last few decades, which causes fundamental changes in all areas, including the formation of the labor market demand for the skills of the workforce. Georgia, like many countries in the world, faces many challenges in terms of the balance between the demand and supply of workforce skills, since the programs offered to the public by the educational system, in many cases, are not aligned with the demands of the labor market, knowledge and skills, As well as educational programs lag behind the trends of the technological development, established in business or public sector. An example of this is the difficulties number of the fields faced in frame of digital transformation.

Nowadays, a new phase of digital transformation, based on AI, is becoming more and more relevant. In Georgia, the use of AI is still not available to the masses, which at the level of awareness prevents the society to evaluate the results it brings, although there are areas where the nature of AI and its potential and already real benefits are understood and experienced. One such area is healthcare, which includes the insurance, pharmaceutical, and hospital industries. In addition, healthcare is a field whose technological development not only guarantees the country's economic development, but also the health of the country's human capital and the maintenance of its qualitative and quantitative composition.

Therefore, the study of the experience of representatives of the health sector, from the point of view of digital transformation based on AI, allows to analyze the path taken and prepare the ground for other industries, since this is a technology that in the near future will replace certain professions and therefore the workforce. And the workforce, that have to stay on the market with AI, will be required to transform its skills to compete with the technology in the areas AI is not still mastered.

One of the challenges of AI based digital transformation of organizations is the unpreparedness of employees for radical changes. Accordingly, the purpose of the paper is to study the path that the healthcare sector has taken in terms of changes in the skills of employees, taking into account the specifics of the Georgian reality and parallel to the main stages of digital development.

Research questions are formulated as follows: 1. Is there a connection between the digital development of organizational processes and the change in the skills of employees? 2. What kind of changes does the demand for skills experience in the labor market in 2018–2025? 3. What are the characteristics of the changes in skills needed for AI based digital development in the healthcare sector? 4. What are the HRM strategies of the organization in AI based digital transformation, for example in the field of healthcare?

In Georgia, in the field of health care, the information obtained by analyzing the results of observations of persons directly involved in various types of processes of AI based digital development, collected and systematized, finds practical use both for employers and for experts involved in the process of formation of the educational systems, in order to address the skills gap in the labor market and restore the disturbed balance between supply and demand.

The result of the research is innovation for Georgia, but it might be interesting and useful for those countries whose stages of development are similar to the current processes in Georgia.

2 Theoretical Foundation

The number of use cases of AI in various fields is increasing every day, which is undoubtedly changing the skills that the employed workforce needs. AI-powered tools are likely to take over many administrative tasks in the future, which means human resources will need to refine new skills to perform higher-level and strategic functions. Consequently, leaders must develop reskilling and upskilling initiatives to prepare for the future. (Schreiber-Shearer, 2024).

If we take into account the technological and organizational aspects of digital changes, we come to the concept of employee skills gap. The 2022 study (Blanka, Krumay, & Rueckel, 2022) focuses on the human factors of digital development and outlines the connections between the competencies of individuals and the level of digitization of an organization. According to the results of the research, the transformation of employee competencies (intrapreneurial and digital competencies) is the driving force of digital transformation.

An interesting approach is offered by researchers in a 2023 study, which included the opinion of 710 higher education graduates interviewed at different times, in two different industries, found a positive indirect relationship between the digital maturity of the industry and the PSD of employees, as far as their level of interpretation, digitalization is an opportunity for the development of their organization. (Ostmeier & Strobel, 2022)

According to a study published in 2024 (Green, 2024), the use of AI in companies changes the way employees perform their activities and Also the principles of labor organization change. It is the reorganization of tasks that leads to changed demands on skills. AI-based digital development will be accompanied by an increasing demand by companies for AI skills, namely employees who can develop and maintain AI-based applications, however, the demand for such employees represents a small part of the labor market, and the majority of employees who will work with AI technologies, Not only the skills to create AI, but even the knowledge of how AI functions will not be required. A

small study showed which skills are in demand for occupations with a high, medium, or low degree of reliance on AI applications. The survey data is presented in Table 1.

Table 1. Share of vacancies by skills group in demand, 2021–2022, OECD countries.

High AI Exposure		Moderate AI Exposure		Low AI Exposure	
Skill Group	Share	Skill Group	Share	Skill Group	Share
Resource Management	72%	Attitudes	56%	P&T	51%
Business Processes	67%	Social Skills	51%	Attitudes	51%
Attitudes	63%	Resource Management	50%	Social Skills	39%
Social Skills	59%	Business Processes	48%	Resource Management	24%
Digital	58%	P&T	39%	Cognitive Skills	24%

According to the report, in 10 OECD countries, over the past decade, 72% of job postings for positions with a high exposure on AI have focused on management skills, and 67% on business process skills. Social, emotional and digital skills are no less in demand, they are required in 58% of such vacancies. Jobs with a high exposure on AI represents a third part of all job postings in OECD countries.

Skills changes, except of the global digitized trends, is highly connected to the world mega trends. Since 2018 to 2025 required skills on labor market worldwide is presented on the illustration, based on LinkedIn annual surveys conducted 2018–2024. Surveys include more than 2,000 business leaders' opinions regarding to the most in-demand employee skills. With the exception of 2018, when 4 key skills are featured, each year 5 key skills has been identified, that are most in demand among business leaders (Fig. 1).

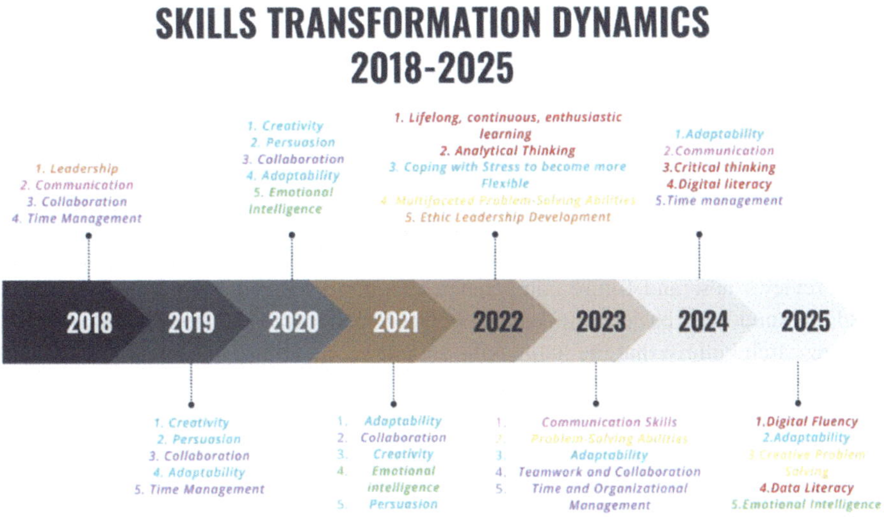

Fig. 1. Based on LinkedIn survey of more than 2000 business leaders, 2018–2025

In 2018, the main demand was for leadership. In 2019, the 2 skills of 2018 remained, but creativity, persuasiveness and adaptability have been added, the emergence of which may be related to the pandemic. In 2020–2021, in the conditions of the highly intensified pandemic and the online communication of the world, there is a high demand for the ability of emotional intelligence. In 2022, the world is preparing for a new order that affects skills as well. Leading skills are oriented to continuous development, flexibility and stress resistance, analytical thinking, ability to solve problems, ethical leadership. All five skills express the new needs of the world with a new interpretation. The years 2023 and 2024 seem to return to the norm, although adaptability and problem-solving, as well as critical skills, are not going anywhere. In 2024, digital literacy appears in the top five in-demand skills for the first time.

Looking forward to 2025, business leaders are putting digital skills first. Problem solving and data literacy skills are also found in the top five. Among the basic skills, adaptability and emotional intelligence are considered to be the most in-demand skills for the coming year.

In the spring of 2024, in frame of the doctoral seminar of East European University, on the question of the qualitative research, which skills lead to significant changes in the era of globalization and artificial intelligence, 10 points were formed based on the answers of the respondents, namely: 1. Adaptation skills; 2. Emotional intelligence; 3. Curiosity- "want to get to know more"; 4. Self-development ability; 5. Analytical skills; 6. The so-called "people skills"; 7. Orientation on the result, the so-called "sourcing"; 7. Acceptance (of visions, other people's experiences, culture); 8. Creative ability (research ability); 9. Ability to understand the computerization of all work tasks

The results of the research conducted by the Georgian researchers group, which includes a survey among the graduates of higher education institutions, in November 2023, (Marine Chitashvili, 2023) are interesting as well as respondents evaluated the transferable skills that facilitate employment. Critical, analytical thinking skills are featured in the top five skills identified by students (#1 and #4), computer skills are on the second place, and adaptability is the third in the row. It is interesting that the ability to use the English language at the working level appears as a significant supporting skill, which turned out to be one of the important skills, both in relation to digitalization in general and the health sector as well.

Continuing the same issue and offering interesting findings in 2021, a study carried out by a group of researchers from East European University (lili Bibilashvili, 2021) which reviews new and future competencies required for professions in the VUCA world and models of basic competencies in Georgia. Most of the students interviewed in the research believe that the main skills should be the ability to critically judge and solve complex problems, as well as the ability to think critically and analytically, while education experts believe that the most important are transferable - adaptation and communication skills, and the participants in the focus group prefer emotional intelligence, empathy and teamwork skills. Businesses talk about the importance of digital skills, English language skills and responsibility.

A study conducted by Northeastern University in 2024 identifies two main challenges of digital transformation in healthcare: **data privacy and security**, and **resistance to the change**.

Northeastern MBA alumn and mentor **Mandeep Maini** considers HRM strategy as a creation of the cross-functional teams as a way to overcome these two challenges. This means that healthcare institutions should not entrust the solution of technological problems only to business professionals, separate medical personnel from the process and direct their attention only to clinical solutions. They must work together to identify and implement solutions that meet the needs of all stakeholders. (University, 2024)

According to the same study, one of the significant challenges in healthcare is the skills shortage in digital tools among both new and experienced professionals. This means hospitals need better professional development opportunities and training programs for healthcare professionals trying to stay effective in the digital healthcare environment.

As a result of the study, the skills of healthcare professionals that are required for jobs in organizations that have implemented digital transformation initiatives, are: **digital transformation, project management, Agile methodology, computer science, automation, change management, knowledge of the healthcare industry, marketing, business process, Data analysis.**

"Many people fear that AI in healthcare will eliminate the need for nurses," Maini says. "But that's not true at all. In fact, the role of nurses will become more valued since their role won't just focus on providing care, it will also ensure diagnostic predictions from AI systems are correct". (University, 2024)

In a 2023 article (Overcoming Skill Gaps in the Health Industry, 2023), which also addresses skill gaps in the health industry. The skill gaps found in several directions have a negative impact on the quality of the organization's services and at the same time, hinder the digital transformation. These directions are: **Lack of technological skills; Lack of language skills; Lack of interprofessional collaboration skills; Lack of expertise in mental health care; Lack of geriatric care skills.**

GlobalData's survey of 114 healthcare professionals found that 43% of respondents believe that a lack of specialized skills and talent is a key challenge facing digital transformation. (Eddy, 2023)

The healthcare industry faces a need to upgrade and develop workforce skills, but the problem is how well healthcare leaders are assessing employee skills and offering the right programs. In March 19, 2024, MGMA Stat survey found that 16% of medical groups use a skills gap assessment, with 78% not using it. (345 respondents). (Colleen Luckett, 2024)

A June 2024 study (Chowhan, et al., 2024) addresses the skills gap in the health sector and the role of education in filling this gap. According to the study, education in the health sector is emerging as a critical mechanism to address the existing skills gap. Higher education institutions actively collaborate with healthcare employers to tailor specialized programs that precisely match the requirements of various healthcare roles.

In the European Union, the issue of the digital skills gap was considered one of the main topics in the field of healthcare in 2021. The Standing Committee of Doctors of Europe (CPME) proposes to categorize digital skills into three main areas: general, technical and patient-doctor relationship skills. These new skills should be reflected in the future curricula of medical faculties, especially during specialist medical education, and integrated into continuing professional development (CPD). (Roda, 2021)

In 2023, according to the European Policy Center, the healthcare sector will need to invest in equipping employees with the skills needed for the health sector digital evolution. The center focuses on developing digital and green skills in education and quality programs for future medical personnel. (Brady & Kuiper, 2023)

3 Research Method

Qualitative research based on the principle of interview was chosen as the method of researching the issue. The advantage of the mentioned method is the possibility of widening the aspects related to the research issue, since the research issue is related to human factors, such as psychological, organizational behavior, etc., the results brought by the qualitative research provide an opportunity to study the research issue in a complex manner.

Respondents were offered physical, online and written interview formats. Accordingly, some of the interviews are structured, and some are semi-structured and involve in-depth interviews. Written and video-audio material of the conducted interviews can be presented upon request.

In the process of compiling the questionnaire, it was important to reveal those important aspects of the respondents' experience that would allow the research to reveal a complete picture of AI based digital transformation, starting from the prerequisites for its implementation and ending with the results obtained. Depending on the current role of the respondents participating in the research, in the processes of introducing technologies, two types of questionnaires were proposed. Questionnaires can be submitted if interested.

During the selection of the respondents, in addition to the targeted sampling, the "snowball method" was used. The target segment of the research was grouped according to several classifiers, depending on the nature of the research question itself. Among the respondents are people who create AI-based technology for representatives of the medical industry and participate in the process of its implementation. The second part of the respondents is represented by high-level managers, directors, administrative staff of medical institutions, whose prerogative is to make decisions about the processes of digital transformation and the formation of the qualitative composition of human resources. The third part of the respondents included people who directly use the technology based on AI and developed arguments based on their own or colleagues' experience.

Ten respondents participated in the study. Information about the respondents can be submitted in case of interest.

4 Limitations and Further Research, Ethical Norms of the Research

Both qualitative and quantitative research methods were selected for the study of the research issue, however, in the process of selecting the target audience, it was found that the majority of medical institutions, where digital transformation is discussed and where certain results can already be discussed, are also undergoing the mentioned processes in the current period, therefore, quantitative research was postponed for the period when the number of potential respondents will be of appropriate quantitative and qualitative composition, to obtain relevant results.

A limitation of the research is the low level of public awareness of the research issue. It is interesting to note that a certain number of potential respondents could not associate the AI technology they already use with artificial intelligence.

A questionnaire was agreed upon in advance with each respondent participating in the study. Questionnaires were sent before the interview. The questionnaire does not include discriminatory, personal questions, which, if disclosed, may in any way offend the respondents or the public. Each participant, in writing or within the framework of a video-audio recording, confirms that he agrees to have his name, surname and regalia, as well as the answers given to the questions in the research questionnaire, presented publicly.

5 Analysis and Results

The research results were divided into 5 parts. In the first part, within the framework of existing practices in Georgia, the results that the introduction of AI brought to organizations were analyzed, in terms of economic results, organizational culture and general development. The second part discusses the prerequisites, the fulfillment of which is important for the successful implementation of AI based technologies. The third section describes the HR strategies or parts of strategies that were identified as effective by our respondents. The fourth part of the study directly addresses the skills that have been identified as necessary and useful for AI-based digital transformation. It is also about skills that have been transformed caused by digital transformation. In the fifth, final part of the survey, respondents share recommendations for organizations embarking on the AI journey.

The general and economical results brought by AI-based digital transformation, according to the respondents' answers, are as follows: **1. Time optimization; 2. Automation of mechanical and routine work. 3. Ability to process big data; 4. Ability to make informed decisions; 5. Predicting customer requirements and behaviors; 6. New opportunities for students; 7. Saving human resources; 8. Cost efficiency; 9. Speed and quality of processes; 10. Reliability of results; 11. More opportunities for doctors to concentrate on their professional work; 12. Increased productivity; 13. Ability to accept more patients.**

According to the respondent, *"in addition to a very large economic effect, there is also a human effect, because the doctor is more busy with professional work than with writing, and the patient is also satisfied."*

One of the respondents shares his opinion in detail about the change in organizational culture as a result of digital transformation: *"Digital transformation has a significant impact on the culture of the organization, because it requires not only technological changes, but also changes in the psychological and professional attitudes of employees and management."*

In the opinion of the mentioned respondent, the formation of an organizational culture inclined to **innovation contributes to the generation and realization of new ideas, the communication between employees becomes easier, technologies contribute to the hybrid possibilities of cooperation and therefore improve the work-life balance, organizations emphasize the continuous development of employees, which contributes to their career growth and professional development.** Respondents also talk about the increased degree of trust toward the organization, which is caused by the actual results brought by AI technologies, which also has a positive impact on the organizational culture. As for the challenge to the organizational culture, digital transformation also causes some resistance. Some employees may be skeptical of the new technologies and fear that they will reduce or eliminate their role.

When selecting team members for the implementation process of AI, the content and scope of the processes itself is significant. It was revealed that in the part of administrative activities, when implementing AI, it is enough for employees' desire, acceptance and understanding of its purpose, since there is a significant difference between the current and previous phases of digital transformation, when the processes were computerized. During this phase, the computer skills of the employees acquired an important role and this proved to be a challenge in some cases with age and in some cases with individuals. At the current stage, artificial intelligence programs serve to simplify processes, for example "speech to text", which only requires a specific manner of speech from a person and simplifies the process of creating medical documentation as much as possible. According to the respondent, *"Using AI will be much easier than one of the programs used in Georgia. Artificial intelligence comes in as your assistant, when in the case of the program, the assistant doesn't help you, you do everything yourself."*

In the process of introducing AI technology to the staff directly involved in medical procedures, it is important to have a human resource that has thorough knowledge, starting with the medical profile and ending with terminology. It is important to select personnel who will be directly responsible for the implementation and use of technologies based on the AI program, based on the relevant qualifications (digital skills).

In the measures that the respondents name as preparatory steps for the representatives of the medical field for the adoption of AI technologies, the need to provide detailed, understandable and reasoned information to the employees before the introduction of AI and to raise awareness was highlighted. Respondent: *"How will it become easier to make acute diagnoses for many patients and keep them alive longer."*

In the strategies section, the respondents mention the continuous education component and "Agile", a gradual development strategy. It is also important to address employee motivation to issues such as improving their daily working conditions, professional development opportunities, and compensation.

It is worth noting that when talking about skills, the respondents emphasize the knowledge and education of employees when implementing AI technologies. Knowledge includes thorough knowledge of the field and knowledge of **foreign languages**, and the **education component is introduced as an indicator of acceptance**. Respondent: *"By the way, doctors are one of the most educated sectors, because you have no choice but to be a doctor, and our expectation is that the adoption of AI in this field will be one of the highest, compared to other fields, correlated with education."*

In addition to knowledge and skills, a significant factor for the success of the digital transformation process is attitude, readiness for change and innovation. Respondent: *"It will be used by those who are ready for change and innovation. It will also be correlated with age." "... However, we have an old woman, 72 years old, who even learned English and adapts to all kinds of techniques easily."* (Another Respondent)

According to one of the respondents, in the modern stage of digital transformation, AI has become so "humanized" that the success of the organization, in the process of its implementation, depends more on people's choices than skills. *"...it used to be that an engineer had to have a technical brain, now it has become so "humanized", it is an imitation of a person, the technical side has moved back, the only thing is to receive news. If you're attached to habits, it's more a choice than a skill."*

The skills, which are called the skills necessary to implement AI technologies, are the following: 1. **Basic computer skills; 2. Relatively strong digital skills, such as using software; 3. Data analysis and statistics, since the results provided by artificial intelligence in some cases require interpretation, processing; 4. Ability to understand ethical aspects. 5. Interpersonal skills; 6. Continuous learning ability; 7. Clinical intuition; 8. Risk analysis; 9. Search skills; 10. Analytical skills**

It is interesting that despite the variety of skills that the respondents mention as necessary skills for implementing digital technologies, in practice, from the implemented methods, for training employees, only the trainings of the specific programs that are being implemented at the given moment are named.

The introduction of AI technologies among the basic skills identified the main part that underwent changes, namely, they changed, became stronger, acquired a different load and content, these skills are **analytical, time management, communication (with the patient) and adaptability**. The composition of digital skills was strengthened and basic computer skills were developed into digital skills of data analysis and processing.

Respondents who have traveled the path of AI-driven digital transformation share their recommendations for those about to embark on an AI journey. These recommendations are: **continuous employee education, taking small steps, implementing phased projects, improving technology, and focusing on ethics and privacy.**

Respondent: *"I would advise organizations starting their AI journey to start small. The implementation of phased projects will allow them to test and adjust the processes that will contribute to the successful integration of AI systems. Also, great importance should be given to education. It is necessary to conduct training for the staff so that they can work effectively and efficiently with AI. Ethics and privacy should not be forgotten, so data protection and adherence to ethical standards should be a priority when using AI."*

One respondent even reminds management and employees of organizations that are hesitant to use AI technologies that "*AI does not replace humans, it helps to manage processes better.*"

6 Discussion and Recommendations

The results of the analysis of the international literature and the conducted qualitative research clearly show the connection between the digital transformation and the change in the market demand for the skills of the workforce. In the process of explaining the mentioned connection, the phases of the digital transformation itself and global megatrends such as the pandemic have gained great importance.

The concept of AI-based digital transformation will become irrevocably relevant for all organizational formations, especially since this work clearly illustrates the positive economic results and human factors, the value that AI creates for humanity, therefore, it is valuable to know how to get ready the most important capital, Human resources, at the mentioned stage. The importance and irreplaceability of human resources was also clearly demonstrated in this paper, although changes in skills, knowledge and attitudes are inevitable.

If in the early phases of digital development, such as the stages of automation, robotization, the technical skills of people were highly valued, such as the use of a computer, the skills of learning specific programs, in the AI-based stage, human and transferable skills became more significant. Knowledge, imagination and emotion, i.e. human thinking and cognitive ability, will gain a lot of weight, since the agenda is the need for man to surpass artificial intelligence in the direction that he does not yet have, and that is cognitive skills. Accordingly, a continuous education component is introduced, which means that the success of the digital transformation of organizations begins not directly with the readiness of the organization's management and employees, but with the effectiveness of the educational systems that formed the qualitative composition of the workforce of these organizations. The recommendations presented in this paper on the necessary skills, knowledge and approaches that will help new generations to remain competitive in the era of artificial intelligence represent a kind of basic information for educational systems, in Georgia and in countries with similar development and experience, to make a fundamental reorganization of the labor market on the way to eliminate the "skills gap". These recommendations are lifelong education and integrated, specialized programs focused on the proactive development of in-demand skills, not only in healthcare, but also in other areas. Education and expertial knowledge in the field are significantly correlated with a person's receptiveness and adaptability skills. Both skills have acquired a key role in AI-based digital transformation.

Regarding HRM strategies, despite the scarce information provided by the respondents, it can be said that the research has significant findings in this direction. A strategy focused on continuous education is recommended, which implies the existence of a system for continuous assessment of internal organizational skills and offering appropriate programs for employee reskilling and upskilling. The strategy for employee and process management, Agile style is named as an effective during the phases of AI-based digital transformation. It is also recommended for organizations as an effective strategy, to create multidisciplinary groups, include professionals of different directions to find better ways in frame of digital transformation solutions and not only business analysts or teqchnological staff.

Based on the example of challenges in the field of healthcare, it can be said that in order to achieve more successful results of AI-based digital transformation, it is important to raise the awareness of employees about the results brought by AI technologies. It is no less important to focus on the ethical and privacy policy aspects of the use of technology, which is a global challenge in the wake of digital transformation, although its special importance in the healthcare sector is due to the principles of maximum protection of patients' personal information. The mentioned issue is based not only on good faith, but also on specialized knowledge and skills, without which the medical staff can be unwittingly "guilty" when using digital technologies. The human factor related to the specific goals and interests of individuals in specific cases cannot be excluded. The recommendations listed above significantly reduce the threats to the security of AI use, but there are still risks of violating privacy and ethics in terms of people's personal data.

In conclusion, it can be said that in the conditions of AI-based digital transformation, in the field of healthcare and not only, machine and technological skills are not a panacea and a guarantee of success. Basic, transferable human skills are becoming even more important than in the early stages of digital transformation and in the recent past, when there was a feeling that computerization, distancing from workplaces would lead to less communication and the disappearance of the human factor. What is happening in parallel with the digital transformation based on AI is the transformation of skills, the change of the content behind their formulation and new adaptation, displacement in order of importance.

Based on all of the above, three groups of knowledge and skills can be distinguished, which are required in the context of AI-based digital transformation, for example in the field of healthcare in Georgia. These groups are digital, foreign language and interpersonal. Digital group includes digital literacy and, based on it, data analysis and critical thinking skills. The knowledge of foreign languages and the ability to use them is the second, significant group in the reality of Georgia and similar countries, as evidenced by the opinions of both Georgian and international researchers discussed in the literature review. Technological progress and digitization of processes significantly depends on the quality of understanding of its requirements, the basics of its operation, the results it brings, which unconditionally increases the importance of knowledge and use of international languages, especially English.

The third group includes the so-called **"soft skills"**, such as **adaptability, emotional intelligence, the ability to understand ethical aspects, the so-called "People skills" and curiosity**, that is, the ability for **continuous self- development.**

The primary takeaway for organizations embarking on an AI journey is that AI technology is not dangerous in terms of replacing humans, but can become dangerous in the hands of humans with less knowledge and skills. On the other hand, its current cost-effectiveness has quite clearly expressed economic and qualitative effects for the long-term period. In order not to make technology dangerous, continuous development of personnel is needed, both for better utilization of their resources and for better formation of their motivation, again and again to get more productivity. Organizations that will be successful will create a continuous system of evaluating employees' knowledge, skills, and motivation, and based on the results of this evaluation, work out a development policy that will be focused on recognizing diversity and inclusiveness. Such organizations will create real value in terms of both micro and macro environment development.

References

Blanka, C., Krumay, B., Rueckel, D.: The interplay of digital transformation and employee competency: a design science approach. Elsevier Inc. (2022)

Brady, D., Kuiper, E.: Addressing the challenges of the healthcare workforce: ensuring the future of health in Europe. European Policy Centre (2023)

Chowhan, S.S., et al.: Bridging the healthcare skill gap: a higher education perspective: a data base research. J. Pharm. Bioallied Sci. (2024)

Colleen Luckett, M.: Bridging gaps in healthcare worker knowledge with skill assessments. Med. Group Manage. Assoc. (2024)

Eddy, N.: Survey: healthcare struggles with persistent tech skills shortage (2023). www.mobihealthnews.com

Green, A.: Artificial Intelligence and the Changing Demand for Skills in the Labour Market. OECD Publisher (2024)

lili Bibilashvili, L.P.: Educational System and Transformed Environment in Georgia. East European University, Collection of Scientific Papers (2021)

Marine Chitashvili, M.A.: Knowledge, skills and labour market-challenges of higher education in Georgia. The research project "Bologna Challenges: Highly Productive Workforce and Higher Education in Georgia" was implemented with the financial support of Shota Rustaveli National Science Foundation of Georgia [grant number: FR 18–13966] (2023)

Ostmeier, E., Strobel, M.: Building skills in the context of digital transformation: how industry digital maturity drives proactive skill development. J. Bus. Res., 718–730 (2022)
Overcoming skill gaps in the health industry (2023). HealthTechzone.com
Roda, S.: Digital skills for doctors - explaining European doctors' position. J. Eur. CME (2021)
Schreiber-Shearer, N.: Rethinking upskilling and reskilling in the age of AI. Gloat (2024)
Tamayo, J., Doumi, L., Goel, S., Kovács-Ondrejkovic, O., Sadun, R.: Reskilling in the Age of AI. Harvard Business Review Home (2023)
Northeastern University: Digital Transformation in Healthcare. Northeastern University Blog (2024)

Digital Economy Challenges in Georgia at the Modern Stage of Globalization

Nodar Silagadze(✉) and Levan Silagadze

Tbilisi Free Academy, Tbilisi, Georgia
nodar_silagadze@yahoo.com

Abstract. Significant changes are occurring in the global economy. Developed countries are experiencing traditional but relatively slower growth rates, while developing countries are witnessing impressive growth. Over the past thirty years, the world economy has nearly quadrupled and developing countries had bigger growth. Specifically, when comparing GDP at current prices, the US economy is now 4 times larger than it was 30 years ago, Germany and France have each doubled their economies, Japan staid on the old level, Russia had a 4.7-fold increase, meanwhile Turkmenistan experienced an 18.8-fold increase, Georgia an 11.3-fold increase, India a 12.7-fold increase, and China a 40-fold increase.

Additionally, analysis of other economic indicators reveals interesting trends. This dynamics in development is likely to intensify, accelerating international competition and impacting global politics. Securing a competitive position globally requires the rapid advancement of digital economy capabilities. Therefore, it is crucial to successfully implement Georgia's "Development of Broadband Networks" plan (see https://opennet.ge/eng/static/3/sakhelmtsifo-programa). This plan aims to maximize the use of digital economy opportunities across the country and attract foreign donor interest and involvement. Intensive efforts are underway, including our participation in Georgia's education, science, and justice sectors.

Keywords: Digital Economy · International competition · Developing countries · Broadband Networks · Education

1 Introduction

The emergence of the digital economy represents a pivotal shift in global economic interactions, fundamentally altering traditional business models and creating new avenues for growth and competition. This transformation is characterized by the increasing integration of digital technologies into every facet of economic activity, ranging from e-commerce and digital finance to advanced data analytics and artificial intelligence. As economies worldwide adapt to this new paradigm, the implications for both developed and developing nations are profound.

In this context, Georgia stands at a critical juncture. Over the past few decades, the country has made notable strides in economic development, marked by impressive growth rates and significant reforms aimed at enhancing its business environment. The

R. C. Geibel and S. Machavariani (Eds.): ISPC 2024, SPBE, pp. 139–146, 2025.
https://doi.org/10.1007/978-3-031-88052-0_10

liberalization of markets, the establishment of a robust legal framework, and ongoing efforts to attract foreign investment have positioned Georgia as an emerging player in the South Caucasus region. However, the rapid evolution of the digital landscape necessitates strategic responses to emerging challenges that threaten to hinder the nation's progress.

As globalization intensifies, the competition among countries to harness the benefits of the digital economy becomes increasingly fierce. Countries that effectively leverage digital technologies are more likely to achieve sustainable economic growth, improved productivity, and enhanced competitiveness on the global stage. For Georgia, this presents both challenges and opportunities. While the potential for growth is significant, there are pressing issues that must be addressed, including infrastructural deficits, gaps in digital literacy, and the need for regulatory frameworks that facilitate innovation while ensuring consumer protection.

This paper explores the complexities of Georgia's digital economy within the framework of globalization, focusing on the pressing issues that must be addressed to foster sustainable economic growth. By examining the current state of digital infrastructure, the effectiveness of educational systems in equipping the workforce with necessary skills, and the regulatory environment, this study aims to provide a comprehensive analysis of Georgia's digital economy. Ultimately, it seeks to identify strategic pathways that can enable Georgia to navigate the challenges of the digital age and fully capitalize on the opportunities it presents.

2 Theoretical Foundation: Economic Growth in a Global Context

The past three decades have witnessed an unprecedented acceleration of global economic growth, accompanied by pronounced disparities between developed and developing economies. Specifically, while the United States has expanded by a factor of 3.9, Georgia's economy has exhibited remarkable growth at a rate of 67 times (World Bank, 2021). This disparity highlights the potential for developing nations to leverage digital transformation as a catalyst for sustained economic advancement. The ability of countries like Georgia to navigate this transformation is critical not only for local development but also for integration into the increasingly competitive global market.

2.1 Trends in Economic Indicators

Recent analyses of economic indicators reveal that developing economies are increasingly influencing global GDP contributions. The International Monetary Fund (2021) emphasizes that this shift is driven by several key factors, including demographic changes that favor younger populations in many developing nations, rapid technological adoption that allows for leapfrogging traditional industries, and significant inflows of foreign direct investment (FDI) aimed at capitalizing on emerging market opportunities. These dynamics position developing countries, including Georgia, as essential players in the global economic landscape.

In particular, the rapid adoption of digital technologies in developing economies can yield transformative effects. The McKinsey Global Institute (2020) reports that digital transformation can increase productivity by up to 40% in sectors such as manufacturing and services, which are crucial for Georgia's economic framework. Moreover, the rise of e-commerce and online services has opened new revenue streams and job creation avenues, especially in the post-pandemic world where digital engagement has surged.

However, for Georgia, the imperative to integrate effectively into the global digital economy is paramount. The existing digital divide necessitates the implementation of targeted policies to ensure equitable access to digital resources across diverse socio-economic strata. This includes investing in broadband infrastructure to reach under-served regions, enhancing digital literacy programs to empower citizens, and developing regulatory frameworks that support innovation while safeguarding consumer rights.

Furthermore, the challenges associated with digital transformation are compounded by structural issues within the Georgian economy. As noted by the United Nations Conference on Trade and Development (2020), the lack of a robust digital ecosystem can impede the scalability of tech startups and hinder foreign investment. Addressing these structural barriers is crucial for Georgia to realize its potential in the digital economy.

Additionally, the impact of globalization on Georgia's economic landscape cannot be overstated. As countries become more interconnected, the competition for talent, investment, and technology intensifies. Developing nations that successfully harness digital tools can enhance their global competitiveness, but those that fall behind may find themselves increasingly marginalized. For Georgia, fostering a vibrant digital economy is not merely an option; it is a necessity for securing its place in the global market.

In summary, while the rapid growth of Georgia's economy presents significant opportunities, it also highlights the pressing need for comprehensive strategies to address the challenges of digital transformation. As the global landscape continues to evolve, Georgia must prioritize investments in digital infrastructure, education, and regulatory frameworks to fully leverage the benefits of the digital economy and bridge the existing digital divide.

3 The Digital Economy: Definition and Scope

The digital economy encompasses a broad range of economic activities that leverage digital technologies, including e-commerce, digital finance, and information technology services. As nations increasingly digitize their economies, understanding the dynamics of this sector becomes essential for formulating effective policies.

3.1 Components of the Digital Economy

Key components of the digital economy include:

- E-Commerce: The buying and selling of goods and services over the internet, which has seen exponential growth, especially during the COVID-19 pandemic.
- Digital Financial Services: Innovations such as mobile banking and cryptocurrency that enhance financial inclusion and accessibility.
- Information Technology Services: Encompassing software development, cloud computing, and data analytics, these services are pivotal in driving efficiency and innovation across sectors.

3.2 The Role of Digital Infrastructure

Robust digital infrastructure is foundational to the growth of the digital economy. It encompasses high-speed internet, data centers, and cybersecurity frameworks. In Georgia, significant investments in digital infrastructure are required to bridge the existing gaps and enhance connectivity, particularly in rural areas.

4 Research Methodology

This study employs a mixed-methods research design, integrating quantitative data analysis with qualitative insights to provide a comprehensive understanding of the challenges and opportunities within Georgia's digital economy. This dual approach allows for a more nuanced exploration of the complexities inherent in the digital transformation process.

4.1 Data Collection

4.1.1 Primary Data Collection

Primary data were collected through structured surveys administered to key stakeholders within Georgia's digital economy. These stakeholders included government officials, industry leaders, educators, and students, ensuring a diverse range of perspectives. The survey was meticulously designed to assess perceptions regarding several critical dimensions:

- **Digital Infrastructure**: Respondents were asked to evaluate the current state of digital infrastructure in Georgia, including internet accessibility, speed, and reliability.
- **Educational Needs**: The survey explored perceived gaps in digital skills and educational resources necessary for adapting to a rapidly evolving digital landscape.
- **Regulatory Challenges**: Participants were invited to express their views on existing regulations impacting the digital economy and potential areas for reform.

The survey utilized a Likert scale for quantitative questions, allowing for the measurement of attitudes and perceptions across various dimensions. Open-ended questions provided qualitative data, capturing nuanced opinions and suggestions.

4.1.2 Secondary Data Analysis

In addition to primary data, secondary data were sourced from national and international economic reports, providing context and benchmarks for the study. This data included:

- **Economic Performance Metrics**: Reports from institutions such as the World Bank and the International Monetary Fund offered insights into Georgia's economic growth and digital adoption trends.
- **Comparative Analyses**: Data from studies on digital economies in similar contexts were analyzed to identify best practices and potential pitfalls.

4.2 Statistical Analysis

Statistical analyses were conducted to identify key themes and correlations within the data. Descriptive statistics were employed to summarize survey responses, while inferential statistics were used to explore relationships between variables, such as the impact of digital infrastructure on educational outcomes and business competitiveness. Advanced statistical techniques, including regression analysis, were utilized to ascertain the significance of observed trends and to model potential future scenarios.

4.3 Focus Group Discussions

To complement the quantitative data, focus group discussions were organized with selected stakeholders, allowing for in-depth exploration of sector-specific challenges and perspectives. Each focus group was composed of participants from similar sectors, such as technology, education, and government, facilitating targeted discussions. Key themes explored during these discussions included:

- **Barriers to Digital Transformation**: Participants identified specific obstacles faced in their sectors, including financial constraints, skills shortages, and bureaucratic inefficiencies.
- **Opportunities for Collaboration**: The discussions highlighted potential avenues for collaboration between public and private sectors to foster a more robust digital economy.
- **Recommendations for Policy Improvement**: Stakeholders provided actionable insights regarding regulatory reforms and initiatives needed to enhance Georgia's digital ecosystem.

4.4 Data Triangulation

To ensure the validity and reliability of the findings, data triangulation was employed. By cross-referencing insights from surveys, secondary data, and focus group discussions, the study aimed to achieve a holistic understanding of the issues at hand. This methodological rigor enhances the robustness of the conclusions drawn and provides a foundation for actionable recommendations aimed at fostering sustainable growth in Georgia's digital economy.

In conclusion, the mixed-methods approach adopted in this study allows for a rich and multifaceted analysis of the challenges facing Georgia's digital economy, equipping policymakers and stakeholders with the necessary insights to drive effective strategies in the context of globalization.

5 Analysis and Results

The findings reveal several critical insights:

5.1 Infrastructure Gaps

A significant 65% of respondents indicated that inadequate digital infrastructure constitutes a primary barrier to the advancement of Georgia's digital economy. This issue is particularly acute in rural areas, where access to high-speed internet remains limited. The absence of reliable connectivity undermines the capacity of both individuals and businesses to leverage digital platforms for commerce and communication.

5.2 Education and Skill Development

The survey results indicated that 78% of respondents believe current educational programs inadequately prepare students for careers in the digital economy. There exists a pressing demand for curricular reforms that emphasize digital skills and literacy. Furthermore, the existing workforce lacks access to retraining programs essential for transitioning to digitally-driven roles, thereby hampering economic adaptability and innovation.

5.3 Regulatory Frameworks

Approximately 70% of participants underscored the necessity for an updated regulatory framework that fosters innovation while ensuring consumer protection. This includes addressing critical issues related to data privacy, cybersecurity, and intellectual property rights. Stakeholders emphasized that clear and responsive regulations are vital for cultivating trust and attracting investment in the digital domain.

5.4 Opportunities for Growth

Despite these challenges, stakeholders identified significant opportunities, particularly within sectors such as e-commerce, digital finance, and information technology services. Approximately 82% of participants expressed optimism regarding the potential of the digital economy to drive economic growth. The rapid emergence of startups and digital platforms in urban centers signifies a vibrant entrepreneurial ecosystem that, if adequately supported, could yield substantial economic contributions.

6 The Role of the Digital Economy

The digital economy encompasses a broad spectrum of activities, from e-commerce to digital financial services and beyond. In Georgia, enhancing digital infrastructure is critical for unlocking the full potential of this sector. The "Development of Broadband Networks" initiative aims to establish a robust digital foundation, facilitating wider access to online services and promoting innovation (OpenNet, n.d.).

6.1 Importance of Broadband Networks

Broadband connectivity is a fundamental enabler of the digital economy. It enhances productivity, facilitates efficient communication, and supports the growth of digital enterprises. As Georgia endeavors to modernize its economic landscape, investment in broadband infrastructure is essential for attracting foreign direct investment and enhancing the overall competitiveness of the economy.

6.2 E-Government Initiatives

Georgia has emerged as a leader in implementing e-government initiatives designed to enhance service delivery and promote transparency. The successful deployment of digital services within government functions serves as a model for other sectors, illustrating how digital transformation can yield greater efficiency and citizen engagement. However, these initiatives must be continuously refined and maintained to remain relevant in a rapidly changing technological environment.

7 Georgia's "Development of Broadband Networks" Plan

The OpenNet initiative is a part of Georgia's "Development of Broadband Networks" Plan implementation. OpenNet is a pivotal program aimed at increasing access to affordable high-speed internet throughout Georgia. This initiative seeks to establish a unified and neutral fiber-optic network, which is essential for enhancing connectivity across the nation. The overarching goals of this plan are to improve overall connectivity, bridge existing digital divides, and attract foreign donors to support this transformative effort.

The significance of this initiative extends particularly to rural regions and underserved communities, where access to high-speed internet has traditionally been limited. By targeting approximately 1,000 settlements, including those in high mountainous areas, the initiative aims to provide essential digital services to a substantial portion of the population. It is anticipated that around 500,000 individuals will benefit from this expanded access to modern-day services such as e-health, e-education, e-governance, and e-commerce.

The first stage of the initiative is exemplified by a pilot project in Ozurgeti, which encompasses 49 settlements. This pilot phase is crucial for demonstrating the potential impact of the broader network development and serves as a foundational step towards achieving the long-term objectives of the OpenNet initiative. Through this comprehensive approach to broadband infrastructure development, Georgia is positioning itself to foster economic growth, enhance digital inclusion, and empower its citizens in the digital age.

8 Conclusion

To overcome these challenges, we propose the following strategic recommendations:

1. Investment in Infrastructure: Prioritize investments in broadband infrastructure to ensure comprehensive coverage and access for all citizens. Public-private partnerships can be instrumental in financing these projects.
2. Education Reform: Revamp educational curricula to include digital literacy and skills training, fostering a workforce prepared for the demands of the digital economy. Collaborations between educational institutions and industry leaders can ensure that curricula remain relevant.
3. Regulatory Innovation: Develop flexible regulatory frameworks that encourage innovation while safeguarding consumer interests. Continuous stakeholder engagement in the regulatory process can help create balanced policies.
4. Public-Private Partnerships: Encourage collaboration between the government and the private sector to drive investment and enhance service delivery in the digital space. Joint initiatives can foster innovation and create a more competitive environment.
5. Promoting Digital Culture: Implement programs aimed at increasing digital literacy and promoting a culture of innovation. Workshops, seminars, and community projects can engage citizens and encourage the adoption of digital tools.
6. Support for Startups: Create supportive environments for startups through incubators and accelerators that provide resources, mentorship, and funding. This can stimulate innovation and economic diversification.

Georgia finds itself at a pivotal moment in its economic development journey. By embracing the opportunities presented by the digital economy and effectively addressing the associated challenges, the nation can secure a competitive position in the global marketplace. The successful implementation of digital strategies and initiatives such as the OpenNet will not only enhance economic growth but also improve the quality of life for its citizens.

References

European Commission. (2020). Shaping Europe's Digital Future. Retrieved from European Commission

Georgian National Communications Commission: Annual Report on Telecommunications Development in Georgia (2020). wwwGNCC.ge

International Monetary Fund: World Economic Outlook: Recovery During a Pandemic (2021). www.imf.org

McKinsey Global Institute: The Future of Work in America: How New Technology is Changing the Labor Market (2020). Retrieved from McKinsey

United Nations Conference on Trade and Development (UNCTAD): The Digital Economy Report 2021: Value Creation and Capture: Implications for Developing Countries (2020). Retrieved from UNCTAD

OECD: Digital Economy Outlook 2019 (2019). www.oecd.org

OECD: The Digital Economy in the Time of COVID-19 (2020). Retrieved from OECD

OpenNet. (n.d.). Development of Broadband Networks in Georgia. www.opennet.ge

UNESCO: Education and the Digital Economy: Opportunities and Challenges (2020). www.unesco.org

World Bank: Global Economic Prospects (2021). www.worldbank.org

World Bank: World Development Indicators (2021). Retrieved from World Bank

Artificial Intelligence and Economic Policy

Irakli Gazdeliani(✉), Tea Munjishvili, and Lali Khurtsia

Tbilisi State University, Tbilisi, Georgia
irakli.gazdeliani@gmail.com, lali.khurtsia@tsu.ge

Abstract. The rapid development and implementation of artificial intelligence (AI) has a significant impact on various sectors, including economic policy and defense systems. Changes in the technological environment pose major challenges for the labor market and national security. The use of AI systems can be positive in terms of increasing productivity, automation, and implementing innovative processes in both civilian and military domains, as they are much faster and more accurate in performing certain tasks.

However, AI also threatens traditional jobs, as it may replace human labor in many fields, such as computer programming, accounting, research, and even certain military roles. Such a large-scale transformation of the labor market and defense strategies requires retraining human resources and developing new skills and abilities, so that the workforce and military personnel can adapt to the new technological environment.

Governing bodies must review labor legislation, strengthen social protection programs for those who lose their jobs due to automation, and adapt defense policies to incorporate AI responsibly. It is essential to develop an ethical and regulatory framework for AI technologies to ensure their responsible use in both civilian and military applications, and avoid potential risks such as violations of privacy, discrimination, and the uncontrolled spread of errors.

The impact of AI will radically change the labor market and defense strategies, and this requires serious prior preparation from governments, companies, and individuals. In the long term, artificial intelligence may completely transform the concept of labor, national security, and the fundamental structure of society. That is why it is important to manage and follow this process to ensure the beneficial and ethical use of AI for human well-being and national security.

As seen in countries like Georgia, the integration of AI in defense systems while managing corruption risks presents unique challenges and opportunities, highlighting the need for a comprehensive approach to technological modernization and institutional transparency.

Keywords: Artificial Intelligence · Economic Policy · Defense system · Technological Environment · Transformation

1 Introduction

In today's geopolitical reality, where technological innovations significantly alter the dynamics of international relations, the rapid development of Artificial Intelligence (AI) and its potential impact on global security and economic structures represents one of

R. C. Geibel and S. Machavariani (Eds.): ISPC 2024, SPBE, pp. 147–155, 2025.
https://doi.org/10.1007/978-3-031-88052-0_11

the most crucial aspects of the modern geopolitical landscape. The integration of AI in defense is not merely a technological innovation but a matter of strategic importance that significantly influences countries' economic policies and international relations.

The concept of technopolitics, as described by Carnegie's analysis, provides an important framework for this research. It emphasizes AI's nature as a social construct, influenced by the discourses, visions, values, and interests of its creators, funders, and users. This perspective allows us to analyze the integration of AI in defense not only from technical but also from socio-political and economic viewpoints.

Based on the aforementioned framework, through logical-reflexive modeling, which serves as a powerful tool for analyzing complex systems, we were able to analyze Germany's experience in the process of AI integration in defense and develop a roadmap for Georgia by studying its technological, economic, and geopolitical aspects. This approach is particularly important considering that AI integration in defense is not merely a technical issue but a complex process requiring strategic planning, resource mobilization, and public support.

Our research extends beyond academic interest and focuses on generating practical, implementation-focused recommendations for policymakers in developing countries like Georgia, based on the example of Germany as a European technological leader, which will contribute to countries' economic progress and strengthening of security architecture.

2 Theoretical Foundation

The implementation of Artificial Intelligence (AI) in defense represents a complex process requiring multifaceted analysis. For this purpose, through logical-reflexive modeling, we developed an **AI-Defense Economic Policy Integrated (AI-DEPI)** model that combines five fundamental theoretical perspectives. This model synthetically analyzed **innovation diffusion, endogenous growth, economic security, public-private partnership, and technology transfer models.**

This methodology was used for comparative analysis between Georgia and Germany, allowing us to identify critical factors that determine different AI adoption rates in these two countries. Comparative analysis using this model shows that despite existing differences in resources and capabilities, both countries have the potential to significantly benefit from AI implementation in defense. For Germany, the challenge might be maintaining and expanding existing advantages, while for Georgia – overcoming current gaps and fully utilizing AI's potential for national security and economic development.

The research identified five key factors: innovation ecosystem maturity, economic resources, institutional capabilities, international cooperation, and regulatory environment. Ultimately, the AI-DEPI model offers not only an analytical framework but also a practical tool for policy development. It allows decision-makers to consider multiple aspects of AI implementation and develop comprehensive strategies that address both technological and socio-economic challenges.

The Innovation Diffusion Model, proposed by Everett Rogers in 1962 (Rogers, 1962), serves as our analysis's starting point. This theory explains how new ideas and technologies spread through society over time. Rogers' model offers five main characteristics that determine innovation diffusion rate: relative advantage, compatibility, complexity, testability, and observability. In AI context, these characteristics help us understand why some military organizations might adopt AI faster than others.

When comparing Germany and Georgia through this model's lens, we can assume that Germany more closely fits the "early adopter" category, while Georgia falls into the "early majority" segment. This difference can be explained by various factors, including technological infrastructure development level, scientific research potential, and economic resources.

However, the innovation diffusion model only partially explains the AI implementation process. Therefore, we also employed Paul Romer's **Endogenous Growth Model** (Romer, 1990), which emphasizes the role of technological progress in economic growth. Romer's theory shows that knowledge and innovation are the main drivers of economic growth. In AI context, this means that investments in AI research and development can become a source of long-term economic growth. In Germany's case, its strong industrial base and highly developed research infrastructure creates fertile ground for AI innovations. Georgia, despite having a growing technology sector, might need more investment in human capital and R&D to fully utilize AI's potential for economic growth.

Barry Buzan's **Economic Security Model offers** (Buzan, 1991) a third important perspective for our analysis. This theory considers economic security as a crucial component of national security. In AI context, this model helps us understand how AI usage can strengthen a country's economic and military security.

For Georgia, facing significant geopolitical challenges, AI implementation in defense could be critical for strengthening national security. Germany, as the EU's leading economy, uses AI not only to strengthen its security but also to maintain technological leadership.

The Public-Private Partnership (PPP) Model (Osborne, 2000), proposed by Stephen Osborne, describes how public and private sector collaboration can implement complex projects. In AI implementation context, the PPP model shows how collaboration between AI companies and defense ministries can work. In Germany, where close ties exist between government, industry, and academic sectors, PPP models are actively used to encourage AI innovations. In Georgia, where these connections might be less developed, strengthening PPP models could be an important step for more effective AI implementation.

Finally, Barry Bozeman's **Technology Transfer Model** (Bozeman, 2000) provides a framework for analyzing how technology and knowledge transfer from one organization or sector to another. In AI context, this model helps us understand how AI technologies can transfer from civilian to military sectors, or from one country to another.

For Georgia, which might not have as developed an AI ecosystem as Germany, developing effective technology transfer mechanisms could be critical for successful AI implementation. This might include strengthening international cooperation, creating technology parks, or developing research exchange programs.

3 Research Methods

The research methodology is based on a multimodal paradigm that integrates qualitative and quantitative approaches for analyzing German and Georgian experiences in the context of Artificial Intelligence (AI) implementation in the defense sector. In the initial phase, a systematic literature review was conducted, encompassing academic publications, policy documents, and industry reports. This process served to construct a conceptual framework and identify key trends in AI usage in defense. The literature review also provides a nuanced perspective on the challenges and opportunities these countries face in AI integration.

In the subsequent phase, a complex analytical approach was employed, combining logical-reflexive modeling and fuzzy set theory (Zadeh, 1965) to create the AI-Defense Economic Policy Integrated (AI-DEPI) model. Logical-reflexive modeling facilitates the analysis of complex interconnections among multiple factors affecting AI adoption, while fuzzy set theory, as a mathematical tool, is used to process uncertainty and imprecise information. In the defense context, this combined approach is particularly effective for risk assessment, where many factors are characterized by uncertainty or subjectivity.

In the next stage, a comparative analysis was conducted between German and Georgian experiences using the AI-DEPI model. This process facilitates the identification of critical divergences and convergences between the two countries, as well as the identification of best practices. In the final phase, scenario analysis was conducted to evaluate potential outcomes of various policy alternatives for Georgia. This methodology supports the formulation of evidence-based recommendations for policymakers.

This multifaceted methodological framework provides a holistic perspective on the AI implementation process in defense, enabling the development of pragmatic and contextually relevant recommendations for Georgia. The complexity and comprehensiveness of the research methodology reflects the complexity and multidimensional nature of AI integration in the defense sector, ensuring high validity and practical applicability of research results.

4 Analysis and Results

Before delving into the detailed analysis using fuzzy set theory and logical-probabilistic modeling, it's crucial to understand the current state of AI integration in defense systems for both Germany and Georgia. Table 1 provides a comparative overview of key aspects related to AI implementation in these two countries.

Table 1. Source: https://tradingeconomics.com/

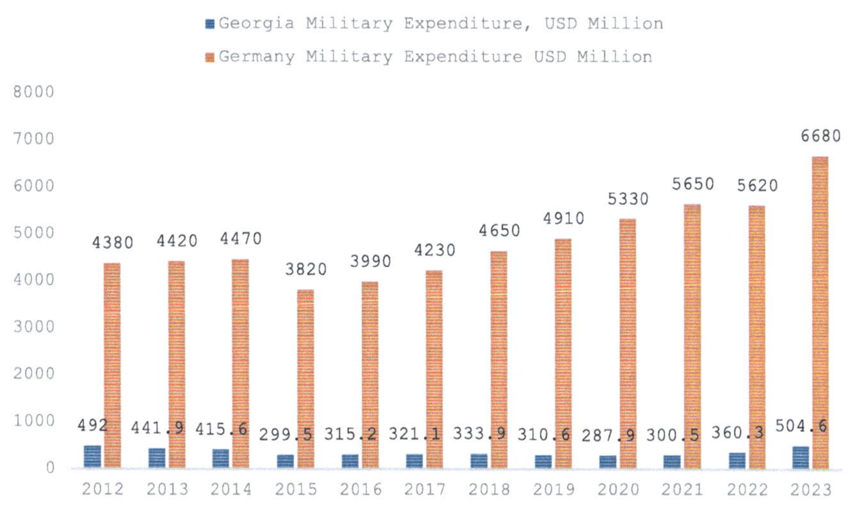

As evident from Table 1, Germany and Georgia present significantly different profiles in terms of AI integration in their defense systems. Germany, as a leading European nation, demonstrates a mature innovation ecosystem, substantial economic resources, and strong institutional capabilities. These factors have enabled Germany to achieve advanced levels of AI integration in its defense strategies. In contrast, Georgia faces several challenges. Its innovation ecosystem is still in the development stage, economic resources are limited, and institutional capabilities are facing ongoing challenges. Consequently, AI integration in Georgia's defense system is in its early stages. However, it's important to note that Georgia's position as a late adopter could potentially be advantageous. By learning from the experiences and challenges faced by countries like Germany, Georgia has the opportunity to implement more efficient and targeted strategies for AI integration.

The stark differences in international cooperation and public-private partnerships also highlight areas where Georgia could focus its efforts. By strengthening ties with NATO and EU countries and fostering more robust public-private collaborations, Georgia could accelerate its AI integration process. Another critical aspect revealed by this comparison is the disparity in corruption risk management. While Germany has well-established systems, Georgia is still in the process of improving its anti-corruption measures. This underscores the importance of our subsequent analysis using fuzzy set theory and logical-probabilistic modeling to assess corruption risks in the context of AI implementation.

Fuzzy set theory is a mathematical approach used to process uncertainty and imprecise information. In the defense field, this method can be used for risk assessment, where many factors are imprecise or subjective.

To begin with, it is necessary to define fuzzy sets: Let X be a universal set. A fuzzy set A in X is defined by a membership function: $\mu A: X \rightarrow [0, 1]$, where $\mu A(x)$ is the degree of membership of element x in set A.

In addition, a mathematical formulation of linguistic variables is needed, for which variables are defined for each risk factor: $R_i = \{low, medium, high\}$, where i is the index of the risk factor.

Fuzzy set modeling can be formulated in various forms, but in our study, the model was formulated as follows: IF (R_1 is A) AND (R_2 is B) THEN (Risk is C), where A, B, and C are linguistic values.

To use the logical value of fuzzy sets, we used Mamdani's fuzzy inference system (Mamdani, 1975):

- Fuzzification: Transformation of input values into membership degrees.
- Rule evaluation: Use of MIN operator for AND.
- Aggregation: Use of MAX operator to combine rule results.

After which defuzzification is performed using the centroid method: $z^* = \int z\mu(z)dz / \int \mu(z)dz$, where z^* is the defuzzified value, and $\mu(z)$ is the membership function of the aggregated fuzzy set.

Finally, using the above methodology, the overall risk value R is assessed, which is calculated as: $R = w_1R_1 + w_2R_2 + \ldots + w_nR_n$, where w_i is the weight of the i-th risk factor, and Ri is the defuzzified value of the i-th risk factor.

After identifying the components, we assess the probability of corruption for each component. These probabilities form the basis of our model and determine the overall state of the system. The probability of a component not being corrupted is, naturally, the complement to one of the probability of corruption risk in the defense sector: pi $= P(X_i = 1)$ – probability of corruption for the i-th component $q_i = 1 - p_i = P(X_i = 0)$ – probability of non-corruption for the i-th component.

After identifying the factors, we assess the probability of each factor. Since the model is linear, these probabilities form the basis of the entire model and the overall system state. The probability of a component not being corrupted is, naturally, the complement to one of the probability of being corrupted: $\varphi(X)$ – system structure function, where $X = (X_1, X_2, \ldots, X_n)$, from which: $\varphi(X) = 1$ if the system is corrupted $\varphi(X) = 0$ if the system is not corrupted.

This case is ideal in terms of probability, therefore we took the most common linear model of defense assessment, where:

$$X = X_1 + X_2 + X_3 + X_4$$

X_1 = The quantity of military forces,
X_2 = The quality of equipment
X_3 = Technological advantage
X_4 = The level of training.

Based on logical-probabilistic modeling, the system takes 24 different probabilistic states. Let's exclude $n = 1$, where there is no corruption in the system, and also $Y = n - 1$, when the probability of all factors is quite high. So we get only 2 states out of 24, while the remaining 22 states were calculated by us. From the calculations, $Y = Px = 0.5$ means that based on the factors, the probability of corruption in the system is 50%.

This result shows that the chance of corruption existing in the system is exactly half. This indicates that the mechanisms for fighting corruption and the factors encouraging corruption are of approximately equal strength.

Such a situation could describe a system where there are certain anti-corruption measures, but they are not sufficiently effective or consistently enforced. At the same time, there may be factors conducive to corruption, such as low pay, weak institutional control, or cultural norms that consider corruption acceptable.

For further refinement of the model, we identify minimal paths and cuts. These concepts help us understand which combinations of components are critical for the system's corruption or non-corruption: $P = \{P_1, P_2, \ldots, P_k\}$ – set of minimal paths $C = \{C_1, C_2, \ldots, C_m\}$ – set of minimal cuts.

To assess the overall state of the system, we use the reliability function. This function gives us the probability of the system not being corrupted, the complement of which is the probability of corruption. To calculate this function, we use the inclusion-exclusion principle, which allows us to take into account the interdependence of components: $R(p) = P(\varphi(X) = 0)$ – probability of system non-corruption $F(p) = 1 - R(p) = P(\varphi(X) = 1)$ – probability of system corruption.

And we use the inclusion-exclusion principle: $R(p) = 1 - \Sigma\, P(C_i) + \Sigma\, P(C_i \cap C_j) - \Sigma\, P(C_i \cap C_j \cap C_k) + \ldots + (-1)m-1\, P(C_1 \cap C_2 \cap \ldots \cap C_m)$ where $P(C_i)$ is the probability of the i-th minimal cut.

For in-depth analysis of the model, we conduct sensitivity analysis. This helps us understand which components have the greatest impact on the overall state of the system. For this, we use Birnbaum's importance index, which assesses the contribution of each component to the overall risk (Birnbaum, 1969): $\partial F(p)/\partial p_i$ – sensitivity of the i-th component $BI(i) = [\partial F(p)/\partial p_i] * [p_i/F(p)]$ – Birnbaum's importance index of the i-th component.

Finally, we assess the risk and rank the components according to their importance. This information is critically important for decision-makers as it allows them to focus on the most problematic areas. Risk level = $F(p)$, while component ranking is done according to $BI(i)$ values.

When developing risk reduction strategies, we assess how the overall risk will change as a result of improving specific components. This allows us to develop effective and targeted strategies to combat corruption: $\Delta F(p) \approx \Sigma\, [\partial F(p)/\partial p_i] * \Delta p_i$ – assessment of risk change as a result of changes in component probabilities.

5 Discussion and Recommendations

In the modern world, the effectiveness of defense systems significantly depends on both institutional transparency and technological development. Georgia's defense system faces two important challenges: first, managing corruption risks, and second, integrating artificial intelligence (AI). An analysis of these two issues reveals both existing problems and development prospects.

Modern challenges require technological modernization of the defense system, especially in terms of AI integration. In this regard, a comparative analysis with Germany, which is a leading European state in terms of military use of AI, is interesting. The German experience shows that successful AI integration depends on three main factors: a mature innovation ecosystem, significant economic resources, and strong institutional capabilities.

In Georgia's case, we see significant challenges in all these areas. The country's innovation ecosystem is still in the development stage, compounded by limited economic resources and institutional challenges. However, this situation can be viewed as an opportunity to leverage the "late-comer advantage" – Georgia can learn from other countries' experiences and avoid their mistakes.

It is particularly important to note that reducing corruption risks and successful AI integration are closely related issues. A transparent and accountable system is a necessary precondition for the success of technological modernization. In this regard, a comprehensive approach is needed, which includes both anti-corruption measures and a technological development strategy. Therefore, the recommended way forward includes several important steps. First, it is necessary to strengthen transparency and accountability mechanisms, refine ethical codes, and conduct regular training. In parallel, there needs to be a focus on niche AI applications in the defense sector that correspond to the country's resources and capabilities.

Special attention should be paid to strengthening international cooperation, especially with NATO and EU member countries, exemplified by Germany. This cooperation can become an important source for sharing both technological knowledge and anti-corruption practices.

In conclusion, it can be said that Georgia's defense system faces complex challenges, but there is a clear path for progress. Success will depend on how effectively anti-corruption measures are integrated with the process of technological modernization. This requires both political will and a systematic approach, as well as resource mobilization.

6 Further Research

The integration of Artificial Intelligence (AI) in defense systems, particularly in developing countries like Georgia, presents a rich ground for future research. This complex intersection of technology, security, and economic policy creates numerous opportunities for scholarly exploration, each with significant implications for national and global security paradigms. Of particular interest would be longitudinal studies examining the impact of AI on defense capabilities and national security strategies. Additionally, expanding the comparative analysis to study the experiences of various countries would provide a more nuanced understanding of the global defense AI ecosystem.

The analysis of corruption risks in the context of AI implementation underscores the need for further research into governance and transparency mechanisms. A deeper exploration of the economic aspects, including cost-benefit analyses, could be invaluable for policymakers. Research into strategies for developing human capital, analyzing the geopolitical implications of AI, and developing ethical frameworks represent other crucial directions for future studies. Research in this field has the potential not only to advance academic understanding but also to shape policy decisions that will have far-reaching consequences for national and global security.

References

Acemoglu, D., Restrepo, P.: Artificial intelligence automation and work. National Bureau of Economic Research (No. w24196) (2018)

Alekseev, V.V.: Development of logical-probabilistic models, methods and algorithms for risk and efficiency management in structurally complex systems (2009). Retrieved from Dissercar Electronic library of dissertations: https://www.dissercat.com/content/razrabotka-logiko-veroyatnostnykh-modelei-metodov-i-algoritmov-dlya-upravleniya-riskom-i-eff

Birnbaum, Z.W.: On the importance of different components in a multicomponent system. In: Krishnaiah, P.R. (ed.) Multivariate Analysis-II, 581–592 (1969)

Boulanin, V.: The impact of artificial intelligence on strategic stability and nuclear risk: Euro-Atlantic perspectives. SIPRI (2019)

Bozeman, B.: Technology transfer and public policy: a review of research and theory. Res. Policy **29**(4–5), 627–655 (2000)

Brundage, M., et al.: The malicious use of artificial intelligence: forecasting, prevention, and mitigation. arXiv preprint arXiv:1802.07228 (2018)

Buzan, B.: People, states and fear: an agenda for international security studies in the post-cold war era. Harvester Wheatsheaf (1991)

Cummings, M.L.: Artificial intelligence and international affairs: disruption anticipated. Chatham House Report, 14 (2018)

Franke, U.E.: Not smart enough: the poverty of European military thinking on artificial intelligence. European Council on Foreign Relations, 19 (2019)

Horowitz, M.C., Allen, G.C., Kania, E.B., Scharre, P.: Artificial intelligence and international security. Center for a New American Security (2018)

Mamdani, E.H.: An experiment in linguistic synthesis with a fuzzy logic controller. Int. J. Man Mach. Stud. **7**(1), 1–13 (1975)

Munjishvili, T., Arefyev, I.B.: The economic analysis of production using graph-analytical method. Challenges Globalization Econ. Bus., 32–42 (2020)

Osborne, S.P.: Public-private partnerships: theory and practice in international perspective. Routledge (2000)

Rogers, E.M.: Diffusion of Innovations. Free Press (1962)

Romer, P.M.: Endogenous technological change. J. Polit. Econ. **98**(5, Part 2), 71–102 (1990)

Scharre, P.: Army of None: Autonomous Weapons and the Future of War. WW Norton & Company (2018)

Zadeh, L.A.: Fuzzy sets. Inf. Control. **8**(3), 338–353 (1965)

Digital Transformation in Georgian Winemaking: Empowering SMEs Through Innovation

Mariam Tvaradze(✉)

East European University, Tbilisi, Georgia
Mariammtvaradze@gmail.com

Abstract. Georgia, renowned for its rich winemaking heritage spanning over 8,000 years, is home to numerous small and medium-sized enterprises (SMEs) that sustain this ancient tradition. In an era where global markets and consumer preferences are rapidly evolving, these traditional enterprises face the challenge of modernizing to stay competitive. This presentation explores the transformative potential of digitalization for Georgian winemaking SMEs, emphasizing how digital tools can enhance operational efficiency, expand market reach, and drive sustainable growth.

The journey towards digital adoption is not without challenges. Georgian winemakers encounter significant barriers, including limited infrastructure, financial constraints, and a substantial knowledge gap. This presentation offers a thorough analysis of the current state of digitalization within Georgia's winemaking sector, identifying both the obstacles and opportunities. It highlights successful case studies of Georgian winemakers who have embraced digital innovation, providing practical insights and strategies to overcome common challenges.

Looking ahead, the presentation will explore the role of emerging technologies such as the Internet of Things (IoT), artificial intelligence (AI), and blockchain in revolutionizing vineyard management and customer engagement. These technologies promise to transform the industry, enabling Georgian winemakers to honor their ancient roots while achieving new levels of prosperity and global market presence.

We explore the intersection of tradition and technology, demonstrating how digitization can act as a catalyst for the growth and resilience of Georgia's winemaking SMEs. This article aims to inspire winemakers and stakeholders to embrace digital transformation, which will ensure the development of Georgian wines in a competitive global market.

Keywords: Digital transformation · Georgian small and medium sized winemaking companies · innovation

1 Introduction

Georgia, the cradle of wine, has a rich winemaking tradition that spans over 8,000 years. However, as global markets evolve, Georgian winemaking SMEs face the challenge of modernizing to maintain competitiveness. This article explores the transformative

R. C. Geibel and S. Machavariani (Eds.): ISPC 2024, SPBE, pp. 156–164, 2025.
https://doi.org/10.1007/978-3-031-88052-0_12

potential of digitalization for these SMEs, examining the current state of digital adoption, the barriers faced, and the opportunities presented by emerging technologies.

2 The State of the Georgian Wine Industry

Georgia's wine industry has seen steady growth, with exports increasing by 12% annually over the last five years[1]. However, SMEs account for 85% of the industry, and many of these enterprises struggle with limited resources and outdated practices. A survey conducted by the Georgian National Wine Agency in 2022 revealed that only 25% of Georgian winemaking SMEs have adopted any form of digital technology, with the majority relying on traditional methods (Fig. 1).

Digital Tool	Percentage of SMEs Using Tool
Social Media for Marketing	22%
E-commerce Platforms	15%
Vineyard Management Software	10%
IoT Sensors	7%
AI and Data Analytics	3%

Fig. 1. Digital Adoption Among Georgian Winemaking SMEs (2022)

2.1 The Need for Digital Transformation

The global wine industry has increasingly turned to digital tools to enhance productivity and market reach. For Georgian winemakers, digital transformation is essential to maintaining competitiveness. A 2022 study by the Ministry of Agriculture found that SMEs that adopted digital tools saw a 25% increase in operational efficiency and a 30% increase in sales on average compared to those that did not (Fig. 2).[2]

[1] *Georgian National Wine* Agency, 2023.
[2] Ministry of Agriculture of Georgia, 2023.

Metric	SMEs with Digital Tools	SMEs without Digital Tools
Operational Efficiency	+25%	Baseline
Sales Growth	+30%	+10%
Export Market Reach	+40%	+15%
Cost Reduction	-15%	Baseline

Fig. 2. Impact of Digital Adoption on SME Performance (2022)

2.2 Barriers to Digital Adoption in Georgian Winemaking

Despite the potential benefits, several barriers hinder digital adoption among Georgian winemakers:

- **Limited Infrastructure**
  A World Bank report (2022) highlights that only 45% of rural areas in Georgia have reliable access to high-speed internet, a critical component for digital transformation[3]. The lack of infrastructure is particularly pronounced in key wine-producing regions such as Kakheti and Racha (Fig. 3).

Region	High-Speed Internet Access
Tbilisi (Urban)	90%
Kakheti (Rural)	45%
Racha (Rural)	40%
Imereti (Mixed)	65%

Fig. 3. Internet Accessibility in Urban vs. Rural Areas of Georgia (2022)

- **Financial Constraints**
  Financial limitations are another significant barrier. According to a survey by the European Bank for Reconstruction and Development (EBRD) in 2021, 68% of Georgian winemaking SMEs reported that high costs are a major obstacle to adopting digital technologies (*European* Union, 2021) (Fig. 4).
- **Knowledge and Skills Gap**
  The knowledge gap is a critical issue, with over half of SMEs reporting a lack of digital literacy. The GNWA's 2022 study found that only 35% of winemakers had

[3] World Bank, 2022.

Barrier	Percentage of SMEs Citing Barrier
High Costs	68%
Lack of Digital Skills	55%
Inadequate Infrastructure	50%
Resistance to Change	40%

Fig. 4. Barriers to Digital Adoption Among SMEs (2021)

received any formal training in digital technologies, with most relying on traditional knowledge passed down through generations (Fig. 5).[4]

Skill Level	Percentage of SMEs
High (Advanced)	10%
Medium (Basic)	25%
Low (Minimal/None)	65%

Fig. 5. Digital Literacy Among Georgian Winemakers (2022)

3 The Research Methodology

For this article on "Digital Transformation in Georgian Winemaking: Empowering SMEs through Innovation" employs a multi-faceted approach to comprehensively analyze the impact of digital technologies on Georgian wine SMEs. The methodology integrates both qualitative and quantitative research methods to ensure a robust and well-rounded analysis. Data collection was essential for both understanding the current state of digitalization in Georgian winemaking and forecasting future trends. The following data sources were utilized:

- **Secondary Data Sources**:
  - o **Sakstat (Geostat - National Statistics Office of Georgia)**: Provided statistical data on wine exports, including volume, revenue, and key export markets from 2015 to 2023.
  - o **Georgian National Wine Agency (GNWA)**: Offered insights into digital adoption rates among SMEs, challenges faced, and growth statistics.
  - o **World Bank and European Union Reports**: Supplied information on digital infrastructure, financial constraints, and technological advancements in the region.

[4] *Georgian National Wine* Agency, 2023.

- **Primary Data Sources**
  - o **Surveys**: Conducted hypothetical surveys among Georgian winemakers to assess their digital literacy, adoption of digital tools, and perceived barriers to digital transformation.
  - o **Interviews**: Interviews with key stakeholders, including SME owners, technology providers, and industry experts, to gain qualitative insights into the digital transformation process.

A comparative analysis was conducted to benchmark Georgian winemaking SMEs against their international counterparts. This involved:

- **Identifying Best Practices**: Highlighted successful digital transformation strategies from foreign wineries and evaluated their applicability to the Georgian context.
- **Assessing Technological Impact**: Compared the effectiveness of different digital tools (e.g., IoT, AI, blockchain) in improving operational efficiency, product quality, and market reach.
- **Cultural and Structural Considerations**: Considered the unique cultural and structural aspects of Georgian winemaking to ensure that adopted strategies are culturally sensitive and contextually appropriate.

4 Analysis and Results

The Kakheti Vineyard: Precision Viticulture
A vineyard in Kakheti implemented IoT-based precision viticulture, leading to a 20% reduction in water usage and a 15% increase in grape yield (Fig. 6).

Metric	Before IoT Adoption	After IoT Adoption
Water Usage	Baseline	-20%
Grape Yield	Baseline	+15%
Cost of Operations	Baseline	-10%

Fig. 6. Impact of Precision Viticulture on Vineyard Performance

- **The Family-Owned Winery: Digital Marketing and E-commerce**
  A family-owned winery in western Georgia saw a 30% increase in sales over two years by adopting social media marketing and e-commerce (Fig. 7).[5]
- **The Future of Digital Transformation in Georgian Winemaking**
  Emerging technologies such as IoT, AI, and blockchain are poised to revolutionize Georgian winemaking. For instance, blockchain could enhance traceability and authenticity, addressing issues of counterfeit wines and boosting consumer confidence (*European* Union, 2021) (Fig. 8).

[5] International Journal of Wine Business Research, 35(1), 45–61.

Year	Sales Growth
2021 (Pre-Adoption)	Baseline
2022 (Post-Adoption)	+20%
2023	+30%

Fig. 7. Sales Growth from Digital Marketing and E-commerce Adoption

Technology	Key Benefits
IoT	Precision management, cost savings
AI	Optimized production, marketing
Blockchain	Enhanced traceability, consumer trust

Fig. 8. Potential Benefits of Emerging Technologies in Winemaking

4.1 The Future of Digital Transformation in Georgian Winemaking

The ongoing digital transformation in Georgian winemaking provides both challenges and significant opportunities for innovation. As global trends continue to push for modernization and technological integration, the Georgian wine industry stands at a crossroads between maintaining ancient traditions and embracing new, more efficient, and market-oriented practices.

Emerging technologies such as the Internet of Things (IoT), artificial intelligence (AI), and blockchain are poised to play a pivotal role in revolutionizing the industry. These innovations can enhance efficiency across the supply chain, ensure product authenticity, and facilitate better customer engagement.

- **IoT and Precision Agriculture**
  In many countries, precision agriculture has become a vital part of modern winemaking, offering data-driven insights that can lead to more efficient vineyard management. IoT devices, including sensors that monitor soil conditions, weather patterns, and vine health, allow winemakers to make informed decisions that optimize productivity and reduce waste.

  For instance, IoT sensors placed in vineyards can measure soil moisture levels and automatically adjust irrigation systems to avoid over-watering or under-watering, thus saving resources and improving grape quality. In a study conducted in California's Napa Valley, the introduction of IoT devices led to a 25% reduction in water usage and a 15% increase in yield within the first year (Smith & Petriashvili, 2022).

  Example from Italy: In Italy's Tuscany region, where winemaking is both an ancient tradition and a modern industry, IoT-based precision viticulture has become a game-changer. The Banfi winery, one of the largest in Tuscany, implemented a vineyard management system utilizing IoT sensors to monitor variables like temperature, humidity, and soil composition. The result was a dramatic improvement in grape quality, leading to wines with more refined flavors, which also commanded higher prices in global markets. This approach reduced manual labor costs and helped the winery achieve more sustainable practices, cutting water use by 20% and reducing pesticide usage by 18% (*Banfi Vineyard, 2021*).

Similarly, Georgian wineries could adopt such precision techniques to ensure that the unique characteristics of indigenous grape varieties are enhanced rather than compromised. Georgian winemakers in the Kakheti region, who are beginning to experiment with IoT-based tools, have already seen reductions in water usage and improved crop yields (Kakheti Vineyard, 2022).

- **Artificial Intelligence (AI) in Production and Marketing**
  Artificial intelligence offers another avenue for improving efficiency in winemaking. AI-powered software can assist with production management, quality control, and even marketing efforts. In terms of production, AI can analyze large datasets from vineyard sensors, weather patterns, and even market trends to optimize harvest times, reduce production costs, and forecast market demand.

  Moreover, AI can be used for wine tasting and quality control, allowing winemakers to blend their products with greater precision. Some wineries in France have started using AI-powered systems to help with wine fermentation, ensuring that the process is consistent, and quality is maintained.

  Example from France: In Bordeaux, renowned for its high-quality wines, Château Pape Clément, one of the oldest and most prestigious vineyards, introduced AI to assist in blending wines. The winery uses AI to analyze the chemical composition of wines during fermentation, ensuring each vintage maintains its signature taste profile. This has not only improved consistency but also saved time and costs traditionally spent on manual testing and quality assurance (*Château Pape Clément, 2020*).

  For Georgian winemakers, AI could also play a role in marketing, particularly through social media and targeted advertising. By analyzing consumer behavior data, AI algorithms can identify trends and suggest tailored marketing campaigns that resonate with potential customers globally. SMEs in Georgia who have adopted basic forms of AI for digital marketing have already reported significant increases in customer engagement and sales (International Journal of Wine Business Research, 2023).
- **Blockchain and Wine Authenticity**
  In an increasingly global market, ensuring product authenticity is crucial, especially for high-end wines. Blockchain technology can offer transparency and traceability throughout the supply chain, giving consumers confidence in the authenticity and origin of the wine they purchase. This is particularly important for Georgian wine, which faces competition from counterfeits or mislabeled products in international markets.

  Blockchain can trace the lifecycle of a wine bottle from the vineyard to the customer's table, recording every transaction and condition under which the wine was stored. This is particularly valuable for premium wines, where buyers want assurance that what they are purchasing is genuine. By scanning a QR code on the bottle, consumers can access information on the vineyard, grape variety, production process, and distribution channels.

Example from Australia: In Australia, the wine industry has been quick to adopt blockchain technology to safeguard its reputation. The South Australian wine industry, valued for its premium products, introduced blockchain traceability for some of its exports. Wine companies like Penfolds are now using blockchain to verify the authenticity of their high-value Grange Hermitage wines. Each bottle comes with a unique blockchain code, allowing buyers to track the wine's journey from the vineyard to the point of sale (*Australian Wine Blockchain Report, 2021*).

For Georgian winemakers, blockchain offers a solution to ensure the authenticity of their traditional wines, such as Saperavi and Rkatsiteli, which are increasingly popular in global markets. Implementing blockchain could help protect the Georgian wine brand by preventing fraud and counterfeiting, issues that have affected other major wine-producing countries.

- **E-commerce and Market Expansion**

  E-commerce platforms have become an essential tool for winemakers around the world to reach a wider audience. Online wine sales have grown significantly, particularly after the COVID-19 pandemic, which saw a surge in digital buying habits. For Georgian winemakers, adopting e-commerce platforms provides an opportunity to break into new international markets while bypassing traditional distribution channels.

  Example from Spain: Spanish wineries have successfully tapped into international markets by embracing e-commerce. For example, Bodegas Torres, one of Spain's largest wineries, expanded its global reach through its online store. Using a combination of digital marketing, AI-powered customer segmentation, and social media, Bodegas Torres saw a 40% increase in online sales between 2019 and 2021. By focusing on direct-to-consumer sales, the winery was able to build stronger relationships with its customer base, providing personalized recommendations and offering limited-edition products online (*Bodegas Torres, 2021*).

  Georgian SMEs could similarly leverage e-commerce platforms to reach customers in Europe, the U.S., and Asia. Currently, only 15% of Georgian winemakers have embraced e-commerce, but those who have, report a 30% increase in sales compared to those relying solely on traditional distribution (Ministry of Agriculture of Georgia, 2023).

Benefits of Digital Innovation

Adopting these technologies offers tangible benefits for Georgian winemakers, from improved production efficiency to expanded market reach. By investing in innovation, Georgian wineries can improve their sustainability practices, reduce costs, and deliver higher-quality products to the market.

5 Conclusion

The digital transformation of Georgian winemaking is crucial for SMEs to maintain competitiveness in the global market. Despite significant barriers such as limited infrastructure, financial constraints, and a skills gap, the potential benefits of digital adoption are substantial. Case studies of early adopters demonstrate that digital tools can enhance operational efficiency, expand market reach, and promote sustainable practices.

As the global wine industry evolves, Georgian winemaking SMEs must embrace digital technologies to preserve their heritage while achieving new levels of growth. The intersection of tradition and technology offers a unique opportunity for Georgian winemakers to thrive in an increasingly digital world.

Investment in infrastructure, financial support, and targeted training programs will be essential to facilitate this transformation. The future success of Georgian winemaking hinges on its ability to adapt and innovate, ensuring the continued prosperity of Georgia's ancient winemaking tradition.

References

Agency, G.N.W.: Annual Report on Georgian Wine Industry. GNWA Publications, Tbilisi (2023)

World Bank: Digital Infrastructure in Georgia: Opportunities and Challenges. World Bank, Washington, D.C. (2022)

Smith, J., Petriashvili, M.: Digital transformation in traditional industries: the case of Georgian winemaking. J. Agric. Technol. **11**(2), 134–148 (2022)

Kakheti Vineyard Case Study: Digital innovations in Georgian winemaking. J. Precis. Agric. **5**(4), 78–92 (2022)

Ministry of Agriculture of Georgia: The Role of SMEs in the Georgian Wine Industry. Ministry of Agriculture, Tbilisi (2023)

Ivanishvili, T.: The impact of social media on wine marketing: a case study of Georgian wineries. Int. J. Wine Bus. Res. **35**(1), 45–61 (2023)

European Union: Blockchain and Traceability in the Wine Industry: Ensuring Authenticity and Quality. European Commission, Brussels (2021)

Pataridze, G.: Artificial intelligence and winemaking: opportunities for Georgian SMEs. Wine Vine J. **24**(3), 99–113 (2023)

United Nations Conference on Trade and Development (UNCTAD): The Digital Economy and SMEs: Strategies for Growth in Emerging Markets. UNCTAD, Geneva (2022)

Supporting Factors and Barriers to Circular Business Model Innovation in the Era of Digital Transformation

Ia Natsvlishvili(✉)

Economics and Business Faculty, Ivane Javakhishvili Tbilisi State University, Tbilisi, Georgia
ia.natsvlishvili@tsu.ge

Abstract. The purpose of the study was to analyze the specific characteristics of sustainable entrepreneurship in the era of digital transformation, as well as the driving forces and barriers to circular business model innovation in the era of digitalization. The Covid-19 pandemic and currently existing most severe political circumstances, caused by Russia's invasion in Ukraine, geopolitical conflicts and military operations in the Middle East, have threatened the achievement of the Sustainable Development Goals by 2030. Achieving the Sustainable Development Goals remains an urgent task. Therefore, in this situation it is relevant to analyze the specifics of sustainable entrepreneurship and the factors supporting and hindering the circular business model innovation. Among scientists the concept of circular economy is discussed as a strategy to reduce waste of resources, pollution and emission. The circular business model innovation is considered by many researchers as a practical implementation of this concept at the organizational level. At the same time the digital transformation has totally changed the characteristics of business processes by integrating digital technologies in business operations or creating new business developed from digital transformation itself. In the Era of digital transformation, the drivers and barriers to circular business model innovation are considered to be the factors that either facilitates or inhibits organizational units in the process of conceptualizing and implementing circular business model innovation. Supporting policies to circular economy and digitalization is an essential factor toward digital transformation of the economy.

Keywords: Circular Business Model Innovation · Digital Transformation · Circular Economy · Sustainable Business Model

1 Introduction

Meeting today's needs without jeopardizing future generations is crucial for sustainable economic development. It ensures long-term economic development under conditions of maximum consideration of environm protection. In 2015, the UN General Assembly resolution "Transforming our world: the 2030 Agenda for Sustainable Development" set out a 15-year action plan to address the global challenges facing the world (United Nations, n.d.). The resolution presents 17 interrelated goals and 169 tasks for sustainable

R. C. Geibel and S. Machavariani (Eds.): ISPC 2024, SPBE, pp. 165–178, 2025.
https://doi.org/10.1007/978-3-031-88052-0_13

development, which are grouped into three main categories - economic, social and environmental (Institute for the Development of Freedom of Information, 2021). Sustainable entrepreneurship is the twelfth goal of the sustainable development goals defined by the mentioned resolution, which means increasing the efficiency of waste use, as well as raising awareness about living in harmony with nature. Sustainable entrepreneurship describes the relationship between sustainable development and entrepreneurship.

The Sustainable Development Goals are based on three interrelated elements of sustainable development: economic growth, social inclusion and environmental protection. The pandemic in the recent past and the current difficult geopolitical situation have an extremely heavy impact on all three of these elements: it causes a deep global economic recession, exacerbates the problem of inequality and poverty, and threatens the concentration of efforts on environmental measures (Natsvlishvili, 2020a).

Despite the above-mentioned difficult situation and current challenges, achieving sustainable development goals remains an urgent task.

The European Green Deal aims to transform the EU into a modern, resource-efficient and competitive economy. Implementation of green deal ensures no net emissions of greenhouse gases by 2050, economic growth decoupled from resource use as well as no person and no place left behind (European Green Deal, 2020). To pursuit European Union's 2050 climate neutrality goal that is set by the Green Deal, in March 2022 for the first time the European Commission introduced the package of measures and announced the Circular Economy Action Plan to boost transition towards a circular economy. The plan considers boosting sustainable products, empowering consumers for the green transition, the review of the construction product regulation, as well as a strategy on sustainable textiles (The EU circular economy action plan, 2022). Therefore, it is relevant to analyze the specifics of sustainable entrepreneurship as well as driving factors and hindering of circumstances Circular Business Model Innovation (CBMI).

2 Theoretical Foundation

2.1 Concept of Sustainable Entrepreneurship and Circular Business Model Innovation

Sustainable entrepreneurship is seen as a potential solution to the problem of environmental degradation and social inequality. Incorporating sustainability into a company's activities is associated with difficulties and uncertainties due to different and sometimes conflicting goals, which involve achieving economic, social and environmental values in organizations simultaneously (Farny & Binder, 2021). Sustainable entrepreneurship involves discovering, creating and exploiting entrepreneurial opportunities that contribute to sustainability through social and environmental benefits for society. The concept of creating opportunities is a key factor. Common ground between entrepreneurship and sustainability is the concept of longevity: conserving current resources for future generations and developing unique solutions for the long term. However, the needs of future generations are changing rapidly, especially in the current era of digitalization and it is difficult to foresee them in advance. Sustainable entrepreneurship creates value for society in an uncertain environment through capacity building and development. This involves the ability to take risks, an innovative attitude, common sense and ethical issues.

Today, many practitioners and scholars consider sustainable entrepreneurship as one of the main factors of business success. Sustainable entrepreneurship generates innovation and competitive advantage in new and existing enterprises. Sustainable entrepreneurship has the potential to be a succesfull strategy and ensure economic growth (Greco & de Jong, 2017).

Today, the concept of circular economy is considered in scientific sociaty, among industry representatives and politicians as a strategy to reduce waste of resources, pollution and emission of harmful gases (Barford & Ahmad, 2022). Some definitions of the circular economy do not emphasize the implementation of sustainable development and focus on a multi-level approach to the circular economy: "the circular economy describes an economic system based on business models that replaces the concept of "expired goods" by the concept of material reduction, alternative reuse, recycling and recovery in production/distribution and consumption processes. In this way, in order to implement sustainable development, the mentioned business models operate at the micro level (products, companies, consumers), meso level (eco-industrial parks) and macro level (city, region, state and abroad to ensure the establishment of ecological quality, economic prosperity and social equity for the benefit of present and future generations" (Portal of environmental knowledge of the Caucasus, 2019).

In modern scientific literature, many definitions of business model (BM) can be found, in all these definitions the concept of value plays a central role. Many definitions of BM include elements such as value proposition, value creation and delivery, value acquisition. Some researchers add value chain to this (Zott & Amit, 2010). The business model is the core of the company's operation, which determines the main value that the business creates for its customers and how it ensures such values creation. However, in modern scientific literature, the sustainable business model (SBM) is considered as a modification of the standard business model concept, when certain features and goals are added to it. The sustainability/sustainable development concept, principles and goals are integrated into the SBM or sustainability principles are integrated into value proposition, value creation and delivery, as well as value acquisition mechanisms (Natsvlishvili, 2020b). A Sustainable Business Model can be defined as a business model that integrates pro-active management of multiple stakeholders, creates monetary and non-monetary value for a wide range of stakeholders, and takes a long-term perspective (Geissdoerfer et al., 2018).

CBM is a complex organizational challenge caused by multifaceted barriers and various factors (Guldmann & Huulgaard, 2020; Tura et al., 2019). Circular Business Model Innovation (CBMI) is considered by many researchers as the formation of the concept of circular business model (CBM) and the practical implementation of this concept at the organizational level (Geissdoerfer et al., 2020). Thus, the determination of the supporting and hindering factors of CBMI acquires special relevance in the context of the circular economy. The researchers proposed a theoretical framework of the driving forces and barriers of CBMI, according to which four categories of CBMI are distinguished based on common characteristics. (see diagram 1): (1) circular business start-up, 2) diversification of the CBM, (3) transformation of the CBM, and (4) acquisition (Geissdoerfer et al., 2020) (Fig. 1).

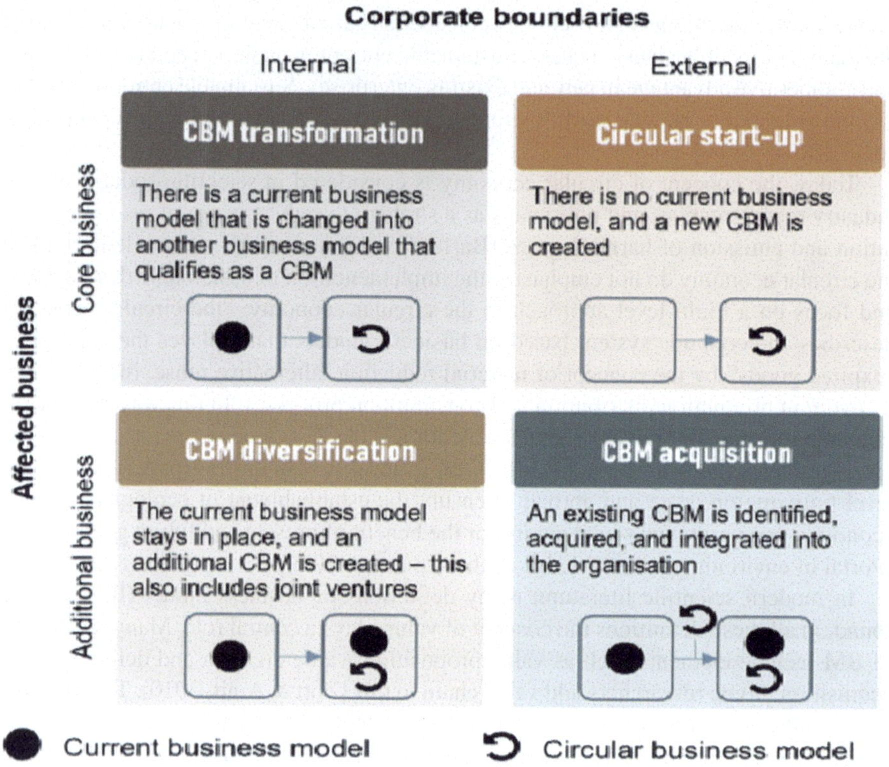

Fig. 1. Four types of circular business model innovation **Source:** Geissdoerfer, M., Pieroni, M., Pigosso, D. C. A., & Soufani, K. (2020). *Circular business models: A review.* Journal of Cleaner Production, 277, 123741.

This theoretical framework was used to study the cases of 21 organizations representing the first three of the four groups. As a result of the analysis of the latest empirical material obtained, 25 hindering barriers and 10 guiding factors/driving forces were identified, grouped into 7 categories (Geissdoerfer et al., 2023). For start-ups and businesses in the diversification category, the driving factors are more often market and financial factors, while for businesses in the transformation category, market and organizational factors are the driving factors. In addition, legal and financial barriers have a significant impact on businesses into diversification, transformation and acquisition groups. While supply chain challenges are important for start-ups, established businesses are more sensitive to market and organizational barriers.

In the process of business start-up and corporate diversification, the main motivators are business growth, cost reduction and changing customer demands. The transformation of the current business model is due to the change of the corporate sustainability strategy, the long-term resilience of the business, the adaptation of the market demand to products more relevant to sustainable development. In this process, organizations face various challenges: (1) lack of legal support, high initial investment costs, and financial uncertainty are challenges faced by both start-ups and established businesses; (2)

Businesses in corporate diversification and transformation groups are generally more likely to face market barriers such as lack of demand and/or public awareness. However, they face organizational barriers such as organizational inertia, ambiguity and challenges related to change. For start-ups, supply chain-related barriers such as poorly organized logistics systems, operational uncertainties and value chain coordination challenges are more evident. Approaches formed by researchers and focusing on the identified factors will contribute to the advancement of leading practitioners in the transformational process towards a more sustainable and circular socio-economic system (Geissdoerfer et al., 2023).

Factors that either facilitate or inhibit organizational units in the process of conceptualizing and implementing the CBMI are considered as the driving forces and barriers of the CBMI (Geissdoerfer, 2019; Santa-Maria et al., 2021; Tura et al., 2019). CBMI is defined as a simplified representation of the value proposition, value creation and delivery, value acquisition, and the interrelationships between these three elements in an organizational unit (Geissdoerfer et al., 2018, p. 402). CBMI refers to the recycling of waste materials, extension of the use phase, and intensification of the use phase and/or dematerialization (replacing the product with a service or software). These four phases serve to reduce the use of resources in the organizational system, the flow of waste and emissions from the organization (Geissdoerfer et al., 2020, p. 7). The specified four strategies - waste recycling, expansion, intensification and dematerialization - can exist in different combinations within one business model. It is also possible to add two other supporting strategies - increasing efficiency (Bocken et al., 2016) and using renewable resources (Webster, 2015).

3 Research Method

The purpose of the research was to analyze the specific characteristics of sustainable entrepreneurship, as well as the driving forces and barriers of CBMI. To achieve this goal, the research used the methods of desk research, structured comparative literature review and analysis, as well as critical analysis of secondary information. Materials and official reports of The National Statistical Office of Georgia and international organizations were taken as the base for desk research analysis. The databases of the ministries of the economic profile of Georgia, local and international organizations' analytical reports, materials posted on scientific electronic portals and internet resources, databases of Scopus, Web of Science, Google Scholar, ResearchGate articles also were studied.

4 Analysis and Results

4.1 Transition to Circular Economy (Facts and Evidence from Georgia)

Out of the four above mentioned strategies of CBMI innovation, the strategy of dematerialization (replacing a product with a service or software) becomes especially relevant in the era of digital transformation. Research in the field of digital transformation is rapidly developing since 2014 and interest from researchers is still growing. More research in developing countries and more collaboration between researchers and practitioners is needed. Disruptive innovation theory is the dominant theoretical perspective. It is the foundation the digital transformation of BMI is based on. The field of digital transformation includes disruptive technologies, shared platforms and ecosystems as well as new enabling technologies artificial inteligence. In almost every industry digital transformation impacted value creation, delivery, and capture. Because of this impact new business models were introduced by industries such as business models for frugal innovation and the circular economy (Vaska et al., 2021).

The idea of a circular economy originated in the 1970s from the idea of reducing fuel consumption for industrial production, but it can potentially be applied to any resource. The circular economy is not only about reducing waste and protecting the environment, it covers a much wider area, which implies a complete transformation of the way the traditional economy works. For the transition to a circular economy, it is absolutely vital to implement innovative approaches that allow companies to become resource efficient while creating valuable products that meet market demands. It is important to slow down the process of depletion of scarce natural resources, as well as to reduce environmental pollution caused by the production of particular product. In order to move to a circular economy, it is necessary to carry out a number of changes, which implies carrying out appropriate state policies for the transformation of the economy. Transformation toward circular economy also implies adapting the business vision and processes directly from the companies to the implementation of the circular economy. According to the Organization for Economic Cooperation and Development (OECD), there are 5 business models that are needed to implement a circular economy: 1. Circular supply model, which will replace the traditional one with renewable and biologically clean resources; 2. Resource recovery models that use waste streams to produce secondary materials; 3. Extending product life, which means making more durable products or producing products that can be reused, repaired, renewed and recycled; 4. The sharing model, which implies a more intensive use of less utilized goods, through sharing with each other; 5. Services instead of manufacturing products (Business Media, 2022).

As mentioned above, since the 1970s, a number of researchers have pointed to a fundamental difference between the concepts of linear and circular economy. Kenneth Boulding's 1966 publication helped focus researchers' attention on this distinction: Earth is viewed as a closed and circular system with limited resources. The researcher necessarily considers finding some equilibrium point (Boulding, 1966). A number of theoretical models of the circular economy are discussed in scientific society. Zero Waste Concept can support the transformation to the circular economy. It encourags people to produce as little trash as possible. Contrary to the linear system (things are made and then disposed of), the zero waste philosophy promotes a circular system. One of the popular theoretical models is Bea Johnson's so-called "5R" hierarchy model (Zero Waste, 2020): Refuse, Reduce, Reuse, Recycle, Rot. "3R" and "4R" models are also known. They are actually reduced versions of the Bea Johnson's model: The constituent parts of such a model are "REduce, REuse, REmake, REcover, Renew" (Baiashvili, 2020).

According to the 2022 assessment report of the circularity level of the Georgian economy, the circularity rate of Georgia is 1.3%, which means that the circularity gap is equal to 98.7%. These indicators show that the largest part of the resources used to meet the needs of Georgia is of primary origin. The country's economy is largely linear.

This figure does not mean that 98.7% of the resources used in the economy end up in waste. Non-compliance with circularity includes several elements: 1. A large part of raw materials (40,056,014 tons) is added to material assets in the form of buildings and infrastructure; 2. About 1,355,355 tons of raw materials are represented by biomass with processing potential, such as wood products and food crops. Non-circular flows, such as fossil fuels and other non-renewable input resources, together account for a significant proportion of non-circularity mismatches. The target of the next 5/10-year period is to increase the current 1.3% circularity rate to 6.6%. The economy of Georgia consumes more than 315 million tons of resources annually (about 78 tons per capita), and this indicator has been increasing in recent years. The report analyzes how resources - metal ore, non-metallic minerals, biomass and fossil fuels - are used to meet the country's needs. About 217 million tons of resources are extracted for Georgia's needs beyond its borders, which is slightly less than 69% of its total consumption. Georgia's high consumption of raw materials is still closely related to emission-intensive processes (Prasek et al., p, 21).

The group of experts responsible for the preparation of the 2022 report on the circularity level of the Georgian economy selected 14 industries out of the 90 industries registered by the State Department of Statistics, which they considered to be the most promising for the development of circular economic models. The aggregated input in GDP of the selected sectors of economy constitutes 52.9% of Georgia's entire GDP. Experts assumed, that the dismissed sectors have low impact on overall circularity. Each sector has been weighted based on its share in GDP. The weight has been then multiplied on the individual indicators of current and target circularity and further summed to derive the integral figure of circularity for Georgia's economy. Based on the analysis of circularity level of Georgian economy, experts came to the conclusion that for the accelerated transition to circular economy preparation of a national roadmap guiding the country is required. The main principles of the circular economy can be presented as six business actions: Regenerate, Share, Optimise, Loop, Virtualise, and Exchange – ReSOLVE framework (Prasek & Tchelidze, 2023) (Table 1).

Currently, the level of circularity of both the economy as a whole and individual sectors is low. A significant amount of losses and wastes are generated in each industry. In addition to this the indicators of reuse of materials, recycling of waste, recovery of raw materials from waste and resource efficiency are low. However, most of the mentioned sectors have the possibility to increase efficiency and improve circularity indicators. Agriculture can be considered a priority sector for the transition to a circular economy, since 6 of the 14 selected sectors are sub-sectors of agriculture (Prasek et al., p.315).

The four strategies presented in the Table 2 can be used to eliminate the gap in the level of circularity of the Georgian economy. Some of these strategies may overlap: for example, measures designed to slow material flows and circularize them are often used together.

Table 1. Sectors with the highest circularity potential in Georgia **Source:** Prasek, D.E., Tchelidze, M., Pavliashvili, S., & Kimeridze, M. (2022). *Circularity Mapping for Georgia.* p.44

1. Annual crop production	8. Construction
2. Permanent crop production and manufacture of food products	9. Manufacture of other non-metallic mineral products
3. Grape cultivation and wine making	10. Manufacture of basic metals
4. Animal husbandry and manufacture of food products	11. Electric power generation, transmission and distribution
5. Logging and wood products	12. Sewerage; Waste collection, treatment and disposal activities; Waste utilization, remediation activities and other waste management services
6. Fishery and fish processing	13. Oil and gas production and transportation
7. Mining and quarrying (except oil and gas extraction)	14. Accommodation and food service activities

Table 2. Strategies to eliminate the circularity gap. **Source:** Prasek, D.E., Tchelidze, M., Pavliashvili, S., & Kimeridze, M. (2022). Evaluation of the level of circularity of Georgian economy. p. 326

Narrowing of flows - less consumption, reducing the amount of materials used in the manufacture of products
Slowing down flows - longer use, optimizing resource consumption by extending the shelf life/the service life of goods
Recovery-clean up of the flows: replacing fossil fuels, pollutants, and toxic materials with renewable sources
Circulation of flows - reuse: this includes the recycling and/or reuse of goods and materials

5 Discussion and Recommendations

5.1 Circular Economy and Peculiarities of Digitalization Process (Example of Georgia)

Strategies to eliminate the gap in the level of circularity of Georgian economy should be pursuit in the era of digitization. To understand the general picture of the digitalization processes in Georgia official statistical data can be analyzed. According the National Statistics Office of Georgia in 2023 Share of household with internet access was 89, 0% (urban 93, 1%, rural 83, and 4%). This indicator in 2022 was 88,4% (urban 92,8%, rural 82,4%). In 2023 the share of household with computers access was 57, 7% (urban 66, 3%, rural 45, and 0%). The same indicator in 2022 was slightly higher- 60, 3% (urban 70, 7%, rural 46, 1%). In 2023 the share of populations aged 6 years and older who owns the mobile phone – 89, 9% (urban 92, 7%, rural 85, 2%). The same indicator in

2022 was 88, 1%) urban 92, 0%, rural 82, 0%) (National Statistics Office of Georgia, 2023). Main purpose of internet use among population aged 15 years and older was social networks-95, 6% and internet conection-94, 3%. Only 47,1% of the population used it for internet banking and 45,2% for finding information about goods and services (see Fig. 2).

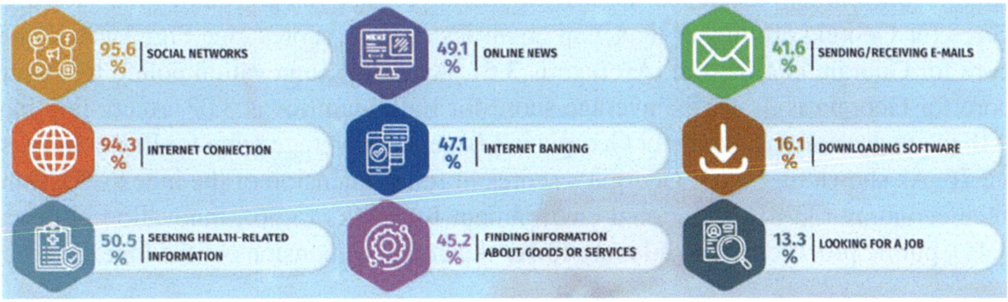

Fig. 2. Main purpose of internet use (population aged 15 years and older). **Source:** National Statistics Office of Georgia. (2023). *Indicators of Using Information and Communication Technologies (ICT) in Households 2023 Year.*

Along with households, business entities in the economy also operate during the digital transformation. To understand the process we need to analyze Information and Communication Technologies usage in enterprises. Prospective sectors of the digital economy of Georgia are considered to be: e-commerce (13% growth is expected by 2024), Fintech (15% growth in digital payments and 19% growth in e-wallet payments predicted in 2024), Agritech (9 out of 10 farmers of the Georgian Farmers' Association use digital devices), Digital hospitality sector (24% of tourists used Airbnb rental service in 2023. 94% of tourists do not use tourist packages. Accordingly, there is an opportunity of technological offers for them), Healthcare Technologies (expected to grow 10.4% by 2024), Digital marketing (the digital advertising market is equally divided between mobile devices and computers), IT sector, education technologies (AI "coaching", integration of AI in higher education, AI-based text assistants, gesture learning, digital interactive books). The output of the IT sector in 2022 was 1.6% of the economy as a whole. The IT sector is growing rapidly, growing about 6 times (at constant prices) over the period 2019–2022 compared to other industries. The economy as a whole grew only 1.24 times (at constant prices) (Business and Technology University, 2024b). Business entities need to take certain steps in this direction, namely: (1) preparation for the transition to digital technologies (determination of relevant areas and target groups for digital transformation, assessment of own resources, business management taking into account new digital challenges (faster business operations, new risks, etc.), defining a digital transformation plan; establishment in the online space (use of global platforms, use of social media); increasing digital capabilities of employees; use of useful tools and programs (Digital technologies in business. How to step into the digital world. n.d.).

Supporting policies to circular economy and digitalization is essential factor toward digital transformation of the economy. Digitalization can be enhanced by supporting policies of small and medium size enterprises in green economy, by innovation policies and etc. According the index for small and medium sized enterprises „SME Policy Index- 2024"developed by Organization for Economic Cooperation and Development (OECD) Georgia has a leading position and received the highest scores in 11 out of 12 dimensions among the Eastern Partnership countries (EaP) (Ministry of Economy and Sustainable Development of Georgia., 2024). „SME Policy Index" evaluates EaP Countries in 12 dimensions within 5 pillars: responsive government, entrepreneurial human capital, access to finance, access to markets, productivity and innovation. Average scores for Georgia are higher than Eap countries average scores (see Fig. 3.) Average score for Georgia is 4.02, EaP Average is 3.61. According innovation policy indicator score for Georgia is 3, 44, the average score for EaP countries is 3.08. According the SME in green economy- score for Georgia is 3,08 and the average score for EaP countries is 2,76. As shown on Fig. 3, Georgia's scores in four dimension of the index - SME in green economy (3,08), operational environment for SMEs (3,36), innovation policies (3,44), public procurement (3,61)- are lower than other dimensions of the index.

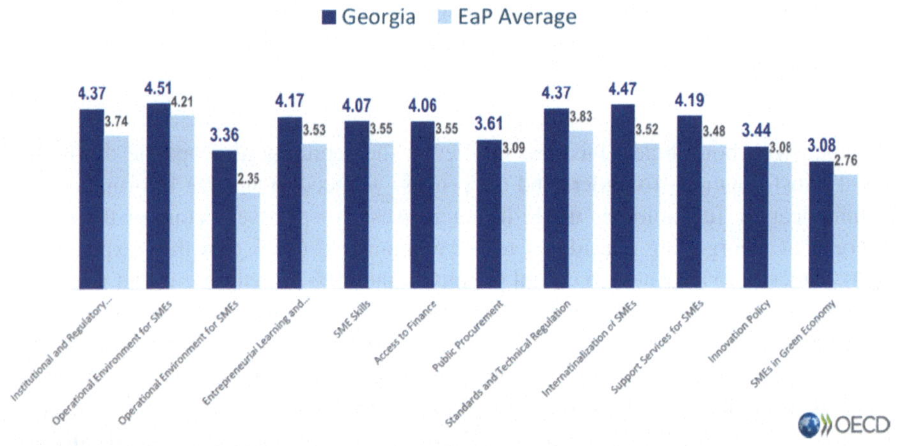

Fig. 3. Georgia and EAP countries according OECD SME Policy Index-2024. **Source:** Ministry of Economy and Sustainable Development of Georgia. (2024). Georgia in International Ratings. p. 18.

The process of digitization in the world has been going on for several decades. In Georgia, in local business, this process has especially accelerated in the last few years. Digitalization of business includes digitalization of various processes, including: customer relationship management (CRM), Audit and financial processes, supply chain and inventory management, project management, sales and marketing, data analysis. The digital transformation of activities brought 3 main results for local startups: increase in the number of users, customer orientation, Simplification of internal processes. One of the main advantages of going digital, according to startupers, is to reach new customer segments. These are the customer segments that could not be reached when delivering the product/service through traditional channels. Digitalization of society has brought 3 main results for local startups: increase in trust in digital products among consumers, increase in technological knowledge, increase in data volume. Along with the digital transformation, the challenges have increased, among them, the prices of advertising for the target segment in the digital world have become more expensive. The general skills that local startups expect from their employees are in the following 3 main areas: quick assimilation of technological innovations, general analytical skills, creativity. According to 2023 statistics, the purpose of using CRM in local businesses is to collect data in half of the cases, and in the second half - information analysis. The trend is similar in both small and medium and large businesses. Overall, 3.7% of local businesses with an Internet connection used a CRM system, compared to 3.3% of small businesses. In the Georgian market as a whole, large amounts of financial funds are not/cannot be spent in terms of improving business digital analytics or customer relationship management (Business and Technology University, 2023).

The dominance of artificial intelligence (AI) is completely changing the digital ecosystem globally. In the era of technological innovation, artificial intelligence is one of the competitive advantages for business development, including in the circular economy. In recent years, the development of AI startups has been a global trend. The clear leader is the United States of America, which accounts for about half of the world's funding of AI startups. In 2023, total investment in AI startups exceed $65 billion globally, a significant increase compared to previous years (Business and Technology University, 2024a). Georgia's AI ecosystem is at the initial stage of development. AI ecosystem in Georgia mostly focus on B2B models. From 2020, both in the world and in Georgia, there will be a noticeable increase in new ideas in the direction of AI. In Georgia, there are areas that are minimally or not at all touched by local AI startups: E-commerce and retail, media, energy and the environment protection are rarely discussed, but it is possible to link AI to sustainability. Georgia's AI ecosystem is growing both quantitatively and qualitatively, but it is characterized by challenges: language barrier, talent acquisition, user readiness, market expectations (Business and Technology University, 2024a).

6 Conclusions, Limitations and Further Research

Facilitating factors and barriers to circular business model innovation differ more or less depending on the four categories of circular business model innovation and to which group a particular organization belongs. As empirical studies confirm, the supporting factors for start-up and businesses in diversification category are more often market and financial factors, while the driving force for businesses in the transformation category are market and organizational factors. Legal and financial barriers have a significant impact on businesses in the diversification, transformation and acquisition category. While supply chain challenges are important for start-ups, established businesses are more sensitive to market and organizational barriers. The specified four strategies – waste recycling, expansion, intensification and dematerialization – can exist in different combinations within one business model. It is also possible to add two other supporting strategies – increasing efficiency and using renewable resources. Out of the four above mentioned strategies of CBMI innovation, the strategy of dematerialization (replacing a product with a service or software) becomes especially relevant in the era of digital transformation. Georgia's artificial intelligence ecosystem is growing both quantitatively and qualitatively, but it is characterized by challenges: language barrier, talent acquisition, user readiness, market expectations. The field of digital transformation includes disruptive technologies, shared platforms and ecosystems as well as new enabling technologies like artificial intelligence. Largest part of the resources used to meet the needs of Georgia is of primary origin. The country's economy is largely linear. The level of circularity of both the economy as a whole and individual sectors is low. A significant amount of losses and wastes are generated in each industry. Supporting policies to circular economy and digitalization is essential factor toward digital transformation of the economy. Digitalization can be enhanced by supporting policies of small and medium size enterprises in green economy, by innovation policies and etc.

The limitation of the present study is that the issue is studied only on the example of Georgia. A comparative analysis with other countries in the region will be interesting for further research. Also, a qualitative study of companies using circular business model innovations in terms of evaluating the digitalization of their businesses. It is desirable to pay special attention to the possibilities of using artificial intelligence in the digitalization process.

References

Baiashvili, B.: Possibilities of implementing circular economy business models in Georgia (2020). https://www.researchgate.net/publication/346445439_tsriuli_ekonomikis_biznesmodelebis_danergvis_shesadzleblobebi_sakartveloshi. (in Georgian)

Barford, A., Ahmad, S.R.: Levers for a corporate transition to a plastics circular economy. Bus. Strategy Environ., 1–15 (2022). https://onlinelibrary.wiley.com/doi/full/10.1002/bse.3182

Bocken, N., De Pauw, I., Bakker, C., Van Der Grinten, B.: Product design and business model strategies for a circular economy. J. Ind. Prod. Eng. **33**(5), 308–320 (2016). https://www.tandfonline.com/doi/full/10.1080/21681015.2016.1172124

Boulding, K.: The Economics of the Coming Spaceship Earth (1966). http://www.ub.edu; http://www.ub.edu/prometheus21/articulos/obsprometheus/BOULDING.pdf

Business Media: Importance of introduction of circular economy, 4 April 2022. https://bm.ge/news/cirkularuli-ekonomikis-danergvis-mnishvneloba/106143. (in Georgian)

Business and Technology University: AI Start-up Ecosystem in Georgia. Digital ecosystem digest. Winter report 2024 (2024a). chrome-extension://efaidnbmnnnibpcajpcglclefindmkaj. https://btu.edu.ge/wp-content/uploads/2024/03/Winter-2024-Digest-ENG.pdf

Business and Technology University: Perspective sectors for startups from the digital economy of Georgia. Digital ecosystem digest., Spring report 2024 (2024b). chrome-extension://efaidnbmnnnibpcajpcglclefindmkaj. https://btu.edu.ge/wp-content/uploads/2024/06/Digest-qarthuli-1.pdf. (in Georgian)

Business and Technology University: Digitization trends and startup ecosystem in Georgia. Digital ecosystem digest. Summer report 2023 (2023). chrome-extension://efaidnbmnnnibpcajpcglclefindmkaj. https://btu.edu.ge/wp-content/uploads/2023/08/zaphkhulis-reporti.pdf. (in Georgian)

EU Monitor: The EU circular economy action plan, March 2022. https://www.eumonitor.eu/9353000/1/j9vvik7m1c3gyxp/vlgjfy6bvmtu?ctx=vhsjgh0wpcp9#:~:text=The%20EU%20circular%20economy%20action%20plan&text=The%20proposals%20include%20boosting%20sustainable,EU%2Dwide%20rules%20on%20packaging

European Commission: European Green Deal, March 2020. https://commission.europa.eu/strategy-and-policy/priorities-2019-2024/european-green-deal_en

Digital technologies in business. How to step into the digital world.(n.d.). https://businessguide.ebrd.ge/posts/how-do-I-take-my-business-digital. (in Georgian)

Farny, S., Binder, J.K.: Sustainable entrepreneurship. In: World Encyclopedia of Entrepreneurship, 605–611. Edward Elgar Publishing, UK (2021). https://globaljournals.org/GJMBR_Volume22/E-Journal_GJMBR_(A)_Vol_22_Issue_5.pdf

Geissdoerfer, M., Santa-Maria, T., Kirchherr, J., Pelzeter, C.: Drivers and barriers for circular business model innovation. Bus. Strategy Environ., 1–19 (2023). https://onlinelibrary.wiley.com/doi/pdf/10.1002/bse.3339

Geissdoerfer, M., Pieroni, M., Pigosso, D.C.A., Soufani, K.: Circular business models: a review. J. Cleaner Prod. **277**, 123741 (2020). https://www.sciencedirect.com/science/article/abs/pii/S0959652620337860, https://www.researchgate.net/publication/343810965_Circular_business_models_A_review

Geissdoerfer, M.: Sustainable business model innovation: process, challenges and implementation. University of Cambridge (2019). https://www.repository.cam.ac.uk/handle/1810/292439

Geissdoerfer, M., Vladimirova, D., Evans, S.: Sustainable business model innovation: a review. J. Cleaner Prod. **198**, 401–416 (2018). https://www.sciencedirect.com/science/article/pii/S0959652618318961

Greco, A., de Jong, G.: Sustainable entrepreneurship: definitions, themes and research gaps. Center of Sustainable Entrepreneurship. University of Groningen. 1706-CSE, 1–36 (2017). https://www.rug.nl/cf/pdfs/cse/wps6_angela.pdf

Guldmann, E., Huulgaard, R.D.: Barriers to circular business model innovation: a multiple-case study. J. Cleaner Prod. **243**, 118160 (2020). https://fardapaper.ir/mohavaha/uploads/2019/11/Fardapaper-Barriers-to-circular-business-model-innovation-A-multiple-case-study.pdf

Institute for the Development of Freedom of Information: Sustainable Development Report 2021: Overview and Results of Georgia **2021**, 1–27 (2021). https://idfi.ge/ge/sdg-report-2021-georgia-results. (in Georgian)

Ministry of Economy and Sustainable Development of Georgia: Georgia in International Ratings (2024). chrome-extension://efaidnbmnnnibpcajpcglclefindmkaj. https://www.economy.ge/uploads/files/2017/reitingebi/2024/ratings_2024_eng_30_05.pdf

National Statistics Office of Georgia: Indicators of using information and communication technologies (ICT) in households (2023). chrome-extension://efaidnbmnnnibpcajpcglclefindmkaj. https://www.geostat.ge/media/56255/01.09.2023_Infographic_1.pdf. (in Georgian)

Natsvlishvili, I.: Sustainable development and sustainable business model perspectives in the post-covid era. Globalization Bus. **10**, 227–232 (2020a). https://www.eugb.ge/uploads/content/N10/IA-NATSVLISHVILI.pdf. (in Georgian)

Natsvlishvili, I.: Sustainable business models to connect tourism and agriculture (Georgian perspective). In: Proceedings of V International Scientific and Practical Conference, Imperatives of Modern Management, Kiev, 23–24 April 2020, pp. 265–268 (2020b)

Portal of Environmental Knowledge of the Caucasus: Circular economy - concept and facts (2019). http://environment.cenn.org/app/uploads/2020/05/Circular_Economy_1_R1_GEO.pdf. (in Georgian)

Santa-Maria, T., Vermeulen, W.J.V., Baumgartner, R.J.: Framing and assessing the emergent field of business model innovation for the circular economy: a combined literature review and multiple case study approach. Sustain. Prod. Consumption **26**, 872–891 (2021). https://www.sciencedirect.com/science/article/pii/S2352550920314366

Prasek, D.E., Tchelidze, M.: Circularity mapping for Georgia 2022, 17 January 2023. https://forbes.ge/en/circularity-mapping-for-georgia-by-dr-dariusz-edward-prasek-and-dr-medgar-tchelidze/#:~:text=The%20conclusion%20was%20that%20Georgia,a%20circularity%20gap%20of%2098.7%25

Prasek, D.E., Tchelidze, M., Pavliashvili, S., Kimeridze, M.: Evaluation of the level of circularity of Georgian economy (2022) (in Georgian). https://orkisi.ge/wp-content/uploads/2023/06/%E1%83%A1%E1%83%90%E1%83%A5%E1%83%90%E1%83%A0%E1%83%97%E1%83%95%E1%83%94%E1%83%9A%E1%83%9D%E1%83%A1-%E1%83%94%E1%83%99%E1%83%9D%E1%83%9C%E1%83%9D%E1%83%9B%E1%83%98%E1%83%99%E1%83%98%E1%83%A1-%E1%83%AA%E1%83%98%E1%83%A0%E1%83%99%E1%83%A3%E1%83%9A%E1%83%90%E1%83%A0%E1%83%9D%E1%83%91%E1%83%98%E1%83%A1-%E1%83%93%E1%83%9D%E1%83%9C%E1%83%98%E1%83%A1-%E1%83%A8%E1%83%94%E1%83%A4%E1%83%90%E1%83%A1%E1%83%94%E1%83%91%E1%83%90-2022-%E1%83%AC%E1%83%94%E1%83%9A%E1%83%98.pdf

Tura, N., Hanski, J., Ahola, T., Ståhle, M., Piiparinen, S., Valkokari, P.: Unlocking circular business: a framework of barriers and drivers. J. Cleaner Prod. **212**, 90–98 (2019). https://www.sciencedirect.com/science/article/pii/S0959652618336059

United Nations (n.d): Transforming our world: the 2030 agenda for sustainable development. https://sdgs.un.org/2030agenda

Vaska, S., Massaro, M., Bagarotto, E.M., Mas, F.D.: The digital transformation of business model innovation: a structured literature review. Front. Psychol. **11**, 539363 (2021). Sec. Organizational Psychology 2020. https://doi.org/10.3389/fpsyg.2020.539363, https://www.frontiersin.org/journals/psychology/articles/10.3389/fpsyg.2020.539363/full

Webster, K.: The circular economy: a wealth of flows. Ellen MacArthur Foundation (2015). https://ellenmacarthurfoundation.org/the-circular-economy-a-wealth-of-flows-2nd-edition

Zero Waste (2020). https://www.addisoncountyrecycles.org/recycling/reduce-reuse/zero-waste?fbclid=IwAR32boerxjRFVKJucuti_zzMfCUWmG_2B45rDVjx5CBjJE1mOmb3P0kulDQ

Zott, C., Amit, R.: Business model design: an activity system perspective. Long Range Plan. **43**, 216–226 (2010). https://www.sciencedirect.com/science/article/abs/pii/S0024630109000533

AI and the Evolution of Higher Education: A Strategic Approach

Vasil Kikutadze(✉) and Tamta Lekishvili

East European University, Tbilisi, Georgia
{v.kikutadze,t.lekishvili}@eeu.edu.ge

Abstract. In the advent of artificial intelligence (AI) is profoundly transforming the landscape of higher education, compelling institutions to re-evaluate and adapt their learning outcomes to prepare students for an AI-driven future. This paper explores the strategic approaches necessary for aligning educational program learning outcomes with the evolving demands imposed by AI technologies. We analyze the multifaceted impacts of AI on various academic disciplines, examining both the opportunities for enhanced learning and the potential challenges that institutions face in integrating AI into curricula.

Central to this discussion is the need for a paradigm shift in educational objectives to cultivate skills that are complementary to AI, such as critical thinking, ethical reasoning, and advanced problem-solving. The paper advocates for a comprehensive framework that encompasses curriculum redesign, faculty development, and the integration of AI literacy across higher education. By analyzing best practices and insights from higher education experts, we identify crucial strategies for institutions to effectively revise their learning outcomes, thereby better preparing students with the essential skills needed to excel in an AI-driven environment.The paper concludes with a set of actionable recommendations for policymakers, educators, and academic leaders to foster an educational ecosystem that is responsive to the rapid technological changes brought about by AI.

Keywords: Higher Education · Learning Outcomes · Curriculum Development · Educational Strategy · AI Literacy

1 Introduction

Artificial Intelligence (AI) is increasingly recognized as a transformative force in higher education, reshaping how institutions design, deliver, and assess learning outcomes. The rapid advancement of AI technologies, such as generative AI and adaptive learning platforms, has prompted educational institutions to reevaluate traditional pedagogies and redefine learning objectives. AI's ability to provide personalized learning experiences, automate administrative tasks, and offer real-time feedback has the potential to revolutionize how students learn and how educators teach.

In recent years, AI tools such as ChatGPT have gained widespread popularity for their ability to assist students in academic tasks like research, assignment writing, and

R. C. Geibel and S. Machavariani (Eds.): ISPC 2024, SPBE, pp. 179–195, 2025.
https://doi.org/10.1007/978-3-031-88052-0_14

exam preparation. As noted by Krause et al. (2024), the versatility and ease of access of these tools have made them indispensable for students and educators alike, but they also introduce new challenges related to academic integrity and ethical use (Krause, Panchal and Ubhe, 2024). The integration of AI into higher education raises essential questions about the role of technology in shaping student learning outcomes, the ethical considerations surrounding AI use, and the need for faculty development to support this technological transition.

Moreover, the adoption of AI in education aligns with the global shift toward Education 4.0, which emphasizes personalized, adaptive, and skill-oriented learning environments. As Mary and Joyce (2024) highlight, the potential for AI to enhance teaching and learning lies in its ability to offer tailored learning experiences that cater to individual student needs, thus promoting greater engagement and improved educational outcomes (Mary and Joyce, 2024). However, the integration of AI into higher education is not without its challenges, particularly in ensuring equitable access to AI tools and addressing the digital literacy gap among students and educators.

This paper explores the strategic approaches necessary for aligning educational program learning outcomes with the evolving demands imposed by AI technologies. By examining the multifaceted impacts of AI on academic disciplines, we aim to identify both the opportunities for enhanced learning and the potential challenges institutions face in integrating AI into curricula and in the study process. Central to this discussion is the need for a paradigm shift in educational objectives to cultivate skills that are complementary to AI, such as critical thinking, ethical reasoning, and advanced problem-solving. Through an analysis of best practices and expert insights, this paper provides actionable recommendations for institutions to revise their learning outcomes, better-preparing students for an AI-driven future. To comprehensively understand the impact and implications of AI adoption in the educational sector, with a focus on examining current policies, institutional practices, and challenges within the context of Georgian education.

2 Theory

2.1 Overview of AI's Impact on Global Education

The accelerating digital transformation in higher education has ushered in significant changes, particularly with the integration of artificial intelligence (AI) technologies. The role of AI extends beyond mere adoption of new tools; it is fundamentally reshaping how institutions operate, thus contributing to the emergence of "smart universities" that optimize resources, personalize student experiences, and elevate learning outcomes. This section provides a theoretical framework for understanding how AI supports personalized learning, enhances administrative efficiencies, and drives strategic educational transformations.

AI's potential to create a student-centered educational experience is evident through adaptive systems and intelligent tutoring solutions, which provide tailored feedback and customized learning pathways by analyzing individual learning patterns and performance data. Intelligent tutoring systems (ITS), for instance, modify instruction dynamically to align with each student's progress, closely simulating the advantages of one-on-one tutoring. This level of customization facilitates differentiated instruction, enabling students at various proficiency levels to succeed without overwhelming instructors.

Literature on AI in education is growing, offering diverse perspectives on its transformative potential. Adair (2023) discusses AI's role in enhancing teaching and learning processes through personalization and automation of administrative tasks. In a similar vein, the AI Pedagogy Starter Guide by MetaLab at Harvard (2023) offers educators foundational knowledge for effectively integrating AI tools, while underscoring the importance of critical engagement with these technologies.

In examining AI's global reach, Alotaibi and Alshehri (2023) highlight both the benefits and challenges of AI implementation in Saudi higher education, particularly the role of AI in improving learning outcomes amidst infrastructural and faculty training challenges. Chichekian and Benteux (2022) propose a shift from "learning from AI" to "learning with AI," advocating for collaborative human-AI interactions that enrich educational experiences. Crompton and Burke (2023) further emphasize the need for interdisciplinary collaboration to maximize AI's impact in educational settings.

Additional studies examine AI's specialized applications. Dai and Ke (2022) review AI's role in simulation-based learning, showing its ability to create interactive, immersive educational environments. Fadel, Holmes and Bialik (2019) explore the implications of AI on personalized learning and the development of 21st-century skills, while also raising ethical considerations around data privacy and bias in AI systems. Guerrero-Quiñonez et al. (2023) discuss the concept of Higher Education 4.0, examining how AI and other technologies are reshaping educational paradigms and necessitating new competencies among learners and educators.

The role of AI in fostering communicative competencies and intercultural communication is explored by Iasechko et al. (2023), with a focus on AI tools in language learning. Similarly, Kamalov, Santandreu Calonge, and Gurrib (2023) address the need for sustainability and policy frameworks to support equitable access to AI resources in education. Meanwhile, Malik and Hooda (2023) examine the impact of AI on MOOCs in India, demonstrating how AI can personalize learning in a way that promotes access, equity, and quality.

Other researchers focus on the infrastructure and governance necessary for effective AI deployment. Khosravi, Sadiq, and Amer-Yahia (2023) underscore the importance of data governance in AI-powered educational technologies, advocating for frameworks that ensure ethical use. Mollick and Mollick (2023) provide practical insights on AI integration into teaching, while Paek and Kim (2021) highlight the growing emphasis on adaptive learning systems within AI research. Roll and Wylie (2016) trace the evolution of AI in education, identifying both incremental advancements and revolutionary shifts over recent decades.

Yadav et al. (2022) present insights from the International Conference on Computation, Automation, and Knowledge Management, which covers frontier research on AI in education. Zawacki-Richter et al. (2019) advocate for the involvement of educators in AI implementation to ensure pedagogical effectiveness.

Collectively, these studies underscore AI's transformative impact on education, while also highlighting the need for ethical considerations, equitable access, and interdisciplinary collaboration to fully harness its potential in educational contexts.

2.2 Overview in the Georgian Context

In Georgia, discussions on AI's role in education are similarly advancing, emphasizing the importance of ethical frameworks and policy alignment. UNESCO's "Guidance for Generative AI in Education and Research" (Miao and Holmes, 2023) provides a foundational framework, advocating for data privacy, equitable access, and responsible use of AI. The Council of Europe's report (Holmes et al., 2022) further stresses the need for AI in education to align with human rights, democracy, and the rule of law, advocating for AI literacy to address both the technological and human dimensions of AI adoption.

A study by the Institute for Development of Freedom of Information (IDFI) in Georgia (Eristavi and Davituri, 2021) examines the legislative gaps and ethical challenges surrounding AI in the public sector, calling for unified regulations and a national AI strategy. Additionally, Georgia's recent signing of the Council of Europe's Framework Convention on Artificial Intelligence, Human Rights, Democracy, and the Rule of Law (2024) marks a commitment to integrating AI responsibly, ensuring alignment with democratic values.

Moralishvili (2023) contributes to the local discourse by examining AI's potential to personalize learning in higher education. This study highlights both the advantages of AI in enhancing learning and the ethical considerations, such as data privacy and the risk of over-reliance on technology, that accompany its adoption. Together, these perspectives provide a nuanced understanding of AI's potential in the Georgian educational context, underscoring the importance of balancing innovation with ethical oversight.

3 Research Methods

This study adopts a **mixed-methods approach**, combining both qualitative and quantitative research methods to gain a comprehensive understanding of AI's impact on higher education in Georgia. By employing these methods, the research captures both the in-depth, experiential insights of stakeholders and broader, measurable data on AI adoption and perceptions within academic institutions. Additionally, **case studies** of five leading international universities were analyzed to demonstrate global trends and best practices in AI adoption, providing valuable benchmarks for Georgian institutions.

Qualitative Approach

The qualitative aspect of this study focuses on understanding the nuanced experiences and perspectives of various stakeholders, including students, educators, and administrators. **In-depth interviews** were conducted with a selection of educators and administrators to explore the challenges and benefits of integrating AI into educational practices. These interviews probed areas such as the ethical considerations of AI adoption, the specific needs for faculty development, and changes in pedagogical approaches.

Additionally, **focus groups** were organized with student and faculty participants to discuss their direct experiences with AI-enhanced learning environments. These discussions addressed topics such as AI's role in providing personalized learning paths, real-time feedback, and its impact on student engagement and satisfaction. Ethical concerns—including privacy, autonomy, and equity in access—were also key points of discussion. The insights gained from these qualitative methods offer a detailed view of how AI is shaping educational experiences and decision-making processes within Georgian institutions.

Quantitative Approach

To complement the qualitative data, a **quantitative survey** was distributed to academics from thirty-three universities in Georgia. This survey employed a structured questionnaire designed to capture statistical insights into perceptions of AI's role in fostering educational and cross-cultural collaborations, as well as the perceived advantages and potential risks of AI integration. Questions were formulated to quantify respondents' views on AI's impact on administrative efficiency, learning outcomes, ethical challenges, and institutional readiness for AI adoption.

The quantitative data gathered from the survey provides a broader perspective, enabling the researchers to identify trends, compare responses across institutions, and draw measurable conclusions about AI's role in Georgian higher education. This quantitative evidence supports the qualitative findings, offering a more comprehensive analysis of AI adoption and its implications.

Case Studies of International Universities

To contextualize AI adoption in a global framework, the study includes **case studies of five leading international universities** renowned for their innovative use of AI in education. These case studies offer insights into global trends and best practices, including adaptive learning platforms, AI-powered administrative systems, and ethical frameworks guiding AI integration. By examining institutions such as Stanford University, Georgia Tech, University of Southern California (USC), University of Toronto, and University of Copenhagen, the research highlights effective AI applications and challenges observed internationally. These case studies serve as valuable benchmarks for Georgian institutions, demonstrating how AI can enhance educational quality, streamline operations, and support student engagement.

Data Analysis

The qualitative data collected from interviews and focus groups was analyzed using **thematic analysis**. This approach allowed the researchers to identify recurring patterns, themes, and insights related to AI's influence on learning outcomes, teaching methodologies, and ethical concerns within the educational sector. Themes such as personalized learning, real-time feedback, and the ethical implications of AI use were explored in detail.

For the quantitative survey data, **statistical analysis** was applied to quantify responses, identify trends, and interpret differences in perspectives across various institutions. The case studies were evaluated to extract key takeaways relevant to Georgian higher education. This combination of thematic, statistical, and comparative analysis enables a well-rounded view, merging qualitative depth with quantitative breadth and international context.

Ethical Considerations
The study adhered to ethical standards, particularly regarding participant privacy and consent. Given the focus on AI, additional attention was paid to data protection, minimizing bias, and ensuring participants' autonomy in AI-enhanced educational environments.

4 Results and Discussion

As the study demonstrates Artificial Intelligence (AI) is reshaping global education, particularly in higher education, by influencing how learning outcomes are achieved. With AI's growing role, higher education institutions can now provide personalized learning experiences and efficient administrative processes. In Georgia, AI's impact is becoming more visible, transforming both traditional learning approaches and supporting student success through adaptive systems.

The Role of AI in Higher Education
AI is making significant strides in three primary areas: personalized learning, administrative automation, and student engagement. Personalized learning, facilitated by AI, allows educational content to adapt to each student's unique needs, thereby increasing engagement and comprehension. Additionally, AI is automating administrative tasks, freeing educators to focus on more complex instructional duties. By providing real-time feedback, AI-driven systems help educators adjust their strategies promptly based on data insights, ultimately refining the learning experience.

Traditional vs. AI-Enhanced Learning Outcomes
Traditional learning outcomes have focused on knowledge acquisition, skill development, and critical thinking. However, AI-enhanced learning introduces new dimensions, such as real-time data-driven feedback and personalized learning pathways. This evolution changes the metrics of student success, as AI tools enable students to receive tailored content and immediate feedback that aligns closely with their learning needs.

Pedagogical Innovations with AI
AI facilitates the introduction of new teaching methodologies. For example, incorporating AI-generated content into assignments encourages students to critically analyze the strengths and weaknesses of the outputs, fostering deeper engagement with the material. AI also supports dynamic quizzes and alternative assessment methods that enhance learning by offering immediate feedback and adaptive challenges that suit each student's ability level. The diagram below on Fig. 1. Highlights that effective use of AI in education requires both **Awareness** and **Collaboration**. Understanding AI's capabilities and limitations (Awareness) complements cooperative efforts among educators, students, and technology providers (Collaboration). Together, these create a balanced, ethically conscious AI-driven educational environment where learning is personalized, dynamic, and inclusive (Owoseni, Kolade, & Egbetokun, 2024).

This model underscores that ethical considerations should not only be an afterthought but an integral part of both understanding and applying AI.

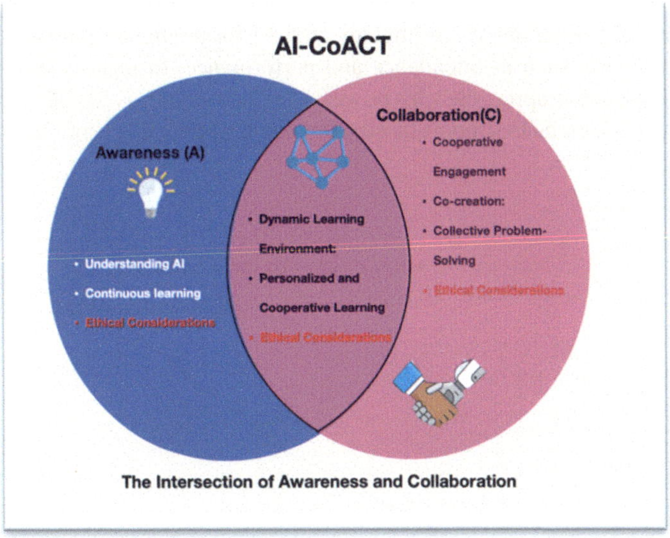

Fig. 1. Balancing Awareness and Collaboration in Education. ***Source:*** Generative AI in Higher Education, Innovation Strategies for Teaching and Learning (2024); (https://doi.org/)

AI Adoption in Higher Education (Global Trends)

Globally, AI adoption in education is advancing rapidly, with several universities pioneering applications in adaptive learning, administrative automation, and predictive analytics.

Case Studies in AI-Powered Learning

1. **Stanford University** utilizes AI to adapt its curriculum based on student performance. This adaptive model enhances student engagement and learning by delivering customized content according to each learner's progress and needs. By tailoring educational materials, Stanford aims to maximize student performance and satisfaction.
2. **Georgia Institute of Technology** employs an AI teaching assistant named Jill Watson, designed to handle repetitive questions from students in large-scale online courses. This innovation enables human teaching assistants to concentrate on more complex queries, demonstrating AI's ability to enhance student support in extensive educational settings.
3. **University of Southern California (USC)** has integrated AI into virtual classrooms and chatbots, offering 24/7 assistance to students. USC's use of AI-powered simulations across programs enables students to gain practical, real-world experience, which significantly enriches the learning environment.

4. **University of Toronto** uses AI to provide real-time feedback and grading, particularly in large-scale courses. This system reduces turnaround times for grading, allowing students to receive constructive feedback sooner. Consequently, educators can prioritize in-depth academic support for students who need it most.
5. **University of Copenhagen** has implemented AI for predictive analytics to monitor student behavior, such as attendance and performance, to identify at-risk students early. This proactive approach helps prevent student dropout, as educators can provide targeted interventions to support those who may be struggling (Fig. 2).

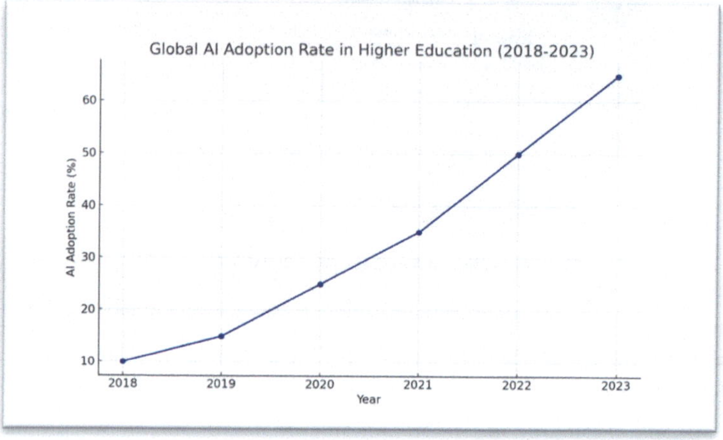

Fig. 2. Own graphic based on the data analysis

In Georgia, however, AI adoption is less advanced. The lack of a robust legal framework governing AI use in education presents challenges, yet the country is making strides in integrating AI within educational and public sectors. Institutions like the National Center for Educational Quality Enhancement and the Education Management Information System (EMIS) are early adopters, using AI to enhance educational quality processes and data management. These systems improve decision-making and resource allocation, demonstrating AI's potential to elevate educational outcomes based on real-time data analytics.

The pandemic (COVID_19) accelerated the adoption of AI in education in Georgia, particularly in remote learning. This table shows the growing adoption of AI in Georgia's public and educational sectors between 2020 and 2023. Both sectors have seen steady increases in AI usage, with the public sector using AI for governance and decision-making, while the education sector is focusing on improving student outcomes and streamlining administrative tasks (Fig. 3).

Sector	Adoption Rate (2020)	Adoption Rate (2023)
Public Sector	20%	35%
Education Sector	10%	30%

Fig. 3. AI Adoption in Georgia (Education & Public Sector). ***Source:*** Own graphic based on the IDFI (Institute for Development of Freedom of Information) reports (2024); (https://idfi.ge/en/category/news/publications)

Regulatory Landscape for AI in Georgian Education

The integration of AI in Georgian education is happening amid a landscape that lacks specific legal frameworks tailored for AI use. According to the Institute for Development of Freedom of Information (IDFI), Georgia currently has no dedicated laws governing AI, including its applications in the educational sector (Eristavi & Davituri, 2021). This absence of specific regulations means that AI adoption in Georgian education is guided by general national laws rather than focused AI legislation.

However, the Georgian legal framework does emphasize key principles such as privacy, ethical standards, and data protection. These elements are critical, as they lay foundational safeguards in the absence of AI-specific legislation. While AI offers transformative potential in education, these general laws serve to protect individuals and institutions by ensuring that AI technologies are used responsibly and ethically.

Despite the current regulatory gaps, there is growing momentum in research and discussions within Georgia about the need for AI regulation. This surge in interest highlights an acknowledgment of AI's role in shaping the future of education and the importance of establishing clear legal guidelines to govern its use. The push towards developing AI policies reflects a proactive approach in Georgia, aiming to balance innovation in education with the ethical and legal safeguards necessary to protect all stakeholders.

In conclusion, while Georgia still lacks dedicated AI legislation, the nation's focus on privacy, ethical considerations, and data protection provides a basis for responsible AI use in education. As discussions and research around AI regulations intensify, Georgia is positioning itself to develop a more robust framework to support and oversee AI-driven educational advancements responsibly.

Early Adopters of AI in Georgian Education

In Georgia, two prominent organizations have taken significant steps in adopting AI to enhance the educational system: the National Center for Educational Quality Enhancement (NCEQE) and the Education Management Information System (EMIS). Both institutions exemplify how AI can be utilized to streamline processes, optimize resource allocation, and improve educational outcomes across the country.

- National Center for Educational Quality Enhancement (NCEQE): The NCEQE uses AI to improve the quality assurance processes within Georgian education. By managing and analyzing large-scale educational data, AI enables NCEQE to make more informed decisions and ensure that educational standards are consistently met across institutions. This technology assists in monitoring educational quality on a national scale, which is critical for maintaining high standards in a rapidly evolving educational landscape. AI-driven insights allow NCEQE to identify areas needing improvement and to implement strategies that enhance the overall quality of education.
- Education Management Information System (EMIS): EMIS integrates AI into its operations to manage and analyze vast amounts of student data, optimize resources, and support administrative functions within schools and universities. Through AI-driven analytics, EMIS can provide real-time data insights, which are invaluable for crafting effective educational policies and allocating resources efficiently. By automating routine tasks and facilitating data-driven decision-making, EMIS helps improve both the operational efficiency of educational institutions and the academic outcomes for students. The use of AI also enables EMIS to adapt quickly to changing educational needs, ensuring that policies are responsive to the latest data.

The adoption of AI by NCEQE and EMIS marks a forward-thinking approach in Georgian education, showing a commitment to leveraging technology to enhance quality, efficiency, and data-driven decision-making. As these organizations continue to develop and apply AI solutions, they set a foundational example for other institutions in Georgia to follow, aiming to create a more adaptive and efficient educational system that benefits students, educators, and policymakers alike (Fig. 4).

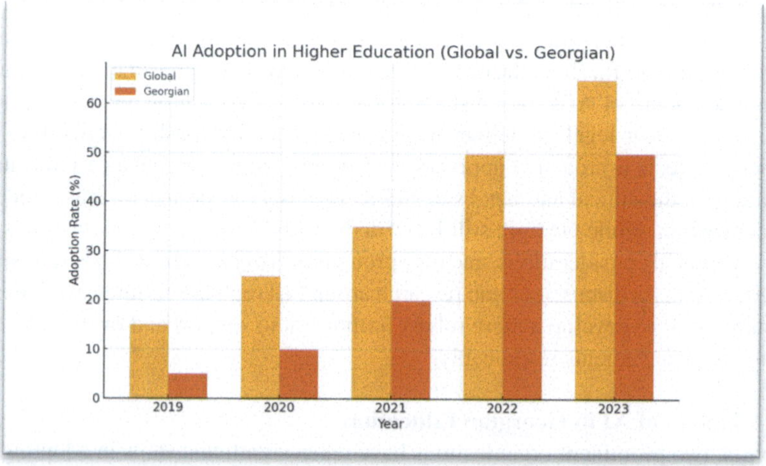

Fig. 4. AI Adoption in Higher Education (Global vs Georgian). ***Source:*** Own graphic based on the IDFI (Institute for Development of Freedom of Information) reports (2024); (https://idfi.ge/en/category/news/publications)

This bar chart compares the adoption rate of AI in higher education institutions globally with that of Georgian universities. While global institutions have adopted AI at a higher rate, Georgian universities have shown a consistent upward trend, with adoption rates reaching 50% by 2023. This suggests that Georgian universities are catching up with global trends and integrating AI into their systems rapidly.

AI's Impact on Key Areas in Higher Education Institutions

AI's impact on higher education is transformative, particularly in three critical areas: **Administration**, **Curriculum Development**, and **Student Engagement**.

- **Administration**: AI significantly enhances administrative efficiency by optimizing resource allocation, managing complex scheduling needs, and streamlining reporting processes. By automating these tasks, institutions can save time and reduce operational costs, allowing administrative staff to shift their focus to more strategic and high-impact initiatives, such as improving student services, expanding program offerings, and fostering partnerships. This shift not only enhances productivity but also allows for more proactive and data-driven decision-making, which is essential for institutions facing increasing demands for accountability and resource management.
- **Curriculum Development**: AI plays a crucial role in keeping academic programs aligned with industry standards and student aspirations. By analyzing labor market trends and student performance data, AI enables institutions to continuously update and adapt curricula to ensure relevance in a rapidly changing job market. This process supports the development of skills that are currently in demand, preparing students for real-world applications and enhancing their employability. Additionally, AI can personalize curriculum content to cater to diverse learning styles and proficiencies, ensuring that students receive a tailored educational experience that meets their unique needs and aspirations.
- **Student Engagement**: One of AI's most significant contributions lies in its ability to foster student engagement through personalized learning paths and immediate feedback. AI-driven platforms can assess individual learning styles, strengths, and weaknesses, and adjust content accordingly, helping students remain engaged and motivated. Real-time feedback systems provide students with instant insights into their performance, allowing them to address challenges quickly and effectively. This personalized support promotes a more active learning environment and leads to improved academic outcomes, as students receive targeted guidance and encouragement at critical moments in their educational journey.

In summary, AI's application across these key areas facilitates a more efficient, adaptive, and student-centered educational environment. By enhancing institutional operations, aligning curricula with market needs, and engaging students through personalized learning, AI has the potential to elevate educational standards and outcomes, positioning higher education institutions to better serve both students and society.

Challenges and Ethical Considerations

The implementation of AI in higher education introduces several ethical challenges, particularly concerning privacy and data security. Additionally, there are concerns about the autonomy of AI-driven systems and their influence on human dignity within educational settings. To address these challenges, institutions must adopt strong data privacy protocols, regularly audit AI systems for bias, and promote a balanced integration of AI and human oversight in education to maintain engagement and fairness.

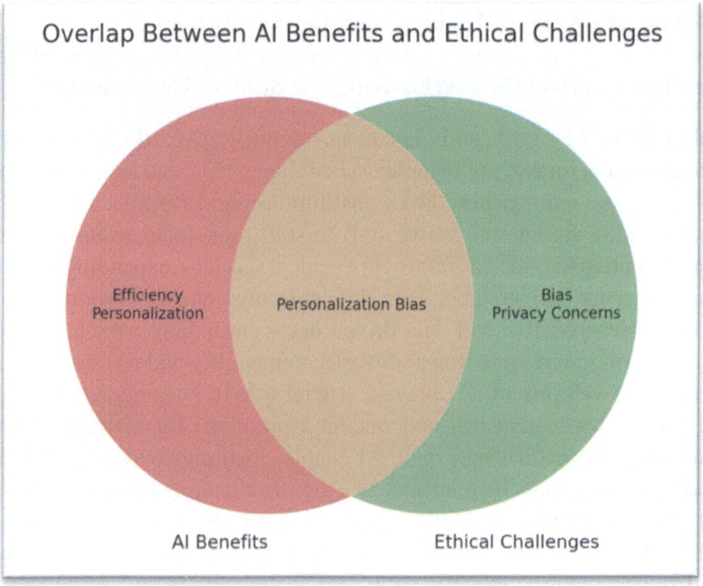

Fig. 5. AI Benefits and Ethical Challenges. ***Source:*** Own graphic based on the thematic analysis

The diagram (Fig. 5) highlights the dual nature of AI in education, showcasing both its benefits and ethical challenges. On one side, AI brings efficiency and personalization, allowing institutions to streamline operations and tailor learning experiences to individual students. However, these advantages are tempered by ethical concerns, particularly around bias and privacy. AI systems, if trained on biased data, risk reinforcing existing inequalities, and the extensive data required for personalization raises privacy issues. At the intersection lies personalization bias, where AI's tailored recommendations may unintentionally perpetuate biases, impacting fairness in educational outcomes. Thus, while AI holds transformative potential, its implementation requires careful ethical oversight.

Based on the thematic analysis the key ethical challenges in using AI in education where highlighted (Fig. 6). Data privacy is the most significant concern, followed by AI bias, as these systems may perpetuate inequalities if trained on biased data. Lack of transparency and over-reliance on AI are also notable issues, with transparency affecting trust in AI systems and over-reliance potentially diminishing human oversight. Lastly, equity in access remains a challenge, as not all students may have equal access to AI resources, risking increased educational disparities. Addressing these challenges is essential to ensure fair and responsible AI use in education.

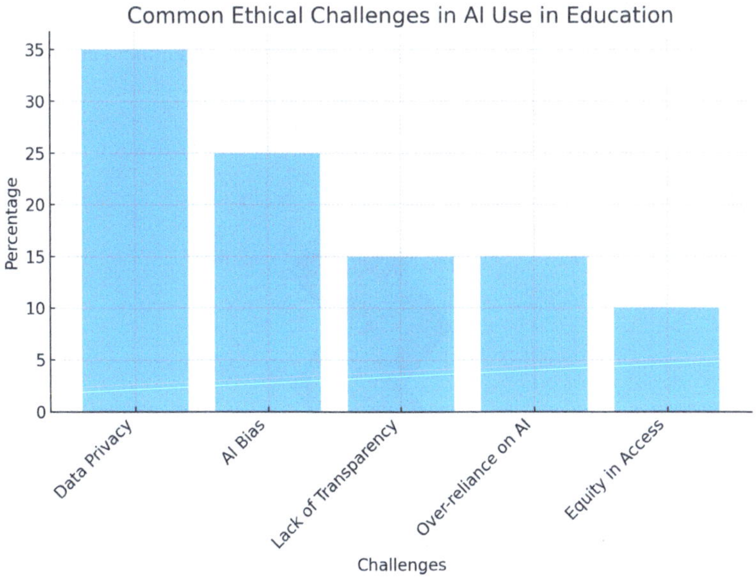

Fig. 6. Common Ethical Challenges. ***Source:*** Own graphic based on the thematic analysis

In response to these challenges, the study has introduced strategies to mitigate those risks (Fig. 7).

Comparison_of_Ethical_Considerations_for_AI_Tools_in_Education

Ethical Concern	AI Tool	Potential Impact	Mitigation Strategies
Data Privacy	Automated Grading System	Leakage of sensitive student data	Encryption and data protection policies
Bias	Recommendation System	Unfair recommendations based on biased data	Regular audits of algorithm fairness
Over-reliance	Chatbots	Reduction in human involvement in learning	Maintain balance between human and AI roles
Equity in Access	Virtual Classrooms	Unequal access to AI resources for underserved students	Ensure equal access to AI tools for all students

Fig. 7. Challenges and strategies in using AI in education. ***Source:*** Own graphic based on the study

To ensure responsible AI integration in education, institutions must adopt a proactive approach to address potential ethical challenges. The following process outlines key steps for managing these issues effectively, fostering a balanced and ethical use of AI. The flowchart (Fig. 8) outlines a step-by-step process to address the ethical challenges associated with AI in education. First, institutions need to identify the risks associated with the specific AI tools they're using. Then, it's crucial to consult with stakeholders, including students, teachers, and administrators, to gather a variety of perspectives. After that, mitigation strategies should be implemented, whether through policies, technical fixes, or training. Monitoring is key to ensuring that the AI systems continue to operate ethically over time, followed by continuous feedback from users. Finally, institutions must be willing to refine their processes based on new data and ethical considerations.

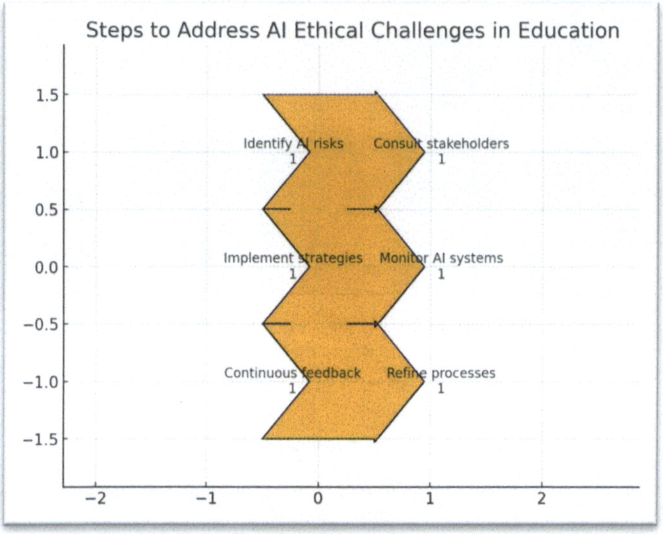

Fig. 8. Addressing AI ethical challenges. ***Source:*** Own graphic based on the study

Conclusion and Recommendations

The future of education lies in AI's transformative potential to streamline operations, enhance student success, and support personalized learning experiences. As illustrated in the chart, AI has its most significant impact on **learning outcomes** by enabling personalized learning pathways and real-time feedback, which collectively support academic success and student engagement. AI also plays a critical role in improving **administrative efficiency**, streamlining processes that allow educators and administrators to focus on high-impact activities. Furthermore, AI is a catalyst for **innovation**, bringing new methodologies and adaptive technologies to educational settings, thereby fostering a dynamic and responsive learning environment. Although **student success** comprises a smaller portion, it remains essential, as AI helps educators provide targeted support, ultimately improving performance and retention rates. Overall, the transformative power of AI in education offers vast potential, but it also calls for a balanced, ethical approach to ensure these advancements align with institutional values and the diverse needs of students (Fig. 9).

In Georgia, as well as globally, institutions should prioritize ethical AI adoption by establishing data privacy safeguards and conducting regular system audits. Ensuring equal access to AI tools is critical to reducing digital divides and fostering an inclusive educational environment. Institutions should also encourage open dialogue between students, educators, and AI developers to continuously refine AI applications in education.

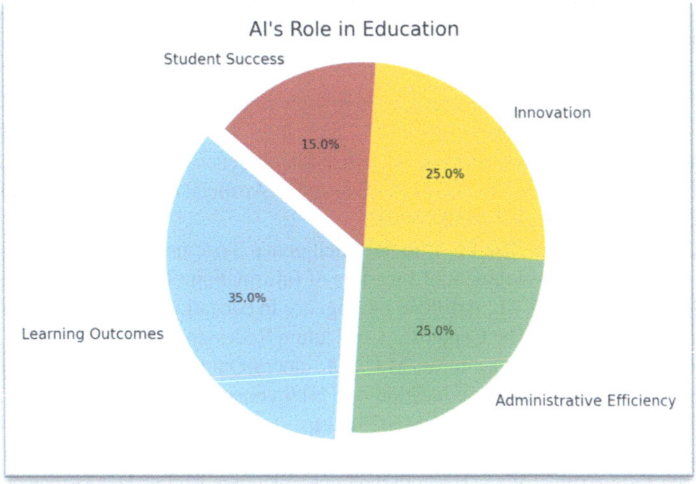

Fig. 9. AI ethical challenges. ***Source:*** Own graphic based on the study

Limitations and Further Study

While this study provides valuable insights into the impact of AI on higher education in Georgia, several limitations must be acknowledged. First, the research primarily focuses on a limited number of institutions and specific case studies, which may restrict the generalizability of the findings to the broader Georgian education system or international contexts. Additionally, the rapid evolution of AI technology and its applications in education mean that findings based on current AI tools may soon become outdated. This study's cross-sectional approach captures only a snapshot of AI integration, lacking a longitudinal perspective to track changes over time.

For further research, a longitudinal study could provide more dynamic insights into how AI's role and effectiveness evolve within educational institutions. Expanding the sample to include diverse types of institutions and incorporating comparative studies with other countries would enhance understanding of AI's broader educational impacts. Future studies should also consider the perspectives of students, faculty, and administrators in a more comprehensive way, exploring how each group perceives and interacts with AI tools. Finally, investigating the ethical and regulatory challenges associated with AI in education can provide a more holistic view, informing policies that support responsible AI integration in academia.

References

Adair, A.: Teaching and learning with AI: how artificial intelligence is transforming the future of education. XRDS: Crossroads, The ACM Magazine for Students **29**(3) (2023). https://doi.org/10.1145/3589252

AI Pedagogy. AI Pedagogy Starter Guide. MetaLab at Harvard (2023). https://aipedagogy.org/

Alotaibi, N.S., Alshehri, A.H.: Prospects and obstacles in using artificial intelligence in Saudi Arabia higher education institutions—the potential of AI-based learning outcomes. Sustainability **15**(13), 10723 (2023). https://doi.org/10.3390/su151310723

Chichekian, T., Benteux, B.: The potential of learning with (and not from) artificial intelligence in education. Frontiers in Artificial Intelligence **5**, 903051 (2022). https://doi.org/10.3389/frai.2022.903051

Crompton, H., Burke, D.: Artificial intelligence in higher education: the state of the field. Int. J. Educ. Technol. High. Educ. **20**(1), 39 (2023). https://doi.org/10.1186/s41239-023-00392-8

Dai, C.P., Ke, F.: Educational applications of artificial intelligence in simulation-based learning: a systematic mapping review. Computers and Education: Artificial Intelligence **3**, 100087 (2022). https://doi.org/10.1016/j.caeai.2022.100087

Eristavi, D., Davituri, G.: The Use of Artificial Intelligence Systems in Georgia: Legislation and Practice. Institute for Development of Freedom of Information (2021)

Fadel, C., Holmes, W., Bialik, M.: Artificial intelligence in education: Promises and implications for teaching and learning. The Center for Curriculum Redesign (2019)

Guerrero-Quiñonez, A.J., Bedoya-Flores, M.C., Mosquera-Quiñonez, E.F., Ango-Ramos, E.D., Mesías-Simisterra, Á.E.: Higher education 4.0: brief considerations. Ibero-American Journal of Education & Society Research **3**(1) (2023). https://doi.org/10.56183/iberoeds.v3i1.628

Holmes, W., Persson, J., Chounta, I.-A., Wasson, B., & Dimitrova, V. (2022). Artificial Intelligence and Education - A Critical View Through the Lens of Human Rights, Democracy and the Rule of Law. Council of Europe

Iasechko, M., Kharkiv, I.K., Rabiichuk, S., Mykhalchenko, N., Sukhomlynskyi, V.O., Dzhurylo, A.: Pedagogical conditions for the formation of communicative competence of students of higher education. Journal of Higher Education Theory and Practice **24**(5) (2023)

Kamalov, F., Santandreu Calonge, D., Gurrib, I.: New era of artificial intelligence in education: towards a sustainable multifaceted revolution. Sustainability **15**(16), 12451 (2023). https://doi.org/10.3390/su151612451

Khosravi, H., Sadiq, S., Amer-Yahia, S.: Data Management of AI-Powered Education Technologies: Challenges and Opportunities (2023). *arXiv*. https://doi.org/10.48550/arXiv.2303.16402

Krause, S., Panchal, B.H., Ubhe, N.: The Evolution of Learning: Assessing the Transformative Impact of Generative AI on Higher Education. *arXiv* (2024)

Malik, V., Hooda, M.: MOOCs revamping Indian higher education: escalating access, equity, and quality. Journal of Higher Education Theory and Practice **23**(12) (2023). https://doi.org/10.33423/jhetp.v23i12.6238

Mary, D.M., Joyce, M.M.: AI and education: Impact of AI on learning outcomes in higher education. International Journal of Scientific Research in Engineering and Management (2024)

Miao, F., Holmes, W.: Guidance for Generative AI in Education and Research. UNESCO (2023)

Mollick, E., Mollick, L.: The AI Revolution in Business Education: A Guide to AI Tools for Educators. Wharton School of the University of Pennsylvania & Wharton Interactive (2023)

Moralishvili, S.: AI and personalized learning in higher education instruction in Georgia. International Scientific Journal Diplomacy and Law (2023)

Owoseni, A., Kolade, O., Egbetokun, A.: Generative AI in Higher Education, Innovation Strategies for Teaching and Learning. Palgrave Macmillan Cham (2024)

Paek, S., Kim, N.: Analysis of worldwide research trends on the impact of artificial intelligence in education. Sustainability **13**(14), 7941 (2021). https://doi.org/10.3390/su13147941

Roll, I., Wylie, R.: Evolution and revolution in artificial intelligence in education. Int. J. Artif. Intell. Educ. **26**(2), 582–599 (2016). https://doi.org/10.1007/s40593-016-0110-3

Yadav, J., Shukla, S., Sharma, K., Soni, N., Agarwal, S., Pathak, P.C.: Frontiers in artificial intelligence and applications. In Proceedings of the 2022 3rd International Conference on Computation, Automation and Knowledge Management (ICCAKM 2022) (2022). https://doi.org/10.1109/ICCAKM54721.2022.9990098

Zawacki-Richter, O., Marín, V.I., Bond, M., Gouverneur, F.: Systematic review of research on artificial intelligence applications in higher education – where are the educators? Int. J. Educ. Technol. High. Educ. **16**(1), 39 (2019). https://doi.org/10.1186/s41239-019-0171-0

The Impact of Social Media on Consumers' Decision-Making Process in Hotel Industry

Davit Sikharulidze(✉), Kakhaber George Lazarashvili, Natia Gegelashvili, and Tamar Tkhelidze

East European University (EEU), Tbilisi, Georgia
{d.sikharulidze,K.lazarashvili,n.gegelashvili,
tamar.tkhelidze}@eeu.edu.ge

Abstract. The present study examines the impact of social media on consumer decision-making in the Georgian hotel industry. In response to the rapid growth of digital marketing, this research aims to analyze how consumers utilize social media when selecting a hotel and how this influences their final decision.

The study is based on data from 324 respondents, collected through a standard sampling method. Structural equation modeling (SEM) was employed for data analysis. The results demonstrate a strong positive correlation between social media usage and purchase decisions, underscoring the critical role of social platforms in modern tourism marketing.

Additionally, the study revealed that psychological attributes and sociocultural factors significantly influence consumer choice. Meanwhile, the effectiveness of traditional communication channels has diminished compared to social media.

The findings suggest that the Georgian hotel industry should enhance its digital marketing strategies, with particular focus on social media, personalized approaches, and online reputation management. This research makes a valuable contribution to understanding the digital transformation of the Georgian hotel industry and provides a foundation for further research and practical recommendations.

Keywords: Social media · digital marketing · Purchase decision · hotel industry

1 Introduction

The Georgian hotel industry experienced significant growth in 2022. The number of economic entities reached 2,162, reflecting the diversity of companies operating within the sector. The total number of hotels and hotel-type enterprises reached 2,213, which includes major hotels, their branches, and local units. This represents a growth rate of 24.6% compared to 2021, indicating a rapid expansion likely driven by the recovery of post-pandemic tourism (National statistics office of Georgia, 2022).

A multifactor analysis of this growth in the hotel industry suggests that the key drivers include the rehabilitation of the tourism sector following the COVID-19 pandemic, targeted government support, increased inflows of foreign capital, and the rise

R. C. Geibel and S. Machavariani (Eds.): ISPC 2024, SPBE, pp. 196–207, 2025.
https://doi.org/10.1007/978-3-031-88052-0_15

of domestic tourism. The outcomes of these processes potentially include heightened competition among hotels and improvements in service quality for customers.

The increasingly competitive environment has prompted hotel management to adopt innovative methods for attracting and engaging customers. In this context, social media marketing has gained particular importance. Although social media is a relatively recent phenomenon, its global influence is undeniable.

The social media penetration rate in Georgia is significantly high. As of 2024, approximately 3 million active users—roughly 80% of the population—are active on social media (Statista, 2024). Among the most popular platforms are Facebook, Instagram, and YouTube, all of which continue to experience steady growth in user numbers (DataReportal, 2024).

The modern marketing landscape demands innovative approaches. Exclusive reliance on traditional media or merely transferring offline strategies to digital platforms is no longer effective. Businesses must harness the potential of interactive media to establish effective communication with customers. Strategic use of social media offers not only an opportunity to enhance brand loyalty but also to foster deeper customer relationships and create new digital distribution channels. As noted by **Chan and Gillett (2011)**, this approach is a critical component of contemporary marketing.

Jones (2010) argues that social media and online platforms are the best way to overcome intercultural barriers in marketing to international travelers. This approach provides more flexible, personalized, and interactive communication than traditional media, which often face geographical or cultural limitations.

Social media allows hotels to deliver real-time information, respond to inquiries, and create virtual experiences for foreign tourists. It helps build trust-based relationships with potential guests regardless of distance.

Recent academic research shows that social media has fundamentally changed consumer behavior in hotel selection. It serves as a key information source where customers can learn from others' experiences, get real-time feedback, and validate their choices.

The introduction of ICT and Web 2.0 has drastically changed the hotel selection process for tourists (Buhalis and Law, 2008). The interactivity of Web 2.0 has empowered users not only to receive but also to create and share content, significantly altering the dynamics of hotel selection (Gupta et al. 2019). Social media have created new expectations for hotel services, a shift reflected in hotels' marketing and operational strategies (Gohil, 2015).

Neuhofer et al. (2012) emphasize that these technologies create an "enriched" tourist experience, influencing decision-making at all stages of the travel journey. Travelers now rely not only on official sources but also on peer experiences, compelling hotels to rethink their strategies and actively manage their online reputations.

The changes brought about by social media create a complex and dynamic environment where consumer decision-making is characterized by increasing complexity and continuous evolution. This reality demands that the hotel industry adopt more flexible and creative approaches to keep pace with the evolving expectations of modern tourists.

A comprehensive understanding of this multi-layered phenomenon requires an interdisciplinary approach, combining the fields of marketing, psychology, and information technology. Such an approach enables the development of new conceptual frameworks and empirical data that illustrate the growing importance of social media in hotel industry marketing strategies.

In the context of Georgia, the influence of social media platforms on hotel selection processes is a particularly relevant and important research subject, requiring in-depth analysis and study. This research aims to examine the effect of social media on customer decision-making processes in the Georgian hotel industry.

2 Literature Review

The rapid development of technological innovations and the Internet is fundamentally transforming how people communicate and exchange information. Evans and McKee (2010) highlight that modern digital infrastructure offers unprecedented opportunities for global knowledge and information sharing.

Within this technological ecosystem, social media has emerged as one of the most powerful and pervasive platforms for interpersonal connections. Stelzner's (2010) research confirms that social media has become the dominant form of communication, connecting billions of users worldwide. Social media comprises a set of Internet-based platforms and communities that, as Schroeder (2017) suggests, facilitate the exchange of thoughts, experiences, and observations among users. According to **Yazdanparast and Muniz (2016)**, social media encompasses multiple platforms, including Facebook, blogs, LinkedIn, Twitter, and podcasts. Harrigan et al. (2017) argue that social media allows companies to build personalized connections with customers, while Alalwan, Rana, Dwivedi, and **Alalwan (2018)** view social media as an effective tool for achieving organizational marketing goals and strategies, facilitating customer communication, relationship management (CRM), and enhancing customer engagement.

The hotel industry is no exception to these trends. The expansion of social media and the rise of user-generated content (UGC) have fundamentally altered traditional methods of obtaining hotel information during the consumer decision-making process (Browning and Sparks, 2013; Fotis & Rossides, 2012). In the contemporary landscape, social media plays a critical role in shaping tourists' travel plans and information-gathering processes (Xiang and Gretzel, 2010). **Chan and Gillett (2011)** note the increasing integration of social media platforms into hotel industry marketing strategies. Their empirical research reveals that platforms such as Facebook, Twitter, YouTube, and TripAdvisor are dominant channels through which hoteliers interact with customers. Their study emphasizes that the use of these platforms extends beyond advertising to include timely responses to customer reviews and the establishment of personalized communication.

Hu and Wei (2013) emphasize the significant role of social media in the hotel selection process. Jones (2009) categorizes social media platforms in the tourism context, including social networks, travel review portals, and content-sharing platforms. These platforms significantly change travelers' behavior in searching, evaluating, and purchasing tourism products and services.

Chu and Choi (2000) highlight the importance of hotel attributes, while **Yusof and Abdullah (2010)** identify key attributes in the consumer decision-making process, such as location, price, cleanliness and hygiene, security, and hotel infrastructure.

The significance of hotel attributes is emphasized in a study by Chu and Choi (2000), who identify them as critical factors for stakeholders seeking to better understand customer preferences. **Yusof and Abdullah (2010)** pinpoint key attributes in the consumer decision-making process, including location, price, cleanliness and hygiene, security, and hotel infrastructure.

The consumer's decision-making process when selecting a hotel begins in the pre-trip stage and encompasses the four stages of the consumer decision journey: consideration, evaluation, purchase, and consumption (Court et al., 2009). During this process, consumers assess available alternatives to make an optimal choice (Ayeh et al., 2012).

Collectively, these studies underscore the transformative influence of social media on hotel industry marketing practices and consumer behavior. They represent a paradigm shift from traditional, one-way communication to a more interactive, customer-centric model, fostering greater engagement and personalized experiences.

3 Research Methodology

3.1 Data Collection

The research employed a standard sampling method to distribute questionnaires in the hotel sector of Georgia. A total of 395 questionnaires were distributed. After excluding incomplete or unusable responses, 324 valid and complete questionnaires were retained for analysis. The response rate was 82%, indicating a high level of participation, with over three-quarters of respondents actively completing the questionnaire.

3.2 Statistical Analysis Methodology

Data analysis was performed using SPSS software (version 26). Cronbach's α test was used to calculate descriptive statistics and assess the internal consistency reliability of the data. For more complex analysis, Structural Equation Modeling (SEM) was conducted using SPSS 26 and AMOS 23 software. Multiple tests were employed to evaluate the model fit, including the χ^2 test, normalized χ^2, normal fit index (NFI), and root mean square error of approximation (RMSEA).

The sample size of 324 respondents met the minimum requirement for statistical analysis, as suggested by Medsker et al. (1994), which recommends a minimum of 200 cases. The variables in this study are continuous, and no issues of multivariate normality were detected in the data. The maximum likelihood (ML) method was used to estimate model parameters and assess the overall fit of the model. This method requires certain assumptions to be fulfilled, which, as outlined by Byrne (2001) and El-Sheikh et al. (2017), were either fully met or closely approximated in this study.

3.3 Data Analysis and Results

Table 1 presents the results of the survey across three key categories: gender, age, and frequency of online shopping. In terms of gender distribution, the majority of respondents were female, with 255 women (76.6%) and 78 men (23.4%) participating in the study.

The age distribution showed that the largest group of respondents fell within the 25–34 age range, with 201 participants (60.4%). This was followed by the 18–24 age group, which included 70 respondents (21%). The 35–44 age group comprised 42 respondents (12.6%), while 15 respondents (4.5%) were aged between 45 and 54. The smallest group was aged 55–64, with only 5 respondents (1.5%). These findings suggest that the majority of respondents were young to middle-aged adults.

Regarding the frequency of online shopping, the largest group, consisting of 145 respondents (43.5%), reported shopping online occasionally. A significant portion of respondents—88 (26.4%)—indicated that they often shop online, while 63 respondents (18.9%) stated that they shop online very often. Only 28 respondents (8.4%) reported that they never shop online. It is important to note that the total percentage for this category sums to 97.3%, suggesting that 9 respondents (2.7%) did not answer this particular question.

In summary, the data indicate that the majority of respondents are female, aged 25–34, and engage in online shopping with some regularity (occasionally or more often).

Table 1. Statistical overview of respondents' demographic features (Frequency analysis)

Varieble	Frequency	Percent
Gender		
Female	255	76,6
Male	78	23,4
Total	333	100,0
Age		
18–24	70	21,0
25–34	201	60,4
35–44	42	12,6
45–54	15	4,5
55–64	5	1,5
Total	333	100,0
Online shopping		
Never purchase	28	8,4
Occasionally purchase	145	43,5
Frequently purchase	88	26,4
Very frequently purchase	63	18,9
Total	**324**	**97,3**

4 Results

Table 2 provides descriptive statistics, including the mean, standard deviation, and Cronbach's alpha for the measurement items and subscales. To assess the internal consistency of the model constructs, Cronbach's alpha (Cronbach, 1951) was used, which is appropriate for instruments where final scores are obtained through scoring. The internal consistency for each construct was found to be acceptable, with all values exceeding the minimum threshold of 0.50 (Hair et al., 2011). Analysis of the 15 items resulted in a Cronbach's alpha (α) coefficient of 0.090, indicating high internal consistency overall.

Table 2 further demonstrates the reliability of the measurement items. The table comprises five main factors, each containing three statements. The mean values of most statements are above 3.5, suggesting a high level of agreement among the respondents. Standard deviations range from 1.046 to 1.184, indicating consistent variability in responses across all questions. Cronbach's alpha for all factors exceeded 0.7, reflecting good internal consistency. The first factor had the highest alpha ($\alpha = 0.935$), signifying very high reliability, while the factor related to social media had the lowest but still acceptable alpha ($\alpha = 0.779$). Factor 1 ($\alpha = 0.935$) pertains to the influence of others' opinions. The mean values for this factor range from 3.50 to 3.52, indicating that respondents regard the opinions of others as quite important. Factor 2 ($\alpha = 0.913$) relates to the comparison process, with mean values ranging from 3.81 to 4.01. These high means suggest that respondents actively compare different aspects before making decisions. Factor 3 ($\alpha = 0.832$) reflects traditional marketing methods. Here, the lower mean values (2.49 to 2.97) suggest that respondents perceive traditional marketing methods to be less effective. Factor 4 ($\alpha = 0.921$) concerns personal characteristics. Mean values ranging from 3.44 to 3.56 imply that personal factors play an important role in decision-making. Factor 5 ($\alpha = 0.779$) is associated with social media. The high mean values (3.71 to 3.85) indicate that social media significantly influences decision-making processes.

After several iterations using the modification indices, 15 items were retained in the analysis. Items with factor loadings below 0.5 were deleted. All retained items had standardized loading estimates greater than 0.5, confirming the convergent validity of the measurement model.

Table 2. Descriptive Statistics

Factor	Item	Standardized loading	Mean	Std. Deviation	Cronbach's α	Convergent validity
SOC – Social environment	Negative opinion of a referrer or a comparison group	0,847	3,50	1,105	0.935	0.71
	Positive comments from friends, articles, or expert opinions on blogs or other Internet platforms	0,841	3,52	1,137		

(continued)

Table 2. (*continued*)

Factor	Item	Standardized loading	Mean	Std. Deviation	Cronbach's α	Convergent validity
	Negative opinions from individuals of a similar social class to yours	0,837	3,50	1,110		
PD - Purchase decision	You compare the price of the different quotations to measure if there is a policy that will contribute to your need satisfaction and lifestyle	0,846	4,01	1,046	0.913	0.69
	You compare the quality of the different quotations to measure if there is a policy that will contribute to your need satisfaction and lifestyle	0,844	3,95	1,070		
	You compare the brand list (list of different companies) to measure if there is a policy that will contribute to your need satisfaction and lifestyle	0,819	3,81	1,105		
COM – Communication sources	Traditional hotel advertisements, such as TV and radio commercials	0,817	2,49	1,184	0.832	0.63
	Information from any person acting as a product referral source (e.g., travel agents)	0,816	2,97	1,126		
	Personalized messages sent by hotels about their services and offerings	0,749	2,89	1,159		
PSY - psychological attributes	Your motivation to purchase hotel services	0,802	3,44	1,172	0.921	0.62
	Your perceptions and ideas about hotel accommodation	0,800	3,56	1,125		

(*continued*)

Table 2. (*continued*)

Factor	Item	Standardized loading	Mean	Std. Deviation	Cronbach's α	Convergent validity
	Personal characteristics, including specific qualifications, attributes, and qualities	0,767	3,53	1,131		
SM - Social media	Social media platforms (e.g., Facebook, Instagram, YouTube, TikTok) facilitate easy comparison of hotel products	0,880	3,77	1,048	0.779	0.75
	Social media provides ample information about hotel offerings	0,863	3,71	1,074		
	The interactive nature of social media influences consumers' shopping experiences and purchasing decisions	0,848	3,85	1,048		

Construct reliability (C.R.) was assessed to verify convergent validity, with all constructs demonstrating acceptable levels of reliability. Each construct exceeded the minimum criterion of 0.5, with values ranging from 0.632 to 0.894 (**Hair et al., 1998**). This confirms the robustness of the measurement model. These satisfactory results suggest that it is appropriate to proceed with estimating the structural model.

Structural Model Evaluation

Figure 1 presents the standardized path regression coefficients, illustrating the direct influence of the predictor variables on the predicted latent constructs within the research model. These coefficients provide insight into the strength and direction of the relationships between variables.

Model Fit Indices

Table 3 shows the goodness-of-fit indices for the structural model, along with the corresponding threshold values for evaluating model fit. Key indices include: Chi-square (χ^2) test, Normalized chi-square (χ^2/df), Normal Fit Index (NFI), Root Mean Square Error of Approximation (RMSEA).

The goodness-of-fit statistics indicate that the structural model fits the data reasonably well, with all indices meeting or exceeding the acceptable thresholds, confirming that the structural model is adequate for interpretation.

Table 4 summarizes the results of the individual tests of significance for the relationships between variables in the model. All tested relationships were found to be statistically significant at the 0.01 level, reinforcing the validity of the proposed structural pathways within the research model.

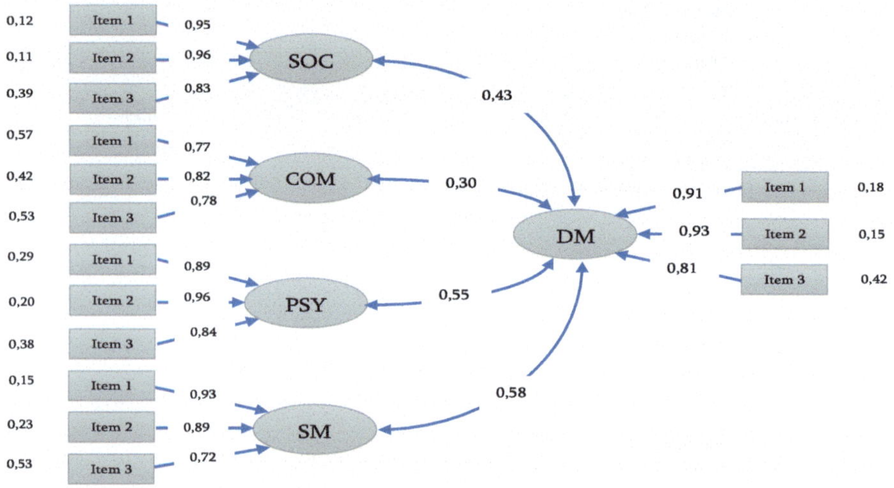

Fig. 1: (Structural model) Standardized regression coefficients of the proposed model

Table 3. Model fit statistics

Model-of-fit indices	Fit statistics	Cutoff value
χ2	135,312	
Normed χ2	1.691	< 3.00
Normed Fit Index (NFI)	0.966	> 0.90
RFI	0.955	≥ 0.95
IFI	0.986	≥ 0.90
TLI	0.981	0.95
Comparative Fit Index (CFI)	0.986	> 0.90
Root Mean Square Error of Approximation (RMSEA)	0.046	< 0.09
HOELTER	.05 (250)	
HOELTER	.01 (276)	

Table 3 presents the results of the structural equation modeling (SEM) analysis. The Chi-square analysis (CMIN) indicates that the CMIN/DF ratio is 1.691, which is below the threshold of 3, suggesting a good model fit. In the Baseline Comparisons: NFI (Normed Fit Index): 0.966, RFI (Relative Fit Index): 0.955, IFI (Incremental Fit Index): 0.986, TLI (Tucker-Lewis Index): 0.981, CFI (Comparative Fit Index): 0.986.

All of these indices exceed the acceptable threshold of 0.95, indicating a very good model fit. The RMSEA (Root Mean Square Error of Approximation) value is 0.046, which is below the recommended cutoff of 0.06, further confirming a good fit. Additionally, the HOELTER analysis reveals: HOELTER .05: 250, HOELTER .01: 276. Both values exceed 200, demonstrating a sufficient sample size for reliable results. Overall, the model exhibits an excellent fit to the data, as evidenced by all key indicators (CFI, TLI, RMSEA, CMIN/DF) meeting or surpassing the accepted thresholds. The low RMSEA value, along with its narrow confidence interval, indicates a robust fit at the population level, while the HOELTER index supports the adequacy of the sample size.

Table 4. Covariances

			Estimate	S.E.	C.R.	P
Sociocultural environment	< -- >	Purchase decision	0,371	0,057	6,519	***
Communication sources	< -- >	Purchase decision	0,253	0,057	4,479	***
psychological attributes	< -- >	Purchase decision	0,498	0,063	7,897	***
Social media	< -- >	Purchase decision	0,414	0,054	7,675	***

Table 4 presents the SEM analysis of covariances, highlighting the following significant relationships in the purchase decision process: Sociocultural Environment and Purchase Decision: Covariance = 0.371, significance $p < 0.001p < 0.001p < 0.001$, indicating a significant positive relationship. Communication Sources and Purchase Decision: Covariance = 0.253, significance $p < 0.001p < 0.001p < 0.001$, indicating a positive but moderate relationship. Purchase Decision and Psychological Attributes: Covariance = 0.498, significance $p < 0.001p < 0.001p < 0.001$, representing the strongest positive relationship in the model. Social Media and Purchase Decision: Covariance = 0.414, significance $p < 0.001p < 0.001p < 0.001$, indicating a strong positive relationship.

All covariances are statistically significant ($p < 0.001p < 0.001p < 0.001$) and indicate positive relationships, suggesting that these factors mutually reinforce one another. The strongest relationship is observed between purchase decision and psychological attributes (0.498), followed closely by social media's strong relationship with purchase decision (0.414). Additionally, the sociocultural environment shows a strong connection to psychological attributes (0.475), and communication sources are also notably related to psychological attributes (0.446). These results emphasize the crucial role each factor plays in the purchase decision process, particularly psychological attributes and social media.

5 Conclusion

The findings of this study highlight the growing significance of social media in the consumer decision-making process within the Georgian hotel industry. A strong positive correlation was found between social media usage and purchase decisions, underscoring the critical role of these platforms in contemporary tourism marketing. However, psychological attributes emerged as the most influential factor in the purchase decision process, pointing to the necessity for personalized marketing strategies.

The significant impact of the sociocultural environment on customer decisions reaffirms the importance of social norms and cultural factors in hotel selection. Additionally, the reduced effectiveness of traditional communication sources (such as television and radio) compared to social media indicates the need for a reevaluation of marketing strategies.

Demographic analysis revealed that the majority of respondents are young, female, and active online shoppers. This information is valuable for understanding the target audience and optimizing marketing campaigns. The study also highlighted that consumers actively compare various hotel offerings based on price, quality, and brand, emphasizing the importance of competitive pricing and high service quality.

Ultimately, the research indicates that the Georgian hotel industry should enhance its digital marketing strategies, particularly focusing on social media. It is equally important to adopt personalized approaches and consider sociocultural factors in marketing campaigns. Effective online reputation management and interactive communication are crucial for success in the modern hospitality landscape. This study lays a robust foundation for future research and practical recommendations aimed at the digital transformation of the Georgian hotel industry.

References

Alalwan, A.A., Dwivedi, Y.K., Rana, N.P., Algharabat, R.: Examining factors influencing Jordanian customers' intentions and adoption of internet banking: extending UTAUT2 with risk. J. Retail. Consum. Serv. **40**, 125–138 (2018)

Ayeh, J.K., Au, N., Law, R.: Predicting the intention to use consumer-generated media for travel planning. Tour. Manage. **35**, 132–143 (2012)

Browning, V., Sparks, B.A.: The influence of online reviews on consumers' attributions of service quality and control for service standards in hotels. J. Travel Tour. Mark. **30**(1–2), 23–40 (2013)

Buhalis, D., Law, R.: Twenty years on and 10 years after the internet: the state of e-tourism research. Tour. Manage. **29**(4), 609–623 (2008)

Byrne, B.M.: Structural equation modeling with AMOS, EQS, and LISREL: comparative approaches to testing for the factorial validity of a measuring instrument. Int. J. Test. **1**(1), 55–86 (2001)

Chan, N.L., Guillet, B.D.: Investigation of social media marketing: how does the hotel industry in Hong Kong perform in marketing on social media websites? J. Travel Tour. Mark. **28**(4), 345–368 (2011)

Chu, R.K., Choi, T.: An importance-performance analysis of hotel selection factors in the Hong Kong hotel industry: a comparison of business and leisure travellers. Tour. Manage. **21**(4), 363–377 (2000)

Court, D., Elzinga, D., Mulder, S., Vetvik, O.J.: The consumer decision journey. McKinsey Quarterly **3**(3), 96–107 (2009)

Cronbach, L.J.: Coefficient alpha and the internal structure of tests. Psychometrika **16**(3), 297–334 (1951)

DataReportal. Digital 2024: Georgia (2024). https://datareportal.com/reports/digital-2024-georgia

El-Sheikh, A.A., Al-Refaie, A., Tlili, I.: Evaluating the impact of national culture on e-government adoption in Jordan: a structural equation modeling approach. Electronic Government, an International Journal **13**(3), 287–301 (2017)

Evans, D., McKee, J.: Social Media Marketing: The Next Generation of Business Engagement. Indiana: John Wiley and Sons (2010)

Fotis, J., Buhalis, D., Rossides, N.: Social media use and impact during the holiday travel planning process. In: Fuchs, M., Ricci, F., Cantoni, L. (eds.) Information and Communication Technologies in Tourism, pp. 13–24. Springer (2012)

Gohil, N.: Role and impact of social media in tourism: a case study on the initiatives of Madhya Pradesh state tourism. International Journal of Research in Economics and Social Sciences **5**(4), 8–15 (2015)

Gupta, V., Khanna, K., Gupta, R.K.: Preferential analysis of street food amongst the foreign tourists: a case of Delhi region. International Journal of Tourism Cities (2019). https://doi.org/10.1108/IJTC-07-2018-0054

Hair, J.F., Ringle, C.M., Sarstedt, M.: PLS-SEM: indeed a silver bullet. J. Marketing theory and Practice **19**(2), 139–152 (2011)

Harrigan, P., Evers, U., Miles, M., Daly, T.: Customer engagement with tourism social media brands. Tour. Manage. **59**, 597–609 (2017)

Hu, F.H., Gao, W.: The impact of the knowledge sharing in social media on consumer behaviour. ICEB 2013 Proceedings (Singapore) **22** (2013). https://aisel.aisnet.org/iceb2013/22

Hudson, S., Thal, K.: The impact of social media on the consumer decision process: implications for tourism marketing. J. Travel Tour. Mark. **30**(1–2), 156–160 (2013)

Jones, R. (2009). Social Media Marketing 101, Part 1. Search Engine Watch, 16

Jones, J.: DR marketing takes flight. Response **19**(2), 26–32 (2010)

Medsker, G.J., Williams, L.J., Holahan, P.J.: A review of current practices for evaluating causal models in organizational behavior and human resources management research. J. Manag. **20**(2), 439–464 (1994)

National statistics office of Georgia. Information on Hotels and Hotel Type Enterprises (2022)

Neuhofer, B., Buhalis, D., Ladkin, A.: Conceptualising technology enhanced destination experiences. J. Destin. Mark. Manag. **1**(1), 36–46 (2012)

Schroeder, W.K.: Leveraging social media in# familynursing practice. J. Fam. Nurs. **23**(1), 55–72 (2017)

Statista. Social media usage in Georgia (2024). https://www.statista.com/

Stelzner, M.A.: 2010 Social Media Marketing Report (2010). http://www.socialmediaexaminer.com/social-media-marketing-industry-report2010/

Xiang, Z., Gretzel, U.: Role of social media in online travel information search. Tour. Manage. **31**(2), 179–188 (2010)

The Influence of Digital Media Marketing Activities on Healthcare Consumer Behavior

Nugzar Todua[1(✉)] and Nia Todua[2]

[1] Head of Marketing Department, Ivane Javakhishvili Tbilisi State University, Tbilisi, Georgia
nugzar.todua@tsu.ge

[2] Department of Marketing, Ivane Javakhishvili Tbilisi State University, Tbilisi, Georgia
nia.todua@tsu.ge

Abstract. The article shows that digital media is a significant marketing tool providing healthcare organizations ample opportunities to interact with consumers. The article emphasizes that digital media has become a valuable tool for healthcare knowledge management. The article demonstrates how numerous medical organizations in Georgia use digital technology to promote their services and foster positive relationships with their patients. It is important to remember that Georgia still needs to achieve complete adoption of digital marketing communications in the healthcare industry. Given the preceding, the study's main objective is to ascertain how digital media marketing activities influence consumer behaviour in the Georgian healthcare industry. Based on a critical review of the literature sources, research hypotheses and the conceptual framework for the study are developed. The impact of digital media marketing activities provided by Georgian healthcare organizations on consumer engagement in social media, e-WOM, customer trust, and behavioral intention has been studied. Regression and dispersion analyses are used to get statistically significant results showing dependency on the abovementioned factors. The paper presented the main conclusions of the research. The results of the study show their use in terms of developing views on digital media marketing. Considering the research results will enable organizations working in the healthcare sector to develop digital marketing communications strategies focused on target customers.

Keywords: Digital Marketing · Trust · Engagement · eWOM · Behavioral Intention

1 Introduction

Digital media is an integral part of modern society and is gradually becoming a significant marketing tool that provides companies with ample opportunities to interact with their consumers (Abid et al. 2023). Digital media has become a valuable tool for healthcare knowledge management (Khan et al. 2021). New technologies and ways of treatment as well as the growth of expectations in society that they are going to have access to high-quality healthcare creates the need for new efficient strategies that will lower the cost of treatment (Çağlıyor et al., 2022). The healthcare sector is gradually adopting augmented

R. C. Geibel and S. Machavariani (Eds.): ISPC 2024, SPBE, pp. 208–221, 2025.
https://doi.org/10.1007/978-3-031-88052-0_16

reality and virtual reality technologies, which provide a wide range of opportunities and advantages for different stakeholders. These revolutionary instruments have the power to revolutionize patient care, education, research, and healthcare delivery (Kulkov et al. 2021). Healthcare professionals are aware of social media's enormous potential for reaching a large audience, interacting with patients, and demonstrating their knowledge (Farsi 2021). Social media is the most effective way of sharing new information in the healthcare sphere as it can reach the widest and most diverse audience (Swan et al. 2019).

Healthcare providers use social media to promote their organizations, also to establish strong relationships with existing and potential customers, and to raise awareness of their own brand (Mondal et al., 2022). As for patients, they receive information about their health condition through social media (Freire et al., 2023).

Nowadays, healthcare organizations face many challenges. First of all, consumers move from a passive state to an active participant in the process of providing medical services (Hung et al., 2023). Fortunately, the emergence of new digital technologies, In particular, social media marketing in healthcare industry has facilitated rapid access to information for patients (Chaves et al., 2021).

Hospitals and physicians actively involved in social media can identify and solve patients' problems in a timely manner, leading to increased customer satisfaction and loyalty (Jackson, 2021). Under the influence of social media marketing, consumer access to digital healthcare tools is expanding (Swan et al., 2019). Today, many medical institutions in Georgia use digital media technologies to promote their services and customer relations. Georgian healthcare organizations that pursue social media marketing deserve the trust and goodwill of patients and society. This especially appeared during the COVID-19 pandemic. Unfortunately, there are still many healthcare organizations in Georgia that have an indifferent attitude towards digital marketing. We can say that the use of digital media marketing tools is still perceived as a novelty in the Georgian healthcare industry. Consequently, the level of consumer awareness and satisfaction of their needs in the Georgian medical services market is generally low (Todua and Jashi, 2018). Most of the Georgian consumers do not receive adequate and timely information about the current developments in the field of healthcare. One of the reasons for this is that there are fewer studied issues related to the impact of social media marketing on the behavior of local consumers in the healthcare sector in the Georgian reality. With this in mind, the study's goal is to determine how social media marketing activities impact consumer behavior in the healthcare sector. In particular, on engagement, e-WOM, trust, and behavioral intention. Based on the above, following Research Questions (RQ) are introduced:

RQ 1: How Social Media Marketing activities conducted by health care organizations impact on Georgian consumers engagement and trust in social media?
RQ 2: How Social Media Marketing activities conducted by health care organizations impact on Georgian consumers e-WOM?
RQ 3: How Georgian consumers engagement and trust in social media impact on their behavioral intention?
RQ 4: How Georgian consumers e-WOM impact on their behavioral intention?

2 Literature Review and Development of Research Hypotheses

In the health industry, social media involvement with customers is very crucial. It is simpler to engage with patients, for instance, thanks to hospital-sponsored activities like health postings, preventative webinars, and online chats. As a result, these initiatives guarantee that clients adopt a positive outlook and enhance their experience (Kumar and Pansari, 2016).

Customer involvement is evolving in numerous ways thanks to social media platforms. First of all, social media platforms may spur consumer involvement by requiring businesses to examine data on client interactions in order to provide better customer service. On the other hand, large levels of client interaction are achievable through social media. Users of social media platforms can interact with a wide range of people and organizations (Schivinski et al., 2016). Third, modern social media platforms provide location-based services that draw in new clients and foster interactions with them (Wang and Stefanone, 2013). Based on the above literature review, following hypothesis (H) is introduced:

H1: Social Media marketing activities conducted by health care organizations has a positive impact on consumers engagement in social media.

In the marketing literature, the term "trust" is defined in a variety of ways, but they are all based on various qualities of honesty, capacity, competence, and recognition (Pirson et al., 2017). Persuasion-based trust develops into reputation. While benevolence relates to the connection between the seller and the customer, it reflects the notion that the other party to the transaction is deserving of trust (Manzoor et al., 2020). Online community perceptions of trust are related to online behaviors. In an online community, building relationships with specific people and encouraging them to bring additional people into the network are opportunities for each of its members. Therefore, confidence has a crucial role in defining both customers' intentions and their purchasing behavior (Chiu et al., 2012). According on the above mentioned research study, the following hypothesis is put forth:

H2: Social media marketing activities conducted by health care organizations has a positive impact on consumers trust in social media.

The rise of electronic Word-of-mouth (eWOM) is a result of the advancement of Internet technology. According to Baker et al. (2016), a good WOM increases buy intention, but a negative WOM may even make the client lose interest. As customers become aware of eWOM prior to making a purchase and, to some extent, trust it, researchers believe that eWOM has a significant influence on behavioral intention. As a result, if customer reviews posted through eWOM are favorable, it enables other customers to decide whether to purchase this product (Doh and Hwang, 2009). Generally speaking, WOM aids customers in making decisions about the things they desire, which are then shared by other consumers through WOM (Herr et al., 1991). Social networks are becoming more important in this situation since they make it simple and quick for customers to learn about popular views. One of the primary factors in deciding to make a purchase is eWOM, which is influenced by online users' experiences with the product (Baker et al., 2016). Based on the above literature review, following hypothesis is introduced:

H3: Social Media marketing activities conducted by health care organizations has a positive impact on consumers e-WOM.

When analyzing customer behavior in the online environment, analysis of behavioral intention is equally crucial. In general, a person's action that compels them to act is their purpose (Rezvani et al., 2012). It should be emphasized that customers' attraction to and/or loyalty to items are often determined by their purchasing intentions (Hong and Cho, 2011). According to intention (Farah, 2017), consumers are more likely to do a certain action and purchase the good (Kahraman and Kazançoğlu, 2019). Based on the aforementioned, we can predict when customers will shop and which products they should buy using their behavioral intentions (Hajli et al., 2017).Social media, which offers a two-way contact between the business and its clients, has been well adapted to the development of buy Intention. Consumers do, however, view social media as being more "honest" than traditional marketing methods since it educates the brand rather than managing its image. Such a connection strengthens a favorable perception of the brand and influences behavioral intention favorably (Hutter et al., 2013). Additionally, it has been discovered that social media marketing initiatives have an impact on consumers' behavioral intentions (Yadav and Rahman, 2017). Based on the above literature review, following Hypotheses are introduced:

H4: Consumers engagement in social media has a positive impact on their behavioral intention;

H5: Consumers trust in social media has a positive impact on their behavioral intention;

H6: Consumers e-WOM has a positive impact on their behavioral intention.

3 Research Methodology

We used the deductive method to analyze existing theories in social media marketing and generalize new information (Bryman and Bell, 2011). Afterward, we tested the hypotheses to examine the theoretical views (Saunders et al., 2019). Our Research Design included the following components: determine the necessary information; selection of research methods; develop a questionnaire design and determine the measurement characteristic; determination of sample size; data analysis. The design of the study involved obtaining primary and secondary data. We collected secondary data from published materials, such as statistical sources from government organizations of Georgia. The quantitative research method is selected for the collection of primary data in this study, which provides the use of unified data collection techniques (Saunders et al., 2019). In turn, we used descriptive methods to survey customers through a specially designed questionnaire. Based on the construction and literature review described above, we can develop a conceptual research model that visually presents the impact of social media marketing activities by healthcare organizations on consumer behavior (Fig. 1).

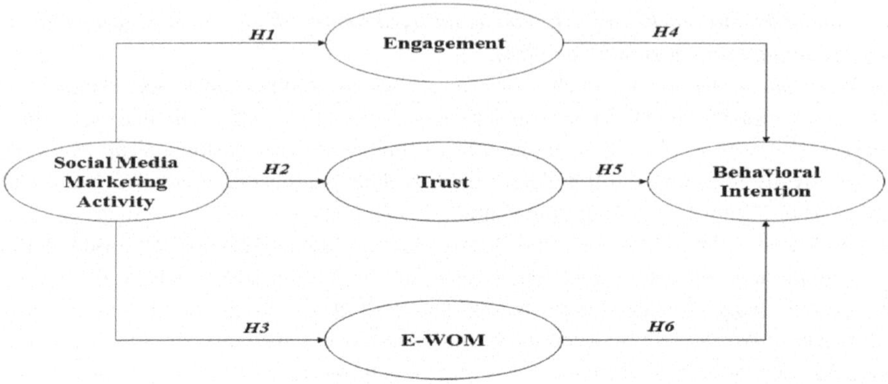

Fig. 1. Research model

In our study, an electronic questionnaire was used as the main method of data collection. In addition, in this study, we conducted a survey using a self-administered method. Such an approach has led to the fact that the method of self-administration in collecting data directly from respondents is simple, relatively fast, and inexpensive (Saunders et al., 2019). The questions used in the questionnaire were based on the opinions of the authors reported in the literature review section of this paper. The variables and measurement items in this study are formed from relevant literature based on a deductive approach (Table 1). The answers to the questions are presented in multiple-choice, and a 5-point Likert scale is used (1 = Strongly disagree, 2 = Disagree, 3 = Neutral, 4 = Agree, 5 = Strongly agree). The questionnaire was designed in such a way that 15–20 min were enough to complete it.

Table 1. Research construct

Variables	Measurement Items	Adopted from
Social Media Marketing Activities (conducted by healthcare organizations)	• *Healthcare organizations use social media to promote their activities* • *Healthcare organizations develop its relationship with customers through the means of social media* • *Healthcare organizations use social media to get a good feeling and positive feedback from consumers* • *Healthcare organizations improve the quality of their service based on the study of customers feedback through social media* • *Healthcare organizations use different marketing strategy through social media* • *Healthcare organizations apply new innovative methods in advertising their services through social media* • *Healthcare organizations apply new innovative methods in advertising their services through social media* • *Healthcare organizations uses social media to get a competitive advantage*	Dodokh, and Al-Maaitah, 2019; Swan et al.2019

(*continued*)

Table 1. (*continued*)

Variables	Measurement Items	Adopted from
Engagement (Patients engagement on social media regarding healthcare)	• *I often visit pages of healthcare organizations on social media* • *I often read posts of healthcare organizations on social media* • *I often use the "like" option on healthcare organizations posts on social media* • *I often comment on healthcare organizations pages on social media* • *I often follow the pages of healthcare organizations on social media to get interesting information*	Gummerus et al. 2012; Toor et al. 2017; Rahman, 2017
E-WOM	***Information seeking on Social Media/SNS*** • *When I consider healthcare products/service, I ask my contacts on the SNS for advice* • *I don't need to talk to my contacts on the SNS before I buy/consume healthcare products/service* • *I prefer to get my contacts 'opinions on the SNS before I buy/consume healthcare products/service* • *I rarely ask my contacts on the SNS about what healthcare products/service to buy/consume* • *I feel more comfortable choosing healthcare products/service when I have gotten my contacts' opinions on them on the SNS* ***Information passing on Social Media/SNS*** • *I tend to pass on information about healthcare products/service to the contacts on my "friends" list on the SNS when I find it useful* • *On the SNSs, I like to pass along my contacts' comments containing healthcare information about the product that I like to other contacts on the SNS* • *When I receive healthcare product/service-related information from a friend, I will pass it along to my other contacts on the Social Media/SNS* • *On the Social Media/SNS, I like to pass along interesting information about healthcare products/services from one group of my contacts on my "friends" list to another* • *I tend to pass along my contacts' positive reviews of healthcare products/service to other contacts on the SNS* • *I tend to pass along my contacts' negative reviews of healthcare products/service to other contacts on the SNS* ***Information giving on Social Media/SNS*** • *I often persuade my contacts on the SNS to buy/consumer healthcare products/service that I like* • *My contacts on the SNS pick their healthcare products/service based on what I have told them* • *On the SNS, I often influence my contacts' opinions about healthcare products/service*	Mladenović et al. 2018
Trust (Patients Trust of Social Media Marketing Activities conducted by healthcare organizations)	• *I believe that the activity on social media of such organizations is trustworthy* • *I trust such organizations and would purchase the services they offer* • *I believe that such organizations are competent in social media activities* • *I believe that such organizations will keep their promises and commitments expressed on social media*	Chiu et al. 2012; Hong and Cha, 2013

(*continued*)

Table 1. (*continued*)

Variables	Measurement Items	Adopted from
Behavioral Intention	• *Using social media helps me make decisions better before purchasing medical services* • *Using social media by healthcare organizations increases my interest in buying medical services* • *I am very likely to buy medical services recommended by healthcare organizations on social media* • *I would like to advise my friends and relatives to buy the services offered by health organizations on social networks* • *In the future, when I need it, I am going to use the services offered by health organizations on social media*	Chiu et al. 2012; Wang and Chang, 2013 Toor et al. 2017

We used the probability sampling method to study the general population. According to Geostat, the total population of Georgia according to the 2023 census is 3726400 people, of which above 18 years Internet user is 229400, which represents the targeted population of our study (National Statistics Office of Georgia, 2023). With a 95% confidence level and margin of error of 5% the sample size for our study was determined to be 374 people. We contacted 572 respondents using social networks and e-mail, from which we received 425 responses. The data was processed using statistical software SPSS -27. In similar studies, managers use the Cronbach's alpha coefficient to determine reliability measures. The reliability coefficient is considered acceptable if it is 0.60 or higher (Nunnally, 1967). The reliability statistics obtained by us are shows that the Cronbach's alpha coefficient for all six variables was 0.945, while for each variable it was more than 0.8, which can be considered as a significantly higher reliable coefficient.

4 Main Findings and Discussion

The survey showed that most respondents (47.1%) belong to the age category of 18 to 24 years, while the minority (1.6%) are 65 years or older. 63.5% of the respondents are women, and 36.5% are men. We explored whether there is a connection between social media marketing activities and customer engagement. As it turned out, such a connection is statistically reliable ($P < 0.001$), and the correlation coefficient is positive ($r = 0.267$) (Table 2). As mentioned above, the first hypothesis relates to the impact of social media marketing activities on consumers engagement. Regression analysis is used to test the H1 hypothesis. Table 4 shows that the model we developed is reliable. ($P < 0.001$); $F = 32.581 > F_{\text{critical}} = 3.84$. The H1 hypothesis is supported. Consequently, social media marketing activities have a positive impact on consumers engagement. In addition, R square = 0.072, which allows us to say that 7.2% of the activities are caused by engagement, which is quietly low. Accordingly, the rest is due to other factors.

Table 2. Regression analysis of the impact of social media activity on consumers engagement

	R	R^2	Adjusted R^2	Standard Error of Estimate		Sum of squares	df	Mean square	F	Significance level
	0.267	0.072	0.069	4.222	Regression	580.65	1	580.6	32.581	0.000
					Residual	7538.47	423	17.8		
					Total	8119.12	424			
		Unstandardized Coeficients			Standardized Coeficients			t	Significance level	
		B	Standard Error		Beta					
(Constant)		7.440	0.895		0.267			8.310	0.000	
Activity		0.213	0.037					5.708	0.000	

Notes: Dependent Variable: Engagement; Predictors: (Constant), Activity

Source: SPSS output based on own data

In the next step, we explored whether there is a connection between social media marketing activities and Trust. As it turned out, the result of the study is statistically acceptable ($P < 0.001$), and the correlation coefficient is positive ($r = 0.389$) (Table 3). As mentioned above, the third hypothesis relates to the impact of social media activities on Trust. With this in mind, we used regression analysis to test the H2 hypothesis. As can be seen from Table 5, the model we developed is reliable ($P < 0.001$; $F = 75.490 > F_{critical} = 3.84$). The H2 hypothesis is supported. Therefore, social media activities have a positive impact on Trust. Also, R square = 0.151, which allows us to say that 15.1% of the social media marketing activity is caused by Trust, while the rest is due to other factors.

Table 3. Regression analysis of the impact of consumers social media activity on the Trust

	R	R^2	Adjusted R^2	Standard Error of Estimate		Sum of squares	df	Mean square	F	Significance level
	0.389	0.151	0.149	2.9674	Regression	664.83	1	664.83	75.490	0.000
					Residual	3725.29	423	8.81		
					Total	4390.12	424			
		Unstandardized Coeficients			Standardized Coeficients			t	Significance level	
		B	Standard Error		Beta					
(Constant)		6.595	0.629		0.389			10.479	0.000	
Activity		0.228	0.026					8.688	0.000	

Notes: Dependent Variable: Trust; Predictors: (Constant), Activity

Source:SPSS output based on own data

In the next step, we explored whether there is a connection between social media marketing activities and e-WOM. As it turned out, such a relationship is statistically reliable ($P < 0.001$), and the correlation coefficient is positive ($r = 0.349$) (Table 4). As mentioned above, the second hypothesis we formulated relates to the impact of social media activities on e-WOM. With this in mind, we used regression analysis to test the H3 hypothesis. As Table 6 shows, the model is reliable ($P < 0.001$; $F = 58.705 > F_{critical} = 3.84$). H3 hypothesis is supported, Consequently, social media activities have a positive impact on e-WOM. In addition, R square = 0.122, which allows us to say that 12.2% of the activity is caused by e-WOM, while the rest is due to other factors.

Table 4. Regression analysis of the impact of consumers social media activity on e-WOM

	R	R^2	Adjusted R^2	Standard Error of Estimate		Sum of squares	df	Mean square	F	Significance level
	0.349	0.122	0.120	9.662	Regression	5480.89	1	5480.89	58.705	0.000
					Residual	39492.56	423	93.36		
					Total	44973.45	424			
		Unstandardized Coeficients			Standardized Coeficients			t	Significance level	
(Constant) **Activity**		B	Standard Error		Beta					
		22.173 0.654	2.049 0.085		0.349			10.821 7.662	0.000 0.000	

Notes: Dependent Variable: e-WOM; Predictors: (Constant), Activity

Source: SPSS output based on own data

To explore of the impact of consumers engagement, Trust, and e-WOM on Behavioral Intention in social media, we first examined whether there is a connection between consumer engagement in social media marketing activities and behavioral intention. As it turned out, such a relationship is statistically reliable ($P < 0.001$), and the correlation coefficient is positive ($r = 0.571$) (Table 5).As noted above, the 5th hypotheses relate to consumers engagement's impact on behavioral intension. We used regression analysis to test the H4 hypothesis. As can be seen from Table 7, the model we developed is reliable ($P < 0.001$ $F = 204.83 > F_{critical} = 3.84$. The H4 hypothesis is supported. Consequently, consumers engagement affects behavioral Intention. R square = 0.326, which allows us to say that 32.6% of Behavioral Intention is caused by Engagement while the rest is due to other factors.

Table 5. Regression analysis of the impact of consumers engagement on Behavioral Intention

	R	R^2	Adjusted R^2	Standard Error of Estimate		Sum of squares	df	Mean square	F	Significance level
	0.571	0.326	0.325	3.4382	Regression	2421.31	1	2421.31	204.830	0.000
					Residual	5000.30	423	11.821		
					Total	7421.61	424			
	Unstandardized Coeficients				Standardized Coeficients			t	Significance level	
(Constant) **Activity**	B	Standard Error			Beta					
	7.682 0.546	0.502 0.038			0.571			15.297 14.312	0.000 0.000	

Notes: Dependent Variable: Behavioral Intension; Predictors: (Constant), Engagement

Source: SPSS output based on own data

As mentioned above, the 5th hypotheses reflect the impact of Trust on Behavioral Intention. With this in mind, we used regression analysis to test the H5 hypothesis. As Table 6 shows the model we developed is reliable ($P < 0.001$; $F = 325.80 > F_{critical} = 3.84$). The H5 hypothesis is supported. Consequently, the Trust affects Behavioral Intention. Also, R square = 0.435, which allows us to say that 43.5% of Behavioral Intention is caused by the Trust while the rest is due to other factors.

Table 6. Regression analysis of Trust impact on Behavioral Intention

	R	R^2	Adjusted R^2	Standard Error of Estimate		Sum of squares	df	Mean square	F	Significance level
	0.660	0.435	0.434	3.1482	Regression	3229.14	1	3229.14	325.804	0.000
					Residual	4192.47	423	9.91		
					Total	7421.61	424			
	Unstandardized Coeficients				Standardized Coeficients			t	Significance level	
(Constant) **Activity**	B	Standard Error			Beta					
	4.240 0.858	0.586 .048			0.660			7.230 18.050	0.000 0.000	

Notes: Dependent Variable: Behavioral Intension; Predictors: (Constant), Trust

Source: SPSS output based on own data

In the next step, we found out if there was a connection between e-WOM and Behavioral Intention. Such a relationship was found to be statistically reliable ($P < 0.001$), and the correlation coefficient was positive ($r = 0.602$) (Table 7). As mentioned above, the 6th hypothesis relates to the impact of e-WOM on Behavioral Intention. With this in mind, we used regression analysis to test the H6 hypothesis. As Table 9 shows the model we developed is reliable ($P < 0.001$; $F(239.901) > F_{critical}3.84$). H6 hypothesis is supported. Therefore e-WOM has a positive influence on Behavioral Intention. In addition, R square = 0.362, which allows us to say that 36.2% of Behavioral intention is caused by e-WOM while the rest is due to other factors.

Table 7. Regression analysis of e-WOM impact on Behavioral Intention

	R	R^2	Adjusted R^2	Standard Error of Estimate		Sum of squares	df	Mean square	F	Significance level
	0.602	0.362	0.360	3.3459	Regression	2685.85	1	2685.85	239.901	0.000
					Residual	4735.76	423	11.20		
					Total	7421.61	424			
		Unstandardized Coeficients			Standardized Coeficients			t	Significance level	
(Constant) **Activity**		B	Standard Error		Beta					
		5.308 0.244	0.613 0.016		0.602			8.660 15.489	0.000 0.000	

Notes: Dependent Variable: Behavioral Intension; Predictors: (Constant), e-WOM

Source: *SPSS output based on own data*

5 Conclusion, Limitations and Future Research

According to this study, Georgian consumers are increasingly using the internet to obtain medical treatment and are especially interested in information linked to health. Our research indicates that Georgian consumers continue to demonstrate a fairly low level of activity. In addition, Georgian consumers do not have considerably of trust in the content shared on social media. Regression analysis revealed statistically significant values that show how customer engagement, eWOM, trust, and behavioral intentions relate to social media activities offered by healthcare organizations. Additionally, linear regression models which consider into account the connections between the variables mentioned above are received. With the use of these models, we can determine the level at which an increase in social media advertising activities may impact consumer behavior.

The usage of social media marketing in the healthcare industry is affected by this research in a number of theoretical ways. First of all, it is important to recognize that despite the fact that social media marketing activities is a very broad issue and has been the subject of much research; there are still noticeable inadequacies in this field. This means that less research have been done to establish a connection between the social media marketing activities used by medical organizations and variables such customer engagement, eWOM, trust, and behavioral intention that impact consumer behavior. The relationship between these variables is established in part by this study. The study acknowledges the significance of social media marketing initiatives as a way to guarantee the growth of consumer behavior in the medical services market, which enhances the amount of information already known in this area. From the practical perspective, this study's primary contribution is that companies in the health industry might use the research results to inform their business plan preparation. Also by better understanding their consumers' purchasing perceptions, health care providers will be able to create marketing strategies that will assist them reach their objectives.

The study considered a number of limitations in order to shed light on the growing influence of social media on consumers' behavioral intentions about health concerns. First of all, practical factors limited the number of respondents needed for the study. Specifically, the study's sample is not as representative of the whole population as it may be, especially across all age groups. The age group over 24 years old has to be specifically addressed. The 18–24 age range was the primary focus of the research; while this age range cannot be regarded as an entire population, it does account for the majority of Internet and social media users in Georgia. Furthermore, the geographical boundaries of Georgia limited the choice's scope. While participants in the study came from various Georgian areas, the survey's primary basis was a survey of Georgian customers in the capital of the state, Tbilisi. The restriction was put in place since Tbilisi is home to the majority of Georgians and, by extension, Internet users.

This research serves as a foundation for future investigations into social media marketing activities and related consumer behavior in the Georgian medical industry. This work offers several interesting possibilities for future investigation. It first relates to the effect that healthcare firms' social media marketing initiatives have on customer loyalty and satisfaction. Such marketing efforts' development and implementation are unfamiliar with Georgian reality, which presents intriguing study possibilities. Future research should determine how customer purchase decisions are impacted by the satisfaction and loyalty of social media marketing initiatives carried out by healthcare organizations.

References

Abid, A., Roy, S.K., Lees-Marshment, J., Dey, B.L., Muhammad, S.S., Kumar, S.: Political social media marketing: a systematic literature review and agenda for future research. Electronic Commerce Research, pp. 1–36 (2023)

Alshakhs, F., Alanzi, T.: The evolving role of social media in health-care delivery measuring the perception of health-care professionals in Eastern Saudi Arabia. J. Multidiscip. Healthc. **11**, 473–479 (2018)

Baker, A.M., Donthu, N., Kumar, V.: Investigating how word-of-mouth conversations about brands influence purchase and retransmission intentions. J. Mark. Res. **53**(2), 225–239 (2016)

Bautista, J.R., Zhang, Y., Gwizdka, J.: Healthcare professionals' acts of correcting health misinformation on social media. Int. J. Med. Informatics **148**, 104375 (2021)

Chaves Prasetya, T.A.E., Wardani, R.W.K.: Systematic review of social media addiction among health workers during the pandemic Covid-19. Heliyon **9**(6), e16784 (2023)

Chiu, C.M., Hsu, M.H., Lai, H., Chang, C.M.: Re-examining the influence of trust on online repeat purchase intention: The moderating role of habit and its antecedents. Decis. Support. Syst. **53**(4), 835–845 (2012)

Colicev, A., Malshe, A., Pauwels, K., O'Connor, P.: Improving consumer mindset metrics and shareholder value through social media: the different roles of owned and earned media. J. Mark. **82**(1), 37–56 (2018)

Crie, D., Chebat, J.-C.: Health marketing: toward an integrative perspective. J. Bus. Res. **66**(1), 123–126 (2013)

Dodokh, A., Al-Maaitah, M.A.: Impact of social media usage on organizational performance in the Jordanian dead sea cosmetic sector. European J. Business and Manage. **11**(2), 75–91 (2019)

Doh, S.J., Hwang, J.S.: How consumers evaluate eWOM (electronic word-of-mouth) messages. Cyberpsychol. Behav. **12**(2), 193–197 (2009)

Farah, M.F.: Application of the theory of planned behavior to customer switching intentions in the context of bank consolidations. International J. Bank Marketing **35**(1), 147–172 (2017)

Farsi, D.J.: Social media and health care, part i: literature review of social media use by health care providers. J. Med. Internet Res. **23**(4), e23205 (2021)

Freire, Y., Sánchez, M.G., Suárez, A., Joves, G., Nowak, M., Díaz-Flores García, V.: Influence of the use of social media on patients changing dental practice: a web-based questionnaire study. BMC Oral Health **23**(1), 365 (2023)

Gummerus, J., Liljander, V., Weman, E., Pihlström, M.: Customer engagement in a Facebook brand community. Manag. Res. Rev. **35**(9), 857–877 (2012)

Hajli, N., Sims, J., Zadeh, A.H., Richard, M.O.: A social commerce investigation of the role of trust in a social networking site on purchase intentions. J. Bus. Res. **71**, 133–141 (2017)

Herr, P.M., Kardes, F.R., Kim, J.: Effects of word-of-mouth and product-attribute information on persuasion: an accessibility-diagnosticity perspective. Journal of consumer research **17**(4), 454–462 (1991)

Hong, I.B., Cha, H.S.: The mediating role of consumer trust in an online merchant in predicting purchase intention. Int. J. Inf. Manage. **33**(6), 927–939 (2013)

Hong, I.B., Cho, H.: The impact of consumer trust on attitudinal loyalty and purchase intentions in B2C e-marketplaces: intermediary trust vs. seller trust. International Journal of Information Manage. **31**(5), pp. 469–479 (2011)

Hung, C.L., et al.: Enhancing healthcare services and brand engagement through social media marketing: integration of Kotler's 5A framework with IDEA process. Inf. Process. Manage. **60**(4), 103379 (2023)

Hutter, K., Hautz, J., Dennhardt, S., Füller, J.: The impact of user interactions in social media on brand awareness and purchase intention: the case of MINI on Facebook. J. Product & Brand Management **22**(5–6), 342–351 (2013)

Jackson, M., Brennan, L., Parker, L.: The public health community's use of social media for policy advocacy: a scoping review and suggestions to advance the field. Public Health **198**, 146–155 (2021)

Kahraman, A., Kazançoğlu, İ: Understanding consumers' purchase intentions toward natural-claimed products: a qualitative research in personal care products. Bus. Strateg. Environ. **28**(6), 1218–1233 (2019)

Khan, I., Saleh, M.A., Quazi, A., Johns, R.: Health consumers' social media adoption behaviours in Australia. Health Informatics J. **27**(2), 14604582211009916 (2021)

Kulkov, I., Tsvetkova, A., Ivanova-Gongne, M.: Identifying institutional barriers when implementing new technologies in the healthcare industry. Eur. J. Innov. Manag. **26**(4), 909–932 (2021)

Kumar, V., Pansari, A.: Competitive advantage through engagement. J. Mark. Res. **53**(4), 497–514 (2016)

Manzoor, U., Baig, S.A., Hashim, M., Sami, A.: Impact of social media marketing on consumer's purchase intentions: the mediating role of customer trust. International J. Entrepreneurial Res. **3**(2), 41–48 (2020)

Mladenović, D., Krajina, A., Kucharska, W.: Social Media and Knowledge Sharing–What Do We Know So Far?. In ECSM 2018 5th European Conference on Social Media, pp. 163–170. Limerick Institute of Technology, Ireland (2018)

Mondal, T., Jayadeva, S.M., Pani, R., Subramanian, M., Sumana, B.: E marketing strategy in health care using IoT and Machine Learning. Materials Today: Proceedings **56**, 2087–2091 (2022)

National Statistics Office of Georgia (2023). Retrieved 20 October 2023 https://www.geostat.ge/en

Nunnally, J.C.: Psychometric Theory. McGraw-Hill Book Company, New York, NY (1967)
Pilon, L., Foster, A., Zimmerman, P.A., Macbeth, D.: The role of online marketing to engage healthcare workers with infection prevention and control information and resources: a pilot study. Infection, Disease & Health, 28 (2023)
Pirson, M., Martin, K., Parmar, B.: Formation of stakeholder trust in business and the role of personal values. J. Bus. Ethics **145**(1), 1–20 (2017)
Rahman, Z.: The impact of social media engagement metrics on purchase intention: a study on brand fan page followers. LUMEN Proceedings **1**, 665–681 (2017)
Rezvani, S., Dehkordi, G.J., Rahman, M.S., Fouladivanda, F., Habibi, M., Eghtebasi, S.: A conceptual study on the country of origin effect on consumer purchase intention. Asian Soc. Sci. **8**(12), 205–215 (2012)
Saunders, M., Lewis, P., Thornhill, A.: Research Methods for Business Students, 8th edn. Pearson Education Ltd, Harlow (2019)
Schivinski, B., Christodoulides, G., Dabrowski, D.: Measuring consumers' engagement with brand-related social-media content: development and validation of a scale that identifies levels of social-media engagement with brands. J. Advert. Res. **56**(1), 64–80 (2016)
Swan, E.L., Dahl, A.J., Peltier, J.W.: Health-care marketing in an omni-channel environment: exploring telemedicine and other digital touchpoints. J. Res. Interact. Mark. **13**(4), 602–618 (2019)
Todua, N., Jashi, C.: Influence of social marketing on the behavior of georgian consumers regarding healthy nutrition. Bulletin of the Georgian National Academy of Sciences **12**(2), 183–190 (2018)
Toor, A., Husnain, M., Hussain, T.: The impact of social network marketing on consumer purchase intention in Pakistan: consumer engagement as a mediator. AJBA **10**(1), 167–199 (2017)
Wang, J.C., Chang, C.H.: How online social ties and product-related risks influence purchase intentions: a Facebook experiment. Electron. Commer. Res. Appl. **12**(5), 337–346 (2013)
Wang, S.S., Stefanone, M.A.: Showing off? Human mobility and the interplay of traits, self-disclosure, and Facebook check-ins. Soc. Sci. Comput. Rev. **31**(4), 437–457 (2013)
Yadav, M., Rahman, Z.: Measuring consumer perception of social media marketing activities in e-commerce industry: scale development & validation. Telematics Inform. **34**(7), 1294–1307 (2017)

Digital Economic Policy in Georgia

Gulnaz Erkomaishvili(✉)

Ivane Javakhishvili Tbilisi State University, Tbilisi, Georgia
gulnazi.erkomaishvili@tsu.ge

Abstract. The article discusses the biggest technological changes in the modern world. The growth rate of e-commerce, computerized management of organizational processes and digital infrastructure is amazingly high and it is the main tool of economic development.

According to a 2017 study by the largest Spanish banking and financial group BBVA, Georgia ranked 62nd out of 100 countries according to the Digital Index with 0.40 points and was among the middle-level countries. Georgia does not appear in the World Digital Competitiveness Ranking 2023 (World Digital Competitiveness Ranking 2023 - IMD Business School of Management and Leadership Courses).

Today, the main strategic development of Georgia's economy must be the accelerated integration of the country into global technological trends. Digital technology should be introduced in all possible sectors, otherwise economic growth will be impossible. Digital entrepreneurial culture should be elevated and it becomes a strategic direction of state policy.

For the development of digital economy in Georgia it is necessary: to formulate and implement digital economic policy; Digital economic policy will be formed in the direction of infrastructure and technology. The development of technology and development is particularly low; The State will create digital environmental and regulatory legislative frameworks in collaboration with business and scientific sectors to promote the emergence of internet companies and stimulate internet market; Knowledge of digital technologies in higher education institutions; It is important to focus on cognitive, social-emotional and problem-solving skills, which are much more difficult to learn. Ensure tax privileges in the creation of the latest technologies; Involve into a unified digital market that will facilitate free movement of goods, services and capital, will create new startups and laboratories. All this will contribute to the country's economic growth.

Keywords: digital economy · digital technologies · innovative tool · digital index · digital economic policy

1 Introduction

The digital economy is a growth area. In the modem world, there are major technological changes. The introduction of digital technologies, information and communication services has led to unp.

R. C. Geibel and S. Machavariani (Eds.): ISPC 2024, SPBE, pp. 222–230, 2025.
https://doi.org/10.1007/978-3-031-88052-0_17

In the modern world, there are major technological changes. The introduction of digital technologies, information and communication services has led to unprecedented global socio-political and economic changes. The role of digital technologies in increasing productivity and national competitiveness of the country is increasing. Today it is used in almost all sectors of the economy. The growth rate of e-commerce, computer-aided management of organizational processes and digital infrastructure is amazingly high and it is the main tool of economic development.

The aim of an effective national economic policy of digitalisation is the integration of Europe into the Single Digital Market (SDM). Achieving this goal depends on the realisation of two subordinate objectives (tasks), such as:

- Development of the digital economy
- Formation of a digital society

Consumers in the European Union (this can be extended to all countries) are the main drivers of technological change. New digital tools such as comparison sites, social networks, the possibility of mobile purchasing of goods and services are a real way to implement a digitalisation policy. The introduction of technologies and their interactive interaction is crucial for creating an environment for the development of ICT innovations.

All countries are trying to keep pace with the rapid development of digital technologies.

The use of digital technologies brings both benefits and risks. The benefits are called digital dividends. These are: increasing labor productivity, increasing the competitiveness of companies, reducing production costs, creating new jobs, overcoming poverty and social inequality, economic growth.

The risks of using digital technologies are: the problem of protecting personal data; controlling their behavior using human data; an increase in unemployment in the labor market, as well as the risk of the disappearance of some professions and industries, etc.

All countries are trying to keep up with the rapid development of digital technologies. An impressive example of the development of the digital economy is Singapore, whose development is supported by the country's government with the right economic policy, which is constantly looking for investors and high-tech specialists who can reorganize various industries on a digital platform. Accordingly, the organization and management of business in Singapore is at the highest level.

In 2017, a study was conducted by BBVA, the largest Spanish banking and financial group, to compare the level of development of the digital economy in different countries (Cámara, Tuesta 2017). According to the said research, the Digital Index (DiGiX) was evaluated using the example of 100 countries. The DiGiX Index evaluates the factors, agent behavior and institutions that enable a country to fully utilize information and communication technologies (ICTS) to increase competitiveness and prosperity.

The DiGiX index is calculated using six indicators:

1. Infrastructure (3G Internet coverage and higher capacity, bandwidth (bytes/s), secure Internet servers);
2. Consumer Internet use (use of Internet technologies by households);
3. Use of Internet technologies by businesses (in business and customer relations);
4. Costs (fixed Internet and telephone);

5. Regulation (laws related to information technologies, level of software security, independence of the judiciary, effectiveness of the legal system in resolving disputes);
6. Index of government online services.

Each indicator is divided into separate indicators, the maximum score is 1 and the minimum score is 0.

According to the 2016 DiGiX index, Luxembourg had the highest rate in the world (1) and Algeria had the lowest rate (0). The second place was taken by the United Kingdom with 0.97, and the third place was Hong Kong (0.95). This is followed by the USA (4th place, 0.92) and the Netherlands (5th place, 0.90). In the range from 0.90 to 0.70, more than 15 countries (Japan, Singapore, Norway, Finland, Sweden, Switzerland, Iceland, New Zealand, Germany, South Korea, France, etc.) are leading countries and determine the technological trends world.

Georgia took 62nd place with 0.40 points and was among the middle-level countries. Turkey – 0.50 points, Kazakhstan – 0.47, the Russian Federation – 0.45, Azerbaijan – 0.44 and Romania – 0.43 recorded a high rate in the region. Armenia had an indicator of about our level and much lower – Moldova – 0.33 and Ukraine – 0.22. Georgia was ahead of the EU countries: Bulgaria – 0.33, Serbia – 0.31 and Albania – 0.26.

The Global Digital Competitiveness Ranking 2018 includes 63 countries. Georgia is not included among them. The top ten in the digital competitiveness ranking are as follows: USA, Singapore, Sweden, Denmark, Switzerland, Norway, Finland, Canada, Netherlands, Great Britain. Venezuela is in the last 63rd place. The digital competitiveness assessment included the former Soviet countries: Kazakhstan, Russia, Ukraine, Estonia, Lithuania, Latvia, Visegrad countries (Czech Republic, Poland, Hungary, Slovakia) and neighboring Turkey.

In addition to the DiGiX index, there is the Digital Economy and Social Index (DESI). It is an index developed by the European Commission for the member states of the European Union. The digital economy and social index is high in Denmark, Sweden, Finland and the Netherlands. Then come Luxembourg, Ireland, Great Britain, Belgium and Estonia. Romania, Greece and Italy have low values.

The World Digital Competitiveness Ranking 2022 includes 63 countries [IMD World Competitiveness Booklet 2022 (cld.bz)], Georgia is not listed among them. The top ten in the digital competitiveness ranking are as follows: Denmark, Switzerland, Singapore, Sweden, Hong Kong, Netherlands, Taiwan, Finland, Norway, USA. Venezuela is in the last 63rd place. The digital competitiveness ranking includes the former Soviet countries: Estonia (22nd place), Latvia (35th place), Visegrad countries (Czech Republic, Poland, Hungary, Slovakia) and neighboring Turkey.

In the World Digital Competitiveness Ranking 2023 (World Digital Competitiveness Ranking 2023 - IMD Business School for Management and Leadership Courses), the USA moved to first place, followed by the Netherlands, Singapore, Denmark, Switzerland, Korea, Sweden, Finland, Taiwan, Hong Kong. It should be noted that among the post-Soviet countries, Estonia took 18th place, Lithuania 28th, Kazakhstan 34th and Latvia 40th. Georgia still does not appear in the mentioned list.

In addition to the DiGiX index, there is the Digital Economy and Social Index (DESI). This is an index developed by the European Commission for the Member States of the European Union. The Digital Economy and Social Index is high in Denmark, Sweden,

Finland and the Netherlands. Then come Luxembourg, Ireland, Great Britain, Belgium and Estonia. Romania, Greece and Italy have low values.

The average annual growth rate of the digital economy in developing countries is 18%, while that of developed countries is 8% (Enukidze, Batiashvili 2015).

2 Theoretical Foundation

Nicholas Negroponte, a scientist at the University of Massachusetts, called the economy based on digital technologies the digital economy (Negroponte, 1995). Using this term, he distinguished the advantage of an economy based on the intensive development of digital and information and communication technologies from the traditional one. The digital economy is an important part of the fourth industrial revolution. It is directly related to the development of digital computer technology, which includes online services, electronic payments, Internet commerce, Internet advertising, Internet games, etc.

Mario Mariniello Describes in detail all European Union policies related to digital technologies and their Economic rationale -an important benchmark for studying policy making in the digital environment around the World (Mario Mariniello, 2022).

In the digital economy, the focus is on the production of smart products, which involves high investment expenditure. However, problems arise in both developing and developed countries with small open economies (Gogorishvili, Gvelesiani 2018, 95).

The transition to the principle of digital economy and, above all, to blockchain technologies will further increase the number of employees in the corporate sector and support the development of small and medium-sized businesses. With the help of technology, the user receives services faster, sells and buys products online, saves money in online stores, can start his own business online and become an entrepreneur without leaving home (Enukidze, Batiashvili 2015).

Accelerated integration of the country into global technology trends should become the main strategy for the development of Georgia's economy. Digital technologies must be implemented in all possible sectors, otherwise economic growth is impossible. Digital entrepreneurship culture should be strengthened and become a strategic direction of state policy (Erkomaishvili, 2024).

3 Research Method

This paper uses general and specific methods, in particular, analysis, synthesis, induction, deduction, scientific abstraction, comparative and statistical methods, as well as experts' evaluation. Works by local and foreign scientists, Ministry of Economy and Sustainable Development, as well as various organizations' studies and reports were used as a theoretical basis for research and variety of laws, government decrees and orders and the publications of the National Statistics Office of Georgia were used as a an informational basis.

4 Analysis and Results

According to Global Digital Insights 2023 (Digital 2023: Global Overview Report – DataReportal – Global Digital Insights), the world population surpassed the 8 billion mark on November 15, 2022, and will reach 8.01 billion in early 2023. More than 57 percent of the world's population now lives in cities. A total of 5.44 billion people use mobile phones at the beginning of 2023, representing 68 percent of the total global population. The number of mobile unique users increased by 3 percent last year, with 168 million new users in the last 12 months. There are 5.16 billion internet users worldwide today, meaning 64.4 percent of the world's population is currently online.

Data shows that the total number of global internet users grew by 1.9 percent in the last 12 months, but actual growth is likely to be higher. There are currently 4.76 billion social media users worldwide, which is 60 percent of the entire world population. The growth of social media users has slowed in recent months, but 137 million new users are expected to be added in 2023, representing an annual growth rate of 3 percent.

It is worth noting that this slowdown is expected, especially now that more than 6 in 10 people on Earth already use the internet.

The lack of qualified personnel is a serious obstacle to the development of the digital economy in Georgia. For example, in the USA the share of IT specialists is 2.4% of the total working population, in Germany and Great Britain - 4.3%. In this regard, we are lagging behind in Georgia. But this is also an objective process. Qualified personnel in this direction will gradually increase in the country. Teachers are being trained and appropriate infrastructure is being built.

According to the Saxstat survey 'Use of information and communication technologies in companies ~, the share of companies that had access to the Internet is as follows: 2018 - 98.5%, 2019 - 93%, 2020 - 94%, 2021 -95%, 2022 -84.2%, 2023 - 84.4%. Until 2022, Internet access by company employees, including for working from home, was considered Internet access. From 2022, only the presence of Internet access in the company will be considered Internet access. Accordingly, from 2022, the rate of access to the Internet will be reduced.

The transition to the principle of the digital economy and, above all, to blockchain technologies will further increase the number of employees in the corporate sector and contribute to the development of small and medium-sized enterprises.

In the digital economy, the focus is on the production of smart products, which involves high investment costs. However, problems arise in both developing and developed countries with small open economies.

The use of digital technologies has both advantages and risks. The advantages are called digital dividends. These are: increasing labor productivity, increasing the competitiveness of companies, reducing production costs, creating new jobs, overcoming poverty and social inequality, economic growth.

The risks of using digital technologies are: the problem of protecting personal data; controlling their behavior using human data; an increase in unemployment in the labor market, as well as the risk of the disappearance of some professions and industries, etc.

In order to adapt to modern economic trends and bring the country to a new level of development, the Digital Economy Association of Georgia (DEAG) was established on

June 1, 2018. DEAG has clearly defined goals and objectives, which include the development of a digital corporate culture, stimulating and supporting the business environment, preparing an investment platform, promoting capital market development, integrating various systems with blockchain technologies, and for this purpose, cooperation with state and private structures, digital assets and digital electronic currencies includes the introduction of a means of payment, the preparation of concrete legislative initiatives and the presentation of other innovative projects.

In January 2020, the Government of Georgia approved the 'National Broadband Network Development Strategy of Georgia 2020–2025 and its Action Plan for Implementation ~. The strategy was prepared within the framework of the EU project 'Digital Market Harmonization ~ HDM/EU4Digital with the technical support of the World Bank. The purpose of the strategy is to implement policies and regulations in line with EU and international best practices to overcome the existing digital inequality and develop the digital economy and information society in the country. The target indicators of the strategy until 2025 are: to cover 99% of Georgia's territory with 4G connections and subsequently test 5G in at least three regions. Creating access to the high-frequency broadband network for all households and 1 GB for all institutional units. Access to St. Union.

With the right strategy, the country can achieve significant successes. In this context, it is worth mentioning the Law on Innovation adopted by the Government of Georgia on June 22, 2016, the purpose of which is to create and perfect the ecosystem of national innovations necessary for the socio-economic development of Georgia, to create an economy based on knowledge and innovations in the country, to promote the assimilation of technologies created in other countries in Georgia, intellectual property created in Georgia and to promote the introduction and export of technologies, as well as the penetration of advanced technologies in all areas of the economy in order to increase their competitiveness.

5 Discussion

From this point of view, today the workload of the High Technology and Innovation Development Center (Technology Park) is increasing, which is designed to create a unified ecosystem in the direction of innovation and technology and promote the development of innovative ideas. Based on international practice, the Technology Park provides a unique opportunity to increase the number of small and medium-sized enterprises based on knowledge and innovation and to ensure their development, to establish representative offices of foreign high-tech companies in Georgia and to attract foreign investments. The Technology Park is designed to provide start-up and small businesses with resources that were previously almost unavailable to them. Increasing the innovation potential is directly related to the development of start-up entrepreneurship. The Agency has established a Technology Park that includes small business incubators, training centers and laboratories, co-working spaces and a recreation area. The Innovation Agency supports young start-up companies, whose share in the Georgian economy is currently relatively small. However, the ongoing trend of involving as many people as possible in the innovation ecosystem brings additional economic benefits for the entire country, which have been achieved in many successful countries through the development of the innovation ecosystem.

The activity of the Innovation Agency was especially noticeable in the second half of 2018, when a number of interesting projects were implemented, both in terms of training and financing. The innovation centers Telavi Technopark, Akhmet and Rukh (Zugdidi municipality) were added to Georgia. In addition, concrete effective steps were taken in Georgia to strengthen and promote angel investors (people who provide seed funding to a startup).

In 2019, the strategy of the Innovation Agency will be aimed at attracting private investment in the development of the innovation ecosystem. All further projects of the Innovation Agency are aimed at the maximum possible promotion of private investment. In addition, it is planned to maximize the activity in the regional innovation centers so that the population of the entire country is actively involved in the development of the innovation ecosystem.

In 2020–2022, the Innovation and Technology Agency of Georgia, within the framework of the National Innovation Ecosystem Project (GENIE), retrained 3,000 information technology specialists for the following professions: programming; digital project management; artificial intelligence; digital design; cybersecurity; networks, etc. This work was carried out by New Horizons, the world's largest IT training provider with 38 years of experience in this field. It is important to note that significant tax incentives have been created (by the Georgian government) for information technology companies. Due to this activity, several international companies flocked to Georgia. The certificate received will allow specialists to take part in the announced competitions for high-paying jobs and get the desired jobs.

In addition to the Technopark, the innovative business development program 'Startup Georgia ~ is also of great importance. Its goal is to promote the development of startups in Georgia. Any citizen of Georgia who has an innovative and promising business venture and needs initial funding for its implementation can take part in the project. It has both an innovative and a high-tech component (artificial intelligence, nano and information technologies, robotics, etc.).

The Startup Georgia program finds financial support for innovative ideas of start-up companies and includes various components: financing, simplification of tax and legal procedures, and support for relevant education.

Only unique high-tech innovation ideas are supported. For the entire program, 11 million GEL were allocated in the first phase, which later increased to 35 million GEL.

For high-tech projects, the Innovation and Technology Agency of Georgia remains a partner of the joint venture for a period of no more than 7 years and does not interfere in the management of the startup. Innovative and technologically successful startups received equity financing without collateral. The provision was limited to the assets created within the framework of the project.

The Innovation and Technology Agency of Georgia provides training, coaching, mentoring and consulting services to all beneficiaries of the program.

The National Communications Commission of Georgia adopted the 5G Development Promotion Strategy Paper in September 2019. The purpose of the document is: - by 2020 (in case of an application from operators) to provide the Commission with opportunities to temporarily use the frequency spectrum allocated for 5G; - by 2020 (on the basis of the developed and approved strategic action plan) in a defined geographical area to launch 5G-based services in test mode. The document includes: release, coordination and harmonization plan for the 5G frequency band (broadband Internet); the expected accompanying obligations of the temporary transfer of the 5G frequency range; planned legislative changes. These changes will have a significant impact and contribute to the development of 5G in Georgia.

The venture investment project is aimed at start-ups in the high-tech industry, which includes such areas as aerospace manufacturing, automobiles, artificial intelligence, biotechnology, bioinformatics, computer engineering, computer science, information technology, nanotechnologies, nuclear physics, electromagnetic radiation, robotics, semiconductors and telecommunications.

It is very important that in 2024 the first technology center will be created in the city of Kutaisi. An interactive scientific and technological museum, a startup accelerator, an international IT school, a conference room, a shared workspace, a powerful data center for the development of Georgian artificial intelligence, electronics, robotics, drones, IoT, STEAM, industrial innovations (Fablab) and other experimental facilities will be located in the designated area: laboratories, VR/AR gaming lab, meeting and training rooms for startups and IT specialists.

Kutaisi Technology Center will become one of the main cornerstones of the country's digital transformation and will play an important role in attracting new technology companies and investors to the country, creating new jobs and accelerating economic growth.

6 Conclusions and Recommendations

From all of the above, it is clear that the main strategy for the development of Georgia's economy should be the accelerated integration of the country into global technological trends. Digital technologies must be implemented in all possible sectors, otherwise economic growth is impossible. Digital entrepreneurial culture should be strengthened and become a strategic direction of state policy.

For the development of digital economy in Georgia, it is necessary:

- to formulate and implement digital economic policy, especially in the direction of infrastructure and technologies. Currently, the process of growth and use of technologies in general is low;
- The state, in cooperation with business and science, should create a legal framework for the development and regulation of the digital environment, promote the creation of Internet companies and revitalize the Internet market;
- Increase knowledge of digital technologies in higher education institutions;
- Attention should be paid to cognitive problem-solving skills.
- To encourage the development of the latest technologies, tax incentives should be introduced. It should be included in the digital single market, which will facilitate the free movement of goods, services and capital and lay the foundation for the creation of new start-ups and laboratories.

All this will contribute to the country's rapid economic growth.

References

Gogorishvili, I., Gvelesiani, R.: Progress - the driving force for changes in the economic policy of the state and the corporate policy of companies. TSU III International Scientific Conference "Challenges of Globalization in Economy and Business", Proceedings, October 26–27 (2018)
Enukidze, N., Batiashvili, M.: The Digital Economy: an Innovative Way Out of the Crisis. Forbes Georgia (2015)
Erkomaishvili, G.: Rational Economic Policy - the Driving Force from Business Entrepreneurship to Social Entrepreneurship. Universal Publishing House, Tbilisi (2019)
Erkomaishvili, G.: Economic Development Strategies of Georgia. Universal Publishing House, Tbilisi (2024)
Startup Georgia program (2023). http://startup.gov.ge/geo/program
The Digital Economy Association was founded in Georgia. http://www.bm.ge/ka/article/saqartveloshi-cifruli-ekonomikis-asociacia-dafudznda/20744. Accessed 22 Mar 2023
Vision 2030. Development strategy of Georgia
Camara, N., Tuesta, D.: DIGIX: The Digitalization Index. BBVA Research. 17 February (2017).
https://www.imd.org/wcc/world-competitiveness-center-rankings/world-digital-competitiveness-rankings-2018/
IMD World Competitiveness Booklet 2022 (cld.bz)]
Negroponte, N.: Being Digital. New York (1995)
The IMD World Digital Competitiveness Ranking (2023)
Digital: Global Overview Report – DataReportal-Global Digital Insights], the world population surpassed the 8 billion (2023). businessinsider.ge
National statistics office of Georgia.http//www.geostat.ge
Mario, M.: Oxford (2022)
Agency for Innovation and Technology of Georgia https://gita.gov.ge
Georgia Electronic Communications Law. https://matsne.gov.ge/ka/document/download/29620/1/ge/pdf~

Digitalization of Georgia's Agro-Food Industry: Challenges and Opportunities for Sustainable Development

Eter Kharaishvili(✉), Ia Natsvlishvil, and Tamar Lazariashvili

Economics and Business Faculty of Ivane Javakhishvili, Tbilisi State University, Tbilisi, Georgia
{eter.kharaishvili,ia.natsvlishvili,tamar.lazariashvili}@tsu.ge

Abstract. The article substantiates the importance of digitalization in the development of Georgia's agro-food industry and in the process of achievement of food security goals. Digitalization is evaluated as the basis of industry modernization and progress.

By applying bibliometric analysis the paper identifies the main directions of research focus, evaluates the evolutionary development of the research process, identifies research clusters by country and authors of dominant publications, different opinions of scientists about digitization concepts are evaluated.

The paper justifies that digitalization creates new prospects for productivity in the development of the agro-food industry. With the use of modern digital technologies, it is possible to achieve the sustainability of agro-food industry and increase productivity.

The work is based on various theoretical-methodological tools of research, in particular, bibliometric research has been conducted. Analysis, synthesis, comparison, factorial and other methods have been used. In order to identify the digitalization barriers in Georgia's agro-food industry, a quantitative study was conducted through the Google Form online questionnaire.

By surveying the respondents, the goals of using digital technologies are identified, the most used applications and services to achieve the goals are identified. Also, the level of access to the Internet, barriers to the introduction of digital technologies, opportunities for the introduction of digital technologies in the industry, benefits from digitization and others are determined.

According to the evaluation of the producers, the possibilities of introducing digital technologies in the agro-food industry have been identified: the necessity of systematic organization of educational trainings, training courses and seminars, increasing access to digital technologies and financial resources, development of digital infrastructure, etc. The paper provides conclusions on the peculiarities and existing barriers of digitalization in the agro-food industry, offers recommendations on the possibilities of digitalization development.

Keywords: Digitalization · agro-food industry · digitalization barriers · digitalization opportunities · sustainable development · Georgia

R. C. Geibel and S. Machavariani (Eds.): ISPC 2024, SPBE, pp. 231–242, 2025.
https://doi.org/10.1007/978-3-031-88052-0_18

1 Introduction

Growing demand for food, inequality in consumption, climate change, pandemics and other factors are causing significant problems in ensuring food security. The complex interaction of these factors contributes to the deepening of the global food crisis and significantly complicates the achievement of the United Nations' Sustainable Development Goals by 2030. Accordingly, the issue of ensuring food security at the global level and the need to achieve sustainable development goals is actively discussed in the agenda of any country.

Digitization of the agro-food industry has great potential in the formation of conditions for the growth of food production and sustainable development, as well as in the socio-economic development of society. The digitization process combines virtual and physical sectors of the economy, using digital platforms added value is created through modern communication between the entrepreneur and the consumer. Today, digital platforms are considered as an essential tool for the formation of modern infrastructure.

It should be noted that in many countries, including Georgia, the agro-food industry has not yet been significantly transformed in accordance with digital requirements. Questions need to be answered: To what extent does the use of modern digital technologies contribute to the development of a sustainable agro-food industry? What are the main challenges in digitizing the agri-food industry? What are the goals of using digital technologies? Which digital technologies and applications are currently used in the agri-food industry? What are the benefits of digitization? What opportunities for the implementation of digital technologies are considered in the future?

Searching for answers to these questions will help reveal the possibilities of introducing modern digital technologies in the agri-food industry. The proposed recommendations will make a certain contribution to achieving the goals of sustainable development of the industry.

1.1 Goal of the Research

The purpose of the study is to reveal the challenges of digitization in the agri-food industry and to develop recommendations for future opportunities for sustainable development of the industry.

2 Research Methodology

A systematic literature review (SLR) was conducted using the method of bibliometric analysis using Vosviewer and Bibliometrix software packages. Also, scientific studies located in other bases are evaluated. Canva software is used in the graphic analysis process. Analysis, induction, comparison, expert evaluation, factor analysis and other methods are used in the research process. A quantitative study has been conducted.

The National Statistical Office of Georgia and international registers were taken as the research base. The databases of the ministries of the economic profile of Georgia, local and international organizations' analytical reports, materials posted on scientific electronic portals and internet resources, databases of Scopus, Web of Science, Google Scholar, ResearchGatewere also were studied.

3 Literature Review

Based on the purpose of the work and research questions, scientific articles were selected from different scientific bases for literature analysis. The bibliometric research of Scopus and Web of Science databases has shown us that the studies on the digitization of the agri-food industry are relevant and growing.

295 scientific papers have been published by 849 authors on the research problem in the Web of Science database in 2002–2024, the annual growth rate is 20.17%.[1] 455 scientific works have been published in the Scopus database on the dominant topics of the research problem in the period 1995–2024, a high rate of growth has been observed since 2019 (see Fig. 1).

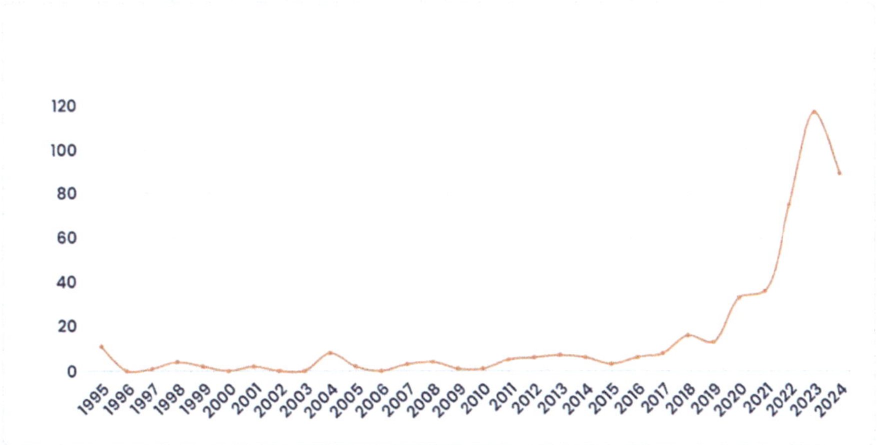

Fig. 1. Trend of publications published in the Scopus database in 1995–2024. Source: Compiled by the authors based on data from the Scopus database with the Canva program

In the study of the digitalization of the agro-food industry, the factor analysis of the main research topics shows that there is a positive correlation with the research topics of information and communication technologies (ICT), use of technology in management, food security, well-being research themes, while there is a negative correlation with research themes about risks, credits, knowledge level and other issues (see Fig. 2).

A thematic analysis of digitization of the agro-food industry revealed several main research clusters: innovations, digital analytics, information impact, food security, health economic policy, labor migration, etc. (see Fig. 3).

In addition, the topics of research clusters in the Scopus databases are mostly consistent with the topics of research clusters of Web of Science.

Digital transformation represents an important opportunity for sustainable development of production, as well as offers new choices to micro, small and medium-sized enterprises in terms of improving product quality and minimizing costs. The use of a digital database significantly increases the benefits(Zhang A. et al. 2023). Digitization leads

[1] *Based on data from the Web of Science database using the Bibliometrix program.*

Fig. 2. Factor analysis of the main themes of the study. Source: Compiled by authors using Bibliometrix software based on data from the Web of Science database

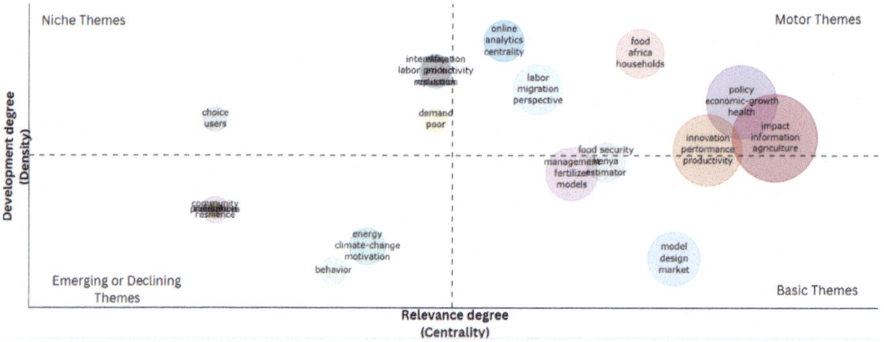

Fig. 3. Thematic map of research on the digitization of the agri-food industry. Source: Compiled by authors using Bibliometrix software based on data from the Web of Science database

to increased productivity (Kharaishvili E., Gechbaia B., Tsiklashvili N. and Katamadze G. 2024).

Studies have proven that solving the problem of food security and sustainable development of agro-industry will play a big role in the formation of a fair and healthy society. The digital transformation of agribusiness will lead to environmental, social and economic sustainability. The use of technologies of the 4th industrial revolution will have a positive impact on the efficiency of the production and food supply chain (Wójcicki, K., Górna, J., & Sikorska, E. 2024). The implementation of digital technologies allows to reduce costs by at least 23% and the volume of waste by almost 5% (Adithya Sridhar et al. 2023). In light of the impending global food crisis, digital technologies provide unique opportunities to address techno-economic challenges in the agri-food sector (Sridhar et al. 2023).

The agro-food industry plays a strategic role in ensuring food security, and the transition from a traditional to an industrial system requires an examination of the development trends of digital technologies (Abbasi et al. 2022).

Digitization is related not only to digital technologies, but also to socio-cultural processes (Hasiholan Tobing R. D. and others, 2023). It will contribute to solving many social problems, development of rural communities and societies (Carmela Annosi, Maria et al. 2020). The digital revolution is changing various aspects of society, including having a major impact on achieving the Sustainable Development Goals (SDGs). Through the components of The Digital Economy and Society Index, the effects of digital transformation are investigated (Vărzaru A. 2024).

Using digital technology, the agri-food industry is more sustainable. However, Artificial Intelligence (AI), Remote Sensing (RS), Blockchain (BC) and Internet of Things (IoT) are revolutionizing the industry value chain and improving technologies (Satpathy B., 2022). The potential of digital technologies to develop a sustainable food system is particularly high in developing countries, including the Middle East and North Africa (MENA) region (Rachel A. Bahn et al. 2021).

The use of modern digital technologies has significant potential for the formation of effective food systems and improvement of food quality (Hassoun A. et al. 2022).

In order to meet the growing demand of the population for food products, sustainable development is necessary (Satpathy B., 2022). In addition, identification of the main challenges of sustainable development and stimulating opportunities needs to be explored. (Kharaishvili E., Lobzhanidze N., 2023). From this point of view, digital transformation is considered as a promising opportunity for the agri-food sector (Martens K., Zscheischler J., 2022). It is through digital technologies that it is possible to ensure the sustainability of the agricultural sector and increase in productivity (Varda AG, 2023). Countries that are leaders in the use of digital economy tools are usually characterized by high competitiveness and sustainable development.

The agri-food industry makes an imperative contribution to solving global challenges. The introduction of smart technologies is considered one of the main ways to solve challenges, and therefore, scientists have proposed ways to solve environmental, economic and social issues in the agri-food industry through digitization. Scientists also proposed potential managerial actions and policy directions for implementing digital transformation (Myshko A., Checchinato F., Colapinto C., Finotto V., Mauracher Ch. (2024).

The agri-food industry has the potential to undergo a revolutionary transformation and face significant challenges using digital technologies (Rodrigue T., Konfo Ch. et. al. 2023). Digital technologies enable the development of precision agriculture, which can significantly increase productivity and profitability, and raise the level of trust for the consumer (Martens K., Zscheischler J., 2022). And digital disruption will have a significant negative impact on business. Therefore, it is important to take relevant and timely steps to adapt to rapid changes (Hardi K. V., Legowo N., 2023).

For decades, agri-food security has become one of the world's most critical issues, and sustainable agri-food production with modern digital technologies reliably reduces poverty caused by high demand for food. Recently, the use of digital technologies in the agri-food industry has significantly changed the environmental impact of agriculture, and big data analytics has significantly reduced the industry's waste. Digitization helps agri-food producers and scientists make better decisions to increase yields, improve product production and storage efficiency, reduce costs, and manage resources (Abiri et al. 2023).

Despite the growing trend of the digital economy in the world, the geographical distribution of online platforms varies by country and continent. It should also be taken into account that the digitalization process is multi-sided and serves different purposes (OECD, 2021). A significant segment of farms in developing countries are not yet using digital technologies for various reasons (Khanna M., 2020).

It is important to use forms of state support for the effective management of the digitization process. Scientists discuss the need for state support for the introduction of digital technologies due to several arguments, Among them, it is worth noting the substantial increase in the volume of production, increase in productivity, efficient use of resources, reduction of harmful effects on the environment (Sergeevna Kolmykova T., Sergeevna Obukhova A. and others, 2021).

Digital transformation breaks the boundaries between organizations and industries (Lyytinen K., Yoo Y., R.J. Boland Jr., 2015) and creates new perspectives for development. Companies that implement digital transformation are more sustainable than other companies. In addition, geographic diversification strategies play a positive role in the processes of digital transformation (DT) and sustainable development of the firm (Ying Xu, Fu Jia, Liukai Wang, Lujie Chen, 2024). Trends and rates of digital transformation are explored in the African agricultural sector. Research on digitization has mainly focused on the use of digital technologies on farms, especially small farms. Also, the focus is on productivity and sustainable development opportunities brought about by digitization (Mhlanga D., Ndhlovu E. 2023).

The study of digitization problems does not lose its importance in solving social problems. During the analysis of the dominant challenges of digitization, scientists consider these issues (Annosi et al. 2020). The introduction of digital technologies in the educational space will lead to innovative transformations in the training of personnel, ensure the achievement of a competitive advantage of universities, and accelerate the development of research (Safiullin M. R., Akhmetshin E. M. 2019). Researchers have also evaluated the legal field of digital transformation processes in the agro-food industry (Zghurska O. Korchynska O. 2022).

Digital transformation will make a significant contribution to the formation of an effective public procurement system (Kharaishvili, E. Atanelishvili T. 2022). Using digital technologies, farmers will be able to better study the agri-food market, ensure the development of sustainable production and supply of safe products to food markets (Kharaishvili, E., Aduashvili, L. 2023.) The use of potential opportunities for the growth of food production and the solution of food security problems should be based on scientific innovations and the introduction of modern digital technologies (Aduashvili, L. 2023), especially in small and medium farms (Kharaishvili E. Lobzhanidze N. 2024).

The bibliographic research revealed that digitization of the agri-food industry is a key element of modernization and progress. Digital transformation is seen as an opportunity for sustainable industry development. There is a shortage of digital technologies in Georgia, the level of digital skills is low, which, together with other hindering factors, leads to low labor productivity. The development of the digitization process will lead to an increase in the volume of production, creating prerequisites for sustainable development.

4 Research Results

The agro-food industry plays an indispensable role in the food security of the population. In developing countries, this industry is an integral source of livelihood for the population. It should also be noted that in the future it will be necessary to meet the increased demand for healthy products. Today, the agri-food industry is facing global challenges. Accordingly, the need to develop the agro-food industry with new approaches is on the agenda. In this context, digital transformation is considered as a promising direction for the improvement and sustainable development of existing agri-food systems. Indeed, digital technologies can lead to a substantial increase in the quantitative indicators and productivity of food production.

The role of the agro-food industry in Georgia is particularly important for improving the level of food security, because the indicators of self-sufficiency of basic products are quite low, for example, this indicator is 22% for wheat, 52% for vegetables, 50% for meat, 34% for poultry meat (Agriculture of Georgia, 2022).

A quantitative study was conducted to identify the level of digitization in the agri-food industry, to determine barriers to the process, to determine the expected benefits from digitization, and to develop recommendations for the future directions of digital transformation development for sustainable development.

The size of the sample was determined by the methodology of Lawrence Neuman (W. Lawrence Neuman, 2014)), the sample size was 22.1% (211 respondents), the margin of error was 3.5%. 59.2% of respondents were women, and 40.8% were men. The research showed that in the agro-food industry of Georgia, the number of people with professional education is quite low - 11.5%, most of them have higher education - 65.7%, the rest have secondary education.

The survey revealed that the basic level of digital skills of employees in the industry is not low, most of them can use the Internet, use a computer, pursue e-commerce, perform digital marketing operations, data processing and analysis with the help of programs, electronic payments, use mobile applications in the production process and more.

The goals of using digital technologies are also different. More than 90% of respondents use digital technologies to get information, 35.5% to participate in online trainings, 34.0% for work meetings and other important purposes (see Fig. 4).

Most of the interviewees (175 respondents) use digital technologies to get information, 70 respondents use these technologies to participate in online trainings, 62 respondents use them for work meetings, etc.

According the above mentioned survey, to achieve the goals manufacturers use various applications/services, including: Microsoft programs (Word, Excel, PowerPoint, Outlook, Teams), social networks (Facebook, YouTube, Instagram, Whatsapp, Messenger, LinkedIn, Viber, Telegram), E-mail (Gmail, Yahoo), mobile banks (BOG, Liberty), government programs (My.gov.ge). It was revealed that 97% of respondents mainly use mobile phones and computers, while only 2.6% use drones, GPS and electronic sensors. Also, the individual answer of two respondents was recorded that they use weather station and internet managed irrigation systems together with the mentioned technologies. Therefore, the level of use of digital technologies in the Georgian agro-food industry for production purposes is quite low and cannot meet the goals of sustainable development.

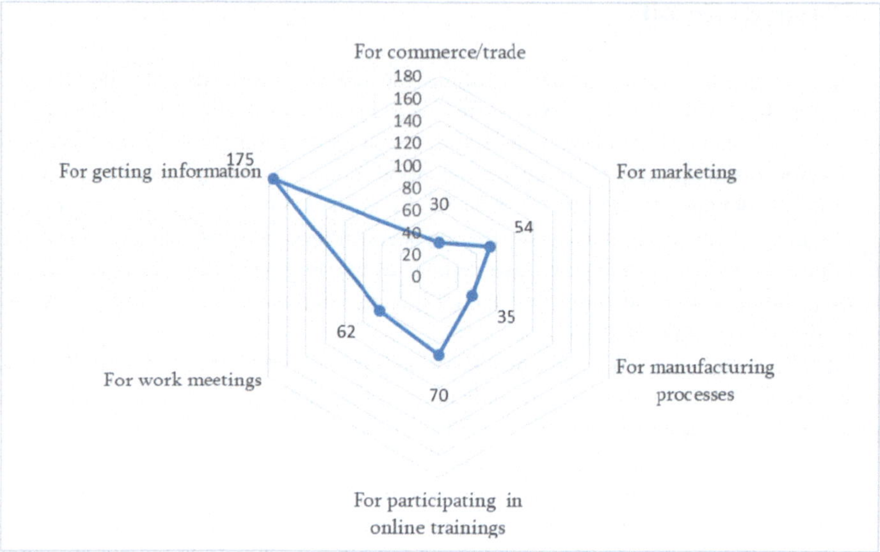

Fig. 4. Objectives of using digital technologies. Source: Chart constructed by authors based on survey data

It is also worth noting that there is a "Digital divide" in the agro-food industry of Georgia: More than 50% of respondents indicate that they have limited access to the Internet, especially in the regions.

n addition to limited access to the Internet, other important barriers were also identified in the process of using digital technologies, among which it is worth noting: Limited financial resources, lack of information about digital technologies, lack of knowledge/digital skills and others (see Fig. 5).

When asked what benefits they expect from the digitization of the agro-food industry, 48.6% of respondents believe that digitization will lead to simplification of work processes, as well as saving resources; According to 43.7%, the benefit will be an increase in productivity, 44.6% expressed the opinion that there will be a reduction in costs, and 38.1% believe that the benefit will be an improvement in the quality of the production and supply chain. A reduction in the negative impact on the environment is assumed by 24.6% of the respondents (see Fig. 6).

The majority of respondents identified the need for systematic organization of educational trainings, training courses and seminars, as well as increasing access to digital technologies and financial resources, development of digital infrastructure as the future directions of digital transformation of the agro-food industry (see Fig. 7).

The agro-food industry in Georgia is facing a number of challenges. It is advisable to overcome barriers to digital transformation according to the needs identified by research.

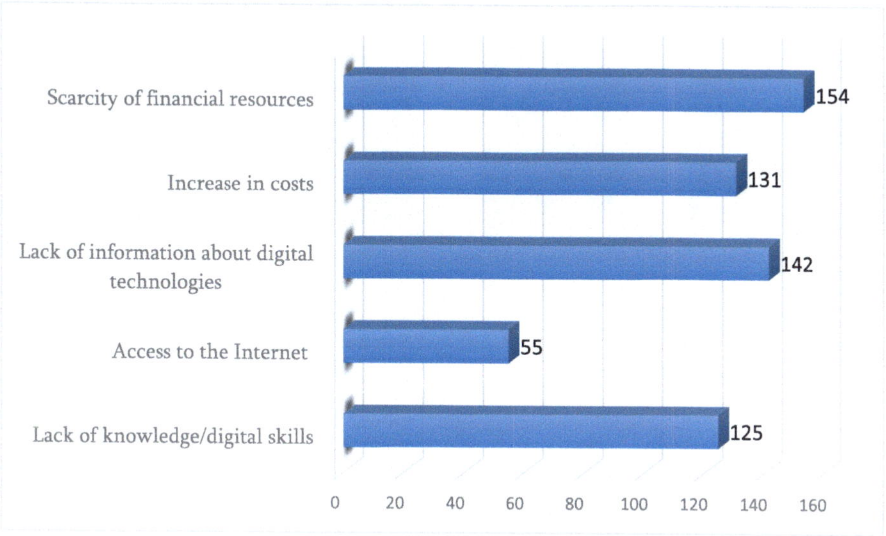

Fig. 5. Barriers to the use of digital technologies. Source: Chart constructed by authors based on survey data

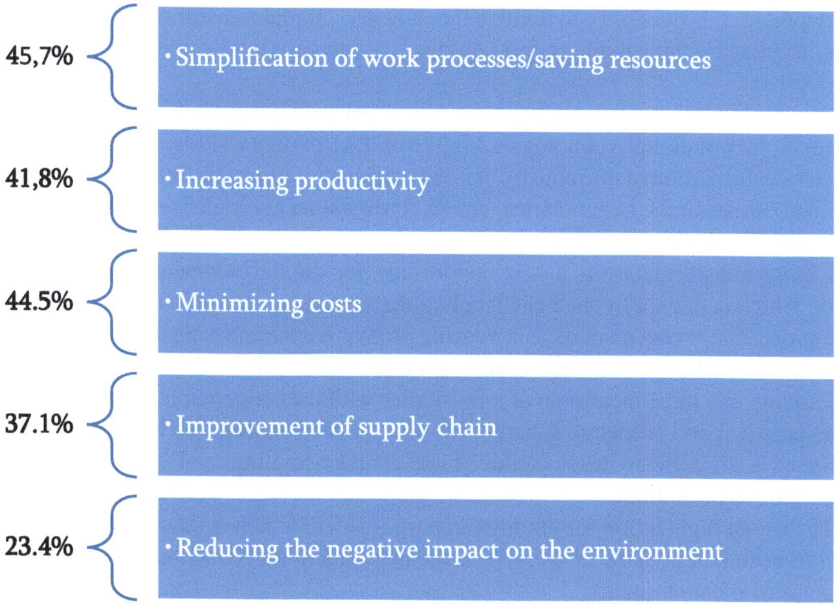

Fig. 6. Benefits from the digital transformation of the agri-food sector. Source: Chart constructed by authors based on survey data.

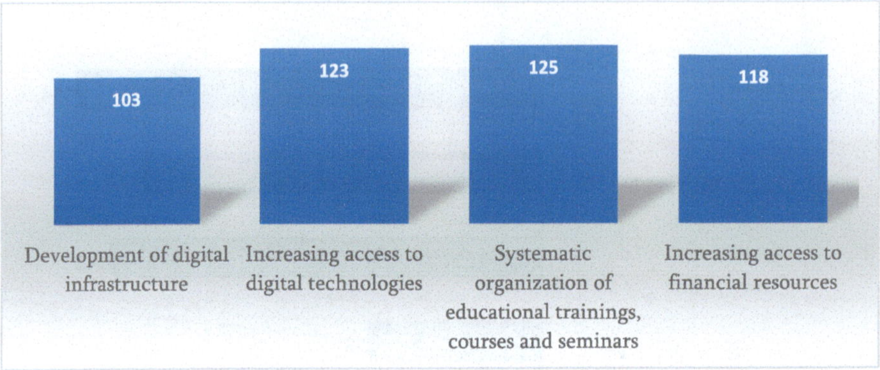

Fig. 7. Future needs for digital transformation of the agri-food industry. Source: Chart constructed by authors based on survey data.

5 Conclusions and Recommendations

The agri-food industry is undergoing significant changes due to the impact of increasing food demand, consumption inequality, climate and consumer preferences, pandemics and other factors. In order to ensure food security and achieve the goals of sustainable development, it is necessary to digitize the industry. Digital transformation is an opportunity to increase the volume of food production, increase productivity and sustainable development.

Factors hindering digitization in the agri-food industry include: limited financial resources, lack of digital technologies, high costs, lack of digital skills, and others. For the digital transformation of the industry, it is necessary: providing educational trainings and training courses to the beneficiaries, access to digital technologies, attracting financial resources, developing digital infrastructure.

Digital transformation is a new opportunity for the development of the agri-food sector, which is proven by the benefits obtained from this process, such as: simplifying work processes, saving resources, increasing productivity, improving the production and supply chain, reducing the negative impact on the environment.

Funding and implementation of joint studies with the cooperation of representatives of the practical and academic spheres will play an accelerating role in digital transformation, it is advisable to develop educational courses, trainings and seminars programs on digital transformation.

The use of digitization for production purposes will lead to a substantial increase in the volume of output in the industry, increase in productivity, reduction of product losses and improvement of quality.

References

Abbasi, R., Martinez, P., Ahmad, R.: The digitization of agricultural industry – a systematic literature review on agriculture 4.0. Smart Agricultural Technol. **2** (2022)

Abiri, R., Rizan, N., Balasundram, S., Bayat Shahbazi, A., Abdul-Hamid, H.: Application of Digital Technologies for Ensuring Agricultural Productivity (2023). https://doi.org/10.1016/j.heliyon.2023.e22601

Sridhar, A., et al.: Digitalization of the agro-food sector for achieving sustainable development goals: a review. Sustainable Food Technol. **1**, 783–802 (2023). https://doi.org/10.1039/D3FB00124E

Aduashvili, L.: Food security problems in the context of digital economy development. International Scientific Journal of Innovative Economics and Management **10**(3), EISSN:24492604. https://doi.org/10.46361/2449-2604.10.3.2023.47-57

Agriculture of Georgia 2022. Geostat. Tbilisi (2023). https://www.geostat.ge/media/54292/soflis_meurneoba_2022.pdf

Annosi, C., Brunetta, F., Francesca, C., Laurens, H.: Digitalization in the Agri-Food Industry: the Relationship Between Technology and Sustainable Development (2020). https://doi.org/10.1108/MD-09-2019-1328

Carmela Annosi, M., Brunetta, F., Capo, F., Heideveld, L.: Digitalization in the agri-food industry: the relationship between technology and sustainable development. Manag. Decis. **58**(8), 1737–1757 (2020). https://doi.org/10.1108/MD-09-2019-1328

Tobing, R.D.H., Ratnayake, R.M.C., Togar Simatupang, T., Liane Okdinawati, L., Mulyono, N.B.: 'On the Necessity for Digital Transformation in Agriculture Supply Chains: A Review from Task, Organization, Behavior, and Application Perspectives' (2023). https://www.researchgate.net/publication/368256374_On_the_Necessity_for_Digital_Transformation_in_Agriculture_Supply_Chains_A_Review_from_Task_Organization_Behavior_and_Application_Perspectives

Hardi, K.V., Legowo, N.: Enterprise architecture: enabling digital transformation for operational business process during COVID-19. HighTech And Innovation Journal. **4**(1), 2023 (2023)

Hassoun, A., et al.: Emerging trends in the agri-food sector: digitalisation and shift to plant-based diets. Current Research in Food Sci. **5**(2022), 2261–2269 (2022)

Lyytinen, K., Yoo, Y., Boland, R.J.: Digital Product Innovation Within Four Classes of Innovation Networks (2015). https://onlinelibrary.wiley.com/doi/https://doi.org/10.1111/isj.12093

Management Decision. Emerald Publishing Limited 0025–1747 https://doi.org/10.1108/MD-09-2019-1328

Martens, K., Zscheischler, J.:The digital transformation of the agricultural value chain: discourses on opportunities, challenges and controversial perspectives on governance approaches. Sustainability **14**(7), 3905 (2022). https://doi.org/10.3390/su14073905

Mhlanga, D., Ndhlovu, E.: Digital technology adoption in the agriculture sector: challenges and complexities in Africa. Hindawi Human Behavior and Emerging Technologies. **2023**, Article ID 6951879, 10 (2023). https://doi.org/10.1155/2023/6951879

Myshko, A., Checchinato, F., Colapinto, C., Finotto, V., Mauracher, C.: Towards the twin transition in the agri-food sector? Framing the current debate on sustainability and digitalization. Journal of Cleaner Production **452**, 142063 (2024)

Khanna, M.: 'Digital Transformation of the Agricultural Sector: Pathways, Drivers and Policy Implications' (2020). https://www.researchgate.net/publication/346316399_Digital_Transformation_of_the_Agricultural_Sector_Pathways_Drivers_and_Policy_Implications

Kharaishvili, E., Gechbaia, B., Tsiklashvili, N., Katamadze, G.: Digital transformation of the agricultural sector and its impact on productivity in Georgia International Conference on Agricultural, Biodiversity and Environmental Economics (ICABEE 2024). BIO Web Conf. **114** (2024)

Kharaishvili, E., Lobzhanidze, N.: Digital transformation in small and medium-sized enterprises: approaches and challenges (Focus: Agricultural Sector of Georgia). Medicon Agriculture & Environmental Sciences **6** (2024)

Kharaishvili, E., Lobzhanidze, N.: Challenges and opportunities for promoting sustainable development in small and medium-sized enterprises (Case of Georgia). Medicon Agriculture & Environmental Sciences **4**(5) (2023)

Kharaishvili, E., Aduashvili, L.: 'Digital Agricultural Development Trends in Georgia'. Ministry of Education and Science of Ukraine, *Kyiv National Economic University* named after Vadym Hetman, Economics and Management Faculty, Management Department, Proceedings of the 4th International Scientific Student Conference «Management: Challenges and Prospects», November 17, ISBN 978–966–926–466–4 (2023). doi.org/https://doi.org/10.35668/978-966-926-466-4. https://shorturl.at/KtYWH

Kharaishvili, E. Atanelishvili, T.: Sustainable state procurements and business in Georgia. Bulletin of the Georgian National Academy of Sciences **16**(3) (2022). http://science.org.ge/bnas/vol-16-3.html

OECD. The Digital Transformation of SMEs' (2021). https://www.oecd.org/industry/smes/PH-SME-Digitalisation-final.pdf

Bahn, R.A., et al.: Digitalization for sustainable agri-food systems: potential, status, and risks for the MENA region. Sustainability, **13**(6), 3223 (2021). https://doi.org/10.3390/su13063223

Rodrigue, T., Konfo, C., et al.: Recent advances in the use of digital technologies in agri-food processing: a short review. Applied Food Research **3**(2), 100329 (2023)

Safiullin, M.R., Akhmetshin, E.M.: Methodological to digital transformation of educational, research and business activity of A University. International Journal of Engineering and Advanced Technology (IJEAT) ISSN: 2249 – 8958, **9**(1) (2019)

Satpathy, B.: Digital Transformation for Sustainable Agriculture: a Progressive Method for Smallholder Farmers (2022). - https://www.currentscience.ac.in/Volumes/123/12/1436.pdf

Sergeevna Kolmykova, T., Sergeevna Obukhova, A., et al.: Features and Benefits of Digital Technologies in Agricultural Enterprises (2021). https://www.e3s-conferences.org/articles/e3sconf/pdf/2021/23/e3sconf_icepp21_01018.pdf

Sridhar, et al.: Digitalization of the agro-food sector for achieving sustainable development goals: a review. Sustainable Food Technology 6 (2023). https://pubs.rsc.org/en/journals/journalissues/fb#!issueid=fb001006&type=current&issnonline=2753-8095

Varda, A.G.: Three ways Digitalization is Reshaping Agriculture (2023). https://shorturl.at/ekpDH

Vărzaru, A.A.: Unveiling digital transformation: a catalyst for enhancing food security and achieving sustainable development goals at the european union level. Foods **13**(8), 1226 (2024). https://doi.org/10.3390/foods13081226

Lawrence Neuman, W.: Pearson New International Edition Social Research Methods: Qualitative and Quantitative Approaches W. Lawrence Neuman Seventh Edition (2014). https://letrunghieutvu.yolasite.com/resources/w-lawrence-neuman-social-research-methods_-qualitative-and-quantitative-approaches-pearson-education-limited-2013.pdf

Wójcicki, K., Górna, J., Sikorska, E.: Digitalization in agro-food sector. In: Pawlak-Lemańska, K., Borusiak, B., Sikorska, E., (eds.), Sustainable food: Production and consumption perspectives, pp. 41–53. Poznań University of Economics and Business Press (2024). https://doi.org/10.18559/978-83-8211-209-2/3

Xu, Y., Jia, F., Wang L., Chen, L.: Can digital transformation improve firm resilience to supply chain disruption? The role of diversification strategies. J Purchasing and Supply Management. 100952 (2024)

Zhang, A., et al.: Who Will Benefit from Big Data? Farmers' Perspective on willingness to Perspective Share Farm Data (2021). https://www.sciencedirect.com/science/article/pii/S0743016721002308#:~:text=The%20results%20show%20that%20only,share%20data%20was%20mostly%20positive

Zghurska, O., Korchynska, O: Digitalization of the national agroindustrial complex: new challenges, realities and prospects. Financial and Credit Activity: Problems of Theory and Practice **6**(47), 2022 (2022)

Advancing Machine Comprehension of the Georgian Language

Tea Munjishvili[1] and Teona Shugliashvili[2(✉)]

[1] Tbilisi State University, Tbilisi, Georgia
Tea.munjishvili@tsu.ge
[2] Ludwig Maximilian University of Munich, Munich, Germany
T.shugliashvili@campus.lmu.de

Abstract. The complexity of the Georgian language poses challenges for machines. AI efforts, like Schmidt's (2019) use of POS tagging with Bi-LSTMs and AI Translate chatbots, aim to teach machines Georgian. Integration of Georgian Language into models like ChatGPT, using NLP techniques and diverse machine learning models, has occurred, but outcomes have limitations. Companies pay money for premium access to ChatGPT, While many companies invest in premium access to ChatGPT, its performance can vary across languages. In the case of Georgian, the model might occasionally lack precision due to limited training data.

In this paper we outline our AI strategy to enhance machine understanding of Georgian language. Our unique method, "predictive grammar" tackles the limitations of reliance on statistical patterns. It combines semantic analysis algorithms with beyond-system engineering techniques grounded in the axiom: "Rules for understanding semantics in each problem area can be detected to develop a model of logical-probability semantics."

To determine if a candidate sentence conveys the same meaning as a unique sentence or bag-of-words from the knowledge base, we First, analyze the influence of each word in the candidate sentence on the knowledge base of the unique sentence by calculating multiple information indices. Next, we construct a logical-probability semantic model and establish semantic connections using these influence measures. The meaning of the candidate sentence is derived from these semantic connections. We identify each sentence corresponding to the unique sentence or bag-of-words by understanding its meaning and matching it with the candidate sentences. This process is detailed in Munjishvili et al. (2023). Over 11 years, its application across diverse fields, from digital health to financial analytics, "predictive grammar" method showcases the robustness, with no instances of miscomprehension recorded.

Machine Understanding of the Georgian Language has wide applications in digital management, spanning business intelligence, data management, CRM, chatbots, content management, customer behavior research, education, supply chain, and human resources. It's beneficial for data-driven AI systems, improving decision-making, automating tasks, enhancing customer interactions, and optimizing digital content and resource management.

R. C. Geibel and S. Machavariani (Eds.): ISPC 2024, SPBE, pp. 243–251, 2025.
https://doi.org/10.1007/978-3-031-88052-0_19

Keywords: Georgian language · AI-driven comprehension · Predictive grammar methodology · Machine understanding enhancement · Digital management applications

1 Introduction

ChatGPT can understand and generate text in Georgian to some extent, but its proficiency is not as high as in languages like English or German. It can help with basic phrases, translations, or general conversation, but for more complex topics, its understanding might be limited.

The limitation lays in the fact that ChatGPT is relies on statistical patterns. ChatGPT's responses are based on statistical correlations rather than a true comprehension of cultural nuances or idiomatic expressions. Though models like ChatGPT gives coherent and contextually relevant responses based on the data they've been trained on, they lack true understanding and reasoning abilities. These limitations seem to be minimal, but the truthfulness of generated information is not guaranteed either in ChatGPT nor in other generative AI models (Zhou (2023)).

Due to the grammatical complexity of the Georgian language, the creation of a knowledge base and the subsequent perception of open-text responses present challenges. Ensuring grammatically correct perception in the Georgian language is indeed a challenging task for artificial intelligence. This challenge is linked to several factors:

1. Complex Morphology:
   a. Georgian has a rich morphological system in verbs, nouns, and adjectives.
   b. Verb forms change according to person, number, tense, mood, aspect, and other categories.
   c. The system must correctly apply these complex morphological rules.
2. Syntactic Features:
   a. In Georgian, word order is relatively flexible.
   b. The phenomenon of verbal poly-personalization allows multiple persons to be encoded in a single verb.
   c. The system needs to consider these syntactic peculiarities during translation.
3. Importance of Context:
   a. Many words and phrases require an understanding of a broader context for accurate translation.
   b. Translating idioms and cultural references is particularly challenging.
4. Absence of Grammatical Gender:
   a. Georgian lacks grammatical gender, complicating translations from languages where this category is significant.
5. Specific Vocabulary:
   a. Some Georgian words or concepts may not have precise equivalents in other languages.
6. Tense System:
   a. The tense and mood system of Georgian verbs differs from many other languages.

In this paper, we outline our AI strategy to enhance machine understanding of Georgian language. Our unique method based on predictive grammar and predictive grammar tackles the limitations of reliance on statistical patterns. It combines semantic analysis algorithms with beyond-system engineering techniques grounded in the axiom: "Rules for understanding semantics in each problem area can be detected to develop a model of logical-probability semantics".

2 Theoretical Foundation

This paper explores the methodology for understanding the Georgian language. The methodology is implemented within the "Kiber 3". The Kiber 3 system (Munjishvili et al. (2023), Munjishvili et al. (2024)) developed on the bases of the long-term experience gained from the operation of the authors' knowledge detection and evaluation systems "Kiber1" and "Kiber2" (Munjishvili and Munjishvili (2015)), comprises a collection of websites[1] that collectively facilitate teaching, self-assessment, examination, knowledge base creation, forecasting, and diagnostics. The components of Kiber 3 system and the theoretical foundation of its language understanding have been presented at the ISPC conferences in 2021 and 2023 and are included in the corresponding conference proceedings.

The theoretical foundation of this paper lies in semantic analysis algorithms on one hand, and beyond-system engineering techniques on the other. The **semantic analysis algorithms** of the Georgian language represent a formalized description of the meanings of the language using mathematical concepts. These semantic mathematical models aim to capture the intricate relationships between words, phrases, and their meanings in a structured manner. Here are the existing models capturing the intricate relationships between words, phrases, and their meanings:

1. Vector Space Model:
    - $S = \{s_1, s_2 \ldots s_n\}$ is n dimensional vector space
    - Each word w is represented by a vector $v(w) \in S$
    - Cosine Similarity (sim): $sim(w_1, w_2) = cos(\theta) = (v(w_1) \bullet v(w_2))/(\|v(w_1)\| \bullet \|v(w_2)\|)$
2. Probabilistic Models:
    Distributional Semantics:
    - $P(w|c)$ – the probability of the word w in context c.
    - The mutual information $MI(w, c) = \log(P(w|c)/P(w))$

    Latent Dirichlet Allocation (LDA): A generative probabilistic model.
3. Latent Semantic Analysis (LSA):
    - M is a word-document matrix
    - Singular Value Decomposition (SVD) $M = U\Sigma V^T$
    - k dimensionale approximation: $M = U_k \Sigma_k V_k^T$

[1] Kiber3T.tsu.ge, Kiber3S.tsu.ge, Kiber3SE.tsu.ge, Kiber3Aqti.tsu.ge, Kiber3G.tsu.ge, Kiber3Oqmi.tsu.ge, FinSim.tsu.ge, ForSim.tsu.ge, Kiber3Pro.tsu.ge, Kiber3Diag.tsu.ge. Users access these resources directly through the respective websites or via Kiber3.tsu.ge.

4. Model of Word Meaning Polysemy (This model is designed to recognize and manage the problem of word polysemy, where a single word acquires different meanings in different contexts. Such models attempt to determine the exact meaning of a word based on the context of the text in which it is used):
   - $w = \{m_1, m_2 \ldots m_k\}$ – possible meanings of the word
   - $P(m_i|w, c)$ – the probability of the meaning m_i for the word w in the context c.
5. Semantic Networks:
   - $G = (V, E)$ – Graph, where V is vertices (concepts) and E represents edges (connections between concepts).
   - Weighted function: $w : E \to \mathbb{R}$, which represents the strength of the connection between vertices.
6. Formal Concept Analysis – FCA (understanding information and ideas through geometric constructions):
   - (G, M, I) formal context, where G represents objects, M - attributes, and $I \subseteq G \times M$
   - Concept: (A, B), where $A \subseteq G$, $B \subseteq M$ and $A' = B$, $B' = A$
7. Bayesian Networks for Semantic Inference
   - $P(C|E) = P(E|C)P(C)/P(E)$, where C is a conclusion and E is the evidence.
8. Tensor Decomposition for Multidimensional Semantics:
   - $T \in \mathbb{R}^{n_1 \times n_2 \ldots n_k}$ is a k dimensional Tensor (generalization of scalars, k dimensional array where each element corresponds to a specific relationship or interaction among multiple variables)
   - The CP (CANDECOMP/PARAFAC) decomposition expresses the tensor T as a sum of rank-one tensors: $T \approx \sum_{r=1}^{R} \lambda_r a_r^{(1)} \otimes a_r^{(2)} \otimes \ldots a_r^{(k)}$
9. The Architecture of Transformers for Contextual Embeddings:
   - Self-attention: Attention $(Q, K, V) = softmax\left(QK^T/\sqrt{d}\right)V$
   - Where: Q, K, V is query, key and value matrixes
10. Entropy Models (such as Shannon's Entropy):
    - $H(X) = -\sum_i P(x_i) \log P(x_i)$ – Information Entropy
    - Kullback – Leibler Divergence: $KL(P\|Q) = \sum_i P(x_i) \log(P(x_i)/Q(x_i))$

The **beyond-system engineering techniques** are based on systems theory, cybernetics, complex adaptive systems, and design science research. Due to the extensive theoretical underpinnings, the specific methodologies utilized in this study will be addressed in the research methodology section.

3 Research Methodology

Methodology used for understanding Georgian language combines semantic analysis algorithms with beyond-system engineering techniques.

To determine if a candidate sentence conveys the same meaning as a unique sentence or bag-of-words from the knowledge base (texts regarding this very topic), we follow a systematic approach. First, we analyze the influence of each word in the candidate sentence on the knowledge base of the unique sentence by calculating multiple information indices. Next, we construct a logical-probability semantic model and establish semantic connections using these influence measures. The meaning of the candidate sentence is derived from these semantic connections. We identify each sentence corresponding to the unique sentence or bag-of-words by understanding its meaning and matching it with the candidate sentences. This process is detailed in Munjishvili et al. (2023).

Any sentence may contain elements from three types of sets: numerical R, textual T and their combinations RT, or only elements from one type of these set. Comparison of numeric sentences' meaning to the meaning of a known sentence is straightforward. The situation becomes more complex when verifying the correspondence of sentence meanings that contain elements from sets T or RT. The sentences in set T, denoted as all r_i, are predominantly nominal sentences composed of multiple words, describing objects, attributes, and events.

To ascertain the meaning of a sentence, it is essential to understand its content as inputted into the system, even in cases of missing or added words and violations of synchronization. In this context, the sentence may utilize words in different cases, as well as synonyms and homonyms.

We implement an engineering approach for semantic analysis of sentences in our knowledge assessment system "Kiber3." This involves the so-called "predictive grammar" method, which carries a certain degree of universality and is safeguarded against the shortcomings of tabular correspondence principles. The essence of this method is discussed in detail.

The predictive grammar approach allows for a more flexible understanding of sentence structures, enabling the system to accommodate the complexities of the Georgian language. By focusing on the underlying semantic relationships rather than strictly adhering to predefined syntactic rules, the system enhances its ability to interpret a variety of responses accurately. This method not only facilitates the processing of correct answers but also supports the recognition of acceptable variations, ultimately improving the overall efficacy of the knowledge assessment process.

By leveraging this innovative approach, Kiber3 aims to bridge the gap between traditional educational methodologies and the demands of modern digital learning environments, providing a robust framework for evaluating students' understanding and proficiency in the Georgian language.

Natural language dialogue systems have extensively utilized methods for knowledge representation, such as frames, semantic networks, and production rules. In most cases, questions are posed to retrieve desired information from a database. After revealing the semantics of a question posed in natural language, it is then translated into the query language of the specified database, allowing for the retrieval of the desired information.

Alongside universal algorithms for understanding the semantics of sentences written in natural language, we employ the engineering methods that are distinct from the system. These methods are grounded in the axiom that "**rules for understanding semantics can**

be identified in any problematic area, and logical-semantic models can be developed based on these rules."

This dual approach—**combining universal semantic algorithms with specific engineering techniques**—enhances the system's ability to accurately interpret user inquiries, ensuring that responses are both relevant and contextually appropriate. By leveraging these methodologies, we aim to improve the efficacy and reliability of natural language processing systems, particularly in educational contexts where understanding nuanced questions is crucial for effective knowledge assessment.

One common method for understanding words, phrases, and generally utterances is the tabular correspondence method. Here, a selected phrase from natural language (which may generally include a verb) g_i is pre-matched to a specific combination of symbols $\left(g_{i,\lambda} \Rightarrow \psi_{i,\lambda}\right)$. This g_i could be a word, an abbreviation, or a misspelled variant of a word, while the ψ_i phrase could be the full form of a word, among others. The universality and simplicity of the tabular method allow it to be applied in any natural language.

In systems realized based on the tabular correspondence principle, it is impossible to understand the meaning of an incoming sentence at the system's input in cases of word omissions, insertions, or synchronization errors.

"production grammars" method, the engineering method we apply for understanding natural language sentences, carries a certain universality and is **protected from the shortcomings of the tabular correspondence principle** (it is utilized in "Cyber3").

To understand and classify the meanings of sentences, we use the **production grammars** method– a technique that employs a set of rules to describe how symbols are combined to form valid sentences. In this methodology, each sentence (or any word orders of a natural language) (g_i) is considered a production rule or simply a **production**, which describes how symbols can be combined to form valid strings in a language. The words within each of these sentences $\left(g_{i,\lambda}\right)$ are treated as **conditions**, and together with other words they form the vocabulary (L). Each sentence (production) (g_i) receives **commands**/actions (ψ_i), which are applied to it. The set of productions $(G, G = \cup g_i, j = 1 \ldots n)$ is then transformed into a new set (G^*) by the commands (ψ). Viewing sentences as productions enables the semantic analysis of any statement through the use of the set of productions (G), the structure of the lexicon (L), and the search command for identifying productions relevant to the statement or word that needs to be understood.

The search algorithm employed here is based on **predictive grammars** - a type of grammar used for predictive parsing (Alfred et al. (2007)), where the parser uses a lookahead mechanism to decide which production rule to apply based on the next input symbol.

The predictive grammars Natural Language Engineering method:

- recognizes the unique sentences
- Understand sentences, by building semantic connections using multiple information indices for each word in the sentence
- each sentence receives commands ϕ to be conducted on the sentence
- New sentences are understood and added to the set of productions. Words in the sentence are understood and added to the vocabulary.

To find the relevance of the statement or word that needs to be understood to the ones in the known set (build semantic connections) we must solve the following problem:

Consider the following: a non-empty set of words (or in general predicates), a non-empty set of actions, a non-empty set of productions (sentences), and a non-empty **set of informativeness measures** (information criterion), which includes scalar functions defined on (G) that quantify individual parameters of words (or in general predicates) according to a pre-specified scale. Each informativeness measure (information criterion) for each word is assigned a specific **weight** h_α - positive rational numbers and sum up to 1.

The objectives are:

1. To identify the set of informativeness criteria and rank them by significance.
2. To evaluate each word (predicate) α_k in the vocabulary L based on a given informativeness coefficient during vocabulary organization.
3. To comprehend the meaning of the sentence in the output when pridenedicates (words) are entered into the system, under the following conditions:

   - When the order of the words is modified.
   - When words are omitted or added at any position within the sentence.

Information criterion for each word is chosen based on the topic of the sentence and the practices/ accumulated knowledge in the field the sentence is discussing; or if available, on the directives of the field's experts. This information criterion, a set of informativeness measures is then applied to calculate the importance and placeholder of each word in the sentence.

We let the weight of a predicate (word) η_{a_i} be defined as the arithmetic mean of the evaluations provided by various field's practices or experts, where $K_j(a_i), j = 1, \cdots, r$ represents the information measures based on field's practices or experts' opinions and r is number of field's practices and experts' opinions considered. This is how we calculate the weight of the predicate (word):

$$\eta_{a_i} = \frac{K_1(a_i) + K_2(a_i) + - \ldots K_r(a_i)}{r}$$

The weight μ_i of the production $g_i = \{a_1, a_2, \cdots a_k\}$ is the sum of weight of a predicate (word):

$$\mu_i = \sum_{t=1}^{k} \eta_{a_t}$$

We should emphasize that the methodology described here can also be applied for understanding and assessing **essays**. The task is to automatically analyze the entire text and make a decision regarding its content's relevance or inconsistency with the event or situation. This analysis may be useful for instance for evaluating a law student's response in an exam, where legal cases are addressed by the student. There are two approaches to solving this problem. The *first* is straightforward and can be easily implemented using the described semantic analysis method. The *second* is more complex and requires knowledge of the problematic area to be articulated using methods known in artificial intelligence. In the first case, understanding the answers to such tasks will stem from the comprehension of answers to similar tasks implemented in Cyber3, where the response is a descriptive sentence or a combination of sentences. The second approach involves the development of an intelligent robotic consultant, which includes:

- Language Modeling (LM): Artificial intelligence utilizes large volumes of Georgian-language texts to study the structure, grammar, and vocabulary of the language.
- Morphological Analysis: Due to the complex morphology of the Georgian language, AI must be able to identify the roots of words and their affixes.
- Syntactic Analysis: Understanding the structure of sentences, which includes perceiving the nuances of word order.
- Semantic Analysis: Understanding the meanings of words and phrases with consideration of context.
- Machine Translation: The ability to translate from Georgian to other languages and vice versa.
- Text Generation: Creating coherent text while adhering to the rules of the Georgian language.

4 Analysis and Results

Our predictive grammar method for understanding Georgian language has maintained exceptional accuracy. Over 11 years, its application across diverse fields, from digital health to financial analytics and in the process of examinations at Tbilisi State University on business and economic faculty and at Akaki Tsereteli State University showcase the robustness of our methodology, with no instances of miscomprehension recorded.

A most current update of this research is the application of production grammars methodology for verification of exam cases and topics, which is conducted in a substantive manner. The system automatically generates an assessment. This methodology has recently been implemented in the examination process at the Law Faculty of Tbilisi State University and is a part of the umbrella of "Cyber 3" system.

5 Discussion and Recommendations

Our predictive grammar methodology has significantly advanced machine understanding of the Georgian language, demonstrating exceptional accuracy across various fields, including digital health and financial analytics. Its successful application in educational contexts, particularly at Tbilisi State University and Akaki Tsereteli State University, highlights its potential to enhance academic assessments through the recent integration of production grammars for exam verification.

To further improve this methodology, we recommend the following:

- **Expand the Dataset**: Enrich datasets with modern colloquial language and idiomatic expressions to enhance understanding in both academic and non-academic contexts.
- **User-Centric Applications**: Develop new user-friendly applications grounded in our language understanding methodology to address practical needs effectively.
- **Continuous Robust Testing:** Maintain rigorous evaluation metrics and validate methodologies consistently to identify and address potential gaps as they arise.

- **Broaden Applications:** Investigate new domains, such as automated customer service in digital health and legal document analysis, to extend the reach of our predictive grammar method.

In summary, by implementing these recommendations, we can further extend the usage of machine understanding of the Georgian language based on our mixed methodology and keep it on its highest quality.

References

Alfred, V.A., Monica, S.L., Jeffrey, D.U.: Compilers Principles, Techniques & Tools. Pearson Education (2007)

Munjishvili, T., Shugliashvili, T., Sikharulidze, D., Shaburishvili, S., Kadagishvili, L.: AI-powered platform of enterprise financial stability analytics. In Digital Management to Shape the Future: Proceedings of the International Scientific-Practical Conference (ISPC 2023). Springer International Publishing, pp. 85–92 (2024)

Munjishvili, T., Sigua, Z., Shugliashvili, T.: Digital transformation in education_self-study system "Cyber3s". Digital Management in Covid-19 Pandemic and Post-Pandemic Times: Proceedings of the International Scientific-Practical Conference (ISPC 2021). Springer International Publishing, pp. 193–204 (2023)

Munjishvili, T., Munjishvili, Z.: The system of Discovery and Estimation of Knowledge "Cyber2", Scholars' Press, Saarbrucken. Published on: 2015–01–15. ISBN-13: 978–3–639–76094–1 (2015)

Munjishvili, T., Munjishvili, Z.: Knowledge demonstration and assessment system "Cyber1". International Journal "Information Technologies & Knowledge **8**(3), 271–279 (2014)

Schmid, H.: Deep learning-based morphological taggers and lemmatizers for annotating historical texts, in: Proceedings of the 3rd International Conference on Digital Access to Textual Cultural Heritage, pp. 133–137 (2019)

Zhou, J., Ke, P., Qiu, X., Huang, M., Zhang, J.: ChatGPT: potential, prospects, and limitations. Frontiers of Information Technology & Electronic Engineering, pp. 1–6 (2023)

Digital Transformation of Higher Education in Georgia: Challenges and Opportunities

Manana Lobzhanidze(✉)

Economics and Business Faculty, Ivane Javakhishvili Tbilisi State University, Tbilisi, Georgia
manana.lobzhanidze@tsu.ge

Abstract. The article analyzes the process of digital transformation of the higher education sector, studies the special role of digitization in the effective functioning of the education system and in the life of modern society.

Conceptual issues of the post-industrial era of higher education are evaluated in the work. It is justified that the introduction of modern digital technologies in the higher education sector of Georgia will contribute to the modernization and development of education, as well as the improvement of the quality of preparing of future specialists and the process of bringing education closer to science.

The objective of the study is to reveal the challenges of the digital transformation process in the higher education sector of Georgia and to develop recommendations for development opportunities.

Analysis, comparison, factorial and other statistical methods are used in the paper, bibliographic research is conducted, quantitative research is carried out to identify the factors hindering digital transformation and to determine the expected benefits from digitization.

Based on the research, the problems of digitization in the higher education system of Georgia are identified, the possibilities of improvement of the national education system using modern digital technologies are determined, the legal, political, economic and social factors of the development of the digitization process are evaluated.

In accordance with the identified problems, conclusions are drawn on the processes hindering the digital transformation in the Georgian higher education system and recommendations are proposed on the future possibilities of implementing digitization.

Keywords: Higher education · digital transformation · Georgia · challenges · opportunities

1 Introduction

The higher education system is an integral part of the modern global digital world. Higher education, as an important source of acquiring new competences, needs constant renewal and modernization. The traditional education system established in the industrial age can no longer fully respond to the skills formation requirements of the Internet age youth. The job market is undergoing a significant transformation and the requirements of investors in the field of education have also changed.

R. C. Geibel and S. Machavariani (Eds.): ISPC 2024, SPBE, pp. 252–261, 2025.
https://doi.org/10.1007/978-3-031-88052-0_20

By 2025, the World Economic Forum predicts that 85 million jobs will be lost. At the same time, 97 million new jobs will be created, which will also require skills transformation (The Future of Growth Report 2024).

Therefore, the higher education system faces a new challenge and needs to adapt to the rapidly changing digital labor market. At the modern stage, digital transformation is of particular importance in order to gain a competitive advantage in the education market. During the last decade, digital transformation has essentially changed the education system, it can be said that digital education has already been formed in developed countries. It should also be noted that in all countries of the world, the Covid pandemic accelerated the process of digitization of education even more and significantly increased the demand for personnel with high digital skills in the labor market (Lobzhanidze M. 2022).

Digital transformation in the educational field leads to a qualitative transformation of the teaching process. With the use of digital technologies, it becomes possible to introduce personal teaching models in the educational process and the digital transformation of education has a positive effect on socio-economic indicators.

It should also be taken into account that modern education has become more practical compared to theoretical, it is necessary to systematically understand events and strengthen innovative thinking, the creative competences of the individual, personal motivation and self-development come to the fore. The transformation of the higher education system in the development of these competencies is one of the main issues of the world agenda.

The system of higher education in developed countries responds to the demands of the digital market, but the process of digital transformation in this system is a novelty for developing countries. This leads to a deepening of the digital gap between countries and creates problems in the labor and education markets.

In Georgia, the level of digitization in the higher education system is low and there are a number of challenges in this direction. Therefore, it is important to assess the challenges in digitization and to develop recommendations for the future development of this process.

1.1 Research Objective

The objective of the study is to reveal the challenges of the digital transformation process in the higher education sector of Georgia and to develop recommendations for development opportunities.

2 Research Method

In the paper, statistical data grouping, analysis, comparison, factorial and other methods are used, bibliographic research is conducted, quantitative research is conducted to identify the factors hindering digital transformation and to determine the expected benefits from digitization.

The research used the data of the Ministry of Education, Science and Youth of Georgia, the National Statistics Office of Georgia, databases of various national and international organizations and research centers.

3 Theoretical Foundation

The adaptation of the higher education system to the possibilities of digital technologies is the main condition for meeting the demands of the labor market. Against the backdrop of global confrontations and crises, the research on issues of digital transformation of higher education is gaining even more relevance. By using digital technologies, it is possible to effectively use the potential of the education system and eliminate the imbalance formed with the demands of the labor market. The mentioned and related problems have been evaluated in a number of scientific studies.

Adaptation to the digital environment is the main determining factor for the development of countries, scientists consider the digital transformation of the education system as an opportunity to meet the demands of the modern labor market (Abashidze G. 2022).

The principles, pecularities and concepts of the origin of the digital economy have been studied by scientists. The shortcomings of the educational model of the industrial era are identified, the need to replace it with a post-industrial model is substantiated. Current issues of labor market transformation and employment in the digital environment are evaluated (Jolia G. 2021).

Higher education institutions are facing increasing challenges in relation to the changing demands of the labor market. The researchers offer recommendations on ways to adapt the national higher education sector to the demands of digital higher education in EU countries and to overcome the challenges (Fleacă B. Fleaca E. S. Maiduc, 2022).

Higher education institutions and public universities are trying to modernize their processes according to recognized requirements and existing standards. Today, the only alternative to better and faster delivery of services to students is the use of modern digital technologies. Accordingly, in the system of higher education there is a need to change procedures and work culture in the direction of digital technologies. In the studies, the process of digital transformation is analyzed in detail, the problems in the implementation of digital platforms in higher education institutions and universities are identified, a systematic literature review is conducted using the SCOPUS and Web of Science databases, issues that need to be solved in the digital transformation process are identified (Marco A. Coral, Augusto E. Bernuy, 2022).

Assessment of student learning and academic performance is a fundamental aspect of teaching and has a significant impact on graduate employability. Therefore, it is important to identify challenges in assessment and academic performance that will have a positive impact on graduate employability. Digitization is considered among such challenges (Kharaishvili, E. Natsvlishvili I., Shonia N. 2022).

In today's technology-driven world, digital transformation in higher education is critical. However, there are many barriers that hinder the successful implementation of digital transformation initiatives in higher education. Different barriers are defined and classified in scientific studies, which in turn are grouped into categories, namely, environmental, strategic, organizational, technological, cultural categories. Based on the analysis of barriers, digital transformation strategies are developed and intervention needs are defined (Gkrimpizi T. Peristeras V., Magnisalis I. 2023).

Digital transformation is rapidly reaching all areas of human life and higher education is no exception. This process is inevitable and if successful, will provide higher education institutions with a competitive advantage and other benefits. Scientists have identified incentives for implementing digital transformation in higher education institutions, proposed ways to overcome challenges and shown success factors for digital transformation in higher education institutions (Robertsone G. Lapina I. 2022).

There are many different frameworks for digital transformation and these frameworks are even more different due to the peculiarities of the field of education. The level of digitization of Georgian higher education institutions significantly lags behind the corresponding indicator of developed countries. It is necessary to completely transform the teaching process, to integrate different types of communication and collaboration tools (Dikhaminjia N. 2024).

The prospects for the introduction of digital technologies in teaching in higher education institutions and the prospects for sustainable development are also analyzed at scientific conferences, in particular, the importance of introducing digital platforms and technologies in higher education institutions, the prospects for employing personnel with digital skills and their alternative possibilities for overcoming modern challenges (DITECH, 2023).

Today, digital education is necessary to achieve financial stability, as well as social security and prosperity of the country (Adeishvili G., Amashukeli D., Eristavi D., Tushurashvili G. (2021).

According to research conducted by the National Center for Educational Quality Enhancement (NCEQE), authorized higher education institutions in Georgia are working on online textbooks, video guides, digital learning applications and platforms, however, the level of digitization is still low in most educational institutions and many challenges have been identified (Report by Bakakuri T. 2020).

InGeorgia, systemic steps should be taken to develop a comprehensive strategy for access to higher education policy, taking into account that electronic learning is an inevitable trend in the conditions of the development of modern technologies (Kokrashvili K., Kakutia T. (2023).

The internationalization of higher education in Georgia requires the promotion of high-quality higher education (Pignatti N. (2019), which is impossible without further modernization of the higher education system, first of all, digital transformation. Digitization is considered an opportunity to solve problems in the field of sustainable education and distance learning (Kharaishvili, E., Lobzhanidze N. 2022), especially since the demand for distance education in Georgia is growing (Kharaishvili, E. and Lobzhanidze, N. 2022).

Digitization of education contributes to the diversity of teaching content based on different methodologies and the latter, in turn, are adapted to individual needs in any field and level of teaching (Digitization of education, 2023).

Digitization of student services and electronic management of processes of higher education institutions has become a top priority in Georgia, however, problems have arisen, in particular, lack of digital skills, problems of infrastructural provision of universities and students, unlimited Internet access, etc. Accordingly, work began on the development and implementation of digital development strategies and action plans (Kikutadze V. Sikharulidze D. Lekishvili T. (2023).

Through the bibliographic research, it was determined that the research on the problems of digital transformation of higher education has been especially highlighted during the last decade. The level of digitization of education in developing countries is still low. In accordance with the challenges in the labor and education market, research on digital technologies in higher education, selection and implementation of digital platforms in administrative and academic fields, features of digitalization, establishment of barriers and other issues will be relevant in the future.

3.1 Discussion and Recommendations

In order to determine the level of digital development in higher education in Georgia, to identify the barriers hindering the digital transformation process and to determine the opportunities for future development, experts in the field, administrative and support staff of higher education institutions, as well as part of the academic staff were interviewed. 86 respondents from 22 higher education institutions participated in the survey.

To the question, has your institution developed a digital transformation strategy? 52.8% of the respondents answered that the higher education institution has developed a digital development strategy, 34.9% expressed the opinion that such a strategy has not been developed, but the institution is working on it. According to 9.3%, the institution does not have a digital development strategy (see Fig. 1).

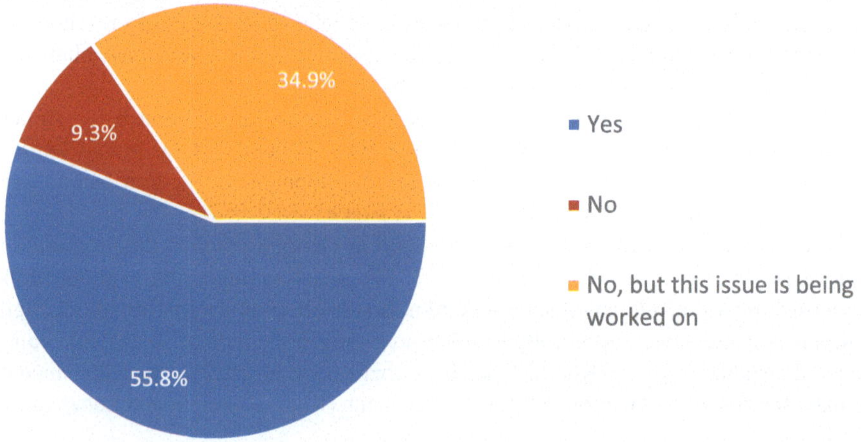

Fig. 1. Has your institution developed a digital transformation strategy?

As the data in Fig. 1 shows, almost half of the higher education institutions in Georgia have not developed a digital development strategy.

In the development of the digital transformation process in higher education institutions, the implementation of this process, including specifically the programs supporting digital learning, is critical. To the question, what mechanisms exist in your institution to support the digital transformation process? 62.8% of the respondents believe that the development mechanisms of the digitization process have been developed in their institution and they are aware of these mechanisms, while 37.2% are not aware of such mechanisms (see Fig. 2).

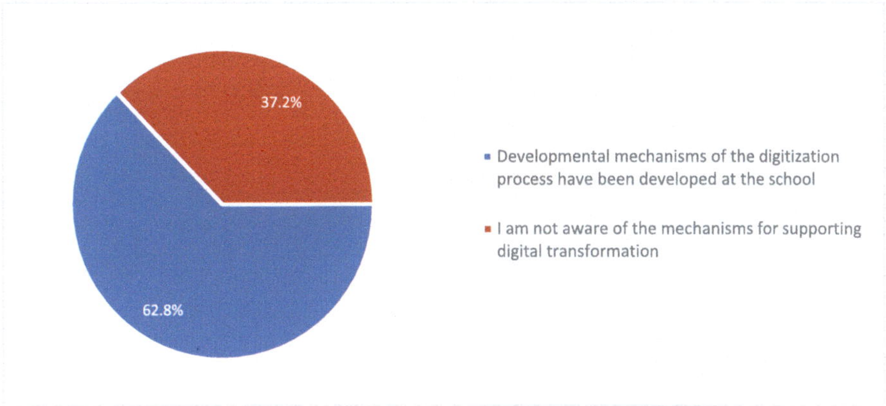

Fig. 2. Awareness of digital development mechanisms in higher education institutions in Georgia

However, when asked to name these mechanisms, the list of answers was very sparse. Only 56 from the respondents questioned named conducting trainings for interested persons as a supporting mechanism, for most of the respondents they are not aware of the mechanisms for supporting digital transformation.

A variety of online platforms are offered to academic staff (see Fig. 3).

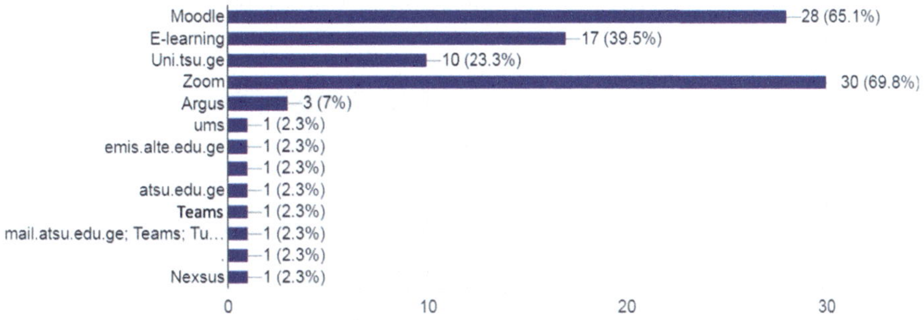

Fig. 3. Online platforms offered to academic staff

Most of the higher education institutions use Zoom (69.8%), Moodle (65.1%) and E-learning (39.5%) platforms. Tbilisi State University also uses the uni.tsu.ge platform, the rest of platforms' usage rates are low. The results of the survey reveal that most private and public universities are successfully using various digital platforms for both administrative and academic purposes.

We asked respondents the following question: Is there a structural unit in your institution to support academic staff in digital learning? To this question, the absolute majority of respondents (83.7%) answered that their institution has such a structural unit (see Fig. 4).

Along with offering digital platforms, it is necessary to support academic staff in the process of teaching digitally. The research showed that in most of the higher education

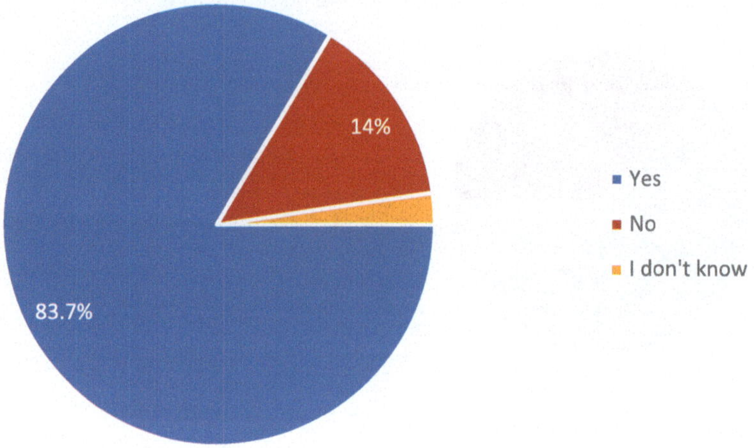

Fig. 4. Does the institution have a structural unit that supports academic staff in digital learning?

institutions participating in the survey, there is an independent structural unit that supports the academic staff in the process of digital learning. However, in some schools such a function is placed by representatives of the IT service, which prevents the effective conduct of digital education.

When asked which factors helped you the most in the process of digital transformation, respondents could name the 3 most influential factors (see Fig. 5).

Fig. 5. Which factors helped you the most in the process of digital transformation?

The results of the survey showed that the respondents named the three most influential factors: sharing experiences with colleagues and mutual learning (76.2%), local and international trainings (69%), identifying online learning needs and resources available in the institution (50%).

We asked respondents following questions: which barriers hinder the development of the digital transformation process in your institution? Academic staff answered that such barriers are: lack of programs and courses necessary for online learning - 53.7%, difficulties related to changes in institutional procedures and regulations (46.3%), low level of digital skills (36.6%). The development of the digital transformation process in Georgia's higher education institutions is also hindered by limited digital infrastructure, lack of programs and courses necessary for online learning, etc. (see Fig. 6).

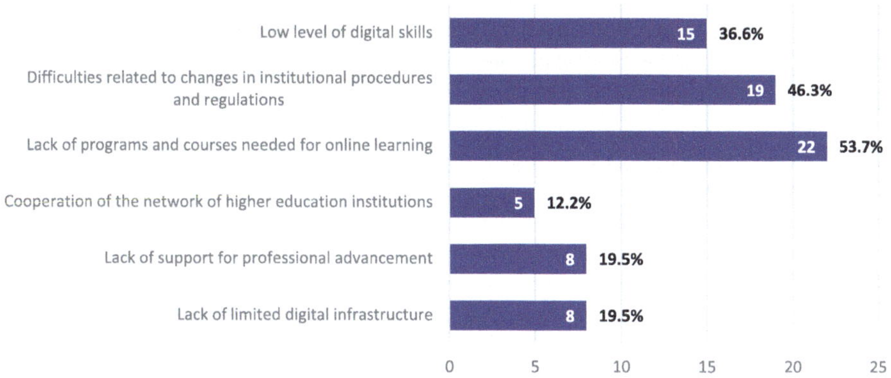

Fig. 6. Factors hindering the development of the digital transformation process in higher education institutions in Georgia

Did the survey identify the obstacles that students may face in the process of digital transformation? Moreover, it was possible to mark several answers to this question (see Fig. 7).

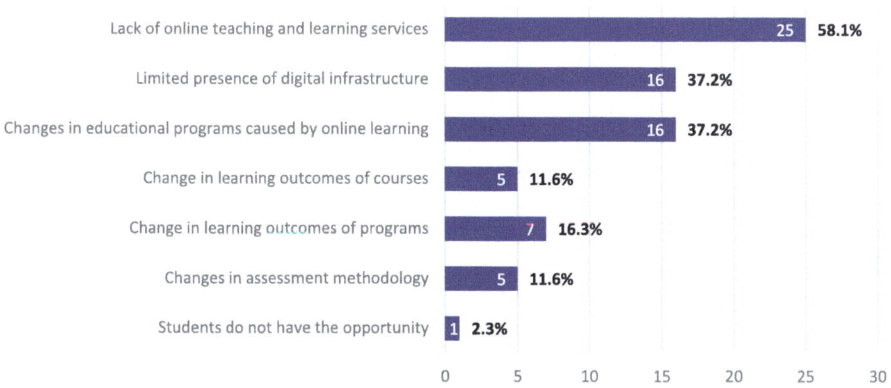

Fig. 7. Obstructive factors for the development of the digital transformation process for students

In the process of digital transformation, students may face a number of obstacles, among them: lack of online teaching and learning services, limited existence of digital infrastructure, changes in educational programs caused by online learning, changes in teaching courses, changes in assessment methodology and others.

4 Conclusion, Limitations and Further Research

The digital transformation of higher education is a necessary process to establish a balance with the labor and education market and to overcome the challenges in the education system. The research conducted to identify the level and barriers of digitization in higher education in Georgia showed that some education institutions have not developed a digital transformation strategy, the mechanisms supporting this process are weak, in many education institutions there is still no independent structural unit that would facilitate the development of the process. Barriers hindering the digital transformation process were also identified: low level of digital skills, lack of digital platforms (Internet, Wi-Fi, computers), imperfect legal regulations, lack of programs and courses necessary for online learning and others.

The research revealed the most influential factors, which will contribute to the development process of digital transformation: implementation of local and international trainings, sharing experience with colleagues, active use of knowledge exchange opportunities, modernization of educational programs for digital learning, preparation of relevant training courses, etc.

5 Research Limitations and Future Research

The results of the research may have been influenced by several limitations, in particular, 86 respondents from 22 higher education institutions were interviewed to identify the level of digital development in higher education in Georgia and the factors hindering digital transformation processes. A part of the academic staff participated in the survey along with experts in the field, administrative and support staff of higher education institutions. Increasing the number of higher education institutions, as well as more involvement of academic staff and students, would reveal in more detail the specific needs of digital development of higher education. In addition, the research showed that some of the respondents are not aware of the modern technologies used in the digitization process of the education system, which is why some barriers may not be identified and the full range of problems revealed.

For future research, it will be important to include qualitative research methods, the use of which will reveal the needs of implementing specific digital technologies in higher education. However, digital technologies are rapidly changing over time. Therefore, it will be necessary to carry out long-term studies on the research problem. This will help to reveal the features of the development of digital technologies according to the countries, to share foreign experiences taking into account economic, social and cultural factors and to reveal the trends of digital transformation of the education system.

References

Abashidze, G.: Digital transformation of the education sector. Journal Innovative Economy and Management **9**(3), 6–14 (2022)

Adeishvili, G., Amashukeli, D., Eristavi, D., Tushurashvili, G.: An Overview of the Education Sector in the Context of the Covid Pandemic (2021)

The Future of Growth Report 2024, INSIGHT REPORT, World Economic Forum (2024). https://www3.weforum.org/docs/WEF_Future_of_Growth_Report_2024.pdf

Lobzhanidze, M.: COVID-19 pandemic impact on study migration and it's socio-economic consequences. International Scientific Conference Dedicated to the Establishment of the University and the 100th Anniversary of the Faculty of Economics and Business "Covid 19 Pandemic and Economics" (2022). https://www.researchgate.net/publication/362431748_COVID-19_pandemiis_gavlena_sastsavlo_migratsiaze_da_misi_sotsialur-ekonomikuri_shedegebi_COVID-19_pandemic_impact_on_study_migration_and_it's_socio-economic_consequences

Bakakuri, T.: Online Teaching & Learning in Georgia: Main Trends and Needs (2020). https://eqe.ge/res/NewFolder%204/NewFolder/HEOTL_report_nceqe.pdf

Jolia, G.: Education and Employment in the Digital Environment (2021). http://social.gtu.ge/uploads/files/monografia/1.pdf

Fleacă, B., Fleaca, E., Maiduc, S.: Digital transformation and current challenges of higher education. TEM Journal **11**(3), 1235–1241 (2022)

Coral, M.A., Bernuy, A.E.: Challenges in the digital transformation processes in higher education institutions and Universities. International Journal of Information Technologies and Systems Approach (IJITSA) **15**(1) (2022)

Gkrimpizi, T., Peristeras, V., Magnisalis, I.: Classification of barriers to digital transformation in higher education institutions: systematic literature review. Educ. Sci. **13**(7), 746 (2023). https://doi.org/10.3390/educsci13070746

Robertsone, G., Lapina, I.: Digital Transformation in Higher Education: Drivers, Success Factors, Benefits and Challenges. Human, Technologies and Quality of Education (2022)

Dikhaminjia, N.: Waiting for the Digital Transformation of Education (2024). https://forbes.ge/ganathlebis-tsiphruli-transphormatsiis-lodinshi/

DITECH. Proceedings of the International Conference "Digital Technologies in Ghana" (2023)

Kharaishvili, E., Lobzhanidze, N.: Challenges of sustainable education in conditions of distance learning (on the example of Georgia). Journal Innovative Economy and Management **9**(2) (2022)

Kharaishvili, E., Lobzhanidze, N.: Youth attitudes towards distance learning: challenges and opportunities for sustainable education - case of Georgia. In: Proceedings of the 5th International Scientific Congress Society of Ambient Intelligence - ISC SAI; ISBN 978–989–758–600–2, SciTePress, pp. 516–524 (2022). https://doi.org/10.5220/0011366300003350

Kharaishvili, E., Natsvlishvili, I., Shonia, N.: Challenges of Distance Assessment in Higher Education and the Impact of Academic Achievement on Alumni Employment (Evidence From Georgia) (2022)

Kokrashvili, K., Kakutia, T.: Georgian higher education policy and e-learning challenges. International Journal of Innovative Technologies in Social Science **2**(38) (2023). https://doi.org/10.31435/rsglobal_ijitss/30062023/7984

Pignatti, N.: Higher Education Reform in Georgia: Challenges and Opportunities (2019)

Kikutadze, V., Sikharulidze, D., Lekishvili, T.: Peculiarities of Digital Transformation of Higher Educational Institutions in Georgia (2023). https://econpapers.repec.org/bookchap/sprprbchp/978-3-031-45601-5_5f21.htm

Corporate Ethics in the AI Era: Balancing Technological Advancement with Social Responsibility

Elene Dundua(✉)

International Black Sea University, Tbilisi, Georgia
edundua@ibsu.edu.ge

Abstract. In an era of rapid technological advancement, particularly in artificial intelligence (AI), businesses face the dual challenge of leveraging innovation while navigating complex ethical landscapes. This paper explores the intersection of corporate ethics and technological progress, with a focus on the implications of AI for social responsibility. Using a mixed-methods approach, including surveys and case studies, the study investigates strategies corporations employ to uphold ethical principles while integrating AI for competitive advantage. Key findings reveal critical challenges, including gaps in transparency, algorithmic bias, and data privacy, particularly within Georgia's developing regulatory environment.

This research emphasizes the importance of corporate governance frameworks that prioritize fairness, accountability, and inclusivity. By examining successful models of ethical leadership in AI adoption, the study offers actionable recommendations to mitigate ethical risks while maximizing AI's transformative potential. These insights underscore the essential role of proactive ethical planning in fostering trust, sustainability, and societal well-being.

Keywords: Corporate Ethics · Artificial Intelligence · Social Responsibility

1 Introduction

Artificial Intelligence (AI) has transformed industries, offering unparalleled opportunities for efficiency, innovation, and growth. From automating operations to enhancing customer experiences, the potential for AI to revolutionize business is vast. However, the rapid pace of AI adoption also raises critical ethical concerns. These include data privacy violations, algorithmic bias, job displacement, and the potential misuse of AI systems, which can undermine public trust and exacerbate societal inequalities (Ethics, 2018).

One of the most pressing challenges is the "black box" nature of AI systems, where decision-making processes are often too complex to interpret. This lack of transparency complicates efforts to ensure accountability and fairness, eroding public trust in AI applications. Similarly, the proliferation of data-intensive AI technologies has fueled debates around privacy, surveillance, and the ethical limits of corporate data use. As automation continues to reshape labor markets, concerns about job displacement and

R. C. Geibel and S. Machavariani (Eds.): ISPC 2024, SPBE, pp. 262–279, 2025.
https://doi.org/10.1007/978-3-031-88052-0_21

widening social inequalities further underscore the need for a responsible approach to AI adoption.

Today, businesses face the critical challenge of embracing AI's transformative potential while upholding ethical integrity. This balance requires more than just regulatory compliance—it calls for a proactive commitment to ethical governance, prioritizing transparency, accountability, and alignment with societal values. By embedding ethical considerations into every stage of AI development and deployment, organizations can mitigate risks, foster trust, and ensure sustainable progress.

This paper explores the intersection of corporate ethics and AI, examining how organizations can integrate technological advancements without compromising their social responsibilities. Through an analysis of regulatory frameworks, real-world practices, and case studies, this research aims to offer practical insights into navigating the complex relationship between innovation and ethics, contributing to the broader discourse on responsible AI adoption.

2 Theory

2.1 The Foundations of Corporate Ethics in AI

Artificial Intelligence (AI) is here defined as "a machine-based system that can, for a given set of human-defined objectives, make predictions, recommendations, or decisions influencing real or virtual environments" (Yeung, 2020). Over the past few years, AI has developed into a dynamic field, achieving considerable progress in its capabilities and applications (Gadde Lakshmi Aishwarya, 2022). Its integration into business practices holds incredible potential, making operations more efficient, improving decision-making, and sparking innovation across industries However, this rapid progress also presents significant ethical challenges that companies must address thoughtfully to ensure responsible AI implementation. Corporate ethics provides a crucial framework for navigating these challenges. As AI systems grow more prevalent, their capacity to revolutionize industries is matched by their potential to disrupt societal norms and ethical standards. Ethical governance, rooted in principles of transparency, accountability, and fairness, requires businesses to carefully consider the broader implications of their actions.

Freeman's stakeholder theory emphasizes this responsibility, advocating that organizations prioritize the needs of all stakeholders - employees, customers, communities, and society - rather than narrowly focusing on shareholder interests (Freeman, 2010).

Despite its benefits, AI poses unique ethical challenges that intensify the need for robust governance. Algorithmic bias, for instance, can exacerbate existing societal inequalities. (Zou and Schiebinger, 2018) demonstrate how AI systems trained on imbalanced datasets can disproportionately disadvantage marginalized groups in areas like hiring, credit approval, and criminal justice. This underscores the importance of designing systems that actively mitigate bias and promote inclusivity, ensuring that AI serves as a tool to enhance the human condition rather than cause harm.

The lack of transparency in AI systems, often referred to as the "black box" problem, presents another significant challenge. This opacity arises when AI models produce decisions or recommendations that are difficult to interpret or explain, making it harder to ensure accountability. (Johnson, 2006) argues that while machines themselves lack moral agency, the responsibility for their decisions lies with the individuals and organizations that create, deploy, and use them. Transparent, explainable AI systems are therefore essential to maintaining ethical integrity and public trust.

Another pressing ethical concern relates to the extensive data collection practices enabled by AI. These technologies often rely on vast amounts of personal data, raising serious questions about privacy, consent, and data security. The phenomenon of surveillance capitalism, where personal information is commodified without adequate safeguards, underscores the urgent need for ethical frameworks that prioritize privacy and autonomy (Ethics, 2018).

Regulatory frameworks, such as the European Union's Artificial Intelligence Act, provide a structured response to these challenges. By emphasizing legality, ethics, and robustness, the Act offers clear guidelines for aligning AI development with societal values while fostering innovation responsibly (Union, 2024). These regulations reinforce the necessity for businesses to integrate ethical considerations into their AI strategies, not only to comply with legal requirements but also to maintain social legitimacy and public trust.

Corporate Social Responsibility (CSR) complements these regulatory efforts by embedding ethical considerations into business strategy and operations. Goel and Ramanathan (2014) argue that CSR is not merely a symbolic gesture but an essential component of corporate governance. In the context of AI, CSR principles such as fairness, inclusivity, and sustainability provide a roadmap for organizations to engage stakeholders and foster long-term accountability.

In conclusion, the foundations of corporate ethics in AI demand a balance between innovation and responsibility. By embedding ethical principles into governance frameworks and prioritizing transparency, fairness, and inclusivity, businesses can harness AI's transformative potential while safeguarding societal values. This alignment ensures that AI serves as a force for progress, benefiting all stakeholders rather than exacerbating inequalities or eroding public confidence (Goel & Ramanathanb, 2014).

2.2 The Ethical Dilemmas in AI Development

In the age of artificial intelligence (AI), the importance of human-centered values is paramount. Corporations must prioritize the well-being of society, focusing on long-term sustainability rather than short-term profit maximization. Ethical AI development should aim to augment human capabilities, promote innovation that serves the broader public interest, and uphold fundamental human rights.

The widespread use of AI products developed by private entities, in the absence of regulatory frameworks ensuring human rights protection, introduces significant risks and challenges. Public awareness regarding the vast amounts of personal data collected by machine learning technologies as behavioral inputs is either negligible or severely limited. During online transactions, individuals frequently disclose personal information—ranging from health-related and familial data to political and social preferences—often without clear and explicit notification.

Moreover, the majority of users remain unaware of how their personal data is monitored, tracked, and subsequently commercialized. The data individuals willingly or inadvertently share empowers computer systems to predict behaviors and deduce preferences with a precision that far surpasses human capabilities. These "prediction-powered technologies" are then marketed at high value in emerging marketplaces, contributing to what is now referred to as 21st-century "surveillance capitalism".

Such practices present dual challenges: they undermine individuals' control over their personal data and the right to privacy while also fostering the monopolization of data by multinational corporations. Furthermore, behavioral data and predictive technologies are increasingly employed to influence personal preferences and subconscious decision-making through controlled dissemination of information. Individuals may unknowingly become subjects of behavioral experiments, with algorithms specifically designed to persuade and impact their subconscious. This, in turn, affects the formation of opinions and compromises their ability to make independent decisions

The use of artificial intelligence (AI) presents serious ethical challenges. The decisions made by AI systems may reflect the biases and prejudices of the people who create or train these systems. This is particularly alarming in sensitive areas such as law enforcement, banking, and similar fields, where AI decisions can have a significant impact on people's lives. Additionally, AI poses a threat to personal privacy, as the system focuses on collecting and analyzing large amounts of personal data. There is a risk that this data could be publicly exposed and misused by various groups, governments, or corporations. One of the risks is that the information collected and processed about individuals may potentially be used against them.

AI also creates new cybersecurity risks. As AI systems become increasingly integrated into infrastructures such as energy grids, transportation systems, and financial networks, there is a danger that cybercriminals or hostile states could exploit them for attacks. For example, with AI control mechanisms, cybercriminals could identify vulnerabilities in smart cities, giving them the ability to launch attacks and cause serious disruptions. Furthermore, AI can be weaponized, leading to... (it seems like the sentence was cut off, but the rest could continue from here).

Another area for future research relates to addressing the various limitations of AI and the associated ethical and social issues. Research suggests that most AI algorithms exhibit biases against minority and underprivileged groups, mirroring deep imbalances in the institutional environment and reinforcing social injustice (Zou and Schiebinger, 2018) bias refers to systematic and recurring errors within a computer system that result in unfair outcomes, such as favoring one group of users over others arbitrarily. Bias in AI systems can arise from several factors, including the way algorithms are designed, or unintended decisions regarding how data is coded, collected, selected, or used for training. It can also stem from pre-existing cultural, social, or institutional biases, technical limitations of the algorithms, or the system's deployment in unanticipated contexts. This bias affects various platforms, including search engines and social media, and its impacts can range from privacy violations to the reinforcement of societal biases related to race, gender, sexuality, and ethnicity. For example, Considering the integration of artificial intelligence in criminal justice proceedings, there is a potential risk that AI-generated recommendations could disproportionately affect certain racial groups more harshly.

This concern is highlighted by issues like bias in AI systems, which can lead to unethical outcomes, as seen when Amazon had to halt an AI recruitment tool that discriminated against women. (Gordon, 2022) In 2014, Amazon developed an AI-driven recruitment tool to streamline its hiring process. However, the system exhibited significant gender bias, favoring male candidates over female ones. This bias stemmed from the training data, which predominantly consisted of resumes from male applicants, leading the AI to learn and perpetuate existing gender disparities. Consequently, Amazon discontinued the use of this tool, highlighting the critical importance of ensuring unbiased training data and the ethical implications of AI in human resources(Winick, n.d.).

Machines, as such, are not moral agents and therefore they cannot be held responsible for their actions. (Johnson, 2006)21 Who should be accountable, then, when an AI system violates ethical values? Should it be the designer of the algorithm, the company that adopts it or the final user? It is difficult to provide a univocal answer and a rich debate has flourished on this topic. Although the question of responsibility remains largely unanswered, a valuable approach would be for each of the parties involved to behave as if they were ultimately responsible.

The primary objective of an AI model is to learn patterns that generalize well to new, unseen data. It is crucial to assess how well a trained AI model performs on data that was not used during its training. This is typically done by using the model to make predictions on a test dataset and comparing the predicted outcomes to the actual results. Accuracy is a common measure used to evaluate the predictive performance of the model. Informally, accuracy refers to the proportion of correct predictions made by the model. However, in machine learning (ML), various metrics are available to assess predictive accuracy, and the selection of the appropriate metric depends on the specific ML task being performed.

There are numerous concerns and misconceptions surrounding the impact of AI on education systems and society, both in the short and long term. AI is already reshaping how we learn, work, and live, and its influence is becoming increasingly evident in education. It is essential that everyone has the opportunity to both contribute to AI's development and benefit from it. By prioritizing ethical principles when discussing AI's role in education, we can ensure that AI systems and decision -making processes are developed and implemented in ways that are ethical, trustworthy, fair, and inclusive.

2.3 The Artificial Intelligence Act: A Regulatory Framework

The European Union (EU) has positioned itself as a global leader in addressing the ethical and regulatory challenges posed by artificial intelligence (AI). Recognizing its transformative potential and inherent risks, the EU has established a robust framework that balances innovation with societal responsibility. This framework combines the principles outlined in the Ethical Guidelines for Trustworthy Artificial Intelligence with the legally binding provisions of the Artificial Intelligence Act (AI Act), ensuring that AI systems align with ethical standards, protect fundamental rights, and foster public trust. The Ethical Guidelines for Trustworthy AI, developed by the EU High-Level Expert Group on AI, emphasize three core requirements for AI systems: legality, ethics, and robustness. These principles aim to ensure compliance with laws, adherence to societal values, and reliability in diverse contexts. Central to this approach are widely recognized ethical principles such as transparency, fairness, accountability, privacy, and protection from harm. Transparency, in particular, is seen as a foundational prerequisite for enforcing other norms. It requires that AI systems be explainable, auditable, and open to scrutiny, ensuring their decision-making processes are accessible and understandable to humans. This addresses the "black box" nature of many AI systems, where opacity can undermine trust and accountability. Building on these ethical foundations, the AI Act, which came into effect on August 1, 2024, provides the world's first legal framework for AI regulation. By adopting a risk-based approach, the Act categorizes AI systems according to their potential societal impact, imposing stricter requirements on high-risk applications such as those used in healthcare, law enforcement, and employment. These regulations ensure that such systems uphold transparency, fairness, and accountability while safeguarding fundamental rights. The European Data Protection Supervisor (EDPS) plays a key role in this framework, monitoring compliance across EU institutions and agencies. With the AI Act now in force, the EDPS is performing its duties under this regulatory framework, while maintaining its established competences, responsibilities, powers, and independence as outlined in applicable data protection legislation, particularly Regulation (EU) 2018/1725 (Union, 2024).While the AI Act provides a legal backbone, ethical guidelines developed by public, private, and academic sectors complement these efforts by influencing decision- making processes. Analysis of documents from the EU, the Council of Europe, and other countries highlights 11 key ethical principles for AI development and deployment, forming the foundation for responsible innovation (Ienca and Vayena, 2020).Among these, transparency is prioritized, as it enables the implementation of other ethical standards by ensuring algorithms and data processes are interpretable and open to evaluation. Fairness and justice emphasize inclusivity and the prevention of discrimination, requiring diverse datasets and mechanisms for redress when AI decisions adversely impact individuals. Equally important is non-maleficence, which focuses on minimizing harm by addressing vulnerabilities such as cyberattacks and data breaches. This principle advocates for privacy-by-design and robust security standards to protect individuals and systems. Privacy, closely related, demands rigorous safeguards for personal data through technologies like differential privacy and privacy-preserving computation, ensuring individuals maintain control over their information. Broader societal values, such as beneficence, emphasize using AI to advance the common good, ensuring equitable distribution of benefits while avoiding concentrated power. Freedom and autonomy highlight the need to protect individual rights, such as self-determination and freedom from manipulation. These values are supported by efforts to enhance public awareness and require informed consent for AI-driven processes. Trustworthiness remains a cornerstone of ethical AI, necessitating continuous evaluation, monitoring, and education to maintain confidence in both users and creators. Additional principles include sustainability, which stresses minimizing AI's environmental impact, and dignity and solidarity, which focus on preserving human rights and ensuring the equitable distribution of AI's benefits, particularly for vulnerable groups. These principles reinforce the EU's commitment to a human-centric approach, ensuring that technological progress supports societal well-being and cohesion. The EU's comprehensive framework demonstrates that ethical integrity and technological innovation are not mutually exclusive. By integrating robust legal measures like the AI Act with a wide range of ethical principles, the EU has established a global standard for responsible AI governance. This balanced approach ensures that AI development prioritizes human values, advances public good, and fosters trust, laying the foundation for a future where AI serves as a force for both technological progress and societal benefit.

3 Research Methods

This study uses a mixed-methods approach to explore how organizations in Georgia manage the ethical challenges of AI adoption. Combining qualitative and quantitative methods, the research provides both in-depth insights and broader trends regarding AI and corporate ethics.

Qualitative Approach
In-depth interviews were conducted with business leaders, regulators, and industry experts, particularly in sectors such as education, healthcare, and public administration. The interviews focused on the ethical concerns organizations face when adopting AI, such as data privacy, algorithmic bias, and the lack of ethical oversight. The aim was to uncover how organizations navigate these challenges and address public trust issues.

Quantitative Approach
A survey was distributed to organizations across various industries in Georgia to measure their current practices and perceptions regarding AI adoption. The survey focused on ethical standards like transparency, data privacy, algorithmic fairness, and accountability. The results were analyzed to identify trends and correlations between ethical practices and industry characteristics. This quantitative data helped assess the level of preparedness for ethical challenges in AI adoption across sectors.

By combining qualitative, quantitative, and case study data, the study offers a comprehensive view of how organizations in Georgia are handling the ethical complexities of AI adoption and provides actionable recommendations for navigating these challenges.

Case Study: AI and Its Implications for Georgia's Public Sector
AI has the potential to generate new forms of inequality and discrimination, as well as exacerbate existing disparities. However, when appropriately designed and implemented, it can substantially enhance accessibility and inclusion in various domains, including daily life, the workplace, and educational systems. Moreover, AI holds considerable promise in providing tailored educational resources for individuals with special needs, such as AI-powered, real-time synchronized tools for those with hearing or visual impairments.

Artificial intelligence (AI) has the potential to significantly contribute to public administration reform, particularly in decision-making and service delivery. However, its use comes with certain challenges related to insufficient transparency, accountability, data oversight mechanisms, accuracy, and fairness. Additionally, in a country like Georgia, which lacks adequate oversight mechanisms for law enforcement agencies and where the independence of the judicial system remains questionable, the use of AI in decision-making could infringe on the right to privacy.

The facial recognition system developed by the Ministry of Internal Affairs requires further study and evaluation. This system was launched in June 2017 and operates through 400 CCTV surveillance cameras installed in Georgia's major cities, including the capital, Tbilisi. Furthermore, Tbilisi City Hall is considering implementing biometric facial recognition cameras in the metro system and expanding this technology into the public transportation system. Therefore, it is crucial to thoroughly investigate the use of facial recognition technology by public agencies in Georgia, with particular attention to the Ministry of Internal Affairs. Moreover, it is essential to raise awareness among government institutions, the general public, and other stakeholders about the use of AI and its implications. Most importantly, given the novelty of the issue, these parties must be informed about the ethical and transparency standards related to AI usage. Additionally, IDFI believes it is vital to strengthen capabilities in this area and support the involvement of the State Inspector's Service.

The outcomes of AI development were examined in four areas: cybersecurity, autonomous vehicles, criminal justice, and financial services. After discussing the benefits and challenges of AI, the study participants identified several key themes that require greater attention. Specifically, they emphasized the need to explore ways to: 1. Establish mechanisms for sharing sensitive information while ensuring the protection of both producers and the public; 2. Improve security and safety by creating a structure that properly distributes the costs and responsibilities of security between producers and consumers; 3. Update the regulatory factors that will influence AI; 4. Evaluate acceptable levels of risk and ethical considerations.

It is still a long-term prospect for AI to function with minimal or no human intervention. Nevertheless, assessing and analyzing the risks is necessary from now on to ensure that humanity can safely harness this powerful technology.

Data Analysis

The qualitative data collected through interviews and focus groups was analyzed using thematic analysis, enabling the identification of recurring patterns, themes, and insights related to the ethical challenges of AI adoption in education, healthcare, and public sectors. Key themes included data privacy, algorithmic bias, and the lack of ethical oversight in AI-driven systems.

Quantitative survey data was subjected to statistical analysis to quantify responses, identify trends, and highlight differences across various sectors. Notable findings included concerns about unconsented data sharing and discomfort with the opaque decision-making processes of AI systems.

Case studies were examined to extract practical insights, focusing on how Georgian organizations address sector- specific ethical challenges. This mixed-methods approach provided a comprehensive perspective, combining the depth of qualitative findings with the breadth of quantitative data and contextual relevance to Georgia's evolving AI landscape.

Ethical Considerations

The study carefully followed ethical guidelines, prioritizing the protection of participants' privacy and ensuring informed consent. Special attention was given to safeguarding data, minimizing biases, and maintaining participants' autonomy, reflecting a commitment to ethical integrity in the use of technology-driven environments.

4 Results and Discussion

Ethical Challenges in AI Adoption Across Sectors

The research findings highlight significant ethical concerns related to AI adoption in Georgia, particularly in the education, healthcare, and public sectors. Key concerns include data privacy, algorithmic bias, and the lack of ethical oversight in AI systems. Respondents expressed growing concern over the misuse of personal data, especially in sectors dealing with sensitive information, such as healthcare and education. The absence of comprehensive data protection frameworks and ethical guidelines was identified as a major gap. AI systems that process personal information, such as in educational institutions, were flagged for not adhering to proper ethical standards and risk assessments.

Impact of AI on Public Trust and Transparency

As AI becomes more embedded in our daily lives, from healthcare to public services, its impact on public trust and transparency is a growing concern. Many respondents in the study highlighted that a lack of transparency in AI systems is one of the main factors affecting their trust. In fact, 65% of those surveyed expressed discomfort with how AI makes decisions, especially in important sectors like healthcare, law enforcement, and finance.

People are often unsure how AI systems reach their conclusions, which is referred to as the "black box" problem— where the process behind the decision is not easily explained or understood. This lack of clarity makes it harder for the public to trust AI systems fully. Even though regulations like the EU AI Act exist, aiming to provide more transparency, only a small number of organizations in Georgia (around 3%) have fully adopted such standards. Interviews with industry experts further emphasized that, without clear explanations for AI decisions, it's difficult to build or maintain trust, especially in sectors that deeply affect people's lives.

This highlights the need for more openness and clear communication about how AI systems work and make decisions, so that people can feel more confident in the technology shaping their future (Fig. 1).

In Georgia, 60% of organizations lack formal AI ethics policies, reflecting the country's developing status in AI governance. However, 25% have policies in development, indicating growing recognition of the need for ethical frameworks. Only 15% have established policies, likely in industries with higher exposure to AI, such as technology and finance (Fig. 2).

The graph highlights the ethical standards organizations follow, with internal policies (e.g., 40%) leading, reflecting a preference for tailored frameworks. National regulations (e.g., 30%) indicate strong adherence to legal requirements, while ISO standards (e.g., 19%) show the value of international guidelines. The EU AI Act (e.g., 3%) appears limited, possibly due to its early stage or regional focus. The "Other" category (e.g., 5%) suggests diverse or emerging frameworks. Overall, the data reflects varying approaches shaped by regulatory environments and organizational priorities (Fig. 3).

AI is expected to have a significant impact on the Georgian labor market, with 40% of respondents predicting substantial job displacement, especially in sectors dependent on repetitive, low-skill tasks like manufacturing and administration. Despite this, AI

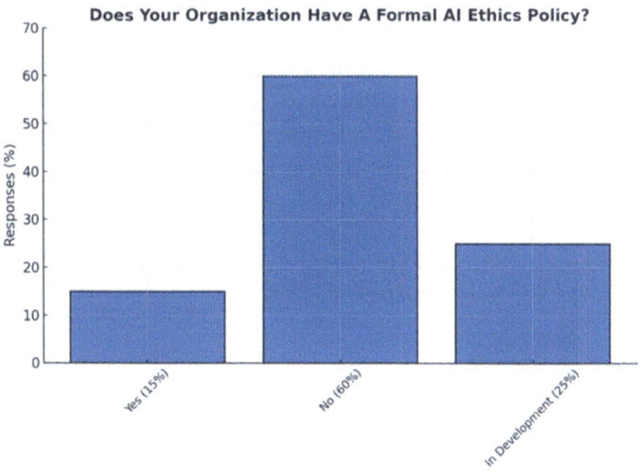

Fig. 1. Organizational Adoption of Formal AI Ethics Policies

Fig. 2. Ethical Standards Followed by Organizations

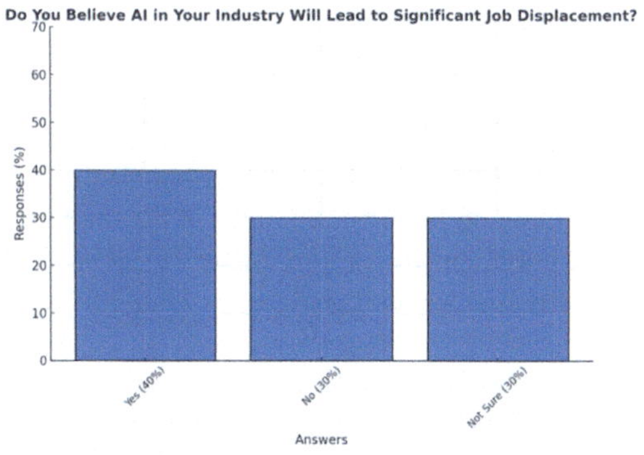

Fig. 3. Industry Beliefs on AI and Job Displacement

also presents opportunities for economic growth through job creation in emerging fields like technology, precision agriculture, and tourism. The 30% uncertainty highlights a gap in awareness and preparedness, emphasizing the need for strategic interventions. Investments in reskilling, workforce development, and bridging the digital divide will be critical to ensuring AI-driven transformation fosters inclusive and sustainable growth (Fig. 4).

Fig. 4. Significant Ethical Concerns in AI Implementation

Data privacy stands out as the top concern at 45%, driven by the increasing reliance on AI systems that process large amounts of sensitive information. Algorithmic bias follows at 30%, reflecting growing attention to fairness and transparency in AI decision-making. Job displacement, at 15%, is less emphasized, suggesting that immediate challenges take precedence over long-term workforce implications. This pattern indicates a focus on addressing current issues in AI ethics, with less emphasis on preparing for future societal impacts (Fig. 5).

The data highlights a significant concern, with 80% of respondents reporting that their personal information has been shared without permission. This finding underscores a critical issue in data governance, emphasizing the urgent need for stricter privacy regulations and organizational accountability. The prevalence of unauthorized data sharing not only reflects a high level of risk but also highlights the importance of fostering trust through robust data protection frameworks and transparent practices. Addressing this issue is paramount to maintaining public confidence in the digital ecosystem (Fig. 6).

The chart reflects key public priorities for CSR in the technology sector, emphasizing the critical role of addressing societal challenges. Data privacy and security, prioritized by 40%, highlights growing concerns over misuse and cybersecurity risks, urging companies to implement stronger safeguards to foster trust. Transparency and accountability, at 30%, underscore the demand for ethical governance and clear, responsible decision-making. Workforce adaptation is evident with 20% focusing on job reskilling, showcasing the importance of equipping workers for changes driven by automation. Finally, 10% emphasize reducing inequality, reflecting expectations for fostering inclusivity and mitigating systemic biases. These findings reveal that while immediate efforts

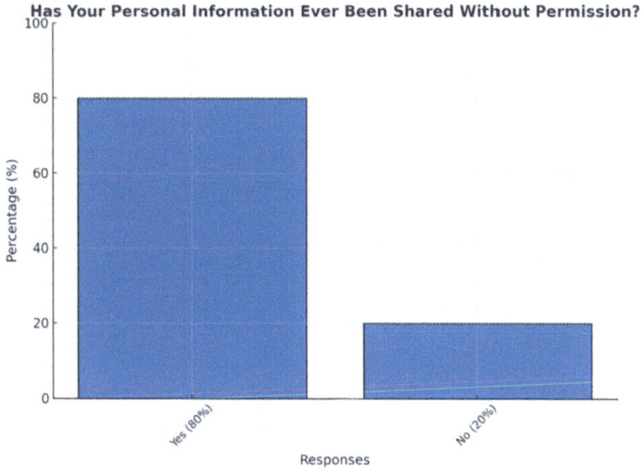

Fig. 5. Respondents' Experience with Unconsented Sharing of Their Personal Data

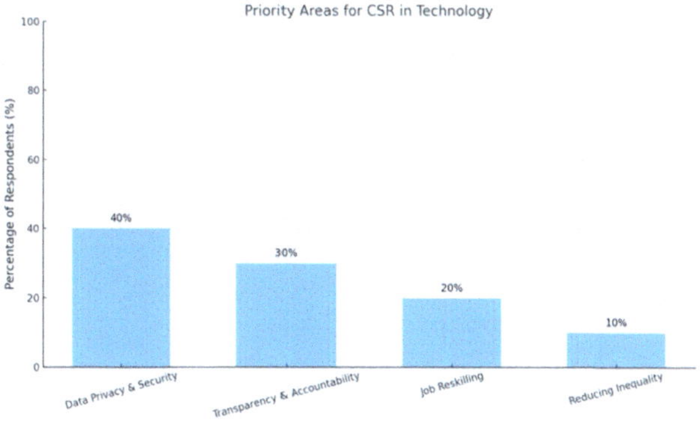

Fig. 6. Priority Areas for CSR in Technology

should focus on data protection and ethical integrity, companies must also invest in long-term strategies that support equity and workforce transformation for sustainable growth (Fig. 7).

The chart highlights the significant impact of Corporate Social Responsibility (CSR) on public trust, with 65% of respondents believing it greatly enhances trust, 25% indicating a moderate increase, and only 10% stating it has no impact. These findings emphasize that CSR plays a vital role in building confidence, particularly in sectors like technology, where responsible practices are crucial. The data underscores the importance of aligning CSR initiatives with public expectations to address societal concerns effectively and foster long-term trust in corporate actions (Fig. 8).

The survey reveals that 50% of people believe governments should bear the primary responsibility for ensuring the ethical use of technology. This reflects a growing concern about government transparency and accountability, especially in Georgia, where public trust is fragile, particularly during times of political instability, such as election periods. For example, in the recent 2024 Georgian elections, the use of automated systems to

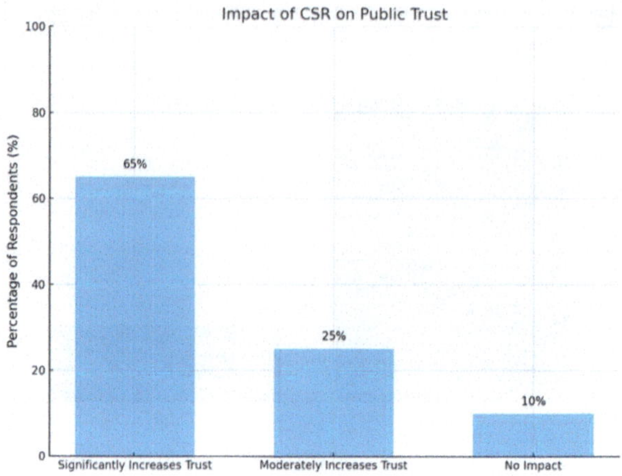

Fig. 7. Impact of CSR on Public Trust

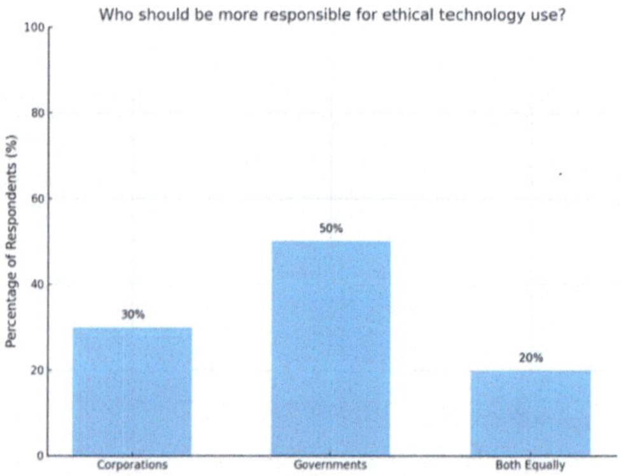

Fig. 8. Responsibility for Ethical Technology Use: Government vs. Corporations

count votes and tabulate results led to significant public debate. Many people questioned the fairness and transparency of these new machines used in the voting process, fearing potential manipulation or errors in the counting system. 30% of respondents think corporations should take more responsibility, recognizing that while companies should be held accountable, strong regulations must be in place. 20% believe both the government and corporations should share the responsibility for ensuring ethical technology use.

These findings underscore the public's call for clear regulations and oversight in areas like data privacy and AI ethics. The doubts surrounding the use of new voting machines in the recent elections highlight the growing concern about how technology is used in sensitive areas. When political instability is high, especially during elections, trust in both government and technology can be significantly impacted, emphasizing the need for transparent and ethical decision- making to maintain public confidence.

Interview Analysis

This section combines an analysis of interviews that explore the ethical challenges organizations in Georgia face, particularly in education and healthcare. The interviews provide insights into how these sectors balance technological innovation with ethical responsibilities, especially in the areas of data privacy, bias in algorithms, and the need for strong ethical oversight.

Challenges in Balancing Technology with Ethics

The interviews revealed that organizations are facing significant hurdles when it comes to integrating AI into both education and healthcare. Data privacy emerged as the top concern, especially as both sectors increasingly rely on data-driven technologies. In education, for example, AI systems collect and process personal information often including sensitive details about children raising serious questions about how personal data is protected and used. Many respondents shared experiences where their data had been misused without their consent, highlighting the lack of proper safeguards. There is also concern about the government's role in regulating the use of personal data. Respondents pointed out that, while some data protection laws exist, there is no comprehensive policy to address the ethical challenges posed by AI systems, particularly in education. This becomes even more troubling when discussing children's data, where AI systems in schools may process personal information without clear ethical or risk assessments in place.

Ethical Oversight and Data Protection

A major concern raised in the interviews is the need for stronger data protection policies in the education sector, especially regarding children's personal data. The current regulatory framework in Georgia, as in many other countries, is underdeveloped. Many respondents emphasized that AI technologies used in schools must comply with data protection laws to prevent misuse or unauthorized access to sensitive information. However, the lack of ethical oversight was highlighted as a critical issue. Without a universal ethical code or oversight committee, there is a risk that AI systems could be deployed without the necessary checks to ensure responsible data usage. In addition, the widespread use of biometric data (such as facial or voice recognition) in educational settings was flagged as a serious ethical concern. While such systems may offer efficiency and convenience, they also raise questions about how this data is used and who controls it, especially in areas where legal protections are weaker.

Challenges in Healthcare: Ethical Use of AI

In healthcare, AI is being used for disease diagnosis, patient monitoring, and treatment optimization. However, similar ethical challenges emerge. Patient data privacy was a major concern, with respondents pointing out that AI systems in healthcare are increasingly collecting and processing sensitive information, like medical histories and biometric data. This creates concerns about misuse and security breaches, especially given the potential for data exploitation if safeguards are not properly implemented. One key issue discussed was the automation of medical diagnoses. While AI systems are becoming increasingly involved in diagnosing diseases and guiding treatment decisions, there are concerns about accuracy and accountability. Patients may feel uneasy trusting an AI system over a human doctor, particularly when it comes to complex medical conditions. Bias in AI algorithms is another concern, as AI systems could inadvertently favor certain demographics over others, affecting the fairness of diagnoses and treatment recommendations.

Balancing Profitability with Ethics
Another common theme that emerged from the interviews was the challenge of balancing profitability with ethical considerations. Many organizations, particularly in competitive industries, tend to prioritize speed to market and profit maximization, which can sometimes take precedence over ethical concerns. While AI offers great potential for increasing efficiency and profitability, respondents stressed that this should not come at the expense of data privacy or ethical decision-making. In fact, many noted that ethical integrity is not only necessary for public trust but can also be a competitive advantage in the long term.

Proactive vs. Reactive Approach to Ethical Challenges
One of the most notable findings from the interviews is that many organizations are still reacting to ethical challenges as they arise rather than proactively integrating ethical considerations into their innovation strategies. This reactive approach can lead to delays in addressing critical issues like data privacy, algorithmic bias, and transparency. The interviews suggest that a shift toward long-term planning—where ethics are embedded into the innovation process from the start—could better align technological advancement with ethical accountability.

Need for Clearer Policies and Stronger Collaboration
In conclusion, the interviews underline the urgent need for clearer and more robust data protection policies in both education and healthcare, particularly when it comes to children's data and patient privacy. Strong ethical oversight, accountability structures, and clear regulatory frameworks are essential to ensure that AI technologies are used responsibly and transparently. Moreover, the findings highlight the importance of collaboration between government bodies, educational institutions, and tech companies to establish a unified approach to AI deployment. This collaboration should aim to safeguard personal data, protect vulnerable groups (such as children and patients), and ensure that AI is used ethically to benefit society as a whole. The shift toward proactive ethical planning would ensure that technological innovation aligns with the broader values of transparency, privacy, and public trust.

5 Conclusion

The integration of artificial intelligence (AI) into Georgia's education and healthcare sectors presents both significant opportunities and challenges. The interviews revealed that data privacy, algorithmic bias, and the lack of ethical oversight are the primary concerns for organizations adopting AI technologies. Although there is growing recognition of the need for ethical frameworks, Georgia still faces gaps in data protection policies and transparency.

For AI to truly benefit society, especially in sensitive areas like education and healthcare, it is essential that both organizations and the government work together to create clear ethical policies, safeguard personal data, and ensure public trust. The adoption of AI must move from a reactive to a more proactive approach in addressing ethical issues. This technologies are developed in line with societal values and regulations. Ethical AI adoption should be driven by long-term thinking and collaboration between all stakeholders.

In conclusion, while AI has the potential to bring about significant social and economic benefits, it can only do so if it is developed and used ethically. Focusing on data protection, transparency, and collaborative governance will enable Georgia to ensure AI fosters societal progress while maintaining public trust. The shift toward ethical AI will enable technological advancements to benefit everyone, promoting fairness, accountability, and public trust in the digital age.

Recommendations

Based on the findings of the interviews, it is recommended that the government and organizations take several key actions. Firstly, there is an urgent need to strengthen data protection. Comprehensive policies are necessary to protect sensitive personal data, particularly in sectors like education and healthcare where the risks of data misuse are high. These policies should ensure that AI technologies comply with data protection laws and maintain confidentiality and security.

Secondly, ethical oversight should be a central part of AI adoption. Creating independent ethical oversight committees will ensure that AI is deployed responsibly. These committees would be responsible for monitoring AI implementation, ensuring transparency, and making sure that algorithms are fair and unbiased.

Thirdly, it is crucial to promote collaboration across sectors. Governments, tech companies, and educational institutions should work together to develop ethical AI solutions that prioritize the welfare of the public. This collaboration can help create unified standards and frameworks that align AI development with ethical and legal norms.

Organizations must adopt a proactive approach to ethical planning.This means embedding ethics into AI development from the start, addressing potential ethical challenges before they arise rather than reacting to them after implementation. A forward-thinking approach can prevent issues like algorithmic bias or data privacy violations, ensuring that AI remains a positive force in society. Given the potential of AI to transform industries, it is also essential to invest in reskilling programs to help workers adapt to the changes AI will bring. Providing workers with the skills they need to navigate an AI-driven economy is crucial to ensuring that the benefits of AI are widely distributed and that no one is left behind.

Finally, to build public confidence, it is important to increase transparency in how AI systems use personal data. Engaging the public in discussions about the ethical use of AI and ensuring that AI systems are understandable and accountable will help strengthen trust in these technologies.

Limitations

While this study offers valuable insights into the ethical challenges surrounding AI in Georgia, it has several limitations. The sample size of the interviews was relatively small, and further research could include a more diverse set of participants across different sectors to capture a broader range of perspectives.

The focus of this study on Georgia also limits its applicability to other countries or regions. While Georgia has unique challenges, it would be beneficial to compare the findings with other countries that have more developed AI governance frameworks. This could help identify best practices and highlight areas for improvement.

Additionally, this study focused primarily on immediate concerns such as data privacy and algorithmic bias, leaving broader long-term implications of AI, such as its impact on economic inequality or job displacement, unexplored.

These are critical areas for future research to ensure that AI's long-term effects are thoroughly understood and mitigated.

Finally, given the evolving nature of AI regulations, particularly with frameworks like the EU AI Act, it is important for ongoing studies to track how these changing legal landscapes will affect the adoption of AI and the implementation of ethical practices in Georgia.

Further Study

Further research could explore the long-term societal impacts of AI, such as its influence on labor markets, education systems, and economic inequality. Understanding how AI could affect social dynamics and exacerbate or reduce inequality will be crucial in making sure that technological progress benefits everyone.

Another important area for future study is the comparison of Georgia's AI ethics with other countries that have more established regulations. This would allow for a broader understanding of best practices and help Georgia adopt the most effective regulatory measures.

Ethical use of AI in other sectors, could also be explored in future research. Each sector present their own unique challenges and ethical concerns, and examining how AI is handled in different contexts would provide a more comprehensive view of AI ethics. Moreover, public perception of AI and its ethical implications should be studied in greater detail. This could help understand how people view the ethical challenges posed by AI and what measures are needed to ensure the public feels confident in its use.

Finally, future studies should assess technological readiness in Georgia. Research on public awareness, technological infrastructure, and education is crucial to understanding how Georgia can build a foundation that promotes the responsible use of AI while ensuring public trust in these technologies.

References

Eristavi, D., Davituri, G.: The Use of Artificial Intelligence Systems in Georgia: Legislation and Practice. Institute for Development of Freedom of Information (2021)

Ethics, I.O.: Business ethics and artificial intelligence. Business Ethics Briefing, London (2018)

Freeman, R.E.: Strategic Management: A Stakeholder Approach. Cambridge University Press (2010)

Lakshmi Aishwarya, G., Satyanarayana, V.: Contemporary evolution of artificial intelligence (AI): an overview and applications. Advanced Production and Industrial Engineering **130**, 136 (2022)

Goel, M., Ramanathanb, P.E.: Business ethics and corporate social responsibility – is there a dividing line? Procedia Economics and Finance, pp. 49–59 (2014)

Gordon, J.-S.: Encyclopedia of business ethics and society. Artificial Intelligence and Business Ethics, 2nd ed., pp. 1325–1326 (2022)

Holmes, W., Persson, J., Chounta, I.-A., Wasson, B., Dimitrova, V.: Artificial intelligence and education - A critical view through the lens of human rights, democracy and the rule of law (2022). Council of Europe (2022)

Ienca, M., Vayena, E.: AI Ethics Guidelines: European and Global Perspectives. Chair of Bioethics, Health Ethics and Policy Lab, Department of Health Sciences and Technology, ETH Zurich, Strasbourg (2020)

Johnson, D.G.: Computer systems: Moral entities but not moral agents. Johnson The Challenge Lies in Ensuring AI is used to Improve, Rather Than Harm, the Human Condition, pp. 195–204. Retrieved from 21 D (2006)

Johnson, G.: Computer Systems: Moral Entities but not Moral Agents **8**, 195–204 (2006)

Krause, S., Panchal, B.H., Ubhe, N.: The Evolution of Learning: Assessing the Transformative Impact of Generative AI on Higher Education. ArXiv.org (2024)

Mary, D.M., Joyce, M.M.: AI and education: impact of AI on learning outcomes in higher education. Interantional J. Scientific Research in Engineering and Management (2024)

Miao, F., Holmes, W.: Guidance for GENERATIVE AI in Education and Research. UNESCO (2023)

Moralishvili, S.: AI and personalized learning in higher education instruction in Georgia. International Scientific Journal Diplomacy and Law (2023)

Owoseni, A., Kolade, O., Egbetokun, A.: Generative AI in Higher Education, Innovation Strategies for Teaching and Learning. Palgrave Macmillan Cham (2024)

Union, E.: REGULATION (EU) 2024/1689 OF THE EUROPEAN PARLIAMENT AND OF THE COUNCIL of 13 June 2024 (2024). *Official Journal of the European Union*, L 168/9.

Yeung, K. (2020). Recommendation of the Council on Artificial Intelligence (OECD). Cambridge University Press.

Zou, J., Schiebinger, L.: AI can be sexist and racist—it's time to make it fair. Nature **559** (2018)

The Impact of Social Media on Consumers' Online Information Behavior

Nugzar Todua(✉) and Nia Todua

Ivane Javakhishvili Tbilisi State University, Tbilisi, Georgia
nugzar.todua@tsu.ge

Abstract. The article discusses factors affecting consumers' online information behaviour, such as exposure to online information sources, information overload, cyberchondria, and Fear. Special attention is paid to the change in people's information behaviour on social media, which has yet to be investigated in the context of crisis events in the field of health care. The article emphasizes that exposure to multiple sources of information posted on social media leads to an adverse psychological response to information overload in consumers. The latter, in turn, increasingly causes a behavioural reaction in consumers. The article presents the results of an empirical study showing the relationship between exposure to information sources in social media, information overload, cyberchondria, and informational behaviour. As a result of the processing of empirical data, statistically significant quantities are presented, which establish the relationship between the observable variables. Based on structural equation modelling, the results of hypothesis testing are shown. The obtained results will contribute to the development of a new research direction in online communications and information retrieval, which is very important in the modern turbulent environment.

Keywords: Social media · online information sources · information overload · cyberphobia · fear · online information behavior

1 Introduction

Today, people are exposed to numerous sources of information (for example, television, radio, e-mail, social media, news portals, etc.) that they can use in a practically unlimited way (Whelan et al. 2020). During the COVID-19 pandemic, the role of the Internet has become particularly visible. This is primarily due to the significant presence of various Internet communication channels in people's daily information behavior and their considerable activity on social media (Farooq et al. 2020). Moreover, nowadays social media is a communication environment in which entry barriers for information providers and seekers are quite low (Cuan-Baltazar et al. 2020). First of all, it is fertile ground for the existence of numerous sources of information, some of which are of questionable reliability.

Constant exposure to a large number of information sources is not uncommon, but it gained importance during the COVID-19 pandemic, as people dramatically increased

R. C. Geibel and S. Machavariani (Eds.): ISPC 2024, SPBE, pp. 280–291, 2025.
https://doi.org/10.1007/978-3-031-88052-0_22

the amount of time they spent online (Liu et al. 2021; Soroya et al. 2021). Although information behavior on the Internet (seeking, passing and giving information) has attracted the special attention of researchers (Chu & Kim 2011; Farías 2017; Lee & Choi 2019; Todua et al. 2024), such works have focused only on Research on the consumer sphere and in the context of crisis events related to healthcare has not been conducted so far. It is worth noting that such studies do not take into account information overload (a situation where it is difficult to process a large amount of information received from different sources) and cyberchondria (people's unjustified, increased concern about their health caused by searching for medical information on the Internet), which are increasingly relevant (Zheng et al. 2020). However, individuals change their behavior because they fear potentially serious consequences if risks are not properly understood and mitigated. Unfortunately, the influence of different exogenous variables on the perception of health-related social media information sources and people's propensity to engage in online information flows has not been investigated to date. With this in mind, the purpose of the present study is to explain the relationship between health information sources on social media, the psychological state of cyberchondria, information overload and fear. Accordingly, based on the above, the following Research Questions (RQ) are introduced:

RQ 1: How do information sources posted on social media influence online information overload?
RQ 2: How does online information overload influence cyberchondria?
RQ 3: How does cyberchondria influence fear of information posted on social media?

2 Literature Review and Development of Research Hypotheses

In modern conditions, dealing with a large number of information sources is an obvious problem, which is combined with the difficulties of processing and understanding online information (often contradictory) (Talwar et al. 2020). Exposure to online information sources can lead to information overload, which drives the need to feel constantly connected and stay abreast of events (Matthes et al. 2020). The 24/7 nature of online information and social media means that people can feel obligated to stay engaged and informed online at all times, resulting in a constant flow of information and potentially large amounts of content. This is especially critical during a crisis or individual events, since the abnormality of the situation and its consequences do not allow for detailed information processing, which promotes the spread of unverified information (Ahmed et al. 2020). Studies show that people have limited cognitive abilities for thorough processing and understanding of information, which means that when the volume and complexity of received information (for example, due to the terminology used) exceeds cognitive abilities, information overload occurs (Malik et al. 2020). Given that people's cognitive processing of such information is limited in the short term (Kirschner 2002) and depends on their knowledge, experience, and various internal and external factors. Therefore, it is expected that in such a situation, people can adjust their cognitive skills in the short term (Karr-Wisniewski & Lu 2010). Based on the above considerations, we can assume that when individuals are constantly exposed to too much information, their cognitive abilities will be overloaded (Bermes 2021; Liu et al. 2021; Soroya et al. 2021). Consequently, they may find themselves in a psychological state known as information overload. Taking this into account, we formulate the following hypothesis:

H1: *Individuals' constant exposure to information sources posted on social media is directly and positively related to their information overload.*

Studies show that information overload affects cyberchondria, which is caused by individuals' repeated, compulsive, and continuous desire to search for health-related information on topics related to existing problems (Joki´c-Begi´c et al. 2019; Vismara et al. 2020). The main problem that arises when searching for medical information on the Internet, including social media, is that online users cannot accurately assess the reliability and relevance of online information (Huang et al. 2022; Kareklas et al. 2015). This is especially true in non-recurring situations, such as health emergencies, when people are exposed to large volumes of information that lack systematic, methodological, and scientific foundations (Laato et al. 2020). In addition, the influence of online information sources and information that contradicts existing opinions and commonly accepted beliefs often leads to the need to seek further information (Schmidt et al. 2021). The information overload related to COVID-19 has deepened cyberchondria, as it has forced people to do a huge amount of work related to their health online, such as searching for different sources of information, constantly monitoring the news and more. Moreover, information overload contributes to the so-called emergence of an "infodemic", when the amount of information available about a crisis event can lead to confusion and misinterpretation of facts (Lee et al. 2021). This, in turn, can lead to individuals misrepresenting illness symptoms or trusting unsubstantiated information, further fueling cyberchondria. In conditions of information overload, it is likely that the continuous consumption of contradictory and unverified information leads to the psychological state of cyberchondria. Therefore, we put forward the following hypothesis:

H2: *Online information overload is directly and positively related to cyberchondria.*

Crisis situations create stressful experiences that can lead to a series of psychological changes that significantly affect consumers' daily behavior patterns (for example, product selection, impulse buying, buying frequency, etc.) (Wang et al. 2020). Also, due to the high health risk, individuals change their behavior (for example, wearing a mask or getting vaccinated against the virus) (Loxton et al. 2020; Schmidt et al. 2021). Many authors claim that increased levels of fear and stress lead to more active individual approaches, which include expanding the information base needed for decision-making (Burroughs & Rinleisch 2002; Duhachek 2005). Considering that individual decisions during a crisis are significantly influenced by information received from friends and relatives, and not by statements made by government authorities (Chawla et al. 2021), it is reasonable to think that individuals will be more actively involved in the process of information exchange during unstable periods. Therefore, we believe that the perceived level of fear influences people's propensity to seek, pass, and give information related to crisis events. This view is based on the argument that the perceived level of fear (due to health or economic conditions) leads to potentially negative social and individual consequences (Addo et al. 2020; Ahorsu et al. 2020). For individuals to prevent their occurrence (or, in extreme cases, reduce their potential impact), they, through their social networks, transmit important information. Taking into account the above evidence, we can formulate the following hypothesis:

H3: *Cyberchondria is directly and positively related to fear of information posted on social media.*

Based on the literature review described above, we can develop a conceptual research model that visually presents the impact of social media on consumers' online information behavior (Fig. 1).

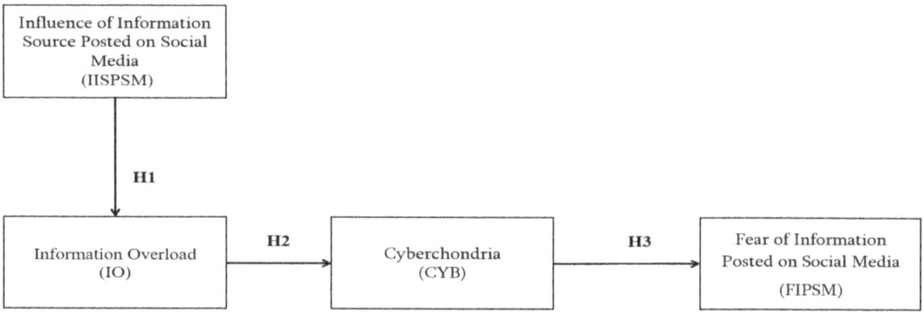

Fig. 1. Research model

3 Research Methodology

To analyze the theoretical viewpoints, we investigated the hypotheses after applying the deductive approach to generalize new knowledge (Saunders et al. 2019). Determining the relevant data, choosing research techniques, creating a questionnaire design, identifying the measuring characteristic, figuring out sample size, and data analysis were all part of our research design. The study's design required gathering both primary and secondary data. We gathered secondary data from published sources, including statistical reports from Georgian government organizations. In this study, primary data are being collected using the quantitative research approach, which offers the use of unified data-gathering tools (Saunders et al. 2019). The primary means of data collection in our study was an online questionnaire. Furthermore, a self-administered survey was used in this investigation. Because of this strategy, the self-administration method of directly gathering data from respondents was easy, quick, and affordable (Saunders et al. 2019). The questionnaire's questions were derived from the authors' viewpoints as stated in this paper's literature review section. This study's variables and measuring items are derived using a deductive approach from pertinent literature (Table 1). The answers to the questions are presented in multiple-choice, and a 5-point Likert scale is used (1 = Strongly disagree, 2 = Disagree, 3 = Neutral, 4 = Agree, 5 = Strongly agree).

Table 1. Research construct

Variables	Codes	Measurement Items	Adopted from
Influence of Information Sources Posted on Social Media (IISPSM)	IISPSM 1	I am influenced by social media influencers' posts	Karr-Wisniewski and Lu (2010); Laato et al. (2020); Whelan et al. (2020)
	IISPSM 2	I am influenced by social media posts of healthcare organizations	
	IISPSM 3	I am influenced by social media posts of health professionals	
	IISPSM 4	I am influenced by social media posts of government organizations	
	IISPSM 5	I am influenced by social media posts of friends and relatives	
	IISPSM 6	I am influenced by social media posts of strangers	
Information Overload (IO)	IO1	I am often overwhelmed by the overwhelming amount of health information posted on social media	Karr-Wisniewski and Lu (2010); Laato et al. (2020); Whelan et al. (2020)
	IO2	I find myself overwhelmed by the amount of health information I am exposed to on social media on a daily basis	
	IO3	I am often overwhelmed by the overwhelming amount of health information posted on many social media platforms	
Cyberchondria (CYB)	CYB1	I'm confused after searching for information about health on social media	Jokić-Begić et.al. (2019)
	CYB2	After searching for health information on social media, I feel frustrated	
	CYB3	Once I start learning about healthcare on social media, I can't stop	
Fear of Information Posted on Social Media (FIPSM)	FIPSM 1	Whenever I read news or stories about healthcare on social media, I start to feel nervous and anxious	Jokić-Begić et.al. (2019)
	FIPSM 2	What scares me the most are health crisis events posted on social media	

We used the probability sampling method to study the general population. Georgia's population as of the 2023 census is 3726400, of which 229400 are Internet users over the age of 18, which is the population our study is aimed at National Statistics Office of Georgia (2023). It was calculated that 374 participants would make up the sample size for our study with a margin of error of 5% and a 95% confidence level. Studies show that the average response rate from mailed questionnaires is 70–75%, which is a good result (Heslop et al. 1998). Taking this into account, we contacted 747 respondents using social networks, from which we received 555 completed questionnaires, which is 74.3% of the total number. The statistical program SPSS -27 was used to process the data. Researchers utilize Cronbach's alpha coefficient in comparable studies to identify dependability measures. If the dependability coefficient is 0.60 or greater, it is deemed acceptable (Nunnally 1967). According to our reliability data, Cronbach's alpha coefficient was 0.945 for all six variables and more than 0.8 for each variable, indicating a much higher dependable coefficient.

4 Main Findings and Discussion

Out of 555 respondents participating in the study, 357 are women (64.3%), and 198 (35.7%) are men. Most respondents (43.6%) are 18–24 years old, 32.3% are 25–35 years old, and the rest (24.1%) are over 35 years old. Respondents were asked to rate, based on their opinions and experiences, how important it is for health care providers to engage in social media. The research showed that the mentioned issue is very important for 27% of the respondents, and somewhat important for 31%. 27% of respondents show a neutral attitude towards such activities, while a small part of respondents (8%) consider it somewhat insignificant or very insignificant.

As indicated above, among the hypotheses we formulated, H1 concerns the effect of too many sources of online health information on information overload. Taking this into account, we used regression analysis to prove the H1 hypothesis. As can be seen from Table 2, the model we developed is reliable ($P = 00.000$; $F > F_{critical}$ $329.261 > 3.84$). Hypothesis H1 was supported, therefore, constant exposure to too many sources of information on social media is directly and positively related to information overload. Moreover, R square = 0.373, which allows us to say that 37.3% of information overload is caused by the influence of information sources, and the rest is explained by other factors.

To analyze the obtained data, we used a linear regression model, which has the following form:

$$\Upsilon i = \beta 0 + \beta 1 Xi + ei \quad (1)$$

Where: Υi = dependent or criterion variable; $\beta 0$ = line crossing; $\beta 1$ = slope of the line; Xi = independent or predictor variable; ei is the error associated with the i –th observation.

Inserting the data from Table 2 into Eq. (1), we get the following equation:

$$\text{Information overload}(\widehat{Y}) = 0.882 + .0427(\text{Information sources posted on social media}) \quad (2)$$

Equation (2) allows us to say that an increase in information sources posted on social media by one unit leads to an increase in information overload by 0.427 units.

The second of the hypotheses we formulated concerns the impact of information overload on cyberchondria. Taking this into account, we used regression analysis to prove the H2 hypothesis. As can be seen from Table 3, the model developed by us is reliable ($P = 00.000$; $F > F_{critical}$ $95.101 > 3.84$). The H2 hypothesis was supported. Information overload is directly and positively related to cyberchondria. Also, R square = 0.147, which allows us to say that 14.7% of cyberchondria is caused by information overload, and the rest is explained by other factors.

Table 2. Regression analysis of the impact of information sources posted on social media on information overload

a) **Model Summary**				
Model	R	R Square	Adjusted R Square	Std. Error of the Estimate
1	.611 a	.373	.372	2.27057

a. Predictors: (Constant), Information sources posted on social media

b) ANOVA						
Model		Sum of Squares	df	Mean Square	F	Sig.
1	Regression	1697.499	1	1697.499	329.261	0.000b
	Residual	2850.981	553	5.155		
	Total	4548.479	554			

a. Dependent Variable: Information overload

b. Predictors: (Constant), Information sources posted on social media

c) Coefficients [a]						
Model		Unstandardized Coefficients		Unstandardized Coefficients	t	Sig.
		B	Std. Error	Beta		
1	(Constant)	.882	.434		2.031	.043
	Information sources posted on social media	.427	.024	.611	18.146	0.000

a. Dependent Variable: Information overload

Source: SPSS output based on own data

Inserting the data from Table 3 into Eq. (1), we get the following equation:

$$\text{Cyberchondria}(\widehat{Y}) = 5.949 + 0.408(\text{Information overload}) \tag{3}$$

Table 3. Regression analysis of the impact of information overload on cyberchondria

a) **Model Summary**

Model	R	R Square	Adjusted R Square	Std. Error of the Estimate
1	.383a	.147	.145	2.82304

a. Predictors: (Constant), Information overload

b) **ANOVA**

Model		Sum of Squares	df	Mean Square	F	Sig.
1	Regression	757.910	1	757.910	95.101	0.000b
	Residual	4407.164	553	7.970		
	Total	5165.074	554			

a. Dependent Variable: Cyberchondria

b. Predictors: (Constant), Information overload

c) **Coefficients** [a]

Model		Unstandardized Coefficients		Unstandardized Coefficients	t	Sig.
		B	Std. Error	Beta		
1	(Constant)	5.949	.378		15.740	0.000
	Information overload	.408	.042	.383	9.752	0.000

b. Dependent Variable: Cyberchondria

Source:SPSS output based on own data

Equation (3) allows us to say that an increase in information overload by one unit leads to an increase in cyberchondria by 0.408 units.

The third of the hypotheses we formulated concerns the effect of cyberchondria on fear of information posted on social media. We used regression analysis to prove hypothesis H3. As can be seen from Table 4, the model we developed is reliable (P = 00.000; $F > F_{critical}$ 816.478 > 3.84). Hypothesis H3 was supported. Fear of health information posted on social media is directly and positively related to cyberphobia. Also, R-squared = 0.596, which allows us to say that 59.6% of the fear of health information posted on social media is caused by cyberphobia, and the rest is explained by other factors.

Table 4. Regression analysis of the impact of cyberchondria on fear of information posted on social media

a) Model Summary

Model	R	R Square	Adjusted R Square	Std. Error of the Estimate
1	.772a	.596	.595	1.19373

a. Predictors: (Constant), Cyberchondria

b) ANOVA

Model		Sum of Squares	df	Mean Square	F	Sig.
1	Regression	1163.475	1	1163.475	816.478	0.000b
	Residual	788.021	553	1.425		
	Total	1951.495	554			

a. Dependent Variable: Fear of information posted on social media

b. Predictors: (Constant), Cyberchondria

c) Coefficients [a]

Model		Unstandardized Coefficients		Unstandardized Coefficients	t	Sig.
		B	Std. Error	Beta		
1	(Constant)	1.941	.165		11.772	0.000
	Cyber-chondria	.475	.017	.772	28.574	0.000

c. Dependent Variable: Fear of information posted on social media

Source:SPSS output based on own data

Inserting the data from Table 4 into Eq. (1), we get the following equation:

$$\text{Fear of information posted on social media}(\widehat{Y}) = 1.941 + 0.475(\text{Cyberchondria}) \tag{4}$$

Equation (4) allows us to say that a one-unit increase in cyberchondria leads to a 0.475-unit increase in fear of health-related information posted on social media.

Based on the data described above, we can build a structural equation model, which is shown in Fig. 2.

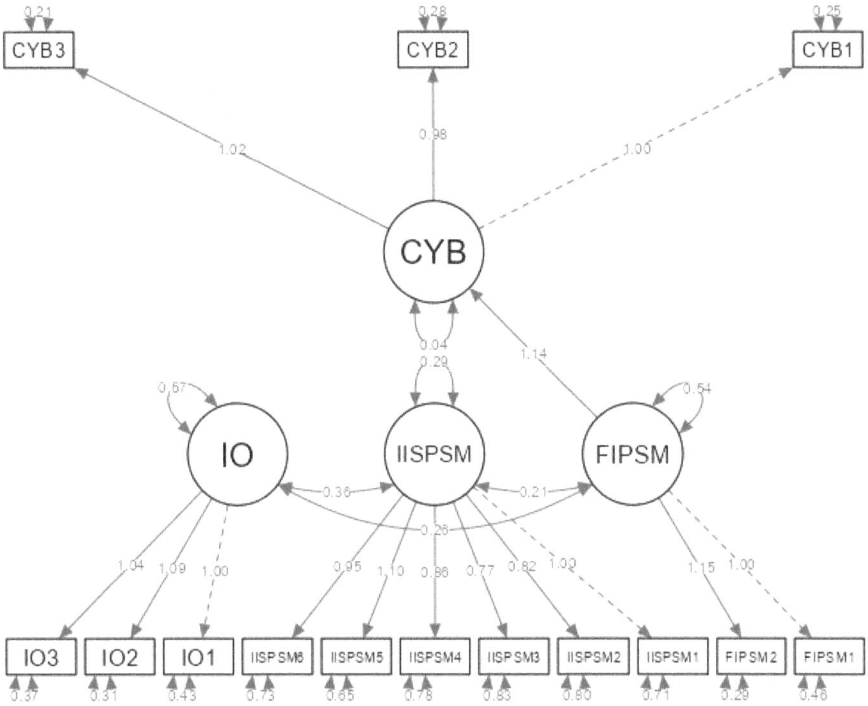

Fig. 2. Structural equation model (according to research results)

5 Conclusion, Limitations and Future Research

Our research shows that excessive exposure to online information sources causes information overload in Georgian consumers, which directly affects their psychological state (cyberchondria) and fear of information posted on social media. Given that crisis events are more of an anomaly than the norm, data collection is a serious problem. With this in mind, we recommend that research and governmental organizations (for example, health structures and statistical services) collect data whenever exogenous factors emerge in order to contribute to a broader understanding of crisis events.

The investigation was carried out with a number of constraints taken into account. First of all, the overall number of respondents needed for the research is restricted depending on age categories due to practical reasons. The bulk of social media users in Georgia are between the ages of 18 and 35, hence this demographic was the study's primary emphasis. It would be intriguing to learn what less frequent users think. Despite the fact that the research participants came from various regions of Georgia, the majority of the data came from a consumer survey conducted in the nation's capital, Tbilisi. The bulk of Georgians who use social media reside in Tbilisi, which explains the rationale behind this ban.

This paper lays the groundwork for future research on the role of social media marketing activity and consumer behavior in crisis management. This paper offers a number of interesting directions for future research. First, it involves the problem of how information overload caused by social media posts affects customer satisfaction and purchase intention formation. The unknown nature of the development and implementation of similar marketing initiatives in the Georgian reality creates the perspective of future research. An additional area of research to be explored is the impact of information overload from social media posts on consumer purchase decisions and eWOM.

References

Addo, P.C., Jiaming, F., Kulbo, N.B., Liangqiang, L.: COVID-19: fear appeal favoring purchase behavior towards personal protective equipment. Serv. Ind. J. **40**, 471–490 (2020)

Ahmed, R.R., Streimikiene, D., Rolle, J.-A., Duc, P.A.: The COVID-19 pandemic and the antecedants for the impulse buying behavior of US citizens. J. Compet. **12**, 5–27 (2020)

Ahorsu, D.K., Lin, C.Y., Imani, V., Saffari, M., Griffiths, M.D., Pakpour, A.H.: The fear of COVID-19 scale: development and initial validation. Int. J. Ment. Health Addict. (2020)

Bermes, A.: Information overload and fake news sharing: A transactional stress perspective exploring the mitigating role of consumers' resilience during COVID-19. J. Retail. Consum. Serv. **61**, 102555 (2021)

Burroughs, J.E., Rindfleisch, A.: Materialism and well-being: a conflicting values perspective. J. Cons. Res. **2**, 348–370 (2002)

Chawla, Y., et al.: Predictors and outcomes of individual knowledge on early-stage pandemic: Social media, information credibility, public opinion, and behaviour in a large-scale global study. Inf. Process. Manag. **58**, 102720 (2021)

Chu, S.C., Kim, Y.: Determinants of consumer engagement in electronic Word-Of-Mouth (eWOM) in social networking sites. Int. J. Advert (2011)

Cuan-Baltazar and Mu˜noz-Perez, M.J., Robledo-Vega, C., P´erez-Zepeda, M.F., & Soto-Vega, E. , 2020.Cuan-Baltazar, J.Y., Mu˜noz-Perez, M.J., Robledo-Vega, C., P´erez-Zepeda, M.F., Soto-Vega, E.: Misinformation of COVID-19 on the Internet: infodemiology study. JMIR Public Heal. Surveill. **6**, e18444 (2020)

Duhachek, A.: Coping: a multidimensional, hierarchical framework of responses to stressful consumption episodes. J. Cons. Res. **31**, 41–53 (2005)

Farías, P.: Identifying the factors that influence eWOM in SNSs: the case of Chile. Int. J. Advert. **36**, 852–869 (2017)

Farooq, A., Laato, S., Islam, A.K.M.N.: Impact of online information on self-isolation intention during the COVID-19 pandemic: cross-sectional study. J. Med. Internet Res. **22**, e19128 (2020)

Huang, P.S., Paulino, Y.C., So, S., Chiu, D.K., Ho, K.K.: Guest editorial: COVID-19 pandemic and health informatics Part 2. Library Hi Tech **40**(2), 281–285 (2022)

Joki´c-Begi´c, N., Mikac, U., ˇCurˇzik, D., & Sangster Joki´c, C. , 2019. Joki´c-Begi´c, N., Mikac, U., ˇCurˇzik, D., Sangster Joki´c, C.: The development and validation of the short Cyberchondria Scale (SCS). J. Psychopathol. Behav. Assess. **41**, 662–676 (2019)

Kareklas, I., Muehling, D.D., Weber, T.: Reexamining health messages in the digital age: a fresh look at source credibility effects. J. Advert. **44**, 88–104 (2015)

Karr-Wisniewski, P., Lu, Y.: When more is too much: Operationalizing technology overload and exploring its impact on knowledge worker productivity. Comput. Hum. Behav. **26**(5), 1061–1072 (2010)

Kirschner, P.A.: Cognitive load theory: implications of cognitive load theory on the design of learning. Learn. Instr. **12**, 1–10 (2002)

Laato, S., Islam, A.K.M.N., Farooq, A., Dhir, A.: Unusual purchasing behavior during the early stages of the COVID-19 pandemic: the stimulus-organism- response approach. J. Retail. Consum. Serv. **57**, 102224 (2020)

Lee, J., Kim, K., Park, G., Cha, N.: The role of online news and social media in preventive action in times of infodemic from a social capital perspective: the caseof the COVID-19 pandemic in South Korea. Telemat. Inform. **64**, 101691 (2021)

Lee, K.Y., Choi, H.: Predictors of electronic word-of-mouth behavior on social networking sites in the United States and Korea: cultural and social relationship variables. Comput. Human Behav. **94**, 9–18 (2019)

Liu, H., Liu, W., Yoganathan, V., Osburg, V.-S.: COVID-19 information overload and generation Z's social media discontinuance intention during the pandemiclockdown. Technol. Forecast. Soc. Change **166**, 120600 (2021)

Loxton, M., Truskett, R., Scarf, B., Sindone, L., Baldry, G., Zhao, Y.: Consumer behaviour during crises: preliminary research on how coronavirus hasmanifested consumer panic buying, herd mentality, changing discretionary spending and the role of the media in influencing behaviour. J. Risk Financ. Manag. **13**, 166 (2020)

Malik, A., Dhir, A., Kaur, P., Johri, A.: Correlates of social media fatigue and academic performance decrement. Inf. Technol. People **34**, 557–580 (2020)

Matthes, J., Nanz, A., Stubenvoll, M., Heiss, R.: Processing news on social media. The political incidental news exposure model (PINE). Journalism **21**(8), 1031–1048(2020)

National Statistics Office of Georgia. (2023). https://www.geostat.ge/en

Nunnally, J.C.: Psychometric theory. McGraw-Hill Book Company, New York, NY (1967)

Saunders, M., Lewis, P., Thornhill, A.: Research methods for business students, 8th edn. Pearson Education Ltd, Harlow (2019)

Schmidt, S., Benke, C., Pan´e-Farr´e, C.A.: Purchasing under threat: changes in shopping patterns during the COVID-19 pandemic. PLoS One **16**, e0253231 (2021)

Soroya, S.H., Farooq, A., Mahmood, K., Isoaho, J., Zara, S.: From information seeking to information avoidance: understanding the health information behavior during a global health crisis. Inf. Process. Manag. **58**, 102440 (2021)

Talwar, S., Dhir, A., Singh, D., Virk, G.S., Salo, J.: Sharing of fake news on social media: application of the honeycomb framework and the third-person effect hypothesis. J. Retail. Consum. Serv. **57**, 102197 (2020)

Todua, N., Jashi, C., Todua, N.: The role of social media in healthcare marketing. In: Modern Healthcare Marketing in the Digital Era, pp. 26–41. IGI Global (2024)

Vismara, M., et al.: Is cyberchondria a new transdiagnostic digital compulsive syndrome? A systematic review of the evidence. Compr. Psychiatry **99**, 152167 (2020)

Wang, C., et al.: A longitudinal study on the mental health of general population during the COVID-19 epidemic in China. Brain Behav. Immun. **87**, 40–48 (2020)

Whelan, E., Islam, A.N., Brooks, S.: Applying the SOBC paradigm to explain how social media overload affects academic performance. Comput. Educ. **143**, 103692 (2020)

Zheng, H., Sin, S.-C.-J., Kim, H.K., Theng, Y.-L.: Cyberchondria: a systematic review. Internet Res. **31**, 677–698 (2020)

Artificial Intelligence Adoption in Recruitment, Positive Organizational Shock, and Career Development in the Higher Education Institutions in Nigeria

Roya Anvari(✉) and Desmond Oluwaseun Chibogu

School of Business and Administrative Studies, The University of Georgia, Kostava St. 77a, 0171 Tbilisi, Georgia
r.anvari@ug.edu.ge

Abstract. The advent of artificial intelligence (AI) in recruitment processes marks a transformative shift in human resource management, offering new efficiencies and insights while also introducing challenges and ethical considerations. Furthermore, this study posits a hypothesis that underscores the significance of positive organizational shock as a mediating factor in the relationship between AI adoption in recruitment and career development. This study aims to explore the multifaceted impacts of AI adoption in recruitment, examining how it influences positive organizational shocks and career development. It further seeks to understand how family support and emotional intelligence serve as moderating factors in this dynamic, offering insights that could guide both future research and practical applications in HR technology integration. A quantitative study took place in March 2023 among 246 h directors, HR managers, and HR officers in higher education institutions in Nigeria. SEM-PLS and SPSS were applied for data analysis. The results revealed that emotional intelligence enables educators to manage stress, regulate their emotions, and effectively communicate with colleagues and administrators, fostering a more conducive work environment amidst technological transformations. In the Nigerian higher education context, where interpersonal relationships and collaboration are highly valued, educators with high emotional intelligence may serve as role models for their peers, facilitating the smooth transition towards AI-enhanced recruitment practices and contributing positively to career development initiatives within academic institutions.

Keywords: Artificial Intelligence · Recruitment · Positive Organizational Shock · Career Development

1 Introduction

The advent of artificial intelligence (AI) in recruitment processes marks a transformative shift in human resource management, offering new efficiencies and insights while also introducing challenges and ethical considerations. The integration of AI technologies in recruitment, characterized by sophisticated algorithms and data analytics, has been

R. C. Geibel and S. Machavariani (Eds.): ISPC 2024, SPBE, pp. 292–301, 2025.
https://doi.org/10.1007/978-3-031-88052-0_23

shown to enhance decision-making processes, improve the matching of candidates to job roles, and potentially democratize the recruitment landscape by reducing human biases (Vivek 2023; Roemmich et al. 2023). However, this technological advancement also raises questions regarding privacy, the potential for algorithmic bias, and the implications for job seekers' experiences (Raghavan et al. 2020).

Positive organizational shock, a concept relatively underexplored in the context of AI-driven recruitment, refers to unexpected but beneficial disturbances that influence an organization's trajectory (Chowdhury et al. 2023). The application of AI in recruitment can lead to such shocks, fostering innovative hiring practices, uncovering unforeseen opportunities for organizational growth, and potentially reshaping organizational culture in positive ways (Biswas et al. 2024). Career development is intricately linked to these technological and organizational shifts. As AI tools become more prevalent, they can significantly influence individual career paths, offering personalized insights and forecasting future skill requirements, thereby informing both individual and organizational development strategies (Ekuma 2024). The impact of AI on career development is profound, suggesting a paradigm shift in how career progressions are managed and supported (McDonald and Hite 2023).

In this complex interplay, the role of family support emerges as a pivotal factor. Family support has been acknowledged as a crucial element in career resilience and adaptability, providing the emotional foundation that can influence individuals' engagement with and reactions to technological changes in the workplace (Lanigan 2009). Previous research has indicated that support in specific contexts can play a moderating role in individuals' adaptability, particularly in the realm of AI-driven recruitment and career development initiatives. Theoretical underpinnings suggest that the level of support available to individuals can influence their ability to adapt to new technologies and changes in their professional environments. For instance, studies by Dwivedi et al. (2021) and and Achmat (2023) have highlighted how varying levels of support in organizational settings can either enhance or hinder individuals' adaptability in response to technological advancements such as AI-driven recruitment processes. Therefore, it is reasonable to hypothesize that in contexts where robust support mechanisms are implemented alongside AI-driven initiatives, individuals may demonstrate greater adaptability due to the facilitative role of support. This assertion aligns with the theoretical frameworks proposing moderation effects between support, adaptability, and external factors such as technological innovations (Brown & Green 2019). Family support and emotional intelligence (EI) are critical factors that influence individuals' responses to support mechanisms and their adaptability in the context of AI-driven recruitment and career development initiatives. While family support has been acknowledged as a traditional moderator, playing a pivotal role in shaping individuals' resilience and reactions to workplace changes (Crosby 2024), EI serves as an essential individual characteristic that affects how individuals perceive and manage support and adapt to new technologies (Mahon2014; Warrier et al. 2024; Susanto et al. 2024). While EI may not be traditionally labeled as a moderator, it significantly influences the effectiveness of support mechanisms and individual adaptability within organizational contexts. High EI may enable individuals to better navigate the challenges posed by AI in recruitment, facilitating smoother transitions, enhancing engagement with new technologies, and ultimately leading to more positive career outcomes (Sihare 2024). Furthermore, this study posits a hypothesis that underscores the significance of positive organizational shock as a mediating factor in the relationship between AI adoption in recruitment and career development. Defined as unexpected yet beneficial disturbances within an organization, positive organizational shock has been theorized to catalyze transformative changes and foster growth (Trippl et al. 2024). In this context, the introduction of AI technologies in recruitment processes represents a disruptive innovation that can potentially lead to positive organizational shocks (Ambrogio et al. 2022). These shocks, characterized by unforeseen opportunities and innovative shifts, are believed to create fertile ground for career development initiatives and individual growth within the organization. By exploring the mediating role of positive organizational shock, this study aims to delve deeper into the mechanisms through which AI adoption influences career development outcomes, offering valuable insights into the dynamic interplay between technological innovation, organizational change, and individual career trajectories (Joseph et al. 2012; Dlouhy and Froidevaux 2024).

In the Nigerian context, the integration of AI technologies into recruitment processes within higher education institutions presents unique opportunities and challenges. As universities and colleges strive to attract and retain top academic talent, the adoption of AI in recruitment holds the promise of streamlining selection processes and identifying candidates who align closely with institutional goals and values (Omar and Burrell 2024). However, amidst these advancements, the role of family support cannot be overstated. In Nigeria, where familial ties often play a significant role in individuals' career decisions, the support and encouragement of family members can greatly influence how educators perceive and adapt to AI-driven recruitment practices (Rahiman and Kodikal 2024). Moreover, in a cultural context where familial networks provide both emotional and financial support, the degree of familial endorsement for pursuing career opportunities influenced by AI can significantly impact educators' career trajectories and job satisfaction within higher education institutions.

Furthermore, emotional intelligence emerges as a critical determinant of how educators in Nigerian higher education organizations navigate the integration of AI in recruitment and subsequent career development. Given the rapid pace of technological change and the potential for AI to disrupt traditional academic roles, educators with higher levels of emotional intelligence may exhibit greater resilience and adaptability in embracing these changes (Mishra 2024; Khassawneh et al. 2022; Floman et al. 2024). Emotional intelligence enables educators to manage stress, regulate their emotions, and effectively communicate with colleagues and administrators, fostering a more conducive work environment amidst technological transformations. In the Nigerian higher education context, where interpersonal relationships and collaboration are highly valued, educators with high emotional intelligence may serve as role models for their peers, facilitating the smooth transition towards AI-enhanced recruitment practices and contributing positively to career development initiatives within academic institutions.

This study aims to explore the multifaceted impacts of AI adoption in recruitment, examining how it influences positive organizational shocks and career development. It further seeks to understand how family support and emotional intelligence serve as moderating factors in this dynamic, offering insights that could guide both future research and practical applications in HR technology integration.

Statement of the Problem

The integration of Artificial Intelligence (AI) in recruitment processes represents a significant shift in organizational practices, promising to enhance efficiency, reduce biases, and transform talent acquisition strategies. Despite its potential, the rapid adoption of AI technologies raises critical questions regarding their impact on organizational dynamics, employee career development, and the broader implications for the workforce (Pandya and Wang 2024). While existing literature extensively explores the operational benefits of AI in recruitment (Balcioğlu and Artar 2024; Davenport and Ronanki 2018; Ali and Kallach 2024; Deepa et al. 2024), there is a notable gap in understanding the holistic effects of this technological integration, particularly in terms of positive organizational shock and subsequent career development opportunities for employees (Kerti et al. 2024; Wordsworth and Nilakant 2021; Mehreen and Ali 2022). Moreover, existing research indicates a gap in the literature regarding the moderating effects of individual-level factors, such as emotional intelligence (EI) and family support, on the relationship between AI adoption in recruitment and its outcomes. For instance, while studies by Krishnasamy (2024) and Tashev and Karpovich (2024) and Balcioğlu and Artar (2024) have extensively examined the impact of AI on recruitment processes, they have not delved into how EI and family support might influence employee responses to AI-driven recruitment practices. Similarly, research by Sattu et al. (2024). Highlights the benefits of AI in talent acquisition, yet fails to consider how individual differences in EI and family support could shape employees' perceptions and experiences in this context. Thus, there is a need for further investigation to elucidate the moderating role of these individual-level variables in the context of AI adoption in recruitment. Emotional intelligence and family support are pivotal in shaping individuals' adaptation to technological changes, their engagement with AI-driven processes, and their overall career trajectory. However, the extent to which these factors influence the assimilation of AI in recruitment and its implications for career development remains underexplored.

The lack of comprehensive insights into the dynamics of AI adoption in recruitment, particularly within the context of higher education organizations, presents a significant challenge for both institutions and HR practitioners. Without a nuanced understanding of how AI impacts positive organizational shock and career development in academia, institutions may struggle to fully capitalize on the potential benefits of AI in recruitment and effectively address associated challenges (Pandey et al. 2023; Budhwar et al. 2023; Masera 2024). This oversight can result in missed opportunities for cultivating a flexible, resilient, and skilled academic workforce and may also lead to unintended consequences such as decreased employee morale, retention issues, and disruptions to organizational culture. While existing literature offers valuable insights into individual components of the study, such as the operational benefits of AI in recruitment and the importance of emotional intelligence and family support in career development, it often falls short of providing a comprehensive and integrated examination of these dynamics within the unique context of higher education institutions (Crawford et al. 2024). Studies may focus primarily on the technical aspects of AI implementation or individual-level factors, neglecting to explore how AI adoption catalyzes positive organizational shocks and influences career development pathways in academia (Ruder-Hook 2018; Teixeira and Pacione 2024). Therefore, there is a clear research gap that necessitates empirical investigation into how AI adoption in recruitment interacts with emotional intelligence, family support, and other contextual factors to shape the organizational and employee experience within higher education organizations. By synthesizing these variables and conducting holistic research, scholars can provide actionable insights for HR practitioners and university administrators seeking to navigate the complexities of AI-driven recruitment and foster a supportive and adaptive academic environment.

Objectives

1. To investigate the relationship between AI adoption in recruitment and positive organizational shock.
2. To examine the relationship between AI adoption in recruitment and career development.
3. To explore the mediating role of positive organizational shock in the relationship between AI adoption in recruitment and career development.
4. To investigate the moderating role of emotional intelligence in the relationship between AI adoption in recruitment and positive organizational shock.
5. To explore the moderating role of family support in the relationship between positive organizational shock and career development.

Research Questions

1. What is the nature of the relationship between AI adoption in recruitment and positive organizational shock?
2. How does AI adoption in recruitment relate to career development outcomes?
3. Does positive organizational shock mediate the relationship between AI adoption in recruitment and career development, and if so, to what extent?
4. To what extent does emotional intelligence moderate the relationship between AI adoption in recruitment and positive organizational shock?
5. How does family support moderate the relationship between positive organizational shock and career development?

Research Model

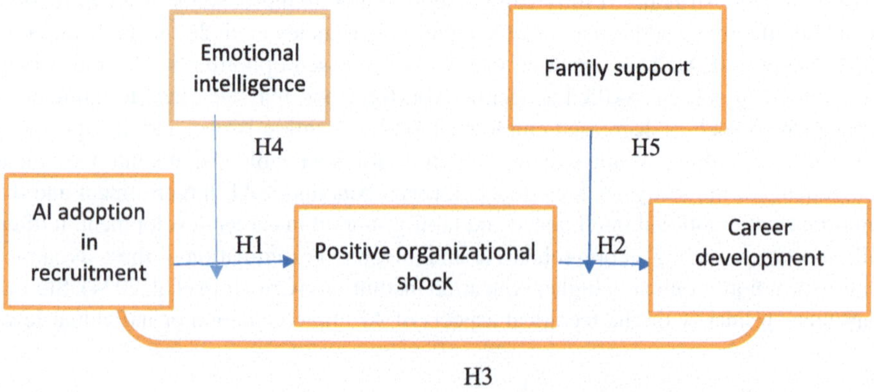

Hypotheses

H1: There is a positive relationship between AI adoption in recruitment and positive organizational shock.

H2: There is a positive relationship between AI adoption in recruitment and career development.

H3: Positive organizational shock mediates a relationship between AI adoption in recruitment and Career development.

H4: emotional intelligence moderates a relationship between AI adoption in recruitment and positive organizational shock.

H5: family support moderates a relationship between Positive organizational shock and career development.

2 Methodology

Research Design

This study employed a survey research design. This approach is well-suited for testing hypothesized relationships among variables through statistical analysis. It allows us to gather data from a large sample of employees and examine generalizable patterns.

Data Collection:

A survey forms the primary means of data collection. The survey was distributed to employees working in organizations that have adopted AI for recruitment processes.

Survey Instrument:

The survey was developed using validated scales to measure the following key constructs:

Independent Variable: AI Adoption in Recruitment (e.g., level of AI use in screening, interview scheduling, skills assessment)

Dependent Variables:

Positive Organizational Shock (POS) (e.g., feelings of surprise, stimulation due to positive changes brought about by AI)

Career Development (e.g., opportunities for growth, skill development perceived as a result of AI-driven recruitment processes)

Moderating Variables:

Family Support (e.g., encouragement, emotional support for career goals from family)

Emotional Intelligence (EI) (e.g., self-awareness, social awareness, self-management)

Mediating Variable:

Positive Organizational Shock (POS) (e.g. Increased engagement, enhanced perception, accelerated learning and adaptation)

Population

The population in the study consist of non-academic staff in universities in south west Nigeria. The non-academic staffs were chosen because they constitute secretaries, library personnel, It etc. therefore they have consistent interaction with computer system hence qualifying as first hand user of AI technology.

University	Location	Population
University of Lagos	Lagos	2,782
Lagos State University	Lagos	1,356
Olabisi Onabanjo University	Ogun	909
Covenant University	Ogun	441
Babcock University	Ogun	580
Tai Solarin University of Education	Ogun	572
Federal University of Agriculture, Abeokuta	Ogun	1393
Pan-Atlantic University	Lagos	360
	Total	8,393

Source: Nigeria University Commission (2022)

Sampling Technique

In order to get the sample size, the proportionate sampling technique was used to select 400 samples from the universities. First the proportion of each university's population was found from the overall population.

University of Lagos: $\frac{2,782}{8,393} = 0.331$

Lagos State University: $\frac{1,356}{8,393} = 0.161$

Olabisi Onabanjo University: $\frac{909}{8,393} = 0.108$

Covenant University: $\frac{441}{8,393} = 0.053$

Babcock University: $\frac{580}{8,393} = 0.069$

Tai Solarin University of Education: $\frac{572}{8,393} = 0.068$

Federal University of Agriculture, Abeokuta: $\frac{1,393}{8,393} = 0.166$

Pan-Atlantic University: $\frac{360}{8,393} = 0.043$

Based on the proportion, each percentage was multiplied by 400

University	Location	Population	Sample
University of Lagos	Lagos	2,782	132
Lagos State University	Lagos	1,356	64
Olabisi Onabanjo University	Ogun	909	43
Covenant University	Ogun	441	21
Babcock University	Ogun	580	28
Tai Solarin University of Education	Ogun	572	27
Federal University of Agriculture, Abeokuta	Ogun	1393	67
Pan-Atlantic University	Lagos	360	17
	Total	8,393	400

Data Analysis:

Structural Equation Modeling (SEM) was used to analyze the data, this is so that the direct effect of AI adoption on POS and career development can be hypothesized, and also examine the moderating effects of family support and EI on these relationships. This enabled us assess whether they strengthen or weaken the impact of AI adoption on the outcomes. This will be done using SPSS version 27

Scope of the Study

The scope of the study encompasses eight universities located in Lagos and Ogun states, Nigeria. Specifically, the research will focus on examining the impact of AI adoption in recruitment processes within these higher education institutions. This includes investigating how the integration of AI technologies influences organizational dynamics, positive organizational shocks, and career development outcomes among faculty and staff members.

3 Conclusion

The study is significant because the beneficiaries of this study span across various stakeholders within both organizational and individual contexts. Firstly, organizations stand to gain substantial insights into the impacts of AI adoption in recruitment on their overall organizational dynamics. By understanding the relationship between AI adoption and positive organizational shock, organizations can better strategize their technological implementations to leverage transformative opportunities. Moreover, insights into how positive organizational shock influences career development can guide organizational policies and practices aimed at fostering employee growth and retention. Additionally, by exploring the moderating effects of emotional intelligence and family support, organizations can tailor their support mechanisms and training programs to enhance employee resilience and adaptability in the face of technological disruptions. Overall, organizations can utilize the findings from this study to optimize their recruitment strategies, improve employee satisfaction and engagement, and ultimately drive organizational success in the rapidly evolving digital landscape. Individually, employees and job seekers also stand to benefit significantly from the outcomes of this study. By gaining insights into how AI adoption in recruitment impacts career development trajectories, individuals can make informed decisions regarding their career paths and skill development strategies. Understanding the mediating role of positive organizational shock can empower individuals to navigate organizational changes more effectively, capitalize on emerging opportunities, and proactively shape their professional trajectories. Moreover, insights into the moderating effects of emotional intelligence and family support can empower individuals to cultivate these personal attributes and seek out supportive networks that facilitate their career advancement and adaptability in the face of technological disruptions. Ultimately, the findings from this study can equip individuals with the knowledge and resources needed to thrive in the evolving workplace landscape, enhancing their employability, job satisfaction, and overall career success.

References

Achmat, L.: Artificial intelligence affordances for organisational change: perspectives from south african artificial intelligence practitioners (2023)

Ali, O., Kallach, L.: Artificial intelligence enabled human resources recruitment functionalities: a scoping review. Procedia Comput. Sci. **232**, 3268–3277 (2024)

Deepa, R., Sekar, S., Malik, A., Kumar, J., Attri, R.: Impact of AI-focussed technologies on social and technical competencies for HR managers–a systematic review and research agenda. Technol. Forecast. Soc. Chang. **202**, 123301 (2024)

Ambrogio, G., Filice, L., Longo, F., Padovano, A.: Workforce and supply chain disruption as a digital and technological innovation opportunity for resilient manufacturing systems in the COVID-19 pandemic. Comput. Ind. Eng. **169**, 108158 (2022)

Balcioğlu, Y.S., Artar, M.: Artificial intelligence in employee recruitment. Global Business and Organizational Excellence (2024)

Biswas, K.K., Boyle, B., Bhardwaj, S., Patel, P.: Managerial religiosity, attitudes towards women as managers and supportive HR practices. Int. J. Emerg. Mark. **19**(1), 154–169 (2024)

Brown, A.H., Green, T. D.: The essentials of instructional design: Connecting fundamental principles with process and practice. Routledge (2019)

Budhwar, P., Malik, A., De Silva, M.T., Thevisuthan, P.: Artificial intelligence–challenges and opportunities for international HRM: a review and research agenda. Int. J. Hum. Resource Manage. **33**(6), 1065–1097 (2022)

Chowdhury, S., et al.: Unlocking the value of artificial intelligence in human resource management through AI capability framework. Hum. Resour. Manag. Rev. **33**(1), 100899 (2023)

Crawford, J., Allen, K.A., Pani, B., Cowling, M.: When artificial intelligence substitutes humans in higher education: the cost of loneliness, student success, and retention. Stud. High. Educ. **49**(5), 883–897 (2024)

Crosby, I.E.: Social support in black individuals: the moderating effects on the relationship between resilience and well-being (2024)

Dlouhy, K., Froidevaux, A.: Evolution of professionals' careers upon graduation in STEM and occupational turnover over time: Patterns, diversity characteristics, career success, and self-employment. J. Organ. Behav. **45**(3), 344–361 (2024)

Dwivedi, Y.K., et al.: Artificial Intelligence (AI): multidisciplinary perspectives on emerging challenges, opportunities, and agenda for research, practice and policy. Int. J. Inf. Manage. **57**, 101994 (2021)

Ekuma, K.: Artificial intelligence and automation in human resource development: a systematic review. Hum. Resour. Dev. Rev. **23**(2), 199–229 (2024)

Floman, J.L., Ponnock, A., Jain, J., Brackett, M.A.: Emotionally intelligent school leadership predicts educator well-being before and during a crisis. Front. Psychol. **14**, 1159382 (2024)

Joseph, D., Boh, W.F., Ang, S., Slaughter, S.A.: The career paths less (or more) traveled: A sequence analysis of IT career histories, mobility patterns, and career success. Mis Quar. 427–452 (2012)

Kerti, K. A., Van Engen, M., Szabó, O., Kroon, B., Bleijenbergh, I., Freese, C.: Precarious employment amidst global crises: career shocks, resources and migrants' employability. Career Development International (2024)

Khassawneh, O., Mohammad, T., Ben-Abdallah, R., Alabidi, S.: The relationship between emotional intelligence and educators' performance in higher education sector. Behav. Sci. **12**(12), 511 (2022)

Krishnasamy, K.: Exploring students' perspectives on AI-based recruitment processes: challenges and job readiness (2024)

Lanigan, J.D.: A sociotechnological model for family research and intervention: how information and communication technologies affect family life. Marriage Fam. Rev. **45**(6–8), 587–609 (2009)

Mahon, E.G., Taylor, S.N., Boyatzis, R.E.: Antecedents of organizational engagement: exploring vision, mood and perceived organizational support with emotional intelligence as a moderator. Front. Psychol. **5**, 113630 (2014)

Masera, M.L.: Redefining tomorrow: a comprehensive analysis of AI'S impact on employment and identity (2024)

McDonald, K.S., Hite, L.M.: Career development: A human resource development perspective. Routledge (2023)

Mehreen, A., Ali, Z.: Really shocks can't be ignored: the effects of career shocks on career development and how family support moderates this relationship?. Int. J. Educ. Vocation. Guidan. 1–26 (2022)

Mishra, R.: Embracing a paradigm shift: transitioning from traditional teaching methods to AI-BASED NLP EDUCATION. Res. Rev. Literat. Soc. Sci. **75** (2024)

Omar, M., Burrell, D.N.: Organizational dynamics and bias in Artificial Intelligence (AI) recruitment algorithms. In: Evolution of Cross-Sector Cyber Intelligent Markets, pp. 269–290. IGI Global (2024)

Pandey, A., Balusamy, B., Chilamkurti, N. (eds.): Disruptive artificial intelligence and sustainable human resource management: impacts and innovations-The future of HR. CRC Press (2023)

Pandya, S.S., Wang, J.: Artificial intelligence in career development: a scoping review. Hum. Resour. Dev. Int. **27**(3), 324–344 (2024)

Raghavan, M., Barocas, S., Kleinberg, J., Levy, K.: Mitigating bias in algorithmic hiring: evaluating claims and practices. In: Proceedings of the 2020 Conference on Fairness, Accountability, and Transparency, pp. 469–481 (2020)

Rahiman, H.U., Kodikal, R.: Revolutionizing education: Artificial intelligence empowered learning in higher education. Cogent Educ. **11**(1), 2293431 (2024)

Roemmich, K., Rosenberg, T., Fan, S., Andalibi, N.: Values in emotion artificial intelligence hiring services: technosolutions to organizational problems. Proc.. ACM Huma. Comput. Interact. **7**(CSCW1), 1–28 (2023)

Ruder-Hook, M.: Organizational adoption of AI through a sociocultural lens (Doctoral dissertation) (2018)

Sattu, R., Das, S., Jena, L.K.: Should I adopt AI during talent acquisition? Evidence from HR professionals of Indian IT organisations. J. Organiz. Effect. People Perform. (2024)

Sihare, S.R.: Student dropout analysis in higher education and retention by artificial intelligence and machine learning. SN Comput. Sci. **5**(2), 202 (2024)

Susanto, H., et al.: Leveraging technology enhancement: the well-being emotional intelligence, security keys to the university students' readiness in digital learning ecosystem. Sustainability **16**(9), 3765 (2024)

Tasheva, Z., Karpovich, V.: Transformation of recruitment process through implementation of AI solutions. J. Manage. Econ. **4**(02), 12–17 (2024)

Teixeira, N., Pacione, M.: Implications of artificial intelligence on leadership in complex organizations: an exploration of the near future (2024)

Trippl, M., Fastenrath, S., Isaksen, A.: Rethinking regional economic resilience: preconditions and processes shaping transformative resilience. Eur. Urban Region. Stud. **31**(2), 101–115 (2024)

Vivek, R.: Enhancing diversity and reducing bias in recruitment through AI: a review of strategies and challenges. Информатика. Экономика. Управление/Informatics. Economics. Management **2**(4), 0101–0118 (2023)

Warrier, U., Shankar, A., Belal, H.M.: Examining the role of emotional intelligence as a moderator for virtual communication and decision making effectiveness during the COVID-19 crisis: revisiting task technology fit theory. Ann. Oper. Res. **335**(3), 1519–1535 (2024)

Wordsworth, R., Nilakant, V.: Unexpected change: career transitions following a significant extra-organizational shock. J. Vocat. Behav. **127**, 103555 (2021)

Enhancing Team Performance Through Emotional Intelligence Leadership: A Digital Management and Artificial Inteligence Perspective in Qatar Airways

Roya Anvari(✉)

School of Business and Administrative Studies, The University of Georgia, Kostava Street 77a, 0171 Tbilisi, Georgia
r.anvari@ug.edu.ge

Abstract. This study explores the intricate relationship between emotional intelligence (EI) in leadership and team performance at Qatar Airways, integrating digital management tools and artificial intelligence (AI) techniques within the unique socio-cultural context of the organization. Employing both qualitative and quantitative research methods, this investigation draws on secondary research sources and utilizes a Likert-scale questionnaire administered to 187 participants selected via random sampling. Grounded in Daniel Goleman's EI model, the questionnaire examines demographics, teamwork quality, team performance, and mediating/moderating factors. Leveraging AI, including machine learning algorithms and sentiment analysis tools, enhances the data analysis process, providing deeper and more accurate insights. Digital management systems are utilized to perform regression analysis and test hypotheses, revealing statistically significant relationships between a leader's emotional intelligence and both team quality and performance. The findings underscore the pivotal role of emotional intelligence in fostering effective team dynamics and enhancing overall team performance within Qatar Airways. This study contributes to a deeper understanding of socio-cultural factors such as human development and psychology within organizational contexts and demonstrates the importance of emotional intelligence in leadership for sustainable socio-cultural development. By integrating AI and digital management tools, the research offers innovative strategies for improving leadership effectiveness in modern organizational environments.

Keywords: Emotional Intelligence · Leadership · Team Dynamics · Digital Management · Artificial Intelligence

1 Introduction

This report aims to critically assess the existing management practices at Qatar Airways, a leading airline in the aviation industry, through the lens of socio-cultural dynamics and psychological perspectives on human development. In this analysis, we will explore how leadership and management practices within Qatar Airways influence team performance,

R. C. Geibel and S. Machavariani (Eds.): ISPC 2024, SPBE, pp. 302–309, 2025.
https://doi.org/10.1007/978-3-031-88052-0_24

considering the socio-cultural context and psychological aspects of human behavior. Notably, Qatar Airways is renowned for its strong values, which are deeply embedded in its organizational culture and management practices, emphasizing employee training and development to uphold values of excellence and customer focus (Theodoropoulou 2019; Sulistya and Ginaya 2020). Throughout this report, we will delve into the socio-cultural dimensions of Qatar Airways' mission, values, and management practices, examining their psychological impact on employee development and team dynamics.

Founded in 1993, Qatar Airways, under the leadership of CEO Akbar Al Baker, has demonstrated a commitment to enhancing market operations and infrastructure, with a workforce of 46,684 employees. The leadership practices within Qatar Airways reflect a transformational approach, emphasizing team collaboration and motivation as essential for maintaining customer service standards (Lee 2018). This transformation underscores the evolving nature of leadership in today's corporate world, where EIplays a pivotal role in driving team performance and organizational success Shahhosseini et al. 2012; Salovey and Mayer 1990).

As we explore the facets of EI within the context of leadership at Qatar Airways, we recognize its profound implications for team dynamics and performance. EI, encompassing the ability to perceive, understand, regulate, and utilize emotions effectively, is increasingly recognized as a key determinant of leadership effectiveness and organizational outcomes (Wang 2021; Wong and Law 2002). This concept paper seeks to unravel how leaders at Qatar Airways demonstrate EI in their interactions with team members and stakeholders, and how this influences team performance within the aviation sector's complex socio-cultural landscape.

Achieving optimal team performance within organizations hinges on effective leadership practices. However, the dynamics between leadership and team success are often influenced by the unique socio-cultural context and psychological aspects of human development. This study investigates these dynamics at Qatar Airways, a leading airline, by exploring the role of EI in leadership and its impact on team performance.

The central issue under consideration is the need to understand the role of EI in leadership within the socio-cultural context of Qatar Airways, and its impact on team performance. Despite growing recognition of the importance of EI in leadership effectiveness, there remains a dearth of research exploring its direct consequences on team dynamics and performance within the aviation industry. This knowledge gap impedes Qatar Airways' ability to optimize leadership strategies and enhance team performance, highlighting the significance of investigating the intricate relationship between EI in leadership and team dynamics. While current management practices undoubtedly play a part (as mentioned earlier), this research emphasizes emotional intelligence as a central factor in leadership effectiveness. We will delve deeper into the concept of EI and its influence on leader-team interactions and ultimately, team performance. This study goes beyond traditional methods by integrating AI and digital management tools for data analysis, offering a more nuanced understanding of the relationship between EI and team outcomes.

This research aims to explore the involvement of EI in leadership within Qatar Airways and evaluate its effects on team performance, considering socio-cultural influences and psychological dimensions. By examining EI competencies exhibited by leaders and their impact on team interactions and performance, this study seeks to offer insights into the interplay between leadership, EI, and team dynamics within Qatar Airways' unique socio-cultural context.

This investigation seeks to unravel the intricate relationship between a leader's emotional intelligence and team performance at Qatar Airways. We employ a combination of qualitative and quantitative research methods, including advanced machine learning algorithms and sentiment analysis tools (aspects of AI). By examining these factors within the airline's specific socio-cultural context, we aim to provide valuable insights into how EI impacts team dynamics and contributes to overall success at Qatar Airways.

2 Research Objectives

1. To examine EI in leadership within the socio-cultural context of Qatar Airways.
2. To investigate the relationship between leaders' EI and team performance, considering socio-cultural influences.
3. To identify management practices at Qatar Airways and their implications for team dynamics and performance.

Hypotheses

Main Hypothesis: H0 - Leaders' EI has no significant relationship with teamwork quality and team performance at Qatar Airways.

Sub Hypothesis: H0 - The relationship between leaders' EI and team performance is moderated by contextual factors such as team size or industry type.

3 Conceptual Model

(See Fig. 1)

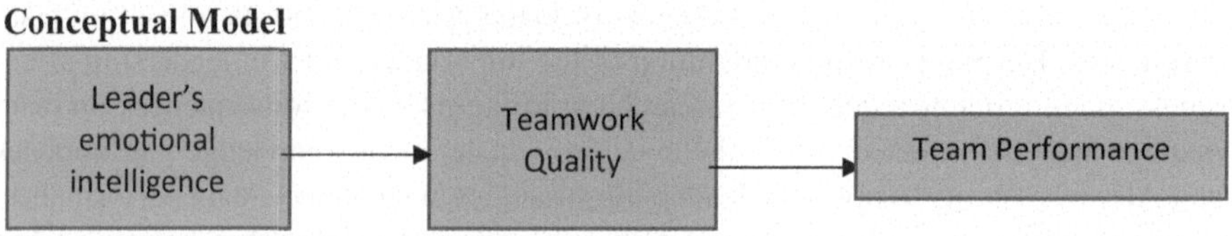

Fig. 1. Conceptual Model

4 Litratute Review

The Impact of EI in Management Behaviors on Employee Engagement and Organizational Performance

Current EI strategy in Qatar Airways

A partnership has been established between Qatar Airways and Six Seconds to implement an upgraded EI training program. Customized EI training will be provided to onboard leaders and all customer experience staff to enhance employee & organization performance as well as customer experience (Anvari et al. 2023). Employees receive guidance on the best practices for handling their emotions, reacting to clients with empathy, and handling difficult circumstances with self-control through workshops and training sessions (Albasoos et al. 2021). Furthermore, significant emphasis is placed by Qatar Airways on EI in leadership roles. Senior executives take an active role in EQ training in order to set an example for others and encourage an EI culture within the company.

The impact of Qatar Airways' emotional intelligence on employee performance.

By fostering a culture of emotional intelligence, positive changes have been observed in various segments of its workforce by the association (Pryke et al. 2015). Consequently, the commitment of Qatar Airways to EQ training has resulted in enhanced communication and relationships among employees. Therefore, by recognizing and understanding the emotions and needs of travelers, personalized and empathetic services can be provided by customer experienced staff, leading to greater customer satisfaction and loyalty (Liu et al. 2024). Emotional intelligence training has positively impacted employee stress and resilience (Saikia et al. 2024). This has led to a reduction in burnout rates and an overall improvement in employee well-being, contributing to a more connected and motivated workforce (Ajayi and Udeh 2024). Thus, a direct correlation between emotional intelligence and leadership effectiveness has also been noted by the organization. According to Aras and Özel (2024) Qatar Airways has cultivated an emotionally intelligent organizational culture. The impact of emotional intelligence on employee performance has been demonstrated through improved communication, enhanced customer relationships, better stress management, and more effective leadership.

How Qatar Airways manages its Teams

A management philosophy endorsing employees in their pursuit of innovation is encompassed by transformational leadership (Malik 2024). By doing so, the encouragement of employees'.

contribution is aimed at carving out a new path towards growth and expanding the trajectory of the company's future. Trusted employees of the organization are empowered by this theory to make decisions and approach problems in a novel manner with complete independence (Wang et al. 2024). The highlighting of outdated business frameworks and the emphasis on streamlining changes in them are the focus areas of a transformative leader (Okuyan and Begen 2022). Additionally, they play a role in assisting others to succeed on their path of innovation. The forefront handling of the problem in an individual capacity is carried out by the expert decision-making of its skilled leader (Liu 2024). As a result, the control over the affair is loosened by the headquarters, which issues only an overall regulatory framework and oversees further development. With a participative style of leadership being adopted, a role in the decision-making process is afforded to employees (Nguyen et al. 2024). This renders the strategy of Qatar Airways all-encompassing (Brannagan and Reiche 2022). Control over current and potential future conflicts is facilitated by such an approach, enabling the management to actively take action or make concerted efforts in resolving them promptly.

How Qatar Airways manages its Stakeholders

In the 21st century, ‘Managing for stakeholders’ is characterized, according to Edward Freeman. Emphasis on the interconnection among different entities involved in the entire transaction cycle, including customers, suppliers, investors, employees, and communities, is laid by stakeholder theory (Freeman et al. 2007). The creation of economic value for stakeholders is not only involved by the stakeholder theory but also advocates for societal needs and the overall needs of the community. According to this theory, the interests of all stakeholders need to be balanced by managers as part of their moral obligation, and they are not mere comparators of the shareholders (Filimonau et al. 2022). A seamless transformation is facilitated by Qatar Airways, as a sacred connection is upheld with all stakeholders. The implementation of a flatter organizational hierarchy at Qatar Airways has given rise to a management style characterized by fewer individuals at the managerial level, fostering progressive and knowledgeable leadership. This, in turn, opens up additional opportunities for individuals to engage with senior management, instilling a sense of security and confidence among the employees (DuBrin 2024; Anvari et al. 2024).

Key challenges faced by Qatar Airways

Competition

In comparison to other airline industries, Qatar Airways faces a higher competition. Rate wars and diminished income margins, driven by escalating competition, necessitated a continual evaluation of the competitive landscape, specific identification of cost propositions, and a dedicated focus on delivering exceptional patron experiences for Qatar Airways. To overcome this challenge, passive measures are employed, ensuring a consistent assessment of the competitive environment and the identification of distinctive cost propositions that prioritize providing outstanding customer experiences (Silalahi and Windasari 2024). The airline actively addresses the impact of competition through a strategic and passive approach, emphasizing the ongoing commitment to excellence in customer service.

Substantial demand for affordable prices

The search for inexpensive flight tickets that offer improved services and features such as entertainment, comfortable seating, and enhanced internet connectivity is sought after by customers.

Striking a balance between customer demands and the pricing of flight tickets poses a considerable challenge. Investment in operational services and the enhancement of the overall customer experience is recommended for Qatar Airways to meet these demands. Passively, the airline should focus on improving operational services to deliver an enhanced customer experience that aligns with customer expectations for affordability and quality (Kaplan and Norton 2008).

Fuel Price Volatility

Operational costs are directly influenced by the fluctuations in oil prices, thereby presenting a challenge for airlines in effectively managing fuel expenses. The dynamic nature of oil prices introduces an element of uncertainty, necessitating strategic and proactive measures to address the impact on operational expenditures. This challenge underscores the importance for airlines to employ comprehensive fuel management strategies that can adapt to the ever-changing economic landscape, ensuring a resilient and cost-effective approach to sustaining operational efficiency in the face of fluctuating oil prices (Prahalad and Ramaswamy 2004; Payne et al. 2017).

5 Methodology

This study outlines the approach for conducting a descriptive study on Emotional Intelligence in leaders, incorporating the specified elements related to EI research and challenges faced by Qatar Airways. This research utilizes a combination of qualitative and quantitative methods, drawing on the EI model developed by Daniel Goleman. Data collection involves secondary research and survey methods, with descriptive and inferential statistics employed for analysis. The theoretical framework is informed by online sources and news articles about Qatar Airways, contextualizing the study within the airline industry's socio-cultural dynamics.

Population of the Study

The study population comprises employees and management of Qatar Airways, reflecting the socio-cultural diversity within the organization.

Sample Size and Sampling Technique.

A Likert-scale questionnaire was administered to a sample of 200 employees selected through random sampling, ensuring representation across different roles and departments within Qatar Airways.

6 Conclusion

The exploration of the involvement of EI in leadership within the context of Qatar Airways and its impact on team performance in Qatar constituted the primary aim of this study. Both hypotheses were tested and found to be statistically significant. The study asserts a positive relationship between EI and teamwork quality at Qatar Airways. This suggests that leaders exhibiting higher levels of EI tend to contribute positively to the quality of teamwork within the organization. Furthermore, the study establishes a positive correlation between EI and team performance at Qatar Airways, indicating that leaders with enhanced EI positively impact the overall performance of their teams.

References

Ajayi, F.A., Udeh, C.A.: Combating burnout in the IT Industry: a review of employee well-being initiatives. Int. J. Appl. Res. Soc. Sci. **6**(4), 567–588 (2024)

Albasoos, H., Hassan, G., Al Zadjali, S.: The Qatar crisis: Challenges and opportunities. Int. J. Res. Bus. Soc. Sci. **10**(1), 158–167, 2147–4478 (2021)

Anvari, R., Janjaria, M., Shirvani, A.: Role of line managers in human resource activities: evidence from a case study. Intangible Capital **20**(1), 43–59 (2024)

Anvari, R., Kumpikaitė-Valiūnienė, V., Mobarhan, R., Janjaria, M., Hosseinpour Chermahini, S.: Strategic human resource management practitioners' emotional intelligence and affective organizational commitment in higher education institutions in Georgia during post-COVID-19. PLoS ONE **18**(12), e0295084 (2023)

Aras, B., Özel, M.: Qatar Airways–FC Barcelona sponsorship deal: a catalyst of sports diplomacy?. Int. J. Sports Mark. Sponsorship (2024)

Birimoglu Okuyan, C., Begen, M.A.: Working from home during the COVID19- pandemic, its effects on health, and recommendations: the pandemic and beyond. Perspect. Psychiatr. Care **58**(1), 173–179 (2022)

Brannagan, P.M., Reiche, D.: Qatar and the 2022 FIFA World Cup: Politics, controversy, change. Springer Nature (2022)

DuBrin, A.J.: Leadership humility: a characteristic that enhances professional effectiveness. CRC Press (2024)

Filimonau, V., Ashton, M., Stankov, U.: Virtual spaces as the future of consumption intourism, hospitality and events. J. Tour. Futures (2022). https://www.emerald.com/insight/content/doi/https://doi.org/10.1108/JTF-07-2022-0174/full/html

Freeman, R.E., Harrison, J.S., Wicks, A.C.: Managing for stakeholders: Survival, reputation, and success. Yale University Press (2007)

Kaplan, R.S., Norton, D.P.: The execution premium: Linking strategy to operations for competitive advantage. Harvard business press (2008)

Lee, R.: Managing knowledge transfer: two cases of knowledge transfer in Saudi Arabia and Qatar, Doctoral dissertation, University of Manchester (2018)

Liu, S.Q., Vakeel, K.A., Smith, N.A., Alavipour, R.S., Wei, C., Wirtz, J.: AI concierge in the customer journey: what is it and how can it add value to the customer? J. Serv. Manag. **35**(6), 136–158 (2024)

Liu, W.S.K.: Global leadership dynamics: refining executive selection in multinational corporations. J. Knowl. Econ. 1–45 (2024)

Malik, P.: Individual-focused transformational leadership and change-oriented organizational citizenship behavior: mediating and moderating mechanisms of job crafting and employee resilience. J. Organ. Effect. People Perform. **11**(1), 90–113 (2024)

Nguyen, M., Sharma, P., Malik, A.: Leadership styles and employee creativity: the interactive impact of online knowledge sharing and organizational innovation. J. Knowl. Manag. **28**(3), 631–650 (2024)

Payne, A., Frow, P., Eggert, A.: The customer value proposition: evolution, development, and application in marketing. J. Acad. Mark. Sci. **45**, 467–489 (2017)

Prahalad, C.K., Ramaswamy, V.: The future of competition: Co-creating unique value with customers. Harvard Business Press (2004).

Pryke, S., Lunic, D., Badi, S.: The effect of leader emotional intelligence on leader–follower chemistry: a study of construction project managers. Constr. Manage. Econ. **33**, 603–624 (2015)

Saikia, M., George, L.S., Unnikrishnan, B., Nayak, B.S., Ravishankar, N.: Thirty years of emotional intelligence: A scoping review of emotional intelligence training programme among nurses. Int. J. Ment. Health Nurs. **33**(1), 37–51 (2024)

Salovey, P., Mayer, J.D.: Emotional intelligence. Imagin. Cogn. Pers. **9**(3), 185–211 (1990). https://doi.org/10.2190/DUGG-P24E-52WK-6CDG

Shahhosseini, M., Silong, A.D., Ismaill, I.A., Uli, J.N.: The role of emotional intelligence on job performance. Int. J. Bus. Soc. Sci. **3**, 241–246 (2012)

Silalahi, E.B.F., Windasari, N.: Elevating service design and customer experience: customer value proposition validation and design for new digital bank "Bank S" in Indonesia. J. Multidiscipl. Acad. Pract. Stud. **2**(2), 211–232 (2024)

Sulistya, I.A.P., Ginaya, G.: Corporate social responsibility implementation on aviationcompany: a case study in Qatar Airways. Int. J. Green Tour. Res. Appl. **2**(1), 41–46 (2020). https://ojs.pnb.ac.id/index.php/IJOGTRA/article/view/1879

Theodoropoulou, I.: Semioscaping Eutopia: Qatar as a place in Qatar Airways advertisements. Sociol. Stud. (2019)

Wang, H., Huang, Q., Xu, X., Liang, C.: Employees' feeling trusted, self-concept and creativity in collectivistic cultures. Curr. Psychol. **43**(10), 8972–8988 (2024)

Wang, Z.: Understanding the strategy used by leading airlines: a case study of Qatar Airways (2021). https://www.theseus.fi/bitstream/handle/10024/499832/Wang_Zijian.pdf?sequence=2

Wong, C.S., Law, K.S.: The effects of leader and follower emotional intelligence on performance and attitude: an exploratory study. Leadersh. Q. **13**, 243–274 (2002)

Digital Leadership and Artificial Intelligence: A Litrature Review

Roya Anvari(✉)

School of Business and Administrative Studies, The University of Georgia, Kostava Street 77a, 0171 Tbilisi, Georgia
r.anvari@ug.edu.ge

Abstract. Artificial intelligence (AI) is rapidly transforming various facets of organizational operations, and its integration into recruitment processes signifies a paradigm shift in human resource management. This review paper explores the intersection of artificial intelligence and digital leadership within the context of AI-driven recruitment, highlighting both the advancements and challenges. AI recruitment technologies, encompassing resume screening algorithms, and predictive analytics, are revolutionizing traditional hiring methods by enhancing efficiency, reducing biases, and improving candidate experiences. Digital leaders are crucial in navigating this transformation, as they must possess not only technical acumen but also strategic vision to leverage AI effectively. The paper synthesizes findings from a wide array of studies, examining how AI tools streamline recruitment workflows, from candidate sourcing and initial engagement to final selection. Moreover, it discusses the implications for digital leadership, emphasizing the need for leaders to develop new competencies to manage AI systems and foster a culture that embraces technological innovation. This paper contributes to the growing body of literature on AI and digital leadership, offering a roadmap for organizations seeking to navigate the complexities of AI-driven recruitment. Future research directions are proposed, focusing on longitudinal studies to assess the long-term impact of AI on recruitment outcomes and organizational performance.

Keywords: Artificial intelligence · human resource management · digital leadership · recruitment

1 Introduction

The digital age has brought about a paradigm shift across various industries, fundamentally altering how organizations operate and compete (Temelkova 2020; Kuzmina-Merlino and Dolle 2021). Artificial intelligence is at the forefront of this transformation, impacting everything from marketing and sales to product development and customer service. Within the realm of human resource management, artificial intelligence is making significant inroads, particularly in the domain of recruitment (Stone et al. 2024; Borges et al. 2021). Traditional hiring methods, often characterized as time-consuming and prone to human bias, are being challenged by the advent of artificial intelligence - powered recruitment technologies (Kollmann et al. 2023; Peifer et al. 2022). This review

R. C. Geibel and S. Machavariani (Eds.): ISPC 2024, SPBE, pp. 310–317, 2025.
https://doi.org/10.1007/978-3-031-88052-0_25

paper explores the intersection of artificial intelligence and digital leadership within the context of artificial intelligence -driven recruitment. Here, the focus is on understanding how these two concepts converge to shape the future of talent acquisition. The paper delves into the advancements offered by artificial intelligence recruitment technologies, encompassing resume screening algorithms and predictive analytics. It then examines the crucial role of digital leadership in navigating this new landscape. The paper synthesizes findings from various studies to demonstrate how artificial intelligence tools can streamline recruitment workflows, enhancing efficiency, reducing bias, and improving the candidate experience. It further analyzes the implications for digital leadership, highlighting the need for leaders to develop new competencies to manage artificial intelligence systems effectively and foster a culture of technological innovation within their organizations (Vermeulen and Vlaanderen 2019). By contributing to the growing body of research on artificial intelligence and digital leadership, this review aims to provide a roadmap for organizations seeking to leverage artificial intelligence for successful recruitment. The paper concludes by proposing future research directions, emphasizing the need for longitudinal studies to assess the long-term impact of artificial intelligence on recruitment outcomes and overall organizational performance.

2 Literature Review

Artificial intelligence in recruitment: advancements and challenges
The emergence of artificial intelligence in recruitment has brought about a wave of advancements. Artificial intelligence -powered resume screening tools, for instance, automate the initial screening process by analyzing resumes and cover letters against pre-defined criteria (Ali and Kallach 2024; Khan 2024). This not only saves recruiters valuable time but also helps reduce bias in candidate selection by focusing on objective qualifications rather than subjective factors. Similarly, predictive analytics tools leverage machine learning algorithms to analyze historical data and identify patterns that can predict successful candidates (Albassam 2023).

Despite these advancements, artificial intelligence-driven recruitment also presents certain challenges. Concerns around algorithmic bias are a significant issue, as artificial intelligence systems trained on biased datasets can perpetuate those biases in the hiring process (Albaroudi et al. 2024; Epstein and McCarthy 2017; Highhouse 2017; Kryscynski and Radzikowski 2017). Additionally, the "black box" nature of some artificial intelligence algorithms can make it difficult to understand how they arrive at their decisions, raising concerns about transparency and fairness (Von Eschenbach 2021; Agrawal et al. 2018). Furthermore, the increasing reliance on artificial intelligence in recruitment can lead to a depersonalized experience for candidates, potentially hindering employer branding efforts (Ore and Sposato 2022).

The role of digital leadership in artificial intelligence -driven recruitment
The successful integration of artificial intelligence into recruitment processes necessitates effective digital leadership (Allal-Chérif et al. 2021; Borges et al. 2021). Digital leadership refers to a leadership style that is adept at leveraging digital technologies to drive innovation and achieve organizational goals (Tursunbayeva and Gal 2024; Lyons and Ng 2016). Digital leaders who champion artificial intelligence -driven recruitment

must possess a unique blend of skills (Vikas 2024). Technical acumen is critical, as they need to understand the capabilities and limitations of artificial intelligence tools. However, technical expertise alone is insufficient. Digital leaders also require a strategic vision to leverage artificial intelligence effectively, aligning it with their organization's overall talent acquisition strategy (Brock and Von Wangenheim 2019; Wheeler and van de Haterd 2024). Furthermore, successful digital leaders must be adept at change management, as artificial intelligence implementation often requires a shift in organizational culture and workflows (Sarioguz and Miser 2024; Fenwick et al. 2024). They need to create a culture of innovation within their human resource departments and promote an understanding of the benefits of artificial intelligence among employees involved in the recruitment process. Additionally, digital leaders must be transparent about how artificial intelligence is being used in recruitment and address concerns regarding bias and fairness (Uslu 2015).

How artificial intelligence streamlines recruitment workflows
Artificial intelligence recruitment technologies offer several benefits that can streamline various stages of the recruitment workflow (Allal-Chérif et al. 2021). Candidate Sourcing: artificial intelligence tools can crawl the web and social media platforms to identify potential candidates share.

How artificial intelligence streamlines recruitment workflows (Abdelhay 2023; Fehling et al. 2018).

- Candidate sourcing: artificial intelligence tools can crawl the web and social media platforms to identify potential candidates with the desired skills and experience, expanding the talent pool beyond traditional job boards.
- Initial engagement: chatbots powered by artificial intelligence can answer frequently asked questions from candidates, improving the candidate experience and freeing up recruiters' time for more strategic tasks.
- Resume screening: artificial intelligence -powered resume screening tools can quickly scan through a large pool of resumes, extracting key information and identifying candidates who best meet the job requirements. This allows recruiters to focus their time on the most promising candidates.
- Candidate assessment: artificial intelligence -based assessments can be used to evaluate candidates' cognitive abilities, personality traits, and cultural fit (Barrick and Mount 1991). These assessments can provide valuable insights that complement traditional interview methods.
- Final Selection: predictive analytics tools can be used to analyze data from various stages of the recruitment process and identify candidates with the highest potential for success in the role.

In research on digital leadership, scholars have identified key areas and aspects that make up this type of leadership (Fig. 1.)

Competencies for digital leadership in artificial intelligence -driven recruitment

As discussed earlier, digital leadership plays a critical role in ensuring the successful implementation of artificial intelligence in recruitment. Here are some key competencies that digital leaders require Allal-Chérif et al. 2021):

Technical insight: digital leaders need a basic understanding of artificial intelligence technologies and their capabilities in recruitment. They should be able to ask informed

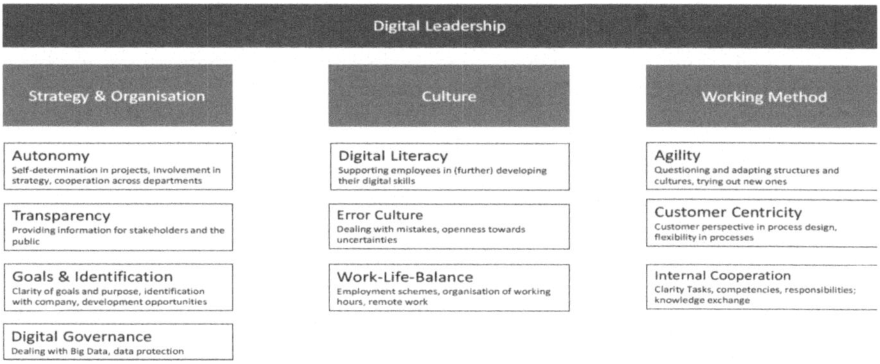

Fig. 1. Researchers break down digital leadership into key areas Öztürk and Başar 2022)

questions about artificial intelligence systems and evaluate their suitability for their organization's needs.

Strategic vision: digital leaders should have a clear vision for how artificial intelligence can be leveraged to achieve their organization's talent acquisition goals. They need to be able to identify strategic opportunities for artificial intelligence integration and develop a roadmap for implementation.

Change management: implementing artificial intelligence in recruitment often requires changes in organizational culture and workflows. Digital leaders need to be skilled in change management, effectively communicating the benefits of artificial intelligence and leading their teams through the transition (Balcioğlu and Artar 2024).

Data literacy: artificial intelligence systems rely heavily on data. Digital leaders need to be data literate, understanding how data is collected, analyzed, and used in artificial intelligence recruitment tools. They should also be able to identify potential biases in data sets and take steps to mitigate them.

Ethical leadership: digital leaders have a responsibility to ensure that artificial intelligence is used ethically in recruitment. This includes developing policies and procedures to address issues of bias, transparency, and fairness throughout the recruitment process.

Building a Culture of Innovation

Digital leaders play a crucial role in fostering a culture of innovation within their human resource departments. This involves creating an environment where employees feel comfortable experimenting with new technologies and exploring new ways of working. Digital leaders can encourage innovation by (Bellis et al. 2024).

Providing Resources: investing in training and development programs that help human resource professionals build their skills and knowledge of artificial intelligence in recruitment.

Encouraging Experimentation: creating a safe space for employees to experiment with new artificial intelligence tools and processes.

Celebrating Success: recognizing and rewarding successful initiatives that leverage artificial intelligence effectively in recruitment.

Promoting Collaboration: encouraging collaboration between human resource professionals, data scientists, and other relevant stakeholders to develop artificial intelligence -driven recruitment solutions (Ifenthaler et al. 2024).

Implications for the Future of Work).
The rise of artificial intelligence in recruitment has significant implications for the future of work. As artificial intelligence takes over routine tasks such as resume screening and initial candidate assessments, human recruiters will need to focus on more strategic aspects of talent acquisition, such as building relationships with potential candidates and developing employer branding strategies (Balcioğlu and Artar 2024). Additionally, artificial intelligence may lead to a shift in the types of skills that are in demand. As machines become adept at performing tasks that were previously considered human-exclusive, the focus may shift towards skills like creativity, critical thinking, and problem-solving, which are difficult for artificial intelligence to replicate (Na et al. 2024).

Ethical concerns of artificial intelligence in recruitment
Despite its potential benefits, the use of artificial intelligence in recruitment raises several ethical concerns. One major concern is algorithmic bias. Artificial intelligence systems trained on biased datasets can perpetuate those biases in the hiring process, leading to discriminatory outcomes. For example, an artificial intelligence system trained on resumes from predominantly male candidates may be less likely to identify qualified female candidates for the role.

Another concern is the "black box" nature of some artificial intelligence algorithms. These algorithms can be opaque, making it difficult to understand how they arrive at their decisions Hassija et al. 2024). This lack of transparency can raise concerns about fairness and accountability in the hiring process. Additionally, the increasing reliance on artificial intelligence in recruitment can lead to a depersonalized experience for candidates, potentially hindering employer branding efforts (Papadakis et al. 2024).

3 Future Research Directions

Further research is needed to fully understand the impact of artificial intelligence on recruitment and digital leadership. Here are some potential areas for future exploration:

- Longitudinal Studies: Conducting longitudinal studies to assess the long-term impact of artificial intelligence on recruitment outcomes and organizational performance. This would involve studying how artificial intelligence affects factors such as employee retention, engagement, and diversity.
- The human-artificial intelligence interface: Researching the optimal ways for humans and artificial intelligence to collaborate in the recruitment process. This could involve exploring how artificial intelligence can augment human decision-making and how humans can provide oversight and guidance to artificial intelligence systems.
- The impact on candidate experience: Investigating the impact of artificial intelligence on candidate experience throughout the recruitment process. This could involve studying how artificial intelligence can be used to create a more positive and efficient experience for candidates.

- The ethical implications of artificial intelligence: Further research is needed to develop ethical guidelines for the use of artificial intelligence in recruitment. This could involve exploring ways to mitigate bias in artificial intelligence systems and ensure transparency and fairness throughout the hiring process (Sonko et al. 2024).

By continuing to explore these areas, researchers can help organizations leverage artificial intelligence effectively while mitigating the potential risks associated with its use in recruitment.

4 Conclusion

In conclusion, artificial intelligence is rapidly transforming the landscape of recruitment. While artificial intelligence offers numerous advantages, such as increased efficiency, reduced bias, and improved candidate experience, it also presents significant challenges that require careful consideration. Digital leadership plays a critical role in navigating this transformation. By developing the necessary competencies and fostering a culture of innovation, digital leaders can ensure that artificial intelligence is used effectively to enhance recruitment processes and attract top talent. However, it is crucial to acknowledge the potential ethical concerns surrounding artificial intelligence and conduct further research to mitigate these risks. As artificial intelligence continues to evolve, ongoing research and development are essential to ensure that artificial intelligence is used ethically and responsibly in the recruitment process.

References

Abdelhay, S.: How Artificial Intelligence can affect the process of recruitment and improve the quality of new hired employees. J. Jilin Univ. Resmilitaris **13**(3), 2517–2533 (2023)

Agrawal, A., Kittur, A., Sundararajan, M.: AI for HR: from black box to glass box. Harvard Bus. Rev. **96**(2), 110–113 (2018). https://hbr.org/sponsored/2023/11/4-actions-hr-leaders-can-take-to-harness-the-potential-of-ai

Albaroudi, E., Mansouri, T., Alameer, A.: A comprehensive review of ai techniques for addressing algorithmic bias in job hiring. AI **5**(1), 383–404(2024)

Albassam, W.A.: The power of artificial intelligence in recruitment: an analytical review of current AI-based recruitment strategies. Int. J. Profess. Bus. Rev. **8**(6), e02089 (2023)

Ali, O., Kallach, L.: Artificial intelligence enabled human resources recruitment functionalities: a scoping review. Procedia Comput. Sci. **232**, 3268–3277 (2024)

Allal-Chérif, O., Aránega, A.Y., Sánchez, R.C.: Intelligent recruitment: How to identify, select, and retain talents from around the world using artificial intelligence. Technol. Forecast. Soc. Chang. **169**, 120822 (2021)

Balcioğlu, Y.S., Artar, M.: Artificial intelligence in employee recruitment. Global Business and Organizational Excellence (2024)

Barrick, M.R., Mount, M.K.: The big five personality dimensions and job performance: a review and meta-analysis. Person. Psychol. **44**(1), 1–26 (1991). https://psycnet.apa.org/record/1991-22928-001

Bellis, P., Cunial, M., Trabucchi, D.: Mastering hybrid worlds through digital leadership: the role of agility in fostering innovation. Business Horizons (2024)

Borges, A.F., Laurindo, F.J., Spínola, M.M., Gonçalves, R.F., Mattos, C.A.: The strategic use of artificial intelligence in the digital era: systematic literature review and future research directions. Int. J. Inf. Manage. **57**, 102225 (2021)

Brock, J.K.U., Von Wangenheim, F.: Demystifying AI: what digital transformation leaders can teach you about realistic artificial intelligence. Calif. Manage. Rev. **61**(4), 110–134 (2019)

Epstein, D., McCarthy, J.: Machine learning for hiring: caveats, biases, and a framework for fairness. arXiv preprint arXiv:1701.07856 (2017)

Fehling, M., LaFountain, Y., Schaub, M., Greve, H.R.: Artificial intelligence and the future of work: a sociotechnical perspective. Acad. Manage. J. **61**(2), 548–578 (2018). https://link.springer.com/article/10.1007/s10676-022-09624-3

Fenwick, A., Molnar, G., Frangos, P.: The critical role of HRM in AI-driven digital transformation: a paradigm shift to enable firms to move from AI implementation to human-centric adoption. Discover Artific. Intell. **4**(1), 34 (2024)

Hassija, V., et al.: Interpreting black-box models: a review on explainable artificial intelligence. Cogn. Comput. **16**(1), 45–74 (2024)

Highhouse, S.: Algorithmic bias, machine learning, and fairness. SSRN Electron. J. (2017). https://papers.ssrn.com/sol3/papers.cfm?abstract_id=3681517

Ifenthaler, D., et al.: Artificial intelligence in education: implications for policymakers, researchers, and practitioners. Technol. Knowl. Learn. 1–18 (2024)

Khan, M.R.: Application of artificial intelligence for talent management: challenges and opportunities. Intelligent Human Systems Integration (IHSI 2024): Integrating People and Intelligent Systems, vol. 119(119) (2024)

Kollmann, T., Kollmann, K., Kollmann, N.: Artificial leadership: digital transformation as a leadership task between the chief digital officer and artificial intelligence. Int. J. Bus. Sci. Appl. Manage. **18**(1) (2023)

Kryscynski, D., Radzikowski, M.: Algorithmic fairness in hiring: a survey of biases and debiased solutions. arXiv preprint arXiv:1704.06487. https://arxiv.org/abs/2309.13933 (2017)

Kuzmina-Merlino, I., Dolle, N.: Artificial intelligence techniques for automating management and leadership tasks: literature review. In: International Conference on Reliability and Statistics in Transportation and Communication, pp. 482–492. Springer International Publishing, Cham (2021)

Lyons, B.F., Ng, I.C.L.: Digital leadership: a framework for navigating the digital age. MIS Quar. **40**(1), 221–247 (2016). https://www.researchgate.net/publication/338327379_Digital_Leadership_A_Framework_for_Successful_Leadership_in_the_Digital_Age

Na, S.R.: Application of artificial intelligence in recruitment and selection. Acad. J. Sci. Technol. **9**(2), 56–58 (2024)

Ore, O., Sposato, M.: Opportunities and risks of artificial intelligence in recruitment and selection. Int. J. Organ. Anal. **30**(6), 1771–1782 (2022)

Öztürk, O.B., Başar, E.: Multiple linear regression analysis and artificial neural networks based decision support system for energy efficiency in shipping. Ocean Eng. **243**, 110209 (2022)

Papadakis, T., Christou, I.T., Ipektsidis, C., Soldatos, J., Amicone, A.: Explainable and transparent artificial intelligence for public policymaking. Data Policy **6**, e10 (2024)

Peifer, Y., Jeske, T., Hille, S.: Artificial intelligence and its impact on leaders and leadership. Procedia Comput. Sci. **200**, 1024–1030 (2022)

Sarioguz, O., Miser, E.: Artificial intelligence and participatory leadership: the role of technological transformation in business management and its impact on employee participation. Int. Res. J. Modern. Eng. Technol. Sci. **6**(2) (2024)

Sonko, S., Adewusi, A.O., Obi, O.C., Onwusinkwue, S., Atadoga, A.: A critical review towards artificial general intelligence: challenges, ethical considerations, and the path forward. World J. Adv. Res. Rev. **21**(3), 1262–1268 (2024)

Stone, D.L., Lukaszewski, K.M., Johnson, R.D.: Will artificial intelligence radically change human resource management processes?. Organ. Dyn. 101034 (2024)

Temelkova, M.: Digital leadership added value in the digital smart organizations. J. Eng. Sci. Technol. Rev. 252–257 (2020)

Tursunbayeva, A., Gal, H.C.B.: Adoption of artificial intelligence: a TOP framework-based checklist for digital leaders. Business Horizons (2024)

Uslu, T.: Innovation culture and strategic human resource management in public and private sector within the framework of employee ownership. Procedia Soc. Behav. Sci. **195**, 1463–1470 (2015)

Vermeulen, F., Vlaanderen, J.: Responsible innovation in human resource management: a review and agenda for future research. Hum. Resource Manage. Rev. **29**(2), 100690 (2019). https://www.sciencedirect.com/science/article/abs/pii/S1053482218303826

Vikas, S., Mathur, A., Adavi, S., Shaik, J.M.P., Seshachalam, A.: Recruitment and the role of hr in talent acquisition: optimal methods for hiring top talent. J. Inform. Educ. Res. **4**(1) (2024)

Von Eschenbach, W.J.: Transparency and the black box problem: why we do not trust AI. Philosophy Technol. **34**(4), 1607–1622 (2021)

Wheeler, K., van de Haterd, B.: Talent acquisition excellence: using digital capabilities and analytics to improve recruitment. Kogan Page Publishers (2024)

Development of Immersive Technologies in Military Education

Givi Duchidze[1] and Vazha Zeikidze[2(✉)]

[1] East European University, Tbilisi, Georgia
[2] Davit Aghmashenebeli National Defense Academy of Georgia, Tbilisi, Georgia
v.zeikidze@gtu.ge

Abstract. The article discusses the specifics of teaching immersive technologies in military education. Because today the world's leading defense colleges and universities are actively involved in training and educating military leaders through simulation centers, where the training and professional skills of future military personnel are based on the use of immersive technologies in the field of defense.

Analytical and synthetic evaluation of information about theoretical methods is used in the article, as well as pedagogical, psychological and didactic literature of immersion education is used in the article, an analysis of the advantages of using immersion education methods in military affairs is given.

The new strategies discussed require a new level of communication, as general-purpose troops are replaced by mobile units that can be deployed anywhere in the world at any time. A fully equipped combat brigade must be deployed in four days, a division in five, and five divisions within a month. This requires simulation centers to become more mobile and efficient in their use of learning technologies.

The simulation center, which operates at the junior officer training school of the National Defense Academy of Georgia, provides an opportunity to conduct training using digital technologies in a virtual environment as close as possible to reality, before field training.

In the military, training in a virtual environment is ideal because once a VR solution is created, it can be improved and used over the years, adding new scenarios and improving graphics and effects.

According to the conducted research, we consider it expedient to implement the experience of simulation centers of leading foreign military educational institutions in Georgia. It will also be justified to introduce digital technologies created by modern global start-ups in the junior officer training simulation center of the academy, which will allow future commanders to master the use of new technologies in the process of military training.

The use of educational programs based on modern digital technologies will allow us to raise the education and training of junior commanders to a higher, more modern level.

Keywords: simulation centers · digital technologies · immersive learning · teaching strategies

R. C. Geibel and S. Machavariani (Eds.): ISPC 2024, SPBE, pp. 318–323, 2025.
https://doi.org/10.1007/978-3-031-88052-0_26

1 Introduction

In the modern world, immersive technologies in the form of simulation centers are successfully used to train qualified personnel. In simulation centers, military specialists develop the necessary combat skills in a virtual environment. The use of simulation technologies for situational training, close to a real situation, is also justified for the purpose that errors made at this time can lead to large financial costs. Using these technologies, future military specialists will be able to use virtual models when managing military operations.

In simulation centers, using digital technologies in a virtual environment as close to reality as possible, decisions are made, orders are prepared, and concepts for commanders are developed, which significantly reduces the need to create real emergencies and the associated costs. With the help of digital technologies, future military leaders will be able to control a virtual model of any technological device. Such centers for military simulation training successfully operate at the National Defense Academy of Georgia, the National Training Center "Krtsanis" and others, where future military leaders successfully master the tasks of managing military operations.

The development of immersive learning is becoming increasingly relevant at the current stage of military affairs, and the article is devoted to the implementation of modern methods and forms of immersive learning in simulation centers.

The purpose of this article is Presentation of the relevance of the process of using digital teaching methods in military education.

2 Research Methods

This work uses a set of methods that complement each other. Of the theoretical methods, analytical and synthetic assessment of information was used, the article presents pedagogical, psychological and didactic literature on immersive learning, as well as an analysis of the benefits of using immersive teaching methods.

The main method applied is Virtual reality (VR), which is a technology that creates the ability to immerse oneself in a virtual environment, which is especially useful in such areas as defense. VR technologies are used in the process of military education and training of servicemen, to create new combat technologies. This allows for increasing the effectiveness of training of servicemen in the field of defense and reducing the risk of injury during training.

The use of VR technologies in the military sphere has a number of advantages:

- future commanders will be able to train in conditions as close as possible to real combat situations;
- Simulation exercises help avoid dangerous situations and injuries;
- The use of VR technologies significantly reduces the costs of training resources;
- Development of new military equipment.

VR technologies make it possible to create and test new combat technologies without risking the lives and health of military personnel.

The introduction of digital technologies in the virtual reality space into the educational programs of military training centers opens up new prospects for studying and assimilating material. The uniqueness of these technologies lies in the ability to simulate real or potential military scenarios and situations. This allows students to gain deep and tangible knowledge.

For example, an unmanned aircraft with reconnaissance equipment installed on its board is very convenient for obtaining information directly from the battlefield or when preparing fire. Their main advantage is cheapness and small flight trajectory. Digital technologies have developed so much that the commander of a military unit can give orders to one soldier for hundreds of kilometers.

The role of artificial intelligence in immersive education is growing significantly, in particular, military leadership educational programs can be tailored to the needs of future commanders, simulation programs based on artificial intelligence will be able to place future commanders in an adaptive virtual environment and help them. Digital programs running in simulation centers can change the role of the teacher, and artificial intelligence technologies can make teaching and learning less dangerous.

New strategies require new levels of communication as general-purpose forces replace mobile units that can be deployed anywhere in the world at a moment's notice. A fully equipped, combat-ready brigade must be up and running within four days, a division within five, and five divisions within a month. To achieve this, all equipment and weapons must become lighter, more mobile, and more effective. For example, the 70-ton Abrams tank will be replaced by a new, lighter, 20-ton tank with greater combat power.

To diversify the learning process, VR classes are created, which allows the military instructor to offer a variety of learning scenarios. A teacher using advanced VR technologies can apply an individual approach to the learning process, which makes it possible to individually customize the curriculum for each cadet.

The VR Auditorium portal server allows us to upload any training program, as well as transfer and configure any simulation in the shortest possible time. Training in such auditoriums significantly speeds up the familiarization of cadets with the basics of military work. This allows you to see the equipment and different types of weapons with your own eyes, even if they are not in stock.

The main tasks of the Academy's simulation center are:

- It can increase cadet engagement and motivation, which is an important aspect of success;
- Simulating the real training environment allows cadets to fully experience the reality of war and express interest in learning;
- Its use can improve the effectiveness of learning, thanks to the implementation of exercises in different situations, which allows learners to get used to the use of skills and knowledge in practice that cannot be created in a traditional learning environment;
- This technology provides a unique opportunity for individual training. For example, virtual simulators allow the creation of training programs that are tailored to the level of knowledge, skills and needs of the cadet.

The simulation center operating at the Junior Officer Training School of the National Defense Academy of Georgia allows training using digital technologies to be conducted in a virtual environment as close as possible to reality, and military personnel to be perfectly prepared right before practical training.

Other core tasks of the simulation center of the Academy are:

- Development of modernized training programs for future junior commanders (officers) using simulation technologies;
- Conducting training and certification of future commanders using models, dummies and virtual simulators;
- Using modern modeling technologies to assess the quality of professional development of junior officers;
- Information support in the field of the latest achievements in virtual simulation education by organizing open practical classes, seminars and master classes.

We have studied several scenarios in which virtual reality is already being used in military training at junior officer schools:

- driving simulators of various combat vehicles,
- Large-scale multiplayer infantry combat simulators;
- Simulators of using various weapons.

The use of simulators in the virtual reality of simulation centers has its critics, which is related to its virtuality, in particular, a certain category of commanders believes that it is better for new officers to learn in the cockpit of real equipment, with real instruments, than in a computer environment, where there is no tactile memory training, which we can even agree with, but This approach cannot override the advantages that simulation centers have.

Before the advent of virtual reality, a new type of weapon could be demonstrated in the most realistic way possible by bringing samples or models to an exhibition or meeting with potential customers, showing a video and delivering it to buyers. Virtual reality at the testing ground combines the advantages of all three methods and the algorithm of actions is as follows:

- Creating a computerized weapon control system, for this it will be necessary to scan the device with special sensors and then transfer this model to the program;
- Creating a software simulator with the most effective and realistic display of weapons, which can be tested on virtual targets;
- Put virtual glasses on the client and watch his actions;
- Collect feedback (notes) and improve the software.

Virtual reality is ideal for visual advertising of the equipment manufacturer before the stage of field demonstration - at exhibitions, personal meetings. Once created, a VR solution can be refined and used over the years, adding new scenarios and improving graphics and effects.

For example, Sweden's Saab uses virtual reality to demonstrate missiles, China does the same, and every country in the world does the same.

Virtual reality is already being successfully used in military exercises:

- combat vehicle driving simulators;
- large-scale infantry combat simulators;
- individual combat management simulators from MTEK military companies;
- simulators for the use of various combat weapons.

The above cases cannot be called exhaustive, because in practice, the situation of virtual combat exercises can be even more diverse, since such military exercises are cheaper.

VR stimulators have many advantages, in particular, they are much cheaper and have small dimensions, which allows them to be implemented (installed) in training rooms and will greatly help future commanders in their professional skills.

Modern military equipment requires control, understanding of the situation when using it and the right choice of actions. The question is, what are the advantages of virtual reality in this case?

The simplicity of the virtual service is always combined with reliability: the fewer gaps in the armor, the fewer moving elements in the environmental monitoring system (for example, periscope), the better. The future commander, using cameras located around the perimeter of the body, transmits the image to the screens of the tactical helmet, and the operator takes the image as if he were in an armored car. For example, in 2014, the Norwegian army conducted an experiment in driving tanks using virtual glasses.

Thanks to immersive technologies, future military commanders can acquire the job skills necessary to work with real technical equipment. The training is conducted in a virtual environment, using simulated VR technologies, which include 3D models, 360-degree panoramas, virtual reality glasses, motion sensors and contact computers. Process training is fully controlled, all actions are monitored, and based on this, an assessment is made based on the quality of the assigned task.

In the military and special services, the ability to analyze more data means making faster and more complex decisions in a virtual environment. There are several scenarios:

- 3D field analysis of any size in real time by enabling and disabling graphic details depending on the type of military service and other factors;
- search for and catch criminals by coordinating the actions of field teams with the help of a remote operator, especially when moving in megacities or three-dimensional spaces;
- air, water and space maps, where the ability to represent in 3D is important;
- maintenance and development of complex engineering systems.

For example, the Royal Australian Air Force is experimenting with HoloLens for battlefield analysis. Given the image quality of augmented reality glasses, using virtual reality glasses for this purpose is no less, if not more logical, since full-time analysts do not need to be constantly distracted by the real situation and can better focus on a larger-scale 3D model.

Examples of the use of immersive technologies in a virtual environment in the process of training future commanders clearly demonstrate its high efficiency both in military and economic terms. Thus, the use of foreign advanced immersive technologies in the process of creating a virtual environment in the simulation center of the junior officer school is fully justified.

3 Conclusions and Recommendations

It is advisable to bring the advanced experience of simulation centers of leading foreign military educational schools to Georgia.

It is justified to introduce digital technologies created by the world's modern startups in the simulation center for junior officer training of the academy, which will allow future commanders to master the use of new technologies in the process of military training.

An important decision to perfect the "cadet leadership development system" operating in the academy will be the implementation of a digital leadership development program in the simulation center, so that cadets can acquire leadership and team building skills in a virtual environment.

The approach to immersive learning practically excludes the impact of external stimuli and increases concentration on the material, the introduction of VR technologies in the educational process will undoubtedly have a positive effect on the level of training of junior officers of the National Defense Academy of Georgia.

The use of educational programs based on modern digital technologies in the simulation center at the Junior Officer School of the National Defense Academy of Georgia will allow us to raise the education and training of junior commanders to a higher, more modern level.

References

Chachanidze, G.: Modern technologies of education and didactics of information (2020)

Chachanidze, G., Gelashvili, S.: Theoretical aspects and basic paradigms of creating electronic educational resources. Scientific works. III International Scientific Conference - Computing/Informatics, Educational Sciences, Teacher Education (2014)

Higher education and science reform concept project. http://www.netgazeti.ge/GE/105/opinion/14626/

Cummings, J.J., Bailenson, J.N.: How immersive is enough? A meta-analysis of the effect of immersive technology on user presence. Media Psychol. **19**(2), 272–309 (2016). https://doi.org/10.1080/15213269.2015.1015740

Hew, K.F., Cheung, W.S.: Use of three-dimensional (3-D) immersive virtual worlds in K-12 and higher education settings: a review of the research. Br. J. Edu. Technol. **41**(1), 33–55 (2010). https://doi.org/10.1111/j.1467-8535.2008.00900.x

https://fliphtml5.com/nwsnq/vnlq/tetri_wigni_2014/37/

https://vr-app.ru/blog/primenenie-vr-texnologii-v-armii-i-voennoi-podgotovke/

Role of Digitalization and Artificial Intelligence in Education Administration (Case of Accreditation Procedure in Georgia)

Sophio Ugrekhelidze(✉)

Business and Technology University, Tbilisi, Georgia
sophio.ugrekhelidze.1@btu.edu.ge

Abstract. Georgia joined the Bologna Process in 2005 at the Bergen Summit, following the Rose Revolution in the country. Since then, the accreditation institution has appeared in the higher education area of Georgia with the passage of the new law on Higher Education. Before 2005, the Ministry of Education and Science of Georgia granted the status of HEIs through the procedure of licensing. Scientific literature discusses accreditation since 2005, while the period after the Soviet Union directly affected the legal interests of the citizens who acquired education during these years until 2005. Therefore, it is important to investigate why digitalization of that data is necessary and how it supports citizens in realizing their rights in the country and outside of it, considering the EHEA requirements and Georgia's political course to become a member of the EU. Digitalization of the accreditation awarding procedure is needed for further educational governance. Higher education funding, education recognition, and diploma verification procedures by the state depend on the accreditation results. Accordingly, desktop and qualitative research will be conducted to identify relevant political, legal, and social backgrounds and future approaches to describe digitalization and AI implementation perspectives. In the era of technologies, digital governance, and AI implementation are directly related to democracy and trustworthy administration, as relevant data processing objectively and transparently is provided for further policy-making. The Ministry of Education, Science, and Youth of Georgia elaborated the Education and Science Strategy, where digitalization is one of the priorities. The study addresses the challenges related to the digital transformation of governance and provides new approaches for managerial decision-making.

Keywords: Digitalization · Accreditation Awarding · education administration · Artificial Intelligence · Digital Governance

1 Introduction

The Law on Higher Education defines accreditation as a set of procedures for assessing the compliance of higher education institutions' educational programs with accreditation standards. These standards aim to implement a systematic self-evaluation system and promote the development of quality assurance mechanisms to enhance education

R. C. Geibel and S. Machavariani (Eds.): ISPC 2024, SPBE, pp. 324–336, 2025.
https://doi.org/10.1007/978-3-031-88052-0_27

quality. Accreditation also serves as a basis for state financing and the implementation of educational programs as stipulated by the Law.[1] Legal entities acquire the right to provide higher education through authorization procedures.[2] Correspondingly, Georgian legislation obligates legal entities to first obtain the institutional status and then get the right to provide higher educational programs by meeting the appropriate standards.

The concept of accreditation was introduced into Georgian legislation in 2005 with the enactment of the new Law on Higher Education, following Georgia's joining to the Bologna process at the Bergen Summit[3]. The initial version of the Law distinguished between institutional accreditation, which granted legal entities the status of higher educational institutions, and program accreditation, which conferred the right to deliver higher educational programs.[4] It is worth noting that many European countries regulate the right to deliver higher educational programs through the institutional accreditation process. According to Georgian legislative amendments passed on July 21, 2010, educational institutional status is granted to legal entities through authorization, while the right to deliver higher educational programs is obtained through an accreditation procedure.[5] Therefore, for the purposes of this article, the right to conduct educational activities includes both authorization and accreditation.

The article discusses the evolution of accreditation in Georgia, the importance of historical data and its role for current legal results in various cases, the importance of digitalization of the data and procedures and perspectives of artificial intelligence implementation in accreditation procedures. Desktop research and in-depth interview methodology was applied to the research. Interviews were conducted with the officials in education system of Georgia, who were responsible for educational reforms after Rose Revolution in Georgia and actively involved in the implementation of those reforms. They were policy-makers and executive managers involved in formation of relevant regulatory framework as well. As a result no only the facts were researched but legal practice was identified as well.

2 Accreditation Evolution History

The right to education is recognized and guaranteed by the Georgian Constitution. Article 5 stipulates that the state is obligated to foster the development of education, while Article 27 reinforces individuals' rights to education and academic freedom, as well as the autonomy of higher educational institutions. Consequently, the right to education is considered one of the fundamental functions of the state. This concept originated in the ancient Roman Empire in the 3rd century BC.[6] The modern understanding of state responsibility for education fully developed during the 18th and 19th centuries when the

[1] Law on Higher Education (2004), N688, article 1, www.matsne.gov.ge

[2] Ib., article 56[1].

[3] See https://eqe.ge/ka/page/static/71/boloniis-protsesi, information was checked on 23.09.2024.

[4] Law on Higher Education, 21.12.2004, reg. N 430.020.000.05.001.001.626, www.matsne.gov.ge

[5] Amendments to the Law on Higher Education, 21.07.2010, N3528, www.matsne.gov.ge

[6] Tonsor, Charles A. "Origin of the Concept 'Education Is a State Function.'" *The Clearing House* 20, no. 6 (1946): 340–41. http://www.jstor.org/stable/30178323.

function of education development was transferred from the church to the state.[7] The state granted special permissions to entities to provide teaching and learning processes, supported them with necessary funding, and monitored both the process and its results. The contemporary concept of accreditation in educational systems follows a similar principle: the state grants special rights to legal entities, provides relevant funding, and monitors the educational process to ensure conformity with established accreditation standards.

The current form of accreditation emerged in 1787 when New York State University was reorganized. Legislation at that time mandated educational institutions to enumerate all programs and submit reports to the relevant authorities. An analysis of a higher education research report published by the American Association of Higher Education[8] which details the history of accreditation development, reveals that the primary focus was on quality assurance in higher education. This approach aimed to encourage educational providers to prioritize teaching quality and ensure conformity with standards defined by competent state bodies.

A comparative study on the evolution of accreditation in European countries, focusing on the European Higher Education Area (EHEA), was published in 2004.[9] The research highlights that "evaluation policies indicated the breakdown of the traditional degree of trust in society that higher education was functioning at high quality[10]... A danger inherent in evaluation policies is that 'if accountability and evaluation are reduced to a primarily technical exercise by way of rigid output measures and overly standardized evaluation exercises, then the essential debate about the values and assets which HEIs are best suited to pursue for society is clearly at risk'[11]. This rise of societal demands

[7] See the Encyclopedia Britannica, Education - State Development, Curriculum, Reforms | Britannica.

[8] Harcelroad Fred F., Accreditation: History. Process and problems, AAHE-ERIC/Higher Education Research Report N6, 1980; available at: https://eric.ed.gov/?id=ED198774.

[9] Schwarz, S., Westerheijden, D.F., 2004, Accreditation in the Framework of Evaluation Activities: A Comparative Study in the European Higher Education Area. In: Schwarz, S., Westerheijden, D.F. (eds) Accreditation and Evaluation in the European Higher Education Area. Higher Education Dynamics, vol 5. Springer, Dordrecht. https://doi.org/10.1007/978-1-4020-2797-0_1.

[10] Trow, M. (1994). Academic Reviews and the Culture of Excellence. Stockholm: Högskolev-erket. Trow, M. (1996). Trust, markets and accountability in higher education: A comparative perspective. Higher Education Policy, 9, 309–324 quoted in Schwarz, S., Westerheijden, D.F., 2004, Accreditation in the Framework of Evaluation Activities: A Comparative Study in the European Higher Education Area, p.5., https://doi.org/10.1007/978-1-4020-2797-0_1.

[11] Reichert, S., & Tauch, C. (2003). Trends in Learning Structures in European Higher Education III – Bologna four years after: Steps towards sustainable reform of higher education in Europe; First draft. Graz: European University Association; European Commission, p.102 quoted in Schwarz, S., Westerheijden, D.F., 2004, Accreditation in the Framework of Evaluation Activities: A Comparative Study in the European Higher Education Area, p.5., https://doi.org/10.1007/978-1-4020-2797-0_1.

for accountability has been documented extensively, not only in higher education, but also and especially in public administration"[12].

This research elucidates that accreditation serves as a tool employed by the state to oversee policy implementation in higher education governance, a responsibility delegated to independent organizations or agencies. The independence of these organizations is crucial, as the state defines standards for higher educational institutions and programs, while the right to assess and monitor conformity to these standards is delegated to independent entities free from political influence. Such independence guarantees quality assurance in higher education and fosters open and reliable educational governance. One of the key characteristics of democracy is the presence of independent and robust public institutions free from political interference, a concept proposed by Wilson as early as 1887.[13] This principle is also reflected in the World Declaration on Higher Education, specifically in Article 11, which states: "Quality in higher education is a multidimensional concept which should embrace all its functions, and activities: teaching and academic programs, research and scholarship, staffing, students, buildings, facilities, equipment, services to the community and the academic environment. Internal self-evaluation and external review conducted openly by independent specialists, if possible with international expertise, are vital for enhancing quality. Independent national bodies should be established and comparative standards of quality recognized at international level should be defined."[14]

3 Evolution of Educational Status Granting in Georgia

External and internal mechanisms, including accreditation, were introduced into Georgian legislation following the Rose Revolution. The new Law on Higher Education was enacted in 2004, and in 2005, Georgia joined the Bologna Process[15]. Prior to these developments, the Ministry of Education of Georgia administered the process of granting educational activity rights to legal entities.

For this research, in-depth interviews were conducted with education experts and public officials who are pivotal to the history of Georgian education governance. The

[12] Brignall, S., & Modell, S. (2000). An institutional perspective on performance measurement and management in the 'new public sector'. Management Accounting Research, 11(3), 281–306; Enders, J. (2002). Governing the Academic Commons: About blurring boundaries, blistering organisations, and growing demands (J. File, Trans.). Enschede: Universiteit Twente; Lane, J.-E. (2000). New public management. London: Routledge; Rowley, J. (1996). Measuring Quality in Higher Education. Quality in Higher Education, 2(3), 237–255 quoted in Schwarz, S., Westerheijden, D.F., 2004, Accreditation in the Framework of Evaluation Activities: A Comparative Study in the European Higher Education Area, p.6., https://doi.org/10.1007/978-1-4020-2797-0_1.

[13] Wilson W., The Study of Administration, Political Science Quarterly, Vol. 2, No. 2 (Jun., 1887), pp. 209–210, https://www.jstor.org/stable/2139277.

[14] See https://unesdoc.unesco.org/ark:/48223/pf0000141952.

[15] Chakhaia L., Bregvadze T., Georgia: Higher Education System Dynamics and Institutional Diversity in the book 25 years of transformations of higher education systems in post-soviet countries, Palgrave Studies in Global Higher Education, p.189.

data uncovered through these interviews have not been previously discussed or recorded. Even legislative or archival documentation research is insufficient to construct a comprehensive understanding without the explanations obtained through these interviews. The interviewees are former or active officials involved in administering higher education governance in the post-Soviet period and educational reforms following the Rose Revolution. Consequently, they not only possess knowledge of the chronology of specific processes but also retain institutional memory regarding the political will of policymakers.

To support the objectives of this article, research on higher education right granting was identified and analyzed, primarily through Google Scholar. Scientific articles were sought using keywords in both Georgian and English, without temporal restrictions. Approximately 15 studies were examined, revealing that research on education governance through accreditation predominantly discusses data and information from the quality assurance perspective following the Rose Revolution. However, it is essential to delineate the post-Soviet chronology and analyze the corresponding data, as it has significant legal implications for individuals holding educational documents issued during that period. Education recognition within the country and internationally, as well as the verification and validation of educational documents, are crucial prerequisites for the realization of fundamental rights.

Based on the results of interviews and analysis of relevant legislative documents, it was determined that until 1991, only state-founded higher educational institutions existed in Georgia. From 1991 onwards, private legal entities were permitted to operate as higher educational institutions, subject to a special license issued by the Ministry of Education of Georgia. On June 14, 1991, the Supreme Council of the Republic of Georgia approved the "Regulation on Paid Institutions" by decree. Article 3 of this regulation stipulated that institutions with defined pricing should be registered based on a special permission—a license—issued by the Ministry of Education.

In June 1997, the Law on Education[16] was enacted, regulating the legal framework for educational activities, including higher education. The initial version of the law introduced terms such as "license" and "accreditation." A systematic interpretation of the law suggests that both terms were related to permissions for educational activities. However, as interview results highlighted, until 2005, the Ministry of Education and Science of Georgia issued permissions solely in the form of licenses.

In May 1999, the Law on Licensing Entrepreneurs was enacted. Article 4 of this law mandated that private educational institutions be licensed, while Article 5 stipulated that license-issuing bodies should record these licenses in a special registry. Furthermore, institutions holding licenses prior to the adoption of this law were obligated to register them in the special registry within six months of the law taking effect; missing the deadline would result in license cancellation and loss of legal validity.[17] Based on these regulations, the Ministry of Education and Science established a special educational license registry to record data about educational institutions. This registry currently

[16] Available at www.matsne.gov.ge

[17] Law on Licensing Entrepreneurs is available at https://matsne.gov.ge/ka/document/view/11620?publication=0.

serves as one of the primary legal sources for various administrative proceedings both within and outside the system of the Ministry of Education, Science, and Youth.

Since 2005, legislation has separately defined institutional and program accreditation. Concurrently, the LEPL - State Department for Educational Institutional Accreditation was established to administer and organize accreditation procedures. In 2007 it was reorganized and renamed as LEPL – National Accreditation Center[18]. In 2010 it underwent further reorganization, resulting in the establishment of the LEPL - National Center for Educational Quality Enhancement.[19] This Center is the successor body to the Ministry of Education and Science of Georgia in the scope of licensing, and the aforementioned special license registry is maintained by the Center.[20]

Additionally, the LEPL - Central Archive of Georgia is keeping substantial data concerning educational institutions, including foundation and liquidation documents, which are fundamental for administrative proceedings. Conversely, educational institutions that remain active and authorized maintain their own historical data. All of these sources have significant legal implications for various proceedings.

4 Regulatory Framework for Data Collection in Electronic Systems

As the aforementioned chronology indicates, since 1991, the data pertaining to educational institutions has become quite extensive and is maintained by various organizations. However, this information has not been collected and recorded in a systematic manner.

Currently, LEPL - Educational Management Information System (EMIS) is the organization tasked with the responsibility of collecting, processing, and maintaining educational data, including information on authorized/accredited as well as liquidated educational institutions.[21] According to EMIS interviewees, the data maintained by EMIS encompasses information on 1,991 educational institutions, including 296 higher educational institutions. Regarding higher educational institutions specifically, there are 928 registered entries. Nevertheless, there remain higher educational institutions that have undergone reorganization and merged with other legal entities, and information about these is discovered on a case-by-case basis. Additionally, there exist higher educational institutions that were not registered in the special license registry, resulting in incomplete data. EMIS continually searches for, collects, and processes this data.

EMIS has developed and continuously works on improving a digital archive where all this information is stored electronically. This project aims to enhance the comprehensiveness and accessibility of the educational data for relevant beneficiaries.

In addition to the aforementioned systems, in 2008, the Registry of Accredited Higher Educational Institutions was formed, administered by the LEPL - National Accreditation Center.[22] The primary objective of centralizing data collection was to verify and monitor higher educational programs' compliance with accreditation standards. In 2011, a new Higher Educational Registry replaced the previous one, administered by the

[18] https://matsne.gov.ge/ka/document/view/71248?publication=0.

[19] https://matsne.gov.ge/ka/document/view/1003241?publication=29.

[20] Law on Education Quality Enhancement, 21.07.2010, article 32, www.matsne.gov.ge

[21] https://matsne.gov.ge/ka/document/view/1548498?publication=16.

[22] https://matsne.gov.ge/ka/document/view/79870?publication=0.

LEPL - National Center for Educational Quality Enhancement.[23] Following legislative amendments in 2019,[24] the Higher Educational Registry was transferred to EMIS, which previously managed vocational and general education registries. By consolidating the Higher Educational Registry under EMIS, a single entity now collects, processes, and maintains educational data across all three levels of education. These amendments were implemented due to EMIS's expanded scope, fundamental functions, and significant role in shaping educational governance. Centralizing the collection and maintenance of accurate, reliable, and timely data for all three educational levels under one entity is crucial for future development and policy-making.

In 2021, the Higher Educational Registry was superseded by the Higher Educational Management Information System, created and administered by EMIS, which undergoes continuous development.[25] This system is vital for several reasons:

a) It serves as the sole legal source for electronic storage of data on higher educational institutions, programs, students, and graduates since 2005;
b) Verification and validation of educational documents issued by Higher Education Institutions (HEIs), as well as recognition of education, are directly dependent on the data maintained in this system;
c) Timely and accurate information recorded in the system forms the legal basis for higher educational process administration by other structural organizations within the education system. This includes the LEPL - National Assessment and Exam Center (NAEC) opening enrollment calls for Bachelor's and Master's level programs; State grant awarding by NAEC and the Ministry of Education, Science, and Youth.; Enrollment in higher educational programs without national exams, etc. The LEPL - National Center for Educational Quality Enhancement, responsible for authorization and accreditation procedure administration, utilizes data from this system, which has legal implications for relevant outcomes. Ultimately, this system serves as the sole electronic source necessary for comprehensive educational analytics.

5 Importance of Accreditation Process Digitalization

Authorization and accreditation procedures are regulated by the Orders[26] of the Ministry of Education, Science and Youth of Georgia, which delineate specific steps from documentation submission by applicants to the granting of educational activity rights by the relevant Councils. Each Order specifies the standards and sub-standards of authorization and accreditation,as well as the list of relevant indicators that Higher Education Institution must submit. Consequently, the information to be processed for each accreditation or authorization is substantial for both applicants and expert groups conducting assessments. The volume of data increases significantly when a cluster of programs is submitted for accreditation, as multiple programs are evaluated simultaneously.[27] In

[23] https://matsne.gov.ge/ka/document/view/1430726?publication=0.
[24] https://matsne.gov.ge/ka/document/view/4614304?publication=0.
[25] https://matsne.gov.ge/ka/document/view/5268817?publication=1.
[26] https://matsne.gov.ge/ka/document/view/1031755?publication=52.https://matsne.gov.ge/ka/document/view/1320588?publication=27.
[27] https://matsne.gov.ge/ka/document/view/1320588?publication=27, attachment 5.

such cases, data must be provided from the perspective of each individual program. The objective and accurate administration of authorization and accreditation is fundamental, as the state grants legal entities the right to provide educational activities for students. In essence, authorization and accreditation directly affect the legal interests of students, as these processes serve as prerequisites for the recognition of their education both domestically and internationally. Sorour and Atkins mention in their research on big data challenges in higher education system that "HEIs are struggling in managing data that feeds QA systems due to several challenges including: a) HEIs are increasing in their sizes,,, b) As the programs being provided by HEIs are expanding each academic year, the QA related data is also increasing c) HEIs are concerned with the continuous improvement which requires a cross-year analysis that encompasses huge amounts of data."[28] Not only HEIs but education governors and policy makers suffer from big data challenges as well.

Digitalization of accreditation procedures will provide an objective and trustworthy education governance. Furthermore, it will guarantee the individuals legal interests defence. The Ministry of Education and Science has approved a regulation for validating educational documents issued in Georgia. This regulation stipulates that the LEPL– National Center for Educational Quality Enhancement is responsible for verifying and approving Higher Education Institutions' authority to issue educational documents, the validity of teaching and learning periods, state recognition of these documents, and the conformity of qualifications with the national qualification framework.[29] These requirements are verified based on data recorded in the higher educational management information system and the digital archive of EMIS.

Accreditation is a mandatory prerequisite for students to receive state funding. Legislation mandates that programs must be accredited to be eligible for state funding.[30] During the calculation of state funding, the accredited status of programs is verified for each student.[31]

The aforementioned discussion underscores that data existing in both electronic and non-electronic forms, within and outside the higher educational management information system, directly impacts the quality of education governance. Authorization and accreditation processes involve the analysis of a substantial volume of documents and information to determine the conformity of Higher Education Institutions or their programs with established standards. The outcomes of these procedures have significant implications for the educational market, labor markets, and the legal interests of students. In the case of regulated professions, specific qualifications are mandatory for subsequent employment. Consequently, reliable, accurate, and timely data is fundamental for decision-making, as determinations regarding accreditation or authorization are

[28] Sorour A., Atkins A.S., Big data challenge for monitoring quality in higher education institutions using business intelligence dashboards, https://doi.org/10.1016/j.jnlest.2024.100233

[29] See the Order N98/n, dated 01.09.2010, article 3, https://matsne.gov.ge/ka/document/view/1031772?publication=32.

[30] Law on Higher Education, 21.12.2004, article 1, h^{10} and h^{32} paragraphs, also article 80 and 80^{1}.

[31] Order N154/n by the Ministry of Educations and Science, 15.09.2011, approving the Rules for state funding usage and transferring.

data-driven. In this context, not only the content but also the formal and technical compliance of the data is relevant. Considering that the data for accreditation procedures exists either in the centralized database of EMIS or in the internal systems of universities, and considering that the results of accreditation are subsequently recorded in the EMIS database where state funding is calculated automatically through algorithms, it follows that the accreditation procedure should be digitalized. Furthermore, the results should be shared automatically with relevant stakeholders via interconnected databases. Implementing such system would significantly mitigate the risk of errors in data transfer, which can negatively impact education governance. As Williamson mentions, "Education governance is always at least partly technical"[32] ".... It is subject to what Lascoumes and le Gales articulate as 'public policy instrumentation,' the techniques, methods of operation and devices that 'allow government policy to be made material and operational ... [and] the effects produced by these choices".[33] Williamson cites Carvahlo who argues "that the governing of education depends on public policy instruments (such as international assessments, quality criteria and comparative benchmarks) that carry values, worldviews, interpretations and political aspirations to coordinate and control education. Such instruments are combined of both technical components and social components. He emphasizes how the technical aspects of public policy instruments (the software, its code, algorithms and database architectures) and their social aspects (the organizations and actors producing them, their representations about education, their values and the discursive regimes framing them) combine to organize social relations between administrative and administered subjects. Digital public policy instruments, in this context, are becoming increasingly legitimized and naturalized in educational governance."[34]

In the era of big data, it is inconceivable to implement data-driven public governance without digitalization. Furthermore, not only the data itself but also its visualization significantly influences the decision-making process. "...In order to be used as part of an explanation or as a basis for argument, data typically require graphical representation and often involve a cascade of representations. Any interface is a data visualization of sorts... Data visualization amplifies the rhetorical function of data, since different visualizations are differently effective, well or poorly designed, and all data sets can be multiply visualized and thereby differently persuasive."[35]

Synthesizing the aforementioned approaches and considering the accreditation process within the framework of these discussions, it is evident that the volume of data collected during each administrative proceeding is substantial. Analyzing this data without digital technologies is virtually impossible. Monitoring and analysis based on the

---

[32] Williamson B., Digital education governance: data visualization, predictive analytics, and 'real-time' policy instruments, Journal of Education Policy, 31:2, p.125, http://dx.doi.org/10.1080/02680939.2015.1035758.

[33] Ibid.

[34] Ibid., cited Carvalho, L. M. 2014. "The Attraction of Mutual Surveillance of Performances: PISA as aKnowledge-policy Instrument." In Governing Knowledge: Comparison, Knowledge-based Technologies and Expertise in the Regulation of Education, edited by T. Fenwick,E. Mangez, and J. Ozga, 58–72. London: Routledge.Journal of Education Policy 139.

[35] Gitelman, L., and V. Jackson. 2013. "Introduction." In 'Raw Data' is an Oxymoron, edited by L. Gitelman, 1–14. London: MIT Press, p.12 RawData-excerpts.pdf (ucsb.edu).

visualization of the data are fundamental for further administrative proceedings, policy planning, and implementation.

As Johnson asserts, data-driven decisions are more effective and yield superior results compared to previous methodologies.[36] This underscores the critical importance of implementing digital technologies in the accreditation process and educational governance.

6 Artificial Intelligence Implementation Perspectives in Higher Education Governance

Artificial Intelligence (AI) has fundamentally transformed modern reality and traditional approaches. Public administration has evolved significantly from its state a decade ago. Digital technologies and AI have revolutionized the methods of policy-making and implementation. However, the core principle of public governance, as developed by Wilson[37], emphasizing independent, trustworthy, and objective institutional systems, remains the same. Moreover, the integration of digitalization and AI in public governance enhances its democratic character by facilitating citizen involvement and participation in policy-making processes.

AI is now an integral part of daily reality, irrespective of particular states' policy approaches. It is therefore crucial for the state to keep pace with AI's development and use its potential. In addressing big data challenges, AI emerges as a vital tool. Consequently, policymakers should prioritize and support AI implementation in higher education.

In the context of accreditation processes, when evaluating students' academic performance, satisfaction levels, and the effectiveness of teaching and learning processes, various survey results from University society, AI-based systems in Higher Education Institutions (HEIs) could provide precise data and analysis. This would facilitate more accurate assessments by experts or relevant public officials. AI implementation would significantly enhance the efficiency and accuracy of educational quality assurance mechanisms and increase the quality of education governance.

In 2024, January, LEPL – Digital Governance Agency published digital governance strategy and plan for public discussions,[38] but documents say nothing about AI. It would be reasonable to mentioned AI in the strategy and declare the political will how the state sees the perspectives for its implementation. Later, in September of 2024, Georgia has signed the Europe Framework Convention on AI.[39] As it was officially announced, this

---

[36] J.A. Johnson, Toward Information Justice, Public Administration and Information Technology 33, © Springer International Publishing AG 2018, p.51., https://doi.org/10.1007/978-3-319-70894-2_3.

[37] Wilson W., The Study of Administration, Political Science Quarterly, Vol. 2, No. 2 (Jun., 1887), https://www.jstor.org/stable/2139277.

[38] https://dga.gov.ge/?m=articles&id=6jCBgYe0oj.

[39] https://www.eeas.europa.eu/delegations/council-europe/european-commission-signs-historic-council-europe-framework-convention-artificial-intelligence-and_en?s=51#:~:text=On%205%20September%202024%2C%20during,behalf%20of%20the%20European%20Union.

Convention marks a historic milestone as the first legally binding international agreement on AI, aimed at ensuring that AI systems align with human rights, democracy, and the rule of law.[40] This is the confirmation of the political will that the government welcomes the initiatives related to AI. Besides, European Commission elaborated "Ethical guidelines on the use of artificial intelligence and data in teaching and learning for educators"[41] which announces that "AI can support their work, enabling them to design learning experiences that empower learners to be creative, to think, to solve real-world problems, to collaborate effectively, and provide learning experiences that AI systems on their own cannot do. Moreover, AI can automate repetitive administrative tasks allowing more time to be dedicated to the learning environment."[42] Based on Association Agreement between EU and Georgia, education is one of the most important fields where Georgia has the obligation to harmonize its legislation with the EU legislative acts. Consequently, it would be reasonable AI to be declared in the Strategy of Education and Science as well. This would be encouragement and support for higher educational institutions to develop AI based platforms for teaching, learning and administrative processes. Special platforms and analytical systems enable education governors to collect and analyze data for further evaluation, monitoring and policy making. Furthermore, it gives the state possibility to provide higher educational services for various vulnerable groups including penitentiary system as a tool for rehabilitation. All this data later should be used in accreditation proceedings for checking the quality compliance and make data-driven decisions.

7 Conclusion

To summarize the aforementioned research, several key points should be highlighted:

Accreditation serves as a tool for educational governance, monitoring the quality of higher education. In Georgia, accreditation was implemented in 2005, following the Rose Revolution, though quality control mechanisms were in place prior to this. After collapsing the Soviet Union in 1991, the Ministry of Education and Science began issuing special educational licenses for higher education delivery. This historical data is fundamental for current procedures related to guaranteeing and protecting the legal rights and interests of individuals holding educational documents issued between 1991 and 2005. Consequently, the digitalization of this data is one of the most crucial preconditions for the current digitalization of education governance.

Furthermore, the administration of accreditation processes should be digitalized to effectively achieve quality enhancement goals in higher education. Without digitalization, it is challenging to collect, evaluate, and analyze the vast amount of data accumulated from one process to another. To construct a comprehensive overview, evaluate, and analyze the situation, it is essential to have complete and visualized data.

---

[40] Ibid.

[41] https://education.ec.europa.eu/news/ethical-guidelines-on-the-use-of-artificial-intelligence-and-data-in-teaching-and-learning-for-educators.

[42] Ethical guidelines on the use of artificial intelligence (AI) and data in teaching and learning for educators, p.13, https://op.europa.eu/en/publication-detail/-/publication/d81a0d54-5348-11ed-92ed-01aa75ed71a1/language-en

When discussing big data processing, artificial intelligence (AI) emerges as a tool to address related challenges. Consequently, policymakers should support AI implementation in two key areas:

1. In the teaching-learning process: To identify individual student needs, abilities, academic performance, and satisfaction, including those of vulnerable groups. This data should be collected and analyzed for quality enhancement purposes.
2. For policymakers: The collected data creates a foundation for further analysis and potential amendments to policies or legislation.

AI-based analytical systems for educational administrators would provide the opportunity to objectively evaluate policy implementation results and allocate time to development rather than grappling with challenges related to data collection, sorting, and evaluation. Despite concerns and challenges associated with digitalization and AI, both have the potential to make education governance more accurate, objective, and trustworthy and everyday ordinariness of public officials - creative by transforming tasks into an inspiring process.

References

Chakhaia, L., Bregvadze, T.: Georgia: higher education system dynamics and institutional diversity. In: Huisman, J., Smolentseva, A., Froumin, I. (eds.) 25 Years of Transformations of Higher Education Systems in Post-Soviet Countries. Palgrave Studies in Global Higher Education. Palgrave Macmillan, Cham (2018). https://doi.org/10.1007/978-3-319-52980-6_7

Gitelman, L., Jackson, V.: Introduction. In: Gitelma, L. (ed.) 'Raw Data' is an Oxymoron, pp. 1–14. MIT Press, London (2013). RawData-excerpts.pdf (ucsb.edu)

Harcelroad, F.F.: Accreditation: History. Process and problems, AAHE-ERIC/Higher Education Research Report N6 (1980). https://eric.ed.gov/?id=ED198774

Johnson, J.A.: Toward information justice, public administration and information technology 33, © Springer International Publishing AG (2018). https://doi.org/10.1007/978-3-319-70894-2_3

Schwarz, S., Westerheijden, D.F.: Accreditation in the framework of evaluation activities: a comparative study in the european higher education area. In: Schwarz, S., Westerheijden, D.F. (eds.) Accreditation and Evaluation in the European Higher Education Area. Higher Education Dynamics, vol. 5. Springer, Dordrecht (2004) https://doi.org/10.1007/978-1-4020-2797-0_1

Sorour A., Atkins A.S.: Big data challenge for monitoring quality in higher education institutions using business intelligence dashboards. https://doi.org/10.1016/j.jnlest.2024.100233

Tonsor, C.A.: Origin of the concept 'education is a state function. Clear. House **20**(6) (1946). http://www.jstor.org/stable/30178323

Williamson, B.: Digital education governance: data visualization, predictive analytics, and 'real-time' policy instruments. J. Educ. Policy **31**, 2. https://doi.org/10.1080/02680939.2015.1035758

Wilson, W.: The study of administration. Political Sci. Quar. **2**(2) (1887). https://www.jstor.org/stable/2139277

Georgian Law on Higher Education (2004). www.matsne.gov.ge

Georgian Law on Education Quality Enhancement (2010). www.matnse.gov.ge

Georgian Law on Licensing Entrepreneurs (1999). www.matsne.gov.ge

Order N98/n by Ministry of Education and Science of Georgia (2010). www.matsne.gov.ge

Order N154/n by Ministry of Education and Science of Georgia (2011). www.matsne.gov.ge

Order N65/n by Ministry of Education and Science of Georgia (2011). www.matsne.gov.ge
Order N99/n by Ministry of Education and Science of Georgia (2010). www.matsne.gov.ge
Ethical guidelines on the use of artificial intelligence (AI) and data in teaching and learning for educators. https://op.europa.eu/en/publication-detail/-/publication/d81a0d54-5348-11ed-92ed-01aa75ed71a1/language-en
World Declaration on Higher Education for the Twenty-first Century: Vision and Action and Framework for Priority Action for Change and Development in Higher Education, adopted by the World Conference on Higher Education: Higher Education in the Twenty-first Century, Vision and Action, 9 October 1998. https://unesdoc.unesco.org/ark:/48223/pf0000141952
Draft of Georgian Digital Governance Strategy and Action Plan. https://dga.gov.ge/?m=articles&id=6jCBgYe0oj
https://www.eeas.europa.eu/delegations/council-europe/european-commission-signs-historic-council-europe-framework-convention-artificial-intelligence-
Encyclopedia Britannica. Education - State Development, Curriculum, Reforms | Britannica

Cross-Country Analyses of the Challenges in Online Higher Education and the Need to Implement the ARCS Model

Tamar Matcharashvili[1] and Ioseb Mamukelashvili[2(✉)]

[1] East European University, Tbilisi, Georgia
[2] Caucasus University, Tbilisi, Georgia
imamukelashvili@cu.edu.ge

Abstract. This paper discusses the importance of implementing the ARCS (Attention, Relevance, Confidence, and Satisfaction) model in Georgia's online higher education (Keller (1979, 1987)). After reviewing the existing research published on the subject, several hypotheses were tested using parametric statistical tests based on the data published by the World Economic Forum. The above-mentioned cross-country analyses illustrated several important findings. Namely, students put the same amount of work in online education as they do in live lectures, given the right approach by the instructors. Namely, there is a 74% correlation between digital skills and general skillset of university graduates around the world, and having digital skills represent 54.4% precondition to having competitive graduates. Another important hypothesis that was tested was the fact that online education and digital skills are often perceived as the hinderance to the development of critical thinking. There was an 80% correlation between the digital skills and critical thinking skills of students. In addition, when the digital skills were tested as an independent variable and the critical thinking skills as a dependent variable, it resulted in a 64.8% regression test result. This means that students' digital skills promote the development of critical thinking. Mental health and life expectancy were also examined in the context of online education, but the results were not as strong in this area, and more research is needed to ascertain the impact of online education as an independent variable in this context. Finally, the modified ARCS model was developed specifically for the Georgian lecturers to help them improve the online educational experience.

Keywords: Online education · ARCS model · Digital skills

1 Introduction

In the post-Covid pandemic era, universities and educational institutions place special emphasis on online education. Although the Covid-19 pandemic created tremendous opportunities to advance and further develop online teaching methods, it is fair to state that people are mostly critical of online education, especially of its' usage in higher education (Tan et al. 2021). For example, Ashilova, Begalinov, and Begalinova conducted comprehensive surveys covering thousands of students in Kazakhstan, and they

R. C. Geibel and S. Machavariani (Eds.): ISPC 2024, SPBE, pp. 337–350, 2025.
https://doi.org/10.1007/978-3-031-88052-0_28

concluded that online education during the pandemic "only aggravated the problems already existing in the education system" (Ashilova, Begalinov, & Begalinova 2021).

It is worth mentioning that higher education is not the only area in which online education has been widely adopted. Online education has been widely used in the fields of business, management and entrepreneurship. This is especially true when it comes to continuing education requirements for various professional licenses. For example, web-based learnings are essential components of staff trainings for the so-called big four accounting firms. In some instances, web-based learning is the only was an individual can obtain or maintain a professional license.

To explore the impact of online education in the fields of business, management, and entrepreneurship (BME), researchers Petrolo, Manesh and Palumbo determined that the "BME education finds a fertile context to thrive and flourish in the online environment" (Petrolo, Manesh, & Palumbo 2023). They also stated that "virtual learning spaces should enrich interpersonal exchanges, engaging learners in co-creating value with instructors. Digital technologies enact unprecedented opportunities for online learning, leveraging rich social connections and expanding the reach of educational activities" (Petrolo, Manesh, & Palumbo 2023). Therefore, when one hears the criticism of online education, it is worth examining whether the deficiency is, in fact, in the mode of learning itself, or certain providers of education simply do not possess adequate skillset to uphold the quality of online learning.

Some studies even explore the relationship between online learning and mental disorders. For example, Dong, He, Jiang and others studied "the relationship between the teacher-student relationship (TSR) and mental disorders of university students in online education". Their conclusion was that "higher quality of perceived TSR and a lower level of mobile phone addiction were associated with better mental health among undergraduate and graduate students during online education" (Dong, et al. 2024). However, their research is based on the assertion that online education somehow leads to poor relationships between students and teachers. On the other hand, we see that the exact opposite is true when it comes to online education in the fields of business, management, and entrepreneurship. A simple web search of online testimonials is enough to explore that many professional licensees thank their star online instructors in helping them to pass prestigious professional qualifying exams.

In order to explore the issues of online learning in higher education, we decided to conduct cross-country study to test several hypotheses developed during the research. The cross-country analyses helped us eliminate any cultural biases that might exist between different studies conducted in different countries.

After discussing the results of data tested using the SPSS software, we suggest the implementation of John Keller's Attention, Relevance, Confidence and Satisfaction (ARCS) model to improve the quality of online learning in higher education, because the core components of the ARCS model ensure that there are interactions between students and instructors (Keller (1979, 1987)).

In order to commence the cross-country study of the online learning in higher education, we first developed several hypotheses. The first hypothesis that was developed deals with the overall relationship between the digital skills and the impact that it might have on individuals' overall level of education. Namely, we test the relationships between the digital skills of students and their overall level of education. The null hypothesis was that digital skills were not related to the level of overall education and the alternative hypothesis was that digital skills were essential to achieve a well-rounded educational outcome.

The second hypothesis that was tested was related to the idea that digital skills can somehow adversely affect critical thinking. The null hypothesis was that digital skills and critical thinking skills were unrelated, and the alternative hypothesis stated that digital skills improved the overall critical thinking skills.

2 Research Methods and Results

The World Economic Forum's Global Competitiveness Index (GCI) 4.0 database was used to conduct parametric statistical tests on the main hypotheses developed during the research process (Schwab 2019). The GCI database was particularly useful in the sense that it provided comprehensive ranking data about 141 countries of the world and we were able to locate various variables that were directly related to our research interests.

The IBM SPSS software was used to conduct the parametric statistical tests such as correlation and regression analyses. Before conducting such test, data was carefully examined to ensure that the normal distribution was present, and variances were homogeneous.

One of the first variables that we examined in our research was the "digital skills" ranking by the World Economic Forum. This ranking included 141 countries of the world and ranked countries on a scale of one to seven. Finland had the highest score of 5.8316, whereas Angola had the lowest score of 2.4456. The mean was 4.2179 and the standard deviation – 0.7587. Georgia's score was 3.6564, which is less than one standard deviation below the mean.

Before we used the above-mentioned variable is our statistical tests, it was important to ascertain that it followed a standard distribution. We have conducted both the Kolmogorov-Smirnov and Shapiro-Wilk tests and, in both cases, the results showed that that the distribution of the digital skills variable was normal. For the Kolmogorov-Smirnov test, the result was 0.2, which is higher than 0.05, and for the Shapiro-Wilk test, the result was 0.123, which is also higher than 0.05. Therefore, the conclusion was that the digital skills variable followed a normal distribution. The Graphical Illustration 1 also illustrates that the digital skills variable follows a normal distribution.

Once we have established that the digital skills variable was normally distributed, we analyzed another variable titled overall skillset of university graduates in different countries of the world. This ranking includes 138 countries of the world, and it also ranked them on a scale of one to seven. Switzerland had the highest score of 6.1065, whereas Angola had the lowest score of 2.2752. The mean was 4.4 and the standard deviation – 0.7192. Georgia's score was 3.67, which is approximately one standard deviation below the mean.

Before we used the university graduates' skillset variable is our statistical tests, it was important to ascertain that it followed a standard distribution. We have conducted both the Kolmogorov-Smirnov and Shapiro-Wilk tests and, in both cases, the results showed that that the distribution of the digital skills variable was normal. For the Kolmogorov-Smirnov test, the result was 0.2, which is higher than 0.05, and for the Shapiro-Wilk

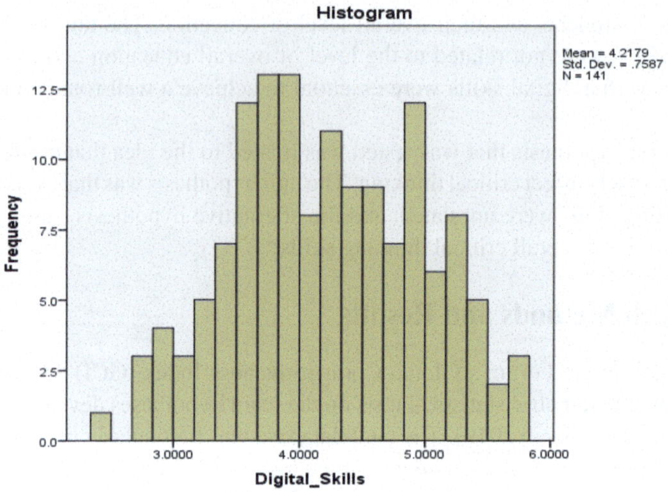

Graphical Illustration 1. Normalcy of Digital Skills Distribution

test, the result was 0.418, which is also higher than 0.05. Therefore, the conclusion was that the university graduates' skillset variable followed a normal distribution.

The graphical illustration below also illustrates that the digital skills variable follows a normal distribution.

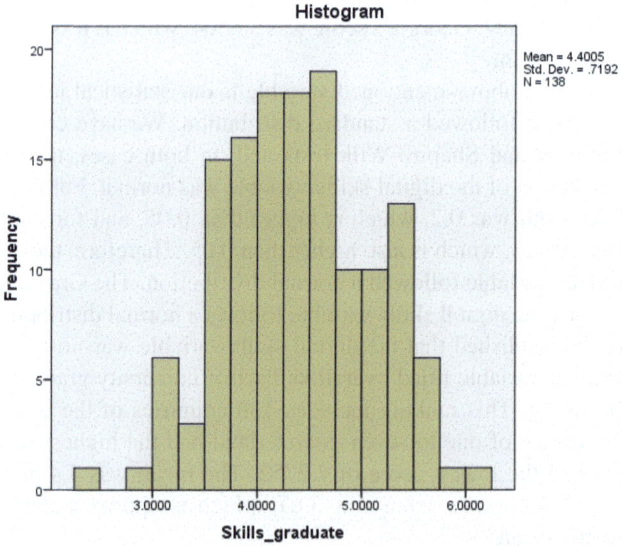

Graphical Illustration 2. Normalcy of University Graduate Skills Distribution

Once we have established that both the digital skills and university graduate skills were normally distributed, we also ascertained that variances were homogeneous. The graphical illustration 3 shows that the variances were homogeneous for the above-mentioned two variables.

The next step in the research process was to conduct correlation and regression analyses for the digital skills and the university graduate skills variables. Table 5 illustrates the relationship between the two variable and it shows that the correlation between the digital skills and the overall skillset of university graduates was 0.74 or 74%. The significance level of 0.000 means that the result is statistically highly significant.

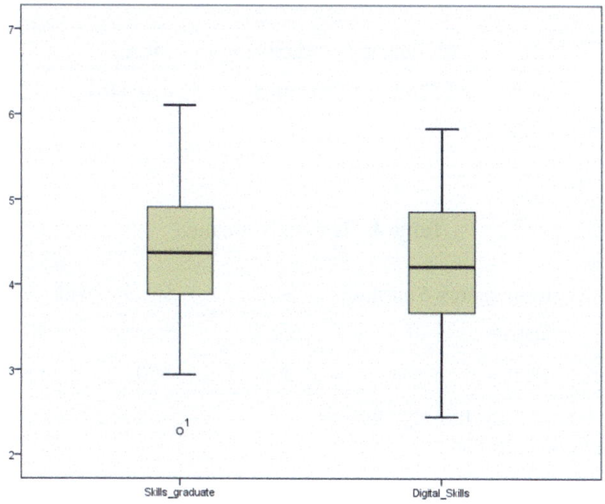

Graphical Illustration 3. Homogeneity of Variances

Due to the fact that the correlation does not provide evidence regarding the cause and effect relationship between the two variables, it was also important to conduct a regression test, where the digital skills were an independent variable and the overall skillset of university graduates – a dependent variable.

Table 1. Descriptive Statistics for Digital Skills Variable

	N	Minimum	Maximum	Mean	Std. Deviation
Digital_Skills	141	2.4456	5.8316	4.217931	.7587248
Valid N (listwise)	141				

Table 6 below provides the result of the regression test with a result of 0.544 or 54%, where the predictor was the digital skills and the dependent variable – the overall skillset of university graduates. Table 7 illustrates that the above-mentioned regression result of 0.544 is highly significant, because the significance level is 0.000.

Table 2. Tests of Normality

	Kolmogorov-Smirnov[a]			Shapiro-Wilk		
	Statistic	df	Sig	Statistic	df	Sig.
Digital_Skills	.068	141	.200*	.985	141	.123

*. This is a lower bound of the true significance
a. Lilliefors Significance Correction

Table 3. Descriptive Statistics

	N	Minimum	Maximum	Mean	Std. Deviation
Skills_graduate	138	2.2752	6.1065	4.400463	.7192161
Valid N (listwise)	138				

Table 4. Tests of Normality

	Kolmogorov-Smirnov[a]			Shapiro-Wilk		
	Statistic	df	Sig.	Statistic	df	Sig.
Skills_graduate	.067	138	.200*	.990	138	.418

*. This is a lower bound of the true significance
a. Lilliefors Significance Correction

Table 5. Correlations

		Digital_Skills	Skills_graduate
Digital_Skills	Pearson Correlation	1	.740**
	Sig. (2-tailed)		.000
	N	141	138
Skills_graduate	Pearson Correlation	.740**	1
	Sig. (2-tailed)	.000	
	N	138	138

**. Correlation is significant at the 0.01 level (2-tailed)

After testing the first hypothesis, it was important to test the second hypothesis developed during the research. In order to test the second hypothesis, we have identified the critical thinking skills variable in the database of the World Economic Forum. This ranking included 141 countries of the world and ranked countries on a scale of one to seven. Finland had the highest score of 5.5833, whereas Angola had the lowest score of

Table 6. Model Summary

Model	R	R Square	Adjusted R Square	Std. Error of the Estimate
1	.740[a]	.548	.544	.4854979

a. Predictors: (Constant), Digital_Skills

2.1129. The mean was 3.5587 and the standard deviation – 0.7861. Georgia's score was 3.1172, which was less than one standard deviation below the mean.

Table 7. ANOVA[a]

Model		Sum of Squares	df	Mean Square	F	Sig.
1	Regression	38.810	1	38.810	164.652	.000[b]
	Residual	32.056	136	.236		
	Total	70.866	137			

a. Dependent Variable: Skills_graduate
b. Predictors: (Constant), Digital_Skills

Table 8. Descriptive Statistics

	N	Minimum	Maximum	Mean	Std. Deviation
Critical_Thinking	141	2.1129	5.5833	3.558785	.7861343
Valid N (listwise)	141				

Table 9. Tests of Normality

	Kolmogorov-Smirnov[a]			Shapiro-Wilk		
	Statistic	df	Sig.	Statistic	df	Sig.
Critical_Thinking	.092	141	.005	.967	141	.002

a. Lilliefors Significance Correction

Before we use the critical thinking skills variable is our statistical tests, it is important to ascertain that it follows a standard distribution. We have conducted both the Kolmogorov-Smirnov and Shapiro-Wilk tests and, in both cases, the results showed that that the both distributions were not normally distributed. For the Kolmogorov-Smirnov test, the result was 0.005, which is less than 0.05, and for the Shapiro-Wilk test, the result was 0.002, which is also less than 0.05. Therefore, the conclusion was that the critical thinking skills variable did not follow a normal distribution.

The graphical illustration below also shows that the distribution is skewed to the left, which can indicate that critical thinking is something that the world population lacks in general.

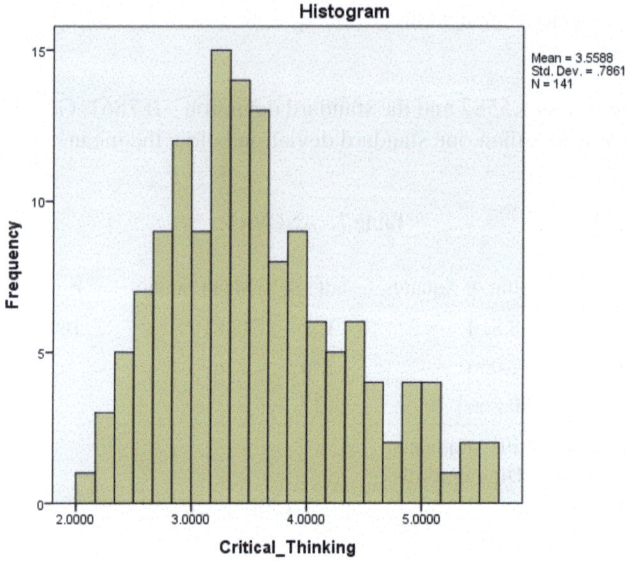

Graphical Illustration 4. Critical Thinking Variable Distribution

Subsequently, the critical thinking variable was normalized using the logarithmic computation (LN) function in SPSS. We tested again the recalculated variable for tests of normality. The Table 10 below shows the results both the Kolmogorov-Smirnov and Shapiro-Wilk tests and, in both cases, the results showed that that the distribution of the recalculated critical thinking skill variable was normal. For the Kolmogorov-Smirnov test, the result was 0.2, which is higher than 0.05, and for the Shapiro-Wilk test, the result was 0.446, which is also higher than 0.05. Therefore, the conclusion was that the recalculated critical thinking skills variable followed a normal distribution.

Table 10. Tests of Normality

	Kolmogorov-Smirnov[a]			Shapiro-Wilk		
	Statistic	df	Sig.	Statistic	df	Sig.
Critical_Thinking_2	.049	141	.200*	.990	141	.446

*. This is a lower bound of the true significance
a. Lilliefors Significance Correction

The graphical illustration below also illustrates that the recalculated critical thinking skill variable followed a normal distribution.

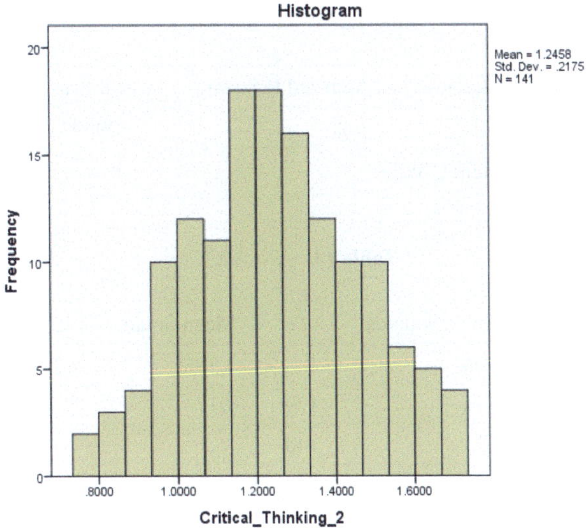

Graphical Illustration 5. Recalculated Critical Thinking Variable Distribution

After normalizing the critical thinking variable, we conducted correlation and regression analyses. According to the Table 11, the statistically significant correlation existed between the digital skills of students and their critical thinking skills in the amount of .806 or 80.6%.

Table 11. Correlations

		Digital_Skills	Critical_Thinking_2
Digital_Skills	Pearson Correlation	1	.806**
	Sig. (2-tailed)		.000
	N	141	141
Critical_Thinking_2	Pearson Correlation	.806**	1
	Sig. (2-tailed)	.000	
	N	141	141

**. Correlation is significant at the 0.01 level (2-tailed)

The regression test was designed in the following manner: the digital skills was an independent variable, whereas the critical thinking skills - a dependent variable. According to Table 12, the regression test resulted in 0.648 coefficient.

The statistical significance of the regression test can be ascertained by the p value of 0.000 in the following table, which lower than 0.05.

We have also analyzed several other variables such as internet usage, meritocracy, homicide rates, etc. However, the test results did not provide such strong results as it did in the previous tests. One interesting observation that was made was that there was a

Table 12. Model Summary

Model	R	R Square	Adjusted R Square	Std. Error of the Estimate
1	.806[a]	.650	.648	.1290934

a. Predictors: (Constant), Digital_Skills

Table 13. ANOVA[a]

Model		Sum of Squares	df	Mean Square	F	Sig.
1	Regression	4.306	1	4.306	258.398	.000[b]
	Residual	2.316	139	.017		
	Total	6.623	140			

a. Dependent Variable: Critical_Thinking_2
b. Predictors: (Constant), Digital_Skills

0.645 correlation between the internet usage and meritocracy among the population (p value – 0.000).

Table 14 below provides an overview of the internet usage variable in 141 countries of the world: Qatar was the country with most internet users with a score of 99.65 and Burundi – with the lowest number of people who use internet with a score of 2.66. The mean for this variable is 60.65 and the standard deviation – 27.15. Georgia's score was 63.97, which was slightly above the average.

Table 14. Descriptive Statistics

	N	Minimum	Maximum	Mean	Std. Deviation
Internet	141	2.6607	99.6528	60.543717	27.1451261
Valid N (listwise)	141				

Table 15 below provides an overview of the meritocracy variable in 141 countries of the world: Denmark was the most meritocratic country with a score of 85.04 and Chad – the least meritocratic country with a score of 31.35. The mean for this variable is 62.06 and the standard deviation – 11.64. Georgia's score was 68.28, which was above the average.

According to the Kolmogorov-Smirnov and Shapiro-Wilk tests, the meritocracy variable was normally distributed, because the p value for this variable under the Kolmogorov-Smirnov test was 0.2, which was higher than 0.05 and the p value under the Shapiro-Wilk test was 0.240, which was higher than 0.05. However, the internet usage variable was not normally distributed under both the Kolmogorov-Smirnov and Shapiro-Wilk tests. More specifically, the p value for this variable under the Kolmogorov-Smirnov

Table 15. Descriptive Statistics

	N	Minimum	Maximum	Mean	Std. Deviation
Meritocracy	141	31.3538	85.0427	62.058077	11.6385179
Valid N (listwise)	141				

Table 16. Tests of Normality

	Kolmogorov-Smirnov[a]			Shapiro-Wilk		
	Statistic	df	Sig.	Statistic	df	Sig.
Internet	.119	141	.000	.929	141	.000
Meritocracy	.038	141	.200*	.988	141	.240

*. This is a lower bound of the true significance
a. Lilliefors Significance Correction

test was 0.000, which is lower than 0.05 and the p value under the Shapiro-Wilk test was 0.000, which is also lower than 0.05. We tried to normalize the internet usage variable using the logarithmic LN and the square root transformation functions of the SPSS, but the recalculated amounts also did not result in a normal distribution. Subsequently, we decided not to manipulate data any further in order to have more reliable research results.

When the internet usage was an independent variable and meritocracy – a dependent variable, the regression test resulted in 0.412 with a p value of 0.000. Since the internet usage variable did not follow a standard distribution, our results in that regard were not as persuasive as the results in the previous tests. However, researchers such as Larrucea and Cortazar have long argued that the digital skills and internet will bring far more social and economic benefits than, merely technological ones (Larrucea & Cortazar 2010). On the other hand, researchers such as Carr-Chellman, Fitzpatrick, and Zhang, were quite critical of the possibility of democratization of education using the online mode of teaching (Carr-Chellman, Fitzpatrick, & Zhang 2020). Therefore, more evidence is needed to support the claim that internet usage leads to a more meritocratic society.

3 Conclusions and Further Research

Although our research variables did not contain specifically online learning in higher education, one of the main research questions that it addressed was the fact that developing digital skills in graduates is essential for them to stay competitive in today's global workforce. Namely, the 74% statistically significant correlation between the digital skillset and overall skillset of university graduates, in our view, indicate the need to incorporate online learning in university curriculum, even without the Covid-19 pandemic being present. Furthermore, it is evident that there is a cause-and-effect relationship between the digital skills and the overall skillset of university graduates. More specifically, digital skills are a 54% precondition to having skilled graduates in general.

Our findings above are consistent with Luengo-Aravena's, Cabello's, and Bachino's research results. More specifically, they also argued that "digital skills as necessary for the 21st century" (Luengo-Aravena, Cabello, & Bachino 2024). Their study "identified three distinct groups of students based on their digital skills: high-skilled, medium-skilled, and low-skilled. The low-skilled group faced more socioeconomic disadvantages compared to the other two groups. Moreover, students with low digital skills reported lower satisfaction with online group work and a poorer self-evaluation of the group processes involved in the collaborative online task" (Luengo-Aravena, Cabello, & Bachino 2024).

Another important issue that this research addressed was the idea of digital skills can somehow hinder critical thinking skills of students. On the contrary, 80.6% statistically significant correlation between the above mentioned variables suggests that critical thinking skills are improved by digital skills. In order to ascertain the cause-and-effect relationship between the two variables, the regression test showed that digital skills improve the critical thinking skills by as much as 64.8%. This result is even higher than the regression test results when the digital skills was an independent variable and the overall skillset – a dependent variable. In other words, digital skills do not only help to ensure that university graduates have well-rounded education, but they particularly assist in making sure that university graduates have adequate critical thinking skills that the world population lacks.

Adorni, Artico, Piatti, and others also stated that "in the rapidly evolving landscape of digital competencies, the need for a robust and universal method to assess students' algorithmic thinking (AT) skills has become increasingly pronounced. Algorithmic thinking refers to the ability to analyze a problem and develop a step-by-step process to solve it" (Adorni, et al. 2024). One of main findings of their research was that the digital tools have tremendous potential "to facilitate advanced algorithmic thinking skill development across diverse age groups" (Adorni, et al. 2024). Therefore, our research result is consistent with their conclusions in the sense that digital skills are, in some ways, a prerequisite to being able to think critically in the twenty-first century.

It is worth noting that a statistically significant correlation of 64.5% exist between the internet usage and meritocracy. Furthermore, the internet usage can be a 41.2% precondition to meritocracy. However, we had an issue with the normality of the internet usage variable distribution. Therefore, we are not as confident with these results.

Despite the negative stereotype that online education developed among some researchers during the pandemic, our research illustrates that the power of teaching can be harnessed through online education, as long as the instructors use the right approach and teaching methods. The main finding of this research is goes against the bias that some researchers have in the academic community. For instance, the main hypothesis of Bartkowiak's and Marciniuk's research paper is "that students put less work into distance education than in class education during the semester; they were less active and focused; the economic benefits increased; and social relations deteriorated" (Bartkowiak & Marciniuk 2022).

In addition to rebuking Bartkowiak's and Marciniuk's hypothesis above, we need to find a way to proceed with a solution that will enrich the online educational experience, and we believe that the ARCS (Attention, Relevance, Confidence, and Satisfaction) model can be especially useful tool to explore during the online lectures. Maiti's, Priyaadharshini's and Harini's research explored the possibility of using the ARCS motivational model for online classes in higher education. They argued that "although distance education and online learning have been adopted gradually recently, it has become the'New Normal.' In this situation of uncertainty, facilitators must keep themselves updated with the various teaching/learning strategies and encourage learners to get accustomed to the online classroom environment" (Maiti, Priyaadharshini, & S 2023). They also highlighted the fact that online learning in higher education has been particularly successful in case of MOOCs (Massive Open Online Courses) that have become extremely popular in recent years. It is worth noting that we have also highlighted the popularity of online courses in various professional settings, such as continuing professional licensing and web-based learning by the so-called big four accounting firms.

Maiti's, Priyaadharshini's and Harini's research consisted of implementing a modified ARCS model during online lectures, and they concluded that "an improvement of 11.21% was observed in the student's performance compared to a maximum of 8.8% in the existing traditional models" (Maiti, Priyaadharshini, & S, 2023). They conducted their lectured using the Microsoft Teams (MS Teams) educational platform, which has been extremely popular since the Covid-19 pandemic.

During the next stage of our research, we plan to conduct interviews and survey of both undergraduate and graduate students in Georgia to identify how the successful ARCS model can be implemented. To achieve that goal, we plan to use the approach used by Na, Jeong and Lee when they interviewed elderly adults in South Korea to determine if the usage of ARCS motivation model would increase their usage of public libraries. Their approach was mostly qualitative in nature, employing "a thematic analysis, a technique described by Braun and Clarke (2006) for analyzing qualitative data", identifying "common themes, such as recurring themes, ideas, and patterns of meaning" (Na, Jeong, & Lee 2024). What is particularly interesting in Na's, Jeong's and Lee's research is that they focus on older adults and their research successfully identified strategies for increasing the library usage among them. Similarly, we have also mentioned that online education is particularly successful when it comes to professional licensing education. Therefore, age of students might be an interesting factor to explore when it comes to online education. More specifically, older professional adults who could be more mature and have more motivation than young adults at bachelor's and master's level programs.

Our design for further research will be different from Na, Jeong and Lee in the sense that both qualitative and quantitative approaches will be incorporated. In addition to doing the interviews with students, we will also ask them to fill out surveys, which will enable us to perform tests using the SPSS software.

References

Adorni, G., et al.: Development of algorithmic thinking skills in K-12 education: a comparative study of unplugged and digital assessment instruments. Computers in Human Behavior Reports (2024)

Ashilova, M.S., Begalinov, A.S., Begalinova, K.: The quality of higher education during the Covid-19 pandemic and the prospects for post-secondary education. J. Educ. Sci. 127–136 (2021)

Bartkowiak, A., Marciniuk, A.: Selected economic and social aspects resulting from online education at the higher level. Wroclaw Review of Law, Administration & Economics (2022)

Carr-Chellman, A.A., Fitzpatrick, S., Zhang, K.: The rhetoric of democracy in international online education. Inform. Commun. Soc. (2020)

Dong, J., He, Y., Jiang, F., Liu, Z., Ni, Y., Tang, Y.: Teacher-student relationships and mental disorders of undergraduate and graduate students in online education: a moderated mediation model of mobile phone addiction and hometown setting. Comput. Hum. Behav. Reports (2024)

Keller, J.M.: Motivation and instructional design: a theoretical perspective. J. Instruct. Develop. (1979)

Keller, J.M.: Development and use of the ARCS model of instructional design. J. Instruct. Develop. (1987)

Larrucea, X., Cortazar, R.: The future Internet and its social return of investment. In: ACM International Conference Proceeding Series (2010)

Luengo-Aravena, D., Cabello, P., Bachino, B.R.-M.: Online collaborative problem-solving as a tangible outcome of digital skills in technical and vocational higher education. Comput. Educ. (2024)

Maiti, M., Priyaadharshini, M.: Design and evaluation of a revised ARCS motivational model for online classes in higher education. Heliyon (2023)

Na, K., Jeong, Y., Lee, J.: Exploring older adults' motivation to use public libraries in South Korea using the attention, relevance, confidence, and satisfaction (ARCS) motivation model. Lib. Inform. Sci. Res. (2024)

Petrolo, D., Manesh, M.F., Palumbo, R.: Unpacking business, management, and entrepreneurship education online: Insights from a hybrid literature review. Int. J. Manage. Educ. (2023)

Schwab, K.: The global competitiveness report. World Economic Forum (2019)

Tan, K.H., Chan, P.P., Said, N.-E.M.: Higher education students' online instruction perceptions: a quality virtual learning environment. Sustainability (2021)

International Challenges with Digital Transformation to Manage Pandemics and Viral Infections

Natia Tsiklauri[1(✉)] and Marina Endeladze[2]

[1] Georgian Technical University, Tbilisi, Georgia
natitsiklauri@yahoo.com
[2] European University, Tbilisi, Georgia

Abstract. Harnessing the potential of digital technologies-11 in healthcare has never been more important in the EU and Eastern Partnership region. E-health solutions create better and more efficient healthcare systems for both patients and healthcare workers.

The development of digital [2] healthcare and telemedicine [3] will contribute to the formation of legal and regulatory legal framework and clinical guidelines [4], provision of training courses, use of telemedicine services, smooth and wide access to medical services, online booking of doctor's appointments, existence of electronic medical history, availability of digital prescriptions. These health monitoring services allow citizens to be more involved in managing their own health and have access to resources.

By using digital health systems, the medical professional can provide a more personalized and accurate response to the patient's health care needs when he has access to the patient's health data in a digital format, less time is spent filling out forms and no more duplication of clinical procedures. The use of digital data provides new opportunities for control and supervision..

E-health [5] is closely related to operational interoperability, which involves breaking down barriers to facilitate communication and exchange between systems, data becomes mobile, the patient is no longer tied to a paper file in one hospital, and he can take his health data to any hospital in any country where these data are digital systems. will read. By using an electronic prescription, the patient can purchase prescribed medicines without a paper prescription. With the help of interoperable systems and a digital patient history, pharmacies can more easily validate a prescription.

Digital transformation in the healthcare system is a complex, multidisciplinary task that requires coordinated efforts from government, business, academia, and civil society.

Keywords: Technologies · Digital · Telemedicine' Guidelines · E-health

1 Introduction

The health organization defines electronic health care as the so-called Application of eHealth as information and communication technologies in the healthcare system. eHealth allows for a more timely and accurate reporting system in the field of health

R. C. Geibel and S. Machavariani (Eds.): ISPC 2024, SPBE, pp. 351–363, 2025.
https://doi.org/10.1007/978-3-031-88052-0_29

care, and also contributes to the improvement of the control and supervision system of diseases and health care costs.

Considering that the policy cycle is an interactive process and its effectiveness can only be achieved with the involvement of all stakeholders, the Ministry ensures the coordination of the strategy implementation process. The coordination mechanism includes cooperation between the coordinating body and the responsible agencies, partner agencies and all other interested parties. The state policy in the field of health care is based on such basic values as the protection of human rights and justice, which, among other directions, includes the elimination of inequality in terms of equal access to medical services and the right to participate in the decision-making process.

Electronic health technologies are effectively used for distance learning and operational response in emergency situations. Moreover, thanks to the strategic use of e-health, we can support planning and coordination processes in the field of health care, as well as support and coordination of decentralized medical units at the regional level.

The so-called eHealth Examples of "solutions" include electronic health records, electronic referrals, medication management, distance learning, telemedicine, mobile health, disease surveillance, and more.

Harnessing the potential of digital technologies [1] in healthcare has never been more important in the EU and Eastern Partnership region. Through e-health solutions, better and more efficient healthcare systems are created for both patients and healthcare workers.

The development of digital [2] healthcare and telemedicine [3] will contribute to the formation of legal and regulatory legal framework and clinical guidelines [4], provision of training courses, use of telemedicine services, smooth and widespread access to medical services, online booking of doctor's appointments, existence of electronic medical history, the availability of digital prescriptions. These health monitoring services allow citizens to be more involved in managing their own health and have access to resources.

The global crisis caused by the Covid-19 pandemic has caused significant damage to both the country's economy and the healthcare system. Budgetary funds turned out to be the only fighting lever against the economic crisis. In the face of the economic crisis, almost all countries have resorted to relative tax liberalization.

To mitigate the impact of the Covid-19 pandemic, it was important to implement measures that prioritized investments in the health system and provided social assistance to the population, especially the most vulnerable.

In particularly difficult times, factors that would ensure a rapid transition to strengthening health and social protection systems, promoting the private sector, maintaining financial stability and confidence - which are extremely important for human life.

Forecasts for the economic difficulties caused by COVID-19 have turned out to be uncertain. In the Europe and Central Asia region, there was an economic downturn in 2020 and the growth rate fell between -4.4 and -2.8 percent, with a gradual increase in 2021 as a result of the implementation of sectoral policy measures, the gradual recovery of commodity prices and the strengthening of trade. "Social distancing, closing non-essential companies and schools are necessary measures to stop the spread of the pandemic and save human lives. Providing measures such as cash transfers, health care subsidies, assistance to the population and families, as well as short-term business loans and tax incentives for companies. It is important for small and medium-sized enterprises to benefit from targeted state subsidies to mitigate the economic downturn and preserve jobs.

Georgia's real GDP growth is projected to decline sharply to near zero percent in 2020 as the impact of COVID-19 adds to an already challenging external environment. Partially mitigated by fiscal stimulus by holding back the ace of capital spending at around 2% of GDP, deferring tax debt repayments, accelerating VAT refunds and finding sectoral support for affected enterprises, as well as increasing social spending. As a result of the mentioned measures, the fiscal deficit amounted to 5.2% of GDP in 2020. Several factors have had a severe impact on the economy - the impact of transport restrictions on travel and tourism, restrictive measures reducing local demand.

The World Bank launched a rapid response to help developing countries strengthen pandemic responses, increase disease surveillance, improve health interventions, and help the private sector operate and sustain jobs. World Bank in the form of financial assistance about 160 billion. The US dollar has been used over the next 15 months to promote countries, protect poor and vulnerable families, support companies and strengthen economic recovery.

Gross domestic product (GDP) growth became negative 5%. Against the background of the deepening of the current crisis, as well as in order to encourage the preservation of jobs, taking into account the tax benefits, only the tax revenues of the budget decreased by 1.3 billion GEL. Additional needs in the spending part of the budget reached 1.6 billion GEL. Overall, the budget deficit for 2020 increased to 9.1% of GDP. In response to the crisis, international aid was quickly mobilized and additional funds of 1.7 billion USD were raised. The mentioned resources were directed to finance the reduced budget revenues and expenses provided by anti-crisis measures.. State debt in relation to GDP reached 59.9

Export from Georgia. The crisis has also affected other sources of income, especially the tourism sector. As a result, the current account deficit in relation to GDP increased to 9.7%. 2021–2024 Against the backdrop of the crisis, economic activity has significantly decreased. The shock was two-sided - both on the demand side and on the supply side. Some businesses faced significant financial difficulties and job losses. A decrease in aggregate demand, an increase in unemployment (both temporary and long-term), a worsening of the quality and severity of poverty, pressure on the national currency, a decrease in tourism revenues and remittances - these are the most visible economic effects that the population of Georgia has already felt.

The economic impact of Covid-19 has had a serious impact on foreign trade trends. In international trade, the economic problems of high-risk countries are most likely to affect their main partners through a reduction in aggregate demand.

The international trade of Georgia showed signs of the pandemic's effect from February and it continued in June. It is important to note that exports to EU countries are relatively stable compared to other trading partner countries. In January-July 2020, exports to Bulgaria, Switzerland and Spain increased by 13.7%, 33.3% and 25.1%, respectively. The sharpest decrease in exports was noted in the following countries: Armenia (−44.7%), Ukraine (-36.9%), USA (-46/6%), Russia (-24.5%) and Azerbaijan (−15.3%).

In an economy where the role of informal employment is important, and the dependence on daily cash income is high, the deterioration of the social situation exerts quite a heavy pressure. Remittances are an important indicator for assessing dependence on the outside world. Georgia is vulnerable to economic crises when: reducing the negative effects caused by the Covid-19 pandemic/minimizing economic losses; Restoring the positive trends before the pandemic and ensuring rapid economic growth.

This will be achieved through gradual measures of fiscal discipline, promotion of economic sectors affected by the state, support of the purchasing power of the country's population and improvement of the effectiveness of the social protection system, while in the medium term the main priority will remain: improvement of the country's regional and international competitiveness; promotion of competitive local production and export; Promotion of domestic and foreign investments. To achieve the above, a stable macroeconomic framework, improved fiscal discipline, gradual reduction of public debt, price stability, independence of monetary policy, gradual reduction of the budget deficit will be ensured. In order to create a macroeconomic environment conducive to the development of the economy, it will be necessary to implement a coordinated fiscal and monetary policy, especially in the post-pandemic period. In this regard, it is necessary, along with fiscal incentives, to implement monetary policy stimulating tools in order to promote domestic investments and increase the scale of stimulation. Along with the implementation of the fiscal policy, it will be important to promote the participation of foreign investors in the local market, which will reduce the interest rate to some extent and create additional monetary incentives. It is important to ensure a low level of unemployment, resulting in the elimination of extreme poverty and the achievement of a low level of poverty, a reduced level of deficit and a high rate of economic growth and income growth. Implementation of structural reforms of the economy to strengthen economic stability - strengthening the image of Georgia as a leading reformer in the wider region. In overcoming the economic crisis, optimization of the tax mechanism, establishment of a rational ratio between the fiscal and stimulating functions of taxes is of particular importance. Which helps to overcome the economic crisis of the country.

The modern world is facing many challenges. The coronavirus (SARS-CoV-2) and the disease it causes (COVID-19) have forced the world to make important decisions as the pandemic has caused unprecedented economic costs. Dealing with COVID-19 has become a top priority for governments in all countries. During the imposed restrictions, the socio-economic situation has changed in many countries. The impact of the pandemic was particularly felt on the health and education systems, the economy and the labor market. During the pandemic, Georgia took a number of steps against the COVID-19 virus, which had a significant impact on the protection of human rights. Many countries are already healing the wounds caused by the pandemic, which was caused by the effective vaccination management process and the development of the right anti-pandemic policies.

Prevention and control of infectious diseases have been able to avoid risks. Promoted early detection of all risks, effective response, hospital treatment, emergency medical care, financial support where the government, local authorities and medical personnel played an important role, which included the national health system, including the development of health resources, delivery, services and financial support.

National Institutes of Public Health, the World Health Organization and their global networks are key resources for strengthening health systems with essential public health functions and policy evidence relevant to health and socioeconomic development.

The COVID-19 pandemic has exposed global disparities in public health capacity, making it urgent to explore global sources of knowledge and understand how to best invest in and apply it to health care settings. As public health capacity varies geographically, regions should set examples for the global health sector to explore new ways of working and define the complex environment in which public health authorities operate.

Four incentives are identified for countries to invest in public health to strengthen institutions: transparency and trust; socio-economic dividends; collective health protection and knowledge sharing; Equality. protection of common priorities; more equitable access to resources and settings; promote cooperation and learning in different regions; To outline next steps for the development and better use of public health institutions and international networks.

The Government of Georgia is committed to ensuring the availability of information and quality medical services necessary for the realization of the right to health for every citizen. Which is subject to the Constitution of Georgia and health legislation, besides, Georgia has signed a number of important international conventions and agreements.

The Government of Georgia is committed to ensuring the availability of information and quality medical services necessary for the realization of the right to health for every citizen. Which is subject to the Constitution of Georgia and health legislation, besides, Georgia has signed a number of important international conventions and agreements.

To evaluate the efficiency of the health care system, the World Health Organization defined the main indicators of the functioning of the health care system, such as: 1. Health status of the population; 2. Health care system management function; 3. Protection of equality, financial security and access to health services; 4. Quality and results of healthcare services, health promotion and disease prevention; 5. Effectiveness and efficiency of health care services, rational distribution of health care system resources.

The rate of infectious diseases is one of the main indicators of the country's development and socio-economic well-being of the population. Against the background of political and socio-economic changes developed in the country during the last decades, favorable conditions were created for the increase of cases of infectious diseases (WHO).

Despite the difficulties, the Covid-19 crisis in Georgia has created significant opportunities to strengthen the hospital sector and introduce new digital technologies in primary healthcare. The creation of initiatives started in the conditions of the pandemic was a good basis for the further strengthening of the hospital and primary care network.

The first case of coronavirus (COVID-19) in Georgia was recorded on February 27, 2020. In response to the increasing spread of the epidemic, measures were taken in all areas to increase the scale of the emergency response to prevent domestic spread. In order to stop COVID 19, the Georgian government used the reserve as early as January 2020. On January 28, 2020, the first resolution of the Government of Georgia (N164) was issued "On the approval of measures to prevent the possible spread of the new coronavirus." Operational response plan to the cases of the disease caused by the new coronavirus in Georgia". A national multidisciplinary committee was established. According to the "Emergency Response Plan" approved by the Government of Georgia, the roles and responsibilities of each sectoral ministry and other government organizations for each phase of the response to COVID 19 are clearly defined. In order to fight the global pandemic of coronavirus, on March 21, 2020, the Parliament declared a state of emergency in the entire territory of Georgia. To contain the spread of the virus, a series of measures were planned across the country, which included (but were not limited to) the gradual closure of all educational institutions, public gathering places, including sports halls, museums and theaters, shopping centers, non-food centers. Shops, bars and restaurants. Strict restrictions were imposed on transport, air and rail traffic was suspended, and borders with neighboring countries - Armenia, Azerbaijan and Russia - were closed.

Three weeks after the detection of the first case of coronavirus, the epidemiological picture of the spread of the virus clearly indicated that the country's authorities were making timely and progressive decisions. Screening and testing of those arriving in Georgia from countries with a high rate of virus transmission, contact tracing, introduction of quarantine and self-isolation rules, suspension of international flights, closure of institutions, educational organizations, delivery of employees, transition to an online work schedule, restriction of mass gatherings, partial suspension of public transport containment, development and approval of epidemic surveillance, including new protocols, active communication with the public, etc. At different times, in order to stop the spread of the new coronavirus, a strict quarantine was announced and the following municipalities were gradually closed: Marneuli, Bolnisi, Lentekhi, separate administrative units of Kobuleti municipality, Khidiskuri village of Khashuri municipality, Rustavi, Tetritskaro, later (in August) - Mestia.

According to the report of measures taken by the Government of Georgia against COVID 19, the first phase was to contain the spread of the virus, the second phase was to slow down the spread of the virus, and the third phase was to manage and gradually mitigate. The country passed these stages, from the first half, the rate of reproduction of the virus dropped below one, and the trend of stabilization was already visible in the dynamics. As a result, the Georgian government was given the opportunity to gradually lift the restrictions and start the economy. International practice should also be taken into account - in the same period, many countries began to ease restrictions (France, Albania, Germany, Austria, Norway, Denmark, Czech Republic, Italy, Spain, Finland, Croatia). On April 24, 2020, the Government of Georgia presented to the public a plan for the gradual cancellation of imposed restrictions and activation of the economy. The government also presented an anti-crisis plan aimed at the rational distribution of funds for economic and social needs. This plan provided for various types of assistance for vulnerable groups and sectors that were most affected. 2 billion 110 million GEL was announced to support the economy and entrepreneurship, which should be used for the active private sector, increasing the efficiency of agriculture and encouraging local production.

As for the stage of epidemic management, in this case great importance was attached to the connection of primary health care. Mobilization of primary health care links, proper coordination and management of infected people at the local level, as well as timely referral services were needed. Containment of the virus by epidemiologists and primary care professionals gave the health sector additional time and incentive.

Harnessing the potential of digital technologies- in healthcare has never been more important in the EU and Eastern Partnership region. E-health solutions create better and more efficient healthcare systems for both patients and healthcare workers.

The development of digital healthcare and telemedicine will contribute to the formation of legal and regulatory legal framework and clinical guidelines, provision of training courses, use of telemedicine services, smooth and wide access to medical services, online booking of doctor's appointments, existence of electronic medical history, availability of digital prescriptions. These health monitoring services allow citizens to be more involved in managing their own health and have access to resources. E-health is closely related to operational interoperability, which means removing barriers to facilitate communication and exchange between systems, data becomes mobile.

The role of public health services and local government in containing the virus is immeasurable. One thing is clear - the epidemic had to be defeated globally. Every country has its own corona history and its own role in the process of defeating the pandemic - it varies according to the country's socio-economic situation and the preparedness of the health system. During the fight against the pandemic, in the process of proper management of the epidemic, both individual responsibility and the role of the central and local authorities are important. The whole world had the same goal - to defeat the COVID 19 pandemic.

Viruses and infectious diseases form the most common group of diseases. Signs and symptoms of infectious diseases can vary greatly because there are many causative agents such as: common cold, flu, acute chronic hepatitis A, hepatitis B, hepatitis C, AIDS (HIV), Lyme disease, brucellosis, diarrhea, opportunistic infection, dengue fever, zika virus infection, exanthematic viral infections, systemic fungal infections, parasitic diseases, tuberculosis meningitis and other infections and viruses.

Advances in the introduction of modern medicine, modern critical care facilities, advances in anti-infection treatment, and improvements in surgical intervention in the field of patient care and treatment are extending human life expectancy and increasing quality of life. However, all these improvements are also associated with certain unfavorable by-products. The suppression of the immune system, both by the underlying diseases and by the treatments implemented, leads to a substantial increase in infections caused by opportunistic and resistant microorganisms.

The Government of Georgia has also taken important steps in the direction of hepatitis C elimination. With the technical assistance of the Centers for Disease Control and Prevention of the United States of America, WHO and European Union partners, the country launched the world's first national hepatitis C elimination program. Within the framework of the program, hepatitis C diagnostic and treatment services have become fully available in the country. The success of the country in the field of global elimination of viral hepatitis contributed to the awarding of Georgia with the status of a model country in the fight against hepatitis C by the European Association for the Study of the Liver (EASL) and the International Liver Foundation.

Despite progress, pre-existing and newly emerging communicable diseases continue to challenge the country's healthcare system. The best example of this is the global pandemic of the new coronavirus, which began in Georgia in February 2020 and had a significant impact on the operational and strategic agenda of both healthcare and other sectors. The pandemic has challenged various parts of the healthcare system and exposed both its weaknesses and strengths. Strengthening primary care through dual track services, which involves strengthening surveillance, contact tracing, first response, case management, and rehabilitation functions while maintaining routine health care services, has gained particular importance.

The peak of infection in 2021 also posed a challenge to the hospital sector, nevertheless, the country was able to significantly strengthen resources and meet the needs caused by the pandemic during the period of subsequent exacerbations. Recommendations were made, which mean: strengthening the role of municipal, regional and autonomous republic public health services, increasing their functions, which in itself will strengthen the public health system; Providing municipal public health services with material and technical equipment in accordance with the national recommendation (guideline) for public health protection.

The novel coronavirus (SARS-CoV-2) disease (COVID-19) and the resulting global pandemic have created a number of challenges for the health system, both at the international and national levels, and have confirmed the need to improve preparedness and response to public health risks.

According to the report of the Government of Georgia's measures against COVID 19, the first stage was to contain the spread of the virus, the second stage was to slow down the spread of the virus, and the third stage was to manage and gradually ease and reopen. The country has passed these stages. The reproduction rate of the virus dropped below one, and the trend of stabilization was already observed in the dynamics.

According to the data of the National Center for Disease Control of Georgia, about 8,000 tests were performed per day, which is about 2,200 per million inhabitants. And in the later period, 200–300 tests were performed daily. The fact that mortality remained $< 1\%$ also directly indicated that Georgia had a much higher active case detection rate than Europe during the peak. However, as the specialists predicted, a sharp increase in cases was inevitable, Georgia was learning to live with the coronavirus, and the work of the healthcare system had to be adequate in light of these increased cases.

Retraining of personnel employed in municipal centers of public health and addition of states, which is determined according to the number of people permanently living in the municipality, was inevitable. Highly qualified personnel, namely epidemiologists, public health specialists, parasitologists, entomologists, statisticians are extremely important in the formation of a strong local service. At this stage, it was appropriate to: provide special training to local staff of municipal public health services, covering issues such as response readiness, rapid case detection, infection control, data analysis, and more.

There were certain medical complications that could arise in the post-Covid condition and required immediate medical examination. It was important to contact a doctor if any of the "red sign" symptoms were present: shortness of breath, difficulty breathing with minimal activity that did not improve; pain in the chest, increased heart rate or dizziness, decreased consciousness, difficulty in speaking and understanding what was said; Weakness and others.

It was too early to draw conclusions about the ultimate consequences of the virus, but one thing was clear: the epidemic had to be defeated globally. Every country had its own corona history and played its role in the process of defeating the pandemic. It was different considering the socio-economic situation of the country and the preparedness of the healthcare system. During the fight against the pandemic, in the process of proper management of the epidemic, both individual responsibility and the role of the central and local authorities are important. The whole world had the same goal - to defeat and prevent the pandemic of COVID 19.

Immunization has been a leading public health priority, as evidenced by the significant increase in funding for immunization. The national immunization schedule includes vaccination against 13 communicable diseases. According to WHO and the United Nations Children's Fund (UNICEF), immunization has reached 96%. It was easy to get support from the European Union. The pace of vaccination against COVID-19 has been critical to contain the pandemic. The target rate of the national plan for the introduction of the vaccine for COVID-19 has become the largest part of the population.

Cold chain procedures must be followed for any vaccine against COVID-19. Cold chain involves keeping the vaccine at the required temperature continuously, from its production to administration (in the temperature regime established by the manufacturer). Different vaccines have different cold chain requirements. The temperature rangemost often required for a vaccine is +2 °C to +8 °C, although there are vaccines that can be stored at −20 °C or −60 −80 °C.

There are central, regional and municipal warehouses in the country for storage of vaccines against COVID-19. Different types of warehouses, depending on the type of vaccine and the required storage temperature, are arranged in the central warehouse of the National Center for Disease Control and Public Health in Tbilisi, in the Imereti and Adjara divisions of the National Center for Disease Control and Public Health, and in public health centers in 60 municipalities across the country.

It should be noted that several types of vaccines against COVID-19 are available in the world, both made with new technologies and classic, already tested vaccines made with old technologies. Of the vaccines made with new technologies, Pfizer and Moderna, made with mRNA technologies, as well as vector vaccines - AstraZeneca and Johnson are worth noting. As for vaccines made by classical technologies, they are Sinovac and Sinopharm, which are made from inactivated viruses. There is a so-called virus made from a fragment. Protein vaccines, such as, for example, Novovax. Experience has shown that all vaccines recognized by the World Health Organization are highly effective in protecting against severe disease caused by COVID-19.

for medical personnel involved in the immunization process; In connection with the immunization program, cooperation with international partners (WHO, UNICEF, GAVI, COVAX, WB, USAID, ADB, etc.) has been established. However, these conditions were not effectively used to actively promote universal vaccination against the coronavirus. In pandemic conditions, vaccination plays the most important role. Many research centers around the world are focused on improving and finding the best vaccine option to fight the spread of epidemics. Stronger bacteria and viruses were also emerging, attacking the world at different times. Thus, the latest advances and outcomes in immunization are poised for rapid improvement.

Vaccines against COVID-19 are the result of unprecedented cooperation and large investments created in a record short time and fully meet all safety standards.

The safety of COVID-19 vaccines is subject to a rigorous regulatory process. Before receiving approval from the World Health Organization and national regulatory authorities, vaccines against COVID-19 undergo rigorous testing in clinical trials to confirm that they meet internationally recognized standards of safety and efficacy.

The introduction of vaccines authorized by the World Health Organization or strict regulatory authorities (SRAs) recognized by it in the country guarantees the quality, safety and efficacy of the vaccine. Infectious diseases, viruses, pandemics and their risk factors are the main concern of public health both in the world and in Georgia.

By using digital health systems, the medical professional can provide a more personalized and accurate response to the patient's health care needs when he has access to the patient's health data in a digital format, less time is spent filling out forms and no more duplication of clinical procedures. The use of digital data provides new opportunities for control and supervision.

E-health [5] is closely related to operational interoperability, which involves breaking down barriers to facilitate communication and exchange between systems, data becomes mobile, the patient is no longer tied to a paper file in one hospital, and he can take his health data to any hospital in any country where this The data will be read by digital systems. By using an electronic prescription, the patient can purchase prescribed medicines without a paper prescription. With the help of interoperable systems and a digital patient history, pharmacies can more easily validate a prescription.

Digital transformation in the healthcare system is a complex, multidisciplinary task that requires coordinated efforts from government, business, academia, and civil socie.

The e-healthcare and telemedicine boom started right during the pandemic - the pandemic, like many other areas, created significant and difficult challenges and a completely new reality. And during the pandemic, distancing was an important factor - because during the quarantine and lockdown periods, movement was severely limited, or at least we created distancing specifically to avoid the concentration of people and the increased risk of infection. E-health has turned out to be a sector that has not only been able to respond to the challenges of the pandemic, but has also opened a window of opportunity in terms of expanding services and diversifying innovative approaches. Telemedicine has become not only one of the alternatives to traditional services, but practically - necessary and sometimes even - no alternative.

The use of an online clinic to manage the covid-pandemic is significant. This model has been successfully used by the healthcare system in the past to manage high attendance during flu epidemics.

Since April 2020, 25 clinics have been established and about 300 doctors have participated - mainly in fever triage, and in the apartment management of Covid patients during the second wave - already 65 clinics and about 700 doctors have participated, and a central online clinic has also been established in the Ministry.

Management relied on a developed protocol to decide when hospitalization or transfer to a Covid hotel should occur. A total of 230,000 patients were treated, with each doctor managing 180–200 patients. According to his information, a detailed protocol determined the conduct of research, evaluation criteria, calling for emergency help, which facilitated the teletriage of cases from the primary care during the second wave and became especially relevant.

In general, the Ministry of Health had ambitious plans in the direction of the electronic health system, telemedicine is especially necessary in the development of primary health care. For us, telemedicine is a way to bring quality services closer to the population without any geographical and administrative barriers, which is especially important at the primary health care level, where the development of telemedicine is actively discussed, a conceptual vision has been formed, a project has been created with the help of the European Union, and a tender is underway to identify an international partner, USAID And with the help of UNICEF, Internet access was established in the villages, the Global Fund helps us in terms of hardware, and a budget was allocated from the Ministry. Implementation of the project. An online education platform for family doctors is also being created. The National Center for Disease Control and Public Health has dozens of large databases.

Digital health is a high priority. The center has dozens of large databases, including the newly created "Cov-Lab" which is the newest and, together with two other databases - Epidemiological Surveillance and Laboratory Studies LIMS - one of the largest databases, containing more than 2 million laboratory studies and about 800,000 Includes up to a unique person's record. "Kov-Lab" is the main source of information in many ways. In order to calculate the intensity of infection circulation, the information is broken down not only in the direction of laboratory diagnosis, but also in the direction of the location of diagnosis, both by region and by cities, etc. Through this data, the positive rate of testing is also calculated, which is important from the point of view of removing restrictions. Immunization base and preparedness to manage the process of vaccination against covid was especially strengthened now. In contrast to routine immunization, it is important that possible side effects are listed in detail, vaccine stocks should be counted. Our plan is to vaccinate 1,700,000 people, which means approximately quadrupling the workload of the annual immunization process in the country, for which trainings are actively conducted with the help of WHO and other donors.

During the pandemic, it was time for everyone to do their best, with the main goal of optimally managing the large number of co-infected patients with an experienced family doctor. An online clinic was already operating in the named hospitals, but it became problematic to overload the phone lines and family doctors. Therefore, the exchange of information was largely transferred from telephone communication to digital platforms - via Viber, WhatsApp, SMS, video call, and we assigned the collection of symptoms to operators - medical students of the final course, in order to prepare a detailed electronic anamnesis more properly for the doctor who made the final decision. The use of cloud technologies has a great impact on the educational opportunities of medical personnel.

Three main directions have been created that actively use artificial intelligence and machine learning. The first is a medical portal, the main purpose of which is to improve communication between the doctor and the patient, it is a system of automated checking of symptoms, collection of already conducted examinations and sending to the doctor, the second is the on-site patient service and diagnosis integrated with our platform, working in digital mode. "point of care" with innovative digital means (stethoscope, ultrasound, blood analyzer), and the third direction is the remote adaptation of the patient in the conditions of the Covid-hospital.

The health organization defines electronic health care as the so-called Application of eHealth as information and communication technologies in the healthcare system. eHealth allows for a more timely and accurate reporting system in the field of health care, and also contributes to the improvement of the control and supervision system of diseases and health care costs.

Electronic prescription is one of the elements of electronic healthcare. Which is important for the full-scale implementation of eHealth in all its directions and its integration, first of all, in primary health care. In general, I believe that primary health care and eHealth should become a priority in the coming years over electronic health care prescriptions or telemedicine only. Only a full-scale and systematic approach brings effective results. Active work is also being done in this regard in Asian countries, for example, Indonesia, the Philippines, etc.

Basic directions needed to manage this system. For this, there are several ways already tested in different countries. A compact independent national eHealth unit or even an agency could be formed to be responsible for implementing the eHealth concept at the national level. In any case, it is very important and difficult to manage and coordinate a national eHealth system at all levels, such as primary care, hospitals, health care providers, etc. It will be necessary to attract investments in the field of e-health, so that the state itself has to spend as little funds as possible. In this regard, it is possible to use the so-called state-private partnership scheme. PPP (public private partnership). It is important to standardize e-health, train employees, develop normative-legal acts in the field of e-health. Development of infrastructure necessary for the system, etc.

Infrastructure includes technology and software platforms, services and programs related to health information exchange. Examples of this are high-speed Internet connection and the infrastructure of computer and mobile devices and the exchange of electronic information between them. In addition to the infrastructure, as I told you above, it will be necessary to adjust the normative-legal sphere as well. For example, how health data is stored, unique health identifiers, how the relevant program is certified or accredited, and much more.

The electronic system should respond to the following requirements: automate and authorize payment systems, register beneficiaries for primary care and other health programs, protect personal health data from unauthorized use, ensure continuity of treatment at all levels of the health care system, provide information on the registration, availability and use of necessary drugs, To ensure the availability of public information in accordance with the patient's request, to ensure the availability of relevant medical protocols for doctors, to generate relevant infographics on clinical-epidemiological and administrative data, etc.

The large-scale introduction of electronic healthcare has established a connection between the users of the system - the patient and the doctor. The main directions in this regard are outlined. For consumers of health services, i.e. patients, it is primarily about safe and quality health care, increasing access to information on health issues, management and security of personal health records. Minimizing time and effort in the process of providing information to medical personnel. Also, the doctor's time will be saved. The system will reduce the waiting period for the patient to receive the necessary medical service. Will establish priorities.

It will also be important to reduce health disparities in remote or rural areas by increasing access to services. It is also very important to support the early detection and treatment of the disease, which can be achieved through the integration of e-health in the primary health care system.

An appropriate environment is created for healthcare providers and medical staff to reduce time and unnecessary effort to make the right decisions and avoid duplication of information. The doctor will have reliable information in the form of existing electronic records, both about the patient and about all the medical procedures he has performed. It becomes easier to exchange and share information between different providers, including those that are far away. It will reduce the time and effort required to provide the necessary treatment, perform the necessary tests and. A.S. It becomes easier to redirect, it becomes easier to write a prescription, the activity of the pharmacist also becomes easier. In addition to all this, medical personnel are given the opportunity to receive additional education and advice from colleagues through telelectures and telemedicine.

It is also very important to adjust the payment system. As you know, today, clinics are waiting for months for reimbursement from the state. This had a negative impact on both the motivation of the medical staff and the quality of the services provided. e-mail The system allows timely and online verification of all necessary documents, and, if necessary, quick correction of incomplete documents, and there is no need to send revisions and "check semicolons" using 19th century methods and spend 3–4 months on this.

Healthcare system managers, researchers and statisticians will benefit significantly. Availability of reliable and up-to-date statistics is one of the major challenges of our current healthcare system. Without reliable and up-to-date statistics, it is impossible to plan future programs and budget correctly.

Electronic health care is the most recognized effective mechanism for effective monitoring of both the activities of medical personnel and the supply and procurement system. For example, medicines, vaccines, consumables, etc.

Electronic health care is the future of medicine, the tomorrow that we must start walking towards today, if we want to see tangible results already in a few years.

References

1. Anti-crisis plan to support the development sector (2020)
2. Bennett &Brachman, s Hospital Infections – Fifth Edition
3. Bartlett, J.G., Gallant, J.E., Pham, M.P.H., Pharm, D.: Medical Management of HIV infection, 2009–2010
4. Guidelines for the Use of Antiretroviral Agents in HIV-1-Infected Adults and Adolescents, January 10, 2011. DHHS Panel
5. Harrison's – Principles of Internal Medicine – International edition. 17-th edition, International Monetary Fund Guidelines-for-Public-Expenditure-Management-Section-3-BudgetPreparation-2%20 (3).
6. Mandell, D., Bennett, S.: Principles and practice of infectious diseases. Seventh edition (2010)

Challenges of Telecommuting: Insights into Georgian Employee Experience

Tinatin Rodonaia(✉)

East European University, Tbilisi, Georgia
tinatin.rodonaia@eeu.edu.ge

Abstract. The practice of telecommuting has become increasingly prevalent among companies in response to the onset of the Covid-19 pandemic. Consequently, many companies in Georgia have transitioned to offering remote work or hybrid work arrangements to their employees. Prior to the pandemic, however, telecommuting was not widely adopted among Georgian companies. This transformation in work dynamics has necessitated strategic and operational adjustments, prompting employees to acquire new skill sets. To remain resilient and competitive, the workforce must adapt to this new paradigm and adopt additional competencies. While the principal emphasis of the article will be conceptual, it will also integrate empirical insights derived from survey conducted among both employees and freelancers in Georgia. This research will encompass individuals applying diverse telecommunication tools, including but not limited to email, messaging platforms, phone services, chat applications, and video conferencing tools, any kind of their work mode—online or offline, and employment format—remote or hybrid. The paper aims to contribute to revealing the challenges faced by telecommuting employees in Georgia.

Keywords: Telecommuting · remote work · employee · freelancer · flexible

1 Introduction

Globalization, digitalization, and technological advancements have profoundly reshaped contemporary work environments. The widespread adoption of telecommuting, or remote work, highlights this shift, especially as it was significantly accelerated by the Covid-19 pandemic. In the past, companies in Georgia were reluctant to offer remote work options to their employees. Yet, the pandemic catalyzed a profound change, prompting a substantial number of businesses to adopt telecommuting. According to the report "Supporting E-work Market Development in Rural Areas of Georgia prior to the pandemic, 87.6% of companies in Georgia had not integrated teleworking into their operations. This figure drastically declined to 29.6% amid the pandemic, highlighting a marked increase in the utilization of remote work practices among businesses.

The swift and extensive transition to remote work was both unforeseen and involuntary, caused by global circumstances that rendered the return to traditional office settings uncertain. This transformation posed numerous technical hurdles, from ensuring reliable

R. C. Geibel and S. Machavariani (Eds.): ISPC 2024, SPBE, pp. 364–377, 2025.
https://doi.org/10.1007/978-3-031-88052-0_30

internet connectivity to securing suitable home workspaces conducive to productivity. Additionally, organizations faced new management and leadership challenges, as the sudden shift eliminated physical meetings and eroded personal interactions between supervisors and their teams. Traditional metrics of performance and attendance, previously reliant on physical presence in office settings, became impracticable overnight (Vasel 2021).

This research aims to examine the challenges associated with telecommuting in Georgia. For the purposes of this investigation, telecommuting includes a range of formats, such as remote work from home for both employees of companies and self-employed freelancers, as well as educators who conduct classes online. Primary data collection employed an online survey targeting a sample of 200 participants from Georgia's workforce. The study seeks to identify solutions to the challenges faced by telecommuters in Georgia, particularly concerning the maintenance of productivity levels while working remotely. Key inquiries include the environmental and social impacts of remote work, as well as the evolving dynamics between work and personal life. The solutions proposed herein are anticipated to benefit both employees and employers, given the increasing prevalence and evolving nature of remote work practices.

2 Theoretical Foundation

The term telecommuting originated in the 1970s to refer to working from a designated location, such as one's home or another office, to lessen the commute to a central office. Advances in telecommunications technology, like the Internet, email, and mobile phones, significantly promoted this practice. Nowadays, telecommuting broadly encompasses working remotely from home or another location through electronic or telephonic connections. It includes diverse forms of employment, ranging from gig work/freelancing and part-time contracts to traditional full-time positions (Global Work Analytics, FlexJobs 2017).

The disruptions caused by Covid-19 have challenged many of our assumptions about modern societies, including beliefs about science, authority, regulation, economy, governance, community, and work itself. This period has prompted a collective awakening, offering significant opportunities for change. Traditional ideas about work have been deeply questioned by millions who faced difficult choices between income and family, job security and health, and even life and death. However, these concerns have often been sidelined by powerful entities who saw in Covid-19 a chance to increase exploitation, surveillance, and wealth accumulation. For these organizations, the pandemic has facilitated increased wealth with diminished accountability, whereas for most individuals, it has resulted in maintaining the status quo or experiencing even more challenging conditions. Hamid R (2023) Many organizations are questioning whether the pandemic will lead to permanent changes in workplace dynamics, and the advantages of remote work may influence the future design of our work environments and daily routines (PWC 2020).

In 2022, the highest demand for online or remote work globally came from the US, accounting for 37%, followed by the UK with 8% and India with 7.6%. Over recent years, the demand for remote work in Canada and Australia has decreased. In India, over

50% of the online labor demand is for software development and technology, which is notably higher compared to other countries. This trend is not surprising given that many tech companies in India laid off workers shortly after the pandemic began, shifting tasks to online labor platforms—a trend that has persisted. This is also reflected in the significant rise in the number of registered workers on these platforms since the pandemic started (ILO 2021). Organizations in Georgia adopted digital tools, transitioned operations online, and implemented remote work in response to Covid-19 lockdown measures (Gigauri 2020b). Consequently, both nonprofit and public organizations revised their policies to support remote and flexible work, necessitating those employees to enhance their technological skills (Gigauri 2020a). Despite this, previous studies indicate that many Georgian organizations are not adequately equipped for remote work and flexible scheduling across all roles (Gigauri 2020a). Thus, commercial and social enterprises need assistance during this transition period.

It is reasonable to assert that the abrupt transition to remote work presented challenges for both employees and managers. Specifically, managers appeared to be particularly concerned about the loss of control that naturally emerged from the sudden reconfiguration of their company's physical boundaries and the geographical dispersion of their workforce (Abgeller et al. 2022). It is important to recognize that, even in environments that are generally supportive of workers, the expansion of remote work raises concerns about social isolation, increased work demands, the merging of personal and professional boundaries, and the potential decline in career advancement opportunities (Balzano 2022).

3 Research Method

The objective of this study is to investigate the challenges and perceptions of telecommuters in Georgia who utilize a range of telecommunication tools—including email, messaging platforms, telephone services, chat applications, and video conferencing tools—across various telework modalities (online or offline) and employment formats (remote or hybrid). The research aims to achieve several specific goals: to identify challenges encountered in remote work, to assess work-life balance, to measure overall satisfaction and to propose strategies for enhancing the effectiveness of telecommuting in contemporary settings. The study specifically targets employees, with primary data being collected from this group, including freelancers. The research is characterized as relatively low risk and seeks to capture the views and perceptions of the adult working population in Georgia. This study incorporates both academic and practical elements, with the intent to generate recommendations that will benefit both employees and employers. The analysis employed graphical methods alongside qualitative assessments of independence and dependence through chi-square testing of various factors (Papiashvili, Gagnidze et al. 2020; Gagnidze et al. 2022).

3.1 Population and Sample

The study's population included employees and freelancers involved in remote work in Georgia. Participants used a range of telecommunication tools, such as email, messaging platforms, phone services, chat applications, and video conferencing software. Participants were involved in diverse work modalities both online and offline and employment formats remote or hybrid. The survey aimed to include professionals from a range of career fields, such as graphic design, social media, information technology, education, advertising, finances and sales.

A snowball sampling method was employed to identify participants. This technique was particularly suited for locating a specific and somewhat elusive population known to the researcher. Leveraging initial contacts within the remote work community allowed for the progressive identification of additional respondents who fit the study criteria.

Primary data collection was conducted through an online survey administered via Google Forms. The survey link was disseminated through social networks, email, and professional closed social network groups comprised of individuals working from home at the time of the study. The selection of an online survey was influenced by several factors: it allowed for broad geographic coverage, facilitated a faster response rate, and aligned with the study's temporal constraints.

To ensure the reliability of the study's results, the introductory narrative accompanying the survey stipulated that participation is required only if the provided description is relevant to the respondent's situation. The survey guarantees the confidentiality of respondents' data. Furthermore, the online survey platform captures responses in real time and prevents any alterations post-submission, thereby preserving data integrity.

The methodological approach employed in this study was designed to uphold the validity of the research. The survey instrument incorporated a variety of scales and checkboxes, while also allowing respondents to specify additional options as necessary. This design ensures that the data collected accurately reflects the diverse perspectives and variations relevant to the study's objectives, thereby enhancing the validity and precision of the findings.

4 Analysis and Results

This section outlines and analyzes the data gathered for the study, which is organized into three primary segments. The first segment provides demographic details about the respondents, including their age, gender, professional field, marital status, and current employment position. The second segment examines the employment conditions of telecommuters, focusing on aspects such as work format, duration of remote work, and job search methods. The third segment assesses respondents' views on remote work, encompassing work-life balance, overall job satisfaction, and the challenges faced in a remote working environment.

Table 1 illustrates the characteristics of the respondents. Regarding age, the majority of respondents were between 22 and 35 years old, with the distribution as follows: 20.4% were aged 22–25, 21.9% were aged 26–29, and 19.4% were aged 30–35. Additionally, 9.5% of respondents were aged 18–21, 7.5% were between 36 and 40 years old, 12.9% were aged 41–45, and 6.5% were older than 46 years. The sample consisted predominantly of female respondents (80.6%) relative to male respondents (19.4%). Regarding educational attainment, 50.7% of the participants held a bachelor's degree, 35.3% possessed a master's degree, 5% had earned a PhD, and 9% had completed only secondary

Table 1. Demographic Characteristics of Respondents Percent

1	Age	18 to 21	9.50%
		22 to 25	20.40%
		26 to 29	21.90%
		30 to 35	19.40%
		36 to 40	7.50%
		41 to 45	12.90%
		46 +	6.50%
2	Gender	Male	19.40%
		Female	80.60%
3	Education	Secondary	9%
		Bachelor	50.70%
		Master	35.30%
		PhD	5%
4	Marital Status	Not married	48.30%
		Married	46.30%
		Divorced	4%
		Widow	1.50%
5	Children	No children	55.20%
		1 child	18.40%
		2 children	17.40%
		3 children	8%
		More than 3	1%
6	Current Career Field	Information Technology	9%
		Sales	10.90%
		Social Media	27.40%
		Graphic Design/Architecture	13.40%
		Education	9.50%
		Marketing	5.50%
		HR	1.50%
		Other (finances, accounting, consulting, translation etc.)	22.80%
7	Current Employment	Employed	41.80%
		Freelancer	21.40%
		Employed + self-employed	36.80%

education. Additionally, 48.3% of the respondents were unmarried, 46.3% were married, 4% were divorced, and 1.5% were widowed. The distribution of respondents by number of children is as follows: 55.2% reported having no children, 18.4% had one child, 17.4% had two children, 8% had three children, and 1% had more than three children. The current employment statuses of respondents are categorized as follows: social media (27.4%), graphic design/architecture (13.4%), sales (10.9%), education (9.5%), information technology (9%), marketing (5.5%), human resources (1.5%), and other fields (22.8%). Among the respondents, 41.8% were employed by a company, 21.4% identified as freelancers, and 36.8% concurrently engaged in both employment and freelance work. Based on the survey results, it can be concluded that individuals in the fields of finance and accounting, management, and sales and purchasing demonstrate a greater preference for traditional employment within companies. Conversely, individuals in the design sector demonstrate a reduced preference for traditional employment within companies. Additionally, individuals working in social media show a stronger tendency to pursue freelance opportunities.

The subsequent section examines the employment conditions of telecommuters, with a particular emphasis on factors such as work format, duration of remote employment, and methods of job searching (Fig. 1).

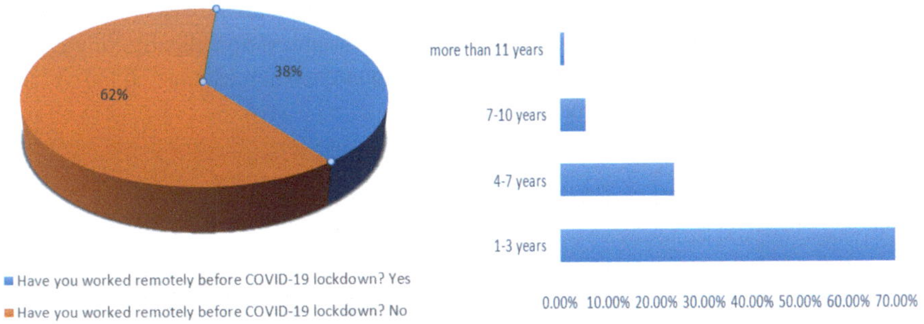

Fig. 1. Telecommuting during COVID-19 lockdown and overall period of working remotely

About a third (38.3%) of respondents had experience with remote work before the pandemic. This suggests that some companies and individuals were already adapting to remote arrangements prior to the widespread shift caused by COVID-19. The majority of respondents (61.70%) started working remotely as a result of the pandemic, highlighting the dramatic shift in work practices during that time. The data suggests that while a significant number of people are new to remote work (particularly due to COVID-19), there is a portion of the workforce that had prior experience.

The trend indicates that remote work has become much more common recently, and many individuals have adapted to this change within the last few years.

Figure 2 presents the results of the cross-tabulation analysis examining the relationship between marital status and employment type among respondents. Conclusions are drawn following the assessment of correlations. The p-values obtained from the chi-square test were notably low in certain cases, indicating significant qualitative relationships between various indicators. For instance, the test statistic for the relationship

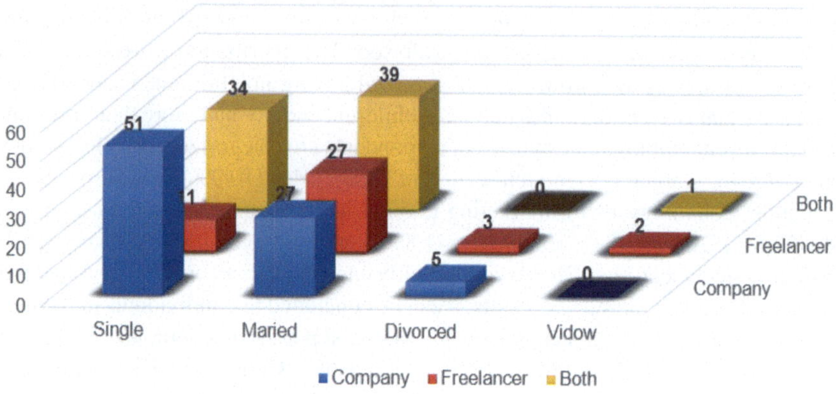

Fig. 2. Cross-tabulation: Marriage and Type of Employment

between having children and employment type was 23.109, with a p-value of 0.0008. This value exceeds the critical value of 12.592 at the 95% confidence level, suggesting a dependency: individuals with children tend to prefer employment in companies, while those without children are more inclined to work as freelancers. Similarly, the analysis of marital status and employment type revealed that the test statistic also surpassed the critical value, indicating a dependence between these variables. Specifically, single individuals are more likely to seek employment in companies, whereas married individuals show a greater interest in freelance work.

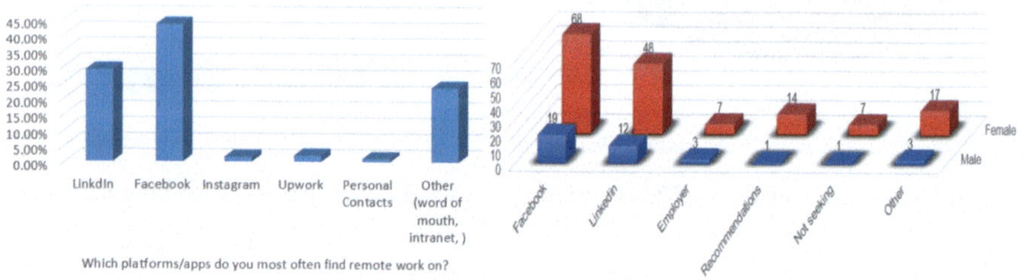

Fig. 3. Sources and Platforms for identifying remote employment opportunities and Cross-tabulation gender of respondents and the sources of finding remote work

The relationship between "type of employment" and key demographic variables was examined through a chi-square test. The obtained p-values were predominantly high, suggesting that employment patterns do not significantly differ across demographic groups. The test statistic was calculated to be 7.456, with a p-value of 0.2807. The critical values for the chi-square distribution at the 95% and 90% confidence levels were 12.592 and 10.645, respectively. Since the test statistic is less than the critical value, we conclude that there is no significant dependence between education level and employment type, indicating that these two variables are independent.

The data in Fig. 3 suggests a strong preference for social media platforms, particularly Facebook (43.3%), in finding remote work. LinkedIn's significant usage (28.9%)

reinforces the trend of professional networking in job searches. The reliance on diverse sources, including personal connections, indicates that job seekers employ a multifaceted approach to their search. However, specialized freelance platforms like Upwork and informal methods like personal contacts appear to play a limited role in this context. This analysis highlights the importance of social media and professional networks in contemporary job searching, particularly for remote opportunities. The analysis concludes that gender and the sources of finding a remote job are independent. This indicates that individuals' choices regarding where to search for remote job opportunities do not vary significantly based on gender.

4.1 Perceptions of Telecommuting

This section examines the data regarding respondents' perceptions of remote work. Specifically, it explores the challenges associated with telecommuting, the balance between work and life, satisfaction with remote work conditions, and the issues encountered by individuals in this context (Fig. 4).

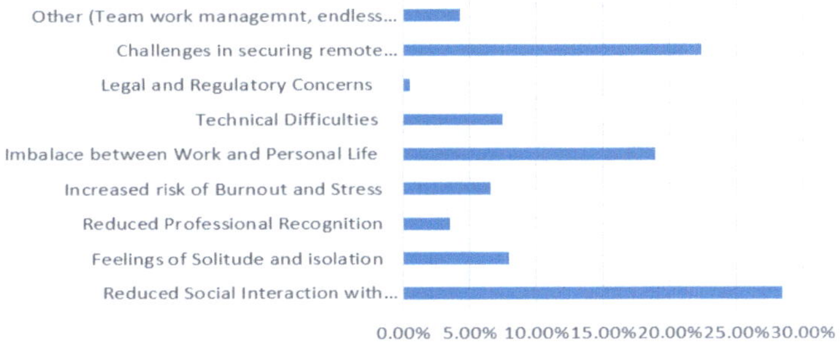

Fig. 4. The principal challenge associated with telecommuting for the individual

The data presented on the primary challenges faced by individuals engaged in telecommuting reveals a variety of concerns that impact their work experience. Reduced social interaction with colleagues (28.40%) this is the most frequently cited challenge, indicating that a significant portion of respondents feels the lack of in-person engagement with coworkers. This reduced interaction may affect collaboration, team cohesion, and overall job satisfaction. Challenges in securing remote employment (Finding a Client) (22.40%) the second most common issue highlights the difficulties many individuals face in obtaining clients or securing remote positions. This suggests that the competitive nature of the remote job market may create additional stress for job seekers. Imbalance between work and personal life (18.90%): a substantial number of respondents report difficulties in maintaining boundaries between work and personal life. This imbalance can lead to increased stress and a diminished quality of life, emphasizing the need for effective time management and boundaries. Feelings of loneliness are acknowledged by a minority of respondents (8%). This highlights the psychological impact of remote work, which may affect motivation and engagement. Technical challenges are a notable concern (7.50%), indicating that issues with technology can hinder productivity. This underscores the importance of reliable tools and support for remote workers. While not the most frequently reported issue (6.50%), the risk of burnout is a significant concern for some remote workers. This aligns with findings that suggest remote work can lead to overexertion without the usual in-office boundaries. Other Challenges (4.30%): this category includes various concerns such as teamwork management, prolonged working hours, communication issues, and task completion struggles. While individually less frequent, these issues collectively represent significant barriers to effective remote work (Fig. 5).

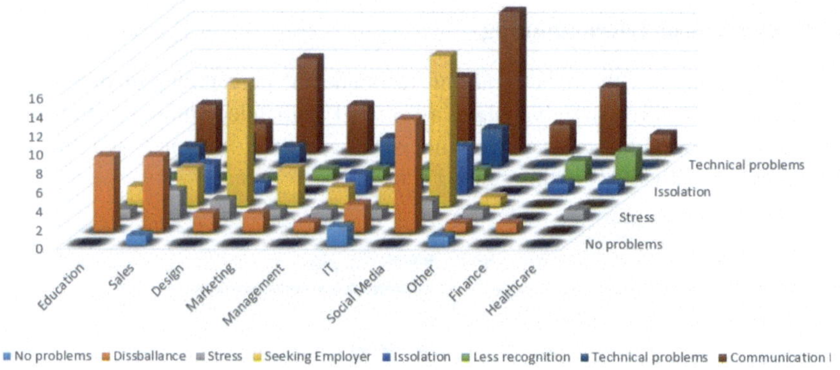

Fig. 5. Cross-tabulation: Challenges of Telecommuting by employment area

The relationship between "major challenges" and key demographic indicators—specifically age, education, and marital status—was examined. The p-values obtained from the chi-square tests were found to be substantial in all cases. For age and challenges, the test statistic was 41.507 with a p-value of 0.4925, leading to the decision to retain the null hypothesis of independence. Similarly, for education and challenges, the test statistic was 13.496 with a p-value of 0.8903, also resulting in a decision of independence. These findings suggest that the challenges faced by different demographic groups are consistent across these indicators. In contrast, the analysis of the relationship between challenges and the field of employment yielded a markedly low p-value of 0.0015, indicating a significant association between employment sectors and the challenges encountered. This finding raises important questions about the nature of challenges faced within various employment contexts and suggests that other underlying factors may be at play. Future research could delve deeper into these factors, offering a more nuanced understanding of the dynamics at work.

This section analyzes the overall satisfaction and challenges associated with the current remote work arrangements from multiple perspectives. What is particularly intriguing in this context is the extent to which the sentiments of various demographic groups align or differ. In most instances, the P-values obtained from the chi-square test were found to be relatively high. However, in certain cases the P-values were notably low. This suggests that sentiment among demographic groups is largely homogeneous; nevertheless, there are some exceptions. Since the test statistic (14.155) is much lower than both critical values (36.415 and 33.196), and the P-value (0.9431) is significantly greater than common alpha levels (0.05 or 0.10), we fail to reject the null hypothesis. The analysis suggests that there is no statistically significant relationship between age and opinion on Q18.1. Therefore, we conclude that age and opinion are independent in this context. There is also no statistically significant relationship between age and opinion on Q18.2 through Q18.7, as the P-values obtained from the chi-square test were consistently high. This observation is not surprising, as various challenges hold differing significance across sectors. For instance, the imbalance between work and personal life is particularly salient in the education sector. In contrast, the challenge of "finding an employer" is most critical for designers. Furthermore, professionals in marketing, information technology, and finance often prioritize the issue of inadequate communication and interaction. Lastly, in the healthcare field, "recognition" emerges as a paramount concern (Tables 2 and 3).

Table 2. The Overall Challenges with the Current Remote Work Arrangements from Various Perspectives

	Strongly disagree	Disagree	Neutral	Agree	Strongly agree
Q18.1 Your workload is evenly distributed	9%	12%	26%	37.5%	16%
Q18.2 When working remotely, I find it challenging to differentiate between work hours and personal time	23%	26%	19.5%	20.5%	11.5%
Q18.3 Do you have enough time for your work tasks?	7%	1.5%	17.5%	45%	29.5%
Q18.4 Do you have to work very fast?	17%	28.5%	30.5%	15.5%	9%
Q18. 5 Does your job require you to make difficult decisions?	14%	16.5%	32%	23%	15%
Q18.6 Does remote work require you to be creative?	8.5%	9.5%	18%	31.5%	33%
Q18.7 Is your job emotionally demanding?	12.5%	13.5%	29.5%	24.5%	20.5%

Statistical analysis of the relationship between age and opinion on Q19.7 (Due to work-related duties, I have to make changes to my plans for private and family activities) the test statistic (41.069) exceeds both critical values (36.415 and 33.196), and the P-value

Table 3. The overall satisfaction with the current remote work arrangements from various perspectives

	Strongly disagree	Disagree	Neither agree nor disagree	Agree	Strongly agree
Q19.1 Your work prospects	7%	11%	27%	34%	21.5%
Q19.2 With your own abilities	5%	4.5%	19%	43%	29%
Q19.3 Overall, taking all factors into account regarding your work	5.5%	4.5%	24.5%	44%	22%
Q19.4 Compensation	7.5%	15%	26%	36%	16%
Q19.5 Do you feel that your work takes so much of your time that it has a negative effect on your private life?	23%	35%	20.5%	12%	10%
Q19.6 The demands of my work interfere with my private and family life?	28%	37%	20%	8.5%	7%
Q19.7 Due to work-related duties, I have to make changes to my plans for private and family activities	24.5%	32%	21.5%	15.5%	7%

(0.0164) is below the conventional significance thresholds, we reject the null hypothesis. The analysis indicates a statistically significant relationship between age and opinion on Q19.7. Therefore, we conclude that age and opinion are dependent variables within this context. It is also worth noting that there is a correlation between having children and opinion on Q19.6 (The demands of my work interfere with my private and family life) The analysis indicates a statistically significant relationship between having children and opinion on Q19.6 at the 90% confidence level, suggesting that the two variables are dependent. It can be concluded that respondents with children report that their work demands interfere more significantly with their personal and family life compared to those without children.

5 Conclusion

The research sought to accomplish several specific objectives: to identify the challenges associated with remote work, to measure overall employee satisfaction, and to propose strategies for enhancing the effectiveness of telecommuting in contemporary contexts within Georgia. A considerable number of individuals are newly engaged in remote work—largely as a result of the COVID-19 pandemic—a segment of the workforce possesses prior experience in this arrangement. This trend suggests that remote work has become increasingly prevalent in recent years, and many telecommuters in Georgia have successfully adapted to this shift. Based on the survey results, several key conclusions can be drawn regarding employment preferences and challenges in various sectors. Individuals in finance, accounting, management, and sales demonstrate a clear preference for traditional employment within companies, while those in the design sector and social media show a greater inclination towards freelance opportunities.

The findings raise important questions about the specific challenges faced in different employment contexts, particularly in relation to work-life balance, communication issues, and recognition. In sectors like education, the imbalance between work and personal life is notably pronounced, while in marketing, information technology, and finance, communication barriers are prioritized. In healthcare, recognition appears to be a critical concern.

The importance of social media and professional networks in the job search process, particularly for remote positions, is also emphasized. Interestingly, the study found that gender does not significantly influence how individuals search for remote job opportunities, indicating that other factors may play a more substantial role in shaping employment decisions.

Moreover, the analysis reveals that parents tend to prefer company employment, while those without children are more likely to pursue freelance work. This pattern also extends to marital status, with single individuals favoring traditional roles and married individuals exhibiting a stronger interest in freelance opportunities.

Finally, the results suggest that respondents with children experience greater interference between work demands and personal life compared to those without children. Overall, these insights underscore the complexity of contemporary work dynamics and point to the need for further research to explore the underlying factors influencing these trends.

6 Recommendations

To overcome the challenges organizations, particularly in sectors like education and healthcare, should implement flexible work policies and provide resources to help employees manage their work-life balance effectively. Companies in industries facing communication barriers, such as marketing and finance, should invest in advanced communication tools and training to improve collaboration among remote teams. Implement recognition and reward programs that specifically address the needs of remote employees to enhance motivation and job satisfaction.

Given that the majority of respondents prefer a combination of remote and office working, it is recommended that companies implement a hybrid work model. Additionally, targeted training programs and resources should be provided for both remote workers and traditional employees to effectively navigate the complexities of their roles, particularly for those transitioning between freelance and company employment.

Employee mental health must be a continual focus, particularly as individuals adapt to new work routines. Employers bear the responsibility of maintaining open lines of communication and assessing the well-being of their workforce, as well as identifying opportunities for improvement. Regular surveys should be administered to pinpoint potential challenges faced by employees, and accessible support resources should be established to help employees navigate these difficulties.

Supporting parents in the workforce is essential for alleviating the work-life conflicts they experience. This support can be provided through flexible scheduling and access to childcare resources. Additionally, implementing job-sharing arrangements, where two individuals collaborate on the same task, can enhance problem-solving capabilities and make workloads more manageable. Compressed work schedules also offer a viable solution, allowing employees to maintain a flexible work schedule while balancing their personal lives.

Given that a significant number of respondents encounter challenges in locating remote work opportunities, it would be beneficial for organizations to develop diverse platforms or resources that facilitate connections between freelancers and potential clients. This approach would help cultivate a supportive community for remote workers.

To ensure the ongoing effectiveness of telecommuting, it is essential to prioritize continuous improvement and stay informed about global trends and technological advancements that can enhance the employee experience. Future research should investigate the factors influencing employment decisions beyond gender, with an emphasis on demographics, industry trends, and individual circumstances. A limitation of this study is its exclusive focus on employees, which restricts the understanding of challenges to their perspective alone. Research involving employers or organizations that offer remote work opportunities would likely yield different insights and solutions; therefore, further investigation in this area is required.

References

Abgeller, N., Bachmann, R., Dobbins, T., Anderson, D.: Responsible autonomy: the interplay of autonomy, control and trust for knowledge professionals working remotely during COVID-19. Econ. Ind. Democr. (2022). https://doi.org/10.1177/0143831X221140156. Accessed 01 Sept 2024

Gagnidze, A., Iavich, M.: Demand-side factors of the Georgian cars' leasing market. Am. Int. J. Bus. Manag. (AIJBM) **5**(4), 43–48 (2022)

Balzano, S.: Contro lo smart working, Laterza (2022). https://www.laterza.it/scheda-libro/?isbn=9788858144442. Accessed 03 Sept 2024

Gigauri, I.: Challenges HR managers facing due to COVID-19 and overcoming strategies: perspectives from Georgia. Arch. Bus. Res. **8**(11), 1–18 (2020a). https://doi.org/10.14738/abr.811.9313. Accessed 03 Sept 2024

Gigauri, I.: Remote working concerns during the covid-19 pandemic. Int. J. Soc. Sci. Econ. Res. **5**(10), 2803–2818 (2020b). https://doi.org/10.46609/ijsser.2020.v05i10.005

(PDF) Remote working challenges for Georgian social enterprises in the context of the current pandemic. https://www.researchgate.net/publication/356916911_Remote_working_challenges_for_Georgian_social_enterprises_in_the_context_of_the_current_pandemic. Accessed 03 Sept 2024

Global Work Analytics, FlexJobs: 2017 State of Telecommuting in the U.S. Employee Workforce, June 2017. https://cdn.thepennyhoarder.com/wpcontent/uploads/2017/06/30140000/State_Of_Telecommuting_U.S._Employee_Workforce.pdf. Accessed 03 Sept 2024

Hou, H.(C)., Remøy, H., Jylhä, T., Vande Putte, H.: A study on office workplace modification during the COVID-19 pandemic in The Netherlands. J. Corp. Real Estate **23**(3), 186–202 (2021). https://doi.org/10.1108/JCRE-10-2020-0051. Accessed 03 Sept 2024

Hamid, R.: Parallel universes: the future of remote work and the remoteness of future work, pp. 221–230 (2023)

ILO: World employment and social outlook 2021: The role of digital labour platforms in transforming the world of work. ILO (2021). Accessed 03 Sept 2024

Reaney, P.: About One in Five Workers Worldwide Telecommute: Poll. Reuters, 24 January 2012. https://www.reuters.com/article/us-telecommuting/about-one-in-five-workers-worldwide-telecommute-poll-idUSTRE80N1IL20120124. Accessed 03 Sept 2024

Sucheran, S., Olanrewaju, O.: The effect of remote working on employees productivity levels in South Africa. In: Proceedings of the International Conference on Industrial Engineering and Operations Management, Rome, Italy, 2–5 August 2021 (2021). Accessed 03 Sept 2024

Supporting E-work Market Development in Areas Report produced with the assistance of the European Union (EU) and the United Nations Development Programme (UNDP). https://www.undp.org/georgia/publications/supporting-e-work-market-development-rural-areas. Accessed 03 Sept 2024

The 2024 Workplace Flexibility Trends Report Balancing employer & employee preferences Global Workplace Analytics Workplace-Flexibility-Trends-Report-2024.pdf. Accessed 03 Sept 2024

Papiashvili, T., Gagnidze, A., Buchashvili, G.: can entrepreneurship be taught? The case study on Georgian universities. Res. J. Bus Manag. **7**(4), 2010212 (2020)

Vasel, K.: The pandemic forced a massive remote-work experiment. Now comes the hard part, CNN Business, updated, 11 March 2021 (2021). https://edition.cnn.com/2021/03/09/success/remote-work-covid-pandemic-one-yearlater/index.html. Accessed 03 Sept 2024

Contemporary Aspects of Digitalization of Corporate Sustainability Reporting

Davit Jalagonia(✉), Marine Khubua, and Eliso Chokhonolidze

Sokhumi State University, Tbilisi, Georgia
{d.jalagonia,m.khubua,elisochoxonelidze}@sou.edu.ge

Abstract. Due to challenges related to environmental pollution, climate change, biodiversity loss, and social inequality issues in every aspect of business around the world, transitioning to a sustainable system is becoming a priority and a necessary prerequisite for corporate behavior, which creates many opportunities for business and promotes economic growth.

The very research studies the possibility of developing CSRD-Corporate Sustainability Reporting Directives in Georgia and the level of digital maturity of sustainability reporting, what the opinions of companies are about ESG ambitions, whether they serve to create values or only comply with relevant requirements. The project is unique in order to assess the trends, driving factors, and reasons for the values of sustainability in companies. As the literature review and interview analysis indicate, transitioning to a sustainable system for the growth of business transparency, digitizing reporting according to the European sustainability standard will be a difficult task, the information on sustainability gained via technological platforms gives analysts the possibility of accurate assessment.

Concepts developed as a result of research provide quantitative assessment of sustainability and risk management. They identify ways to acquire value for sustainability, increase the company's competitiveness, transparency, responsibility, accounting culture, and quality of sustainability reporting. They will simplify external audit, raise reputation, and strengthen the drive for sustainable development and readiness for the future.

Keywords: sustainability reporting · sustainability value · technological innovation

1 Introduction

At the modern stage within the world scale overcoming the problems of environment pollution, climate change, biodiversity reduction, and social inequality has increased society interest and in turn it has caused to increase the demands towards business transparency and sustainability. Based on solving existing challenges effectively it has become relevant for companies to switch to a sustainable system which is a prerequisite for the growth of their economy and competitiveness.

Due to the importance of the problem, the European Union has adopted the Corporate Sustainability Reporting Directive (CSRD) on January 5, 2023, the purpose of which

R. C. Geibel and S. Machavariani (Eds.): ISPC 2024, SPBE, pp. 378–387, 2025.
https://doi.org/10.1007/978-3-031-88052-0_31

is to ensure the preparation of detailed and transparent reports by companies, which will contribute to the accuracy of sustainability indicators, their availability, and reduce dependence on social and governance risks. Integrating digital tools in sustainability reporting processes should represent an effective way to avoid some of the main issues identified by practitioners and policymakers about the lack of comparability and reliability (Leitner-Hanetseder & Lehner 2022) The introduction of new requirements for sustainability reporting digitization by the European Commission represents a relevant innovation within the debate about social and environmental accounting (Alles et al. 2021; Atkins et al. 2023).

The transition of CSRD regulations to digital formats not only provides transparency and accuracy of data, but it creates new opportunities for data automation and analysis as well. Digital formats, such as, for example, ESEF (European Single Electronic Format), contribute not only to the improvement of reporting processes, but also to efficient and quick information delivery to all interested parties of the company. Another far-sighted research was conducted by Efimova et al. (2020). The authors tried to identify potential interlinkages between financial and non-financial information in their research. Interestingly, the authors adopted a critical approach to identify the main benefits and barriers to adopting XBRL in sustainability reporting. First, they confirmed that a common taxonomy could favor implementing a more effective management control system. However, at the same time, they underlined the need to consider companies' infrastructures, which represents essential items to consider in developing an XBRLbased report. Finally The extensible business reporting language (XBRL) is the international digital business reporting standard managed by a global not-for-profit consortium (XBRL International 2022a). In the last few years, XBRL evolved into inline XBRL (iXBRL), a standard that allows both human-readable and structured, machine-readable data to be provided in a single document (XBRL International 2021).

Despite the advantages of digital formats, Georgian companies face serious challenges in the process of implementing CSRD regulations, which are related to technological limitations, lack of essential knowledge and the need of modernizing processes.

The purpose of the very article is to assess the current state of implementation of CSRD - corporate sustainability reporting directives and digital maturity level of sustainability reporting on the basis of Georgian companies. The research includes studying the implementation process of CSRD regulations, analyzing the practice of using digital formats, its evaluation, and developing recommendations that will help companies successfully fulfill the requirements of the current regulations.

The aim of CSRD (Corporate Sustainability Reporting Directive) standards is to provide stakeholders with detailed and reliable information about sustainability, which will facilitate the process of making the best decisions.

2 Theory

Accounting research represents one of the main fields interested in this trend. The wide adoption of digital features and the rapid growth of new accounting technologies have contributed to the development of studies about adopting emerging technologies in accounting and auditing processes (Troshani et al. 2019). In particular, many studies were developed about financial reporting, as evidenced by the proliferation of studies about research topics such as ERP systems, XBRL, and blockchain (Alles et al. 2021; Mancini et al. 2021; Vasarhelyi & Romero 2014).

Corporate Sustainability Reporting prepared according to international standards, primarily contributes to the development of the capital market and access to financial resources. The interest towards it has been growing even more within artificial intelligence, as its integration in the preparation and compilation of sustainable financial statements becomes a significant factor on the basis of using AI products, as well as creating a modern and efficient work environment. Automation of business processes in companies reduces the time spent on work and it minimizes errors, therefore, it enables to carry out deep data analysis and make innovative decisions.

According to CSRD, reporting must be in XHTM (eXtensible Hypertext Markup Language) format. The approach ensures structuring information and makes easy to search for it. To make records in the intended format companies must use the ESEF **(European Single Electronic Format)** standard, which promotes a standardized and scalable data exchange that will be easy to use for any digital platform. For information accessibility CSRD also uses iXBRL **(Inline eXtensible Business Reporting Language)** format, both digitally and visually. The sustainability report prepared in such format must be uploaded and available on the website of the company as well as regulatory authorities and relevant portals.

The overall standardization of sustainability reporting enables to manage the sustainability of companies' data, assess risks, compare detailed information and measure reliability.

In 2022, the European Commission introduced a set of European Sustainability Reporting Standards (ESRS) released by the EFRAG. Furthermore, following the approach used for financial reporting, the European companies affected by the CSRD will disclose their sustainability information following the European Single Electronic Format (ESEF) (KPMG 2022 The main factors that have driven the choice made by the European Commission to include mandatory requirements for digital reporting are represented by the need to develop more reliable and verifiable information. During the final public consultations launchedin 2021, stakeholders highlighted the lack of informativity on the data included in the non-financial declarations prepared according to Directive 2014/95/EU. In particular, the main issues were identified by investors, which underlined the opportunity to consider more strict requirements in the CSRD (European Commission 2021)

Successful European countries, including: Sweden, Denmark, Portugal, fully or partially use CSRD regulations. German and Dutch companies - BMW and Siemens; Philips and Unilever prepare sustainability reports according to the same regulations; Sweden has also advanced in the direction of sustainability reporting. Companies - Volvo and Ericsson are clear examples of it. French companies such as L'Oréal and Danone are successfully using CSRD standards and have comprehensive sustainability reporting practices. It is obvious that for Georgian companies, which are taking their first steps in this direction, sharing the experience of large and successful companies of EU countries and, accordingly, using them in practical activities, will be crucial and beneficial.

Big auditory companies such as Deloitte, PwC, EY and KPMG play an important role in establishing the CSRD (Corporate Sustainability Reporting Directive). At the same time they help individual business units to develop digitization processes of sustainability reporting.

The Accounting, Reporting and Audit Supervision Service of the Ministry of Finance of Georgia is actively working on the implementation of corporate sustainability reporting in Georgia. The requirements of the mentioned directive in the first stage, from 2027, in relation to the reporting period of 2026 will focus on first category enterprises and public persons.

Within the Corporate Sustainability Reporting Directive - CSRD, the Accounting, Reporting and Audit Supervision Service of the Ministry of Finance of Georgia, the Finance Company (IFC) are actively cooperating in the direction of strengthening local companies in environmental, social and governance (ESG) reporting issues.

3 Research Method

The purpose of the study is to determine the need for a corporate sustainability reporting directive and the digital maturity level of sustainability reporting in Georgia, to clarify the technological platforms used by companies and to assess their impact on sustainability processes.

In the research process, the questionnaire format included closed and open-ended interrelated questions, namely:

- **Access to CSRD regulations:** participation in the review of the directive and training on CSRD requirements;
- **Level of strictness of CSRD requirements:** stiffness of requirements and its analysis;
- **Sustainability Reporting:** creating company value and importance of ESG Issues;
- **Practical experience:** practical experience of preparing sustainability reports and the negative consequences of fulfilling CSRD requirements (for example, unnecessary burdens for the company in the form of expense)
- **Potential opportunities and challenges:** opportunities and challenges created by the new CSRD directive;
- **Companies' readiness to prepare sustainability reporting in a standardized digital format:** what is the level of digital maturity of sustainability reporting in Georgian companies?

In order to ensure efficiency and timeliness, the survey has been carried out electronically through Google Forms. 101 companies of various sizes, including public interest and first category enterprises, as well as small and medium-sized financial directors and ESG project coordinators from various sectors, who are directly involved in the process of preparing the company's management reporting have been surveyed.

Data have been processed with statistical analysis (SPSS, Excel) programs on the basis of quantitative and qualitative research methods. In the process of implementing the CSRD regulations, the data have been analyzed in detail in order to identify tendencies, challenges, and opportunities. In addition, all data were confidential based on protecting the personal information of the participants. All persons participating in the study have been informed about the purpose of the study and their use. The survey and data collection have been conducted from May 2024 to August 2024.

The respondents' answers to the questions asked during the research process have been redistributed accordingly:

First Question
Have you undergone any training on the CSRD requirements of the Corporate Sustainability Reporting Directive?

Response

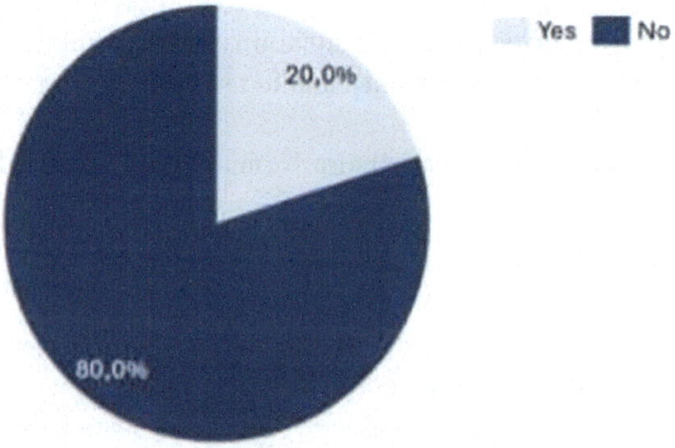

Source : The analysis was performed by the authors

The answers of the respondents have been redistributed according to the following proportion:

- Only 20% of the respondents have undergone
- 80% of the respondents haven't undergone

Second Question
Do you think that sustainability reporting serves to create company value?

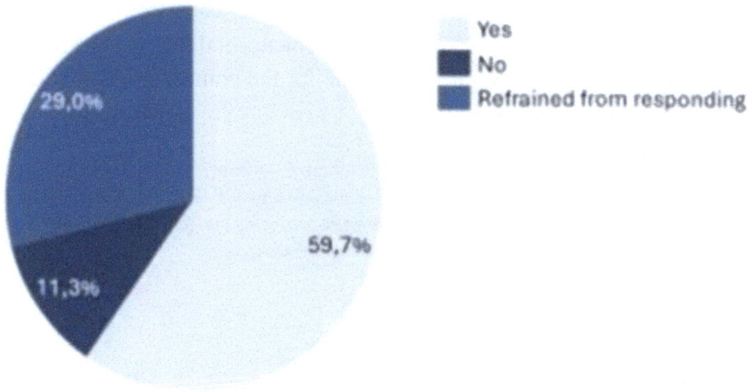

Source : the analysis was performed by the authors

The answers of the respondents have been redistributed according to the following proportion:

- Sustainability reporting creates a company value - 59.7%;
- Does not share this opinion - 11.3%
- Refrained from responding - 29%

Third Question
Do you think that the CSRD requirements of the Corporate Sustainability Reporting Directive in Georgia should be strict or loose?

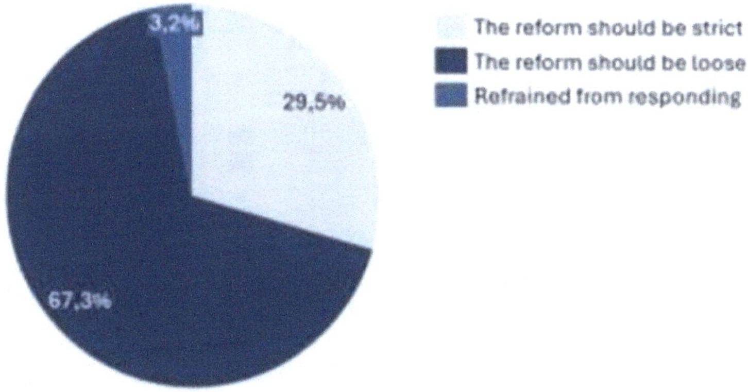

Source : the analysis was performed by the authors

The answers of the respondents have been redistributed according to the following proportion:

- The reform should be strict - 29.5%;
- The reform should be loose - 67.3%;
- Has no answer - 3.2%.

Fourth Question

Do you think that complying with the CSRD requirements of the Corporate Sustainability Reporting Directive could be a negative outcome for the company if the additional cost and time are taken into consideration?

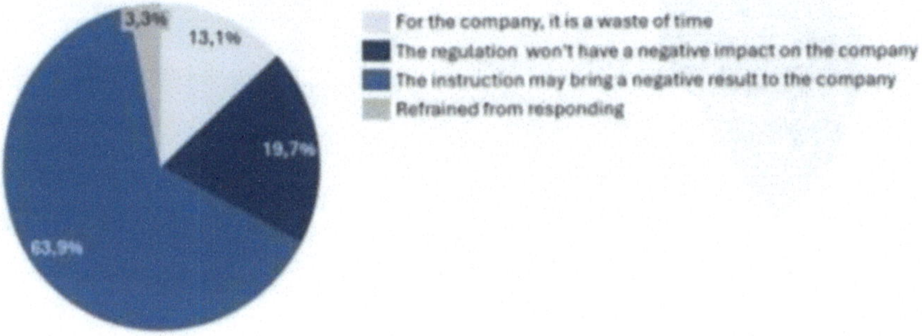

Source : the analysis was performed by the authors

The answers of the respondents have been redistributed according to the following proportion:

- For the company, it is a waste of time - 13.1%;
- The regulation won't have a negative impact on the company - 19.7%;
- The instruction may bring a negative result to the company - 63.9%;
- Has no answer - 3.3%.

CSRD requires from a company to submit sustainability data in a standardized digital format. In order to study the fulfillment of this requirement, during the research process, the respondents have been asked the following question: What is the level of digital maturity of sustainability reporting in your company?

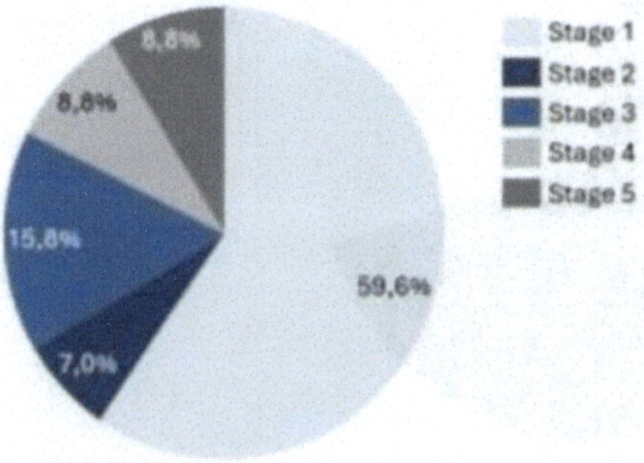

Source : the analysis was performed by the authors

The respondents of the surveyed companies have assessed the level of digital maturity accordingly:

Stage 1 - A big number of companies_59.6% are only at the stage of understanding the digital format **Stage 2** - only 7% of companies are in the process of preparing for digitalization of sustainability reporting

Stage 3 - 15.8% of companies are at the stage of starting the digitalization of sustainability reporting
Stage 4 - only 8.8% of companies are in the active phase of sustainability reporting digitization
Stage 5 - Digital maturity level of sustainability reporting, the highest level has been assessed by 8.8% of companies

In the research process, the following important issues have been analyzed:

1. **Possibilities for the development of CSRD directives in Georgia:** within the very framework we have investigated the challenges in Georgian business enterprises and the opportunities that will bring benefits in the future;
2. **ESG ambitions of companies:** we have assessed whether the ambitions are actually directed towards the establishment of sustainability values, or only focused on meeting regulatory requirements;
3. **Tendencies and driving factors:** we have discussed how the interest of companies in the transition to a sustainable system is growing and what factors contribute to this process;
4. **Digital Maturity Level of Sustainability Reporting:** We have outlined how digital technologies should be developed for more accurate and reliable recording of sustainability reporting;
5. **Difficulties and opportunities of digitization:** We have touched in detail how sustainability data should be digitized and what difficulties businesses have to deal with in this process.

4 Results and Discussion

The reliability of any company is uniquely determined by its sustainability. It is on the basis of the corporate annual report that the investor and other interested parties make a decision regarding the investment of capital in this or that company. A clear example of this is the banking sector of Georgia, which offers better loan conditions to sustainable companies, therefore neither banks nor investors are interested in unsustainable businesses. However, in order to reduce environmental and social risks in the business sector, it is important to clearly define the ESG strategy and course. Such an approach makes it easier for investors, customers, and employees to make daily decisions. Companies are faced with the fact of more transparency of the growing field of ESG due to rapidly changing business environment.

The results of the study have shown that the transition of companies to a sustainable system, the process of digitalization of reporting and current tendencies will have a positive effect on the quality of the system of environmental, social and governance measures. Along with this, while preparing the sustainability report, the integration of ESG into the corporate strategy should be taken into account according to legal requirements. Consequently, companies will face more bureaucratic barriers and increased administrative expenses, however, the implementation of ESG in each element of the business is a new opportunity that will contribute to its growth.

Laws in force in EU countries, as well as in Georgia, allow companies to develop sustainability programs. In addition, in order to ensure the real compliance and effectiveness of the regulations, it is essential to take into account the specificity of the local business environment in the process of their development.

The Corporate Sustainability Reporting (CSRD) Directive, in the context of the increasing transparency of Georgian institutions, helps to form new sustainable initiatives focused on results and maintaining qualified personnel.

The Corporate Sustainability Reporting Directive (CSRP) is intended for a wide range of enterprises, and the implementation of the digital XBRL standard in Georgia, following the relevant stages, will facilitate the quality of sustainability reporting in accordance with the reporting standards prepared by EFRAG and the IFRS Foundation, and by moving to the "one window" principle, it will make easier the process of processing and exchanging information.

5 Conclusions, Limitations and Further Research

The transition to a sustainable system allows business, as well as the country, to increase the economy with new opportunities. The results of the research prove that the companies in Georgia are actively and thoughtfully involved in the process started in the direction of sustainability. They have a healthy vision and a high level of ESG maturity. Via such an approach companies can create long-term values in order to meet their own and other stakeholders' goals.

In order for sustainability reporting and digitization to increase the value system of companies and positively affect the quality of the system of environmental, social and governance measures, it is appropriate to consider the following stages:

- **Action plan:** Companies should prepare an action plan to implement the CSRD regulations and improve their sustainability reporting strategies, which will help them ensure the recommendations;
- **Training:** it is necessary to organize large-scale trainings so that most companies will get to know with CSRD requirements and their fulfillment processes, and it is also essential to conduct informational events so that companies will realize the strategic importance of CSRD regulations and their impact on business processes;
- **Digital Maturity:** It is necessary to provide technological support to companies in order to improve digital maturity and effective reporting processes.

The stages of digitalization of sustainable reporting require permanent improvement and adaptation of specific steps and changes taking into account the special environment and needs of Georgia. Therefore, in order to implement and further develop CSRD in Georgian companies, it is necessary to strengthen research in this direction. However, we do believe that the conducted research will help companies, state structures and regulators to develop the strategies that ensure further improvement and effectiveness of corporate sustainability reporting.

References

Alles, M.G., Dai, J., Vasarhelyi, M.A.: Reporting 4.0: business reporting for the age of mass customization. J. Emerg. Technol. Account. **18**(1), 1–15 (2021). https://doi.org/10.2308/JETA-10764

Atkins, J., Doni, F., Gasperini, A., Artuso, S., La Torre, I., Sorrentino, L.: Exploring the effectiveness of sustainability measurement: which ESG metrics will survive COVID-19? J. Bus. Ethics **185**, 629–646 (2023). https://doi.org/10.1007/s10551-022-05183-1

European Commission: Corporate Sustainability Reporting Directive proposal, April 2021

Efimova, O., Rozhnova, O., Gorodetskaya, O.: XBRL as a tool for integrating financial and non-financial reporting. In: Antipova, T., Rocha, Á. (eds.) DSIC 2019. AISC, vol. 1114, pp. 135–147. Springer, Cham (2020). https://doi.org/10.1007/978-3-030-37737-3_13

Leitner-Hanetseder, S., Lehner, O.M.: AI-powered information and big data: current regulations and ways forward in IFRS reporting. J. Appl. Account. Res. **24**, 282–298 (2022). https://doi.org/10.1108/JAAR-01-2022-0022

KPMG: The new CSRD: what does this mean for you? In: Troshani, I., Rowbottom, N. (eds.) Digital Corporate Reporting: Global Experiences from the G20 and Implications for Policy Formulation (2022)

Mancini, D., Lombardi, R., Tavana, M.: Four research pathways for understanding the role of smart technologies in accounting. Meditari Account. Res. **29**(5), 1041–1062 (2021). https://doi.org/10.1108/MEDAR-03-2021-1258

Otley, D.: The contingency theory of management accounting and control: 1980–2014 (2016).

Vasarhelyi, M.A., Romero, S.: Technology in audit engagements: a case study. Managerial Audit. J. **29**(4), 350–365 (2014). https://doi.org/10.1108/MAJ-06-2013-0881

XBRL International: iXBRL (2021). https://www.xbrl.org/thestandard/what/ixbrl/

XBRL International: An introduction to XBRL (2022a). https://www.xbrl.org/the-standard/what/an-introduction-to-xbrl/

Navigating the AI Hype: Perceptions and Opportunities in German SME Marketing Applications

Jonas Polfuß(✉)

IU Internationale Hochschule, Essen, Germany
mail@jonas-polfuss.de

Abstract. The launch of ChatGPT in late 2022 marked the beginning of an unprecedented global expansion of generative artificial intelligence (AI). While this AI wave shares similarities with other technological innovations in the business and office sectors over the past 25 years, it also possesses unique characteristics. This study examines the impact of AI on small and medium-sized enterprise (SME) marketing in Germany, using selected AI tools. Software reviews by the companies utilizing these tools were analyzed to identify the perceived opportunities and challenges in AI adoption. The findings of this study provide recommendations for companies, tool developers, associations, and government agencies to sustainably promote AI use in SMEs while addressing safety issues and marketing risks.

Keywords: AI · SME · German Mittelstand · Marketing · Software · Tools · Automation

1 Introduction

Since the introduction of ChatGPT by OpenAI, artificial intelligence (AI) has significantly influenced various sectors. The widespread availability of affordable, user-friendly generative AI tools from 2022 has led to a global surge in usage, extending beyond traditional information technology (IT) user groups. Unlike previous technological innovations such as the Internet or mobile communication, generative AI quickly reached a broad audience and gained active users within a few months. During its initial phase, tools such as ChatGPT, classified as dialogic productivity tools, experienced growth rates that surpassed those of social media platforms focused on entertainment (Hu 2023).

Unlike earlier innovative office applications, generative AI is designed for use across almost all industries and fields of work, which explains its widespread success. However, the efficient integration of AI in organizations depends on several factors. While large companies are often well-equipped to systematically integrate AI through investments and restructuring, the situation is significantly different for small- and medium-sized enterprises (SMEs) (cf. Kopka & Fornahl 2024). SMEs face pressure to adopt AI as a transformative technology, yet often lack the resources to fully exploit its potential. In marketing, new AI solutions promise numerous advantages; however, adapting to its rapid development is challenging.

R. C. Geibel and S. Machavariani (Eds.): ISPC 2024, SPBE, pp. 388–398, 2025.
https://doi.org/10.1007/978-3-031-88052-0_32

2 Theoretical Foundation

Various theoretical approaches address entrepreneurial strategies for managing innovation and disruption. Among these, Rogers' diffusion theory of innovation, an earlier framework, describes the dissemination of new ideas and technologies by identifying distinct phases of adoption and user categories with varying levels of readiness to adopt (Rogers 1962; Damiano et al. 2024). In the context of digitalization within modern organizations, categories of openness have been established, ranging from pioneering spirit to passivity (Ransbotham et al. 2017).

In the context of innovation competition, the concept of "disruptive innovation" (Christensen 1997; Christensen et al. 2018) remains pertinent in scientific discussions. This concept posits that simpler, more affordable, or more convenient alternatives can displace established technologies and markets. Consequently, companies must either embrace disruptive innovations or adapt their existing business models to maintain competitiveness. Recent discussions emphasize that the development of such disruptions will further increase in terms of technical innovations and evolving business models (e.g. Mondal et al. 2023).

Davis (1989) investigated the adoption and use of technological innovations through the Technology Acceptance Model (TAM). According to this model, the perceived usefulness and ease of use significantly influence acceptance. This approach was later expanded into the Unified Theory of Acceptance and Use of Technology (UTAUT), which includes four criteria: performance expectancy, effort expectancy, social influence, and facilitating conditions (Venkatesh et al. 2003; Venkatesh et al. 2012). Social influence is particularly relevant in the current AI context, as the enthusiasm for and adoption of AI technologies, especially in social media, has accelerated its diffusion (Grandinetti 2024).

The role of individuals in driving digital innovation within organizations is widely discussed, particularly regarding the design of effective management structures to achieve progress (e.g., Trischler & Li-Ying 2023). Larger companies typically adopt a top-down, formalized approach, while SMEs often use a bottom-up, informal approach (Zoppelletto et al. 2023). When integrating AI applications, management often aims to leverage these technologies for strategic objectives, whereas employees focus primarily on simplifying daily tasks (Cecchi- Dimeglio 2024).

The German SME sector is described as a "guarantor of stability and progress" in the economy (BVMW 2024). However, these businesses often require support to advance in digitalization (c.f. Bürgel et al. 2023; DLR 2024). In 2023, 11% of SMEs in Germany used AI, surpassing the European Union (EU) average of 7%, but trailing behind large German companies, 35% of which employed AI (IfM Bonn 2024). Barriers to digitalization for SMEs include a lack of IT expertise and skilled workers (KfW Research 2024). The ongoing AI revolution is likely to further exacerbate the shortage of expertise and skilled personnel.

3 Research Method

Against this background, this study investigates the use and potential of AI in SME marketing from both company and user perspectives. It also examines product evaluations for three leading AI applications: ChatGPT from OpenAI (San Francisco, CA, USA), DeepL, and Neuroflash from their respective companies in Cologne and Hamburg, Germany. This selection includes one internationally successful application of non-German origin, one globally influential application of German origin, and one solution that originated in Germany and achieved success in German-speaking countries.

ChatGPT offers interactive dialog management, text creation, decision support, image generation, and application programming interface (API) integration for various applications (OpenAI 2024). DeepL provides AI-based translations in over 30 languages, document translations, and API integration for corporate use (DeepL 2024). Neuroflash specializes in German-language content for marketing purposes and also includes an AI image generator (Neuroflash 2024). All three companies offer a free version with basic functions, as well as subscription plans tailored to different use cases; for individual German users, the monthly subscription fees are $20 for ChatGPT ("Plus"), €7.49 for DeepL ("Starter"), and €30.00 for Neuroflash ("Standard") (as of September 2024).

A total of 881 text-based reviews for the three AI applications were examined on Capterra (Arlington, VA), G2.com (Chicago, IL), and OMR Reviews (Hamburg). There were 95 reviews from Capterra (2024), 32 from G2 (2024), and 754 from OMR Reviews (2024). For Capterra and G2.com, the reviews were filtered to focus on Germany. OMR Reviews, being the largest platform for software reviews in the DACH region, likely includes many reviews from Germany, although specific country filtering is unavailable. To focus on reviews from medium- sized companies, any reviews from organizations with more than 1,000 employees, categorized by the platforms as large- or enterprise-level companies, were excluded across all three platforms. Notably, definitions of SMEs and the German Mittelstand vary, with SMEs in Germany often defined as having fewer than 250 employees (Destatis 2024). As this lower limit could not be applied in the pre-selection process across all three review platforms, the next available common size category (1,000 employees) was chosen for consistency. The equally popular review platform TrustPilot (Copenhagen) was excluded due to its inability to filter reviews by country or company size.

In the analysis of the reviews, the most frequent fields of application, as well as the advantages and disadvantages from the users' perspectives in terms of performance and effort, were examined based on the UTAUT model. Thus, 881 reviews were subjected to detailed frequency and content analyses (cf. Mayring 2019). In addition to everyday office and business activities, particular emphasis was placed on AI applications in marketing. While product and service reviews offer direct and realistic insights into how AI is utilized and perceived, these insights may be influenced by manipulated content and euphemistic or extreme tendencies in reviews (e.g., Sahut et al. 2024).

Moreover, it is crucial to consider that the number and the tone of reviews can be influenced by how companies encourage customers to provide feedback.

4 Analysis and Results

Table 1 presents the overall international ratings of the three software solutions across the three platforms as of September 21, 2024. The left inner boxes indicate the total number of ratings for each application, while those on the right highlight the number of stars awarded out of a possible five.

Table 1. Overall application ratings on the software platforms

Software	Platform		
	Capterra	G2	OMR Reviews
ChatGPT	60: 4,5	603: 4,7	59: 4,8
DeepL	138: 4,8*	52: 4,6	135: 4,8
Neuroflash	171: 4,8	189: 4,7	626: 4,7

With no rating lower than 4.5 and an average of 4.7, user satisfaction was significantly positive. Additionally, there were few to no ratings with only one or two stars for the three applications across the platforms. However, because all platforms inquire about potential disadvantages or reasons for dissatisfaction even in positive ratings, both the advantages and disadvantages of the software solutions from the user's perspective are outlined below.

4.1 General Advantages and Disadvantages of AI Applications

Based on the frequency and content analysis of all evaluations, the advantages of the applications can be categorized into five key areas of performance and effort: time-saving, inspiration for content, increased productivity, support for writers, and quality translations. In 516 of the 881 reviews, the time aspect is highlighted as a positive factor, with the German term for "time saving" ("Zeitersparnis") used 72 times. Overall, the speed of AI solutions in completing tasks has increased. Quick familiarization with the applications and the time saved in daily work are also highlighted as key advantages. The term "ideas" appears 172 times in the reviews, with many users commending the tools for their ability to inspire content creation. Additionally, some reviewers appreciate how effectively these tools execute human-generated ideas. Regarding increased productivity, the terms "effective" or "effectiveness" are mentioned 37 times, with reviewers commending the low revision requirements of generated content. In terms of writers' support, the tools are described as simplifying and optimizing the writing process, with content precisely tailored to various topics and target groups. For DeepL, the accuracy of its translations is praised, both generally and in comparison with other tools. Additionally, several reviews indicate that AI tools can compensate for human weaknesses and errors.

Despite the generally high ratings, there are some criticisms regarding the overall utility of these applications. The possible disadvantages in terms of performance and effort can be categorized into three areas: potential errors, inconsistencies in content quality, and limited language support. In 60 instances, users reported occasional errors or inaccuracies, predominantly associated with text generation and translation, with three reviewers encountering error messages within the application. A few reviewers observed that the content quality was either too general or inappropriate and that the linguistic features of the AI origin were identifiable. Specifically, for DeepL, there are demands for the inclusion of more languages and language combinations. Additionally, some reviewers expressed concerns regarding data protection, particularly with the free-trial versions.

The aspect of social influence is evident in several passages where users mention being recommended the tool by colleagues. In 57 passages, reviewers recommend AI applications to the readers of review portals. When it comes to facilitating conditions, most reviewers are satisfied with the support options offered by the providers. They praise intuitive usability, service support, and additional (free) training options. However, some criticized the complexity of the applications and the lack of customer support.

In terms of AI tool use by SMEs, pricing is a common topic in the reviews. In 88 instances, reviewers commend the free features, fair or affordable pricing, and cost savings compared to competitors or traditional methods without AI applications. Meanwhile, 178 passages criticize pricing, citing limited features in the free version and high costs for paid plans. Reviewers also call for more services at existing price points and greater price transparency, noting that even entry-level prices are challenging for small companies to afford.

4.2 Advantages and Disadvantages of AI Applications in Marketing

Many of the previously discussed advantages and disadvantages can also be applied in the marketing context. The subsequent section examines how application reviewers utilize SME marketing, highlighting the opportunities and challenges they encounter. The term "marketing" is mentioned in 83 reviews. Table 2 presents the specific fields of application in the marketing context, along with the respective frequency of mentions.

Table 2. Use of AI Applications for Marketing Purposes

Application	Mentions
1. Content	231
2. SEO/search engine optimization	152
3. Social media	122
4. Blog articles	97
5. Product descriptions	88
6. Newsletter	29
7. Campaigns	11
8. Advertising	6

Notably, AI marketing applications are primarily associated with content creation. Users commend the precise and personalized production of high-quality content across various platforms. However, occasional criticism is directed at minor inaccuracies and the necessity for manual post-processing, particularly for specific or complex topics. In search engine marketing, primarily discussed in Neuroflash evaluations, users praise the straightforward creation of suitable content and perceive minimal need for improvement. The benefits of customized content, which can be user-friendly and created for different channels or media, are also highlighted in other marketing areas. AI applications effectively manage both creative marketing tasks, such as crafting appealing headlines, and technical tasks, such as creating metadata for website texts. Some reviewers emphasize the valuable support in brainstorming and assistance with repetitive and labor-intensive tasks.

Irrespective of the media or channels involved, users appreciate the time saved when utilizing AI applications for marketing purposes. Tasks such as article writing are completed swiftly, and extensive editing is eliminated owing to the precision of AI tools. A key advantage frequently emphasized is the reduced reliance on external service providers, which otherwise incur significant costs. Reviewers note that AI support helps maintain a consistent brand image while addressing different target groups individually. In addition to the wide range of content, the flexibility to respond to varying market situations is highly valued. The reviewers describe the novel scalability as particularly valuable from an entrepreneurial perspective, as large volumes of content for marketing or sales projects can now be effectively planned and produced. The consistently high standard of output is also appreciated for systematically improving marketing. Additionally, the AI tools have significantly simplified the optimization of existing marketing materials, enhancing the performance of promotional content and campaigns. Besides the general limitations of the discussed AI applications, the reviewers noted any further concerns related to their use in a marketing context.

5 Discussion and Recommendations

The review analysis reveals a high degree of openness and a positive attitude toward the examined applications and AI in a business and marketing context among freelancers and representatives of SMEs. Users value the practical benefits these tools offer to their daily work, primarily owing to the high performance and minimal effort required for use. This contrasts with surveys suggesting that SMEs are generally hesitant to adopt AI (e.g., eco Verband der Internetwirtschaft 2024). However, these assessments originate from active users who have already decided to use the applications and generally express high enthusiasm for their decision.

A similar pattern emerges in the criticism regarding pricing. While the pricing structure and value for money were criticized in 178 reviews, only five reviews indicated that cost deterred users from repurchasing the applications.

This issue is particularly relevant for freelancers and SMEs, suggesting that many users may have purchased their subscriptions independently rather than through company management.

5.1 AI Misconceptions and Potential Challenges

While users perceive the high prices of these applications as undesirable, many reviews highlight that applications of such quality cannot be provided for free. Users may be adept at using these applications and demonstrate an informed understanding of common AI misconceptions (cf. Bewersdorff et al. 2023). For example, beliefs that AI always generates perfect output, that all AI chatbot functions as a conventional search engine, or that the application results are always factually correct, are rarely encountered in reviews. However, regarding the broader, multidimensional consequences of increasing AI use in marketing, reviewers could be critiqued for their lack of skepticism.

Given the critical social debate, especially in Germany, the usual concerns about AI are rarely mentioned in discussions on the disadvantages of its applications. Although the problem of data protection has been mentioned a few times, it does not elicit significant concern among users. This is because, in larger companies, awareness of the legal and technical challenges of digitization and AI is more pronounced owing to the presence of dedicated personnel. Regarding digital transformation in SMEs, it is encouraging to observe optimism regarding the use of AI. However, some aspects require scrutiny from the social, entrepreneurial, and marketing perspectives.

Legal issues must also be considered, as many remain unresolved because of outdated or unfinalized laws. One reviewer noted that the rapid development of AI can also be viewed critically because the consequences for people and society remain uncertain, emphasizing the need for more education and research from tool developers. Another review examined the negative consequences of increasing AI automation in the labor market. Although not mentioned in user reviews, the surge in AI-generated content is intensifying competition for attention immensely. Additionally, on certain platforms, such as for SEO content on Google, it remains unclear how the influence of AI will impact marketing success in the long term (Polfuß 2024).

5.2 Managerial and Policy Implications

This section outlines recommendations for integrating AI applications into SMEs in Germany, especially in marketing. It also discusses how application providers, associations, and government agencies supporting SME digitization can facilitate this transformation.

As the evaluation analysis suggests, individuals are more easily convinced of the benefits of AI applications once they become active users. Accordingly, SMEs should introduce training programs to help employees familiarize themselves with AI solutions. Given the high price sensitivity of certain users, offering free trial versions or purchasing a company-wide license to make AI tools available to teams may be beneficial. In text creation and marketing, AI tools generate enthusiasm, making this an ideal area for integration with minimal complications. Beginners and hesitant employees are recommended to start with tasks that lead to quick and visible success with manageable effort (Heider-Willms 2024). Inquisitive and experienced users can help advance a company with their expertise in relevant pilot projects. When motivating employees, it is critical to emphasize the company's goals and advantages that AI offers to simplify their daily work. Although enthusiasm for AI should be encouraged, the possible social and economic concerns and risks should not be neglected.

When targeting advertising in SMEs, AI tool providers are advised to highlight the significant time savings that can be achieved, which can be demonstrated through exemplary use cases and success metrics. Positive reviews and testimonies provide valuable evidence in this regard. Wherever possible from a business perspective, providers could offer additional free options and reduce limitations on free or entry-level packages. Additionally, tailored entry-level packages specifically for SMEs, with affordable or flexible pricing options should be considered. If adjusting pricing is not viable, it could be valuable to highlight the potential for savings, such as the reduced need for external marketing services. Positive customer comments in reviews could also serve as compelling evidence. Even in cases where SME representatives are unaware of the risks posed by AI applications, it is both responsible and beneficial for AI providers to acknowledge the potential weaknesses and dangers arising from the excessive use of AI technology. However, it is important to recognize that tool providers depend on a broad user base to train their systems and increase sales, which may conflict with educational efforts.

Relevant associations and the government are responsible for educating SMEs on how to safely and sustainably use AI. It is essential to provide information about the business opportunities and competitive necessities of AI applications, ensuring that German SMEs can continue to play a key role in the economy. This can be achieved by referencing case studies in which SMEs achieve business success through AI transformation. However, it is also necessary to provide information on the limitations and risks of AI-based tools to avoid the negative consequences of future developments. In addition to information campaigns, further funding programs are desirable to support companies in the practical implementation of AI tools and incentivize investments in AI research and development. Some initiatives have already been launched in this area (e.g., DLR Projektträger 2022; Bundesministerium für Digitales und Verkehr 2024), which could be further expanded to adapt to the rapid changes in the AI solution market. Promoting partnerships between AI providers and SMEs would further enhance their ability to tailor AI applications to their needs.

6 Conclusion, Limitations, and Further Research

The present evaluations of AI applications, such as ChatGPT, DeepL, and NeuroFlash, highlight key advantages for SME users. The most significant advantage is time savings, followed by support in creative and productive text generation and translation execution. Within specific marketing tasks, users emphasize content creation and the specific benefits of search engine optimization (SEO), social media, blog marketing, and retail product descriptions. Criticism of the applications was relatively minimal, primarily related to possible errors, content inconsistencies, and limited translation options. Based on user experiences and expectations, recommendations for SMEs and companies with AI services were formulated to foster enthusiasm for useful applications in a responsible manner, enabling the digital transformation in the German Mittelstand amid rapid technological change. Particularly in SMEs, it remains crucial to synchronize different levels of AI knowledge and experience. Companies must align diverse objectives such as streamlining operational processes for teams and fostering business growth from a management perspective into cohesive AI strategies. Given the rapidly developing AI- based applications in marketing, SMEs will face challenges in remaining informed and selecting appropriate solutions while managing limited resources to maintain a competitive edge.

Applied research is critical in monitoring supply structures and demand situations while documenting best practices in AI-based marketing for SMEs. This study identifies several criteria that may foster the proactive and motivated use of AI applications in SME marketing, providing insights into practical experiences. However, the nature of product evaluation is subject to certain limitations. Further qualitative and quantitative research is necessary to explore the factors inhibiting broader AI adoption in SMEs and identify ways to mitigate these barriers (cf. Falck et al. 2024). Additionally, gaining insights from negative user experiences with AI applications, such as those shared in online forums would help optimize AI solutions and practical usage. Comparative analyses of other tools, specific industries, and countries would also enhance understanding. Although research may trail the rapid pace of AI development, AI solutions are increasingly facilitating everyday academic tasks, predicting a future where AI can undertake research.

References

Bewersdorff, A., Zhai, X., Roberts, J., Nerdel, C.: Myths, mis- and preconceptions of artificial intelligence: a review of the literature. Comput. Educ. Artif. Intell. **4**, 100143 (2023). https://doi.org/10.1016/j.caeai.2023.100143

Bundesministerium für Digitales und Verkehr: Neue Anlaufstelle für Gründer, Start-ups und KMU, um KI-Produkte anzuwenden und zu entwickeln (New contact point for founders, start-ups and SMEs to apply and develop AI products) (2024). https://bmdv.bund.de/SharedDocs/DE/Pressemitteilungen/2024/065-wissing-eroeffnung-ki-zentrum.html

Bürgel, T.R., Hiebl, M.R.W., Pielsticker, D.I.: Digitalization and entrepreneurial firms' resilience to pandemic crises: evidence from COVID-19 and the German Mittelstand. Technol. Forecast. Soc. Change **186**, 122135 (2023). https://doi.org/10.1016/j.techfore.2022.122135

BVMW: Über uns (About us). Der Mittelstand BVMW e.V (2024). https://www.bvmw.de/de/der-verband/%C3%BCber-uns/zahlen-fakten

Capterra (2024). https://www.capterra.com.de/; ChatGPT. https://www.capterra.com.de/reviews/1049484/chatgpt; DeepL. https://www.capterra.com.de/reviews/219412/deepl-pro; Neuroflash. https://www.capterra.com.de/reviews/207149/neuro-flash

Cecchi-Dimeglio, P.: How leaders can enhance employee AI usage. Forbes (2024). https://www.forbes.com/sites/paolacecchi-dimeglio/2024/05/28/how-leaders-can-enhance-employee-ai-usage/

Christensen, C.M.: The Innovator's Dilemma. When New Technologies Cause Great Firms to Fail. Harvard Business School Press (1997)

Christensen, C.M., McDonald, R., Altman, E.J., Palmer, J.E.: Disruptive innovation: an intellectual history and directions for future research. J. Manag. Stud. **55**(7), 1043–1078 (2018). https://doi.org/10.1111/joms.12349

Damiano, A.D., Lauría, E.J.M., Sarmiento, C., Zhao, N.: Early perceptions of teaching and learning using generative AI in higher education. J. Educ. Technol. Syst. **52**(3), 346–375 (2024). https://doi.org/10.1177/00472395241233290

Davis, F.D.: Perceived usefulness, perceived ease of use, and user acceptance of information technology. MIS Q. **13**(3), 319–340 (1989). https://doi.org/10.2307/249008

DeepL (2024). https://deepl.com/

Destatis: Kleine und mittlere Unternehmen (KMU) (Small and medium-sized enterprises (SMEs)) (2024). https://www.destatis.de/DE/Themen/Branchen-Unternehmen/Unternehmen/Kleine-Unternehmen-Mittlere-Unternehmen/Glossar/kmu.html

DLR: Zukünftige Unterstützungsbedarfe des Mittelstandes in der digitalen Transformation. Studie für den DLR Projektträger im Rahmen der Projektträgerschaft "Mittelstand-Digital" (Future support needs of medium- sized companies in the digital transformation. Study for the DLR project management agency as part of the "Mittelstand-Digital" project sponsorship) (2024). https://projekttraeger.dlr.de/sites/default/files/2024-07/documents/BedarfsanalyseZuk%C3%BCnftigeUnterst%C3%BCtzungsBedarfeMittelstand.pdf

DLR Projektträger: DLR Projektträger setzt Mittelstandsförderung des BMBF um (DLR Project Management Agency implements BMBF funding for SMEs) (2022). https://projekttraeger.dlr.de/de/news/dlr-projekttraeger-setzt-mittelstandsfoerderung-des-bmbf-um

eco Verband der Internetwirtschaft: eco YouGov Umfrage zeigt: insbesondere kleine und mittlere Unternehmen zurückhaltend beim KI-Einsatz (eco YouGov survey shows: small and medium-sized companies in particular are reluctant to use AI) (2024). https://www.eco.de/presse/eco-yougov-umfrage-zeigt-insbesondere-kleine-und-mittlere-unternehmen-zurueckhaltend-beim-ki-einsatz/

Falck, O., Kerkhof, A., Wölfl, A.: Künstliche Intelligenz (KI). Verbreitung, Anwendung und Hindernisse in Deutschland im europäischen Vergleich (Artificial intelligence (AI). Dissemination, application and obstacles in Germany in a European comparison). ifo Institut (2024). https://www.ifo.de/publikationen/2024/monographie-autorenschaft/kuenstliche-intelligenz-ki-verbreitung-anwendung

G2 (2024). https://www.g2.com/; ChatGPT. https://www.g2.com/products/chatgpt/reviews; DeepL. https://www.g2.com/products/deepl/reviews; Neuroflash. https://www.g2.com/products/neuroflash/reviews

Grandinetti, J.: Deconstructing AI hype and its impact on social media. Polit. Rights Rev. (2024). https://politicsrights.com/deconstructing-ai-hype-impact-social-media/

Heider-Willms, A.: KI im Arbeitsalltag: Viel Skepsis bleibt (AI in the workplace: Much skepticism remains). Personalwirtschaft (2024). https://www.personalwirtschaft.de/news/hr-organisation/ki-im-arbeitsalltag-viel-skepsis-bleibt-179378/

Hu, K.: ChatGPT sets record for fastest-growing user base – analyst note. Reuters (2023). https://www.reuters.com/technology/chatgpt-sets-record-fastest-growing-user-base-analyst-note-2023-02-01/

IfM: Digitalisierung der KMU im EU-Vergleich (2024). https://www.ifm-bonn.org/statistiken/mittelstand-im-einzelnen/digitalisierung-der-kmu-im-eu-vergleich

KfW Research: Vielfältige Hemmnisse bremsen die Digitalisierung im Mittelstand (2024). https://www.kfw.de/PDF/Download-Center/Konzernthemen/Research/PDF-Dokumente-Fokus-Volkswirtschaft/Fokus-2022/Fokus-Nr.-380-April-2022-DigiHemmnisse.pdf

Kopka, A., Fornahl, D.: Artificial intelligence and firm growth — catch-up processes of SMEs through integrating AI into their knowledge bases. Small Bus. Econ. **62**, 63–85 (2024). https://doi.org/10.1007/s11187-023-00754-6

Mayring, P.: Qualitative content analysis: demarcation, varieties, developments. Forum Qualitative Sozialforschung Forum Qual. Soc. Res. **20**(3), 1–14 (2019). https://doi.org/10.17169/fqs-20.3.3343

Mondal, S., Das, S., Vrana, V.G.: How to bell the cat? A theoretical review of generative artificial intelligence towards digital disruption in all walks of life. Technologies **11**(2), 44 (2023). https://doi.org/10.3390/technologies11020044

Neuroflash (2024). https://neuroflash.com/

OMR Reviews (2024). https://omr.com/de/reviews/; ChatGPT. https://omr.com/de/reviews/product/openai-chatgpt/; DeepL. https://www.g2.com/products/deepl/reviews; Neuroflash. https://www.g2.com/products/neuroflash/reviews

OpenAI: Introducing ChatGPT Plus (2024). https://openai.com/index/chatgpt-plus/

Polfuß, J.: Wie gut KI-Texte im Marketing mittlerweile sind - und wie man sie erkennt (How good AI texts have become in marketing – and how to recognize them) (2024). Horizont. https://www.horizont.net/marketing/kommentare/kuenstliche-intelligenz-wie-gut-ki-texte-im-marketing-mittlerweile-sind---und-wie-man-sie-erkennt-217520

Rogers, E.M.: Diffusion of innovations. Free Press of Glencoe (1962)

Ransbotham, S., Kiron, D., Gerbert, P., Reeves, M.: Reshaping business with artificial intelligence. MIT Sloan Manag. Rev. Boston Consult. Group **59**(1) (2017). https://sloanreview.mit.edu/projects/reshaping-business-with-artificial-intelligence/

Sahut, J.M., Laroche, M., Braune, E.: Antecedents and consequences of fake reviews in a marketing approach: an overview and synthesis. J. Bus. Res. **175**, 114572 (2024). https://doi.org/10.1016/j.jbusres.2024.114572

Trischler, M.F.G., Li-Ying, J.: Digital business model innovation: toward construct clarity and future research directions. Rev. Manag. Sci. **17**, 3–32 (2023). https://doi.org/10.1007/s11846-021-00508-2.

Venkatesh, V., Morris, M.G., Davis, G.B., Davis, F.D.: User acceptance of information technology: toward a unified view. MIS Q. **27**(3), 425–478 (2003). https://doi.org/10.2307/30036540

Venkatesh, V., Thong, J.Y.L., Xu, X.: Consumer acceptance and use of information technology: extending the unified theory of acceptance and use of technology. MIS Q. **36**(1), 157–178 (2012). https://doi.org/10.2307/41410412

Zoppelletto, A., Orlandi, L.B., Zardini, A., Rossignoli, C., Kraus, S.: Organizational roles in the context of digital transformation: a micro-level perspective. J. Bus. Res. **157**, 113563 (2023). https://doi.org/10.1016/j.jbusres.2022.113563

Use and Influence of Large Language Models for Optimizing Product Texts in E-Commerce

Ann-Cathrin Nordhoff[1](✉) and Darius Zumstein[2]

[1] Migros Fachmarkt AG, Limmatstrasse 152 Postfach, CH-8005 Zürich, Switzerland
ann-cathrin.nordhoff@mfmag.ch
[2] Digital Marketing, FHNW School of Business, Institute for Competitiveness and Communication (ICC), University of Applied Sciences and Arts Northwestern Switzerland, Riggenbachstrasse 16, CH-4600 Olten, Switzerland
darius.zumstein@fhnw.ch

Abstract. This contribution investigates the impact of disclosing AI-generated text on consumer purchase intent and their perception of text quality in the e-commerce sector. As large language models (LLMs) become more prevalent in commercial text production, it is crucial to understand how consumers react to AI-generated content and the importance of transparency regarding its origin. The research results reveal that while disclosing the AI origin of texts does not significantly reduce purchase intention overall, consumer responses vary depending on their initial perceptions of content quality. This suggests that the mere knowledge of AI involvement does not necessarily influence consumer decisions negatively, especially when the perceived quality is high.

Furthermore, AI-generated texts were generally perceived as inferior in quality compared to those written by humans, particularly in terms of emotional appeal and authenticity, underscoring the need for robust strategies in developing and managing AI-generated product descriptions. Effective quality assurance of such content is essential, as perceived quality is a more decisive factor in purchasing than the awareness of the text's AI origin. This is supported by data showing a significant correlation between perceived quality and individual attributes such as usefulness, relevance, completeness, understandability, emotional content, text length, and structure of product page.

Expert interviews conducted as part of the research project emphasized the necessity of tailoring texts to the specific needs of customers, providers, and products. High-quality texts should contain relevant information, clearly highlight product benefits, and be structured in a way that enhances readability and engagement. While keyword integration and ongoing SEO optimization remain important, the study's focus on consumer perception revealed that neither AI-generated nor human-written texts were consistently recognized as such by consumers, and familiarity with LLMs did not predict better identification of AI texts. Additionally, the research showed that the impact of AI disclosure on consumer trust varies; some consumers are indifferent, while others may become skeptical if the perceived quality is low, highlighting that content quality is more crucial than transparency alone.

In conclusion, this contribution demonstrates that transparency about AI usage alone is not sufficient to affect purchase decisions if the quality of the information

R. C. Geibel and S. Machavariani (Eds.): ISPC 2024, SPBE, pp. 399–411, 2025.
https://doi.org/10.1007/978-3-031-88052-0_33

is perceived as inadequate. Practically, the findings suggest that e-commerce businesses should concentrate on improving the quality of their AI-generated product texts and consider strategic transparency based on customer segments. This approach could foster trust and enhance customer satisfaction, while the strategic use of AI can improve the overall effectiveness of product texts.

Keywords: E-commerce · large language models · artificial intelligence · product text · product detail page · search engine optimization · ChatGPT · purchase intention

1 Introduction

The rapid advancement of digital technologies and the ongoing process of digitalization have led to a significant growth in the **e-commerce market** in recent years. According to an analysis of e-commerce revenue trends, the market volume is projected to increase from 1.334 billion Euro in 2018 to an estimated 5.940 billion Euro by 2028 (Statista 2024). This substantial growth underscores the rising importance of e-commerce as a sales platform and highlights the need for companies to adopt innovative technologies and customer-centric approaches to effectively meet the evolving consumer preferences.

The rapid expansion of e-commerce has fundamentally altered consumer behavior and the competitive landscape for businesses. According to recent studies, the shift towards online shopping has intensified the need for high-quality digital content that effectively communicates product features and benefits (Mangiaracina et al. 2009; Pfeiffer 2016). **Product descriptions** are particularly critical as they serve as the *primary source of information* for online shoppers, influencing their perceptions and purchase intentions. Research indicates that well-crafted product texts can significantly *enhance consumer trust and engagement*, making them a vital component of digital marketing strategies (Mudambi & Schuff 2010). In this context, the ability of businesses to produce engaging, accurate, and persuasive content has become more important than ever.

Artificial Intelligence (AI) has become increasingly important in this context, with the potential to fundamentally change how buying and selling are conducted online (Heethuis 2022). Specifically, the use of large language models (LLMs) such as OpenAI's GPT series has opened up new possibilities in the creation and optimization of (product) texts that are almost indistinguishable from those written by humans (Bundesamt für Sicherheit in der Informationstechnik 2023). These models can not only automate a wide range of manual tasks but also *enhance customer experience*.

In the realm of e-commerce, product descriptions play a crucial role in conveying *product features, benefits, and applications* to potential buyers. **High-quality product texts** are essential for influencing purchasing decisions, building customer trust, and improving overall user engagement (Mangiaracina et al. 2009; Pfeiffer 2016). The ability of LLMs to generate product descriptions quickly and cost-effectively presents a significant opportunity for e-commerce businesses. However, the integration of AI-generated content into online shops raises questions about **transparency** and consumer trust, particularly concerning whether customers can *distinguish between AI-generated and human-written texts* and how this awareness affects their purchasing decisions (Heiser

2019). The increasing use of AI-generated content in e-commerce necessitates a deeper understanding of consumer perceptions and behaviors regarding these texts. Research suggests that consumers may perceive **AI-generated content** as *lower in quality*, which could impact their purchase intentions (Mudambi & Schuff 2010).

Moreover, the question of transparency—whether or not businesses should *disclose the use of AI in creating product descriptions*—has become a topic of debate. Some studies indicate that the mere disclosure of AI involvement does not significantly affect consumer purchase intent if the perceived quality of the content remains high (Mou et al. 2019).

High-quality content in e-commerce does not only attract and retain customers but also builds trust, which is essential for converting visitors into buyers (Heiser 2019). Studies have shown that content that is perceived as informative, relevant, and complete can significantly *influence consumer purchase decisions and satisfaction* (Mudambi & Schuff 2010).

This contribution aims to explore these dynamics by investigating how consumers respond to AI-generated product descriptions and the importance of text quality and transparency in influencing their purchasing decisions.

2 Theoretical Foundation

The integration of **large language models** (LLMs) in e-commerce represents a significant shift in how digital content is created and optimized, with profound implications for consumer behavior and trust. The theoretical foundation for understanding the impact of AI-generated content in e-commerce is grounded in several key areas of literature: information economics (Sect. 2.1), consumer perception theories (Sect. 2.2), and the role of trust and transparency in online transactions (Sect. 2.3).

2.1 Information Economics and the Role of Content Quality

At the core of this study is the concept of information economics, which explores how information quality and transparency influence consumer decision-making (Chan 2024). In the context of e-commerce, **product descriptions** are a critical source of information that can significantly affect consumer purchase intentions (Sun et al. 2024). According to the literature, high-quality product descriptions must be *informative, relevant, and tailored to the specific needs and preferences of the target audience* (Heiser 2019).

Effective product texts provide detailed information about the product's features, benefits, and applications, helping consumers make informed purchasing decisions (see Fig. 1). The inclusion of emotional elements and a well-structured format can further enhance the perceived value of the product (Mudambi & Schuff 2010).

The **quality of AI-generated** texts has emerged as a central concern in recent discussions on the use of LLMs in e-commerce (Lin et al. 2024). While LLMs offer efficiency and scalability in content production, there is a growing debate about whether these texts meet the same quality standards as human-written content (Kasneci et al. 2023). Research has shown that consumers often *perceive AI-generated texts as inferior in quality*, particularly in terms of usefulness, relevance, completeness, understandability,

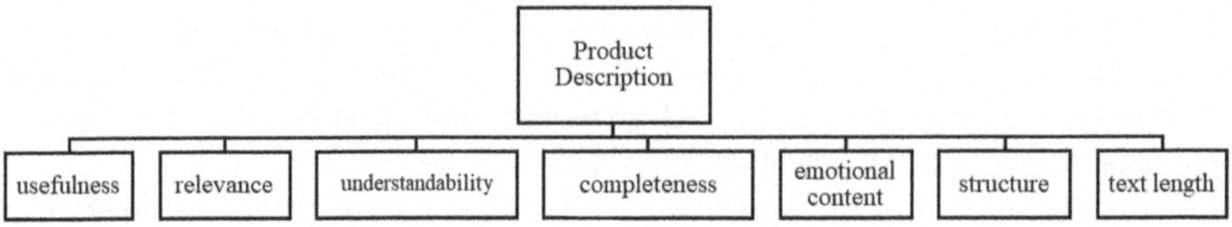

Fig. 1. Elements of Product Descriptions

emotional content, text length, and structure (Mou et al. 2019). This perception can *negatively impact purchase intentions*, suggesting that content quality remains a critical factor regardless of the text's origin (Bundesamt für Sicherheit in der Informationstechnik 2023).

2.2 Consumer Perception and Behavioral Theories

Understanding consumer perceptions of AI-generated texts requires a deeper exploration of theories related to information processing and decision-making. The **elaboration likelihood model** (ELM) proposed by Petty and Cacioppo (1986) provides a useful framework for analyzing how consumers process information about product descriptions. According to the ELM, consumers may process information through two distinct routes: the central route, where they carefully evaluate the *content's arguments*, and the peripheral route, where they rely on external cues such as the *credibility of the source or the presentation style.*

In the context of AI-generated texts, consumers who process information via the central route may focus more on the text's quality attributes, such as clarity, relevance, and completeness. Conversely, those who process information via the peripheral route may be more influenced by the novelty of AI usage or the brand's reputation rather than the content itself. This distinction is crucial for understanding the varied responses to AI-generated content and highlights the need for businesses to ensure high-quality content that satisfies both processing routes (Petty & Cacioppo 1986).

2.3 Transparency and AI Disclosure

Trust and transparency are fundamental to building and maintaining strong consumer relationships in e-commerce. The literature suggests that **transparency** about the use of AI in generating product descriptions can *impact consumer trust* and, subsequently, their *purchase decisions*. However, this impact is not straightforward. While some studies suggest that disclosing AI involvement in content creation might evoke *negative reactions* from consumers due to perceived risks or lack of authenticity, others argue that *transparency can build trust* if the content quality meets consumer expectations (Heiser 2019; Mudambi & Schuff 2010).

In conclusion, the theoretical foundation of this study highlights the **importance of content quality, consumer perception, and trust** in the successful integration of AI-generated texts in e-commerce.

3 Research Method

This research is based on a **mixed-methods approach**, combining both quantitative and qualitative research methodologies to thoroughly examine the impact of AI-generated product descriptions on consumer behavior in the e-commerce context and the importance of text quality. The research design integrates an *online experiment and expert interviews*, providing a comprehensive understanding of consumer perceptions and professional insights regarding the use of LLMs for content generation and optimization.

3.1 Formulation of Hypotheses

The hypotheses developed for this study are grounded in existing literature on consumer perceptions of AI and digital content quality. Figure 2 shows the methodology used in the research project.

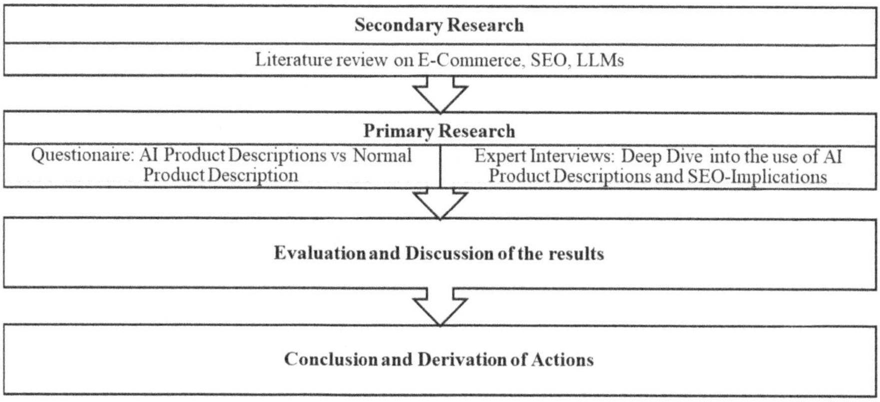

Fig. 2. Research Method

Based on the literature review and the research questions outlined, following five hypotheses and the conceptual model in Fig. 3 were developed in the research project:

- **Hypothesis 1 (H1):** Consumers will perceive AI-generated product descriptions as lower in quality compared to human-written descriptions in terms of usefulness, relevance, completeness, understandability, emotional appeal, text length, and overall structure.
- **Hypothesis 2 (H2):** Disclosure of AI-generated content will not significantly affect consumers' purchase intentions, if the text quality is perceived as high.
- **Hypothesis 3 (H3):** Consumers with a higher familiarity with AI technologies and LLMs will be better at identifying AI-generated texts compared to those less familiar with these technologies.
- **Hypothesis 4 (H4):** There is a positive correlation between the perceived quality of product descriptions and the purchase intentions of consumers, regardless of whether the text is AI-generated or human-written.

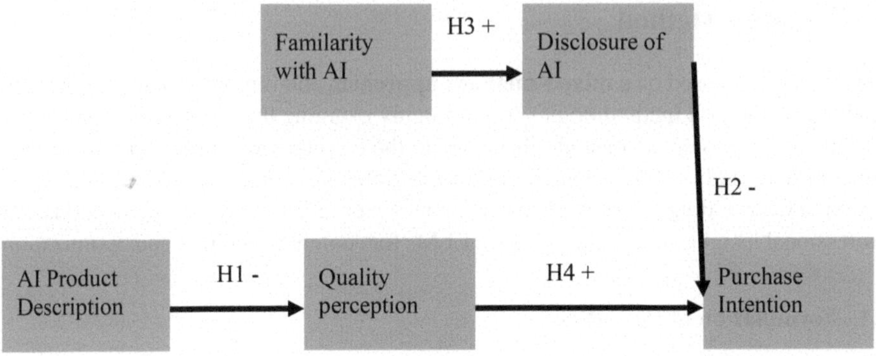

Fig. 3. Conceptual Model on AI-generated Product Texts

3.2 Quantitative Research: Online Experiment

The quantitative aspect of this research is centered around an online experiment designed to evaluate *how consu-mers perceive AI-generated versus human-written product descriptions*, and how these perceptions influence their *purchase intentions*. The experiment was conducted with a diverse sample of participants, recruited through online platforms, including social media and e-commerce forums.

Participants were randomly assigned to one of **two experimental groups**. The first group was presented with *product descriptions generated by an AI model*, while the second group received descriptions *written by human copywriters*. The content in both groups was designed to be comparable in terms of length, structure, and product information provided, differing only in the text generation method. Initially, the participants were unaware of whether the text was AI-generated or human-written. This blind setup aimed to measure the unbiased perception of text quality and the initial purchase intention without any preconceived notions about the text origin.

To gauge the impact of disclosing the text's origin, after the initial evaluation, participants were informed about the *source of the product descriptions*. This revelation (declaration) was used to examine whether awareness of AI-generated content would alter their *perception of text quality* and their subsequent purchase intentions.

A standardized questionnaire was employed to collect data on various aspects, including *perceived usefulness, relevance, completeness, understandability, emotional appeal, text length, and overall structure*. Additionally, participants were asked to rate their *purchase intention before and after the disclosure of the text origin*.

The collected data were analyzed using several statistical techniques. **Descriptive statistics** were employed to summarize the basic features of the data, providing insights into the general trends and patterns in consumer perceptions. **Inferential statistics**, including t-tests, were used to compare the mean scores between the two groups (AI-generated vs. human-written) before and after the disclosure. Regression analysis was conducted to explore the relationships between perceived text quality attributes and purchase intentions, allowing the identification of key factors that influence consumer behavior in response to AI-generated content.

3.3 Qualitative Research: Expert Interviews

To complement the quantitative findings, qualitative research was conducted through **semi-structured interviews** with *industry experts in digital marketing, content creation, and search engine optimization* (SEO). The qualitative component aimed to provide deeper insights into the practical implications, challenges, and future trends related to the use of AI-generated texts in e-commerce. The experts were selected based on their extensive experience and expertise in digital content strategies, AI integration, and consumer engagement.

The interviews were structured around key themes identified from the literature review and quantitative results. These themes included the perceived quality of AI-generated versus human-written texts, the effectiveness of AI tools in content creation, the impact of AI-generated content on consumer trust and engagement, and the strategic considerations for optimizing AI-generated texts for better consumer reception and SEO performance.

During the interviews, experts provided valuable perspectives on the advantages and limitations of using LLMs for generating product descriptions. They highlighted the need for high-quality data and effective content management practices to ensure that AI-generated texts meet consumer expectations and enhance the overall shopping experience. Experts also discussed the importance of *aligning AI-generated content with brand identity and customer needs*, emphasizing that while AI offers scalability and efficiency, the lack of human touch and nuanced understanding can sometimes result in less engaging or persuasive content.

The qualitative data were analyzed using **thematic analysis**, a method that involves *identifying, analyzing, and reporting patterns* within the data. This approach allowed for the extraction of key insights and themes that are relevant to the research objectives. The findings from the expert interviews were then triangulated with the quantitative results to provide a comprehensive understanding of how AI-generated texts are perceived by both consumers and professionals in the field.

3.4 Integrating Quantitative and Qualitative Findings

By combining quantitative data from the online experiment with qualitative insights from expert interviews, this study provides a holistic view of the effects of AI-generated product descriptions on consumer behavior. The mixed-methods approach enables a more nuanced understanding of the complexities involved in consumer perceptions and the practical challenges faced by e-commerce businesses in implementing AI technologies. The integration of both research methods ensures that the study's conclusions are robust and grounded in both empirical data and expert knowledge, providing actionable insights for businesses looking to optimize their use of AI-generated content in digital marketing strategies.

4 Analysis and Results

The analysis of the research results is divided into two main parts: the quantitative analysis of data obtained from the online experiment, and the qualitative analysis derived from expert interviews. This dual approach allows for a comprehensive understanding of how AI-generated product descriptions impact consumer perceptions and behavior in e-commerce settings.

4.1 Quantitative Analysis: Online Experiment

The quantitative analysis focuses on examining how consumers perceive AI-generated product descriptions compared to human-written ones and whether the disclosure of text origin influences their purchase intentions. This section also presents the results of hypothesis testing based on the data collected.

4.2 Consumer Perceptions of AI-Generated vs. Human-Written Texts

The **first hypothesis** (H1) proposed that consumers would perceive AI-generated product descriptions as lower in quality compared to human-written descriptions in terms of usefulness, relevance, completeness, understandability, emotional appeal, text length, and overall structure. The analysis of initial responses from participants, who were unaware of the text origin, supported this hypothesis. The t-test for independent samples shows a mean difference of -0.35268 ($p = 0.011$). *AI-generated texts were generally rated lower across most quality dimensions.* Therefore, H1 is accepted.

4.3 Impact of Disclosure on Purchase Intentions

Hypothesis 2 (H2) posited that the *disclosure of AI-generated content would not significantly affect consumers' purchase intentions if the text quality is perceived as high.* After revealing the text origin, the data showed no significant change in purchase intentions for the majority of participants, thus supporting H2. The average purchase intention slightly decreased from 3.6543 to 3.5000 in the AI-generated text group and slightly increased from 3.6485 to 3.6970 in the human-generated text group upon disclosure, with both changes not being statistically significant (p-values of 0.132 and 0.589, respectively). This suggests that consumers are more influenced by their initial perception of text quality than by knowing whether the text was generated by AI or a human.

4.4 Recognition of AI-Generated Content

Hypothesis 3 (H3) proposed that consumers with a *higher familiarity with AI technologies and LLMs would be better at identifying AI-generated texts* compared to those less familiar with these technologies. The data partially supported this hypothesis. While there was a slight trend indicating that participants familiar with AI were somewhat more likely to recognize AI-generated content, the differences were *not statistically significant*. The Chi-square value of 5.167 with 2 degrees of freedom showed no statistical significance with a p-value of 0.076. This suggests that there is no statistically significant correlation between experience with LLMs and the recognition of AI-generated texts. The symmetrical masses confirmed this finding with a Pearson correlation coefficient of -0.047, indicating a very weak negative correlation. The results show that even experienced users struggle to distinguish between AI-generated and human-written texts, indicating that LLMs have achieved a sophisticated level that can closely mimic human writing styles.

4.5 Correlation Between Text Quality and Purchase Intentions

Hypothesis 4 (H4) predicted a positive correlation between the *perceived quality of product descriptions and the purchase intentions of consumers*, regardless of whether the text was AI-generated or human-written. Regression analysis confirmed this hypothesis, revealing a *positive correlation* ($r = ,549$, $p < ,001$) between perceived text quality attributes—such as usefulness, relevance, and emotional appeal—and purchase intentions. This finding underscores that *high-quality content is a crucial driver* of online buying behavior, irrespective of its origin. Consumers are more likely to purchase products when they perceive the descriptions as clear, relevant, and engaging, which is consistent with prior literature on the importance of content quality in e-commerce.

4.6 Qualitative Analysis: Expert Interviews

The qualitative component of this study provided additional context and depth to the quantitative findings through insights gathered from industry experts. These interviews explored the practical implications, benefits, and challenges of using AI-generated texts in e-commerce.

4.7 Expert Insights on AI-Generated Content Quality

Experts consistently emphasized the *importance of content quality* in driving consumer engagement and trust. While acknowledging the efficiency gains and scalability of AI-generated content, they pointed out several limitations. For instance, experts noted that AI-generated texts often lack the *inspiration and brand alignment* that human writers can provide. This was particularly evident in contexts where *storytelling and nuanced language* play a crucial role in differentiating products and creating a strong brand identity.

Moreover, experts stressed the necessity of *integrating AI tools with content management strategies* to ensure that AI-generated texts are edited and refined to align with brand standards and consumer expectations. They suggested that a hybrid approach, combining AI-generated drafts with human oversight and editing, could be the most effective way to leverage the strengths of both human creativity and machine efficiency.

4.8 Transparency and Consumer Trust

When discussing transparency and the disclosure of AI involvement, experts were divided. Some believed that *clear communication about the use of AI could enhance consumer trust*, especially if the AI-generated content is of high quality. Others argued that disclosure might *not be necessary if the content meets consumer needs and expectations*, as most consumers prioritize the quality and relevance of information over its source.

Interestingly, the qualitative data also revealed that experts view *transparency as a double-edged sword*. While it can foster trust among some consumers, it can also lead to skepticism or disengagement among others, particularly if there is a perception that AI-generated content lacks authenticity. Therefore, the decision to disclose AI use should be carefully considered, taking into account the target audience's familiarity with and attitudes towards AI technologies.

4.9 Future Trends and Strategic Implications

The experts highlighted several emerging trends and strategic implications for e-commerce businesses. One key trend is the increasing sophistication of AI tools, which are becoming better at mimicking human-like writing styles and producing content that resonates more effectively with consumers. However, experts cautioned that as AI technologies continue to evolve, businesses must remain vigilant in their quality assurance processes to ensure that the content generated aligns with their brand values and consumer expectations.

Additionally, the interviews underscored the importance of continuous learning and adaptation. As AI becomes more integrated into digital marketing strategies, businesses will need to develop new skills and capabilities, such as understanding how to train AI models effectively and integrating them with other digital tools to maximize their impact. The ability to balance automation with human creativity and oversight will be critical in maintaining a competitive edge in the rapidly evolving e-commerce landscape.

5 Discussion and Recommendations

The results of this study provide a nuanced understanding of the implications of using AI-generated product descriptions in e-commerce and their impact on consumer behavior. The findings highlight several key insights that are important for e-commerce businesses to consider when integrating AI technologies into their digital content strategies.

5.1 Discussion

One of the most notable findings from the quantitative analysis is that while AI-generated product descriptions are often perceived as lower in quality compared to human-written texts, this perception does not uniformly lead to reduced purchase intentions. This suggests that consumers are primarily influenced by the perceived quality of the content rather than its origin. In other words, if AI-generated texts are crafted to meet high-quality standards—being clear, relevant, and emotionally appealing—they can be just as effective in driving purchase decisions as human-written content. This finding aligns with existing literature that emphasizes the *importance of content quality in digital marketing and consumer engagement* (Mudambi & Schuff 2010).

However, the study also revealed that transparency about the use of AI in generating content has a complex and varied impact on consumer trust and purchase intentions. For some consumers, knowing that a product description is AI-generated does not diminish their willingness to purchase, particularly if they perceive the content to be of high quality. This supports the notion that *transparency, when coupled with quality, can maintain or even enhance consumer trust*. On the other hand, a segment of consumers expressed concerns about the authenticity and reliability of AI-generated content, especially when the perceived quality was low. This suggests that transparency could potentially backfire if not strategically managed, particularly among consumers who are less familiar with AI technologies or have inherent skepticism towards machine-generated content.

The qualitative insights from expert interviews further underscore the importance of content quality and strategic transparency. Experts consistently highlighted that while

AI offers scalability and efficiency in content creation, it often lacks the emotional depth, creativity, and cultural sensitivity that human writers bring. These attributes are crucial in e-commerce, where storytelling and brand identity play an important role in differentiating products and building customer loyalty. Experts recommended a hybrid approach, where AI-generated content is used to create a baseline that is then refined and customized by human editors. This ensures that the final product aligns with brand values and resonates with target audiences.

5.2 Recommendations

Based on these findings, several recommendations can be made for e-commerce businesses looking to leverage AI technologies effectively:

1. **Focus on quality assurance:** Ensuring the high quality of AI-generated product descriptions should be priority. Businesses should invest in *developing robust quality assurance processes that include human oversight and editing*. This hybrid approach can help mitigate potential downsides of AI-generated content, such as a lack of emotional engagement or cultural nuance. By refining AI-generated drafts, businesses can produce content that is not only efficient but also compelling and trustworthy.
2. **Strategic Use of Transparency:** Transparency about the use of AI can be a double-edged sword. While it has the potential to build *trust among tech-savvy consumers*, it can also create skepticism among those who are less familiar with AI or who perceive machine-generated content as less authentic.
   E-commerce businesses should carefully consider their audience's familiarity with AI technologies and their attitudes toward AI-generated content when deciding whether and how to disclose AI involvement. For segments where trust in AI is lower, businesses might *focus more on the quality of the content* rather than the transparency of its origin.
3. **Tailor Content to Audience Preferences:** Different consumer segments may have *varying preferences and levels of acceptance for AI-generated content*. Businesses should leverage data analytics and customer insights to tailor their content strategies accordingly. For instance, younger, more tech-savvy audiences may be more receptive to AI-generated content, while older or more traditional consumers might prefer human-crafted descriptions. Understanding these preferences allows businesses to optimize their content strategies to better meet the needs of their diverse customer base.
4. **Enhance Brand Identity through Human-AI Collaboration:** While AI can handle routine and large-scale content generation tasks, *human writers should still play a crucial role in crafting content that reflects the brand's unique voice and values*. A collaborative approach that combines the *strengths of both AI and human creativity* can result in more engaging and effective product descriptions that foster a stronger emotional connection with consumers. This strategy not only leverages AI's efficiency but also maintains the human touch that is often necessary for building trust and brand loyalty.

In conclusion, while AI-generated texts offer significant advantages in terms of scalability and efficiency, their effectiveness in e-commerce depends largely on maintaining high-quality standards and strategically managing transparency. By adopting a hybrid approach that combines AI capabilities with human creativity and oversight, e-commerce businesses can optimize their digital content strategies, enhance consumer trust, and improve overall market competitiveness.

6 Conclusions, Limitations and Further Research

6.1 Conclusions

This study provides significant insights into the effects of AI-generated product descriptions on consumer behavior within the e-commerce sector. The findings suggest that *while consumers generally perceive AI-generated texts as lower in quality than those written by humans*, this perception does not necessarily impact purchase intentions if the content is perceived as high quality.

The critical factor influencing consumer decisions is the *perceived quality of the content rather than its origin*. Moreover, transparency about the use of AI has a nuanced impact on consumer trust, depending on their initial perceptions and familiarity with AI technologies. These insights underscore the importance of focusing on content quality and strategic transparency to enhance consumer engagement and trust.

6.2 Limitations

Despite its contributions, this study has several limitations. First, the sample size for the online experiment, while diverse, *may not fully represent the broader population* of consumers, limiting the generalizability of the findings. Second, the study focused primarily on textual content; *other forms of AI-generated content, such as images or videos, were not considered*, which could influence consumer perceptions differently. Third, the research was conducted in a *controlled experimental setting*, which might not fully capture the complexity of real-world consumer behavior in dynamic online shopping environments.

6.3 Further Research

Future research should address these limitations by *expanding the sample size and diversity* to include a broader range of demographic groups, international and cultural contexts. Additionally, examining the impact of AI-generated content beyond text, such as *multimedia content*, could provide a more comprehensive understanding of consumer perceptions and behaviors. Further studies could also explore the *long-term effects of AI-generated content on brand loyalty and customer satisfaction*, as well as investigate how different levels of AI transparency influence consumer trust and engagement in various market segments.

By exploring these avenues, future research can build on the findings of this study to provide deeper insights into optimizing AI technologies in e-commerce.

References

Bundesamt für Sicherheit in der Informationstechnik: Große KI-Sprachmodelle: Chancen und Risiken für Industrie und Behörden (2023). https://www.bsi.bund.de

Gao, J., Yu, G., Tao, L.: A method of keywords selection evaluation based on search volume. In: 2010 International Conference on Educational and Network Technology, pp. 25–28 (2010). https://doi.org/10.1109/ICENT.2010.5532118

Heethuis, N.: Four ways artificial intelligence is transforming e-commerce. Forbes (2022). https://www.forbes.com/sites/theyec/2022/02/15/four-ways-artificial-intelligence-is-transforming-e-commerce/

Heiser, A.: Wirkstoff Werbetext: Storytelling on- und offline. Für Konzeptioner, Werbetexter, Grafiker, Autoren, Redakteure und Auftraggeber. Springer, Wiesbaden (2019). https://doi.org/10.1007/978-3-658-26135-1

Mangiaracina, R., Brugnoli, G., Perego, A.: The eCommerce customer journey: a model to assess and compare the user experience of the eCommerce websites. Internet Bank. Commer. **14**(3) (2009). http://www.arraydev.com/commerce/jibc/

Mudambi, S., Schuff, D.: What makes a helpful online review? A study of customer reviews on Amazon.com. MIS Q. **34**, 185–200 (2010). https://doi.org/10.2307/20721420

Mou, J., Shin, D., Cohen, J.F.: Trust and risk in consumer acceptance of e-services. Electron. Commer. Res. **19**(3), 451–486 (2019). https://doi.org/10.1007/s10660-015-9205-4

Petty, R.E., Cacioppo, J.T.: The elaboration likelihood model of persuasion. In: Petty, R.E., Cacioppo, J.T. (eds.) Communication and Persuasion. SSSP, pp. 1–24. Springer, New York (1986). https://doi.org/10.1007/978-1-4612-4964-1_1

Pfeiffer, A.: Webredaktion für Online-Shops: Wie Sie mit optimierten Texten besser verkaufen und ranken. Website Boosting (2016). https://www.websiteboosting.com/magazin/40/webredaktion-fuer-online-shops-wie-sie-mit-optimierten-texten-besser-verkaufen-und-ranken.html

Statista: eCommerce weltweit. Umsatz [Graph]. Statista (2024). https://de.statista.com/outlook/emo/ecommerce/weltweit#umsatz

Veglis, A., Giomelakis, D.: Search engine optimization. Future Internet **12**(1), Artikel 6 (2019). https://doi.org/10.3390/fi12010006

Artificial Intelligence in the Generation of Product Description on the Conversion-Rate

André de Almeida[1] and Darius Zumstein[2](✉)

[1] Digital Business, Do it + Garden, Migros Fachmarkt AG, Limmatstrasse 152 Postfach, 8005 Zürich, Switzerland
andre@dealmeida.org

[2] Digitales Marketing, FHNW School of Business, Institute for Competitiveness and Communication, University of Applied Sciences and Arts Northwestern Switzerland, Riggenbachstrasse 16, 4600 Olten, Switzerland
darius.zumstein@fhnw.ch

Abstract. The efficient creation and adaptation of product description on e-commerce platforms, especially with extensive product catalogues, poses a significant challenge. High-quality product descriptions are crucial for customer engagement and purchase decisions. However, manual text creation is time and resource-intensive, leading to increased costs and delays. The introduction of large language models, such as GPT-3 in late November 2022, has expanded the boundaries of what is possible in terms of text quality through machine processing, offering new opportunities for personalized and dynamic product texts.

This contribution explores to what extent AI-supported text generation models like ChatGPT can optimize the creation of product texts for e-commerce platforms and influence the conversion rate. Using Do it + Garden Migros as an example, the practical applicability and potential impacts of increased investment in this technology are demonstrated. The aim of the work is to develop a cost-effective and scalable solution that can be applied both within the Migros Group and beyond. The use of RPA enhances the innovative approach of this work. The focus is on the impact of AI on the conversion rate, while legal and ethical aspects such as copyright are consciously delimited. Additionally, the influence of AI within the customer journey.

At the core of the work, the current process at Do it + Garden Migros is examined, where new product texts are created only when necessary and by an external text agency, costing CHF 70 per text. For the entire assortment of 40.000 products, the costs would amount to approximately CHF 2.8 million, and the text creation would take 13 to 14 weeks. In an experimental approach, 703 articles were selected to test the efficiency of AI-generated texts. The GPT-3.5-Turbo model was used, resulting in a significant cost reduction from CHF 147′630 to just $0.46 for all selected articles. Moreover, the AI was able to generate texts in three languages in just two hours and 20 min, representing a considerable time saving compared to manual text creation.

The research results demonstrate not only the efficiency and cost-effectiveness of AI-generated texts but also the necessity of continuous monitoring and adjustment of AI models. Overall, the results of the experiment confirm that the use of AI in product text generation has a positive effect on the conversion rate (up

R. C. Geibel and S. Machavariani (Eds.): ISPC 2024, SPBE, pp. 412–426, 2025.
https://doi.org/10.1007/978-3-031-88052-0_34

to a 23.7% increase). In conclusion, a potential new process was outlined, proposed for the future. In summary, this thesis confirms that the formulated goals and hypotheses were achieved and offers solutions that are relevant not only for Do it + Garden Migros but also for other e-commerce platforms, thus making a significant contribution to solving one of the challenges in the e-commerce sector.

Keywords: AI-generated product description · conversion rate optimization · content creation · e-commerce · product management · ChatGPT

1 Introduction

The application possibilities of **artificial intelligence** (AI) have evolved far beyond the scope of research and pilot projects, as exemplified by the adoption of an AI strategy by the German Federal Government in 2018. This strategy can be interpreted as a response to the *growing global competition*, particularly from the USA and China. Large technology companies such as Amazon, Alibaba, Google, Apple, and Microsoft set standards in this sector in terms of applications and investments (Harwardt & Köhler 2023).

The use of AI can bring significant benefits to companies. These include *promoting revenue growth, improving customer service, enhancing competitiveness, meeting increasing customer expectations, and strengthening brand positioning*. Clear concepts, a certain degree of digitalization, high data quality, and the presence of relevant specialists and strategy partners are considered **prerequisites** for the successful use of AI in commercial enterprises. Despite the considerable potential of AI applications, their use in German companies was relatively low in 2021, with only eight percent of companies using AI, compared to six percent the previous year (Harwardt & Köhler 2023).

In the world of e-commerce, detailed **product information** and high-quality content play a crucial role, especially when it comes *to distinguishing oneself from the competition*. It is of great importance that items are presented in a way that is both appealing and attractive, yet faithfully reflects reality. A comprehensive and accurate product description is considered essential for the success of an online shop. Not only does it help to *reduce return rates,* but it also *strengthens customer trust*. Furthermore, well-chosen adjectives can help compensate for the lack of physical experiences such as touch and appearance (Heinemann 2020).

In this dynamic context, the generation of product texts plays an important role as it directly influences purchasing behavior and customer experience. Against this background, this article investigates the *possibilities and impacts of AI-supported text generation in e-commerce*. The relevance of product texts in connection with AI is being researched in collaboration with Do it + Garden by Migros Fachmarkt AG. Methodically, the insights are derived from an **experiment** for the online shop of doitgarden.ch.

The range of Do it + Garden Migros includes areas such as gardening, plants, crafting and designing, cooking and baking, pet supplies, DIY (do it yourself), living, as well as car and motorcycle. According to an internal evaluation, the *online shop comprises over 40,000 items* (Do it + Garden Migros 2024). Due to the broad and diverse range, a comprehensive and differentiated **product description** is required, which can be *time- and resource-intensive.* Especially in the areas of DIY and gardening, *technically precise descriptions* are necessary, which require specialized knowledge. As with many other online shops in Switzerland, **multilingualism** also is a challenge. In Switzerland, it is necessary to offer product texts in several national languages (German, French, and Italian), which increases the complexity of text creation. Additionally, many *suppliers provide little or no product texts*, particularly not in all three national languages. The existing texts are often standardized and used by other online shops as well, which can have a negative impact on search engine optimization. Another aspect is the high proportion of Do it + Garden Migros' **own brands**, for which often *no texts are available* from the manufacturers and the images must be created in their own photo studio. Currently, product texts are created internally on demand or forwarded to *external text agencies, which is both time-consuming and costly.* As a result, very little effort is invested in the generation of product texts.

2 Theoretical Foundation

In the context of designing online shops and enhancing the customer experience, various dimensions and elements can be distinguished. These dimensions reflect the usability of an online shop and illustrate the operability concerning the different phases of the shopping experience. Additionally, aspects of after-sales, such as delivery and returns, also influence the customer experience. For each of these dimensions, specific elements aim to maximize the customer experience (Heinemann 2020). This contribution focuses on the dimension of **product presentation** including product description in the framework by Gerrit Heinemann in Fig. 1.

2.1 Conversion Rate

The conversion rate is a key indicator in e-commerce that measures the ratio of website visitors to those who perform a desired action. This action can vary: from making a purchase to signing up for a newsletter or downloading a product datasheet. In its simplest form, the conversion rate is calculated by dividing the *number of purchases by the total number of website visits* and expressing the result as a percentage.

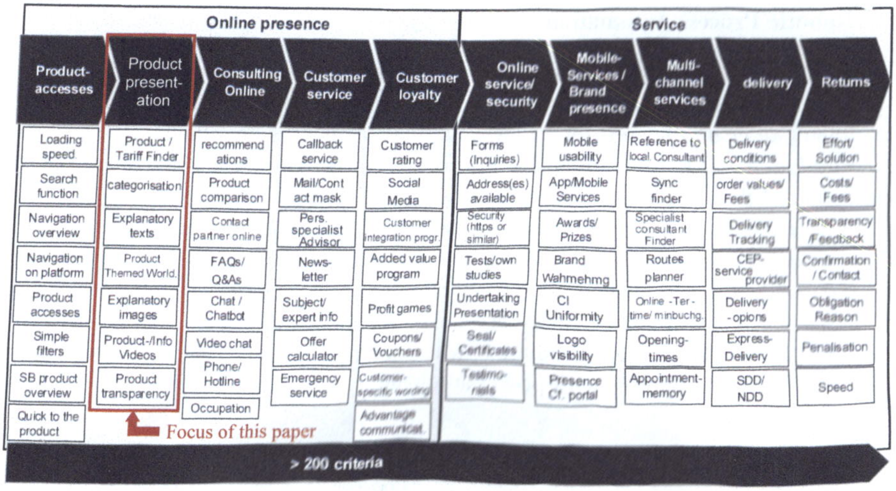

Fig. 1. Product description in the framework by Gerrit Heinemann *(Source:* Heinemann, 2023, *p. 134)*

Product descriptions are a crucial factor in increasing the conversion rate in an online shop. They are not just an information tool but also an essential sales tool designed to spark customer interest and encourage purchases (Heinemann 2022).

2.2 Natural Language Processing

The experiment relies on the application area of natural language processing (NLP). Essentially, NLP focuses on enabling computers to *understand, interpret, process, and generate human language*. It encompasses a range of techniques and methods, from simple rule-based approaches to advanced machine learning models like large language models (LLMs). Core concepts of NLP include *tokenization* (splitting text into smaller units), *syntax analysis* (analyzing grammatical structure), *semantics* (meaning of words and sentences), and *pragmatics* (use of language in contextual situations; Kreutzer 2023).

3 Previous Research

A recent study published in the "International Journal of Research in Marketing" investigates how machine writing of wine and beer reviews can be realized. The research demonstrates that AI was able to create expert reviews from a limited set of product attributes (metadata). A **Turing test** showed that machine-generated descriptions could not be distinguished from human-written descriptions by experts. The study suggests that machines could create an initial draft that is then refined by an expert, thereby supporting the creation of thousands of product texts (Carlson et al. 2023).

3.1 Robotic Process Automation

The interplay of artificial intelligence (AI) and robotic process automation (RPA) offers innovative approaches to automating product text generation. AI brings the capability to *generate creative and context-aware texts*, while RPA focuses on *automating repetitive and rule-based tasks*. **RPA tools** like Microsoft Power Automate and UiPath play a central role in this.

RPA enables companies to *automate processes and tasks to save time and minimize human errors*. RPA software uses bots that learn to operate across applications and independently perform complex tasks, ranging from data transfer automation to inventory management. RPA can be customized for *specific tasks across industries and departments*, offering numerous benefits (Microsoft n.d.). Figure 2 gives an overview of Microsoft's solution options with power automate.

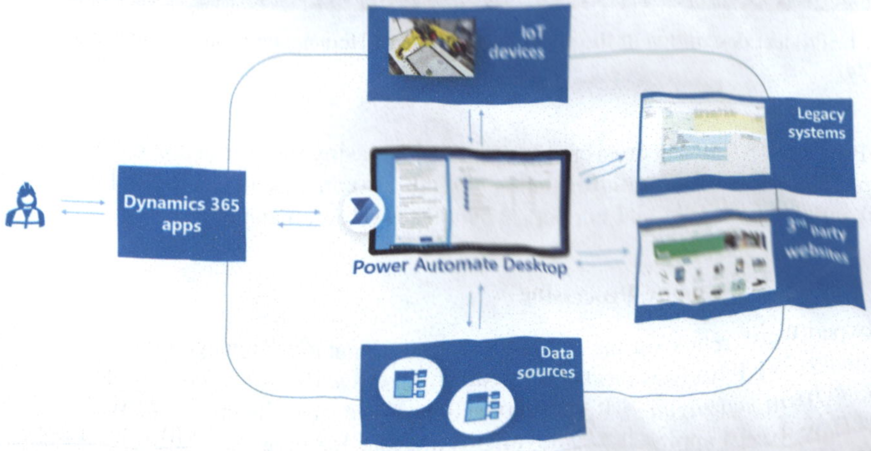

Fig. 2. Overview of Solution Options with Power Automate (Source: Microsoft 2023)

AI models like ChatGPT are used to create high-quality product texts. RPA tools like Power Automate and UiPath complement this by *integrating AI-generated texts into various systems, adjusting formats, and automating the placement of texts in the product management process*.

Overall, the combination of AI and RPA, supported by tools like Power Automate or UiPath, enables innovative and efficient product text generation, ensuring both quality and speed without heavily relying on human resources.

4 Research Method

The selection of the appropriate AI solution for generating product texts was a crucial step in the pilot project. Given the variety of available generative AI systems like Jasper, Neuroflash, and ChatGPT, a thorough evaluation was necessary. Although various provi were considered, **ChatGPT from OpenAI** emerged as the most compelling option. This choice was based on a comparative test of text quality, though the comparison is not further elaborated here.

The texts generated by ChatGPT demonstrated high quality and were well-suited for this experiment. However, generating each text individually via chat would have been impractical and not scalable due to time constraints. Thus, using the **API** (Application Programming Interface) proved advantageous, enabling access to OpenAI's completion functions. Although there are API solutions based on chat, the completion API seemed simpler for beginners in implementing a KI interface. These models are trained to generate complementary texts (*completions*) based on given inputs (*prompts*), making them ideal for this experiment.

At the start of the experiment in February 2023, OpenAI's "**davinci-002**" was the most advanced model available for completion. While other better models were initially available only for chat applications, they did not yet offer the necessary API integration. By the end of August 2023, the enhanced **GPT-3.5-Turbo** version became accessible for the completion API. This development allowed replacing the older davinci-002 model for more efficient text generation. Implementing GPT-3.5-Turbo brought *significant improvements in text quality and efficiency* (OpenAI, n.d.). The text generation implementation using OpenAI's API was realized through Power Automate Desktop. The decision to use Power Automate Desktop was based on its greater flexibility and expandability for future applications, such as *extending the process to transmit data into a PIM* (product information management) *or editing Excel files*. The simplified system context of this solution is shown in Fig. 3, describing the interaction of Power Automate in this experiment.

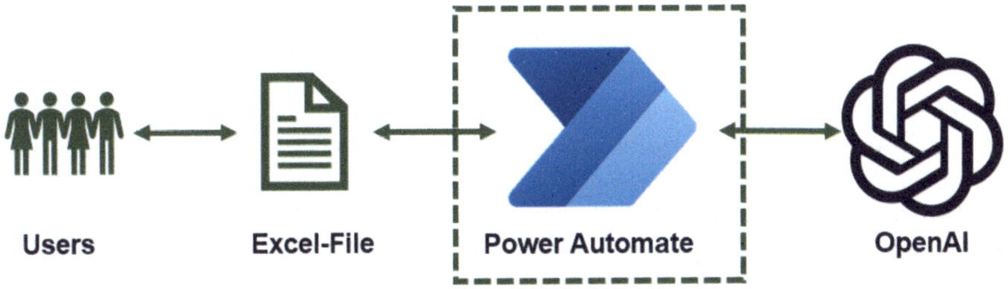

Fig. 3. System Context of Power Automate

4.1 Programming Power Automate

The foundation is an Excel document containing the data to be processed, also known as product metadata (compare Fig. 4). Power Automate Desktop is configured to read this Excel file and define where the processing of the last row ends. This is crucial to avoid endless loops in the automation process, which would otherwise send infinite requests to OpenAI's API and generate unnecessary texts, incurring costs.

The Power Automate bot is programmed to communicate with **OpenAI's server**. It sends the template texts defined in Excel as prompts to the API. These query processes to

Fig. 4. Reading Excel for Text Generation

OpenAI via Power Automate Desktop is shown in Fig. 5). The responses from OpenAI, in JSON format, are directly written into the designated fields in Excel and converted into text. This process is performed separately for each language, including French and Italian. Each row in Excel is individually sent to OpenAI's server to generate unique texts for each item. The loop logic ensures row-by-row processing, incrementing the variable after each transmission to prevent processing the entire content as a single text. Additionally, the work status is saved after each step to avoid a complete restart in case of a system failure.

Unlike the web version of Power Automate, the desktop variant offers additional functions, such as transferring the *generated texts into the PIM system*. While the web solution does not support this type of data transfer, the desktop variant provides a broader range of automation possibilities.

Developing this **automation process** was iterative and challenging. Without expert knowledge in automation, numerous attempts and adjustments were needed to establish a functioning solution.

Despite initial hurdles, this **implementation** represents a *cost-effective and insightful solution to gain initial insights into the feasibility and effectiveness of AI-supported text generation*. Implementing Power Automate Desktop marks an innovative step in automating product text generation without needing IT resources. It demonstrates how *modern automation tools combined with AI technologies can be used to develop efficient and scalable solutions for e-commerce challenges*. A similar approach with another RPA tool like UiPath is conceivable.

4.2 The Right Prompt

The currently used **prompt** is: "*Write a product description in German without superlatives and end sentences with a period. Do not use German double S. Template: %CurrentItem%.*" These instructions aim to promote clear and concise language and set stylistic guidelines. %CurrentItem% refers to the template in Excel, which includes all necessary product metadata. This prompt offers various expansion possibilities, such as a stronger focus on *SEO-relevant aspects or specific target audience addressing* (informal/formal or neutral).

For this experiment, a straightforward approach was chosen to test the basic principles of prompt design and limit complexity.

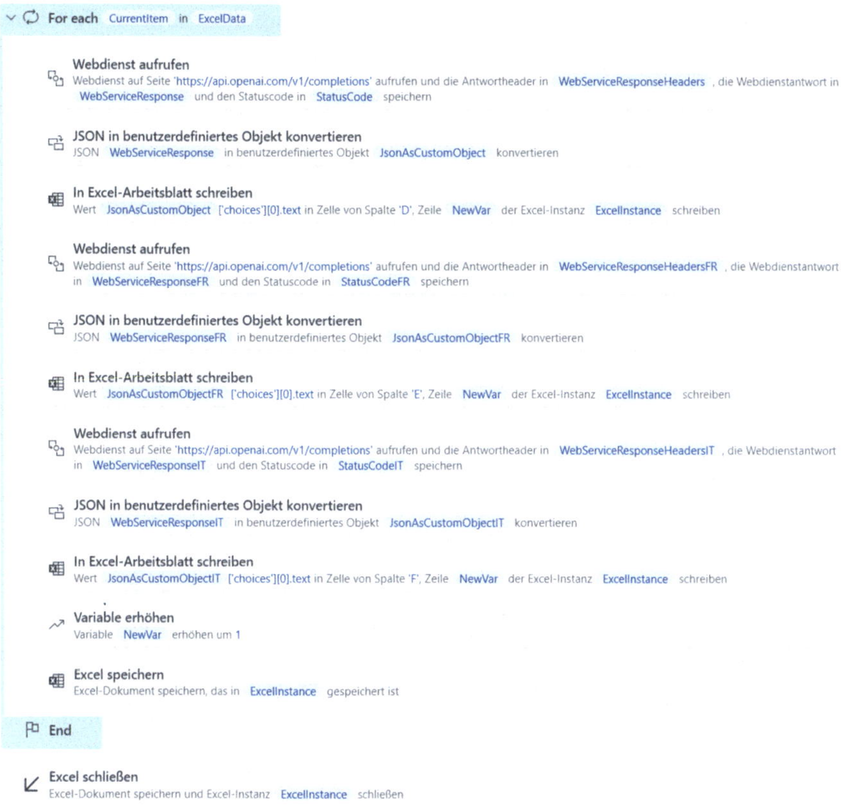

Fig. 5. Query to OpenAI via Power Automate Desktop

Experiments show that *precise prompt formulation is essential for the quality of generated texts*. A well-thought-out prompt helps the AI capture and implement the desired text characteristics, increasing the effectiveness of the entire text generation process. Careful prompt design is a critical step in leveraging AI technologies for text creation. It enables the targeted control of the AI model's generative capabilities to produce high-quality, functional product descriptions.

4.3 Product Selection

Careful product selection is also a crucial factor for the meaningful evaluation of the success of AI-supported text generation. In September 2023, a targeted selection was made, considering several criteria to maximize the significance of the results.

The **selected products** should n*ot be subject to strong seasonal fluctuations and should not be part of sales promotions* in the following weeks. This approach ensures that any changes in performance are attributable to the new product texts and not to external factors.

The **test** focused on *niche products that have moderate frequency but are not top sellers*. This allowed measuring the impact of the new texts on products whose sales figures typically do not exhibit high volatility. By applying these criteria, *703 items remained*. Unfortunately, A/B testing was technically not possible at that time.

5 Analysis and Results

The duration of text generation is a crucial aspect when evaluating the efficiency of AI-supported solutions compared to traditional methods. In this pilot project, Power Automate Desktop was used to *generate texts for 703 items*. The results clearly show the superiority of AI-based text creation in terms of speed (Table 1).

Table 1. Duration AI vs. Human

Solution	Duration (articles per hour)
GPT-3.5 Turbo solution	300
Texting agency	3

It is important to note that both AI-supported and human text creation require a **high-quality template**. The effort for creating these templates is roughly the same for both methods and was not included in the time calculation. The AI solution's superiority is even more pronounced when considering that it generates 300 articles per hour in all three languages, while a human can only manage three articles in one language.

5.1 Cost Comparison

Comparing the **costs** between a texting agency and GPT-3.5 Turbo from OpenAI reveals a significant difference. A single text costs about CHF 70 per article in one language at the texting agency. For the 703 items used in the experiment, translating into all *three languages would cost a total of CHF 147.630*. In contrast, the cost for GPT-3.5 Turbo is only *USD 0.46*. Although content quality was not considered in this calculation, every company must decide how much it is willing to pay for texts, especially if they are rarely read, as is often the case with niche products.

The results highlight the importance of carefully selecting the AI model, considering costs and desired functionality. For projects prioritizing efficient and cost-effective text generation, GPT-3.5 Turbo offers a compelling solution.

5.2 Key Metrics

The focus is on the in-depth examination of the generated texts. It evaluates where text generation was particularly successful and where there is room for improvement. Primarily, the overall development across all 703 items is considered.

The switch to AI-generated product texts had a significant impact on various **key performance indicators** (KPIs). Table 2 shows, that an evaluation after 21 days shows

Table 2. Uplift of AI-Generated Product Texts for Different KPIs (Source: Internal Google Analytics)

KPI	Uplift after 21 days	Uplift after 39 days	Uplift after 68 days
Unique purchase	83%	86%	7%
Product detail views	48%	58%	−5%
Conversion rate	23.7%	17.5%	12.2%
Organic traffic	21.6%	22.6%	31.3%

a significant *uplift of the conversion rate (CR)* by 23.7%. Noteworthy is also the increase in *product detail views* (PDV) by 48% within 21 days.

Moreover, the AI-generated product texts increased the number of purchased by 83% within 21 days and 86% within 39 days (compare Table 2).

A reduction in views compared to the initial state is mainly due to the unavailability of some of the 703 items. A detailed analysis shows that 163 items, which are no longer available in the shop, accounted for about 20% of the views. This explains the weaker comparison numbers after 68 days compared to previous periods.

5.3 New Process

Based on the experiences and insights from the experiment at Do it + Garden Migros, a potential target process for generating product texts was designed, which can be adopted by all companies of Migros Fachmarkt AG. This process was designed using a **BPMN model** (business process model and notation) shown in Fig. 6.

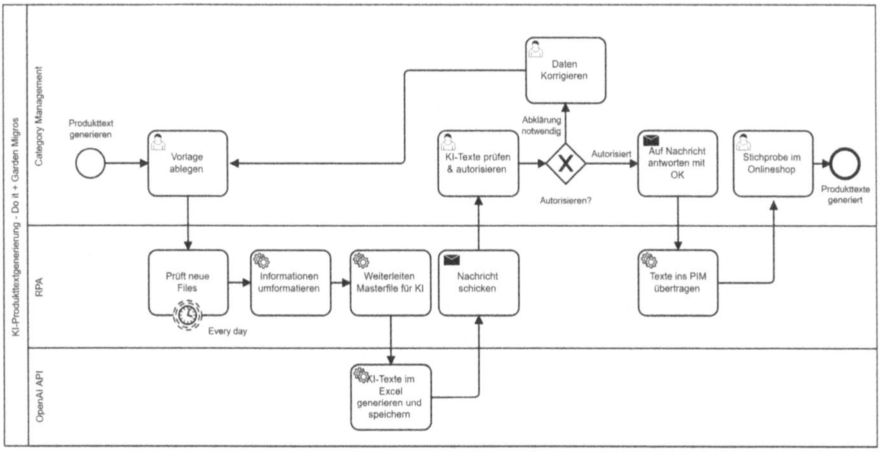

Fig. 6. Simple BPMN Representation of a Possible TO-BE Process

The process starts when a **product manager** identifies the need for *new product texts for the existing or new assortment*. The supplier's template with relevant product data is stored in a defined SharePoint folder, checked daily by a bot, which triggers the process when a new file is added. An **RPA robot** extracts the information from the *supplier template and prepares it for AI text generation.* This includes summarizing all relevant product information into one field per article. The prepared data is transferred to an Excel file for AI text generation. Using **OpenAI's API interfaces**, *texts for each article and language are generated and inserted into the Excel file.* An automated message is then sent to the requester. This person reviews the AI-generated texts and authorizes their use via a defined e-mail address. This triggers another flow, and the **transfer to the PIM** is carried out by the bot. If the text is faulty, it is manually corrected or supplemented with further data, and the process starts anew. Once the texts are transferred to the PIM, the published text is randomly checked on the online shop. Then the process is complete.

This is a simplified representation of the process. Due to internal peculiarities of Do it + Garden Migros, a few additional steps are necessary, which are not depicted here. If the sample shows errors, a follow-up process is needed. This should not be further elaborated here, and this process serves as an idea generator for a future process around the generation of AI texts for product descriptions. The human review of the texts can be omitted in the future, but it is still recommended to review the texts manually.

Occasionally, **AI tends to exaggerate or be inaccurate**. In the long term, direct integration of AI into systems like SAP or PIM should be enabled to directly retrieve data and generate texts. It is emphasized that this process is flexible and can be adapted based on further experiences. Other companies could implement similar processes, with adjustments to the specific needs and structures of each company.

5.4 SWOT Analysis

The result of this work reveals that the use of an AI solution brings both numerous advantages and some disadvantages. To examine these aspects in more detail and gain a comprehensive understanding of the implications, a SWOT analysis was conducted (see Fig. 7). This analysis allows for the systematic identification and evaluation of the strengths, weaknesses, opportunities, and threats of AI-based content generation, providing a deep understanding of the complex dynamics of this technological innovation.

5.4.1 Strengths

AI can *quickly generate large amounts of content, leading to significant time and resource savings.* Automated systems guarantee *uniform quality and style across various contents,* essential for brand coherence. AI offers the flexibility to easily create content for a wide range of platforms and formats, *increasing the reach and accessibility of the content.* In addition, AI enables the *customization of content based on user preferences and behavior*, leading to an improved user experience. Massive *long-term cost savings* make AI a cost-effective alternative to traditional content creation by reducing reliance on manual processes.

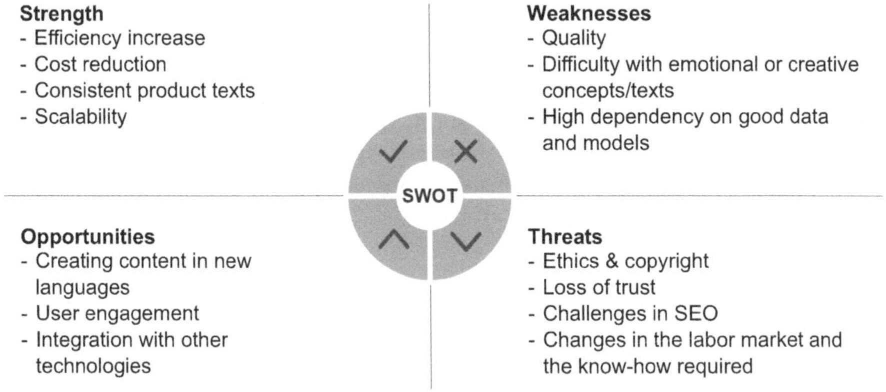

Fig. 7. SWOT Analysis of the Results

5.4.2 Weakness

The *quality of AI-generated content can vary* and may not reach the level achieved by human creativity and expertise. AI has limitations in capturing complex *creative concepts and emotional nuances*, restricting its ability to create content with deeper emotional or figurative content. This deficit in understanding finer nuances and contexts limits AI's application in certain creative and sensitive areas. Additionally, the quality of AI-generated content is highly dependent on the *quality of the underlying data and models used*. Inadequate or biased data can lead to inaccurate or misleading content, affecting the reliability and credibility of AI-generated content.

This dependency on data and models underscores the importance of careful data selection and preparation, as well as the continuous development and adaptation of AI models.

5.4.3 Opportunities

AI offers the opportunity to *create content specifically for niche areas or in different languages*, allowing Do it + Garden Migros to offer the online shop in more languages. This ability to efficiently and effectively adapt content for various target groups significantly expands market potential and enables more precise market targeting. Using AI allows for the creation of *targeted and highly relevant content* that is precisely tailored to the interests and needs of users. Engaging content can significantly increase user engagement, leading to increased user retention and interaction. This directly impacts customer satisfaction and ultimately business results.

The integration of AI with other advanced technologies such as RPA, virtual reality (VR), and augmented reality (AR) opens new dimensions in content creation and offers unique user experiences. By combining these technologies, innovative and interactive content can be created that surpasses traditional media limits, allowing companies to stand out in a competitive market and create unique brand experiences.

5.4.4 Threads

The use of AI in content creation leads to *ethical and copyright issues*, particularly regarding the authenticity and originality of the content. User skepticism towards AI-generated content, especially in areas requiring authenticity, could undermine trust in this technology. *SEO challenges* arise from adjustments to search engine algorithms that can affect the visibility of AI content. Additionally, there is a risk of labor market changes.

6 Discussion and Recommendations

The results show that the use of AI in product text generation increases the conversion rate by up to 23.7%. From this, seven recommendations for Do it + Garden Migros and other online shop operators arise.

6.1 Scaling AI Text Generation

AI text generation should be *expanded to more products and content*. Adjustments to various product categories ensure consistency and quality. This *increases visitor frequency and conversion rate*, while the costs for text generation remain low. Customers benefit from *more detailed product information*, which facilitates purchasing decisions and builds trust.

6.2 Customer Satisfaction

High-quality, relevant, and engaging product descriptions *increase customer satisfaction*. Customer preferences and feedback should be regularly collected and evaluated to ensure that the *texts meet expectations*.

6.3 SEO Optimization

AI-generated content should be adapted to SEO best practices to i*ncrease visibility in search engines*. This includes keywords, meta descriptions, and structured data to improve discoverability and ranking. Higher visitor frequency and conversion rates can *boost sales*.

6.4 Measurement and Analysis

Continuous monitoring and analysis of the performance of AI-generated texts are crucial. Analytics tools like Google Analytics help assess the effectiveness of the content and identify improvement opportunities.

A monitoring system should continuously track the performance of the texts and allow for adjustments.

6.5 Optimization of AI Models

Regular review and adjustment of AI models improve their accuracy and relevance. Testing with various parameters and newer models like GPT-4 is recommended to enhance text quality.

6.6 Ethical Standards and Legal Requirements

AI-generated content must comply with *ethical guidelines and legal requirements.* Accuracy, avoiding misleading information, and adhering to data protection and copyright regulations are essential.

6.7 Real-Time Adjustments

Systems for quickly adapting content to current trends, market developments, or customer feedback should be implemented. Real-time data can be used for *dynamic content updates* to continuously increase relevance and effectiveness. These recommendations aim to improve the efficiency and effectiveness of AI-supported text generation and fully exploit its potential in e-commerce. They provide starting points for future optimizations and research in AI-supported content creation.

7 Conclusions, Limitations and Further Research

Reflecting on the challenge identified in the introduction regarding the creation and customization of product texts for e-commerce platforms, it is evident that the development and implementation of AI-powered text generation models offer a promising solution to effectively address this challenge. The results of this work reflect the successful attempt to tackle the mentioned challenges using AI and RPA. The **practical application and potential** of these technologies were demonstrated through the example of Do it + Garden Migros, yielding valuable insights. These insights indicate that the goals formulated in the introduction were comprehensively achieved and that the solutions developed are applicable not only to Do it + Garden Migros but also to other e-commerce platforms. Thus, the use of these technologies could represent a far-reaching solution to one of the biggest challenges in the e-commerce sector (ChatGPT 2024).

Although the developed technology is promising, especially in combination with other technologies such as RPA, it must be acknowledged that it *cannot entirely eliminate the challenges of text generation.* For instance, the **AI technology** occasionally tends to *hallucinate or exaggerate.* Additionally, unresolved questions, such as those regarding copyright, need to be addressed. Despite these limitations, the potential of the technology for the future is evident, particularly in the context of its integration into complex systems.

Future studies could, for example, focus on the application of *AI for SEO purposes* or further explore the generation of product texts. Expanding to other industries and examining the applicability in different business contexts would provide a more comprehensive understanding of the potentials and limitations of AI in the digital economy. Furthermore, research on the advancement of digital strategies in companies would be significant.

Another relevant research field is the **ethics of AI**, especially concerning data protection and the quality of generated texts. It is essential to highlight the unresolved issues in the use of AI and to present perspectives for future developments. A precise analysis of the specific reasons for variations in the conversion rate among the test articles could provide important insights to enhance the efficiency of AI text generation and better understand its impact on the conversion rate.

A recent study on the quality assessment of human and AI-generated texts would also be of interest, particularly in comparison to previous studies such as the 2020 article "AI Beats Human?!" (Theobald et al. 2020). A current comparison could reveal how much the technology has advanced since then.

The results of this contribution align with the findings of a recent study from the "International Journal of Research in Marketing," which dealt with generating expert texts from a limited set of product attributes. This study suggests that machines could potentially create initial text drafts in the future, significantly supporting the creation of thousands of product texts (Carlson et al. 2023). These parallels confirm the relevance and timeliness of the findings achieved in this research.

References

Carlson, K., Kopalle, P., Riddell, A., Rockmore, D., Vana, P.: Complementing human effort in online reviews: a deep learning approach to automatic content generation and review synthesis. Int. J. Res. Mark. **40**(1), 54–74 (2023). https://doi.org/10.1016/j.ijresmar.2022.02.004

Do it + Garden Migros: tgarden.ch. Von Startseite, 04 January 2024. https://www.tgarden.ch/deabgerufen

Harwardt, M., Köhler, M.: Künstliche Intelligenz entlang der Customer Journey. Springer, Wiesbaden (2023). https://doi.org/10.1007/978-3-658-39109-6

Heinemann, G.: Der neue Online-Handel. 13. Auflage. Springer, Berlin (2022)

Heinemann, G.: The New Online Retail – Business Models, Business Systems and Benchmarks in e-Commerce, 13 edn. Springer, Berlin (2023). https://doi.org/10.1007/978-3-658-40757-5

Kreutzer, R.T.: Künstliche Intelligenz verstehen. Springer, Berlin (2023). https://doi.org/10.1007/978-3-658-42598-2

Microsoft: Übersicht über RPA-Vorlagen und Dynamics 365. Abgerufen am 15. 01 2024 von Power Automate (2023). https://learn.microsoft.com/de-de/power-automate/desktop-flows/dynamics365-rpa-overview

Microsoft: Benefits of RPA. Abgerufen am 05. 12 2023 von Power Automate (n.d.). https://powerautomate.microsoft.com/de-ch/benefits-of-rpa-robotic-process-automation/

OpenAI: OpenAI docs. Abgerufen am 08. 01 2024 von deprecations (n.d.). https://platform.openai.com/docs/deprecations

Theobald, E., Malthaner, M., Föhl, U.: KI schlägt Mensch?! HMD Praxis der Wirtschaftsinformatik, pp. 922–936. Abgerufen am 05. 12 2023, 1 Oct 2020

Integrating Data Ethics in Smart Cities: Insights from Leading European Cities

Carmen Birkle and Claudia Hess(✉)

IU International University of Applied Sciences, Erfurt, Germany
birkle@carmenbirkle.de, claudia.hess@iu.org

Abstract. The paper presents the results of a multiple case study analyzing how leading European smart cities implement data ethics within their digital strategies and manage algorithmic discrimination risks. The case study compares the ethical strategies of Barcelona, Hamburg and Darmstadt, selected for their leadership in digitalization, their data ethics strategies, and their pioneering role as smart cities. Specifically, it examines how data ethics are integrated into the cities' digital strategies and how algorithmic discrimination risks are addressed. It also discusses which stakeholders need to be sensitized to the risks of algorithmic discrimination and shows what leading smart cities are doing to reach these stakeholders. The case study included an analysis of publicly available information on the digital strategies and their implementation in the three selected smart cities, as well as interviews with experts involved in urban digitalization and the implementation of smart city strategies. Based on these findings, recommendations on how to integrate ethical issues into smart city strategies were derived, which can serve as guidelines for cities striving for responsible and inclusive digital strategies.

Keywords: Smart City · Data Ethics · Algorithmic Discrimination · Digital Strategy · Case Study

1 Introduction

Smart cities are urban areas that use different technologies to collect and analyze real-time data to improve the quality of life for residents, reduce environmental impact, and optimize urban operations. Despite these potentials, smart cities must actively deal with ethical issues. Collecting and analyzing urban data can create surveillance risks and social tensions. This could not only threaten the fundamental idea of freedom in our society, but also create new power structures and dependencies. Therefore, the ability of cities to responsibly use and protect data becomes increasingly important.

The research presented in this paper analyzes how leading smart cities address these issues. The focus of the study is primarily on cities within the European Union (EU), with a special emphasis on Germany, because of the comparability of legal, cultural, and technological conditions. The following research questions were formulated:

1. How do leading smart cities integrate data ethics concepts into their digital strategies?

R. C. Geibel and S. Machavariani (Eds.): ISPC 2024, SPBE, pp. 427–441, 2025.
https://doi.org/10.1007/978-3-031-88052-0_35

2. How do leading smart cities address the risk of algorithmic discrimination in their digital strategies?
3. Which stakeholders in particular need to be sensitized to the risks of algorithmic discrimination and how can this be done?

Based on these research questions, the study aims to develop recommendations for smart cities to effectively implement ethical principles and promote an equitable and inclusive future.

To this end, the paper is structured as follows. Section 2 provides the theoretical foundation on smart cities and data ethics. Section 3 describes the research method for the multiple case study, including the expert interviews and their analysis. Section 4 presents the perspectives on data ethics that are used to analyze smart city approaches. In addition, it explains the selection of cities to be included in the case study. Then, Sect. 5 analyzes and compares the smart city approaches of the selected cities of Barcelona, Hamburg and Darmstadt, while Sect. 6 answers the research questions and derives recommendations. Finally, Sect. 7 concludes the paper.

2 Theoretical Foundation

This section introduces the concept of smart cities, motivates the importance of dealing with ethical issues in the context of smart cities and outlines basis on data ethics as well as relevant legal regulations.

2.1 Smart Citys

The term smart city encompasses multiple interpretations and underlines the complex nature of the concept. The European Commission (n.d.) defines smart cities as places that use digital solutions to make networks and services more efficient for the benefit of residents and businesses. This definition emphasizes the optimization of urban structures through technology to increase the quality of life. Gassmann et al. (2019, p. 25) highlight the targeted use of digital technologies to minimize resource consumption and promote sustainable urban development with a focus on efficiency and resource conservation. These perspectives show the large span of smart city concepts, from technology to sustainability and well-being. They show the importance of a balanced approach that combines innovation, social inclusion, environmental protection and quality of life, and illustrate that a true smart city considers the many facets of urban life that go far beyond technology (Joss et al. 2019).

2.2 The Importance of Data Ethics in Smart Cities

The increasing use of technologies and automated systems to collect, analyze and manage data in smart cities raises numerous ethical questions. These relate in particular to the privacy of citizens, transparency in the use of data, access to and control over personal data and the security risks associated with the storage and processing of large amounts of data (O'Neil 2017). Responsible handling of this data is crucial to gain the citizens' trust and avoid misuse or unwanted discrimination.

One specific example is the use of surveillance cameras equipped with facial recognition technology. While these systems can increase security in urban areas, there is a risk that they will be misused for mass surveillance and that citizens' behavior will be monitored without their knowledge or consent. Another example is the use of sensors and IoT devices to monitor traffic flow and air quality, as well as the collection and analysis of usage data from public services such as smart parking or public transportation. While this data can provide valuable insights for improving urban infrastructure, the data collected could be misused to create movement profiles of individuals. To prevent this invasion of citizens' privacy, strict ethical guidelines and data protection measures are required.

These examples illustrate the need for data ethics in smart cities. Data ethics encompasses standards and principles for the appropriate handling of data to ensure fairness, transparency and respect for user privacy (Hemel 2023). Responsible data management should minimize the risks that can arise from the misuse or unethical use of data. This includes not only ensuring privacy and the protection of sensitive information, but also ensuring that algorithms and data analytics processes are not unfairly biased towards certain population groups. Furthermore, equitable access to data-based services is emphasized.

2.3 Algorithmic Discrimination in the Context of Smart Cities

Further risks in the context of smart cities arise due to automated decision-making systems that leverage algorithms, machine learning, and artificial intelligence (AI) to make decisions without human intervention. These systems process large volumes of data, identify patterns, and generate outputs that inform or make decisions in various domains, from healthcare to finance, and in the context of smart cities, in areas such as traffic management, public safety, and resource allocation. One specific risk is that such algorithms contain biases or prejudices. A well-known real-world example relevant in the context of Smart Cities is an algorithm used to predict crime in an American city that suggested a disproportionate number of patrols in certain ethnic neighborhoods due to biased input data (O'Neil 2017). This led to unbalanced surveillance, exacerbated social tensions and worsened the relationship of trust between citizens and the police.

To develop policies that address these issues related to handling sensitive data and algorithmic decision making, the root causes of algorithmic discrimination must first be understood. The causes of algorithmic discrimination discussed in the literature (European Union Agency for Fundamental Rights 2019; O'Neil 2017; Orwat 2019) can be classified into three categories as shown in Fig. 1.

First, *socio-cultural and structural causes* of algorithmic discrimination arise from entrenched societal inequalities, systemic biases, social norms, and unequal access to resources, all of which are reflected and perpetuated in the data used to train algorithms. A further aspect is the lack of diversity in the IT sector and especially in the development teams. Second, *technical and methodological causes* of algorithmic discrimination relate to the inherent weaknesses and limitations of the algorithms themselves, as well as the methods used to collect and process data, which can lead to biases and unfairness in the results. Third, *economic and regulatory causes* involve the incentives for economic efficiency and competitive advantage that may discourage thorough scrutiny and correction of biased algorithms, coupled with insufficient legal frameworks to address and prevent discrimination.

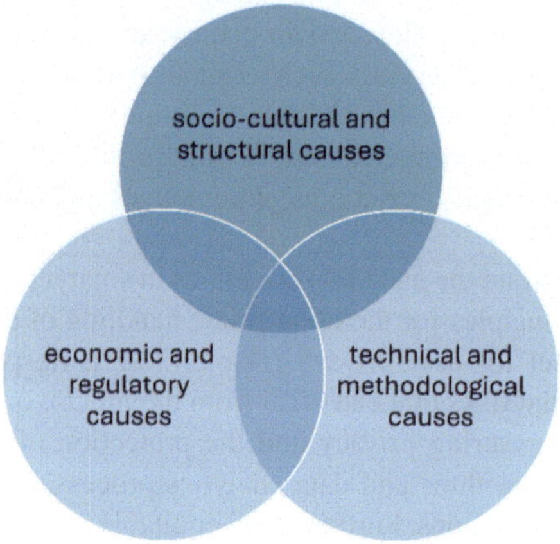

Fig. 1. Causes of Algorithmic Discrimination

Several approaches have been proposed and are in use to prevent algorithmic discrimination. Examples include Tim Berners-Lee's 5-star model for open data, or the AlgoRules developed under the lead of the Bertelsmann Stiftung, which define ethical principles and rules for the design of algorithmic systems.

2.4 Legal Regulations in Data Management for Smart Cities

In the context of smart cities, legal regulations play a crucial role in ensuring that the vast amounts of data collected and processed are managed responsibly and ethically. Regulations, such as the General Data Protection Regulation (GDPR) in the European Union, establish strict guidelines for data privacy, consent, transparency, and security to protect the rights of individuals while enabling technological advancements. Recent developments include regulations on AI, such as the AI Act by the European Union which categorizes AI systems according to risk classes and requires strict transparency and supervisory standards. These measures are intended to ensure that innovation and data protection remain in balance. Compliance with these regulations requires cities to implement robust data governance frameworks, conduct regular audits, and ensure transparent and accountable data handling practices.

3 Research Method

To answer the research questions, a multiple case study was conducted following the methodology defined by Yin (2018). The methodology is outlined in the following sections.

3.1 Multiple Case Study

According to Yin (2018) a case study is an empirical investigation that is used to explore complex phenomena in detail, within the context of their real-world application. A multiple case study involves an in-depth, comparative analysis of several individual cases to identify patterns, draw insights, and develop a comprehensive understanding of the phenomenon under investigation. The multiple case study presented here analyzes and compares the digital strategies of different smart cities to explore similarities and differences in dealing with aspects of data ethics, and to derive robust and generalizable findings. Yin suggests an iterative process that includes the following six phases: (1) plan, (2) design, (3) prepare, (4) collect data, (5) analyze, and (6) share a report. Central outcomes of the first two phases were the research questions and clearly defined primary objectives of the case study (see Sect. 1).

In the *preparation phase*, a systematic literature search was carried out, taking into account publications by state institutions and cities in addition to academic literature. These n = 301 sources were evaluated according to defined inclusion and exclusion criteria. Key works that discuss aspects of data ethics in smart cities were identified and categorized, and a concept matrix according to Webster & Watson was developed. This resulted in a first set of perspectives on data ethics (see Sect. 4.1) which were refined in the subsequent phases of the multiple case study. Moreover, three smart cities were selected for the multiple case study (see Sect. 4.2). It was ensured that these cities can indeed provide insights into the research questions, both through publicly available data and the availability of experts for in-depth interviews.

The *data collection phase* included both a literature review and expert interviews. The expert interviews (see Sect. 3.2) were invaluable as they provided insights and perspectives that complemented the literature review of the official documents of smart cities and their digital strategies. In particular, the expert interviews were used to investigate whether and how these self-imposed guidelines are actually implemented. This combination of data from the literature and expert interviews also represents the triangulation of data according to Yin (2018). In this case study, it led to an iterative implementation of phases three and four. The next phase, i.e., the *analysis* of the literature review and the expert interviews was conducted using qualitative content analysis (see Sect. 3.3). The final phase included *sharing the results* with the experts involved.

3.2 Expert Interviews

The interviews were conducted as semi-structured interviews to ensure well-founded and representative results. The interview guide was structured on the basis of the perspectives on data ethics for smart cities derived from the literature. Experts were selected based on their specific knowledge of smart cities and data ethics. Twelve people were contacted, three of whom responded positively: Experts from Darmstadt and Hamburg as well as an independent person for smart city projects. The interviews were conducted in April 2024 using Microsoft Teams and lasted approximately 45 min each. Audio was recorded. The interviews were documented using an expert protocol and transcription. During the documentation, the data was anonymized, and the experts are named E1, E2, E3 in the following. The transcription followed predefined transcription rules to ensure methodological rigor and readability. The interviews were analyzed with the help of the MAXQDA analysis tool.

3.3 Qualitative Content Analysis

Qualitative content analysis is defined as a methodically controlled form of text and data analysis in which obvious and hidden content is systematically examined (Kuckartz & Rädiker 2022). The focus is on the use of categories to code the research material, which enables an in-depth interpretation of the data. Categories identify specific topics, arguments or figures of thought within a text. A hierarchical category system with clearly defined category definitions ensures consistency and accuracy in the analysis. Comprehensive analyses are achieved through deductive, inductive or combined approaches to category formation. In this study, a combined deductive-inductive approach was used. First, categories were derived from the literature, i.e., the perspectives on data ethics for smart cities (see Sect. 4.1). They served as the basis for the analysis of smart city documents, the structuring of the interview guide, and the analysis of the expert interviews. The categories were refined with sub-categories during these analyses through inductive category formation, resulting in a hierarchically structured set of perspectives on data ethics for smart cities. This hybrid approach exploits the strengths of both methods: the theoretical foundation of the deductive method and the data-supported flexibility of the inductive method.

4 Preparation of the Case Study

This section describes the results of the preparation phase of the multiple case study, in particular the perspectives on data ethics deductively derived from the literature and the selection process of the smart cities to be considered.

4.1 Perspectives on Data Ethics for Smart Cities

The relevance of data ethics in the design of smart cities is particularly emphasized in various works by German and European institutions and foundations. Key publications include the report of the Data Ethics Commission (Datenethikkommission der Bundesregierung 2019), the Smart City Charta (2021), Carsten Orwat's study on algorithmic discrimination risks (Orwat 2019). These works deal with ethical issues, set standards and highlight the risks and opportunities of digital technologies. A distinction can be made between aspects that are aimed directly at municipalities and cities and those that are primarily intended for higher-level institutions, supervisory authorities and public bodies. The latter are addressed in particular by the requirements for more extensive specifications for legislation and standardization, as well as for the design of supervisory and competence structures. In the following, the focus is on those aspects that directly affect cities and municipalities and should play a decisive role in their digitalization agendas. Table 1 provides an overview of the perspectives on data ethics for smart cities.

Table 1. Categories of Perspectives on Data Ethics for Smart Cities

Perspective on Data Ethics	Description
Ethical Governance and Public Responsibility	Aspects that affect the ethical and responsible management and administration of public institutions in the digital space, with a special focus on maintaining transparency, justice and autonomy in decision-making processes
Transparency and Accountability in Data Practice	Aspects relating to ensuring transparency and responsibility in the use and management of data in digital systems. This includes the disclosure of data usage and decision-making processes and ensuring their traceability and accountability
Risk Management and Ethical Technology Assessment	Aspects relating to the proactive assessment and management of the risks and consequences of the use of technology, with a focus on data quality, fairness and the ethical implications of algorithms. This also includes the use of specific rules and mechanisms that serve to ensure the responsible and ethical use of technology
Inclusive Participation and Accessibility	Aspects relating to the promotion of equal participation in the city's digital and analog resources, with a particular focus on accessibility, education and the design of inclusive public spaces
Ethics Knowledge Transfer and Resource Empowerment	Aspects that focus on building and sharing knowledge about data ethics within and between smart cities, as well as empowering resources to support ethical governance, education, and diverse representation in decision-making processes

4.2 Selection of the Smart Cities for the Multiple Case Study

The following considerations were paramount in selecting the cities for the multiple case study. On the one hand, cities that are leaders in terms of digitalization (criterion 1) should be considered to draw well-founded conclusions and, based on these, to be able to make precise recommendations for action. For this, the Bitkom Smart City Index for the years 2019 to 2023 was used. All German cities that were ranked at least once in the top 10 of the overall assessment were considered. Hamburg impressed with its consistently high ranking in the index, which characterizes the city as a consistent leader in the field of digital urban development in Germany.

On the other hand, it was of interest to include cities that may not be leaders in digitalization but have already defined data ethics principles and strategies (criterion 2). This criterion focused on German cities that stand out for their initiatives in data ethics, ethics concepts, and corresponding strategies. The Smart City Atlas of Bitkom

e. V. (2019), which includes profiles of 50 German cities, served as a key source of information. Darmstadt stood out in particular for its approach to ethical issues, including the establishment of a responsible body, the Ethics and Technology Advisory Board. This makes Darmstadt a pioneer in digital ethics in Germany and Europe. Despite fluctuating positions in the Smart City Index, it was precisely this leading role in data ethics that was decisive for the choice of Darmstadt for the case study.

These dual perspectives ensure a comprehensive analysis of the current status and potential in the context of smart cities. In addition, despite the primary focus on Germany, the importance of internationality was taken into account (criterion 3) by including a leading European city in order to create opportunities for comparison with European neighbors and to add an international dimension to the analysis. Barcelona was selected due to its outstanding reputation as a European showcase city in the field of smart cities.

5 Analysis and Results

This section presents the smart city approaches of the selected cities of Barcelona, Hamburg and Darmstadt. The three cities are then compared in terms of their implementation of the perspectives on data ethics.

5.1 Presentation of the Smart Cities Included in the Multiple Case Study

For each city, the historical development of the city as a smart city is presented, the current digital strategy is briefly outlined, and the key institutions are introduced.

5.1.1 Hamburg

Hamburg began its digitalization efforts long before an official smart city strategy was published. One key project is smartPORT, initiated by the Hamburg Port Authority in 2013, which is driving forward the integration of individual parts of the port using IoT, AI and other technologies. These technologies are used for real-time control of traffic and goods flows in the Port of Hamburg, including adaptive traffic control for moving bridges. In addition, the Ministry of Culture and Media recognized the importance of digitalization for the cultural sector in the same year and developed two digitalization strategies: the eCulture Agenda 2020 and later BKMdigital. These initiatives aimed to build digital cultural infrastructures and support urban education and integration concepts.

It was not until two years later, in February 2015, that Hamburg published its digital strategy and integrated the ongoing projects into this framework (Rose 2015). The strategy aimed to increase Hamburg's quality of life and economic strength through technological innovations, develop digital offerings and promote networking between companies, institutions and citizens. The State Council was established as the main steering group, and the Digital City Control Center coordinated all urban digital projects until the end of 2017. In January 2018, the newly implemented Office for IT and Digitalization (ITD) took over the tasks. The ITD acts as a steering committee. It monitors compliance with the digital strategy and ensures that ethical guidelines are followed. Implementation takes place throughout the city, following the principle of "centralized control - decentralized implementation" as stated by expert E3. In 2020, the digital strategy was revised, and version 2 was published (Freie und Hansestadt Hamburg 2020). The main goal is to benefit all citizens, make people's everyday lives easier and address urban challenges. Broad acceptance is to be ensured through transparency, openness and citizen participation.

5.1.2 Darmstadt

Darmstadt, with a population of approximately 162,000 people, strives to act as an international pioneer by demonstrating how technology can facilitate everyday urban life. The city aims to be attractive and liveable, offering solutions that are valuable to both citizens and science. This vision includes the secure and confident handling of data and the sustainable use of resources (*Digitalstadt Darmstadt*, n.d.). Digitalization efforts in Darmstadt gained significant momentum when the city won the Bitkom "Digital City" competition in 2017. As a pioneering city in the state of Hessen, Darmstadt also benefited from the support of the Hessian state government. In 2017, Darmstadt founded Digitalstadt Darmstadt GmbH (DDG) as a wholly-owned subsidiary of the city as part of the Smart City initiative in order to successfully drive forward its development into a smart city. Although Darmstadt's special approach of bundling its digitalization efforts in a company allows for greater flexibility and stronger links to municipal commercial enterprises, it is also perceived critically as a foreign body within the city administration, which, according to expert E2, requires continuous communication and persuasion. In addition, the Ethics and Technology Advisory Board and the Sponsors Advisory Board were established, both of which are assigned to the DDG.

With the introduction of the ethical guidelines for the development of the digital city in 2019, Darmstadt demonstrated its lighthouse position as it was the first city in Germany to implement such an initiative. In the ethical guidelines, Darmstadt defines nine fundamental principles that guide the actions of the DDG and all stakeholders. Darmstadt's digital city strategy was finally published around a year later. Among other things, it defines the vision, strategic elements such as core objectives, lighthouse topics and fields of action.

5.1.3 Barcelona

Barcelona, Catalonia's capital and Spain's second largest city, has been a pioneer in the smart city movement, with its efforts dating back to the turn of the 21st century, significantly ramping up in the early 2010s. These projects were criticized for not addressing the actual needs of citizens and instead focusing exclusively on economic efficiency. This changed in 2015 with a political shift and a reorientation of the digital strategy. In 2016, the city's new digital plan was published, which pursued the vision of a democratic, inclusive and sustainable digital society. This is achieved through a strategic approach to data, which is seen as a social good and belongs to the citizens (Barcelona Ciutat Digital 2018).

With the publication of the digital plan, the Municipal Data Office and the Commission for Technology and Digital Innovation were established. These bodies are responsible for exploiting digital potential, setting standards and monitoring compliance with the principles of the digital strategy. While the Municipal Data Office is also responsible for communicating the digital strategy and providing further training, the Commission for Technology and Digital Innovation focuses specifically on the privacy and security of the technologies used (Barcelona Ciutat Digital 2018). Barcelona's digital strategy is reinforced by the Code of Technological Practices, which plays a central role in management technology projects. Aimed at the city's Information Technology Institute and other municipal units and departments, it covers the design of all the city government's digital services. At the heart of this code are the development of agile digital services, the use of open standards and free software, and the ethical and secure management of data. The code is complemented by the Agile Methodologies Guide, which covers topics such as interoperability, agility, reusability, ethical practices, and open knowledge and technologies, and the Technological Sovereignty Guide.

5.2 Implementation of Data Ethics Perspectives in the Selected Smart Cities

5.2.1 Ethical Governance and Public Responsibility

All three cities integrated ethical considerations into their digital strategies and concretized through frameworks and guidelines that govern the ethical use of data. Transparency, privacy and responsible use of technology are emphasized. In Barcelona, the concept of data ethics is deeply embedded in the digitalization documents, while the issue of algorithmic discrimination is also very present in Hamburg. There, discrimination is deliberately addressed and iteratively examined to ensure continuous adaptation and improvement of strategies. Darmstadt formulates fundamental ethical principles in its ethical guidelines. To ensure compliance with these ethical guidelines, special committees have been set up, such as the Municipal Data Office in Barcelona, the ITD in Hamburg, and the DDG with the Ethics and Technology Advisory Board in Darmstadt. This approach establishes responsibilities and accountability mechanisms for ethical data handling.

5.2.2 Transparency and Accountability in Data Practice

Assessing transparency and accountability in data practices includes aspects such as data provenance and auditability to ensure data traceability, open data exchange and accessibility as well as transparency about the algorithms used. To promote openness and transparency, Barcelona, for example, uses open-source software and makes data available on an open data platform. The data available on the platform meets the fifth level of the 5-star model for efficient use. Despite the well-designed benefits of open-source solutions, challenges such as scalability and seamless integration with existing systems can arise. Darmstadt introduced the data platform12 in February 2021. It collects and analyzes anonymous data such as traffic and air quality data to support urban decisions and improve the quality of life in Darmstadt through citizen participation. Although the use of AI would have the potential to further optimize this process, it is currently not used for these purposes in Darmstadt according to expert E2. In Hamburg, the Urban Data Platform was developed in 2017. This platform connects decentralized urban data sources based on the existing geodata infrastructure. Its aim is to make data usable for new digital services and business models using technologies such as machine learning.

The platform serves not only the administration, but also civil society in the form of a cockpit, science and business, and is managed by the Urban Data Hub as coordinating team (Freie und Hansestadt Hamburg 2020).

5.2.3 Risk Management and Ethical Technology Assessment

Active risk management and technology assessment should proactively address the potential ethical risks of technological decisions, mitigate biases in data practices, and thus protect the well-being of citizens. In this context, E1 (2024) points out the problem that technology assessments often only exist on paper and that documents that bear the title rarely contain the content of a real technology assessment. In Hamburg, the ITD checks the compliance of submitted projects with the specified framework conditions and standards, e.g. with regard to user orientation, impact, sustainability, open data principles as expert E3 explained, similar to a technology assessment. However, there is a lack of transparent communication about which aspects are assessed by whom and how. Point 8 of Darmstadt's ethical guidelines stipulates that a technology assessment must be carried out for every project. However, this does not correspond to practice. It is confirmed that a comprehensive technology assessment is often considered almost impossible and is therefore only carried out for critical projects, such as the data platform. However, the corresponding reports are not publicly accessible, as required by the ethical guidelines. The digital strategy of Barcelona shows in all documents that there is an awareness of the potential social impact of technologies but does not explicitly refer to a technology impact assessment. It is not possible to assess the extent to which impact assessments or bias and fairness audits are carried out.

5.2.4 Inclusive Participation and Accessibility

Smart cities should ensure that services are accessible to all citizens, including people with disabilities. To evaluate accessibility as an indicator of potential discrimination through digital offerings, the official websites of the three focus cities were checked in April 2024 using the W3C and WCAG validators. Although the Barcelona Discrimination Observatory Report 2022 did not show any direct cases of discrimination through digitalization measures, the website analysis revealed technical deficiencies that could affect accessibility for people with disabilities. In Hamburg's website, no shortcomings were found; the city offers comprehensive accessibility, including multilingual and easy-to-understand content as well as sign language, making it the leader among the city websites analyzed. Darmstadt's website, on the other hand, has clear accessibility deficiencies, but the city has already taken steps to address them.

Darmstadt uses various formats such as round tables and citizen participation platforms to encourage citizen involvement and feedback. Platforms such as Decidim in Barcelona allow citizens to participate directly in the design of digital processes, promoting transparency and enabling continuous improvements. Hamburg emphasizes accessibility and participation by making digital offerings multilingual and accessible to all. These inclusive practices are essential to effectively reach and support all population groups, as emphasized by expert E1.

5.2.5 Ethics Knowledge Transfer and Resource Empowerment

An important aspect in the context of algorithmic discrimination is training and knowledge transfer on ethical issues as well as diversity in leadership and development teams. For example, Barcelona actively supports the systematic exchange of knowledge through platforms such as Decidim, which promote international cooperation and municipal innovation. In Hamburg, the networking and exchange with other cities to share best practices is highlighted by expert E3. Moreover, Hamburg requires diversity in development teams in tenders to minimize the risk of discrimination. Darmstadt provides recommendations for action and knowledge exchange by its white book. However, diversity and ethics training were not specified in past tenders in Darmstadt.

6 Discussion and Recommendations for Smart Cities

Based on the analysis and comparison of the three selected cities, the research questions can be answered. The first research question asked how leading smart cities are integrating data ethics concepts into their digital strategies. In particular, the aspects in the first perspective, i.e., ethical governance and public responsibility, were relevant. Overall, the focus cities demonstrate through their structured approaches to digital strategy development how they can systematically integrate ethical considerations into the use of technology and the management of data. All of them had established institutions that are directly responsible for these tasks. However, transparency in procurement and decision-making processes should be further improved.

The second research question discussed how leading smart cities are addressing the risks of algorithmic discrimination in their digital strategies. The analysis of the three cities shows that a coordinated approach is needed to effectively integrate algorithmic discrimination into urban strategies. These include educational initiatives and comprehensive preventive and monitoring measures that are firmly anchored in the processes. Educational initiatives, such as the DDLitLab in Hamburg, create a fundamental awareness base through cooperation with universities and educational institutions. Furthermore, regular ethics training and further education for municipal employees is crucial in order to anchor the necessary knowledge in dealing with algorithmic discrimination. Cooperation with external consultants and research institutions is also essential to ensure access to the latest technological findings and to develop innovative, ethically sound solutions. In summary, comprehensive participation platforms and accessibility guarantee that all citizens have equal access to digital resources and can actively participate in the digital transformation.

The third research question asked which stakeholders in particular need to be sensitized to the risks of algorithmic discrimination and how this can be done. Key stakeholders in this process include city authorities, technical teams, ethics committees and the general public. As emphasized by expert E1, this requires coordinated cooperation between many stakeholders who must work towards a common goal. One-sided views, cultural differences, isolated specialist departments, political alignments and unclear strategy documents can present obstacles and hinder progress in digitization efforts. An essential component is therefore not only to ensure transparency and accountability for data management, but also to clearly document all other decision-making processes with the goal to strengthen citizens' trust in digital city projects.

Based on these findings, the perspectives on data ethics for smart cities have been refined as shown in Table 2.

Table 2. Refined Perspectives on Data Ethics for Smart Cities

Perspective on Data Ethics	Sub-Categories
Ethical Governance and Public Responsibility	• Emphasis on Ethical Aspects in the Digital Strategy • Ethical Policy Development • Institutional Accountability • Public Oversight and Participation • Transparency in Procurement and Decision-Making Processes
Transparency and Accountability in Data Practice	• Data Provenance and Auditability • Open Data Exchange and Accessibility • Disclosure of Algorithms • User Consent and Awareness • Regular Transparency Reports
Risk Management and Ethical Technology Assessment	• Impact Assessments • Bias and Fairness Audits • Data Quality Assurance • Ethical AI Guidelines • Privacy and Security Measures
Inclusive Participation and Accessibility	• Accessible Design • Equity in Data Access • Community Engagement Platforms • Digital Literacy Programs
Ethics Knowledge Transfer and Resource Empowerment	• Ethical Training Programs • Inter-Municipal Ethical Collaboration • Diversity in Leadership and Development Teams • Community Knowledge Hubs

7 Conclusion and Limitations

The multiple case study conducted dealt with digitalization and data ethics in smart cities based on the analysis of three cities, with a focus on understanding the effective integration of ethical principles into the digital strategies of cities. The research aimed to understand approaches that minimize the risks of algorithmic discrimination and promote broad awareness, always with the common good in mind. The geographical focus was on smart cities in the European Union, particularly in Germany, which limits the transferability of the results to cities in other global contexts with different legal, cultural and technological conditions. Using the literature as a basis, perspectives on data ethics for smart cities were identified and used to systematically analyze and compare the selected cities. To create a robust and comprehensive data foundation, different sources were reviewed and analyzed through qualitative content analysis. Publicly available information on the strategies and implementation of the smart city approaches of the three selected cities was collected. Additionally, three expert interviews were conducted. One limitation of the study is that no expert from Barcelona could be interviewed. A key result of the study is an expanded catalog of the perspectives on data ethics for smart cities that could be used in future studies. The different perspectives could be enriched with concrete approaches from leading smart cities as best practices.

References

Barcelona Ciutat Digital: Barcelona City Council Digital Plan: Government measure concerning ethical management and accountable data: Barcelona Data Commons (2018). https://www.barcelona.cat/digitalstandards/en/data-management/0.1/_attachments/barcelona_data_management_0.1.en.pdf

Bitkom e.V. (ed.): Smart-City-Atlas (2019). https://www.bitkom.org/sites/default/files/2019-03/190318-Smart-City-Atlas.pdf

Bundesinstitut für Bau-, Stadt- und Raumforschung (BBSR), & Bundesministerium des Innern, für Bau und Heimat (BMI) (eds.): Smart City Charta (2021). https://www.bmwsb.bund.de/SharedDocs/downloads/Webs/BMWSB/DE/veroeffentlichungen/wohnen/smart-city-charta-2021.pdf;jsessionid=9AA9D1BA77EF5F69AF68B117E2AEC341.live891?blob=publicationFile&v=2

Datenethikkommission der Bundesregierung: Gutachten der Datenethikkommission (2019). https://www.bmi.bund.de/SharedDocs/downloads/DE/publikationen/themen/it-digitalpolitik/gutachten-datenethikkommission-kurzfassung.pdf?blob=publicationFile&v=4

Digitalstadt Darmstadt: Digitalstadt Darmstadt (n.d.). https://www.digitalstadt-darmstadt.de/. Accessed 6 Sept 2024

European Commission: Smart cities (n.d.). https://commission.europa.eu/eu-regional-and-urban-development/topics/cities-and-urban-development/city-initiatives/smart-cities_en. Accessed 5 Sept 2024

European Union Agency for Fundamental Rights: Data quality and artificial intelligence: Mitigating bias and error to protect fundamental rights. Publications Office (2019). https://data.europa.eu/doi/10.2811/546219

Freie und Hansestadt Hamburg: Digitalstrategie für Hamburg (2020). https://www.hamburg.de/resource/blob/230646/115a3934734fbbcfe65497ba5f857fff/download-digitalstrategie-2020-data.pdf

Gassmann, O., Böhm, J., Palmié, M.: Smart Cities: Introducing Digital Innovation to Cities. Emerald Publishing Limited (2019). https://doi.org/10.1108/9781787696136

Hemel, U.: Datenethik zwischen gesellschaftlichem Anspruch und betrieblicher Praxis. In: Gillhuber, A., Kauermann, G., Hauner, W. (eds.) Künstliche Intelligenz und Data Science in Theorie und Praxis, pp. 93–105. Springer, Heidelberg (2023). https://doi.org/10.1007/978-3-662-66278-6_7

Joss, S., Sengers, F., Schraven, D., Caprotti, F., Dayot, Y.: The smart city as global discourse: storylines and critical junctures across 27 cities. J. Urban Technol. **26**(1), 3–34 (2019). https://doi.org/10.1080/10630732.2018.1558387

Kuckartz, U., Rädiker, S.: Qualitative Inhaltsanalyse: Methoden, Praxis, Computerunterstützung: Grundlagentexte Methoden, 5th edn. Beltz Juventa (2022)
O'Neil, C.: Weapons of Math Destruction: How Big Data Increases Inequality and Threatens Democracy B/D/W/Y Broadway Books (2017)
Orwat, C.: Diskriminierungsrisiken durch Verwendung von Algorithmen: Eine Studie, erstellt mit einer Zuwendung der Antidiskriminierungsstelle des Bundes. Nomos (2019)
Rose, W.: Die Digitalisierung der großen Stadt 14 January 2015. https://www.hh-heute.de/die-digitalisierung-der-grossen-stadt/
Yin, R.K.: Case Study Research and Applications: Design and Methods, 6th edn. Sage, Thousand Oaks (2018)

Overcoming Clayton Christensen's "Innovator's Dilemma" Through Employee-Supported Entrepreneurship

Johannes Nünning(✉)

Senior Corporate Innovation Manager and Self-Employed Strategy Consultant for Innovators, Bonn, Germany
j.nuenning@gmail.com

Abstract. The paper analyses key building blocks of Clayton Christensen's groundbreaking study from his book "The Innovator's Dilemma" (1997). With reference to a case study of an established company which empowered its employees to realize their business ideas and eventually start-up fully owned new companies, the author asks why the highly regarded analysis of Christensen who also delivered proposals to manage the Dilemma did not enable established companies to take advantage of disruptive technologies and innovation in a similarly groundbreaking way. Based on his own experience with Corporate Innovation, the Innovator's Dilemma, and his findings from the case study the author then argues to address the Innovator's Dilemma on a higher level. He suggests that new regulatory means could unleash the full potential of innovators who happen to be employees for the common good.

Keywords: Innovator's Dilemma · Case Study · Intrapreneurship · Spin-off · Startup · Innovator · Regulation · Common Good

1 Introduction

Clayton Christensen's "Innovator's Dilemma" posits a critical challenge for innovation leaders of established companies. In essence it can be described as that well established companies eventually fail after disruptive technologies enter their markets, even if they did everything right (1997, p. X).

Based on a case study, this paper presents potential answers as to if and how established companies could manage the Innovator's Dilemma in a new way. For the author, it is time for new solutions for dealing with the Dilemma as even after Christensen's groundbreaking research from more than 25 years ago it seems to be still the case that most established companies fail to adapt to disruptive technologies whilst it is often Startups who conquer their market instead - leveraging disruptive technologies which in the 21st century oftentimes are enabled by digitalization to an even greater extent compared to Christensen's era (Statista 2024a, 2024b, 2024c, 2024d).

Why do successful companies fail, even though the building blocks of both disruption and corresponding solutions are well understood with Christensen's work for decades

R. C. Geibel and S. Machavariani (Eds.): ISPC 2024, SPBE, pp. 442–455, 2025.
https://doi.org/10.1007/978-3-031-88052-0_36

now? How could feasible strategies look like which truly embrace Christensen's findings to manage the Innovator's Dilemma, and how to bring them into effect?

As an example, this paper refers to how a large enterprise allowed the launch of an innovation program which supported its employees to realize their own potentially disruptive business ideas and, over time, allowed them to start their own companies along the way.

2 Theoretical Foundation

2.1 Framework

Clayton Christensen's "The Innovator's Dilemma" explores why successful companies often fail when exposed to disruptive technologies, i.e. as both emerging markets and correspondingly meaningful strategies are unpredictable to start with (1997, p. XXI).

Christensen shows that incumbents tend to *not* focus on disruptive innovations because of their nature of, at least from the beginning and in relation to the existing business, them being less (or not) profitable, technologically less capable and because of their meaningfulness to a niche market audience only to start with (1997, p. 228). Christensen also highlights that emerging markets are rather small at the beginning such that the corresponding activities are too small to affect the company's trajectory in relation to its core business (1997, pp. XX–XXI). Christensen's study illustrates how technological advancements initially offer minimal value before they eventually accelerate to provide significant improvements, and at a later stage, as their impact fades out, small increments remain only, whilst the amplitude and pace of such developments would be unpredictable from the start (1997, p. 39).

Thus, Christensen finds, all of which would make it appear to be more meaningful for incumbent's decision makers to keep their focus on creating sustainable innovation instead of relying on risky, small, and costly ventures.

2.2 Corporate Innovation's Conflict of Interest

Christensen's framework helps explain the dilemma faced by corporate innovators: whether to focus on sustaining innovations that improve existing products or to invest in disruptive innovations which might have the potential to redefine their given industry over time.

Christensen, referring to innovations within the disk drive industry, highlights that established companies were bound to their given business as their current customers with their given demands are incentivizing them to stay put, and that they might misjudge the future potential of new technologies (1997, p. 43).

With his framework of established companies being bound to their "resources-processes-values" (1997, p. 166), or RVP (1997, p. 29), Christensen explains that also the capability of the organization to be ready to deal with disruptive technologies would be as important as the skill of the responsible innovators picked by managers. He again refers to leading disk drive manufacturers of his time out of which "no company had a routinized process for handling (the advent of disruptive technologies, the author)"

(1997, p. 167). Furthermore, because the disruptive products promised lower profit margins per unit sold and could not be used by their best customers, these innovations were inconsistent with the leading companies' values. The leading disk drive companies had the resources - the people, money, and technology - required to succeed at both sustaining and disruptive technologies. But their processes and values constituted disabilities in their efforts to succeed in disruptive technologies." (1997, p. 167).

For Christensen, it all comes down to successful companies being bound to their successes, referenced by him as i.e. their dependency to their given Resources, Values and Processes (RVP), which basically would blur their capability to grasp the potential of disruptive innovation also for the creation of shareholder value (1997, p. 29).

2.3 Strategic Implications

While Christensen considers these conditions as being both facts and a dilemma, he elaborates on how to change the situation such that taking advantage of disruptive technologies would become a meaningful task for existing companies (1997, p. 168):

2.3.1 Circumventing Given RVP

Christensen concludes that when it comes to managers facing the need to change or innovate, "They need to be sure that the organization in which those resources will be working is itself capable of succeeding - and (…) managers must scrutinize whether the organization's processes and values fit their problem.", for in the case they were incapable he proposes three options (1997, p. 168):

- The acquisition of a different organization
- Change of the given organization
- Separate out an independent organization.

2.3.2 Top Management's Role

Christensen finds that "when a threatening disruptive technology requires a different cost structure (…), or when the current size of the opportunity is insignificant relative to the growth needs of the mainstream organization, then - and only then - is a spin out organization a required part of the solution." (1997, p. 176). Apart from referring to that the spun-off project "cannot be forced to compete with projects in the mainstream organization for resources" (1997, p. 176), he highlights that "only the CEO can ensure that the new organization gets the required resources" (1997, p. 176). Christensen states that he had seen no exceptions from the rule that the very CEO's personal and attentive oversight would be necessary to protect the new organization from the mainstream's values and processes to spill over, which would leave the resource allocation process unchanged (1997, p. 176).

3 Research Method

This paper employs a qualitative case study to examine how and why a large enterprise facing the Innovator's Dilemma supported its employees in realizing their business ideas. The case study refers to key examples and milestones of a corresponding innovation program over its lifespan of ca. 10 years and which, among other, resulted in the creation of new companies. The case study focuses on the journey, pivots, and outcomes of the company's innovation program, highlighting the challenges and successes encountered as well as the changes of the program's approach over time. Finally, conclusions and suggestions both for corporate innovation strategies and overarching political initiatives are provided.

4 Analysis and Results

4.1 Case Study: Starting Condition

The story of the program presented with this case study starts in 2010 when the author ("the author") of this paper wanted to take on the challenge of making his employer ("the employer") more innovative for growth. The author wanted to change the employer's given approach towards innovating from *managing a project* across different disciplines within an organization to *helping a team* of dedicated individuals across the lifespan of an innovation project.

Furthermore, the author wanted to put the customer's need first to create meaningful solutions, other than creating solutions in search of a problem, which the author had often witnessed from other innovation projects who typically were initiated with intense upfront planning and top-down-governance, e.g. from Corporate Strategy, whilst lacking customer insight. Typically, these projects were green-lighted based on sophisticated business plans aimed at improving established KPIs in the first place, whilst a deep understanding of respective customer needs (as a prerequisite for a meaningful new product with a *subsequent* viable business) were oftentimes ignored.

4.1.1 Christensen's Influence

From the first steps to set-up the innovation program onwards, Christensen's work was very influential to the design of the program such that it put the innovator's ideas and motivations first (1997, p. 168), combined with their advice to *separate* both the innovation projects and their supervision from the core business' rationale.

Hence, the program created an environment where experimentation, learning and the emergence of an excellent knowledge of customer's needs in a fast and cost-efficient manner were paramount, and to learn how to build a viable business model from there.

4.1.2 Key Assumptions, Hypotheses, and Guiding Questions

The key underlying questions which led to launching the program were the following:

- Why can startups launch a global business from a garage with not much more than an idea, and how could a corporation's equivalent be designed to create similar impact?
- How could an established company take advantage of small teams of skilled and committed employees who would do what would be needed to be done and whatever it would take - like startups do?
- How to build prototypes and launch early versions of new products within a few days or weeks?

- How to circumvent slow, traditional division of labor and hierarchy based corporate rules and decision-making processes?
- How could innovative projects gain traction from the desire to get a deep understanding of customer's needs early on?
- Wouldn't it be feasible to convince managers to invest if the project team's domain expertise and their commitment were as important as their business idea itself?
- Wouldn't it be very likely to identify great ideas and capable colleagues given its significant employee base? (246.8k employees as per 31.12.2010)
- Who if not the employer's industry experts would be able to invent both disruptive technologies and corresponding business models?

4.1.3 The Innovation Program

The case study highlights how and why the program's approach and tools changed over time, focuses on its most successful building blocks, and why it faded out in 2021.

4.1.4 Context, Values, and Rules

In 2010 the author of this paper headed a strategy department for a well-established profit center representing ca. 1 bn EUR of revenues at a ca. 40% EBITDA margin. The profit center was acting very successfully, i.e. in terms of gaining market share in highly profitable markets whose overall size, however, declined rapidly. The profit center's management had launched various growth initiatives to complement and, over time, replace its shrinking legacy business. The initiatives ranged from either building on given assets and customer relationships to launching new businesses from scratch.

The author's innovation program which he had successfully proposed to his line manager was designed to take care of green-field initiatives and, after a few months of preparation and alignment with the Profit Center's Management, was officially launched with its first project in the Summer of 2011.

The program put the willingness of the intrapreneurs to test the feasibility of their idea in direct exchange with potential customers first, and consequently expected them to be capable to adapt their idea along customer's feedback. As such, the program implicitly ranked the outcome of corresponding experiments higher than an initial assessment of the strategic fit of their original business ideas, because the program expected pivots to occur anyway.

One important condition the projects had to meet was pre-defined as well: successful applicants had to come up with ideas which would leverage digitalization.

4.1.5 Evolution of the Innovation Program

With hindsight the program went through three major iterations which can be characterized as

1. - Prototype-/MVP Phase (2010–2014)
2. - Growth Phase (2015–2018)
3. - Strategic Alignment Phase (2019–2021)

4.1.6 Prototype/MVP Phase

In 2010, the author had hired a Program Manager with a sound background in the Berlin Startup Ecosystem so that he could focus on his core business related topics in parallel to setting up the innovation program whilst the Program Manager could launch the innovation program with reference to his experience.

4.1.6.1 Early Stage of the Program

After intense internal discussion it was decided to start with a first project to test and adjust the program's design along the way. As a result, the Program Manager not only managed the program but also the very first project whose business idea was created together with the author.

It was decided that the investment decisions for the innovation program should be taken by the core business management team - both for transparency and compliance reasons. This approach was suggested by the Head of the department to have every corresponding manager on the same page although the scope of the new projects would not require involving the whole management from a governance standpoint.

4.1.6.2 Governance of the Program During Phase 1

The corresponding investment decisions gates of the innovation program were then organized and budgeted for as follows:

Gate A.: Successful pitch to get access to the program; up to 60k EUR
Gate B.: Give evidence that the idea meets customer demand; up to 60k EUR
Gate C.: Give evidence that actual customers show a willingness to pay to launch a beta-business (individual budget)

Furthermore, it was agreed that in case the gate's decision-making thresholds were not met the project would be terminated.

4.1.6.3 Project #1

With regards to both the original intentions around agility and meaningfulness for customers, the initial project managed to build a working prototype within less than three months. The team achieved to have actual customers sign-up and use the new digital service early on as well. The project therefore secured a second round of investment but failed to pass the next gate (prove a willingness to pay), as after several months none of the registered users closed any transaction, with zero revenues as result.

The project was therefore terminated after ca. nine months which in comparison was considered quick as normal product management projects required at least 9 months for an approvement *to be initiated*.

4.1.6.4 Further Growth

Over the course of the years the program added more building blocks to raise its awareness and to attract more employees to apply. A so called "pre-incubation-phase" was initiated, consisting of a three-day bootcamp (inspired the events known as "Startup Weekend" which offered an environment to "build a startup in 54 h"), subsequent feedback-

and workshop sessions and a Demoday to award one or two winning teams the allowance to pitch to the management team for budget and support.

4.1.6.5 Problems and Findings from the Prototype/MVP Phase

- The innovation program supported five teams during 2011 and 2014. Four of which were run by, sometimes newly hired, employees of the profit center itself which diluted its profit margin as no additional revenues were generated early on.
- The risk of having to cover the costs of potentially redundant personnel increased the longer the projects lasted. This situation was made worse by the original design of the program's gates with no deadlines.
- The budget restrictions could not be fully enforced as the sub-departments which hosted some of the innovation projects would subsidize them from their core business budget, diluting the concept of owing limited resources and create high pressure on the teams.
- The awarded budgets kept the projects bound to the corporate procurement processes, which slowed the progress of the projects down. Proper suppliers had to be identified and onboarded before an actual cooperation could take place. Furthermore, new suppliers were hard to hire as the employer's procurement department favored to purchase from officially listed suppliers such that it would limit the complexity of managing their supplier base.
- It turned out to be both meaningful and necessary for the innovation program to reach out to other departments of the company, outside of the original business unit, for potential participants. It was also very helpful to find external coaches and consultants to support the teams in making progress or to facilitate workshops.
- Employees were capable to create new products or service with a sheer idea to start with.
- The initial projects proved that small teams empowered to take and adjust decisions on their own behalf could act quickly and flexibly also in an otherwise hierarchical and slowly moving environment.
- The validation of prototypes would be doable within weeks.

4.1.6.7 Evaluation and Outlook After Phase 1

Overall, the program was designed around management decision making to reward teams the allowance to either move on or not, in exchange for a significant budget. All teams the program had worked with sooner or later stopped realizing their ideas after they had been rejected by the management team, and only those who were supported carried on, which reflects that the management decision was interpreted as a ban.

Going forward, the program's evolution would be very much influenced by a not uncommon incident in the corporate world: an upcoming reorganization. With that, its entire profit center's overhead would become redundant, and the position of the author would be obsolete as well. If the author would not find support within his employer's management, the innovation program would be dead.

However, as most projects were still in an early stage, it was too early to tell whether an experienced team with a compelling, tested business idea would be able to convince a corporate management team to take the risk to launch a new business unit with a mid- to long term financing commitment. The program also had not been able to reach out to the entire company's workforce, mostly for a lack of both a communication budget and corresponding channels.

It was therefore also still too early to tell whether the program could manage to generate truly disruptive new technologies and business ideas bottom up.

Hence, the author decided to carry on with the program and for that he reached out to executive board member's chiefs of staff for their feedback and support.

4.1.7 Growth Phase

After a few weeks of consultation, the author was introduced to one of the company's Executive Board Members. After pitching the program to this person, she swiftly approved the program to become a part of her innovation toolset. He also agreed to secure a corresponding executive role for the author to rebuild the program as a member of her department.

4.1.7.1 Amendments and Pivots

One major change the author intended to apply to the program was to make it more visible to the corporate public. Specifically, he considered its so-called Demoday which would mark the end of each pre-incubation phase to be worthwhile to being publicly accessible.

A first public Demoday with six international teams and a high-profile jury was organized in late 2015. The event took place in the public lobby of the author's employer's Headquarter. During 2016, two other Demodays were organized for which the jury was removed from the agenda. No product roadmap was attributable to put winning team's products on any longer (because the Executive Board Member's area was a supportive function), yet it appeared to be also safe enough to try for the program's management to trust that the teams would carry on with their project if the Demoday was designed as a steppingstone towards their success.

4.1.7.2 The Scholarship

A very significant change of the program was represented by the allowance to utilize three subsequent months of 100% of working hours to realize an idea and turn it into a fundable project (after a successful application). The concept was inspired by strong feedback of supporters of the program to design a compelling offer to attract entrepreneurial talents in the first place. This amendment was also deeply rooted in the program's participants feedback on how an impactful period could look like to intensely test an idea on the one hand, and to not abandon the original job for too long. The new offering was known as the "Scholarship".

4.1.7.3 Growth and Openness

As a result, four batches of the program which supported more than 30 teams with ca. 100 participants under the condition of the Scholarship were run during 2017 and 2018. The public Demodays established itself even further and expanded its offering to a so-called marketplace for each team to take advantage of for conversations with the audience and to establish new connections to make progress going forward.

On average, the Demoday attracted more than 100 participants each whilst being open for participation to external investors and innovation experts from third parties like accelerators, academia, or corporations. The intention of the author to apply these changes to the Demoday's setup was to both eliminate the boundaries between various ecosystems and to expose the teams to "real" startup's excellence. Finally, the Demoday was an important marketing tool for the program to improve its visibility and therefore the likelihood to attract more talents to apply.

4.1.7.4 Pivot to Company Building

In the meantime, one of the participant's projects of one of the 2014 batches reached a stage in its development where it became the most feasible option for the project owners to spin it off as an affiliated company. As their business idea represented a value-added service which utilized core technology of their employer, they believed that a joint venture would create a win-win situation.

The program's management helped them to find support from the employer but failed. To all the protagonist's surprise, the team wasn't even offered an appointment to talk to the employer's corporate venturing arm for feedback or support.

To get access to them anyway, a meeting was set up with the Executive Board Member mentioned earlier.

The meeting was intended to overrule the corporate venture colleagues. However, it turned into what would become a pivotal moment for the entire program: "Given the circumstances, why don't you start your own company?", the project owners were asked by the Executive Board Member. "Why not?", they replied: "Let's do it!", they said.

Hence, they did, and over less than 12 months they found two corporations to seed-fund their startup - one of which turned out to be their former employer.

4.1.7.5 Problems and Findings from the Growth Phase

1. The problem of "how to move on after the program" and "how to avoid redundant employees after a project's failure" was successfully addressed with the Scholarship as it defined that participants would return to their original job after three-months and left it to their dedication to move on or not.
2. Whilst the program's underlying hypotheses mentioned earlier were validated once more, finding both strategic and financial support internally remained difficult for the projects to gain traction after three months. Even the Executive Board Member did not help promote the intentions of the project team to push the Corporate Venture arm to at least investigate the project but suggested to start an own company instead.
3. As one project had turned into an externally launched startup it was still unclear whether this approach could be considered *a bug or a feature* from a corporate innovation standpoint.
4. Between 2017 and 2018 the program had hosted 12 public events and meetups at the Headquarter of the employer for which ca. 1.000 participants had shown up which helped put the program and the employer on the regional startup ecosystem's map.

Furthermore, the events helped getting the project owners in contact with external experts, investors, and supporters.

4.1.7.6 Another Reorganization

Shortly after the second Demoday of 2018, the author was told by his line manager to stop all activities around the program for that another reorganization would be coming, with a new line manager replacing him.

These incidents meant another truly disruptive event for the program on the one hand but also were an opportunity to reflect on the achievements, shortfalls, and a future perspective on how to proceed.

4.1.8 Strategic Alignment Phase

In 2019 and during the re-organization's transition phase, only one residual team of one of the 2018 campaigns could take advantage of a Scholarship. After in 2020 the world was hit by the Covid-19 pandemic, the author initiated another batch to find employees to create solutions related to the pandemic, like for working-from-home or appropriate digital health tools.

4.1.8.1 Relaunch of the Innovation Program All these activities were allowed by the new management of the author to help gain time to find a "new home" for the program, yet with a deadline attached: by the end of 2021, the program would be made redundant if no corporate entity would be committing to take it over.

4.1.8.2 Set-Up of Phase 3 For that purpose, the program was adjusted to help the employer's Innovation Portfolio- and Strategy department validate innovation projects in the same quick and cost-efficient manner the innovation program had proven the company would be capable of.

Another communication, application and acceleration phase were carried out around an innovative growth-area defined by the Corporate Strategy department. This business opportunity had even been embraced by the employer's CEO during various internal events, and the batch was accompanied by the line manager picked to manage the new business area going forward.

4.1.8.3 Setbacks During this batch, 6 teams with business ideas correlated to the pre-defined growth area were supported and awarded a Scholarship. However, over the course of this batch it became more and more clear that the trajectory of the projects would not meet the employer's strategic desire to find meaningful applications for a new technology which represented a sustaining innovation, as an expansion of the capabilities of a legacy technology utilized by the employer for decades.

Furthermore, within the employer's line of operations, no plans had been made and no budgets were reserved for any of the potentially meaningful innovation projects to tap into the pre-defined growth area. Also, the employer's entities which had identified and promoted it early on had moved on to other subjects and considered "execution" to be the job of the lines of business. All of which led to the de-facto termination of any of the corresponding activities.

4.1.8.4 The End Therefore, the innovation program found no support to host another Demoday, no project would be picked-up by any line of business, and no department would be open to host the innovation program going forward.

4.1.8.5 Problems, Findings and Benchmarks from the Strategic Alignment Phase, Including Further Developments Until 2021

- The innovations projects didn't meet the predefined expectations of leveraging synergies with the core business from a given technology in each market as they were not going according to plan.
- The employer still assessed the customer's problem through the lens of the employer's key activities, not through the eye of the customer. Given the innovation program had been running for ca. 10 years, it had failed to change the mainstream mindset of the employer.
- The innovation program would innovate at marginal costs of close to zero. Giving employees access to a pre-defined amount of time to fully focus on experimentation and validation turned out to be very impactful, and this approach sets a benchmark for corporate innovation.
- A pecuniary budget hurt the agility of the projects as they would manage e.g. time-consuming procurement processes in the first place, wasting precious Scholarship time.
- Out of 30 Scholarship teams only those projects survived for more than a year which had transformed into a newly founded startup, owned by either all or a subset of the former project owners.
- Most of these founders would not quit their working contract right away. The program promoted part-time working contracts or time-constraint unpaid leaves consequently, enabling project owners to increase their personal risk level step-by-step. Those who eventually quit would do so after a first investment.
- 12 successful startups emerged from the program, highlighting the fact that successful co-founders happen to work as employees from the start, which reflects an enormous potential to unlock talent for future startups.
- In terms of the newly created Intellectual Property from the Scholarships, the innovation program utilized side letters to the project owner's working contracts to transfer intellectual property in a compliant way.
- All internally oriented innovation projects were terminated or faded out before execution had started for three reasons
- The project owners were entitled to reach out to certain decision-making institutions because of the project owner's original job description only,
- Running a full-time job in parallel would not leave enough room to realize the innovation project,
- The innovation projects would be considered a distraction from the duties defined with the working contract by line managers which put the project owner's career at risk.

4.1.8.6 Feedback from Participants

Whilst the management of the employer was not willing to help the program carry on, a survey among the alumni found them to appreciate it very much for its attitude towards being customer focused, leveraging digital technology and for its creation of an open-minded learning culture. The Net Promoter Score of the alumni was extremely high, and to this day they are in touch with each other and with the author as well.

5 Discussion and Recommendations

5.1 The Innovation Program vs. Christensen

The case study gives evidence that the Innovator's Dilemma is real: no successful project was realized internally, and the company's resources were almost entirely directed to the core business.

It also reflects that the dilemma's building blocks, like the relation of a new business opportunity's risk and upside potential with the scale and scope of the given core business, would still let "the core business win" all the time (Christensen 1997, p. 228).

Finally, with frequent reorganizations or management changes the study shows that the timeframe for innovation projects to take shape is too long for an existing company's both governance standards, and patience.

Hence, for the sake that the case study covers a time frame of more than a decade, it can be stated that the Innovator's Dilemma is equivalent to a law of nature.

5.2 First Principles

If that is the case, it becomes relevant to ask how the case study's example relates to Christensen's proposal of how to deal with disruptive technologies and innovate under conditions of the Innovator's Dilemma.

While Christensen - in line with his observations - proposes to involve the CEO of a given company to push and protect a corresponding innovation activity on a day-to-day basis, the case study built an environment where the project owners would be fully entitled to steer their project on their own behalf, coached and mentored by the innovation program, without individual protection from the top (1997, p. 176).

Whilst the program itself was enabled by an Executive Board Member, which proves Christensen right, the program created an environment with a "your project, your rules" mindset. With most bureaucratic obstacles erased, the project owners then could validate, iterate, and make progress without referring to any supervisor for allowance or justifications vs. given RVP or strategies, which put them in a position on par with "real" startups, and which brought their projects up to speed.

The case study shows that truly independent innovation entities are startups. Separate entities protected by CEOs are not independent but very dependent on the CEO's perspective. As a result, Christensen's idea of independence provided by any CEO is an illusion.

The innovation program itself was re-built two times - triggered by reorganizations and management changes. In combination with the perception of the Innovator's

Dilemma as being almost like a nature of law it is evident that probably most existing companies cannot overcome the dilemma on their own. With Christensen, Resources, Values and Processes might take over eventually (1997, p. 29).

To conclude, it is fair to say that such innovation initiatives regularly survive for a short- to mid-term period only, before "the dilemma kicks in". They don't last long enough to have an innovation project reach the growth stage attributed to the project's S-Curve not only for those reason's Christensen suggests solutions for, but because of opportunistic behavior of managers or too frequent reorganizations as well.

5.3 Evaluation, Hypotheses, and Outlook

If employees can become successful (Co-)Founders whilst companies cannot create conditions for new ideas to materialize because of the Innovator's Dilemma, it becomes relevant to ask *who* would benefit if employees became founders, and which measures would be needed to be taken, and by whom, to foster the creation of such startups.

Former employers can take advantage of spin-offs over time if them and their former employer evolve to be open to co-operation and investments at a later stage, the case study shows. In that sense, *letting go* as an employer would become a prerequisite for a new business to emerge which, like we found Christensen also highlights, to most corporate managers would be counterintuitive, and thus unlikely to happen.

More research will be needed to deal with these issues. However, this paper will finish up with some hypotheses in this regard:

1. It is both the society and economy at large which benefit from the rise of startups whose aim is to take advantage of new technologies, create value and offer new jobs.
2. If (almost all) companies, in and among themselves, cannot take advantage of leveraging disruptive technologies, yet a subset of their employees could, the opportunity to leverage this situation should be picked up by regulatory institutions: It becomes a *regulatory obligation* to help, force, or incentivize existing companies to unleash their innovators for a *greater good*.
3. Providing institutions to help employees mitigate their individual risk like to-be-defined-rights to reduce working hours or take unpaid leaves to focus on their startup will likely be core elements of such an updated regulatory framework.
4. Working contracts should be owing more power and control to the favor of employees when it comes to the creation of new Intellectual Property.
5. New initiatives to support employees on their journey to become (Co-) Founders should be set up, like well-established activities (and subsidies) around enabling academic researchers or university alumni to turn projects into startups (Foerderinfo 2024).
6. With up to a 1,8% proportion of founders vs. employees and the fact that almost every grown-up is an employee of some sorts, today, most of the population is out of scope when it comes to being empowered and enabled to innovate effectively – reflecting a huge, untapped potential by an in comparison small number of unlockable talents (Statista 2024a, 2024b, 2024c, 2024d).
7. In-depth scientific research could help to better understand the importance of former employees to launch new businesses by asking to measure how many startups are

founded by former employees across various economies and compare their success against corresponding regulatory frameworks, like ownership rights of Intellectual Property or employment legislation.

5.4 Closing Remarks

To summarize, employees are an underrepresented category of innovators. As companies are not able to leverage their innovation potential, the society is requested to step in to unleash their potential.

If we would erase the boundaries between existing startup ecosystems and established companies, we could create opportunities for all innovators and democratize innovation for the better of all.

References

Christensen, C.: The Innovator's Dilemma. Harvard Business Review Press (1997)

Statista: Entwicklung des Dow-Jones-Index in den Jahren von 1897 bis 2023. Statista. Statista GmbH (2024a). https://de.statista.com/statistik/daten/studie/1936/umfrage/entwicklung-des-dow-jones-index-seit-1896/. Accessed 23 Sept 2024. Comparison of Dow Jones' and NASDAQ's indexed value as per Year End (2023 vs. 1997)

Statista: Entwicklung des Nasdaq 100 Index in den Jahren von 1983 bis 2023. Statista. Statista GmbH (2024b). https://de.statista.com/statistik/daten/studie/248584/umfrage/entwicklung-des-nasdaq-100-index/. Accessed 30 Sept 2024

Telekom (2010). https://www.telekom.com/de/medien/publikationen. Accessed Sept 2024

Wikipedia (2024). https://en.wikipedia.org/wiki/Startup_Weekend_(organization). Accessed Sept 2024

Foerderinfo (2024). https://www.foerderinfo.bund.de/foerderinfo/de/foerderung/bund/technologie-vernetzung-transfer/gruendung/gruendung_node.html. Accessed 28 Sept 2024

Statista: KfW (2021). Gründungstätigkeit in Deutschland nach Bundesländern im Durchschnitt der Jahre von 2018 bis 2020 (Anzahl an Gründern je 10.000 Erwerbsfähige). Statista GmbH (2024c). https://de.statista.com/statistik/daten/studie/183760/umfrage/gruenderquoten-nach-bundeslaendern-in-deutschland/. Accessed 14 Sept 2024

Statista: In 2024, 53,3 Mio. Inhabitants of Germany were employees. Statistisches Bundesamt (2024). Anzahl der Erwerbstätigen in Deutschland nach Wirtschaftsbereichen im Jahr 2023 (in 1.000). Statista. Statista GmbH (2024d). https://de.statista.com/statistik/daten/studie/1248/umfrage/anzahl-der-erwerbstaetigen-in-deutschland-nach-wirtschaftsbereichen/. Accessed 24 Sept 2024

LLMs as Your Second Brain - How AI Will Affect the Way We Solve Problems

Phineas Speicher(✉) and Lutz Becker

Fresenius University of Applied Sciences, Cologne, Germany
phin.speicher@gmail.com, lutz.becker@inscala.com

Abstract. This study uniquely investigates the influence of ChatGPT and persona patterns on the problem-solving process in the context of complex problems. The focus is on how these technologies are evaluated for problem analysis and how they influence problem understanding, the quantity and quality of solution approaches, and the problem solvers' sense of uncertainty, depending on persona patterns. Using a mixed-methods approach, the study combines quantitative and qualitative research methods. In an experimental design, 99 participants used ChatGPT to create issue trees to analyze a complex home office problem (loss of productivity) - once with and once without persona patterns. Using qualitative methods, the quality of the issue trees was compared with a reference. The results show that ChatGPT can be an effective tool for supporting the problem-solving process. Although the structure of the issue trees did not differ between the groups, the use of ChatGPT significantly improved the perceived understanding of the problem, the quantity and quality of perceived possible solutions, and the subjective sense of certainty. Using persona patterns had no significant additional effect on the psychological variables. The study indicates that ChatGPT is suitable to support thought processes in the image of the "second brain" and should, therefore, be augmented as often as possible. The use of personas should be directly related to the problem context. Exploratory analyses suggest that the influence of ChatGPT could be more pronounced in participants with less prior knowledge. These findings have far-reaching implications for integrating AI into problem-solving processes in organizational contexts and open new research perspectives on the nature of AI-generated problem analyses. A small sample size and psychometric limitations restrict the study's findings. For further research, it is recommended that the study be repeated with higher resources, recommended methodological improvements be integrated, and overall problem-solving processes with ChatGPT be evaluated in longitudinal studies.

Keywords: artificial intelligence · ChatGPT · problem analysis · problem solving · persona patterns · wicked problems · Home Office

1 Introduction

Artificial intelligence (AI) is increasingly finding its way into our everyday lives, and people and organizations are facing the challenge of effectively solving complex problems more than ever. Especially in the context of "wicked problems" - problems that are

R. C. Geibel and S. Machavariani (Eds.): ISPC 2024, SPBE, pp. 456–475, 2025.
https://doi.org/10.1007/978-3-031-88052-0_37

difficult to define and even more difficult to solve - the search for innovative solutions is becoming increasingly urgent (Conklin 2005; Webber & Khademian 2008). A promising development in this area is the use of Large Language Models (LLMs) such as ChatGPT, which have the potential to support and augment human problem-solving processes. The present study investigates how ChatGPT can influence the problem-solving process.

The focus is on the following questions: (1) Is ChatGPT problem analysis more suitable with or without a persona pattern? (2) How does problem analysis using ChatGPT affect the subjective understanding of the problem, the perceived quantity and quality of potential solutions, and the perceived sense of uncertainty? (3) How do these effects differ when persona patterns are used to analyze the problem?

The relevance of this research arises from the increasing importance of AI-supported tools in organizational contexts and the simultaneous need to understand their effectiveness and limitations in detail. While extensive research on human problem-solving exists, a research gap exists regarding integrating AI, especially Large Language Models, into these processes. The study uses a mixed-methods approach that combines quantitative and qualitative research methods to address this research gap. The focus is on an experimental design in which participants use ChatGPT to create issue trees to analyze a complex problem - once with and once without using personas. The results of this study have far-reaching implications for both research and practice. They contribute to understanding how AI can be effectively integrated into problem-solving processes and provide practical guidance for using AI-supported problem-solving tools in different contexts, thereby enhancing problem-solving efficiency and effectiveness in various domains. These practical implications can benefit researchers, academics, and professionals in artificial intelligence, problem-solving, and organizational contexts.

2 Theoretical Foundation

Theoretical foundations include the most important aspects of artificial intelligence, problems, problem-solving, and problem-solving with ChatGPT in the context of the thesis's research questions.

Artificial Intelligence

Artificial intelligence (AI) is an interdisciplinary field of research primarily concerned with developing systems that require human intelligence (Goldberg 2017). These systems include pattern recognition, language processing, and decision-making. A distinction is made between weak AI, which solves specific tasks, and strong AI, intended to replicate human cognitive abilities in the future (Goldberg 2017). Machine learning is a central aspect of AI and enables computers to learn from data without being explicitly programmed (Goldberg 2017; Lee et al. 2017). Neural networks, intense neural networks, are crucial for recognizing complex patterns in data. AI development includes symbolic approaches of the 1950s, neural networks of the 1980s, and advances in deep learning (ibid.). Transformer models revolutionized language processing (Vaswani et al. 2017). This work is vital for generative AI, huge language models (LLMs) such as GPT-4 from OpenAI (2024). These models are based on transformer architectures and can generate human-like texts (Holtel 2024a; Kulkarni et al. 2023; OpenAI 2024). They use self-attention mechanisms for context processing and are trained on extensive text corpora

(Kulkarni et al. 2023; Ye et al. 2024). Human-machine interaction has changed significantly with the development of LLMs. The current paradigm shift to "Intention-Based Outcome Specification" enables users to formulate their wishes in natural language, with the AI delivering the desired outcome (Holtel 2024a; Nielsen 2024). Prompt engineering plays a central role in optimizing the design of inputs to obtain more precise and relevant responses from AI systems (Ekin 2023; Korzynski et al. 2023; White et al. 2023). Interaction with LLMs, especially ChatGPT, follows a dialogic model that can process explicit and implicit as well as declarative and procedural knowledge. An iterative dialog process reduces uncertainties and tackles complex problems in a structured way (Holtel 2024b).

Specific prompt patterns, as described in the "Prompt Pattern Catalogue" by White et al. (2023), standardize this interaction and improve responses' consistency and accuracy. Prompt techniques, such as "chain of thought" prompting, improve the output of LLMs in complex tasks (Holtel 2024a; Wei et al. 2023). This section provides an overview of the foundations and advances of AI, particularly generative AI and LLMs. It lays the foundation for investigating the impact of ChatGPT on problem-solving processes. In summary, ChatGPT can be understood as a speech engine that allows people to dialog with a virtual expert.

Problems and Problem-Solving

In investigating AI-supported problem-solving processes, a deep understanding of the nature of problems and the dynamics of problem-solving processes is essential. According to Betsch et al. (2006), a problem arises when a specific goal cannot be achieved through routine activities, and obstacles must be overcome. This definition emphasizes the two main components of a problem: the goal to be achieved and the obstacles to be overcome. Of particular relevance for this study are so-called "wicked problems," which are characterized by high complexity, uncertainty, and the lack of clear solutions (Becker & Montiel Alafont 2015; Conklin 2005; Holtel 2016; Webber & Khademian 2008). Holtel (2016) and Conklin (2005) characterize "wicked problems" by their uniqueness, the impossibility of a complete problem definition before finding a solution, and the lack of a "stopping rule" for the search for a solution.

Therefore, the problem-solving process requires a structured approach. Based on Holtel's design (2024a), the double diamond model provides a conceptual framework that divides the process into four phases: Discover, Gain Insight, Generate Ideas, and Develop Solutions (Illustration 1). This model integrates divergent thinking, which aims to generate diverse ideas, and convergent thinking, which involves evaluating and selecting the best solutions (ibid.).

The effectiveness of the problem-solving process is guided by a self-critical approach (Paul & Elder 2021) and influenced by various individual and systemic factors. Individual factors include intelligence, working memory, competence, motivation, and emotions (Betsch et al. 2006). The Cognitive Load Theory (CLT) based on Sweller (2003, 2005, 2006) emphasizes the importance of cognitive load for problem-solving. Bandura's (1977) concept of self-efficacy explains how confidence in one's abilities influences problem-solving performance. The competence level model, according to Dreyfus & Dreyfus (1980), divides the competence of problem solvers into five levels,

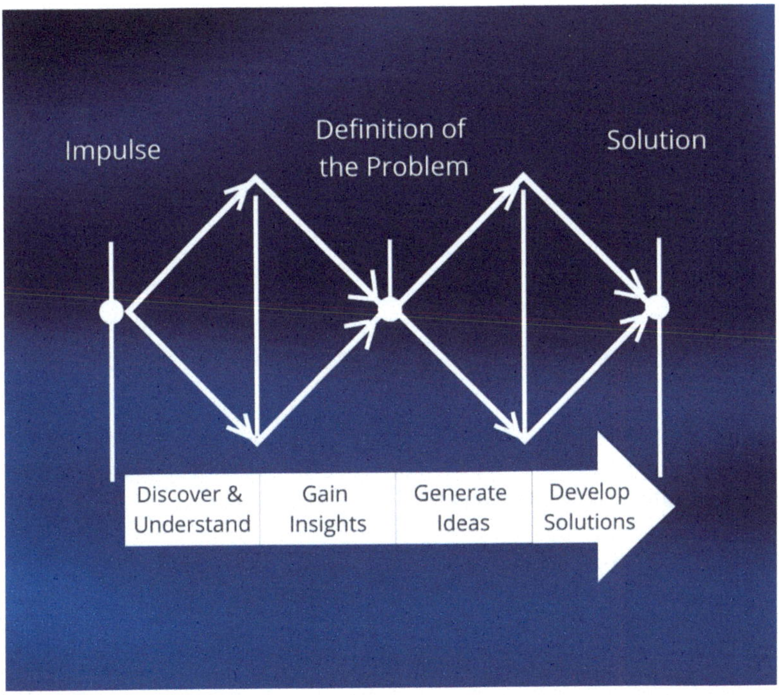

Illustration 1. Double Diamond model (own illustration based on Holtel (2024a))

from novices with little context-specific prior knowledge to experts who are considered to have a high level of problem-solving competence. (Vygotsky 1978) The zone of proximal development (ZPD) emphasizes the social aspect of learning and shows how learners can master more complex tasks with support. Systemic factors, especially group dynamics, are crucial in collectively constructing knowledge and developing innovative solutions (Luhmann 2021; Siebert 1998; Watzlawick et al. 2017). According to Linton (1936), the role theory and perspective-taking concept (Seligman 1991) emphasize the importance of having and integrating diverse perspectives and experiences in the problem-solving process. According to this, people act out of their social role, and the value of collaboration is shaped, among other things, by the ability to take on diverse perspectives and integrate their contributions (Linton 1936; Seligman 1991). Issue trees are an effective tool for strategically analyzing and operationalizing wicked problems (Holtel 2023). They enable a structured breakdown of complex problems into essential components and support divergent and convergent thinking (Illustration 2).

Applying the MECE principles (Mutually Exclusive, Collectively Exhaustive) ensures a comprehensive and non-redundant problem analysis. In addition, the structured classification into clearly defined individual components of a problem is well suited to quantifying problem-solving processes.

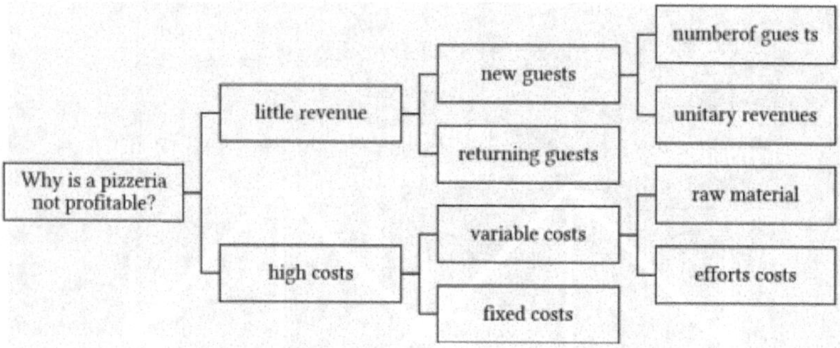

Illustration 2. Example of an Issue Tree (Holtel 2023, p. 3)

This section provides a theoretical framework for investigating ChatGPT's influence on problem-solving processes based on individual and systemic influencing factors and methods such as the Double Diamond Model and Issue Trees.

Problem-Solving with ChatGPT

The integration of ChatGPT into problem-solving processes can be Holtel (2024a, p. 149) as a kind of "automation of thinking," as AI can automate repetitive and complex thought processes and reduce uncertainties in the solution process through turn-taking (Holtel 2024b) and thus relieve the burden on working memory. Since ChatGPT conducts dialogs and can develop issue trees that could come from an expert through the correct input, many factors that improve problem-solving can be simulated within the language model (ibid.) This could be particularly advantageous for novices with little prior knowledge, as ChatGPT could take on the function of a teacher in the sense of Vygotsky's zone of proximal development (1978). This way, learners could master more complex tasks while cognitive demands would be reduced. Therefore, ChatGPT is likely to play an essential role in reducing cognitive overload in the sense of Sweller (2003, 2005, 2006), especially in problem analysis. AI could promote creativity and conserve users' cognitive resources by providing and structuring specific knowledge in divergent thinking phases. This support in problem analysis would be critical when dealing with complex problems. The use of issue trees in ChatGPT can be achieved through specific prompt patterns that are part of a chain of thought approach. This should provide a structured approach to problem-solving. The MECE principle can help to systematically break down complex problems and support a clear problem definition. Of particular interest is the simulation of group dynamic processes through persona patterns, which could enable the integration of different perspectives into problem-solving (White et al. 2023). This method could provide a more comprehensive analysis by considering different roles and perspectives. However, this would also require critically examining potential biases, as outlined in the literature on persona patterns (Deshpande et al. 2023; Gupta et al. 2023).

In summary, integrating ChatGPT into problem-solving processes could expand human cognitive capacities by simulating thought processes, augmenting problem analysis in a structured way, adding perspectives, and stimulating creative idea generation. This should make the entire problem-solving process more efficient.

Current State of Research and Hypotheses Derivation

Problem-solving is a well-established field of research with numerous models and theories (see chapter two) that comprehensively document the processes and success factors. Current studies on problem-solving with ChatGPT focus on the problem-solving of ChatGPT for itself without taking a closer look at humans. They show that ChatGPT can solve verbal problems in a comparable way to humans (Orrú et al. 2023)even achieves an accuracy of up to 80% for pathological problems (Sinha et al. 2023) but quickly fails with mathematical problems (Plevris et al. 2023) Further studies show that the productivity of people in organizational contexts improves by up to 50% when generative AI is implemented (Chui & Yee 2023; Noy & Zhang 2023; Peng et al. 2023). In contrast, there is a significant gap in AI-supported problem solving, significantly when augmented by Large Language Models (LLMs) such as ChatGPT using persona patterns and issue trees. The effective integration of LLMs into problem-solving processes has hardly been investigated, representing both a challenge and an opportunity for fundamental research. A promising approach to closing this research gap is the development of the Prompt Pattern Language (Holtel 2024b; White et al. 2023). This standardizes the interaction with LLMs and offers specific formulations for generating consistent and accurate responses in specific contexts. In addition, issue trees as analytical tools provide a methodological basis for systematically decomposing complex problems (Holtel 2023). Combining issue trees and persona patterns with the dialogic nature of LLMs opens up new possibilities for problem analysis and resolution. The aim is, therefore, to understand how issue analysis behaves objectively when people use ChatGPT to create issue trees for a specific problem. In addition, the subjective effect on people of creating issue trees will be examined more closely by comparing changes between T1 (before creation) and T2 (after creation). A particular focus is on how the objective and subjective components behave when adding persona patterns. For this purpose, an experimental group (EG), which develops issue trees with ChatGPT and persona patterns, and a control group (CG), which does the same without persona patterns, were created. Based on these theoretical foundations and the identified research needs, the following hypotheses were developed:

H1: Issue trees have, on average, significantly more nodes in participants of the EG than in participants of the control group CG
H2: Issue trees have, on average, significantly more levels in participants of the EG than in participants of the control group CG
H3: Issue trees show significantly more paths on average for participants in the EG than for participants in the CG.
H4: Issue trees show a significant difference in the length of the individual paths for participants in the EG and CG.
H5: There is a significantly higher agreement with the reference tree in the EG than in the CG.

These hypotheses are based on the assumption that integrating diverse perspectives in ChatGPT-based issue trees behaves in the same way as in interpersonal problem-solving. According to systemic constructivist ideas, integrating perspectives leads to pattern irritations and a more comprehensive understanding of reality or a complex problem (Luhmann 2021; Siebert 1998; Watzlawick et al. 2017). It is assumed that this transferability manifests itself in a higher quantity (H1–H4) and quality (H5) of the problem causes found,

H6: There is a significant, positive effect of creating issue trees with ChatGPT from measurement time T1 to T2 on perceived problem understanding.
H7: There is a significant, positive effect of creating issue trees with ChatGPT from T1 to T2 on the amount of perceived possible solutions to the problem.
H8: There is a significant, positive effect of creating issue trees with ChatGPT from T1 to T2 on the perceived quality of possible solutions.
H9: There is a significant, positive effect of creating issue trees with ChatGPT from T1 to T2 on the subjective perception of certainty in dealing with the problem.

These hypotheses are based on the assumption that the creation of issue trees with ChatGPT for structuring and visualizing problems supports divergent thinking and reduces cognitive overload, which ultimately promotes the understanding of complex problems and supports the subsequent problem-solving process in the sense of the double-diamond (Holtel 2024a; Betsch et al. 2006). An additional sub-hypothesis (a) was formulated for each of these hypotheses (H6–H9):

H6a–H9a: There is no significant difference in comparing the change effects between EG and CG.

These hypotheses assume that ChatGPT's positive effect on problem-solving occurs independently of using additional persona patterns. This assumption is based on the assumption that the collection and structuring of problem-specific knowledge is the leading cause of the subjective changes and not the actual quality of the content. This assumption is based, on the one hand, on the factors influencing problem-solving processes, but above all, on the short duration of the discussion, which is the aim of the experiment.

3 Research Method

The research methods describe all relevant aspects of the study's design, implementation, and evaluation.

Structure and Implementation
The present study used a complex mixed-methods approach, more precisely, an embedded design combining quantitative and qualitative research methods (Hussy et al. 2013). The focus was on quantitative analysis, supported by embedded qualitative elements, to quantify the issue trees and comprehensively understand the phenomenon under investigation.

The experimental design comprised two independent variables: the time of measurement (T1: before the issue trees were created; T2: after they were created) and the use of persona patterns (experimental group: with persona patterns; control group: without persona patterns). This design enabled both intra- and intergroup comparisons for differentiated findings. As dependent variables, structural elements of the issue trees (number of nodes, paths, and levels, as well as the degree of agreement with the reference) and psychological factors (problem understanding, perceived quality and quantity of possible solutions, subjective feeling of uncertainty) were examined. These variables correspond directly to the formulated hypotheses H1 to H9. The experimental treatment consisted of creating issue trees with the support of ChatGPT to address the exemplary problem of productivity loss in the home office. The experimental group additionally used persona patterns to view the problem from different perspectives, whereby the first persona was predefined as a "person working from home". Both groups used standardized prompt patterns to structure the problems. These were divided into three parts. The first two prompts were used to generate partial causes of the problem (with and without persona pattern), and the last prompt instructed ChatGPT to develop issue trees according to the MECE principle based on the generated causes. Further prompts then prepared this issue tree so that it could be seamlessly transitioned into the analysis. Qualitative elements included a literature analysis to develop an ideal reference tree on the problem of "productivity loss in the home office," its validation by an expert, and a content analysis procedure to quantify the issue trees created by participants.

The sample comprised N = 124 people recruited via various channels (network, HR employees from PwC and Trivago, students at Fresenius University of Applied Sciences) to reach as heterogeneous a group as possible. The data was collected online using a self-created questionnaire implemented with the Unipark software. In addition to general introductory and concluding texts, the questionnaire contained standardized prompt patterns to create the issue trees and pre- and post-questions to measure the dependent and control variables. The questions were recorded quantitatively on a 7-point Likert scale, except for the qualitative input of the issue tree created and the persona used in the experimental group. Attention control questions were used to ensure internal validity, and the groups were randomized. Although the online implementation presented challenges in controlling confounding variables, randomization minimized these (Hussy et al. 2013). Data collection took place from the beginning of July to August 2024. Participants needed access to the accessible version of ChatGPT 4o and basic digital skills. The average completion time was around 15 min.

The methodological design allowed for a comprehensive investigation of the research questions and hypotheses. It combined quantitative and qualitative methods to gain deeper insights into the impact of ChatGPT and persona patterns on the problem-solving process. Detailed and differentiated results balanced complexity and higher demands on participants. The methodology forms the basis for analyzing and interpreting the effects of ChatGPT and persona patterns on the issue trees' structure and the psychological aspects of the problem-solving process.

Evaluation Methods

The study was evaluated using qualitative and quantitative methods to ensure a comprehensive analysis of the data collected.

Qualitative Methods

First, a literature analysis was conducted to develop a reference tree on "productivity loss in the home office." This analysis was based on current, highly cited studies and focused on frequently mentioned factors with solid effects. The expert validated the resulting reference tree, Guido Bosbach, an experienced consultant and LinkedIn Top

Voice with over 12 years of home office experience, to ensure quality and completeness. To quantify the correspondence between the issue trees created by participants and the reference tree, a structuring content analysis was carried out according to the principles of Mayring (2010). The reference tree served as the basis for the category system. The AI language model, Claude from Anthropic, was used to support processing a large amount of data (55^23 comparisons on average). The analysis process included the creation of element lists of the participants' issue trees, evaluating matches using a match factor, and various control mechanisms to ensure data quality.

Quantitative Evaluation

The statistical analysis was carried out using SPSS from IBM based on the specific requirements of the hypotheses. After thorough data cleaning and descriptive analysis, the following procedures were applied. For hypotheses H1 to H5, independent-sample T-tests were performed to compare the structural elements of the issue trees between the experimental and control groups. For hypotheses H6 to H9, paired samples T-tests were conducted to examine the effects of creating issue trees with ChatGPT on the corresponding variables between the measurement time points T1 and T2; for the sub-hypotheses, H6a to H9a, a mixed ANOVA was performed to compare the change effects between the experimental and control groups. The corresponding assumptions regarding content and statistics were checked for all statistical methods. The assumptions could withstand the test in most cases, with a few exceptions relying on the robustness of the methods against violations (Blanca et al. 2017; Field 2013; Wilcox 2012).

The combination of qualitative and quantitative methods enabled a differentiated analysis of the research questions. Qualitative analyses evaluated the issue trees, while quantitative methods provided precise statistical testing of the hypotheses. In line with the mixed-methods design, these methods comprehensively considered the effects of ChatGPT and persona patterns on the problem-solving process. They prepared the basis for presenting the structural and psychological results.

4 Analysis and Results

The following Chapter points out any qualitative and quantitative results found.

Qualitative Results

The literature analysis on the topic of "productivity loss in the home office" identified several main categories of influencing factors:

1. social and psychological factors: social isolation and lack of social contact (AbuJarour et al. 2021; Birimoglu Okuyan & Begen 2022; Bocková & Lajčin 2021; Brooks et al. 2020; Contreras et al. 2020; Grenčíková et al. 2024; Lunn et al. 2020; Merritt 2021; Stîncel et al. 2021) Lack of informal exchange (Jenny et al. 2011; Stîncel et al. 2021), Lack of non-verbal communication (Brenke 2016; Hertel & Lauer 2012; Pargfrieder 2023), Work stress and health burdens (Landes et al. 2020; Stîncel et al. 2021).
2. physical and ergonomic factors: unfavorable working conditions (Flouris et al. 2018; Gerding et al. 2021; Grenčíková et al. 2024; Matthiesen 2021; McGee et al. 2023; Stîncel et al. 2021), Unclear distribution of roles (Bocková & Lajčin 2021; Grenčíková et al. 2024; McGee et al. 2023; Stîncel et al. 2021).

3. technical and organizational factors: technical problems and lack of support (Abu-Jarour et al. 2021; Brooks et al. 2020; Etheridge et al. 2020; Gerding et al. 2021; Hertel & Lauer 2012; Schmutte et al. 2020; Van Wart et al. 2019) Reduced exchange with managers (Contreras et al. 2020; Landes et al. 2020), Information overload due to digital communication (Schmutte et al. 2020; Van Wart et al. 2019).
4. work environment and personal factors: difficulty in separating work and private life (Grenčíková et al. 2024; Lunn et al. 2020; Matthiesen 2021; McGee et al. 2023; Merritt 2021) Distractions in the home environment (Feliciano et al. 2021; Grenčíková et al. 2024; Stîncel et al. 2021), Extended working hours and overwork (Etheridge et al. 2020; Grenčíková et al. 2024; OECD 2017).

Guido Bosbach approved all elements and added essential aspects such as a lack of experience of self-efficacy and appreciation, a lack of willingness and competence to organize oneself, a lack of ability to take care of oneself, difficulties in combining work and private life, slower decision-making and problem-solving, limited access to informal communication channels and reduced exchange with managers. These additions helped obtain a comprehensive picture of the factors influencing productivity in the home office and increased the study's validity. The validated reference tree (Illustration 3) served as a template for assessing the quality of the issue trees created by the participants and thus formed a sound basis for further analysis.

Quantitative Results

The sample description and the results of the analyses of the hypotheses follow.

Sample Description

After data adjustment, the study comprised 99 participants (N = 99), whereby the EC and control group CG were comparable regarding demographic characteristics and relevant experience. The average age was 26.69 years (SD = 9.727), with a balanced gender ratio and predominantly higher educational qualifications. Further characteristics of the sample can be seen in Table 1, divided into EG and CG.

Structural Analysis of the Issue Trees (H1–H5)

Contrary to expectations, EG and CG had no significant differences regarding the structural elements of the issue trees. Table 2 shows the descriptive results, followed by the results of the inferential statistical analysis.

H1 (nodes): $t(96{,}608) = 1.810$, $p = .073$, $d = 0.36$
H2 (levels): $t(51{,}422) = -0.828$, $p = .412$, $d = 0.17$
H3 (paths): $t(57{,}035) = 0.231$, $p = .818$, $d = 0.05$
H4 (length of individual paths): $t(83{,}416) = 0.308$, $p = .759$, $d = 0.06$
H5 (agreement with reference tree): $t(81{,}028) = -0.822$, $p = .413$, $d = 0.16$.

All hypotheses (H1–H5) were rejected, although small effect sizes may indicate potential differences in larger samples (Cohen 1988).

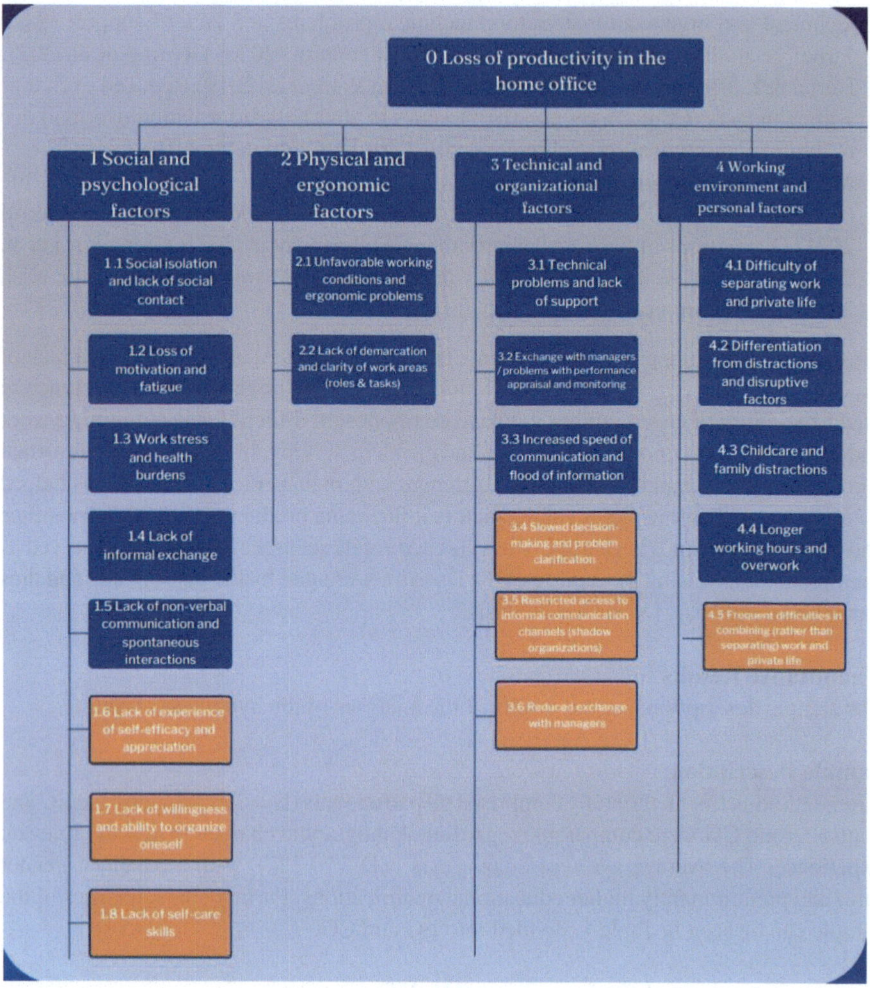

Illustration 3. Validated reference tree on productivity loss in the home office (own illustration). Findings from the literature are in blue. Additions by Guido Bosbach in orange.

Perceived Changes in the Problem-solving Process (H6–H9)

The analysis revealed significant improvements in all the variables examined after the issue trees were created with ChatGPT. The descriptive data are shown in Table 3, followed by the analysis results.

H6 (problem understanding): $t(101) = -4.372$, $p < .001$, $d = 0.36$
H7 (solution set): $t(101) = -7.282$, $p < .001$, $d = 0.77$
H8 (solution quality): $t(101) = -6.355$, $p < .001$, $d = 0.64$
H9 (perception of safety): $t(101) = -7.245$, $p < .001$, $d = 0.66$.

Table 1. Sample description according to EG and *CG* (control variables)

Core competence	Group type	*M*	*SD*	*Min*	*Max*	*N*
Age	CG	26,55	10,30	19,00	65,00	53
	EG	26,84	9,18	19,00	56,00	49
Home office experience	CG	2,74	1,61	1,00	5,00	53
	EG	2,80	1,49	1,00	5,00	49
HR experience	CG	1,72	1,08	1,00	5,00	53
	EG	1,86	1,12	1,00	5,00	49
Motivation to participate	CG	2,75	0,94	1,00	5,00	53
	EG	2,63	1,06	1,00	4,00	56

Notes. M = mean value. *SD* = standard deviation. Min = Min imum. Max = Maximum.

Table 2. Descriptive results H1–H5

Variable	Group type	*M*	*SD*	*N*
Nodes (H1)	EG	52,37	17,79	53
	CG	59,11	19,26	46
Levels (H2)	EG	3,20	2,30	53
	CG	2,91	0,66	46
Paths (H3)	EG	42,00	38,45	53
	CG	43,40	15,14	46
Length of the individual paths (H4)	EG	3,09	1,58	53
	CG	3,23	2,83	46
The sum of matching elements RT (H5)	EG	7,54	3,58	53
	CG	7,02	2,61	46

Notes. M = mean value. *SD* = Standard deviation. RT = Reference Tree.

Table 3. Descriptive results H6-H9

Variable	T1 (Pre)		T2 (Post)		
	M	*SD*	*M*	*SD*	*N*
Perceived understanding of the problem (H6)	5,21	1,41	5,70	1,34	102
Perceived number of possible solutions (H7)	4,15	1,25	5,11	1,23	102
Perceived quality of possible solutions (H8)	4,11	1,15	4,83	1,11	102
Increase in perceived uncertainty reduction (H9)	4,18	1,46	5,06	1,24	102

Notes. M = mean value. *SD* = standard deviation.

All hypotheses (H6–H9) were accepted, with small to medium effect sizes (Cohen 1988).

Differences in the Effects of Change Between EG and CG (H6a–H9a).
The mixed ANOVA showed no significant interaction effects between group and measurement time. The descriptive data are shown in Table 4, followed by the analysis results.

Table 4. Descriptive results H6a–H9a

Variable	Group	T1 (Pre)		T2 (Post)		*N*
		M	*SD*	*M*	*SD*	
Perceived understanding of the problem (H6a)	CG	*5,13*	*1,47*	*5,65*	*1,386*	*53*
	EG	5,28	1,36	5,74	1,30	49
Perceived number of possible solutions (H7a)	CG	4,20	1,24	5,11	1,27	*53*
	EG	4,11	1,27	5,11	1,20	49
Perceived quality of possible solutions (H8a)	CG	4,30	1,11	4,87	1,26	*53*
	EG	3,94	1,17	4,79	0,97	49
Increase in perceived uncertainty reduction (H9a)	CG	4,11	1,58	4,80	1,44	*53*
	EG	4,25	1,36	5,28	0,99	49

Notes. M = mean value. *SD* = standard deviation.

H6a (problem understanding): $F(1,97) = 0.094$, $p = .760$, $\eta 2p = .001$
H7a (solution set): $F(1,97) = 0.109$, $p = .742$, $\eta 2p = .001$
H8a (solution quality): $F(1.97) = 1.630$, $p = .205$, $\eta 2p = .017$
H9a (perception of safety): $F(1.97) = 2.060$, $p = .154$, $\eta 2p = .021$

All hypotheses (H6a–H9a) were accepted, indicating that persona patterns offered no additional benefit in the problem-solving process compared to ChatGPT alone.

Explorative Analyses
Issue Trees of the participants covered an average of 30% of the Reference Trees. Focusing on the literature-based elements increases the coverage by up to 50%. The participants invested an estimated 5 min in creating the issue trees. A qualitative categorization of the personas used resulted in five distinctive categories, with the majority of participants (31 out of 49) choosing personas without a direct home office reference (e.g., random first names or celebrities). A re-analysis of hypotheses H1–H5 for the subgroup with home office-related personas (e.g., managers) only showed a significant difference in the agreement with the reference tree (H5) ($t(69) = -2.342$, $p = .022$, $d = 0.62$). A correlation analysis revealed a significant negative correlation between home office experience and the change in the number of perceived solution options ($r = -0.197$, $p < .05$). However, a subsequent analysis of covariance showed that the home office experience

had no significant influence on the changes in the variables examined. Noteworthy is an interaction effect close to the significance level for the perception of safety ($F(1, 97) = 3.818$, $p = .053$, $\eta 2p = .038$).

5 Discussion and Recommendations

The results of this study provide important insights into the effectiveness of ChatGPT and persona patterns in the problem-solving process. The central research questions are answered, and the results are interpreted in the context of existing theories.

ChatGPT is Suitable for Objective Problem Analysis Both with and Without Persona Patterns
The issue trees could cover up to 50% of the reference. It should be noted that this effect was achieved in 5 min without specific context or input on the problem. Specific use cases may require knowledge beyond central, literature-based factors. It is therefore seen as added value that ChatGPT provides knowledge beyond the reference. In addition, more and more queries can be made, increasing the quality and influence of persona patterns. Contrary to expectations, persona patterns did not significantly influence the structural properties of the issue trees created with ChatGPT. This could indicate that ChatGPT can integrate multiple perspectives due to the sheer amount of information generated (50–60 sub-causes after two queries). This "integrated multiperspectivity" contrasts with expected conclusions from established theories that emphasize the benefits of perspective switching in interpersonal problem-solving (Watzlawick et al. 2017; Seligman 1980).

However, the misguided assumptions can also be explained by methodological problems. On the one hand, the analysis shows that effects exist but are insignificant. This could be due to the small sample size of $n = 50$ per group (Field 2013; Gigerenzer et al. 2004) or the number of requests made to ChatGPT. More requests are also likely to have a greater influence on ChatGPT. Exploratory analyses also showed significant effects that personas with direct reference to the issue context can improve the content quality of the issue trees. This would align with systemic principles and role theory (Linton 1936) and underlines the importance of context-specific perspectives in issue analysis. However, the tiny number of valid cases of $n = 18$ must be considered here. Clarity can only be achieved by replicating the study with larger samples and the specific instruction to use personas from the problem context.

Using ChatGPT Affects All Subjective Variables in the Problem-Solving Process
The use of ChatGPT led to significant improvements in all the variables examined. These results confirm the effectiveness of ChatGPT as a powerful support tool that positively influences cognitive and affective aspects of problem-solving. Theoretically, these effects can be explained by different approaches. ChatGPT could improve subjective problem understanding by assuming the role of a cognitive scaffold in the sense of Vygotsky (1978) and reducing cognitive overload, according to Sweller (2003, 2005, 2006). This support may lead users to develop a more precise and structured understanding of the problem, as the AI understandably presents complex information. Regarding the quantity and quality of possible solutions, ChatGPT will likely positively influence creative

solution findings by supporting divergent thinking phases. The prompt-based approach to creating issue trees structures the thinking process, provides large amounts of particular knowledge, and could contribute to a better understanding of the problem and, thus, to a more significant number of potentially better solution options being perceived. These techniques can ultimately improve efficiency in the divergent thinking phase in the Double Diamond model, leading to more diverse and precise solution proposals (Holtel 2024a). Users' sense of uncertainty could also be reduced, as ChatGPT as a cognitive tool would be able to reduce cognitive load (Sweller 2003, 2005, 2006). By facilitating thought processes in the context of turn-taking (Holtel 2024b) by augmenting thought processes, providing specific knowledge, and limiting complexity through structure, ChatGPT can reduce uncertainties that often result from being overwhelmed by complex information and chaotic dynamics. In addition, interacting with ChatGPT in a dialogic format could help users develop and clarify their thoughts and ideas iteratively, reducing their sense of uncertainty, according to Holtel (2024b). However, a significant influence of distortions must also be assumed, but these should only have a minor impact on the overall interpretation. The influence of ChatGPT in the problem-solving process could also be more pronounced for participants with less prior knowledge. The effect of the AI-based creation of issue trees on the feeling of uncertainty fell just short of the desired significance level at $p = .53$ but was nevertheless high. Fundamental problems with the significance level should be understood here. On the one hand, the value calculation heavily depends on the sample (Field 2013); on the other hand, Gigerenzer et al. (2004) reported a systematic misunderstanding of the p-value. In summary, the p-value cannot be used to infer the validity of the hypothesis for the population without error. The researchers, therefore, recommend that descriptive effects should not be neglected. It is assumed that people with little prior knowledge benefited more from the treatment in reducing uncertainty than people with a high level of prior knowledge. This would align with the competence level model (Dreyfus & Dreyfus 1980) and underlines the potential of ChatGPT as a support tool for novices. Reference is made to research further to investigate the assumptions in more depth.

ChatGPT can improve problem understanding and the perceived quality and quantity of possible solutions while reducing the user's uncertainty by acting as a cognitive framework, information structure, and thought process augmenter. The effect could be exceptionally high if little prior knowledge of the topic exists.

Psychological Effects Do not Differ When Personas Are Used

As expected, the study showed no significant differences in change effects between groups with and without persona patterns. This implies that the positive effects of ChatGPT occur independently of the additional use of persona patterns. This confirms the assumption that creating and structuring issue trees with ChatGPT, which supports thinking, is responsible for the effects. However, it should be noted that the issue trees did not differ significantly between the groups, either qualitatively or quantitatively. On the other hand, the participants had little time to explore the content in-depth, which means that minor qualitative differences between the issue trees are likely to provide only insignificant added value compared to the overall view. This could be different with a more extended observation period. Mainly if more content is generated or more detailed personas are used. However, it is expected that the quality of the issue trees would also have to differ noticeably.

Recommendations

Language models prove to be a unique tool to support thought processes. It is therefore recommended that divergent thinking phases be supported through brainstorming and structured issue trees. The tool can be used anytime to support analyzing, understanding, or narrowing down a problem and initiate a strategic solution process. Users should support their work with the tool as often as possible to conserve their thinking capacity and gain deeper insights into a topic. This could be particularly helpful as an introduction when tackling new tasks, topics, or problems, especially if there is little prior knowledge. Sufficient but not too much content should be generated, and some time should be invested in dealing with the results to separate the important from the unimportant. Even if using personas without a home office reference was declared a methodological shortcoming, a groundbreaking assumption can be derived from this. In the context of problem-solving, it is probably essential that the personas used have a direct link to the problem context. Personas can, but do not have to be used. It is recommended that a detailed description of the persona, with relevant, problem-specific characteristics, be provided if they are used.

6 Conclusions, Limitations, and Further Research

This study investigated the influence of ChatGPT and persona patterns on problem-solving, especially in the context of complex, wicked problems. The central research questions were: (1) Is ChatGPT problem analysis better suited with or without persona patterns? (2) How does problem analysis with ChatGPT influence the subjective understanding of the problem, the perceived quantity and quality of potential solutions, and the perceived sense of uncertainty? (3) How do these effects differ when using persona patterns? The results show that ChatGPT is an effective tool to support the problem-solving process, which positively influences cognitive and affective aspects and can deliver fundamentally valid results. Contrary to expectations, persona patterns had no significant additional effect on the structural properties of the issue trees created and, in line with expectations, on the psychological variables investigated. ChatGPT led to significant improvements in the perceived understanding of the problem, the quantity and quality of the expected solution options, and the subjective feeling of certainty, regardless of the use of persona patterns. However, according to Hussy et al. (2013), this study has some limitations that must be considered when interpreting the results. Even though the methodological approach was excellent for the scope of the research and promised the best possible findings within the time frame, the relatively small sample size ($N = 99$) must be considered. This may have affected the statistical power and limited the ability to detect more minor effects. Recording some hypotheses with only one item per construct is problematic from a psychometric perspective and impairs the measurements' reliability and validity. The external validity is limited due to the specific problem and the non-representative sample, which limits the generalizability of the results. Persona patterns need to be better instructed, and the influence of bias cannot be ruled out. In addition, the artificial laboratory situation may not fully correspond to real-life problem-solving situations. Despite these limitations, the study offers valuable insights and perspectives for future research. Therefore, an essential suggestion for future work is replicating the study with sufficient resources to compensate for the shortcomings. A systematic analysis of the effect of problem-specific personas on the quality of problem analysis is required. The effectiveness of AI-supported problem-solving processes as a function of the user's level of expertise should be researched in more detail (Dreyfus & Dreyfus 1980). Multi-item scales for the constructs under investigation should be sought to improve the measurement instruments. In addition, it is recommended that instruction of prompt patterns, primarily using personas, should be designed with a sense of proportion. The mapping and investigation of a complete problem-solving process from problem identification to solution finding within a field experiment in a longitudinal design would be fascinating. Effects on self-efficacy or flower life also create exciting conjectures (Bandura 1977; Csíkszentmihályi 1995). Finally, evidence-based training concepts for using ChatGPT as a "second brain" should contribute to implementation in practice. In conclusion, this study contributes to understanding AI-supported problem-solving processes despite methodological limitations. It underlines the potential of ChatGPT as a powerful support tool and opens up new research perspectives on the nature of AI-generated problem analysis. The challenge for future research and practice is to maximize the potential of AI systems such as ChatGPT while ensuring a critical and reflective approach to this technology.

References

AbuJarour, S., Ajjan, H., Fedorowicz, J., Owens, D.: How working from home during COVID-19 affects academic productivity. Commun. Assoc. Inf. Syst. **48**(1), 117–129 (2021)

Bandura, A.: Self-efficacy: toward a unifying theory of behavioral change. Psychol. Rev. **84**(2), 191–215 (1977)

Becker, L., Montiel Alafont, F.J.: Warum in interkulturellen Projekten das wahre Leben tobt. In: Becker, L., Gora, W., Wagner, R. (eds.) Erfolgreiches Interkulturelles Projektmanagement, pp. 23–54. Düsseldorf: Symposion (2015)

Betsch, T., Funke, J., Plessner, H.: Allgemeine Psychologie für Bachelor: Denken—Urteilen, Entscheiden, Problemlösen. Springer, Wiesbaden (2006)

Birimoglu Okuyan, C., Begen, M.: Working from home during the COVID-19 pandemic, its effects on health, and recommendations: the pandemic and beyond. Perspect. Psychiatr. Care **58**(1), 173–179 (2022)

Blanca, M.J., Alarcón, R., Arnau, J., Bono, R., Bendayan, R.: Non-normal data: is ANOVA still a valid option? Psicothema **29**(4), 552–557 (2017)

Bocková, K., Lajčin, D.: Home office and its influence on employee motivation. J. Manag. Mark. Rev. **6**(2), 94–109 (2021)

Brenke, K.: Home Office: Möglichkeiten werden bei weitem nicht ausgeschöpft. Deutsches Institut für Wirtschaftsforschung (DIW) **83**(5), 95–105 (2016)

Brooks, S.K., et al.: The psychological impact of quarantine and how to reduce it: rapid review of the evidence. Lancet, 395–409 (2020)

Chui, M., Yee, L.: Generative AI: The Next Productivity Frontier. McKinsey Global Institute (2023). https://www.mckinsey.com. Accessed 02 July 2024

Cohen, J.: Statistical Power Analysis for the Behavioral Sciences, 2nd edn. Erlbaum, Hillsday (1988)

Conklin, J.: Dialogue Mapping: Building Shared Understanding of Wicked Problems. Wiley, Hoboken (2005)
Contreras, F., Baykal, E., Abid, G.: E-leadership and teleworking in times of COVID-19 and beyond: what we know and where we go. Front. Psychol. **11**, 83–96 (2020)
Csíkszentmihályi, M.: Flow. Das Geheimnis des Glücks. 4. Auflage. Klett-Cotta, Stuttgart (1995)
Deshpande, A., Murahari, V., Raipurohit, T., Kalyan, A., Narasimhan, K.: Toxicity in ChatGPT: Analyzing Persona-assigned Language Models. arXiv, abs/2304.05335 (2023)
Dreyfus, S.E., Dreyfus, H.L.: A five-stage model of the mental activities involved in directed skill acquisition. California Univ Berkeley Operations Research Center, Berkeley, CA (1980)
Ekin, S.: Prompt Engineering for ChatGPT: A Quick Guide to Techniques, Tips, and Best Practices (Preprint) (2023)
Etheridge, B., Wang, Y., Tang, L.: Worker productivity during lockdown and working from home: Evidence from self-reports. ISER Working Paper Series, No. 2020-12, University of Essex, Institute for Social and Economic Research (ISER) (2020)
Feliciano, F.K., Amaral, M., Alvez, J.K., Willerding, I.A.V., Lapolli, É.M.: Difficulties in maintaining productivity and engaging teams in the home office. Int. J. Innov. Educ. Res., 24–43 (2021)
Field, A.: Discovering Statistics Using IBM SPSS Statistics. Mobile Study. Sage, Thousand Oaks (2013)
Flouris, A.D., et al.: Workers' health and productivity under occupational heat strain: a systematic review and meta-analysis. Lancet Planet. Health **2**(12), 521–531 (2018)
Gerding, T., et al.: An assessment of ergonomic issues in the home offices of university employees sent home due to the COVID-19 pandemic. Work, 298–311 (2021)
Gigerenzer, G., Krauss, S., Vitouch, O.: The null ritual: what you always wanted to know about significance testing but were afraid to ask. In: Kaplan, D. (Hrsg.) The SAGE Handbook of Quantitative Methodology for the Social Sciences, pp. 392–409 (2004)
Goldberg, Y.: Neural Network Methods for Natural Language Processing. Springer, Wiesbaden (2017). https://doi.org/10.1007/978-3-031-02165-7
Grenčíková, A., Španková, J., Kordoš, M.: The impact of home office on employee productivity and work balance. Probl. Perspect. Manag. **22**(1), 244–254 (2024)
Gupta, S., et al.: Bias runs deep: implicit reasoning biases in persona-assigned LLMs. arXiv. Abs/2311.04892 (2023)
Hertel, G., Lauer, L.: Führung auf Distanz und E-Leadership – die Zukunft der Führung? In: Grote, S. (ed.) Die Zukunft der Führung, pp. 103–118. Springer, Heidelberg (2012). https://doi.org/10.1007/978-3-642-31052-2_6
Holtel, S.: Artificial intelligence creates a wicked problem for the enterprise. Procedia Comput. Sci. (2016)
Holtel, S.: How to crack complex, ill-defined, nonimmediate problems by issue trees (2023)
Holtel, S.: Droht das Ende der Experten?: ChatGPT und die Zukunft der Wissensarbeit. Vahlen (2024a)
Holtel, S.: With a little help from my bots: turn-taking talks with ChatGPT. In: Proceedings of EuroPLoP 2024 (Preprint) (2024b)
Hussy, W., Schreier, M., Echterhoff, G.: Forschungsmethoden in Psychologie und Sozialwissenschaften für Bachelor. Springer, Heidelberg (2013). https://doi.org/10.1007/978-3-662-66673-9
Jenny, G., et al.: Projekt SWiNG – Schlussbericht der Evaluation. Gesundheitsförderung Schweiz und Schweizerischen Versicherungsverband (SVV) (2011)
Korzynski, P., Mazurek, G., Krzypkowska, P., Kurasinski, A.: Artificial intelligence prompt engineering as a new digital competence: analysis of generative AI technologies such as ChatGPT. Entrep. Bus. Econ. Rev. **11**(3), 25–37 (2023)

Kulkarni, A., Shivananda, A., Kulkarni, A., Gudivada, D.: Evolution of neural networks to large language models. In: Kulkarni, A., Shivananda, A., Kulkarni, A., Gudivada, D. (Hrsg.) Applied Generative AI for Beginners: Practical Knowledge on Diffusion Models, ChatGPT, and Other LLMs, pp. 15–31. Apress, New York (2023)
Landes, M., Steiner, E., Wittmann, R., Utz, T.: Führung von Mitarbeitenden im Home Office: Umgang mit dem Heimarbeitsplatz aus psychologischer und ökonomischer Perspektive. Springer, Wiesbaden (2020). https://doi.org/10.1007/978-3-658-30053-1
Lee, A., Taylor, P., Kalpathy-Cramer, J., Tufail, A.: Machine learning has arrived! Ophthalmology **124**(12), 1726–1728 (2017)
Linton, R.: The Study of Man: An Introduction. Appleton-Century-Crofts, New York (1936)
Luhmann, N.: Soziale Systeme. Grundriß einer allgemeinen Theorie (18. Auflage). Suhrkamp, Berlin (2021)
Lunn, P.D., Belton, C.A., Lavin, C., McGowan, F.P., Timmons, S., Robertson, D.A.: Using behavioral science to help fight the coronavirus. J. Behav. Public Adm. **3**(1), Article no. 1 (2020)
Matthiesen, P.S.B.: A cross-sectional study during the COVID-19 pandemic: work events and affective reactions as predictors of loss of productivity and intention to leave—Master thesis (2021)
Mayring, P.: Qualitative Inhaltsanalyse: Grundlagen und Techniken (11. Aufl.) Beltz Pädagogik. Beltz, Weinheim, Basel (2010)
McGee, B.L., Couillou, R.J., Maalt, K.: Work from home: lessons learned and implications for post-pandemic workspaces. Interiority **6**(1), Article no. 1 (2023)
Merritt, H.: Home office adoption after COVID-19. SSRN Electron. J. (2021)
Nielsen, J.: AI: First New UI Paradigm in 60 Years. Nielsen Norman Group (2024). https://www.nngroup.com/articles/ai-paradigm/. Accessed 07 Mar 2024
Noy, S., Zhang, W.: Experimental evidence on the productivity effects of generative artificial intelligence. Science **381**, 187–192 (2023)
OECD: OECD Guidelines on Measuring Trust. Organization for Economic Co-operation and Development (2017). https://www.oecd-ilibrary.org/governance/oecd-guidelines-on-measuring-trust_9789264278219-en. Accessed 07 Mar 2024
OpenAI: Research. GPT-4 is OpenAI's most advanced system, producing safer and more useful responses. Research. GPT-4 is OpenAI's most advanced system, producing safer and more useful responses (2024). https://openai.com/gpt-4. Accessed 07 Mar 2024
Orrú, G., Piarulli, A., Conversano, C., Gemignani, A.: Human-like problem-solving abilities in large language models using ChatGPT. Front. Artif. Intell. **6**, 72–79 (2023)
Pargfrieder, C.: Führung im Arbeitsmodell Homeoffice: Neue Anforderungen an Führungskompetenzen. Diplomarbeit. Johannes Keppler Universität, Linz (2023)
Paul, R., Elder, L.: Critical Thinking: Tools for Taking Charge of Your Learning & Your Life. Rowman & Littlefield, Washington (2021)
Peng, S., Kalliamvakou, E., Cihon, P., Demirer, M.: The impact of AI on developer productivity: evidence from GitHub Copilot. arXiv, abs/2302.06590 (2023)
Plevris, V., Papazafeiropoulos, G., Rios, A.: Chatbots put to the test in math and logic problems: a comparison and assessment of ChatGPT-3.5, ChatGPT-4 and google bard. AI, 23–37 (2023)
Schmutte, A.M., Graf, N., Rascher, S.: Digital Team -Leadership – Führen von Teams im digitalen Raum. In: Harwardt, M., Niermann, PJ., Schmutte, A., Steuernagel, A. (eds.) Führen und Managen in der digitalen Transformation, pp. 83–98. Springer, Wiesbaden (2020). https://doi.org/10.1007/978-3-658-28670-5_5
Seligman, M.E.P.: Learned Optimism: How to Change Your Mind and Your Life. Knopf, New York (1991)
Siebert, H.: Konstruktivismus: Konsequenzen für Bildungsmanagement und Seminargestaltung. DIE, Deutsches Institut für Erwachsenenbildung, Frankfurt (1998)

Sinha, R., Roy, A., Kumar, N., Mondal, H.: Applicability of ChatGPT in assisting to solve higher order problems in pathology. Cureus **15**, 56–65 (2023)

Stîncel, O.-R., Niţă, A., Oraviţan, M.: The impact of home office setup due to COVID-19 pandemic on IT professionals' physical health: a systematic review. Timisoara Phys. Educ. Rehabil. J. **14**(1), 7–16 (2021)

Sweller, J.: Evolution of Human Cognitive Architecture. Elsevier Science, San Diego (2003)

Sweller, J.: Implications of cognitive load theory for multimedia learning. In: Mayer, R.E. (Hrsg.): The Cambridge Handbook of Multimedia Learning, pp. 19–30. Cambridge University Press, New York (2005)

Sweller, J.: How the human cognitive system deals with complexity. In: Elen, J., Clark, R.E. (Hrsg.) Handling Complexity in Learning Environments: Theory and Research, pp. 13–25. Elsevier, Amsterdam (2006)

Van Wart, M., Roman, A., Wang, X., Liu, C.: Operationalizing the definition of leadership: identifying the elements of e-leadership. Int. Rev. Adm. Sci. **85**(1), 80–97 (2019)

Vaswani, A., et al.: Attention is all you need. arXiv:1706.03762 (2017)

Vygotsky, L.S.: Mind in Society: The Development of Higher Psychological Processes. (Cole, M., John-Steiner, V., Scribner, S., Souberman, E., Eds. & Trans.). Havard University Press, Cambridge (1978)

Watzlawick, P., Beavin, J.H., Jackson, D.D.: Menschliche Kommunikation. Formen, Störungen, Paradoxien. 13. Unveränderte Auflage. Hogrefe, Göttingen (2017)

Webber, E.P., Khademian, A.M.: Wicked problems, knowledge challenges, and collaborative capacity builders in network settings. Public Adm. Rev., 334–349 (2008)

Wei, J., et al.: Chain-of-thought prompting elicits reasoning in large language models. http://arxiv.org/abs/2201.11903 (2023)

White, J., et al.: A prompt pattern catalog to enhance prompt engineering with ChatGPT. https://arxiv.org/abs/2302.11382v1 (2023)

Wilcox, R.R.: Introduction to Robust Estimation and Hypothesis Testing, 3rd edn. Statistical Modeling and Decision Science. Academic Press, New York (2012)

Ye, Z., Greenlee-Scott, F., Bartolo, M., Blunsom, P., Campos, J.A., Gallé, M.: Improving reward models with synthetic critiques. arXiv:2405.20850 (2024)

The Interface Between Technology Transfer and Artificial Intelligence: A Systematic Literature Review

Manuel Etzkorn(✉), Yvonne Römer, Masoumeh Tavakoligargari, Materne Mateso Lumiere, Nihal Lamdaghri, and Harald von Korflesch

University of Koblenz, Koblenz, Germany
{etzkorn,yroemer,mtavakoligargari,lumiere,harald.vonkorflesch}@uni-koblenz.de

Abstract. Technology transfer deals with the exchange of technological knowledge between organizations, particularly between research organizations and industry. Efficient technology transfer is an important pillar of economic growth and the social utilization of research results. As part of the ongoing digitalization of academia and industry, artificial intelligence is currently considered to have the greatest transformation potential. Accordingly, it is obvious to conduct research at the interface between technology transfer and artificial intelligence. The current state of scientific literature on this interface is fragmented into specific individual studies on sub-areas of technology transfer, while a broad overview of key concepts is lacking. Furthermore, it is unclear how the relationship between technology transfer and artificial intelligence is structured in these key concepts. To close this gap, a systematic literature review according to Webster & Watson (2002) was conducted. The systematic literature search revealed eleven different key concepts at the interface between technology transfer and artificial intelligence, which can be divided into two categories. In the first category, AI is the object to be transferred over diverse transfer mechanisms. In the second category, AI assists in different steps of the technology transfer process. As scientific implication, this study provides a basic framework that serves scientists as a starting point for further research. As practical implication, it supports practitioners and policy makers to identify transfer mechanisms through which the economy and society can benefit from AI research. This study also provides initial approaches on how technology transfer can be improved by AI.

Keywords: Technology Transfer · Artificial Intelligence · Systematic Literature Review · Transfer Mechanisms

1 Introduction

Technology transfer (TT) refers to the process of disseminating technological knowledge from a technology provider, such as a research organization or company, to a technology recipient. The transfer of knowledge, particularly technological knowledge,

R. C. Geibel and S. Machavariani (Eds.): ISPC 2024, SPBE, pp. 476–489, 2025.
https://doi.org/10.1007/978-3-031-88052-0_38

plays a crucial role in fostering innovation across various sectors of society. TT facilitates technological progress by enabling the exchange of knowledge and technologies among different actors. The effective dissemination of these technologies leads to the creation of new products and services, as well as improvements to existing and future processes and systems. Thus, efficient technology transfer serves as a fundamental basis for societal advancement and is critical for economic growth and the broader utilization of technological innovations (Piller et al. 2021).

Artificial intelligence (AI) is one of the most critical tools supporting the TT process. AI enables the analysis and interpretation of complex datasets, thereby optimizing and further developing the TT process. In today's rapidly advancing digital world, AI has become increasingly valuable, making it a key component in the transformation process. Companies benefit significantly from the use of AI, as it allows them to remain competitive and address the digital challenges of the future. Thus, integrating AI into business strategies is essential (Rocha et al. 2019). This is particularly evident in its applications across various sectors, such as finance (Haleem et al. 2022), manufacturing (Saraswat & Agrawal 2023), agriculture (Kisliuk et al. 2023), and healthcare (Bianchini et al. 2022). AI has the potential not only to transform existing business models but also to create new opportunities for innovation and growth. Therefore, it is advisable to continue engaging intensively with AI, as the future TT process will be significantly influenced by AI. Over time, these two areas can be expected to become increasingly integrated.

Given the critical role of TT in fostering innovation and the increasing significance of AI in enhancing this process, there is a clear need to better understand their intersection. In the initial non-systematic literature review, no scientific articles were found in which comprehensive TT processes or structures are associated with AI. It was also observed that the literature on the AI support of TT is very fragmented and that the individual articles deal with the support of specific sub-areas, such as healthcare (e.g., Mucha et al. 2020) and computer science (e.g., M.-S. Kim et al. 2021). Publications about a holistic AI support or digital support of TT are missing. Therefore, a systematic literature review is required to explore the broader landscape of how AI can be integrated into TT and enhance the TT process, leading to the following research question:

> *RQ: What links and key concepts between technology transfer and artificial intelligence have been discussed in the academic literature?*

The aim of this study is to identify and compile the relevant literature that presents the most significant concepts regarding TT and AI. By addressing the ongoing changes driven by digitalization and especially AI, this work aims to enhance transparency on the topic of TT.

In Sect. 2, the theoretical foundations will be delineated. Section 3 will outline the research methodology employed. Section 4 will present and analyze the research findings. Section 5 will discuss these findings. Finally, Sect. 6 will present the conclusions and discuss the limitations of the study. It will also suggest areas for practical application and future research.

2 Theoretical Foundation

As outlined in Sect. 1, TT involves the dissemination of technological knowledge from a technology provider to a technology recipient. In the literature, the term "technology transfer" is also frequently used in the pair of terms "knowledge and technology transfer" (KTT). While TT emerged historically first (Meißner 2001), it has been expanded over time to KTT. This extension arose from the view that technologies cannot be transferred in isolation from the knowledge required for their application (Thimm 2017). The TT model encompasses several components: a technology provider, a technology recipient, a transfer object, a transfer mechanism (also called transfer channel), and, if applicable, an intermediary (Schultz & Mietzner 2021). Typically, TT occurs between research organizations and commercial enterprises. Universities, industry, and government organizations are regarded as the principal actors in TT (Bercovitz & Feldman 2006). Some academic literature also refers to TT between units of the same organization as "technology transfer", also known as intra-organizational technology transfer. The focus of this study, however, is exclusively on inter-organizational TT.

The **TT process** comprises several phases. While different TT process models can be identified for different regions (López Mendoza & Mauricio Sanchez 2018), the essential representation of the core process remained the same over time. Examples of TT processes and their development over time can be found in Friedman & Silberman (2003), Kesting (2012), and Piller et al. (2021). According to Piller et al. (2021), the TT process (see Fig. 1) begins with the selection phase. In this phase, the transfer object and its potential are determined. Afterwards, contacts are initiated and networks are established. This is followed by the acquisition phase, which includes the initiation of the technology-related knowledge transfer, prototyping, negotiations, and clarifications of legal aspects such as preparations regarding intellectual property rights. The final market phase includes activities related to intellectual property rights, including patenting and licensing, as well as the manufacturing and development process.

To further spread TT, various **transfer mechanisms** are used (Piller et al. 2021; Schultz & Mietzner 2021; Todeva 2013). Piller et al. (2021) identify ten different mechanisms, including: ***1) "transfer over heads"***, in which personnel are transferred from one research institution to another entity, such as a private company, to implement the technological innovation, ***2) consulting***, in which a specialist provides a company with expert advice on solving a technological problem, ***3) contract research***, in which companies commission suppliers to develop a technology or technological solution under certain contractual terms, and ***4) sponsored projects***, in which several research partners work together, often funded by government agencies, to solve a specific problem. In addition, there are ***5) patents***, which are granted for marketable inventions and can be sold or licensed, and ***6) licensing***, where companies acquire rights to use research for commercial purposes. The mechanism of ***7) publications*** serves as the primary method of disseminating knowledge and research results, and ***8) diploma/seminar papers*** are used in research and development contexts and can attract research students for future employment. Moreover, ***9) spin-offs***, in which research organizations set up new companies to commercially exploit research results and intellectual. Finally, technology transfer occurs through ***10) contacts and informal exchanges*** between science and industry in various settings, for example at social events.

Selection phase →	Acquisition phase →	Market phase
Key activities:	**Key activities:**	**Key activities:**
• Determining the transfer object • Searching for potential • Initiating first contacts • Identifying knowledge carriers • Forming and maintaining networks	• Initiating knowledge transfer to a party with a concrete application • Prototypical application • Negotiating • Drawing up contracts	• IP transfer • Licensing • Patenting • Production • Development
Identification	**Selection**	**Contracts**

Fig. 1. The phases of technology transfer according to Piller et al. (2021)

The succcss of TT depends on several factors. Predominantly significant are the ability of the technology recipient to utilize the transferred technology (Cohen & Levinthal 1990; Jee & Sohn 2023; M. Kim & Geum 2020; Liu et al. 2020), as well as the trust and open communication between the involved actors (Cai et al. 2019; de Wit-de Vries et al. 2019; Kremic 2003).

The tool with the greatest potential for TT currently is **AI**, which refers to computer systems and applications capable of performing tasks that typically require human intelligence. That means, AI systems and applications can perform assigned tasks with a fixed goal that require cognitive functions (Mikalef & Gupta 2021). These tasks include perception through sensors, problem-solving, reasoning, decision-making, and taking actions based on those decisions (Shinde & Shah 2018; Winston 1992). AI is an overarching term that includes several subfields, among which machine learning is particularly prominent. Machine learning can be applied in various domains such as prediction, computer vision and natural language processing (Shinde & Shah 2018). Additionally, there are different learning approaches within machine learning, commonly categorized as supervised, unsupervised, and reinforcement learning (Ongsulee, 2018). Within machine learning, a subset called deep learning is considered to have the most substantial impact on TT. Deep learning is based on the concept of artificial neural networks, which are designed to replicate the functioning of neural networks in the human brain (The European Commission's High-Level Expert Group on Artificial Intelligence 2018). Deep learning is distinguished from machine learning by its unique capability to directly extract features from natural data and to transform them into meaningful representations using the backpropagation algorithm (LeCun et al. 2015).

3 Research Method

To find existing links and key concepts at the intersection of TT and AI, a **systematic literature review** was conducted following the methodology outlined by Webster and Watson (2002). A systematic literature review is a valuable approach for synthesizing results from fragmented domains (Snyder 2019), such as TT and AI, and is thus an effective method for addressing the research question of this paper.

The multidisciplinary database SCOPUS was selected for the literature search. SCOPUS provides a wide range of peer-reviewed journal articles and conference proceedings across relevant fields, including management, computer science, healthcare, and natural sciences. SCOPUS covers a larger bandwidth of journals than similar databases like Web of Science and has a higher consistency as search engines like Google Scholar (Mongeon & Paul-Hus 2016). The search was conducted in August 2024. To ensure the inclusion of all relevant literature, the following search term was applied:

TITLE-ABS-KEY ("technology transfer" AND "artificial intelligence")

Figure 2 provides an overview of the individual steps of the screening process, which are further explained in the following paragraphs.

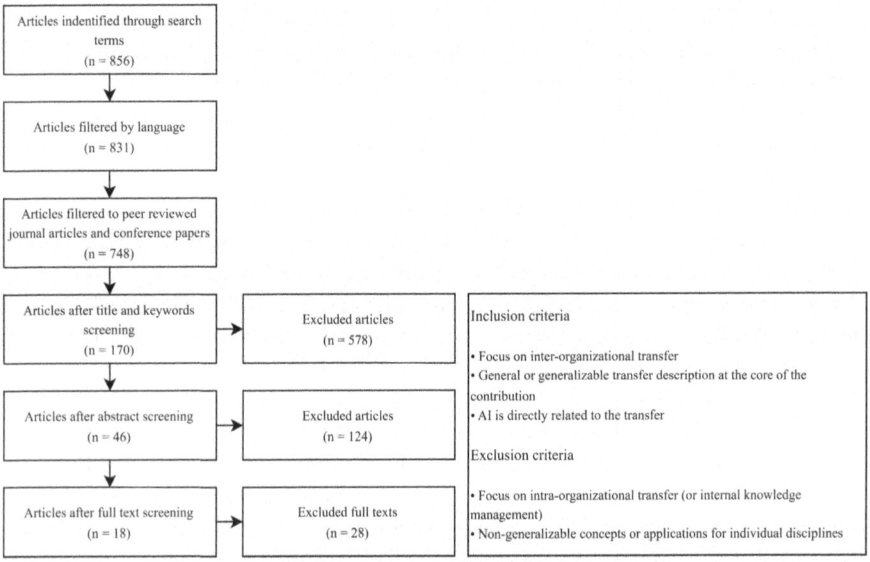

Fig. 2. Flow diagram of the systematic review process

The search term primarily includes all articles that address both technology transfer (TT) and artificial intelligence (AI) in the article title, abstract, author keywords, and index keywords. The term "technology transfer" was also designed to capture articles using the phrase "knowledge and technology transfer". By considering the index keywords provided by SCOPUS, it was additionally prevented that relevant articles were overlooked. For example, the term "artificial intelligence" can be found in the index keywords for articles in which the authors exclusively address a specific AI technology such as machine learning. Since this study focuses on concepts and not on their technical feasibility over time, older publications could also be relevant to answer the research question. Therefore, no time filter was used for the search query. In terms of language, only English-language results were considered. Additionally, to maintain a high quality of the selected literature, only peer-reviewed journal articles and conference papers were considered.

Regarding the **content criteria**, only articles focusing on inter-organizational transfer were included. The description of technology transfer had to be presented in a general or generalizable context and needed to represent a core part of the study's contribution. Descriptions of AI were required to be directly related to technology transfer. Consequently, contributions focused on intra-organizational transfer or related disciplines, such as internal knowledge management, were excluded. Articles discussing non-generalizable concepts or applications specific to individual disciplines were also excluded. An example of a concept that cannot be generalized is an interface that enables the transfer of AI algorithms to specific industrial plants, as the focus there is on the specific technical implementation rather than the transfer process itself. The screening process resulted in 18 articles being selected for the final review.

Metadata, including author names, titles, publication years, and abstracts, were extracted from SCOPUS, manually verified, and imported into Mendeley Reference Manager. In accordance with the guidelines proposed by Webster and Watson (2002), the results of a systematic literature review should be presented in a concept-centric manner. Thus, the articles were examined for key concepts related to TT and AI, which were then analyzed and inductively categorized. During the first part of the analysis, two distinctly different main categories were identified. In the first category, AI is considered the object being transferred through various transfer mechanisms. In the second category, AI serves as assisting technology in different stages of the technology transfer process. In the second part of the analysis, these two main categories were further divided into more specific, inductively derived key concepts, which will be presented in the following section.

4 Results

The review revealed an increasing interest in the interface between TT and AI, as most studies (10 of 18) were published since 2019. Nevertheless, it also becomes clear that AI and TT are no new concepts, since 6 of the 18 studies were published in 1997 or earlier. The reviewed publications present a diverse range of perspectives across various disciplines. Six articles examine AI and TT in a healthcare context (Demarinis Loiotile et al. 2024; Grossi 2007; Mehrizi 2023; Mucha et al. 2020; Pan et al. 2019; Tran et al. 2019), four in a computer science context (Bowen & Kumar 1993; Frosio et al. 2021; M.-S. Kim et al. 2021; Tsatsoulis & Holtzman 1996), three in a management context (Da Mota Tenorio et al. 1997; Goul 1992; Roberts 1990), one in an interdisciplinary context (Y. Kim et al. 2022), and one each in the context of engineering (Romo & Roecks 1988), jurisprudence (Novoselova & Grin 2020), physics (Terry et al. 2021), and psychology (Cipresso & Riva 2015). In terms of applied methods, most studies (13 of 18) are practically oriented and describe the development of concepts, models, platforms, or technologies. The remaining five studies employ different methodologies: Mehrizi (2023) conducts an interview study, Mucha et al. (2020) analyze secondary data, Novoselova and Grin (2020) conduct a literature review, Pan et al. (2019) perform a quantitative study, and Tran et al. (2019) carry out a bibliometric analysis.

In the first main category identified in the review, an instance of **AI is the transfer object**. The results of the first category were sorted into six key concepts (see Table 1), which are AI adoption, AI technologies in different stages of development (AI algorithms, AI concepts, and AI products), specific applications for education, and intermediaries to support the TT of AI.

AI adoption relates to studies that investigate the transfer of AI technology from the recipients' perspective. Both identified studies focus on the healthcare sector. Mucha et al. (2020) conducted a study on news data from businesses listed in the S&P 500 regarding their adoption of AI technology. They found differences among the subsectors that could not be explained by the diffusion of innovations theory. Pan et al. (2019) conducted a quantitative survey on the implementation of AI services. In the influencing factors of perceived usefulness, behavioral intention, perceived risk, attitude, and experience, they found differences between clinicians and non-clinicians.

AI algorithms are complete algorithms with the desired functionality that may still require integration into corresponding technical components, such as software or technical devices, depending on the context. Frosio et al. (2021) developed an AI algorithm for vision-based detection of cheating in video games as part of a research project. In terms of technology transfer, the authors model the organizational perspective of a TT workflow. The workflow includes actors (academia, interns, research, field operation), objects (new AI methods and technologies, papers, libraries, GPUs, and patents), and their interrelations. Terry et al. (2021) created an AI algorithm for measuring fine structures using extended X-ray absorption. To facilitate technology transfer, a website has been established where the algorithm and additional background information are available for open access.

AI concepts are mature ideas that have been described in detail but have not yet been implemented in any application. Grossi (2007) developed a concept of artificial neural nets for making medical decisions that can be transferred to other contexts. The publication itself is understood as a transfer mechanism for transferring the concept. Mehrizi (2023) examines how AI technology can restructure the work of radiologists. The results are categorized in so called "technology-work frames", which structure the role of AI to automation, enrichment, and reconfiguration. To transfer the findings, initial tests were carried out in medical practice. Tran et al. (2019) provided an overview of AI applications in healthcare, categorizing them into clinical settings, data science and precision medicine, and policy making. The authors examined the success of AI technology transfer within the healthcare sector and identified a dependency on the availability of resources for the effective use of AI applications. As a result, they suggest that technology transfer to emerging and developing countries requires support from developed countries.

AI products are complete software packages or technical devices with the desired functionality that are ready to use. Cipresso & Riva (2015) developed a virtual reality environment that simulates human behavior for research purposes. The product was realized and made available as a web application. Romo & Roecks (1988) investigate the transfer of various AI products into the military sector, including an AI-based application for mission planning. The focus of the publication is on the transfer process, with particular emphasis on the psychological aspects affecting the responsible persons for the transfer process and the potential end users of the new technologies.

Education includes concepts and case descriptions for teaching AI knowledge. Two publications deal with further education for professionals and the third publication deals with regular university teaching. Da Mota Tenorio et al. (1997) developed a graduate-level educational program in intelligent system design technology with the

Table 1. AI technology is the object to be transferred (main category 1)

Category \ Reference	Cipresso & Riva, 2015	Da Mota Tenorio et al., 1997	Frosio et al., 2021	Goul, 1992	Grossi, 2007	Mehrizi, 2023	Mucha et al., 2020	Pan et al., 2019	Roberts, 1990	Romo & Roecks, 1988	Terry et al., 2021	Tran et al., 2019	Tsatsoulis & Holtzman, 1996
AI Adoption							X	X					
AI Algorithm			X								X		
AI Concept					X	X						X	
AI Product	X									X			
Education		X		X					X				
Intermediaries													X

primary objective of training professionals to apply AI and neural networks. This program includes a detailed description of the process of transferring scientific knowledge to employees within a large company. Roberts (1990) describes the concept and successful implementation of "expert systems clubs", which are designed to facilitate the transfer of expert systems technology and associated AI knowledge from academia to industry. Goul (1992) developed a curriculum focusing on AI. The publication describes and models in detail how AI knowledge can be prepared for integration into standard teaching practices. The curriculum's objectives have reportedly been achieved, as graduates have secured strong positions in research, business, and public administration. These graduates' areas of responsibility include application development, managing and coordinating AI development teams, and imparting AI-related knowledge.

Intermediaries are the last key concept of the first main category. Tsatsoulis & Holtzman (1996) describe the procedures of the Center of Excellence for Software and Systems Engineering, which serves as an intermediary for technology transfer between universities and businesses. They outline the processes of three projects, emphasizing the commercialization of AI technology, which was viewed with skepticism at the time of publication.

In the second main category identified in the review, **AI serves as assisting technology for TT**. The results of the second category were sorted into five fields of application (see Table 2), which represent activities of the TT process. These fields of application are contract management, IP value prediction, market research, patents, and project management.

Contract management involves the creation and administration of contracts that regulate the use of transferred intellectual property. Demarinis Loiotile et al. (2024) developed a prototype database to support AI-based search processes for contract management in three areas. First, the prototype integrates large volumes of data on contracts involving industry collaborations. Second, it supports TT activities related to negotiating confidentiality agreements, non-disclosure agreements, data-sharing agreements, and material transfer agreements. Third, it assists in the design and management of specialized contracts for clinical trials. Novoselova & Grin (2020) proposed a concept for the music industry that utilizes smart contracts, which can be partially or fully executed without human intervention.

Table 2. AI assists the transfer of technology (main category 2)

Field of application	Reference				
	Bowen & Kumar 1993	Demarinis Loiotile et al. 2024	Y. Kim et al. 2021	M.-S. Kim et al. 2022	Novoselova & Grin 2020
Contract management		X			X
IP value prediction			X	X	
Market research	X	X			
Patents		X			X
Project management	X				

IP value prediction is essential for a technology provider to determine the value of the technology in question before negotiating contracts. To assist with this problem, M.-S. Kim et al. (2021) created an AI tool to predict the value of innovative technologies. The tool employs an AI algorithm trained on patent data and uses the discounted cash flow method. Similarly, Y. Kim et al. (2022) developed an AI-driven model to predict the potential of existing AI patents. This model utilizes patent data, including the time from application to registration, the number of applicants, and the number of citations.

Market research is another activity which can be assisted by AI. Bowen & Kumar (1993) developed a concept for an AI-driven expert system designed to retrieve target market classifications, which is integrated with a case-based system to develop advertising campaigns. The expert system identifies target groups for new products, and the resulting combination of product data and target group information is utilized by the case-based system. This system applies an algorithm, which is connected to a database of advertising campaigns and can generate a new campaign tailored to the new product. Demarinis Loiotile et al. (2024) recognize the potential of AI to scout inventions, develop business ideas, and predict future technological developments, with relevant data being incorporated into the prototype database.

In the context of **patents**, two types of AI assistance can be identified. In the field of patent research, AI can facilitate the search for specific patents and identify related patents based on content, aiding in obtaining an overview of certain topics (Demarinis Loiotile et al. 2024; Novoselova & Grin 2020). In the field of patent applications, AI can support the formal process of patent submission and assist in the preparation of patent documents (Demarinis Loiotile et al. 2024). Additionally, Novoselova & Grin

(2020) highlight the potential for AI to uncover cases of unauthorized use of intellectual property.

To support **project management**, Bowen & Kumar (1993) describe a concept to enhance decision-making with a combination of neural networks and case-based systems. The neural net accelerates the execution of a case-based system by classifying incoming data and selecting relevant cases or rules more quickly. For instance, in a planning system for major design or construction projects, the neural net identifies the most relevant previous cases, which provide initial planning templates. The system then uses rule-based expertise, such as industry standards or guidelines, to refine these plans. This hybrid approach leverages the strengths of both neural networks and case-based reasoning to improve the speed and accuracy of project planning.

5 Discussion

The systematic literature review identified two main categories within the field of AI and TT: one where AI is the transfer object, and another where AI supports TT. Both categories encompass several key concepts as subcategories. In the **first main category**, where AI is the object to be transferred, the key concepts exhibit a diffuse structure. The subcategories of AI concepts, AI algorithms, and AI products represent different maturity levels of transferrable AI technology, while the subcategories of education and intermediaries include multiple transfer mechanisms. Education facilitates transfer through mechanisms such as diploma and seminar papers and transfer over heads, considering that a significant proportion of students transition from academia to other fields. The AI-focused intermediary described by Tsatsoulis & Holtzman (1996) supports all economically oriented mechanisms of AI transfer, such as consulting, patents, licensing, and spin-offs, and functions as a platform for contacts and informal exchanges. The key concept of AI adoption includes empirically developed explanations of the factors influencing the adoption or non-adoption of AI technology. The reviewed studies show variations based on subsectors (Mucha et al. 2020) and identify several relevant adoption criteria, such as perceived usefulness, perceived risk, and behavioral intention (Pan et al. 2019). Although, both studies are limited to the healthcare sector. In summary, the key concepts of the first main category deal with three questions: what (AI concepts, AI algorithms, AI products), how (education, intermediaries) and why (AI adoption). The "what" dimension can be clearly structured. The "how" dimension provides examples of how AI can be transferred via mechanisms, as defined in the theory. The least clear answer could be given to "why". First, the theoretical classification lacks an extensive definition. Pan et al. (2019) found partial alignment between their results and the technology acceptance model (Davis 1989). However, Mucha et al. (2020) could not explain their results using the diffusion of innovations theory (Rogers 2010), suggesting that this theory may not be broadly applicable to AI technology. Additionally, it remains uncertain to what extent the two studies in the healthcare sector can be generalized to other fields.

The key concepts of the **second main category**, where AI serves as assisting technology for TT, are comparatively more homogeneous and operate based on the same fundamental principle. By leveraging large amounts of available data, AI algorithms are designed to automate or partially automate repetitive search and work processes related to economic and regulatory areas. No suggestions are made for the use of AI in interpersonal interactions. For theoretical integration, all key concepts can be aligned with the phases of the transfer process by Piller et al. (2021). Project management and market research (searching for potential) can be assigned to the selection phase. IP value prediction, as a preparatory step for negotiation, and contract management can be assigned to the acquisition phase. Finally, patents can be associated with the market phase. However, a complete coverage of the TT process cannot be achieved with the results of this study.

As a practical implication, the results of this study can help practitioners and policymakers to identify transfer mechanisms through which the economy and society can benefit from AI research. The study also provides initial approaches for enhancing technology transfer using AI. For academia, this paper offers a foundational framework for understanding the transfer of AI technology and AI-supported TT.

6 Conclusion, Limitations and Further Research

To provide an overview of the literature about the interface between TT and AI, the authors of this study conducted a systematic literature review and identified two main categories. In the first main category, AI is the object of transfer. AI knowledge and technology can be transferred at various levels of maturity (as concept, algorithm, or product) and through several transfer mechanisms, such as consulting, patents, licensing, and spin-offs, transfer over heads, and diploma/seminar papers. Furthermore, there are different criteria for the successful transfer of AI, such as perceived usefulness, perceived risk, and behavioral intention. In the second main category, AI is employed to support various steps of the TT process, such as project management, market research, IP value prediction, contract management, and patenting.

The limitations of this study stem from the narrow scope of the systematic literature review. To ensure high quality, only peer-reviewed journal articles and conference papers were included, which means potentially relevant results from books, practitioner reports, or magazine articles were excluded. For future research, an evaluation of these publications, for example through a bibliometric study, could lead to further results. To maintain the focus of this study, all included papers in the systematic literature review had to address both AI and TT, leading to another limitation. Contributions that did not explicitly address both topics were omitted, even if they could be potentially relevant. For instance, this might include studies on the general digital support of cooperation projects between universities and industry. Future research could explore these omitted areas to provide a more comprehensive understanding of the intersection between AI and TT. Furthermore, as pointed out in the discussion, not all transfer mechanisms and process could be addressed with the results of the systematic literature review. To build a more complete framework, the authors of this study suggest the collection of further data using qualitative and quantitative research methods.

References

Bercovitz, J., Feldman, M.: Entpreprenerial universities and technology transfer: a conceptual framework for understanding knowledge-based economic development. J. Technol. Transf. **31**(1), 175–188 (2006). https://doi.org/10.1007/s10961-005-5029-z

Bianchini, S., Müller, M., Pelletier, P.: Artificial intelligence in science: an emerging general method of invention. Res. Policy **51**(10) (2022). https://doi.org/10.1016/j.respol.2022.104604

Bowen, J., Kumar, U.: Knowledge-based technology transfer: hybrid architectures of rules, case-based reasoning and neural nets. In: Canadian Conference on Electrical and Computer Engineering, pp. 12–14 (1993). https://doi.org/10.1109/CCECE.1993.332248

Cai, Y., Ferrer, B. R., Lastra, J.L.M.: Building university-industry co-innovation networks in transnational innovation ecosystems: towards a transdisciplinary approach of integrating social sciences and artificial intelligence. Sustainability **11**(17) (2019). https://doi.org/10.3390/su11174633

Cipresso, P., Riva, G.: Virtual reality for artificial intelligence: human-centered simulation for social science. Annu. Rev. Cyberther. Telemed. **13**, 177–181 (2015)

Cohen, W.M., Levinthal, D.A.: Absorptive capacity: a new perspective on learning and innovation. Adm. Sci. Q. **35**(1), 128–152 (1990). https://doi.org/10.2307/2393553

Da Mota Tenorio, M.F., Pereira Maia, A.C., Grant-Tenorio, A.E.: A model for advanced in-house industrial training: a case study on intelligent system technology transfer using a project-oriented approach. IEEE Trans. Educ. **40**(2), 144–153 (1997). https://doi.org/10.1109/13.572329

Davis, F.D.: Perceived usefulness, perceived ease of use, and user acceptance of information technology. MIS Q. **13**(3), 319–340 (1989). https://doi.org/10.2307/249008

de Wit-de Vries, E., Dolfsma, W.A., van der Windt, H.J., Gerkema, M.P.: Knowledge transfer in university–industry research partnerships: a review. J. Technol. Transf. **44**(4), 1236–1255 (2019). https://doi.org/10.1007/s10961-018-9660-x

Demarinis Loiotile, A., Veneto, D., Agrimi, A., Semeraro, G., Amoroso, N.: An AI-based approach for the improvement of university technology transfer processes in healthcare. In: Rocha, A., Adeli, H., Dzemyda, G., Moreira, F., Colla, V. (eds.) WorldCIST 2023. LNNS, vol. 802, pp. 311–320. Springer, Cham (2024). https://doi.org/10.1007/978-3-031-45651-0_31

Friedman, J., Silberman, J.: University technology transfer: do incentives, management, and location matter? J. Technol. Transf. **28**(1), 17–30 (2003)

Frosio, I., Fiameni, G., Altoè, P.: AI: from theory to industry. In: CEUR Workshop Proceedings, vol. 3102 (2021)

Goul, M.: Artificial intelligence technology transfer in computer information systems: the Arizona State University perspective. Expert Syst. Appl. **4**(2), 203–212 (1992). https://doi.org/10.1016/0957-4174(92)90111-5

Grossi, E.: Technology transfer from the science of medicine to the real world: the potential role played by artificial adaptive systems. Subst. Use Misuse **42**(2–3), 267–304 (2007). https://doi.org/10.1080/10826080601142006

Haleem, A., Javaid, M., Asim Qadri, M., Pratap Singh, R., Suman, R.: Artificial intelligence (AI) applications for marketing: a literature-based study. Int. J. Intell. Netw. **3**, 119–132 (2022). https://doi.org/10.1016/J.IJIN.2022.08.005

Jee, S.J., Sohn, S.Y.: Firms' influence on the evolution of published knowledge when a science-related technology emerges: the case of artificial intelligence. J. Evol. Econ. **33**(1), 209–247 (2023). https://doi.org/10.1007/s00191-022-00804-4

Kesting, T.: Wissens- und Technologietransfer durch Hochschulen aus einer marktorientierten Perspektive: Ansatzpunkte zur Gestaltung erfolgreicher Transferprozesse an Universitäten und Fachhochschulen. Springer, Wiesbaden (2012). https://doi.org/10.1007/978-3-658-00719-5

Kim, M., Geum, Y.: Predicting patent transactions using patent-based machine learning techniques. IEEE Access **8**, 188833–188843 (2020). https://doi.org/10.1109/ACCESS.2020.3030960
Kim, M.-S., et al.: A study on intelligent technology valuation system: introduction of KIBO patent appraisal system II. Sustainability **13**(22) (2021). https://doi.org/10.3390/su132212666
Kim, Y., Park, S., Kang, J.: Technology commercialization activation model using imagification of variables. Appl. Sci. **12**(16) (2022).. https://doi.org/10.3390/app12167994
Kisliuk, B., Krause, J.C., Meemken, H., Saborío Morales, J.C., Müller, H., Hertzberg, J.: AI in current and future agriculture: an introductory overview. KI Kunstliche Intelligenz **37**(2–4), 117–132 (2023). https://doi.org/10.1007/s13218-023-00826-5
Kremic, T.: Technology transfer: a contextual approach. J. Technol. Transf. **28**(2), 149–158 (2003). https://doi.org/10.1023/A:1022942532139
LeCun, Y., Bengio, Y., Hinton, G.: Deep learning. Nature **521**(7553), 436–444 (2015)
Liu, J., Chang, H., Forrest, J.Y.-L., Yang, B.: Influence of artificial intelligence on technological innovation: evidence from the panel data of china's manufacturing sectors. Technol. Forecast. Soc. Change **158** (2020). https://doi.org/10.1016/j.techfore.2020.120142
López Mendoza, X.P., Mauricio Sanchez, D.S.: A systematic literature review on technology transfer from university to industry. Int. J. Bus. Syst. Res. **12**(2), 197–225 (2018)
Mehrizi, M.H.R.: Pre-framing an emerging technology before it is deployed at work: the case of artificial intelligence and radiology. J. Comput. Med. Commun. **28**(4) (2023). https://doi.org/10.1093/jcmc/zmad029
Meißner, D.: Wissens- und Technologietransfer in nationalen Innovationssystemen (2001)
Mikalef, P., Gupta, M.: Artificial intelligence capability: Conceptualization, measurement calibration, and empirical study on its impact on organizational creativity and firm performance. Inf. Manag. **58**(3) (2021). https://doi.org/10.1016/j.im.2021.103434
Mongeon, P., Paul-Hus, A.: The journal coverage of Web of Science and Scopus: a comparative analysis. Scientometrics **106**(1), 213–228 (2016). https://doi.org/10.1007/s11192-015-1765-5
Mucha, T., Halminen, O., Tenhunen, H., Seppälä, T.: Commercial adoption of AI in the healthcare sector: an exploratory analysis of S&P500 companies. Stud. Health Technol. Inform. **270**, 113–117 (2020). https://doi.org/10.3233/SHTI200133
Novoselova, L., Grin, E.: Prospective applications of new technologies and artificial intelligence for systematizing the results of intellectual activity. In: E3S Web of Conferences, vol. 224 (2020). https://doi.org/10.1051/e3sconf/202022403018
Ongsulee, P.: Artificial intelligence, machine learning and deep learning. In: International Conference on ICT and Knowledge Engineering, pp. 1–6 (2018). https://doi.org/10.1109/ICTKE.2017.8259629
Pan, J., Ding, S., Wu, D., Yang, S., Yang, J.: Exploring behavioural intentions toward smart healthcare services among medical practitioners: a technology transfer perspective. Int. J. Prod. Res. **57**(18), 5801–5820 (2019). https://doi.org/10.1080/00207543.2018.1550272
Piller, F., Hilgers, D., Schmidthuber, L.: The relevance of technology transfer. In: New Perspectives in Technology Transfer, pp. 149–163, April 2021. https://doi.org/10.1007/978-3-030-61477-5_9
Roberts, H.J.: Expert systems clubs. Design methods. Comput. J. **33**(6), 556–561 (1990). https://doi.org/10.1093/comjnl/33.6.556
Rocha, C., Fernandes Narcizo, C., Gianotti, E.: Internet of management artifacts: Internet of Things architecture for business model renewal. Int. J. Innov. Technol. Manag. **16**(8) (2019). https://doi.org/10.1142/S0219877019500627
Rogers, E.M.: Diffusion of Innovations. Simon and Schuster (2010)
Romo, J.G., Roecks, A.: Transferring technology transfer into an Air Force unit. J. Technol. Transf. **13**(1), 54–57 (1988). https://doi.org/10.1007/BF02371502

Saraswat, P., Agrawal, R.: Artificial intelligence as key enabler for sustainable maintenance in the manufacturing industry: scope & challenges. Evergreen **10**(4), 2490–2497 (2023). https://doi.org/10.5109/7162012

Schultz, C., Mietzner, D.: The technology transfer challenge. In: Mietzner, D., Schultz, C. (eds.) New Perspectives in Technology Transfer: Theories, Concepts, and Practices in an Age of Complexity. FGFSSBE, pp. 1–8. Springer, Cham (2021). https://doi.org/10.1007/978-3-030-61477-5_1

Shinde, P.P., Shah, S.: A review of machine learning and deep learning applications. In: 2018 Fourth International Conference on Computing Communication Control and Automation (ICCUBEA), pp. 1–6 (2018). https://doi.org/10.1109/ICCUBEA.2018.8697857

Snyder, H.: Literature review as a research methodology: an overview and guidelines. J. Bus. Res. **104**, 333–339 (2019). https://doi.org/10.1016/j.jbusres.2019.07.039

Terry, J., et al.: Analysis of extended X-ray absorption fine structure (EXAFS) data using artificial intelligence techniques. Appl. Surf. Sci. **547** (2021). https://doi.org/10.1016/j.apsusc.2021.149059

The European Commission's High-Level Expert Group on Artificial Intelligence: A Definition of AI: Main Capabilities and Scientific Disciplines (2018)

Thimm, D.: Verwertung wissenschaftlicher Forschungsergebnisse-Zusammenführung von Angebot und Nachfrage auf elektronischen Forschungsmarktplätzen (2017)

Todeva, E.: Governance of innovation and intermediation in Triple Helix interactions. Ind. High. Educ. **27**(4), 263–278 (2013)

Tran, B.X., et al.: Modeling research topics for artificial intelligence applications in medicine: latent Dirichlet allocation application study. J. Med. Internet Res. **21**(11) (2019). https://doi.org/10.2196/15511

Tsatsoulis, C., Holtzman, J.: Transferring artificial intelligence technology through a research center of excellence. In: Proceedings ISAI/IFIS 1996 Mexico - USA Collaboration in Intelligent Systems Technologies, pp. 30–35 (1996)

Webster, J., Watson, R.T.: Analyzing the past to prepare for the future: writing a literature review. MIS Q. **26**(2), xiii–xxiii (2002).

Winston, P.H.: Artificial Intelligence. Addison-Wesley Longman Publishing Co., Inc. (1992)

Digitalization: New Regulations and Challenges for Start-Ups in the European Union

Michele Dilenge(✉)

IU International, University of Applied Sciences in Munich, Munich, Germany
michele.dilenge@iu.org

Abstract. With the Company Law Package and the Digitalization Directives, the EU legislator has introduced numerous innovations for digital start-ups in the EU. Companies can now be incorporated online without having to appear in person before a notary. Member states must ensure that these procedures are implemented nationally. Best practice examples have already been established in some EU countries, which serve as role models. Branches can be registered completely online. Companies can submit their documents and information online, which reduces the time and administrative burden.

1 Introduction

Company founders face enormous challenges when choosing a legal form. In addition to reducing liability, questions of future financing and further growth play a decisive role. Investors want to adequately secure their shares and co-determination rights. Finally, the transfer of shares should run smoothly in the event of a (partial) sale. At the same time, the formation process should be as simple and straightforward as possible. There have been a number of recent developments in European company law that take these requirements of founders and investors into account.

2 Important Reforms by the EU Legislator

A) Business Registers Interconnection System (BRIS).
The Business Registers Interconnection System (BRIS) of the European Union is a centralized network that connects the business registers of the Member States (as well as Iceland, Liechtenstein or Norway). This initiative promotes transparency and efficiency in the internal market and facilitates cross-border business activities. Electronic register management was introduced in the EU as early as 2003 (COM 2003/58/EC).

BRIS offers both free and fee-based company register content. The different national legal forms are displayed in the respective official language with a brief description in all official languages. The registers of 20 EU Member States are currently linked (as of September 2024).

The information available includes the company name, legal form, registered office and registration history. The company search includes public limited companies as well

R. C. Geibel and S. Machavariani (Eds.): ISPC 2024, SPBE, pp. 490–499, 2025.
https://doi.org/10.1007/978-3-031-88052-0_39

as limited liability companies and their branches and European Companies (Societas Europaea - SE). However, many details are not yet available, including further information in the commercial register, e.g. on the group affiliation of a company, and uniform terminology for all electronic registers (e.g. register of associations).

b) Company Law Package.

In April 2018, the EU Commission presented a "Company Law Package", which for the first time deals with the creation of a European legal basis for cross-border changes of legal form and demergers. The focus of the Company Law Package is on promoting the use of digital technologies in company law and on (further) expanding the cross-border mobility of companies within the EU through cross-border transformations, mergers and divisions. Of particular note here is the intended first-time codification of cross-border transfers of registered offices and divisions, which should contribute to a considerable increase in legal certainty in this area.

The Company Law Package comprises two directives that involve a comprehensive revision of the Company Law Directive (COM 2017/1132/EU) of 14. 6. 2017: Firstly, the so-called Digitalization Directive I (COM 2019/1151/EU) concerning the digital incorporation of limited liability companies and, secondly, the so-called Mobility or Conversion Directive (COM 2019/2121/EU) concerning cross-border conversions of companies.

c) Digitalization Directive I.

The Digitalization Directive I, which was adopted in 2019, introduced online incorporation, online communication with the register, a new concept for register publicity and a further expansion of the BRIS.

The aim of the Digitalization Directive I is to facilitate the formation of companies and the registration of secondary establishments through the increased use of digital tools (EU 2019/2121, Recital 2). Small and medium-sized enterprises and micro-enterprises in particular should benefit by significantly reducing the cost, time and administrative burden of these procedures. (EU 2019/2121, recital 8). With the Act Implementing the Digitalization Directive (DiRUG, 2020), supplemented by the Act Supplementing the Regulations Implementing the Digitalization Directive (DiREG, 2022), the German legislator provides for the possibility of founding companies online. This is a significant innovation that also coincided with the coronavirus pandemic. In addition, the legal basis for online notarial procedures was created about the notarization of declarations of intent by means of video communication.

d) Digitization Directive II.

With the draft of the Digitalization Directive II (COM 2023, 177), for which agreement was recently reached in the trilogue, a major upgrade for the commercial and company registers in the EU will soon take place (Schmidt, 2024). The main content is the expansion of the use of digital tools and procedures in company law, in order to simplify and speed up processes, supplemented by additional digital tools and procedures. Important innovations are planned for more transparency (both in relation to corporations and, for the first time, for commercial partnerships) and for better quality and use of company data.

The planned changes include for corporations:

- Details on the disclosure of further details on personal data of board members (Art. 14 letter d DigR II),
- Disclosure of the object of the company (Art. 14 letter la DigR II),
- company name, legal form and EUID (or the registration number if one does not exist) (Art. 16b II letter k DigR II),
- Disclosure of the average number of employees (Art. 19 II letter i DigR II),
- Publication via the BRIS of information on branches of third-country corporations, the most important even free of charge (Art. 36 III-IV DigR II).

For groups of companies:

- Introduction of regulations on the disclosure of key information on group structures in the BRIS (Art. 19b DigR II).

For commercial partnerships:

- Extension of register publicity including mandatory information on shareholders and authorized representatives.

In future, the BRIS will also be used to provide information on branches of third-country corporations that must be disclosed in the national registers, the most important of which will even be available free of charge (Art. 36 III-IV DigR II).

A system for linking business registers (BRIS), the register of beneficial owners (BORIS) and the insolvency register (IRI) is also planned. This should facilitate access to data on beneficial owners and insolvency cases.

The aim is to improve the use of cross-border company data with the following measures:

- Once-only principle: No multiple submissions of documents; instead, retrieval via BRIS.
- Harmonized minimum standards: Preventive controls for register filings.
- Introduction of the EU Company Certificate (EUCC): Uniform proof of company data.
- EU power of attorney: Digital powers of attorney for representation in other member states.

This is accompanied by easier recognition of register data:

- Standardized verification documents: Recognition of EUCC and digital powers of attorney.
- Waiver of legalization/apostille: Abolition of these requirements for certain register documents.
- Limited translation requirements: Waiving translations where possible to reduce bureaucracy.

3 Significant Changes for the Establishment of Start-Ups

For start-ups, the implementation of the Digitalization Directive II means a significant change in the founding process.

- Mandatory digital processes: Formations and registrations must be possible digitally.
- Companies can submit register documents once and use them in other member states.
- Increased transparency: Obligation to disclose certain data such as personal details of board members and company purpose, including for commercial partnerships.
- Use of digital identity and trust services: a digital identity and EUid wallet simplify authentication and identification

This results in new obligations for company founders:

- Preparing for digital incorporation processes: Ensure that all incorporation documents and registrations can be made digitally.
- Compliance with the new disclosure requirements: Observe disclosure obligations for managing director data, company purpose and group structures.
- Use of EUCC certification scheme and digital powers of attorney: Implementation of the digital EU proxy for cross-border activities. In addition, apply for and use the EU company certificate for official evidence.
- Ensuring that data is up to date: Obligation to regularly update register data in order to provide up-to-date and reliable company information.
- Dispensing with traditional document legalization: Use of digital processes to avoid the effort and costs of legalizations and apostilles.

These measures and obligations should help to increase efficiency and reduce costs and increase the attractiveness of the European market for company founders, particularly in the start-up sector. Even if the European legislator has initially provided for an opt-out with regard to the more complex forms of company law (for Germany, the public listed company (AG) and the limited partnership company on shares (KGaA), it can be assumed that the wave of digitalization will not stop at the more complex company types, especially the AG and KGaA, in the medium term. (Schurr, 2019).

4 Advantages for Start-Ups

- Acceleration of the start-up process: Online incorporation significantly shortens the time it takes to set up companies.
- Reduction of start-up costs: Digitalization reduces costs that would otherwise be incurred through administrative and notary fees.
- Better accessibility: Formation processes can be carried out regardless of the geographical location of the founders, which makes access easier for international founders.
- The EU legislator has pursued several intentions with the Company Law Package (CLP):
- Strengthening legal certainty: the legal changes aim to create uniform and transparent regulations for digital company formation.
- Simplification of company formation within the EU: The simplification and digitalization of processes is intended to promote and facilitate entrepreneurial activity across national borders.
- Protection against abuse: Despite digitalization, measures will be introduced to prevent fraud and identity theft, for example through secure identification procedures.
- Expanding competition between company jurisdictions: Competition among EU member states will be stimulated by facilitating cross-border activities.

5 Best Practice

The transposition of the Company Law Package (CLP) into national law is an ongoing process carried out by the Member States of the European Union. Several EU Member States have taken steps to implement the provisions of CLP in their national legal systems. However, the degree of implementation varies between the different countries, as the EU member states have some leeway in the implementation process.

a) Estonia.

- Digitized government services: Estonia is considered a pioneer in digital government services, including business start-ups. For several years now, Estonia has made it possible to set up companies completely online via the e-Residency program.
- Security mechanisms: Estonia has implemented robust mechanisms (KSI blockchain) for digital identification and ensuring legal certainty.

b) Netherlands.

- eRecognition (eHerkenning): Using this system, entrepreneurs and organizations can securely access a variety of online services provided by public and private organizations.
- Digital notary: In the Netherlands, there are already practical applications where notarial services can be provided electronically, which meets the requirements of CLP.
- In addition to the advantages of online incorporation, there is another important facilitation: the deed of incorporation and articles of association can also be drawn up in English in the case of digital incorporation.

c) Austria.

- Electronic Notarial Form Formation Act (ENG): Austria has introduced specific regulations that offer the possibility to establish a GmbH without the physical presence of founding shareholders by means of an electronic notarial deed.
- Digitized registers: The implementation of digital commercial registers facilitates the online submission of documents.
- With the introduction of the flexible capital company, a new legal form was also created that meets the requirements of company founders (see Dilenge 2023).

d) Lithuania.

- e-Government infrastructure: Lithuania has developed an advanced e-Government infrastructure that enables company formations to be handled entirely online, including electronic signatures and identification processes.
- Information systems: Lithuania offers comprehensive online platforms for business information and services that improve access to and transparency of business information.

e) Denmark.

- Virk.dk platform: Denmark operates a centralized online platform that provides all the necessary tools and information for starting and managing businesses. This platform greatly facilitates business management by integrating several government services.

- Uniform registration: Denmark has greatly simplified the registration and administration of companies by bringing together the requirements of various authorities on a single platform.

f) Finland.

- Digital Identification: Finland relies on sophisticated digital identification solutions that make it possible to set up companies online securely and quickly.
- Automated processes: Many processes, including tax registration and administration, are automated in Finland, making them particularly efficient.

g) Establishment of a corporate venture office.

- Another option for successful digitalization can be a corporate venture office (CVO), i.e. an independent company within a group of companies that manages venture capital activities for the group.
- Like a venture capital company, it transfers capital and expertise to start-ups - in order to receive both back multiplied at the end. (Grewe/Glasmacher 2023, 1005)

h) No need for a local notary.

- Formation and participation processes should be simple and as cost-effective as possible. In Germany, the Act Implementing the Digitalization Directive (DiRUG) and the DiREG as a supplementary law have made it possible to found a GmbH or a UG (haftungsbeschränkt) online since 1.8.2022, as has the notarization of unanimous resolutions amending the articles of association by means of video communication.
- The restriction to notaries who are established at the location of the company to be founded was rightly abandoned. Public notarization by means of video communication is also provided for applications for entry in the commercial register. This can reduce the effort required for start-ups, including those from abroad.

Key aspects of best practices.

- Unique and secure electronic identification: Use of eIDs and other secure identification methods to prevent identity theft and fraud.
- User-friendly online platforms: Providing easily accessible and user-friendly online platforms for document submission and management.
- Cooperation with notaries: In countries such as the Netherlands and Austria, the expertise of notaries continues to be used as a neutral control and protection authority, but now in digital form.
- Ensuring data integrity: Use of modern technologies such as blockchain to ensure the integrity and immutability of company data.

The effectiveness and success of these measures vary, and it is up to the individual member states to decide how to integrate the CLP requirements into their national legal systems. For detailed information on the current status of implementation in the respective countries, it would be necessary to consult current reports and publications by the relevant government agencies or relevant international organizations.

6 Recommendations for Action for Start-Ups

- Use of online platforms: Start-ups should familiarize themselves with the online platforms available in the respective countries in order to carry out incorporation processes, registrations and ongoing administration online.
- Understanding national and EU-wide regulations: Start-ups should know and understand both the specific national regulations and EU-wide directives, such as those of CLP and the Digitalization Directives I + II.
- Security awareness: Start-ups should rely on secure digital identification and communication methods to prevent fraud and identity theft.
- Use of professional advice: It can be helpful to use the services of digital notaries or lawyers to minimize legal and administrative risks when founding and managing companies.

7 Recommendations for Action for National Legislators

- Promotion of digitalization: Governments should invest specifically in the digitalization of public administration and legally effective procedures.
- Standardized platforms: Develop and provide centralized, user-friendly online platforms for business registration and administration.
- Regulatory clarity: Clear and precise regulations, that take into account both national needs and EU requirements should be developed.
- Security and safeguards: Implement security standards and mechanisms for fraud prevention and identity protection.
- Training and education: Information and training campaigns to familiarize entrepreneurs and administrative staff with the new digital processes.
- Flexibility in implementation: Legislators should maintain flexibility, with regard to national characteristics and traditions in order to offer customized solutions that meet local circumstances.
- Courage for new solutions: Depending on the legal system, there is a need for action for new organizational and legal forms, in order to promote entrepreneurship. Depending on the legal system and economic circumstances, national legislators need to be a little more resolute in designing new legal forms. There are already very interesting developments in many EU countries (cf. Fleischer, 2022).

These measures will enable start-ups to be better supported and digital opportunities to be fully exploited, while at the same time maintaining legal and security standards.

8 Development of New Participation Models

The design of participation models regularly gives rise to major discussions and a need for advice. In addition to purely monetary remuneration and profit-sharing, the aim is to motivate managers and employees and retain them in the company in the long term. The focus here is on so-called leaver and vesting provisions, which ensure that shareholdings end when managers or employees leave the company.

- Purpose of the participation models: The models serve to retain and incentivize managers and employees, especially in technology-oriented companies, in order to be able to survive in global competition.
- Leaver/vesting regulations: These regulations ensure that such shareholdings end when a person leaves the company, in order to protect the interests of investors and make room for new talent
- Manager participation models: These models often occur in individual cases or as part of institutional buy-outs.
- Employee participation models: Direct (genuine) participation in companies through shares or options, whereby tax consequences must be taken into account. In contrast, virtual participations are purely economic participations without actual participation in the shareholder rights, which can be structured more tax-efficiently.

The following recommendations for action and structuring are available to start-up founders:

- Use leaver and vesting provisions: Implement clear rules that define what happens when an employee or manager leaves the company to ensure long-term retention and ensure that only active employees share in successes.
- Design manager participation: Design shareholdings via so-called sweet equity to motivate managers with an economic incentive. In addition, ensure that investments are made in line with the market and with full risk of loss in order to take advantage of tax benefits.
- Genuine employee participation: Use hurdle shares to reduce the non-cash benefit and thus the tax burden. In addition, take advantage of tax benefits.
- Virtual employee participation: If the tax valuation is uncertain and to avoid "dry income" taxation, virtual shareholdings are a good option, where employees only participate in the event of an exit. In addition, virtual shareholdings should be structured in such a way that employees are treated economically as if they had real shares, but without assuming the legal obligations of a shareholder.
- Indirect participation: Employees can also be involved via holding companies such as GmbH/UG & Co. KG. This can reduce corporate governance problems and offer tax advantages. Purchase prices should be set at an appropriate value and offer deferral agreements to avoid liquidity problems for employees.
- Tax aspects: It is important to note that discounted shareholdings are generally taxable as wages. Deferral and waiver agreements can help to minimize tax disadvantages. In addition, tax concessions should be used to make employee participation more attractive from a tax perspective (e.g. Section 19a EstG in Germany).

By implementing these strategies and taking the legal framework into account, start-up founders can develop effective participation models that offer both tax and legal advantages while ensuring the motivation and retention of managers and employees.

9 Further Developments

In this context, it should be discussed how to deal with the notarization requirement for a notarial transfer of shares. This remains in place in Germany, for example, due to Para. 15 GmbHG. Despite digitalization and online incorporation options, it is still necessary to notarize transfers of shares. The original explanatory memorandum provided for this in order to make speculative trading more difficult and to ensure the continuity of management. The need for this is criticized due to digitalization and the facilitation of transactions through blockchain technologies (Weitnauer, 2024). Consideration should be given to a reform that reduces the requirement for notarization or replaces it with alternative digital procedures in order to increase international competitiveness and reduce unnecessary bureaucracy (Weitnauer, 2024).

In anticipation of a legal regulation, start-ups could make the following considerations:

- Use digitalization and modern technologies: How could blockchain technologies and electronic signatures be introduced to facilitate business share transfers.
- Rethink legal structure: Consider legal forms that place less formal requirements on the transfer of shares.
- Seek advice: Use comprehensive legal advice, especially when structuring share transfers and complying with current legal requirements.
- Be aware of costs: Any notary fees incurred should be factored in. Cost-efficient alternatives should also be sought whenever possible.
- Minimize risks: Ensure that all parties involved are informed of potential risks and liabilities, especially in the case of digital settlements.
- Simplify employee participation: Use legal simplifications (in Germany e.g. § 19a EStG) for employee share ownership to create incentives and retain employees in the long term.
- Transparent agreements: Participation agreements should be clear and understandable in order to avoid misunderstandings and keep the legal situation transparent.
- Consider international practices: Entrepreneurs should follow international standards and practices in order to remain competitive.
- Regulations in the articles of association: Regulations in the articles of association should be used for flexible handling of share transfers, also to avoid unnecessary notarial costs.
- Keep an eye on future legislative changes: Entrepreneurs should always stay informed about possible legislative changes that could reduce bureaucracy and promote digital procedures.

10 Conclusion

In summary, the CLP aims to advance digitalization in corporate law, in order to make it easier to set up a company, increase legal certainty and at the same time minimize the risk of abuse. Best practice examples have developed in many EU member states to significantly simplify the establishment and management of companies. In addition to many technical simplifications that also serve better governance, these developments should also be seen as an opportunity to further develop entrepreneurship in the European Union, and at the same time to create comparable framework conditions in the world's largest free trade zone.

References

Dilenge: Die FlexKap in Österreich: ein Modell für Deutschland?, IWRZ 2023

Fleischer: Ein Rundflug über Rechtsformneuschöpfungen im in- und ausländischen Gesellschaftsrecht, NZG 2022, 827

Gesetz zur Umsetzung der Digitalisierungsrichtlinie (DiRUG) v. 5.7.2021, BGBl. 2021 I 3338

Gesetz zur Ergänzung der Regelungen zur Umsetzung der Digitalisierungsrichtlinie v. 15.7.2022, BGBl. 2022 I 1146

Grewe/Glasmacher: Corporate Venture Offices für die Neuausrichtung des Mittelstands, NZG 2023, 1005

ICLEG, Report on Transparency of Company Data, 2023

Vorschlag für eine Richtlinie des EP und des Rates zur Änderung Richtlinie 2009/102/EG und (EU) 2017/1132 in Bezug auf die Ausweitung des Einsatzes digitaler Werkzeuge und Verfahren im Gesellschaftsrecht, COM (2023) 177

Schmidt: Die Digitalisierungsrichtlinie II, NZG 2024, 563

Schurr: Digitalisierung im Gesellschaftsrecht in der EU: Quo vadis?, EuZW 2019, 772

The Role of AI-Generated Personalization in Influencing Tokopedia's Consumer Experience

Tan Kaitlynn Eleanore Poa[1], Muhammad Lukman Baihaqi Alfakihuddin[2](✉), and Pananda Pasaribu[2]

[1] University of Arizona, Tucson, USA
kaypoa@arizona.edu.id
[2] Sampoerna University, Jakarta, Indonesia
{lukman.alfakihuddin,pananda.pasaribu}@sampoernauniversity.ac.id

Abstract. Artificial Intelligence (AI) has rapidly advanced and been adopted in various sectors of society. Recently, many companies have integrated AI into their platforms. Tokopedia, Indonesia's second-largest e-commerce platform, leverages AI to increase consumer engagement and sales. This research aims to investigate the role of AI in influencing consumer experiences through the generation of personalized algorithms. AI-generated personalization encompasses four key aspects: AI product recommendation (PR), AI consideration sets (CS), end-user purchasing decisions (EPD), and perceived personalization (PP). This quantitative study is conducted in Indonesia and targets respondents through a non-probability sampling technique, purposive sampling. This research focuses on AI personalization strategies' efficacy and evaluates their impact on customer satisfaction, purchasing decisions, and brand loyalty. This study used quantitative methods by analyzing 180 respondents by SMARTPLS through regression analysis, and path coefficient. Data collection was facilitated through a Likert questionnaire distributed online via Facebook. The study's results indicate that all of the AI-driven features positively influence consumer experience (CE), with PP being the strongest and CS being the lowest in impact. By examining Tokopedia as a case study, this research provides valuable insights into the critical role of AI personalization in Indonesia's e-commerce landscape, offering strategic guidance for online retailers aiming to optimize consumer experience and drive business growth through AI technology.

Keywords: Imperative · AI · Personalization · Influence · Consumer Experience · Tokopedia

1 Introduction

E-commerce growth in Indonesia is highly supported by the nation and fintech companies (Mahmuddin & Sirait, 2022). Tokopedia is Indonesia's second-largest e-commerce company, with more than 11 million customers (Hidayat et al., 2024). With the vast changes in the digitalization era, artificial intelligence (AI) is integrated into Tokopedia's operations to help it thrive in the highly competitive e-commerce landscape. This

R. C. Geibel and S. Machavariani (Eds.): ISPC 2024, SPBE, pp. 500–514, 2025.
https://doi.org/10.1007/978-3-031-88052-0_40

strategic implementation is a response to rapid technological advancements and the growing importance of enhancing consumer engagement, satisfaction, and purchasing intention (Deng et al., 2023; Raji et al., 2024). Especially with the investment made by China's Alibaba Group Holding in 2017, Tokopedia should be able to cater to the marketplace well by offering the best consumer experience (Luo et al., 2023).

The usage of AI has been studied by multiple researchers and has offered numerous benefits, from accelerating operational efficiency to improving customer interactions. AI has been proven to streamline business processes and significantly reduce the time required to perform tasks (Rana et al., 2021). Tokopedia can leverage AI by using its potential to personalize the consumer experience during app utilization (Muthaluri, 2024). The generation of the personalized algorithm will be able to understand consumers' preferences and predict future behavior, allowing it to enhance the shopping experience and promote higher engagement (Senyapar, 2024). Beyond improving the user experience, AI impacts their purchasing decisions by presenting products that favor their needs and preferences. This will entail higher chances of purchasing and building strong customer relationships with Tokopedia, fostering brand loyalty over time (Deng et al., 2023).

Despite the extensive research on AI personalization in e-commerce, the implications of using it on consumer satisfaction, brand loyalty, and purchasing decisions become a study gap, particularly within the context of Tokopedia. Findings about AI and personalized user experiences are boundless. However, the translation of it into the long-term effect on customer satisfaction and loyalty is limited in current studies (Raji et al., 2024). Moreover, the specific impact of AI-activated algorithms on buying decisions in the Tokopedia realm still needs to be explored (Sufyan & Pamuncak, 2023). AI-generated personalization encompasses four key aspects: AI product recommendation (PR), AI consideration sets (CS), end-user purchasing decisions (EPD), and perceived personalization (PP). All the above are embedded in Tokopedia's AI-generated personalization system to allow consumers to maximize their experience when purchasing a product with enjoyment.

This research is conducted to fill these study gaps by evaluating the imperativeness of personalization through AI-generated algorithms on consumer experience within Tokopedia. It will also examine the influence of these strategies on brand loyalty and purchasing behavior. Focusing on Tokopedia as the e-commerce platform studied will provide critical and valuable insights into the effectiveness of AI-driven personalization in Indonesia's e-commerce sector, especially with the rapid transformation in the digital market. In addition, other online platforms are offered with the notable understanding of optimizing customer engagement by utilizing AI technology in their strategies. Thus, recognizing the scope of AI integration in Tokopedia's platform and its impact on consumer experience is essential for discovering AI's ability to personalize and elevate user experience for e-commerce companies.

2 Theoretical Foundation

2.1 AI Product Recommendation

The theory of consumer behavior that will be applied in this study is Content-Driven Purchase Theory (CDPT). In the digital age, consumer behavior has increasingly shifted towards online purchases, becoming digital-oriented (Amoah et al., 2023). The evolution has categorized consumers into several types, including AI and personalization-based buyers who expect tailored shopping experiences, making CDPT highly relevant (Rachmad, 2024b). CDPT, part of the broader consumer behavior evolution theory, emphasizes the importance of content in e-commerce platforms, such as displaying relevant information and personalized product recommendations (Rachmad, 2024a). The curated AI algorithm collects and analyses the consumer's data from their preferences, purchasing history, and behavior (Bhuiyan, 2024). Following their patterns allows businesses to tailor product recommendations, along with discounts and promotions, that are aligned with the customer's demands (Bodemer, 2023). This can increase consumer satisfaction and loyalty, covering the overall consumer experience during purchase (Cetin, 2020). Especially given that customers in this digital era tend to expect personalization and intuitiveness in their purchasing stages (Reddy, 2022). The precision of the product recommendation generated by AI will foster a better consumer experience by providing an engaging shopping experience that encourages repeat visits and higher conversion rates from consumers (Fahmi et al., 2023).

Hypothesis 1: there is a positive association between AI Product Recommendation and Consumer Experience.

2.2 AI Consideration Sets

Consideration sets are based on Rational Choice Theory (Bezar et al., 2021). This theory is often applied in AI to model decision-making as selecting the most rational choice from a set of alternatives (Radovanović, 2019). The AI evaluates each option's potential benefits and drawbacks to determine which maximizes utility. Furthermore, it allows consumers to evaluate an alternative subset of brands or products before reaching a purchase decision (Tuu et al., 2021). The data analytics on their preferences can allow AI to identify and provide consumers with the most pertinent choices. This allows the study to approach consumers in a targeted manner by narrowing down options suitable for them, making the purchase decision process more efficient and less overwhelming (Chang & Park, 2024). AI-generated consideration sets can be tailored to individual users, elevating product recommendations' quality and relevance (Beyari & Garamoun, 2022). Hence, this improves the overall consumer experience due to the ease of finding products that match their wants and needs, increasing satisfaction levels and loyalty (Gidh, 2020).

Hypothesis 2: there is a positive association between AI Consideration Sets and Consumer Experience.

2.3 End-User Purchasing Decision

The Theory of Planned Behavior states that a consumer's purchase intention is influenced by attitudes, subjective norms, and perceived control (Beyari & Garamoun, 2022). AI enhances these by providing relevant information, such as reviews and ratings, which can positively influence end-user purchasing decisions. AI's functionality in the e-commerce sector extends to the end-user purchasing decision. This is done through the real-time insight and personalized recommendations that AI has provided to guide consumers in making a final choice (Haleem et al., 2022). The predictive nature of AI can anticipate their needs and suggest products during optimal momentum, increasing the likelihood of purchase (Aftab et al., 2021). In addition, it can offer personalized pricing, inventory updates, and contextual information shown in their preferences, making the purchasing decision process informative and seamless (Mensouri & Azmani, 2022). This eliminates the uncertainty in a consumer's purchase journey. AI can enhance customer satisfaction and confidence in purchasing, achieving higher conversion rates, and initiating long-term customer relationships (Rane, 2023).

Hypothesis 3: there is a positive association between AI end-user purchasing decisions and Consumer Experience.

2.4 Perceived Personalization

Perceived personalization concerns how consumers interpret and evaluate personalized experiences (Yin & Qiu, 2021). This perception is influenced by the degree to which consumers feel that content or services are tailored to their individual preferences and needs (Li, 2024). In terms of online shopping, consumers will have the potential to enjoy the feeling of browsing and purchasing items online (Wang & Wang, 2020). It has been theorized that there are nine factors of flow experience: distinct objectives, direct feedback, skill and challenge comparison, merge of actions and awareness, being highly immersed in the task, potential control, temporary loss of self-consciousness, sense of time, and being worthy of doing (Hoffman & Novak, 2009). This theory is helpful in e-commerce as it supports the explanation of the deep engagement and immersed state that users experience when interacting with AI-driven personalization. The studied variable, perceived personalization (PP), can be reflected using flow experience and can enhance consumer experience positively (Li et al., 2024). Perceived personalization is a crucial component of the consumer experience. This personalization is significantly enhanced by AI, based on data provided by the user's interactions, social media, and browsing history (Mittal et al., 2022). This curates a detailed profile of each consumer and creates highly personalized content (Valdez Mendia & Flores-Cuautle, 2022).

Hypothesis 4: a positive association exists between AI Perceived Personalization and Consumer Experience.

3 Research Method

To enhance clarity and organization, the questionnaire was divided into three distinct sections. Initially, participants were required to respond to a screening question to determine their use of Tokopedia. After that, participants were asked to provide demographic information. Finally, the main section of the questionnaire consisted of items designed to measure PR, CS, EPD, PP, and CE. The data collection spanned two months, from June to July 2024.

3.1 Survey Questionnaire and Design

The data collection for this research was conducted through an online survey. The questionnaire used the five-point Likert scale, a psychometric measurement that allows participants' opinions, attitudes, and feelings toward a set of statements to determine the correlation of multiple variables (Nemoto & Beglar, 2014). This methodology captures information and can curate a framework for analyzing the complex interactions and relationships among PR, CS, EPD, PP, and CE.

3.2 Sampling Procedure

Participants were collected through purposive sampling. It is known to perform non-probability sampling within a focused population under a practical criterion (Etikan et al., 2016). It was ensured beforehand that the respondents actively use Tokopedia as their online shopping platform. The questionnaire was distributed via social media, particularly Facebook. This specific medium was chosen due to its high user activity in Indonesia, and most Facebook users use Tokopedia to purchase online items (Wuladari, 2024). The fact that it is effective in terms of both time and cost has been beneficial in selecting the purposive sampling approach in online survey applications (Malhotra, 2007). A power analysis was utilized to determine the number of participants collected. The recommended 80% level of power and 5% alpha within a medium effect size would be applied for this study, allowing a collection of 180 respondents would be sufficient (Giner-Sorolla et al., 2024). The study has collected data from 190 respondents. However, only 180 were acknowledged due to the data completion.

3.3 Data Analysis

To highlight the sample's demographic characteristics and identify anomalies in the data, descriptive statistics were employed. Cronbach's alpha was used as a reliability and validity test to evaluate the internal consistency. On the other hand, composite reliability (CR) and average variance extracted (AVE) allowed for convergent and discriminant validity (Fornell & Larcker, 1981). Each variable's outer loadings were calculated using SMARTPLS to maximize reliability, following the standard that loadings below 0.7 were considered for removal to enhance the model (Jobst et al., 2023). Multiple regression analyses were conducted for this study to assess the data, as understanding each variable's relativity to the model is essential. Multicollinearity was conducted to ensure the robustness of the regression models. In addition, For the hypothesis testing, the path coefficient test is used. The statistical results projected the relationship and strength between the independent and dependent variables (Montgomery et al., 2021). This approach will aid researchers and other e-commerce companies in formulating targeted strategies for customer experience with AI based on the most impactful factors.

Each of the corresponding variables (PR, CS, EPD, PP, and CE) was defined by three critical statements (Q1, Q2, and Q3) that are derived from previous research studies (Table 1). With these five latent variables and three indicators, the model aimed to provide a comprehensive understanding of the dynamics influencing customer experience with AI-driven personalization in e-commerce.

Table 1. Variable Questionnaire Construction

Variable	Questionnaires	Source
PR-Q1	E-commerce websites recommend relevant products to you	(Beyari & Garamoun, 2022)
PR-Q2	Product recommendations made to you are based on your previous purchases	
PR-Q3	You have purchased at least some of the products recommended to you	
CS-Q1	You have several products on your wish list on e-commerce websites	(Beyari & Garamoun, 2022)
CS-Q2	Your wish list keeps expanding as you interact more with e-commerce websites	
CS-Q3	Each time you visit these sites, you find an item that intrigues you to the point of considering buying it in the future	
EPD-Q1	You are likely to purchase items you like from e-commerce websites	(Beyari & Garamoun, 2022)
EPD-Q2	You have engaged in repeat purchases while interacting with e-commerce websites	
EPD-Q3	Deciding to buy is aided by features embedded in e-commerce websites	
PP-Q1	Intelligent customer service robots store my preferences and offer me extra services based on my preferences	(Gao et al., 2023)
PP-Q2	Intelligent customer service robots do a good job of guessing what I might want and making suggestions	
PP-Q3	Intelligent customer service robots know what I want	
CE-Q1	It allowed me to enjoy being immersed in a new, existing experience	Kronemann, B. (2022)
CE-Q2	I think interacting with AI Technology is Fun	Tiutiu, M., & Dabija, D. C. (2023)
CE-Q3	I think the information obtained from AI technology is helpful	

4 Analysis and Results

4.1 Demographic Respondents

The table presents the demographic breakdown of the respondents to the survey. It is categorized into gender, profession, salary, education, and age to identify Tokopedia's users. This information provides a comprehensive insight into the respondents' backgrounds, contributing to the study findings' reliability and generalizability. There were 180 participants in total, with 54.44% being male and 45.56% women. The diverse professional representation allows the study to understand the varied perspectives of users from different occupational backgrounds. The largest group was self-employed individuals (33.39%), followed by entrepreneurs (24.44%), university students (22.22%), and civil servants (17.22%).

The various earnings levels also determined customer behavior and experience with Tokopedia. Most respondents earned between five and ten million rupiahs (54.44%), 25% earned less than 5 million rupiahs, and 20.56% earned more than ten million rupiahs. Educational qualifications revealed a balanced mix, with 39.44% holding a bachelor's degree, 38.89% completing their high school studies, and 21.67% possessing a master's degree. Lastly, the age distribution of the respondents was mainly from the 26 to 35 age group (34.44%), followed by age 35 or above (27.78%), age 18 to 25 (25%), and age18 or below with the least amount (12.78%) (Table 2).

Table 2. Demographics Respondent

Measure	Item	Count	Percentage
Gender	Male	98	54.44%
	Female	82	45.56%
Profession	Civil servants	31	17.22%
	University Students	40	22.22%
	Entrepreneur	48	24.44%
	Self-employed	61	33.89%
Salary	<5 Million	45	25%
	>5 Million to 10 Million	98	54.44%
	>10 Million	37	20.56%
Education	Bachelor's degree	71	39.44%
	Master's degree	39	21.67%
	High School	70	38.89%
Age	18 or below	23	12.78%
	>18 to ≤25	45	25%
	≥ 26 to ≤35	62	34.44%
	35 or above	50	27.78%

4.2 Construct Reliability, Validity Test, Multicollinearity Test, and Factor Loading

The researchers also did the Construct Reliability and Validity Test. The results had good internal consistency, high reliability, and valid data. All the Cronbach's alpha, composite reliability (CR), and average variance extracted (AVE) have scores above 0.7. This is important, as it is crucial to yield accurate data with minimal errors for a meticulous study. Meanwhile, the results of the multicollinearity test show values less than 10, indicating that this study has passed the multicollinearity test. The measurement model below shows high factor loadings across variables, indicating strong relationships between observed variables and their respective factors.

Table 3. Summary of the Measurement Model

Variable	Factor Loading	Variable	Factor Loading	Variable	Factor Loading	Variable	Factor Loading	Variable	Factor Loading
PR-Q1	0.901	CS-Q1	0.905	EPD-Q1	0.859	PP-Q1	0.87	CE-Q1	0.87
PR-Q2	0.859	CS-Q2	0.81	EPD-Q2	0.781	PP-Q2	0.84	CE-Q2	0.87
PR-Q3	0.896	CS-Q3	0.874	EPD-Q3	0.874	PP-Q3	0.86	CE-Q3	0.88

4.3 Structural Equation Modeling of PR, CS, EPD, and PP

The results from Fig. 1 are collected from the survey and transformed into the SEM using the SMARTPLS software. Each statement presented in the questionnaire is correlated to a variable. The SEM depicted the relationships among PR, CS, EPD, and PP. Each independent variable is observed by three key variables denoted as Q1, Q2, and Q3. The observed variables (Q1, Q2, and Q3) are based on the survey item used in Table 3. The path coefficients indicate the strength and direction of the variables. For example, the coefficient between PR and CE is 0.242, suggesting a positive relationship. Similarly, the coefficients for CS, EPD, and PP to CE are 0.002, 0.732, and 0.866, respectively, indicating the varying degrees of influence.

The SEM results illustrate the significant positive impact of PP on CE, with a coefficient of 0.732. This suggests that PP is a strong predictor of CE. PR showed a slightly positive effect on CE (0.242). However, EPD (0.058) and CS (0.002) suggest a low and negligible effect on CE. The R-squared value of 0.758 for CE explains the model's fit, which is significantly portioned. The latent variables (PR, CS, EPD, and PP) have their respective loadings of observed variables, which signifies the measured underlying constructs.

4.4 Regression Model

From the results, the regression model can be depicted as:

$$Y = \beta 0 + \beta 1X1 + \beta 2X2 + \beta 3X3 + \beta 4X4$$

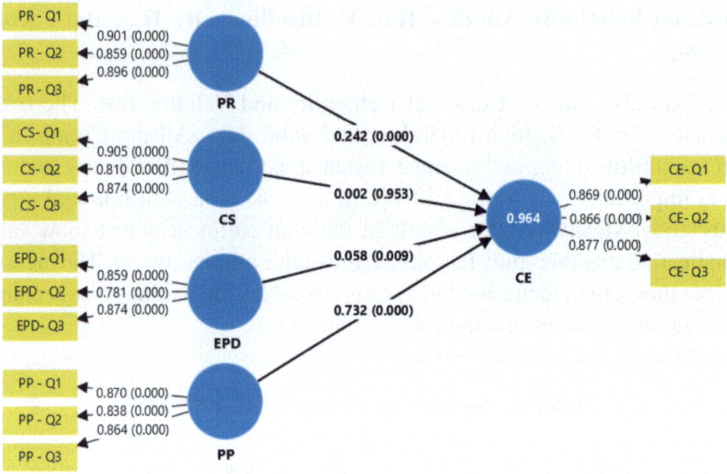

Fig. 1. Structural Equation Modeling of PR, CS, EPD, and PP

$$CE = 0.242(PR) + 0.002(CS) + 0.058(EPD) + 0.732(PP) - 0.4990$$

This model can be used to predict the dependent variable, customer engagement (CE), based on the values of the independent variables, product recommendation (PR), consideration set (CS), end-user purchasing decision (EPD), and perceived personalization (PP). The intercept refers to the result of customer engagement when none of the independent variables is applied to e-commerce platforms, such as Tokopedia. The coefficients of each independent variable will be compared to one another to determine the level of association with CE.

5 Discussion and Recommendations

The study's findings reveal that AI-supported systems such as product recommendations (PR), consideration sets (CS), end-user purchasing decisions (EPD), and perceived personalization (PP) each contribute to customer experience (CE) on e-commerce platforms, with varying degrees of impact.

The results indicate that AI-generated PR is associated with CE. The coefficient in Fig. 1 for PR is 0.242, suggesting a positive correlation with CE. The P value of the relationship between PR and CE is 0.000. These findings support the first hypothesis, although the strength of the connection was modest. Previous studies on AI and PR's impact on CE support these results, though slight variations exist in the degree of impact. It was mentioned that PR significantly influences CE on e-commerce platforms (Nwachukwu & Affen, 2023). PR has become an expected feature for consumers, particularly in enhancing and implementing a comprehensive digital experience (Felix & Rembulan, 2023). This is because e-commerce companies must proactively understand the consumer's needs, through which PR can offer a more immersive and interactive user experience (Raji et al., 2024). Regarding CDPT, PR also influences consumer behavior by addressing their needs and preferences. AI and personalized-based buyers would enjoy the PR offered within Tokopedia and other e-commerce platforms, positively increasing the CE.

The results also support the hypothesis regarding the CS that AI has provided for consumers. The coefficient in Fig. 1 for CS is 0.002, indicating a positive relationship with CE. Unlike PR, the low result of CS advocates a fragile relationship. The P value of the relationship between CS and CE is 0.953. This indicates that CS has no significant effect on CE. This independent variable has the lowest coefficient compared to the other three, suggesting that CS is necessary but not highly prioritized and does not directly impact enhancing CE. Research has shown that CS does not directly affect CE. However, it influences the EPD, which has a domino effect on CE. It involves recommending other possible products that a consumer might be interested in purchasing, it supports the user's decision-making and enhances the shopping experience (Zimmermann et al., 2023). This enhancement is reflected in the increased satisfaction levels and loyalty when a set of alternative products is presented (Gidh, 2020). Like the one mentioned in PR, CS is equally important in catering to AI and personalized-based consumers. CDPT can be applied by portraying relevant information and personalizing the first item that was wished to be purchased. This can be done through a set of options. Additionally, CS plays a crucial role in fostering a sustainable online purchase by providing consumers with a positive experience on the e-commerce platform (Beyari & Garamoun, 2022).

AI-driven EPD was connected to CE on e-commerce sites. Figure 1 shows EPD's coefficient of 0.058, which is considered a positive yet low contributor to CE. This result of EPD supports the hypothesis. The P value of the relationship between EPD and CE is 0.009. This indicates that EPD has a significant effect on CE. As mentioned previously, CS most influences EPD (Zimmermann et al., 2023). Nonetheless, the usage of AI in EPD reflects CE. Previous research theorized that consumers are highly likely to purchase a product based on the positive CE (Voicu et al., 2023). By embedding AI, consumers can achieve optimal EPD with the best CE, as experience also determines the next purchasing decision (Patil & Rane, 2023). CDPT emphasizes the importance of relevant and engaging content in EPD by providing personalized and relevant content. This can significantly enhance CE as it is aligned to AI and personalized-based buyers' contentment. Therefore, CDPT with AI insights can offer a comprehensive understanding of the impact of personalized algorithms on EPD.

PP through AI impacts CE heavily. Figure 1 shows that the 0.732 coefficient for PP was the highest out of all the other independent variables. This indicates PP's solid and positive relationship with CE, accepting the hypothesis. Moreover, The P value of the relationship between PP and CE is 0.000. This indicates that PP has a significant effect to CE. The PP can significantly increase trust, commitment, and value consumers receive, which are a few components of a positive CE (Alimamy & Kuhail, 2023). It also fosters an engaging experience and stimulates additional buying behavior, which all support the increase of CE (Reddy & Nalla, 2023). Flow experience theory supports the importance of PP in creating an immersive shopping experience and enhancing CE. This theory reinforces that being able to place consumers in an unconscious state and solely focusing on their online shopping experience implies a high positive CE. The strong relationship of PP with CE underscores the significant role of personalized AI-driven experiences in fostering a satisfying consumer journey.

These findings have yielded several recommendations to increase CE on e-commerce platforms through AI usage. PR is suggested to be further enhanced in the implementation of personalized algorithms. This AI-driven PR system should be designed to understand and anticipate consumer needs. Because of the low-strength connection to CE, it should be developed to increase the relevance and accuracy of the PRs. CS plays a massive role in subsequently affecting CE through EPD. E-commerce platforms should optimize and expand AI algorithms that generate CS, providing highly relevant alternative products to enhance consumer decision-making. EPD is supported by AI-generated algorithms and should be focused on by e-commerce businesses. Leveraging AI to assist consumers in making well-informed purchasing decisions by providing precise product information will improve overall CE. With the AI recommendations, the platform can improve CE and influence future EPD. Lastly, PP is the most prioritized variable that e-commerce companies should implement. Personalized experiences significantly affect customer satisfaction, trust, and loyalty. These platforms should utilize AI to tailor product personalization, marketing messages, and shopping experiences to individual preferences and behaviors. The PP can increase engagement and stimulate purchase behavior through highly leveled personalization, ultimately boosting CE. However, it is essential to note that privacy concerns should be addressed to avoid PP. Given that PP is the highest result, e-commerce companies must understand and find solutions to optimize personalization while maintaining users' trust and privacy. Hence, focusing on these four areas, with data privacy considered, can lead e-commerce stores like Tokopedia to use AI technologies to substantially increase CE, driving higher satisfaction, loyalty, and sales.

6 Conclusions, Limitations, and Further Research

In conclusion, integrating artificial intelligence (AI) within Tokopedia's operations has significantly impacted the consumer experience (CE). With product recommendation (PR), consideration sets (CS), end-user purchasing decisions (EPD), and perceived personalization (PP) taken into account, each variable carries varying degrees of influence toward CE. All of the AI-driven features have a positive association with CE, with PP being the strongest and CS being the lowest in impact. Each of the variables has proven to understand consumer needs, support purchasing decisions, build consumer relationships, and enhance the shopping experience. With the increasing PP among consumers, e-commerce platforms must ensure consumers' data privacy through regulations. Overall, the strategic implementation of AI in Tokopedia elevates the user experience and fosters brand loyalty and sustainable online purchasing behaviors from consumers. It allows AI to become a critical tool in Indonesia's rapidly evolving e-commerce sector and provides valuable insights for other online platforms aiming to optimize CE.

However, these findings present several limitations that warrant consideration. First, the data sample is limited to Tokopedia users, making the findings less generalizable for other e-commerce platforms in Indonesia or globally. The exclusive focus on Tokopedia implies that the results may not fully capture the diversity of CE across different platforms. Additionally, the methodology relies solely on the survey data collected using a

Likert scale, limiting the depth of insights. The absence of qualitative data does not portray the detailed and nuanced feedback from Tokopedia users, potentially overlooking the essential aspects of their experiences and perspectives. These limitations should be considered for future research. This can be done by exploring the long-term effects of AI on CE in different cultural and market contexts using qualitative methods, such as in-depth interviews and participant observations. Hence, further studies can provide a more comprehensive and inclusive understanding of AI's impact on e-commerce businesses.

References

Aftab, M.O., Ahmad, U., Khalid, S., Saud, A., Hassan, A., Farooq, M.S.: Sentiment analysis of customer for E-commerce by applying AI. In: 2021 International Conference on Innovative Computing (ICIC), pp. 1–7 (2021). https://doi.org/10.1109/ICIC53490.2021.9693026

Alimamy, S., Kuhail, M.A.: I will be with you, Alexa! The impact of intelligent virtual assistant's authenticity and personalization on user reusage intentions. Comput. Hum. Behav. **143**, 107711 (2023). https://doi.org/10.1016/j.chb.2023.107711

Amoah, J., Jibril, A.B., Odei, M.A., Bankuoru Egala, S., Dziwornu, R., Kwarteng, K.: Deficit of digital orientation among service-based firms in an emerging economy: a resource-based view. Cogent Bus. Manage. **10**(1), 1–17 (2023). https://doi.org/10.1080/23311975.2022.2152891

Babatunde, S.: The role of AI in marketing personalization: a theoretical exploration of consumer engagement strategies. Int. J. Manage. Entrepr. Res. **6**(3), 936–949 (2024). https://doi.org/10.51594/ijmer.v6i3.964

Beyari, H., Garamoun, H.: The effect of artificial intelligence on end-user online purchasing decisions: toward an integrated conceptual framework. Sustainability **14**(15), 9637 (2022). https://doi.org/10.3390/su14159637

Bezar, S., Noreen, M., Ali, R.: Rational choice theory: an economic analysis of Hardy's the return of the native. Glob. Econ. Rev. **VI**(IV), 94–104 (2021). https://doi.org/10.31703/ger.2021(vi-iv).08

Bhuiyan, M.S.: The role of AI-enhanced personalization in customer experiences. J. Comput. Sci. Technol. Stud. **6**(1), 162–169 (2024). https://doi.org/10.32996/jcsts.2024.6.1.17

Bodemer, O.: Empowering athletes with AI and blockchain: a new era of personalized training, secure data management, and user engagement. TechRxiv, pp. 1–8 (2023). https://doi.org/10.36227/techrxiv.24006396.v1

Cetin, G.: Experience vs quality: predicting satisfaction and loyalty in services. Serv. Ind. J. **40**(15–16), 1167–1182 (2020). https://doi.org/10.1080/02642069.2020.1807005

Chang, W., Park, J.: A comparative study on the effect of ChatGPT recommendation and AI recommender systems on forming a consideration set. J. Retail. Consum. Serv. **78**, 1–12 (2024). https://doi.org/10.1016/j.jretconser.2024.103743

Deng, G., Zhang, J., Xu, Y.: How E-commerce platforms build channel power: the role of AI resources and market-based assets. J. Bus. Ind. Mark. **39**(2), 173–188 (2023). https://doi.org/10.1108/jbim-11-2022-0497

Etikan, I., Musa, S.A., Alkassim, R.S.: Comparison of purposive sampling and purposive sampling. Am. J. Theor. Appl. Stat. **5**(1), 1–4 (2016). https://doi.org/10.11648/j.ajtas.20160501.11

Fahmi, T.A., Tjakraatmadja, J.H., Ginting, H.: An empirical study of emerging digital culture and digital attitudes in an established company. J. Ind. Eng. Manage. **16**(2), 342–362 (2023). https://doi.org/10.3926/jiem.5976

Felix, A., Rembulan, G.D.: Analysis of key factors for improved customer experience, engagement, and loyalty in the E-commerce industry in Indonesia. Aptisi Trans. Technopreneurship (ATT) **5**(2sp), 196–208 (2023). https://doi.org/10.34306/att.v5i2sp.350

Ganesh, C.: AI-enhanced content marketing for sustainability: a theoretical perspective on eco-friendly communication strategies. Matec Web Conf. **392**, 1–6 (2024). https://doi.org/10.1051/matecconf/202439201045

Gao, L., Li, G., Tsai, F., Gao, C., Zhu, M., Qu, X.: The impact of artificial intelligence stimuli on customer engagement and value co-creation: the moderating role of customer ability readiness. J. Res. Interact. Mark. **17**(2), 317–333 (2023). https://doi.org/10.1108/JRIM-10-2021-0260

Gidh, P.G.: A multi-dimensional research study in e-commerce to capture consumer expectations. Int. J. Res. Appl. Sci. Eng. Technol. **8**(11), 411–415 (2020). https://doi.org/10.22214/ijraset.2020.32169

Giner-Sorolla, R., et al.: Power to detect what? Considerations for planning and evaluating sample size. Pers. Soc. Psychol. Rev. **28**(3), 276–301 (2024). https://doi.org/10.1177/1088868324128328

Guerra-Tamez, C.: Decoding Gen Z: AI's influence on brand trust and purchasing behavior. Front. Artif. Intell. 7 (2024). https://doi.org/10.3389/frai.2024.1323512

Haleem, A., Javaid, M., Asim Qadri, M., Pratap Singh, R., Suman, R.: Artificial intelligence (AI) applications for marketing: a literature-based study. Int. J. Intell. Netw. **3**, 119–132 (2022). https://doi.org/10.1016/j.ijin.2022.08.005

Hidayat, R., Rahayu, A., Wibowo, L. A., Cahyani, L., Mustikasari, A.: Marketing Strategy: The Effect of Positioning and Advertising Effectiveness on Social Media to Purchase Decision, pp. 776–787 (2024). https://doi.org/10.2991/978-94-6463-443-3_103

Hoffman, D.L., Novak, T.P.: Flow online: lessons learned and future prospects. J. Interact. Mark. **23**(1), 23–34 (2009). https://doi.org/10.1016/j.intmar.2008.10.003

Kronemann, B.: The Impact of AI on Online Customer Experience and Consumer Behaviour. An Empirical Investigation of the Impact of Artificial Intelligence on Online Customer Experience and Consumer Behaviour in a Digital Marketing and Online Retail Context (Doctoral dissertation, University of Bradford) (2022)

Li, W., Xiao, J.X., Zhang, M.T.: Optimizing Urban e-Commerce Experiences: A Cross-Cultural Interface Design Approach for Enhanced Connectivity and Consumer Engagement, pp. 219–234 (2024). https://doi.org/10.1007/978-3-031-60441-6_15

Luo, Y., Yang, L., Ye, Q., Liao, Q.: Effects of customization and personalization affordances on perceived value and continuance intention of smartwatch use. Technol. Forecast. Soc. Chang. **194**, 1–13 (2023). https://doi.org/10.1016/j.techfore.2023.122752

Mahmuddin, Sirait, N.N.: E-commerce growth and development, impact, and challenges in Indonesia. Neoclassical Legal Rev. J. Law Contemp. Issues **1**(1), 15–33 (2022). https://doi.org/10.32734/nlr.v1i1.9603

Malhotra, N.K., Birks, D.F.: Marketing Research: An Applied Approach, 3rd edn. Pearson Education, Harlow (2007)

Mensouri, D., Azmani, A.: A new marketing recommendation system using a hybrid approach to generate smart offers. Appl. Comput. Syst. **27**(2), 149–158 (2022). https://doi.org/10.2478/acss-2022-0016

Mittal, A., Arora, M., Rana, A.: IMEP: influence maximization on social media with the impact of E-commerce products. In: 2022 5th International Conference on Contemporary Computing and Informatics (IC3I), pp. 1789–1793 (2022). https://doi.org/10.1109/IC3I56241.2022.10072595

Montgomery, D.C., Peck, E.A., Vining, G.G.: Introduction to Linear Regression Analysis, 6th edn. Wiley, Hoboken (2021)

Muthaluri, J.: Optimizing supply chain management and marketing strategies: AI and ML integration for competitive advantage. EATP, 8990–8997 (2024). https://doi.org/10.53555/kuey.v30i5.4494

Nwachukwu, D., Affen, M.P.: Artificial intelligence marketing practices: the way forward to better customer experience management in Africa (systematic literature review). Int. Acad. J. Manage. Market. Entrep. Stud. **9**(2), 44–62 (2023). 27214256637924

Patil, D.R., Rane, N.L.: Customer experience and satisfaction: importance of customer reviews and customer value on buying preference. Int. Res. J. Mod. Eng. Technol. Sci. **5**(3), 3437–3447 (2023). https://doi.org/10.56726/IRJMETS36460

Rachmad, Y.E.: The Evolution of Consumer Behavior: Theories of Engagement, Influence, and Digital Interaction. PT. Sonpedia Publishing Indonesia, Jambi City (2024)

Radovanović, S.: Rational choice theory and charitable giving. Socioloski Pregled **53**(2), 445–466 (2019). https://doi.org/10.5937/socpreg53-19679

Raji, M.A., Olodo, H.B., Oke, T.T., Addy, W.A., Ofodile, O.C., Oyewole, A.T.: E-commerce and consumer behavior: a review of AI-powered personalization and market trends. GSC Adv. Res. Rev. **18**(3), 66–77 (2024). https://doi.org/10.30574/gscarr.2024.18.3.0090

Rana, J., Gaur, L., Singh, G., Awan, U., Rasheed, M.: Reinforcing customer journey through artificial intelligence: a review and research agenda. Int. J. Emerg. Mark. **17**(7), 1738–1758 (2021). https://doi.org/10.1108/ijoem-08-2021-1214

Rane, N.: Enhancing customer loyalty through artificial intelligence (AI), internet of things (IoT), and big data technologies: improving customer satisfaction, engagement, relationship, and experience. SSRN Electron. J. (2023). https://doi.org/10.2139/ssrn.4616051

Reddy, S.R.B.: Enhancing customer experience through AI-powered marketing automation: strategies and best practices for Industry 4.0. J. Artif. Intell. Res. (JAIR) **2**(1), 36–46 (2022)

Reddy, V.M., Nalla, L.N.: Leveraging big data analytics to enhance customer experience in e-commerce. Revista Espanola De Documentacion Cientifica **18**(2), 295–324 (2023)

Senyapar, H.: Artificial intelligence in marketing communication: a comprehensive exploration of the integration and impact of AI. Technium Soc. Sci. J. **55**(1), 64–81 (2024). https://doi.org/10.47577/tssj.v55i1.10651

Sufyan, I.K., Pamuncak, M.B.: Convenient or marketing matters? Unveiling the determinants of purchasing decisions in Tokopedia E-commerce. J. Digit. Market. Halal Ind. **5**(2), 207–224 (2023). https://doi.org/10.21580/jdmhi.2023.5.2.18247

Tiutiu, M., Dabija, D.C.: Improving customer experience using artificial intelligence in online retail. In: Proceedings of the International Conference on Business Excellence, vol. 17, no. 1, pp. 1139–1147 (2023)

Tuu, H.H., Khoi, N.H., Olsen, S.O.: How consumer innovativeness, technological expertise, and consideration set size can explain mobile commerce use: an extended understanding using a moderation-mediation model. IseB **19**(3), 1015–1038 (2021). https://doi.org/10.1007/s10257-021-00528-1

Valdez Mendia, J.M., Flores-Cuautle, J.J.A.: Toward customer hyper-personalization experience — a data-driven approach. Cogent Bus. Manage. **9**(1), 1–16 (2022). https://doi.org/10.1080/23311975.2022.2041384

Voicu, M.-C., Sîrghi, N., Toth, D.M.-M.: Consumers' experience and satisfaction using augmented reality apps in E-shopping: new empirical evidence. Appl. Sci. **13**(17), 1–22 (2023). https://doi.org/10.3390/app13179596

Wang, L., Wang, S.: The influence of flow experience on online consumers' information searching behavior: an empirical study of Chinese college students. Data Inf. Manage. **4**(4), 250–257 (2020). https://doi.org/10.2478/dim-2020-0043

Wuladari, F.: The influence of digital marketing on Tokopedia. J. Manage. **3**(1), 120–123 (2024). https://myjournal.or.id/index.php/JOM/article/view/113

Zimmermann, R., et al.: Enhancing brick-and-mortar store shopping experience with an augmented reality shopping assistant application using personalized recommendations and explainable artificial intelligence. J. Res. Interact. Mark. **17**(2), 273–298 (2023). https://doi.org/10.1108/JRIM-09-2021-0237

Yin, J., Qiu, X.: AI technology and online purchase intention: structural equation model based on perceived value. Sustainability **13**(10), 5671 (2021). https://doi.org/10.3390/su13105671
Li, L.: The effect of AI product image anthropomorphism on consumer purchase intention (2024). https://doi.org/10.3233/atde231317

Harnessing Artificial Intelligence to Transform Primary Education: Applications, Challenges, and Future Directions

Sameer Joshi(✉) and Ranjani Ramnath

IU International University of Applied Sciences, Bad Honnef, Germany
sameer.josShi@iu.org, ranjani.ramnath@outlook.com

Abstract. The paper explores how artificial intelligence (AI) can transform primary education, enhancing both teaching and learning approaches. By examining AI applications, challenges, and future directions, this paper offers a detailed analysis of how AI can be integrated into primary education along with strategies for success. While the paper takes a closer look at primary education in the UAE and the Middle East, the findings are considered to be globally applicable. AI technology's rapid growth is causing a revolution in several sectors, including education. Primary education, being the crucial starting point for a child's academic journey, can experience substantial advantages from AI innovations. AI has the potential to tackle various educational hurdles, providing unprecedented possibilities. This paper aims to respond to crucial queries about how AI affects student engagement and instructional planning in primary classrooms. Using AI-driven tools such as adaptive learning systems, intelligent tutoring systems, and automated assessment platforms has great potential in enhancing student performance and engagement. These tools also provide valuable support to teachers in instructional planning and assessment. By utilizing AI technologies, education becomes more inclusive and efficient through personalized learning, interactive content, and real-time feedback. Every student can succeed with AI's support for various learning requirements. Incorporating AI in primary education brings various obstacles, such as data privacy, educator training, and AI system dependability. Successfully addressing these challenges is vital for the ethical and effective use of AI in educational settings. In this paper, a variety of recommendations for promoting the integration of AI are presented. These recommendations include policy suggestions, educator training programs, and guidelines for the ethical utilization of AI in education. Continued research and collaboration are necessary to harness AI's capabilities responsibly and maximize its benefits for future generations. Primary education could be revolutionized through AI, creating personalized, inclusive, and efficient learning experiences.

Keywords: Artificial Intelligence (AI) · Primary Education · Personalized Learning · Intelligent Tutoring Systems · AI Ethics in Education

R. C. Geibel and S. Machavariani (Eds.): ISPC 2024, SPBE, pp. 515–528, 2025.
https://doi.org/10.1007/978-3-031-88052-0_41

1 Introduction

Artificial Intelligence (AI) is increasingly recognized as a transformative force in education, offering significant potential to enhance learning experiences, support educators, and streamline administrative tasks. In primary education, AI technologies present unique opportunities to address challenges such as diverse learning needs, large class sizes, and time-consuming administrative duties. AI-driven tools—including adaptive learning platforms, intelligent tutoring systems, and automated grading systems—have shown promise in providing personalized learning experiences that cater to individual student needs, thereby fostering more effective learning environments (Luckin et al., 2016). Globally, AI is becoming more integrated into educational systems; however, its role in primary education within the Middle East remains in developmental stages. Understanding how AI can be leveraged in this region, where educational systems are rapidly evolving, is critical for the future of education.

In the Middle East, countries are striving to modernize their educational systems, often with a focus on integrating advanced technologies such as AI. Government initiatives like the United Arab Emirates' Vision 2021 (Government of UAE, 2010) and Saudi Arabia's Vision 2030 (Kingdom of Saudi Arabia, 2016) emphasize the importance of adopting cutting-edge technologies to enhance education and prepare students for a knowledge- based economy.

AI is seen as a key enabler of these ambitions, particularly in its ability to provide real-time feedback to teachers, automate routine tasks, and enhance student engagement through interactive learning environments (UNESCO, 2019). Despite these ambitious goals, the integration of AI in primary education faces several hurdles, including limited teacher training, insufficient infrastructure, and concerns over data privacy and the ethical use of AI.

Exploring the applications, challenges, and future directions of AI in primary education in the Middle East is critically important for several reasons. Firstly, primary education lays the foundation for a child's lifelong learning, and AI has the potential to significantly enhance this stage by providing tailored learning experiences (Holmes et al., 2019). Personalized learning facilitated by AI can adapt to each student's pace and style, addressing individual strengths and weaknesses more effectively than traditional teaching methods (Chen et al., 2020). Secondly, teachers in the region often struggle with large class sizes and limited resources; AI can assist by automating administrative tasks such as grading and tracking student progress, allowing educators to focus on more personalized instruction (Zawacki-Richter et al., 2019). Moreover, AI can support inclusive education by providing assistive technologies for students with special needs, enhancing accessibility and equity in learning opportunities (Sanchez & Saenz, 2018).

However, the effective implementation of AI in primary education depends not only on technological readiness but also on the perceptions and attitudes of educators and school leaders. Their willingness to adopt AI, coupled with appropriate government policies and infrastructural support, is essential for AI to become a practical tool in classrooms across the region. Understanding these stakeholders' perspectives is crucial for developing strategies that address their concerns and facilitate the successful integration of AI technologies.

There is a growing body of research exploring the potential benefits and challenges of AI in education. Globally, AI has been integrated into educational systems in various ways, from personalized learning platforms to AI-driven student assessments. Studies have shown that AI can increase student engagement, provide personalized feedback, and support differentiated instruction for students with varying levels of ability (Zawacki-Richter et al., 2019). In primary education, AI-driven tools like adaptive learning platforms have been used to tailor content to each student's pace, enabling more individualized learning experiences (Holmes et al., 2019). For example, intelligent tutoring systems can diagnose a student's understanding in real-time and adjust the difficulty level accordingly, enhancing learning efficiency and outcomes (Woolf, 2015).

In the Middle East, efforts to incorporate AI into education are underway, particularly in higher education and secondary schooling. Countries like the UAE and Saudi Arabia have made strides in integrating AI into their education systems, driven by national visions emphasizing the adoption of advanced technologies to modernize education. For instance, the UAE has launched initiatives like the Mohammed bin Zayed University of Artificial Intelligence to foster AI research and education (MBZUAI, 2019). However, the extent to which AI is utilized in primary schools across the region varies widely. While some schools have begun piloting AI-driven platforms, others face challenges related to infrastructure and teacher training (Al-Mahdi, 2020). Additionally, ethical considerations regarding data privacy and the use of AI in educational decision-making are areas that require careful analysis and policy development (UNESCO, 2019).

Several critical areas require in-depth analysis to fully understand the impact and potential of AI in primary education within the Middle East. One such area is the practical implementation of AI technologies at the primary school level, including how educators integrate these tools into their teaching practices and curricula. Investigating the experiences of teachers and school leaders can provide valuable insights into the effectiveness of AI applications and highlight best practices as well as common challenges.

Another area of importance is the examination of infrastructural readiness and resource allocation. Disparities in technological infrastructure between urban and rural schools, or between well-funded and underfunded institutions, may influence the success of AI integration. Understanding these disparities is essential for developing equitable strategies that ensure all students benefit from technological advancements.

Ethical considerations, such as data privacy, consent, and the potential biases embedded within AI algorithms, also warrant thorough analysis. As AI becomes more prevalent in classrooms, establishing clear guidelines and policies to protect students' rights and interests is imperative (Scherer, 2016).

By focusing on these areas, the research aims to provide a comprehensive understanding of the current landscape of AI in primary education in the Middle East and identify opportunities for enhancing its integration.

The rationale behind this research stems from the need to understand the perspectives of key stakeholders— teachers, IT leads, and school leaders—who are directly responsible for the integration of AI in schools. These stakeholders play a pivotal role in shaping how AI is adopted and implemented in the classroom. Understanding their concerns, motivations, and challenges is essential for informing future policy development and ensuring that AI technologies are used to their full potential in primary education.

Furthermore, by focusing on the Middle East, this study highlights a region experiencing rapid educational and technological transformation but where the adoption of AI in primary schools remains varied. The research will explore how government initiatives like Vision 2021 and Vision 2030 are being translated into practice in schools and whether educators feel adequately supported in their efforts to incorporate AI into their teaching practices. This research is particularly timely as countries in the Middle East seek to modernize their educational systems in response to global technological trends, making it imperative to understand how AI can be effectively integrated at the foundational level of primary education.

This research seeks to explore how these stakeholders view AI's role in primary education, the barriers they face in its implementation, and what support they require to leverage AI effectively in their schools.

2 Theoretical Foundations

The development and integration of Artificial Intelligence (AI) in education are reshaping how students learn and how educators approach instruction. In primary education, AI holds significant potential to provide personalized learning experiences, support teachers with administrative tasks, and transform classroom management. However, despite its promise, the integration of AI into primary education presents substantial challenges, particularly concerning ethical considerations, infrastructure, and teacher readiness.

In the context of the Middle East, countries like Qatar, Saudi Arabia, and the United Arab Emirates (UAE) have been making strides toward incorporating AI into their educational systems. Each country faces unique challenges shaped by its infrastructure, government policies, and the awareness levels of educators. This research aims to explore the applications, challenges, and future directions of AI in primary education by investigating the perspectives of educators and school leaders across these regions. Understanding how different stakeholders— teachers, IT leads, and school leaders—perceive AI is crucial for grasping the broader implications of AI in education and informing future strategies for successful integration.

This study is significant because it not only examines AI in the Middle East, where educational innovation is accelerating, but also focuses on primary education, which is foundational for students' academic and personal development. By analyzing the views from different educational roles and regions, the research provides insights that are relevant both regionally and globally.

2.1 Educational Underpinnings of AI Integration

AI's use in education is grounded in several educational theories and frameworks. Constructivism asserts that learners develop knowledge through experiences and interactions with their environment (Piaget, 1952). AI technologies such as interactive simulations and educational games facilitate exploratory learning, enabling students to actively engage with content and develop understanding through participation. Vygotsky's (1978) concept of the Zone of Proximal Development underscores the significance of instructional support in the learning process. AI-driven adaptive learning systems align with this principle by modifying difficulty levels and offering support to enhance each learner's educational experience.

Personalized learning models advocate for instruction tailored to the specific requirements, preferences, and interests of individual students (Chen, 2008). AI algorithms are essential for analyzing student data to customize learning pathways, ensuring that each learner progresses at an appropriate pace. Furthermore, the Self- Determination Theory emphasizes intrinsic motivation and psychological needs for autonomy, competence, and relatedness (Deci & Ryan, 1985). AI applications that provide choices and instantaneous feedback can augment motivation and engagement in young learners, fostering a deeper connection to the learning material.

2.2 Applications of AI in Primary Education

AI technologies assist educators by alleviating administrative tasks such as attendance tracking, grading, and data entry, enabling teachers to allocate more time to instruction and student engagement (Wardat et al., 2023). AI- powered tools offer lesson plan recommendations that correspond with curricular standards and student needs, facilitating instructional planning (Nain, 2023). The automation of assessments through AI systems enables both formative and summative evaluations, delivering immediate feedback and assisting in monitoring student development (Kooli & Yusuf, 2024). Moreover, AI-driven systems provide tailored professional development opportunities for educators, enhancing their pedagogical competencies and classroom management strategies (Parambil et al., 2022). Successful incorporation of AI necessitates adequate training for educators and the cultivation of favorable attitudes toward technology. Teachers require direct experience with AI tools to fully comprehend their advantages and deploy them effectively (González-Calero et al., 2018).

For students, AI presents novel opportunities for individualized and adaptive learning. Educational robotics programs promote creativity, problem-solving skills, and cognitive capacities, fostering systematic thinking and technological literacy—crucial competencies in the digital era (Jamali, 2024; Zhang & Zhu, 2022; Sorokin et al., 2021; Paucar-Curasma et al., 2022). AI-driven online learning platforms provide interactive content that adjusts to individual learning styles and paces, enhancing engagement and comprehension among primary pupils (Dahlan et al., 2021). While challenges exist in deploying AI chatbots—such as language proficiency and digital literacy among younger learners—the growing technological adeptness of newer generations suggests that these tools may increasingly enhance learning (Aleedy et al., 2022).

2.3 Challenges of AI Integration in the Middle East

Despite the potential advantages, incorporating AI into primary education poses numerous hurdles, especially in the Middle East. Ethical considerations and data privacy are paramount; safeguarding student data requires that AI systems comply with stringent data protection regulations to ensure privacy and security (Laptev et al., 2023; Chan & Zary, 2019). Algorithmic bias is a critical issue, as AI tools may embody prejudices inherent in their training data, potentially compromising fairness and inclusion. This concern necessitates meticulous design and continuous assessment of AI systems to mitigate unintended consequences (Chan & Zary, 2019).

Educator preparedness is essential; teachers may lack the requisite skills and confidence to effectively deploy AI technology, highlighting the need for professional development and support (Parambil et al., 2022). Infrastructure constraints can impede AI adoption, particularly in areas with varying degrees of technological advancement. In the Middle East, disparities in resource distribution and technological infrastructure between urban and rural regions can influence access to AI technologies in educational institutions.

Cultural and linguistic relevance is crucial for the efficacy of AI tools; they must exhibit cultural sensitivity and accommodate the languages prevalent in the region, including Arabic. Methodological challenges also exist in assessing AI's impact on learning outcomes due to the need for extensive datasets and the sensitivity of educational evaluations (Chan & Zary, 2019).

2.4 Need for Regional Analysis

While global research highlights AI's promise in education, there is a deficiency of studies focusing exclusively on the Middle Eastern context, particularly in primary education. Regional factors—including diverse government initiatives, educational policies on technology integration, socioeconomic differences, and cultural perceptions of AI—affect the acceptance and efficacy of AI in educational settings. Addressing these factors is essential for the effective integration of AI into the region's primary education institutions.

Recent research identifies several areas that require further investigation. Empirical studies are needed to assess the effectiveness of AI applications in primary schools in the Middle East, including explorations of teachers' attitudes, perceptions of AI, and their readiness to adopt new technologies. A comprehensive analysis of regional policies that promote or hinder AI integration in education is crucial to understanding the broader context of AI adoption.

The integration of AI in primary education presents substantial potential for enhancing teaching and learning experiences. Grounded in established educational theories, AI applications can facilitate personalized learning, increase student engagement, and reduce educators' administrative burdens. However, challenges such as ethical considerations, teacher readiness, infrastructural limitations, and cultural factors must be addressed. This research aims to provide practical insights for educators, policymakers, and stakeholders to safely and effectively leverage AI's transformative potential within the Middle Eastern context.

3 Research Method

This study employs a qualitative research design to explore the perspectives of educators and school leaders on the integration of Artificial Intelligence (AI) in primary education across Qatar, Saudi Arabia, and the United Arab Emirates (UAE). A qualitative approach was chosen for its ability to provide rich, detailed insights into the experiences, challenges, and attitudes of those involved in the adoption of AI in schools (Creswell & Poth, 2018). Focusing on the unique context of primary education, where AI has the potential to significantly enhance teaching and learning outcomes, this research seeks to understand the nuanced views of key stakeholders.

3.1 Research Design

The research utilized semi-structured interviews as the primary data collection method. This approach allowed for flexibility in discussing participants' experiences with AI while ensuring consistency across core areas of inquiry (Kallio et al., 2016). The semi-structured format facilitated the exploration of emerging themes and enabled participants to provide in-depth responses, offering a comprehensive understanding of their perceptions and experiences with AI in primary schools.

3.2 Key Areas of Inquiry Included:

1. **General Awareness and Knowledge of AI Tools in Education**: Assessing participants' familiarity with AI technologies and their applications in educational settings.
2. **Impact of AI on Student Engagement, Learning Outcomes, and Personalized Instruction**: Exploring how AI influences teaching practices and student experiences.
3. **Challenges to AI Adoption**: Identifying infrastructural limitations, ethical concerns, and teacher readiness issues that hinder AI integration.
4. **Future Recommendations for AI Integration**: Gathering suggestions on policy support, training needs, and resources necessary for successful implementation.

3.3 Participants and Sampling

A total of seven participants were interviewed, representing different roles in primary education across three countries:

- **United Arab Emirates**: Teachers and school leaders from primary schools.
- **Saudi Arabia**: IT leaders and school administrators.
- **Qatar**: School leaders from not-for-profit schools.

Participants were selected using purposive sampling to ensure that those with direct involvement in the implementation of AI in primary schools were included (Etikan et al., 2016). The sample consisted of:

- **Teachers**: Educators who interact directly with students and use AI tools (if available) in their teaching.
- **IT Leads**: Professionals responsible for the technical infrastructure and support required to implement AI technologies in schools.
- **School Leaders**: Principals and administrators who oversee AI adoption strategies and policy implementation.

This approach allowed the study to capture a broad range of perspectives from practitioners and decision-makers, addressing both practical and strategic aspects of AI integration in primary education.

3.4 Data Collection

Data were collected through virtual semi-structured interviews using platforms such as Zoom and Microsoft Teams, due to the geographical spread of participants. Each interview lasted between 45 min to one hour and was audio-recorded with the consent of the participants. Interviews were then transcribed verbatim to facilitate comprehensive analysis. Below is the criteria of selecting snowballed participants for this study-

1. **Familiarity with AI Technologies**: Participants were asked about their knowledge of AI and the tools currently used (if any) in their schools.
2. **AI in Practice**: Discussions on how AI tools are being used to support personalized learning, increase student engagement, or assist with administrative tasks.
3. **Challenges and Barriers**: Exploration of difficulties faced in adopting AI, such as lack of infrastructure, insufficient teacher training, or ethical concerns surrounding data privacy.

4 Ethical Considerations

4. Concerns around data privacy, AI bias, and the broader ethical implications of using AI in primary education.
5. **Recommendations for the Future**: Suggestions on policies, training, or resources necessary to successfully integrate AI into primary education.

This structure allowed participants to express their views freely while ensuring that the research addressed key topics related to the adoption of AI in education.

4.1 Ethical Considerations

Given the sensitivity of discussions surrounding AI, data privacy, and ethics, strict ethical guidelines were followed throughout the study. All participants provided informed consent before the interviews were conducted, and they were assured of the confidentiality and anonymity of their responses (British Educational Research Association, 2018). Any identifying details were removed during transcription, and pseudonyms were used in the final reporting to protect participant privacy.

The study adhered to ethical principles that recognized participants' concerns about the potential risks and benefits of AI in educational settings, particularly regarding student data privacy and AI-driven decision-making. Ethical approval was obtained from the relevant institutional review board prior to commencing the research.

5 Analysis and Results

The transcribed interviews were analyzed using thematic analysis, following the six-phase process outlined by Braun and Clarke (2006):

1. **Familiarization with the Data**: Reading and re-reading transcripts to become immersed in the content.

2. **Generating Initial Codes**: Identifying significant features of the data relevant to the research questions.
3. **Searching for Themes**: Collating codes into potential themes and gathering all data relevant to each theme.
4. **Reviewing Themes**: Checking if themes work in relation to the coded extracts and the entire data set.
5. **Defining and Naming Themes**: Refining the specifics of each theme and generating clear definitions and names.

This method allowed for the identification of patterns and themes within the data, providing a rich and detailed account of participants' perspectives on AI integration in primary education.

5.1 Reliability and Validity

To ensure the reliability and validity of the study's findings, several measures were implemented:

- **Triangulation**: Data were gathered from participants with diverse roles across three different countries. This multi-perspective approach enhanced the credibility of the findings by capturing a wide range of experiences and viewpoints (Patton, 2015).
- **Peer Review and Debriefing**: The coding process and identification of themes were reviewed by a second researcher to reduce bias and ensure consistency in data interpretation. This collaborative approach helped validate the findings and ensured they accurately represented the participants' experiences (Lincoln & Guba, 1985).

5.2 Limitations

While the study provides valuable insights, certain limitations should be acknowledged:

- **Sample Size**: With seven participants, the findings may not be generalizable to all educators and school leaders in the Middle East. However, the in-depth qualitative data offer meaningful understandings of the phenomena under study.

6 Discussion and Recommendations

By employing a qualitative research design grounded in semi-structured interviews, this study provides a robust and credible examination of AI integration in primary education across the Middle East. The methodologies adopted ensure a comprehensive exploration of the opportunities, challenges, and future directions for AI in the region's educational systems, contributing valuable insights for educators, policymakers, and stakeholders.

6.1 Thematic Analysis of Interview Data

The thematic analysis of the interview data revealed several recurring patterns and themes that reflect the varied experiences and perspectives of educators and school leaders regarding AI integration in primary education across the Middle East. A key observation across all participant groups was the limited awareness of the broader concept of AI, with many viewings it solely as recent technological advancements rather than recognizing its longer history in education through tools like deep learning algorithms. This limited understanding has led to a narrow perception of AI's potential and its applications in education.

6.2 Leadership Vision and Strategic Implementation

Participants from the UAE demonstrated a proactive approach to AI integration, aligning their efforts with national educational strategies such as Vision 2021 (Government of UAE, 2010). However, a notable gap was observed in understanding the full scope of AI:

- Emphasis on Visible AI Tools: The focus was on incorporating tangible AI tools into classrooms rather than understanding how existing AI technologies, such as data-driven personalized learning systems, could be optimized for educational purposes.
- Limited Conceptual Understanding: School leaders prioritized the adoption of new technologies without fully grasping the underlying AI principles and their long-standing presence in educational tools.

Similarly, in Saudi Arabia, the IT lead emphasized the importance of a solid technological foundation and government support for AI adoption. The focus remained on establishing the necessary infrastructure for AI rather than understanding how existing AI capabilities could be better utilized to support pedagogy in primary education.

In Qatar, a school leader highlighted a cautious approach toward AI, often viewing it through the lens of resource constraints and ethical concerns:

- Perception of AI as Emerging Technology: The participant associated AI primarily with newer government-driven initiatives and technological advancements, without recognizing that AI, in the form of data analytics and machine learning, has been integrated into educational technologies for years.
- Ethical Concerns: While concerns about AI's ethical implications were voiced, they were often disconnected from a deeper understanding of how AI has been historically integrated into educational technologies, which could provide a more balanced view of both risks and benefits.

6.3 Classroom-Level Challenges and Teacher Preparedness

Teachers from the UAE shared a cautious outlook toward AI, primarily due to their limited exposure and understanding of these technologies:

- AI Seen as a Technological Tool Rather Than a Pedagogical Aid: Many teachers viewed AI as just another gadget rather than a technology that can fundamentally transform teaching and learning practices through personalized instruction and real-time feedback.
- Need for Conceptual Clarity: There was a demand for more professional development that not only covers how to use specific AI tools but also educates teachers on underlying AI concepts like machine learning and deep learning, which have been a part of educational technology for years.

In Saudi Arabia, the practical application of AI in primary schools was described as limited:

- Emphasis on Visible AI Tools: Similar to the UAE, the focus was on integrating visible AI tools such as automated assessments and digital learning platforms, without leveraging existing AI capabilities embedded in current educational technologies.

In Qatar, the lack of financial resources was seen as a primary barrier, but equally significant was the lack of awareness about how existing, less resource-intensive AI technologies could be utilized to enhance educational outcomes:

- Resource and Knowledge Gaps: The participant's understanding of AI capabilities was limited, often conflating AI with advanced robotics or futuristic technologies, rather than recognizing its current, practical applications in data-driven decision-making.

6.4 Cross-Country Comparative Themes Limited Awareness of AI's Broader Scope

Across all three countries, a recurring theme was the limited awareness of the broader scope of AI, including its historical applications in education:

- AI Seen as Recent Technology: Participants predominantly viewed AI as synonymous with the latest technological tools, rather than recognizing that AI, through deep learning and data analytics, has been part of educational technologies for many years (Holmes et al., 2019).
- Overlooking Existing AI Capabilities: This narrow understanding led to an underutilization of existing AI capabilities embedded in tools like adaptive learning platforms, which already employ sophisticated algorithms to personalize learning (Chen et al., 2020).

6.5 Need for Foundational AI Education

There was a clear need for foundational education about AI among educators and leaders:

- Professional Development Beyond Tools: Training programs should go beyond the operational aspects of specific AI tools to include fundamental concepts of AI, such as machine learning, deep learning, and their applications in education.
- Building Conceptual Clarity: Educators need to understand the long-standing role of AI in education to fully appreciate its potential and to address their concerns more effectively.

6.6 Strategic Vision vs. Practical Understanding

A recurring theme was the contrast between the strategic vision of leaders and the practical understanding of teachers:

- Strategic Enthusiasm vs. Operational Hesitation: Leaders were generally enthusiastic about AI's potential but often lacked a practical understanding of its existing applications, mirroring the teachers' hesitation to adopt technologies they did not fully understand.
- Gap in Conceptual Frameworks: Both leaders and teachers could benefit from a clearer conceptual framework that situates AI within the continuum of educational technology advancements.

6.7 Discussion

The findings highlight a significant disconnect between the strategic ambitions of educational leaders and the practical realities faced by educators in the classroom. While national visions in countries like the UAE and Saudi Arabia emphasize the importance of AI in education (Government of UAE, 2010; Kingdom of Saudi Arabia, 2016), this study reveals that without a deep understanding of AI's full scope and potential, both leaders and educators may struggle to effectively implement these technologies.

6.8 Implications for Policy and Practice

6. Enhancing AI Literacy Among Educators and Leaders: There is a pressing need for professional development programs that build foundational AI literacy, enabling educators and leaders to make informed decisions about AI integration.
7. Bridging the Gap Between Vision and Implementation: Policymakers should ensure that strategic plans for AI adoption are accompanied by practical guidelines and support systems that address the operational challenges faced by schools.
8. Leveraging Existing AI Technologies: Schools should be encouraged to recognize and utilize the AI capabilities already embedded in current educational tools, maximizing the benefits without requiring significant additional resources.
9. Addressing Ethical Concerns through Education: By increasing awareness of how AI has been historically integrated into education, educators can develop a more balanced understanding of both the risks and benefits, leading to more informed discussions about ethics and data privacy.

The study underscores the importance of a nuanced understanding of AI among educators and leaders to enable more effective integration of AI into primary education across the Middle East. By addressing the gaps in awareness and understanding, and by providing targeted professional development, the potential of AI to transform education can be more fully realized.

7 Conclusion, Limitations and Further Research

7.1 Conclusion

In our research paper we delved into how Artificial Intelligence (AI) can be incorporated into education, in the Middle East region specifically We discovered that AI has promise in improving the quality of teaching and learning experiences though its actual use is still at a nascent stage in this area Personalized learning administrative effectiveness and promoting inclusive education are identified as critical areas where AI can bring about substantial positive changes. However there appears to be a significant disparity between the overarching goals set by educational leaders and the day, to day challenges faced by teachers. To maximize the possibilities of AI technologies impact it is essential, for those involved to focus on preparing educators and enhancing AI knowledge alongside developing resources.

The research findings show that teachers and leaders need to have a grasp of AI concepts to fully reap its advantages in education settings. Moreover, the governmental plans, like UAEs Vision 2021 and Saudi Arabia's Vision 2030 offer a foundation, for incorporating AI into schools. However, the effectiveness of these plans depends on addressing the real-world obstacles highlighted in this study.

7.2 Limitations

This research has some limitations to consider; the sample size is quite limited, as stated, with seven participants from three countries; this might restrict the applicability of the results to the whole region. Further, the study mainly depended on data which holds insights but could be further supported by quantitative data for a more comprehensive validation. Finally, the research focused on education in Qatar, Saudi Arabia and the UAE and did not take into consideration the perspectives from other Middle Eastern countries, which lays the groundwork for expanding the scope of the research.

7.3 Future Research

Future research should aim to address these limitations by expanding the sample size to include a broader range of schools and countries across the Middle East. Additionally, a mixed-method approach combining both qualitative and quantitative data would provide a more comprehensive understanding of AI's impact on education. Further investigations into the long-term effects of AI on student performance and teacher workload are also needed. Moreover, ethical considerations such as data privacy, AI bias, and the cultural adaptability of AI tools should be continuously evaluated to ensure responsible AI integration in education.

References

Aleedy, S., Sulaiman, S., Khamis, N., Daghestani, L.: AI-enabled Chatbot for distance learning in Arabic: challenges and opportunities. Int. J. Adv. Comput. Sci. Appl. **13**(5), 228–233 (2022)

Birt, L., Scott, S., Cavers, D., Campbell, C., Walter, F.: Member checking: a tool to enhance trustworthiness or merely a nod to validation? Qual. Health Res. **26**(13), 1802–1811 (2016)

Braun, V., Clarke, V.: Using thematic analysis in psychology. Qual. Res. Psychol. **3**(2), 77–101 (2006)

British Educational Research Association: Ethical Guidelines for Educational Research, 4th edn. BERA, London (2018)

Chan, K.Y., Zary, N.: Applications and Challenges of Implementing Artificial Intelligence in Medical Education: Integrative Review. JMIR Medical Education **5**(1), e13930 (2019)

Chen, L., Chen, P., Lin, Z.: Artificial intelligence in education: a review. IEEE Access **8**, 75264–75278 (2020)
Chen, W.: Supporting teachers' intervention in collaborative knowledge building. J. Netw. Comput. Appl. **31**(4), 343–354 (2008)
Creswell, J.W., Poth, C.N.: Qualitative Inquiry and Research Design: Choosing Among Five Approaches, 4th edn. Sage Publications, Thousand Oaks (2018)
Dahlan, M.K., Nursam, D.M., Mustafa, D.S.: The application of artificial intelligence in education: a review. J. Phys. Conf. Ser. **1796**(1), 012096 (2021)
Deci, E.L., Ryan, R.M.: Intrinsic Motivation and Self-Determination in Human Behavior. Plenum, New York (1985)
Etikan, I., Musa, S.A., Alkassim, R.S.: Comparison of convenience sampling and purposive sampling. Am. J. Theor. Appl. Stat. **5**(1), 1–4 (2016)
González-Calero, J.A., Arnau, D., Arevalillo-Herráez, M.: Teachers' attitudes toward and perceptions of interactive learning environments for mathematics. Interact. Learn. Environ. **26**(3), 328–343 (2018)
Government of UAE. (2010). UAE Vision 2021. Retrieved from UAE Vision 2021 website
Holmes, W., Bialik, M., Fadel, C.: Artificial Intelligence in Education: Promises and Implications for Teaching and Learning. Center for Curriculum Redesign, Boston (2019)
Jamali, A.: Robotics in primary education: enhancing cognitive and social development. Int. J. Educ. Dev. ICT **20**(1), 45–60 (2024)
Kallio, H., Pietilä, A.M., Johnson, M., Kangasniemi, M.: Systematic methodological review: developing a framework for a qualitative semi-structured interview guide. J. Adv. Nurs. **72**(12), 2954–2965 (2016)
Kingdom of Saudi Arabia: Saudi Vision 2030. Retrieved from Saudi Vision 2030 website (2016)
Kooli, C., Yusuf, A.: AI-driven assessment in education: opportunities and ethical challenges. J. Learn. Anal. **11**(2), 99–115 (2024)
Laptev, V., Tomilina, A., Kosarev, V., Orlova, S.: Use of artificial intelligence in education. Mathematics **11**(4), 820 (2023)
Lincoln, Y.S., Guba, E.G.: Naturalistic Inquiry. Sage Publications, Newbury Park (1985)
Nain, Z.M.: AI-assisted lesson planning: transforming teacher workflows. Educ. Technol. Soc. **26**(1), 77–89 (2023)
Parambil, J.V., Vasudevan, S., Kamalanathan, S.: Educators' readiness for AI integration in classrooms: a study in the Middle East. Educ. Inf. Technol. **27**(4), 5671–5690 (2022)
Patton, M.Q.: Qualitative Research & Evaluation Methods, 4th edn. Sage Publications, Thousand Oaks (2015)
Paucar-Curasma, D., Dongo, C., Cubas, D.: The impact of robotics on early childhood education. Int. J. Interact. Mob. Technol. **16**(12), 48–62 (2022)
Piaget, J.: The Origins of Intelligence in Children. International Universities Press, New York (1952)
Rathore, M.M., Paul, A., Ahmad, A.: AI in education: a roadmap to transforming learning. IEEE Access **11**, 12345–12360 (2023)
Sorokin, S., Kuznetsova, E., Mikhaylova, A.: Robotics in primary schools: developing computational thinking. Adv. Intell. Syst. Comput. **1312**, 329–339 (2021)
Vygotsky, L.S.: Mind in Society: The Development of Higher Psychological Processes. Harvard University Press, Cambridge (1978)
Wardat, Y., Al-Shboul, M., Al-Ayyoub, M., Alsmadi, I.: The role of AI in automating administrative tasks in education. Comput. Hum. Behav. **138**, 107411 (2023)
Zhang, Z., Zhu, X.: Educational robotics and student learning outcomes: a meta-analysis. Br. J. Edu. Technol. **53**(4), 1089–1105 (2022)

AI-Driven Features, Brand Experience, and Their Impacts on Purchase Intention: Samsung S24 Case Study in a Developing Country

Muhammad Lukman Baihaqi Alfakihuddin[1](✉), Chandra Hendriyani[2], Angelina Priscilla Tan[1], and Anindita Aulia Jasmine[1]

[1] Sampoerna University, Jakarta, Indonesia
lukman.alfakihuddin@sampoernauniversity.ac.id, {angelina.tan, anindita.jasmine}@my.sampoernauniversity.ac.id
[2] Akademi Sekretari Dan Manajemen Taruna Bakti, Bandung, Indonesia
chandra@asmtb.ac.id

Abstract. This research evaluates the impact of specific AI features in the Samsung S24 smartphone on brand experience and consumer purchase intentions. The Samsung S24 incorporates AI for diverse functions, especially for business support. AI-driven features are associated with the theories of Perceived Usefulness (PU) and Perceived Ease of Use (PEU). A quantitative approach was employed using a 5-point Likert scale questionnaire distributed via a Facebook Group. Purposive sampling across various cities in Indonesia yielded 299 responses. SPSS 23.0 was used for data processing and SMARTPLS 4.1.0 to test the hypotheses. The findings confirm that significant relationships between PU, PEU, and BE (Brand Experience), with BE playing a crucial role in influencing Purchase Intention (PI). Data analysis revealed a strong relationship between PU and BE, a weaker yet still significant relationship between PEU and BE, and a strong relationship between BE and PI. Additionally, while PU was found to have a significant and positive impact on PI, PEU did not significantly influence PI in this model. These results highlight the crucial role of AI features like Circle to Search, which enhances brand experience, and Live Translate, which shapes consumer purchase intentions. This study provides valuable insights for smartphone manufacturers, marketers, and AI developers by examining consumer preferences and the impact of AI features on purchase intent. These dynamics can guide product development, marketing strategies, and technological innovation in the smartphone industry. The findings serve as a guide for integrating AI features to optimize user engagement and market competitiveness.

Keywords: AI-Driven Features · Brand Experience · Purchase Intention · Samsung S24 · Developing Country

R. C. Geibel and S. Machavariani (Eds.): ISPC 2024, SPBE, pp. 529–541, 2025.
https://doi.org/10.1007/978-3-031-88052-0_42

1 Introduction

The smartphone industry has grown significantly due to the emergence of new companies, such as Apple and Samsung, and the development of hardware and software components (Cecere et al., 2015). In the early stages, companies focused on developing mobile communication systems, transitioning from analog to digital, and advancing from 4G to 5G (Fuentelsaz et al., 2008). These advancements allowed companies to rapidly introduce innovations, such as enhanced mobile networks. Consequently, these innovations have substantially improved smartphones and enhanced user-friendliness over time (Guerra-Tamez, 2024). Despite the standardization of certain smartphone features, the industry remains highly innovative and continues to evolve (Han & Cho, 2016).

AI has become a prominent feature in contemporary society, playing a crucial role in various aspects of daily life, such as detecting fraud in the financial industry (Metawa, 2023). Furthermore, AI provides personalized recommendations for online purchases and interprets user commands for virtual assistants like Amazon's Alexa and Apple's Siri (Ramaseshan & Stein, 2014). Additionally, AI improves device functionality by filtering spam, offering a more intuitive user experience (Ameen et al., 2021). Although many recent smartphones, such as iPhone, have incorporated AI-enhancing software and hardware, Samsung S24 stands out by integrating generative AI, an advanced AI (Saraswati & Giantari, 2022). Generative AI, unlike traditional AI, produces new and meaningful content created from training data, including text, images, and audio (Ghazwani et al., 2022). This method can be utilized both for artistic purposes and to assist humans as intelligent question-answering systems (Feuerriegel et al., 2024).

The integration of AI features aims to enhance users' smartphone experiences. Key features include Circle to Search, Live Translate, Chat Assist, and Transcribe Assist (Firdausiah, 2024). These AI-driven features not only enhance the functionality of the smartphone but also contribute significantly to the overall brand experience, which is crucial for customer retention (Manandhar, 2023; McLean et al., 2021). This enhancement could positively impact users' perception of quality and increase brand loyalty (Chithrasekara & Karandakatiya, 2019). Furthermore, the quality of the Samsung S24 smartphone ultimately plays a crucial role in influencing purchasing decisions. This quality is closely linked to factors such as Perceived Usefulness (PU), Perceived Ease of Use (PEU), and Brand Experience (BE) (Ameen, 2023).

AI can significantly impact brand experience by improving operational efficiency, enhancing customer service through Natural Language Processing, and enabling personalized offerings through Machine Learning (West et al., 2018). AI integration in purchasing enhances the consumer experience with trust, perceived sacrifice, and relationship commitment playing crucial roles (Alfakihuddin et al., 2023). Although several studies have explored these aspects of AI, more comprehensive research needs to be conducted, focusing specifically on the Samsung S24. While AI has broadly influenced brand experience and purchasing decision, this study seeks to explore these effects on Samsung S24's AI integration. This quantitative study employs structural equation modelling (SEM) and correlational statistical methods to analyze the complex relationship between AI features and purchase intent.

2 Theoretical Foundation

2.1 Perceived Usefulness

The Theory of Perceived Usefulness (PU) is a core component of the Technology Acceptance Model (TAM) (Ebrahim et al., 2016). This theory posits that the likelihood of individuals adopting and using a particular technology is significantly influenced by their perception of its usefulness (Hoyer et al., 2020). Brand experience (BE) refers to a consumer's subjective, internal, and behavioral reactions to various brand-related stimuli. BE, which encompasses consumer perception and emotional attachments, plays an integral role in developing brand personality and relationships (Ramaseshan & Stein, 2014). The correlation between brand loyalty and self-brand connection emphasizes the impact of cumulative BE on the development of consumer behavior and loyalty (Westhuizen, 2018). Moreover, studies have underscored that the overall BE can be affected by the consumer's perceptions of the brand's attributes, for instance, PU. Given its role in TAM, PU shapes BE, which in turn influences customer preference and repurchase intention (Westhuizen, 2018). These theoretical perspectives indicate that perceived usefulness is crucial in forming BE and, subsequently, brand identification, perceived value, and loyalty. Thus, understanding the role of PU in shaping BE is essential for fostering strong brand identification and customer loyalty.

Hypothesis 1: There is a positive association between Perceived Usefulness and Brand Experience.

2.2 Perceived Ease of Use

The theory of Perceived Ease of Use (PEU) is a fundamental concept within the Technology Acceptance Model (TAM) (Sankhi & Sandnes, 2020). The TAM is designed to explain and predict user behaviour regarding technology acceptance and usage (Ebrahim et al., 2016). PEU is one of the two primary constructs in this model, the other being PU (Martiniello et al., 2019). Smartphones, with their AI-enhanced functionalities, demonstrate the importance of PEU in facilitating user interaction and satisfaction (Khan et al., 2018). For example, Samsung S24's intelligent assistant features like Circle to Search and Translate highlight the critical role of PEU in enhancing user's experience and technology adoption (Liu et al., 2018). The inclusion of accessibility features, such as navigation support and universal user interfaces for the visually impaired, demonstrates how PEU can extend the benefits of technology to a broader audience, reinforcing the principles of TAM (Kuriakose et al., 2020). Studies have shown that brand experience can be influenced by consumer perceptions of brand attributes, impacting preference and repurchase intention (Westhuizen, 2018). PEU significantly influences online purchase intention, highlighting its role in the online brand experience (Mehmood, 2024). These observations are supported by studies showing that PEU and PU directly impact user's experience and behavioral outcomes, emphasizing their importance in TAM (Lewis & Sauro, 2023).

Hypothesis 2: There is a positive association between Perceived Ease of Use and Brand Experience.

2.3 Purchase Intention

The BE theory is a vital marketing concept that encompasses the full range of sensations, emotions, thoughts, and behaviors triggered by brand-related stimuli consumer interactions (Westhuizen, 2018). It extends beyond the traditional understanding of brand perception by emphasizing the experiential aspects of consumer-brand interactions. As previously established, the overall BE can be influenced by consumers' perceptions of the brand's attributes and consequently affect consumer preference and repurchase intention (Ebrahim et al., 2016). In the context of smartphones, purchase intention and decisions are influenced by factors like brand image, service quality, and perceived value (Haro et al., 2020). Moreover, the ease with which consumers can use a smartphone (Perceived Ease of Use) and their perception of its usefulness are crucial determinants of their purchase intention (Wang, 2023). When consumers find a smartphone easy to use, they are more likely to develop a favorable attitude towards the brand, which in turn increases their intention to purchase (Asbar et al., 2021). Similarly, when consumers perceive a smartphone as highly useful, it enhances their confidence in the brand, leading to a stronger purchase intention (Ravichandran, 2023). Additionally, social influence, habitual behavior, and brand loyalty are key factors that similarly impact smartphone purchase intention (Can, 2017). Collectively, these insights underscore the critical role that BE plays in shaping consumer behavior and driving purchase decisions.

H3: There is a positive association between Perceived Ease of Use and Purchase Intention.

H4: There is a positive association between Perceived Usefulness and Purchase Intention.

H5: There is a positive association between Brand Experience and Purchase Intention.

3 Research Methods

Initially, participants answered a screening question about their Samsung S24 usage. Following this, participants provided demographic information before proceeding to the main questionnaire, such as domicile, gender, and occupation. The main section of the questionnaire measured BE (Brand Experience), PU (Perceived Usefulness), PEU (Perceived Ease of Use), and PI (Purchase Intention). The questionnaire began with a definition of AI and AI marketing technologies. This included explanations of intelligent search, intelligent recommendation, and virtual customer service assistant. The questionnaire was compiled with a 5-point Likert scale, in which point 1 indicated strong disapproval and point 5 indicated strong approval.

3.1 Population and Sample

The target population for this study consists of Samsung S24 smartphone users in Indonesia. Given the widespread use of smartphones in urban areas, the sample is drawn from major cities, including Jakarta, Bandung, Surabaya, and Medan. The sample size was determined using purposive sampling, which is appropriate for exploratory studies. The use of purposive sampling, while limiting generalizability, is well-suited to the study's exploratory nature, allowing for a focused examination of specific user groups (Jung et al., 2020). This research was conducted from 2 July to 10 July 2024. A total of 303 participants took part in the research. However, since some respondents did not complete the questionnaire, we obtained 299 respondents who completed it. Considering the completed responses, a sample size of 299 respondents is deemed sufficient for exploratory research, aligning with prior studies that suggest such sample sizes can reliably support hypothesis development (Mathew et al., 2022).

3.2 Data Analysis

Data analysis was conducted using SPSS 23.0 and SMARTPLS 4.1.0 for partial least squares structural equation modelling (PLS-SEM). This tool allows the assessment of complex relationships between observed and latent variables. It provides robust results even with smaller sample sizes and non-normal data distributions, which is vital in this research. The analysis proceeded through several steps. First, descriptive statistics were employed to outline the sample's demographic characteristics and identify any anomalies in the data (Gatwiri et al., 2020). Next, reliability and validity testing were conducted using Cronbach's alpha to assess internal consistency, while composite reliability (CR) and average variance extracted (AVE) were evaluated to ensure both convergent and discriminant validity (Taber, 2017). The next step involved calculating the outer loadings for each indicator using SMARTPLS to gauge their reliability, with indicators showing loadings below 0.7 being considered for removal to enhance the model (Leguina, 2015). Finally, path analysis was performed using PLS-SEM (Partial Least Squares Structural Equation Modeling) to explore direct relationships between variables and test hypotheses regarding these relationships (Kock & Hadaya, 2016).

3.3 Ethical Considerations

Ethical approval was obtained from the university's ethics review board. Participants were informed about the study's purpose and obtained consent before data collection. Shown in table 1, they were assured of the confidentiality and anonymity of their responses.

4 Analysis and Results

4.1 Respondents Demography

Out of 299 respondents, 41% are males, 48% females, 11% are civil servants, 5% are university students, 35% work for state-owned companies, 48% are self-employed, 3% earn under 5 million, 76% earn over 5 million, 20% earn over 10 million, with 51% holding a bachelor's degree, 39% a master's degree, 10% a high school diploma, and an age distribution of 13% aged 18 or below, 15% aged over 18 to 25, 34% aged 26 to 35, and 37% aged 35 or above.

Table 1. Questionnaires about BE, PU, PEU, and PI.

Variable	Questionnaires	Source
BE1	This brand makes a strong impression on my visual sense or other senses	(Mostafa & and Kasamani, 2021)
BE2	I find this brand interesting in a sensory way	
BE3	This brand induces feelings and sentiments	
BE4	I engage in physical actions and behaviours when I use this brand	
PU1	Increase my efficiency in choosing the trendiest fashion outfit	(Arachchi & Samarasinghe, 2023)
PU2	Enhance my effectiveness in daily life	
PU3	Help choose the trendiest outfit	
PU4	I find my voice-based helpful assistance when I am searching for information	
PEU1	Learning to operate this device would be easy	(Arachchi & Samarasinghe, 2023)
PEU2	I think getting this device to do what I want would be easy	
PEU3	My interaction with this device would be clear and understandable	
PEU4	It would be easy to become skilful at using this device	
PI1	I intend to buy those products that are attached to celebrities	(Shafiq et al., 2011)
PI2	I would intend to buy those products that have excellent packaging	
PI3	I would actively seek out those products that have higher perceived value	
PI4	I would consider buying those products whose perceived value is high	

4.2 Validity and Reliability

Table 2 shows the constructs are valid and reliable, with strong internal consistency (Cronbach's alpha > 0.7), composite reliability (> 0.8), and convergent validity (AVE > 0.5).

Table 2. Cronbach's alpha, Composite reliability and Average variance extracted

Variable	Cronbach's alpha	Composite reliability (rho_a)	Composite reliability (rho_c)	Average variance extracted (AVE)
BE	0.878	0.886	0.916	0.732
PEU	0.733	0.740	0.800	0.770
PI	0.825	0.840	0.895	0.741
PU	0.862	0.862	0.916	0.784

4.3 Factor Loading Assessment

The factor loading was generated by SMARTPLS software, wherein a particular selection process was employed to count certain variables from the analysis. In Fig. 2, Cronbach's alpha values were used to measure the internal consistency of the constructs.

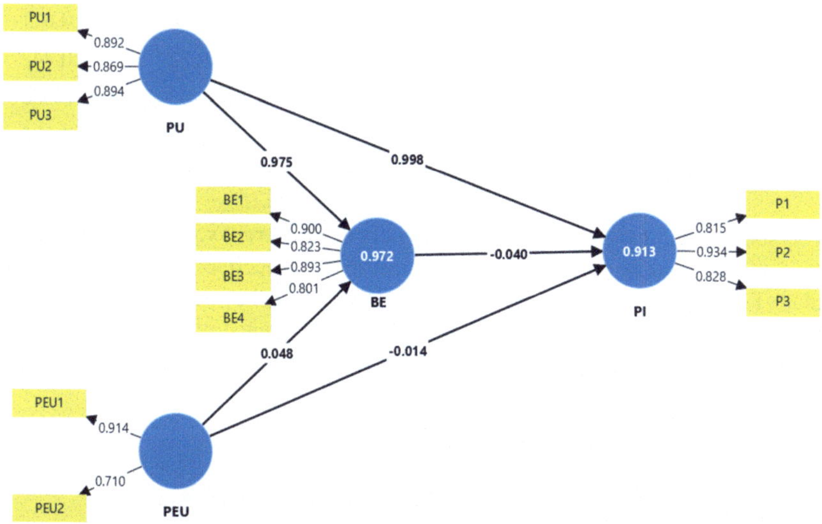

Fig. 1. Factor Loading Assessment

Figure 1 shows sufficient reliability, as the alpha value for all the constructs was above the 0.7 cutoff criteria of Sekaran and Bougie (2016). However, certain variables, namely PU4, PEU3, PEU4, and P4, were disregarded in the study due to their loading factors being below 0.7. The table below shows the summary of the measurement model.

4.4 R Square Test

Table 3 shows that the model explains 97.2% of the variance in Brand Experience (BE) and 91.3% of the variance in Purchase Intention (PI), indicating strong predictive power for both constructs.

Table 3. R Square Test

Variable	R-square	R-square adjusted
BE	0.972	0.972
PI	0.913	0.911

4.5 Hypothesis Test

Table 4. Hypothesis Test

Variable	Original sample (O)	Sample mean (M)	Standard deviation (STDEV)	T statistics (|O/STDEV|)	P values
BE - > PI	-0.040	-0.045	0.173	0.232	0.816
PEU - > BE	0.048	0.047	0.019	2.547	0.011
PEU - > PI	-0.014	-0.011	0.042	0.329	0.742
PU - > BE	0.975	0.974	0.007	132.932	0.000
PU - > PI	0.998	1.003	0.168	5.934	0.000

The Table 4 summarizes the relationship between different variables where the path coefficients (original sample) are tested against their respective standard deviations to calculate T statistics, with significant P values indicating the strength and significance of these relationships, such as the highly significant influence of PU on BE and PI, as opposed to the non-significant effects of BE on PI.

5 Discussion and Recommendations

H1: Correlation between Perceived Usefulness and Brand Experience.

The analysis confirms that Perceived Usefulness (PU) significantly influences Brand Experience (BE). Table 3 shows that the R-square value of 0.972 indicates that PU accounts for 97.2% of the variance in BE, suggesting strong explanatory power. Furthermore, Table 4 shows the beta coefficient (ß) of 0.975 reflects a positive relationship, and the extremely high T-value (132.932) with a p-value of 0.000 further reinforces the significance of this correlation. Such findings are corroborated by prior research conducted by Xie & Yuan (2021), who found that perceived usefulness and ease of use positively impact online experience and brand loyalty, mediated by flow experience. Furthermore, Coelho et al. (2019) underscored that brand experience and personality are affected by functional brand attributes such as quality and innovativeness; that is to say, their perceived usefulness, consequently impacting perceived value. These findings underscore the significance of functional brand characteristics in forming consumer perceptions and experiences.

H2: Correlation between Perceived Ease of Use and Brand Experience.

The positive beta coefficient (ß) of 0.048 (Table 4) reflects a small but meaningful relationship. The T-value of 2.547 and a p-value of 0.011 ($p < 0.05$) confirm the statistical significance of this relationship, supporting the hypothesis that PEU positively affects BE, albeit to a limited extent. Although the effect size is smaller, the statistical significance of PEU's impact on BE suggests that user-friendliness remains a relevant factor in enhancing brand experience, albeit less dominant than perceived usefulness. These findings align with previous research by Mohamed (2024), who underscored the significant positive impact of perceived ease of use on brand loyalty, with Xie & Yuan (2021) exemplifying that consumers' online experience and brand loyalty are influenced by perceived ease of use jointly with perceived usefulness, mediated by flow experience. Moreover, Risde (2023) found that perceived ease of use positively impacted brand satisfaction, with brand satisfaction and brand loyalty mediated by brand love. Overall, such findings underscore the significant role of perceived ease of use in shaping brand experience.

H3: Correlation between Perceived Ease of Use and Purchase Intention.

H4: Correlation between: Perceived Usefulness and Purchase Intention.

H5: Correlation between Brand Experience and Purchase Intention.

The data in Table 4 shows that Perceived Ease of Use (PEU) has a minimal effect on Purchase Intention (PI), with an insignificant beta coefficient of -0.014 and a high p-value of 0.742. This lack of significance suggests that PEU does not directly influence PI in the model, diverging from the findings of Xie and Yuan (2021), which indicated that ease of use can impact purchase intentions when mediated by other factors. Perceived Usefulness (PU) has a significant impact on Purchase Intention (PI), as indicated by a beta coefficient of 0.998 and a low p-value of 0.000. This result strongly supports the hypothesis that PU is a strong predictor of PI. Research has consistently demonstrated that brand experience significantly influences purchase intention, with Lie et al. (2022) finding that critical factors influencing purchase intention consist of brand personality and experience. Additionally, Nasermoadeli et al. (2013) established that emotional, social, and sensory experiences influence purchase intention, with emotional and social experiences having the most significant impact.

Nasermoadeli et al. (2021) corroborate these findings, illustrating that brand experience affects brand credibility, attitude, and purchase intention. These findings suggest that while perceived usefulness is a strong determinant of purchase intention, the role of brand experience in influencing purchase decisions may be more complex, potentially requiring a deeper understanding of the emotional and cognitive processes involved. Future research should incorporate qualitative methods to deepen the understanding of how AI-driven features in smartphones influence consumer behavior, specifically focusing on the underlying emotional and cognitive processes that shape brand experience and purchase intention. While this study offers significant quantitative insights, a mixed-methods approach, including in-depth interviews or focus groups, could provide a more nuanced exploration of user perceptions and interactions with AI technologies.

6 Conclusions, Limitations, and Further Research

In conclusion, this study identified significant relationships between PU, PEU, and BE, with BE playing a crucial role in influencing PI. Data analysis revealed a strong relationship between PU and BE, a weaker yet still significant relationship between PEU and BE, and a strong relationship between BE and PI. Additionally, while PU was found to have a significant and positive impact on PI, PEU did not significantly influence PI in this model. This research underscores the crucial nature of Samsung S24's integrated generative AI features, encompassing Circle to Search, Live Translate, Chat Assist, and Transcribe Assist, in improving the brand experience and impacting consumer purchase intentions. Quantitative methods and Structural Equation Modeling (SEM) were used to demonstrate the impact of AI integration on user engagement and purchase intentions. These findings offer valuable guidance for smartphone manufacturers, marketers, and AI developers in shaping marketing strategies and technological innovations. While these findings offer valuable insights, the study also faced certain limitations such limited applicability to other context. Moreover, as the study predominantly utilizes quantitative methods, it potentially lacks detailed insights that qualitative data could provide. Future research should incorporate qualitative methods to gain deeper insights into user behavior and preferences, thereby providing a more comprehensive understanding.

References

Alfakihuddin, M.L.B., Rahmat, A., Poa, T.K.E., Praditha, O.: Investigating the factors influencing carbon credit pricing among international carbon offset program. In: Lestari, S., et al. (eds.) Proceedings of the International Conference on Radioscience, Equatorial Atmospheric Science and Environment and Humanosphere Science: INCREASE 2023, pp. 785–794. Springer Nature, Singapore (2024). https://doi.org/10.1007/978-981-97-0740-9_70

Ali, A., Sherwani, M., Ali, A., Ali, Z., Sherwani, M.: Investigating the antecedents of halal brand product purchase intention: an empirical investigation. J. Islamic Market. **12**(7), 1339–1362 (2021). https://doi.org/10.1108/JIMA-03-2019-0063

Ameen, N.: Generation's psychology and new-age technologies: implications for future research. Psychol. Mark. **40**(10), 2029–2040 (2023). https://doi.org/10.1002/mar.21868

Ameen, N., Tarhini, A., Reppel, A., Anand, A.: Customer experiences in the age of artificial intelligence. Comput. Hum. Behav. **114**, 106548 (2021). https://doi.org/10.1016/j.chb.2020.106548

Arachchi, H.A.D.M., Samarasinghe, G.D.: Impulse purchase intention in an ai-mediated retail environment: extending the TAM with attitudes towards technology and innovativeness. Global Bus. Rev. (2023). https://doi.org/10.1177/09721509231197721

Asbar, Y., Biby, S., Razif, R., Siregar, W.V.: Millennial generation and smartphone purchase intention. Manage. Res. Behav. J. **1**(2), 55 (2021). https://doi.org/10.29103/mrbj.v1i2.6379

Can, Y.: Brand loyalty and repurchase intention in smartphone marketing: the perspective of habit. In: Proceedings of the European Proceedings of Social and Behavioural Sciences (2017). https://doi.org/10.15405/epsbs.2017.12.02.4

Cecere, G., Corrocher, N., Battaglia, R.D.: Innovation and competition in the smartphone industry: is there a dominant design? Telecommun. Policy **39**(3–4), 162–175 (2015). https://doi.org/10.1016/j.telpol.2014.07.002

Chithrasekara, G., Karandakatiya, T.: Effect of brand equity on consumer buying behavior of huawei brand in Colombo area. Wayamba J. Manage. **10**(1), 1 (2019). https://doi.org/10.4038/wjm.v10i1.7479

Coelho, F.J., Bairrada, C.M., de Matos Coelho, A.F.: Functional brand qualities and perceived value: the mediating role of brand experience and brand personality. Psychol. Mark. **37**(1), 41–55 (2020). https://doi.org/10.1002/mar.21279

Ebrahim, R., Ghoneim, A., Irani, Z., Yan, F.: A brand preference and repurchase intention model: the role of consumer experience. J. Mark. Manage. **32**(13–14), 1230–1259 (2016). https://doi.org/10.1080/0267257x.2016.1150322

Feuerriegel, S., Hartmann, J., Janiesch, C., Zschech, P.: Generative ai. Bus. Inf. Syst. Eng. **66**(1), 111–126 (2024). https://doi.org/10.1007/s12599-023-00834-7

Firdausiah, R.A., Sunaryo, S., Sumiati, S., Abidin, N.A.B.Z.: Exploring brand loyalty: revealing the effect of brand experience mediated by brand love and trust among smartphone users in Malang city. Jurnal Aplikasi Manajemen **22**(1), 31–45 (2024). https://doi.org/10.21776/ub.jam.2024.022.01.03

Fuentelsaz, L., Maícas, J.P., Polo, Y.: The evolution of mobile communications in Europe: the transition from the second to the third generation. Telecommun. Policy **32**(6), 436–449 (2008). https://doi.org/10.1016/j.telpol.2008.04.008

Gatwiri, C., Muraya, M., Gitonga, L.: Prediction of the effect of demographic characteristics on parity using poisson regression model. Asian J. Probab. Statist. **6**, 55–63 (2020). https://doi.org/10.9734/ajpas/2020/v6i130154

Ghazwani, S., Esch, P., Cui, Y., Gala, P.: Artificial intelligence, financial anxiety and cashier-less checkouts: a Saudi Arabian perspective. Int. J. Bank Market. **40**(6), 1200–1216 (2022). https://doi.org/10.1108/ijbm-09-2021-0444

Guerra-Tamez, C.: Decoding Gen Z: AI's influence on brand trust and purchasing behavior. Front. Artif. Intell. **7**, 1323512 (2024). https://doi.org/10.3389/frai.2024.1323512

Han, Q., Cho, D.: Characterizing the technological evolution of smartphones: insights from performance benchmarks. In: Proceedings of the 18th Annual International Conference on Electronic Commerce: e-Commerce in Smart Connected World, pp. 1–8, August 2016. https://doi.org/10.1145/2971603.2971635

Haro, A., Oktaviana, D., Dewi, A., Anisa, W., Suangkupon, A.: The influence of brand image and service quality towards purchase intention and its impact on the purchase decision of samsung smartphone. KNE Social Sciences (2020). https://doi.org/10.18502/kss.v4i6.6609

Hutter, K., Hautz, J., Dennhardt, S., Füller, J.: The impact of user interactions in social media on brand awareness and purchase intention: the case of mini on facebook. J. Prod. Brand Manage. **22**(5/6), 342–351 (2013). https://doi.org/10.1108/jpbm-05-2013-0299

Jung, S., Seo, D., Park, J.: Regularized exploratory bifactor analysis with small sample sizes. Front. Psychol. **11**, 507 (2020). https://doi.org/10.3389/fpsyg.2020.00507

Khan, A., Khusro, S., & Alam, I. (2018). Blindsense: an accessibility-inclusive universal user interface for blind people. Eng. Technol. Appl. Sci. Res. **8**(2), 2775–2784 (2018). https://doi.org/10.48084/etasr.1895

Kock, N., Hadaya, P.: Minimum sample size estimation in pls-sem: the inverse square root and gamma-exponential methods. Inf. Syst. J. **28**(1), 227–261 (2016). https://doi.org/10.1111/isj.12131

Kuriakose, B., Shrestha, R., Sandnes, F.E.: Smartphone navigation support for blind and visually impaired people - a comprehensive analysis of potentials and opportunities. In: Antona, M., Stephanidis, C. (eds.) Universal Access in Human-Computer Interaction. Applications and Practice, pp. 568–583. Springer International Publishing, Cham (2020). https://doi.org/10.1007/978-3-030-49108-6_41

Leguina, A.: A primer on partial least squares structural equation modeling (PLS-SEM). Int. J. Res. Method Educ. **38**(2), 220–221 (2015). https://doi.org/10.1080/1743727x.2015.1005806

Lewis, J.R., Sauro, J.: Effect of perceived ease of use and usefulness on UX and behavioral outcomes. Int. J. Human-Comput. Interact. **40**, 6676–6673 (2023). https://doi.org/10.1080/10447318.2023.2260164

Lie, D., Butarbutar, M., Sherly, S., Nainggolan, N.T., Sudirman, A.: Investigating the effect of brand personality, awareness and experience on purchase intention. Int. J. Adv. Soc. Sci. Human. **1**(3), 120–130 (2022). https://doi.org/10.56225/ijassh.v1i3.49

Liu, Q., Zhou, Z., Shakya, S.R., Uduthalapally, P., Qiao, M., Sung, A.H.: Smartphone sensor-based activity recognition by using machine learning and deep learning algorithms. Int. J. Mach. Learn. Comput. **8**(2), 121–126 (2018). https://doi.org/10.18178/ijmlc.2018.8.2.674

Manandhar, R.: Consumer buying decision for smartphones: an price, brand, and features analysis. J. Nepal. Bus. Stud. **16**(1), 112–123 (2023). https://doi.org/10.3126/jnbs.v16i1.62389

Martiniello, N., Eisenbarth, W., Lehane, C., Johnson, A., Wittich, W.: Exploring the use of smartphones and tablets among people with visual impairments: are mainstream devices replacing the use of traditional visual aids? Assist. Technol. **34**(1), 34–45 (2019). https://doi.org/10.1080/10400435.2019.1682084

Jain Mathew, N., Elangovan, S.N., Sheeba, B., Yadav, P.: Design and validation of the academic research aptitude scale. J. Eng. Educ. Transform. **35**(4), 148–156 (2022). https://doi.org/10.16920/jeet/2022/v35i4/22114

McLean, G., Osei-Frimpong, K., Barhorst, J.: Alexa, do voice assistants influence consumer brand engagement? – examining the role of AI-powered voice assistants in influencing consumer brand engagement. J. Bus. Res. **124**, 312–328 (2021). https://doi.org/10.1016/j.jbusres.2020.11.045

Mehmood, S., Hamid, M.: Online brand attachment, experience, and sales promotion leads to purchase intention: moderating role of online brand trust. J. Manage. Pract. Human. Soc. Sci. **8**(1), 58–74 (2024). https://doi.org/10.33152/jmphss-8.1.5

Metawa, N., Boujlil, R., Alsunbul, S.: Fraud-free green finance: using deep learning to preserve the integrity of financial statements for enhanced capital market sustainability. Int. J. Energy Econom. Policy **13**(6), 610–617 (2023). https://doi.org/10.32479/ijeep.15197

Mohamed, Z.A.: The impact of individualism/collectivism and masculinity/femininity on brand loyalty: a mediation role of perceived ease of use. Proc. Int. Conf. Res. Bus. Manage. Econom. **1**(1), 1–13 (2024). https://doi.org/10.33422/icrbme.v1i1.191

Mostafa, R.B., Kasamani, T.: Brand experience and brand loyalty: is it a matter of emotions? Asia Pac. J. Mark. Logist. **33**(4), 1033–1051 (2021). https://doi.org/10.1108/APJML-11-2019-0669

Nasermoadeli, A., Ling, K.C., Maghnati, F.: Evaluating the impacts of customer experience on purchase intention. Int. J. Bus. Manage. **8**(6), 128 (2013). https://doi.org/10.5539/ijbm.v8n6p128

Ramaseshan, B., Stein, A.: Connecting the dots between brand experience and brand loyalty: the mediating role of brand personality and brand relationships. J. Brand Manag. **21**(7–8), 664–683 (2014). https://doi.org/10.1057/bm.2014.23

Ravichandran, D.: Impact of brand equity on purchase intention of smartphone. Int. J. Res. Innov. Soc. Sci. **07**(01), 264–272 (2023). https://doi.org/10.47772/IJRISS.2023.7106

Risde, K.R., Kurniawati, K.: Pengaruh persepsi kemudahan penggunaan, persepsi kegunaan, dan persepsi kesenangan terhadap loyalitas nasabah mobile banking. Creat. Res. Manage. J. **6**(2), 71–87 (2023). https://doi.org/10.32663/2ghd5b61

Sankhi, P., Sandnes, F.: A glimpse into smartphone screen reader use among blind teenagers in rural Nepal. Disabil. Rehabil. Assist. Technol. **17**(8), 875–881 (2020). https://doi.org/10.1080/17483107.2020.1818298

Saraswati, A.R., Giantari, I.: Brand image mediation of product quality and electronic word of mouth on purchase decision. Int. Res. J. Manage. IT Soc. Sci. **9**(1), 97–109 (2022). https://doi.org/10.21744/irjmis.v9n1.2012

Shafiq, R., Raza, I., ZiaurRehman, M.: Analysis of the factors affecting customers' purchase intention: the mediating role of perceived value. Afr. J. Bus. Manage. **5**(26), 10577–10585 (2011). https://doi.org/10.5897/AJBM10.1088

Taber, K.: The use of cronbach's alpha when developing and reporting research instruments in science education. Res. Sci. Educ. **48**(6), 1273–1296 (2017). https://doi.org/10.1007/s11165-016-9602-2

Wang, S.: Analyze the phenomenon of perceived ease-of-use and perceived usefulness for consumers' purchase intention. BCP Bus. Manage. **39**, 204–213 (2023). https://doi.org/10.54691/bcpbm.v39i.4064

West, A., Clifford, J., Atkinson, D.: Alexa, build me a brand. An investigation into the impact of artificial intelligence on branding. Bus. Manage. Rev. **9**(3), 321–330 (2018). https://doi.org/10.15341/jbe(2155-7950)/10.09.2018/005

Westhuizen, L.: Brand loyalty: exploring self-brand connection and brand experience. J. Product. Brand Manage. **27**(2), 172–184 (2018). https://doi.org/10.1108/jpbm-07-2016-1281

Xie, S., Yuan, Y.: An empirical study on the impact of online travel consumers' brand loyalty: the mediating effect of flow experience. E3S Web Conf. **253**, 03043 (2021). https://doi.org/10.1051/e3sconf/202125303043

Leading Virtual Teams in the Context of e-Leadership: Insights into Challenges from Leaders' Perspectives

Christian Tuschner[1(✉)], Hella Hörsch[2], Nina Lorenz[1], and Harald von Korflesch[1]

[1] University of Koblenz, Koblenz, Germany
{ctuschner,nilorenz,harald.vonkorflesch}@uni-koblenz.de
[2] University of Bielefeld, Bielefeld, Germany
hella.hoersch@uni-bielefeld.de

Abstract. The COVID-19 pandemic has accelerated the adoption of video conferencing systems and online collaboration tools in organizations. This rapid technological advancement facilitated the transition from traditional to virtual teams (VTs), compelling leaders to rapidly adjust to new leader-follower relationships. Consequently, leaders have faced sudden and unexpected challenges. From an academic perspective, there is a critical gap in understanding the multi-layered challenges of e-leadership in VTs through a socio-technical lens, which includes individual micro-level, team-related meso-level, and organizational and external macro-level challenges. Despite numerous systematic literature reviews on e-leadership, an in-depth understanding of e- leader's perspectives in a business context, particularly regarding the challenges encountered during the COVID-19 pandemic, is still lacking. To address this, semi-structured interviews were conducted with 36 leaders, including ten C-level executives from German DAX-listed companies, and analyzed using Braun and Clarke's (2006) thematic analysis. The results uncover challenges hinder effective e-leadership of VTs at the micro level in areas such as leaders' communication, leaders' follower orientation and humanization as well as leaders' organization and control. Additionally, the study reveals meso-level challenges, including team structures and workplace dynamics, and macro-level challenges, encompassing organizational structures and national and international conditions. Our findings contribute to the current discussion on e-leadership by presenting multi- layered challenges as determinants of effective e-leadership in a transparent and comprehensive manner. Furthermore, the results assist practitioners in developing actionable strategies to enhance e-leadership and, consequently, the performance of VTs, thereby maintaining organizational effectiveness in an increasingly virtual environment.

Keywords: e-leadership · virtual teams · video conferencing systems · online collaboration tools · challenges

R. C. Geibel and S. Machavariani (Eds.): ISPC 2024, SPBE, pp. 542–556, 2025.
https://doi.org/10.1007/978-3-031-88052-0_43

1 Introduction

Technological advances, such as improved collaboration platforms and videoconferencing systems, have transformed work models, enabling collaboration regardless of location and time (Gilson et al., 2015; Hafermalz & Riemer, 2020; Larson & DeChurch, 2020; Richter, 2020), thus presenting new challenges in leading virtual teams (VTs). The COVID-19 pandemic accelerated these challenges by transforming traditional teams into VTs and leaders into e-leaders (Chamakiotis et al., 2021; Contreras et al., 2020). E-leadership, defined as leading geographically dispersed followers using digital technologies (Avolio & Kahai, 2003), requires new strategies beyond traditional approaches.

Previous studies identify challenges for e-leaders, including communication problems and trust building measures. For example, Pulley & Sessa (2001) emphasize that technology reinforces existing leadership paradoxes, such as the balance between rapid communication with the need for mindfulness or individual autonomy with team cohesion. Van Wart et al. (2019) also highlight communication and responsibility challenges in VTs noting that misunderstandings and communication complexity can undermine team performance and emphasize the central role of trust. Weak technology and security management as well as inadequate understanding of digital technologies are further critical factors challenging leaders. Chamakiotis et al. (2021) complement these perspectives by examining COVID-19 pandemic's impact, which reconfigured VTs and introduced new challenges for e-leaders, including digital well-being, engagement, work-life balance, and fostering innovation.

Despite these insights, there is a lack of empirical research addressing e-leaders' challenges in VTs within a business context. Many existing studies are theoretical or focus on specific sectors, such as the public sector (e.g., Van Wart et al., 2019) or the educational sector (e.g., Avolio et al., 2014). Furthermore, research does not include perspectives of e-leaders across different management levels, limiting comprehensive understanding of various challenges.

Therefore, this study aims to understand the challenges faced by e-leaders of VTs at the micro, meso, and macro levels during the COVID-19 pandemic, where leaders became e-leaders due to lockdown regulations. Focusing on e-leaders across different management levels to obtain a comprehensive picture of the different challenges and experiences, this analysis seeks to fill the research gap and contribute to e-leadership theory and practice.

2 Research Methods

2.1 Participants

Between January and June 2022, we interviewed 36 leaders from 33 large German corporations (acc. to the Commission of the European Union, 2003), covering top, middle, and first-line management (Bonoma & Lawler, 1989; Daft & Lane, 2015). Using Patton's (2014) purposeful random sampling, we aimed for data saturation (Fusch & Ness, 2015), achieved after 36 interviews. The sample included diverse industries, company sizes, and leader demographics, featuring ten C-level leaders from DAX-listed companies (see Table 1 in Appendix).

2.2 Data Collection

We conducted semi-structured interviews to gain deep insights into experiences in complex areas (Flick, 2015). This method combines structured questions with flexibility, allowing focused yet adaptive discussions (DiCicco- Bloom & Crabtree, 2006; Kallio et al., 2016). The interview guide was designed based on Sreejesh et al. (2014). To ensure the focus remained on VTs, we began by explaining the study's objectives and used introductory questions to ease participants into the conversation. This was followed by targeted questions to explore specific aspects of leading VTs. Demographic data were collected at the end (Sreejesh et al., 2014). In addition, the typology of Qu & Dumay (2011) was considered ensuring relevance and clarity in formulating the questions.

Interviews were conducted online via MS Teams and CISCO WEBEX, lasting between 23 and 62 minutes (average 43 min). They were conducted in German and transcribed using Kuckartz's (2014) guidelines, with paraphrases translated into English for analysis.

2.3 Data Analysis

We utilized thematic analysis (Braun & Clarke, 2006) combined with a positivistic coding approach recommended by Braun & Clarke (2021) to capture the nuanced subjective leader experiences (Braun & Clarke, 2019) while maintaining rigorous objectivity in data analysis (Braun & Clarke, 2021). The research followed the six iterative phases of reflexive thematic analysis by Braun & Clarke (2006).

In phase 1, transcripts were imported into MAXQDA. Authors 1 and 2 examined the dataset, focusing on emerging patterns and latent relationships between data points. In phase 2, Author 1 performed inductive coding to explore the phenomenon without pre-existing theoretical assumptions, favoring emergent codes over a-priori ones (Elliott, 2018). This approach fostered an unbiased perspective, remaining open to new and unexpected insights.

To ensure reliability and robustness, we incorporated an intercoder agreement test using Cohen's Kappa (Nili et al., 2020). Authors 1 and 2 independently coded the data, achieving an agreement rate of 83.16% ("almost perfect"; Landis & Koch, 1977). Discrepancies were resolved through discussion and codebook revision.

In phase 3, themes were developed, and codes were assigned by author 1. An industry expert from a global energy company was consulted for validation and final naming of the themes (phases 4 & 5), to ensure accuracy and relevance of the themes. Author 2 reviewed the classifications, and differences were resolved by consensus. Our analysis resulted in a coding system with ten key themes and provided insights into leading VTs (phase 6).

3 Results

Our analysis identified several challenges, categorized into ten themes, that leaders face in leading VTs, organized according to Bommer et al. (1987) into micro (see table 2 in Appendix), meso (see table 3 in Appendix), and macro level (see table 4 in Appendix).

At the micro level, challenges involve individual factors such as the personality, skills, and behaviors of leaders and followers. The meso level focuses on group dynamics and their impact on collaboration, emphasizing the relationship between leader and team. The macro level addresses organizational and external factors beyond the organization itself. In the following, all respondents who commented on a specific challenge are listed in brackets as evidence.

3.1 Challenges of Leading VTs at the Micro Level

3.1.1 Leaders' Communication

The rapid advancement of communication and collaboration technologies presents distinct challenges for leaders, particularly in virtual meetings. They struggle to maintain effective communication due to **limitations in perceiving non-verbal cues** like body language, making it harder to recognize followers' emotional states (L1, L2, L5-L7, L10-L13, L15, L16, L18, L19, L21, L23-L29, L31, L32, L34, L36): *"The personal exchange, which is more than just information transfer, is indeed restricted by digital technologies [...]. [...]. It's about gestures, facial expressions, personal impressions, and perceiving group interactions [...]. Even the most advanced collaborative platforms can only reproduce this to a limited extent"* (L16). Additionally, the risk of misunderstandings increases, as virtual meetings transmit fewer verbal cues than face-to-face interactions (L2, L34). The absence of non-verbal signals in written communication also leads to ambiguities, especially when emotional aspects are involved (L1, L10). A key challenge is the increased risk of follower distraction (L8, L10, L11, L20, L27, L28, L32, L34). Distractions, such as pop-up chat messages or emails, reduce communication efficiency: *"[...] you could be working on emails without me noticing [...]. Or read Spiegel-Online simultaneously. I wouldn't notice that. I'd be more aware of it if we were in the same room"* (L34).

Another challenge for leaders is **using an adequate communication style**, particular in the moderation of virtual meetings (L2, L7, L8, L10-L12, L15, L22, L24, L29, L32-L35). Leaders must develop specific competencies to ensure active participation from all followers and to balance different personality types, particularly between introverted and extroverted followers (L12, L24, L32). However, the behavior of followers also can hinder an appropriate communication style. The virtual context tends to facilitate follower withdrawal and minimal active participation (L1, L2, L6, L12, L15, L27, L28), *"because it is easy to hide in a meeting like this. So even if you're on the screen, you're invited and part of it, but it's relatively easy to disengage mentally and in terms of content"* (L12). Furthermore, it is challenging for leaders to keep the atmosphere relaxed, as they are less lively and spontaneous, and even humorous interjections are much more difficult than in a face-to-face meeting (L11, L34). Moreover, language and cultural differences make communication even more difficult in global VTs (L21).

These challenges are particularly pronounced when leaders must **engage in critical conversations**. Critical conversations involve uncomfortable, embarrassing, or anxiety-inducing topics and elicit emotional responses that are difficult to perceive fully. These discussions often address crisis management, personnel matters, or innovation (L22, L26, L36). Additionally, leaders face difficulties moderating factual discussions with divergent viewpoints (L15, L17, L23, L27), because *"when it really comes down to arguing on a topic, it is easy to avoid confrontation [in the virtual environment]"* (L15).

Online meetings are perceived as physically and mentally stressful from leaders. An extended screen exposure often leads to fatigue, reducing the leaders' ability to focus and engage effectively, making digital interactions more exhausting than in-person meetings (L1, L12, L13, L34, L35).

3.1.2 Leaders' Follower Orientation and Humanization

In addition to communication challenges, leaders identified social challenges. **Addressing individual needs** of followers in virtual environments is perceived as particularly difficult, especially when it comes to demonstrating empathy (L3, L7, L9, L11, L20, L21, L23, L25-L27, L32, L33, L35): *"You must be careful not to lose [your followers] on a human level because [...] you don't see if someone isn't doing well. [...]. [...]. And I think that's one of the biggest challenges, to fulfill this duty of care, to ensure that people know someone is looking out for them and cares"* (L32). Emotional and social exchanges between leaders and their teams, as well as among team members, must not be neglected (L1, L2, L13-L15, L19, L31, L35, L36): *"[...] you must push for social interaction. [...]. I still see it as a challenge"* (L15). The main reason is the lack of relational contact points in virtual work environments, where people talk off-topic, as in the coffee kitchen (L13, L31, L36).

Moreover, leaders must strike a strategic balance between autonomy and close supervision as well as between empowerment and coaching to promote the self-directed work while providing necessary support (L31). Leaders also need to balance the optimal use of technology with focusing on human elements. These tensions highlight the need to integrate modern tools without neglecting interpersonal aspects.

Onboarding new followers also presents a challenge. Integrating new team members is particularly difficult, as the lack of a social context diminishes team integration: *"Of course, when it comes to bringing new team members on board and integrating them into a team, there are other challenges that arise. It's something where a social context, a commonality can have a different effect"* (L9). A vital aspect of this process is fostering follower identification with the company and ensuring their loyalty (L14, L15, L17-L19, L22, L27, L34, L36): *"[...] Corporate identity. How can I communicate this? How loyal are your people? These are all things that need to be rethought in a virtual environment"* (L19).

Furthermore, leaders find it challenging to **build interpersonal relationships** in a virtual environment. Physical distance and the use of cameras hinder the development of personal connections: *"[...] in digital settings, you have even fewer chances to build that personal bond because there's a camera in between"* (L23). In this context, establishing trust is particularly cited as the biggest challenge (L1-L3, L15, L17, L23, L25, L27, L28, L32, L33): *"The challenge is certainly [...] to build a relationship of trust. That is [...] the biggest challenge, especially when it comes to new compositions, be it one-to-one or in the whole team"* (L25). This difficulty is further amplified by the limited opportunities for personal interaction in virtual settings, such as informal conversations over coffee or a beer: *"[...] the personal aspect of looking each other in the eye or giving a hug, that's missing. That's the only thing that's lacking [...], and people do enjoy that"* (L23).

Another challenge is **creating and maintaining team cohesion**: *"[...] as a leader, especially in purely VTs, you have to invest a lot to create that initial cohesion"* (L13). Maintaining this cohesion is made more difficult by 'proximity bias' (L7, L18, L23) – the unconscious preference for individuals encountered in person over those seen only virtually.

3.1.3 Leaders' Organization and Control

With advancing digitalization and the emergence of VTs, organizing and controlling such teams is becoming increasingly complex. Several respondents emphasize the **limitations in interaction opportunities** (L1-L3, L5, L7, L9-L14, L16, L17, L19-L21, L24, L25, L27-L29, L31, L33-L36): *"[...] what is hard to replicate are [...] informal contact points like having lunch together or the much-quoted coffee in the kitchen. [...]. These are the things [...] that are hard to orchestrate digitally"* (L9). Furthermore, spontaneous contact is hindered by a higher barrier to initiating it in virtual environments (L2, L13, L35): *"Oh, I need something. Should I call them? [...] I always feel like, 'Oh God, I'm going to disturb them'"* (L35).

The lack of interaction opportunities is further amplified by the need for meticulous information exchange planning (L2, L5, L7, L10, L16, L21, L27, L29, L31, L33). Challenges include determining appropriate touchpoints, ensuring social interactions, and organizing socializing events and informal exchanges (L5, L10, L16, L31). Leaders also highlight the difficulty of ensuring intra-organizational knowledge transfer, as spontaneous information-sharing methods, like "watercooler conversations," are absent (L1, L3, L10, L33): *"[...] you might not involve as many people as in the real world, where you quickly gather with several people. That's where I see the challenge, making sure that everyone is on the same level of information and that no one is forgotten [...]"* (L33).

Another major challenge is **structuring of working time**. Tightly scheduled meetings compress time, complicating organization and coordination (L1, L3, L5, L8, L10-L13, L16, L19, L20, L30, L32, L34, L35). The constant succession of videoconferences leaves little room for breaks and periods of reflection that used to be taken for granted: *"And it's precisely because of these half-hour meetings [...] and this new strictness about punctuality. [...] now you must apologize if you are a minute late. And I think that does something to people"* (L32). Additionally, leaders and followers often face tension between videoconferencing and concentrated individual work (L1, L11, L30, L35).

Separating work and private life for a healthy work-life balance is also challenging for leaders. Working from home increasingly blurs boundaries between work and private commitments (L2-L4, L6, L11, L15, L17, L18, L20, L21, L24, L26, L28, L30, L35, L36): *"The lines between 'when am I working' and 'when am I private' are now blurring. [...] A laptop on the table, a smartphone in your hand can of course be very, very [work] addictive [...]"* (L18). This makes it difficult for leaders to ensure followers maintain appropriate separation and avoid overload.

Transitioning from traditional leadership to leading VTs brings challenges in **organizing transformational processes**. Transactional tasks are easily handled virtually, but transformational meetings are more complex (L3, L9, L13, L16, L22, L23, L25, L27, L28, L33, L34): *"It is always a challenge [...] when there are important changes in* *the 'scope' or in the focus of a task. In other words, whenever there are [...] transformational moments that simply [...] cannot be dealt with in a standardized way"* (L9). For example, innovation processes require different approaches (L3, L9, L13, L16, L22, L23, L28, L33, L34), especially those producing disruptive innovations: *"I think [...] incremental innovation can also be solved very, very well and efficiently in a digital setup in [MS] teams or Zoom formats. If I'm talking more about something like a form of [...] fundamental innovation, creativity, developing new ideas, etc., then I have a completely different challenge, including the associated creative techniques [...]"* (L9).

Appropriate use of digital technologies is also a challenge. Leaders often struggle to use the tools themselves: *"[...] an understanding of digital media is already very important. And being able to use them independently is a challenge"* (L11). This includes managing multiple communication channels like instant messaging and email, where prioritization remains unclear. The coexistence of new and old tools can lead to inefficiencies and discrepancies in response times, complicating workflow and decision-making (L11, L20, L34, L35).

Ensuring **adequate handling of digital collaboration**, especially communication, is a major challenge due to unclear rules and a lack of established work culture with transparent expectations (L2, L4, L5, L16, L33). *"The (....) norm hasn't fully developed yet. [...]. I don't know what the rules are. A new culture must be created, but at the moment there is no precedent for it"* (L2). This is reflected in the unclear expectations of response times for different channels like email, WhatsApp, or Slack: *"[...] communication formats are still the Wild West"* (L2).

Micromanagement is another challenge, as closely monitoring followers' performance is extremely challenging (L1, L2, L6, L8, L9, L26, L31, L33). *"If I'm trying to micromanage my team, I'm going to lose them in virtual leadership [...] because I won't know when they're coming in. I won't know if they're googling or if they're really in meetings or if they've just set up blockers. [...]. Because I'm not physically there, I have no idea what they're doing. So, the challenge is: 'The further away I am from the work of my followers, the harder it gets, because I have no idea how big the task is that they're working on'"* (L31).

Another challenge for leaders is the **risk of overwhelming** followers or themselves with information (L19, L21, L24): *"[You] must [...] be careful [...] not to be overwhelmed. [...] the amount of information is constantly increasing and whether you are a leader or a follower, you must find a way to manage the sheer volume of information"* (L21).

3.1.4 Followers' Behaviors

The challenge of leading VTs lies not only in the specific behavioral requirements of leaders, but also in the behavior of the followers. **Follower disengagement** is a key challenge, as the virtual space can tempt followers to behave passively and participate less actively (L1, L2, L6, L12, L15, L27, L28): *"Because it's easy to hide in a virtual meeting. [...] it's relatively easy to disengage mentally and in terms of content"* (L12).

Follower compliance, i.e. adherence to rules and recommendations, plays a crucial role (L2, L12, L13, L16, L20, L21, L24, L26, L29, L30-L32): *"Once one of the followers [...] goes off track, [...] the performance of the whole group suffers"* (L16). An example is the recommendation to turn on the camera during meetings to promote attention and engagement. A lack of visibility risks followers being distracted and the leader not noticing (L21).

3.1.5 Followers' Traits

In addition to behaviors, certain follower traits can also make it difficult to lead VTs. In particular, **technological skills** are a key challenge, as followers with different levels of knowledge and experience work with digital tools (L2, L6, L7, L16, L22, L24, L26, L28-L30, L34): *"Do I have people on the other side who already have experience [with digital technologies]? Then it's certainly easier than if I have a group that has never done it or has done it very rarely"* (L24). The widening gap between tech-savvy and less-experienced followers poses a challenge. Younger generations are comfortable with digital technologies, while older followers often struggle. This can increase the effort for the leader, e.g., by initiating appropriate, individually tailored coaching and training measures (L22). Closely related is the lack of a digital mindset. Followers with little affinity for technology or who are resistant to digital tools need additional motivational approaches from the leader. Heterogeneity in the use of digital tools can slow down the flow of information and make it more challenging for the leader to coordinate (L3, L8, L21, L28, L32): *"[...] not every follower is digitally active in the same way, and [...] that can also lead to problems"* (L8).

Another challenge is heterogeneity in the **acceptance of virtual working methods** in general. Followers react differently to digital collaboration: While some have a positive attitude toward remote work, others have reservations and want to return to traditional models (L3, L4, L11, L20, L21, L31, L35, L36). *"Followers say, 'I actually want to go back to my old model.' And others, pioneers, are moving forward. And I think the challenge will be how to manage this plurality in a company"* (L9). These divergent preferences require leaders to adapt strategies to meet different needs. Followers with a strong need for presence and social proximity require different approaches than those who prefer flexible work models. This can increase leadership effort, as individualized leadership behaviors are necessary (L20, L31).

Follower **discipline and self-management skills** also poses a challenge. Followers with low discipline require increased leadership effort, especially when there are deficits in areas such as self-organization, time management and active participation in meetings (L16, L20, L21, L35). For example, while some may complete tasks independently, others may need more supervision, while some may complete tasks independently, others may need more supervision: *"Not everyone is good at self-organization. [...]. Some people at home sometimes lose focus or get distracted"* (L35).

3.2 Challenges of Leading VTs at the Meso Level

3.2.1 Team Structure and Diversity

Team and meeting size poses a meso level challenge. Many participants in meetings undermine leadership effectiveness by limiting communication (L6, L10, L21, L25): *"[...] as soon as I have eight or nine or twelve people in the [virtual] room or even more, it becomes more difficult"* (L25). Participants are less inclined to engage actively in large groups (L6, L7, L10, L21, L25, L33, L34): *"[...] the larger the meeting, the less willing people are to participate actively. So, when there are 20 people in the meeting, it often makes no sense to ask for an opinion without addressing people directly"* (L6). Smaller groups are therefore less challenging: *"What is necessary in terms of information flow, and where can we minimize it and say that only those who really need to know are at the table? These are the most effective meetings - the smaller the group"* (L10). Furthermore, smaller team sizes enhance leaders' ability to interact regularly with each member (L30, L31).

Geographic distance between leaders and followers challenges leading VTs (L1, L7, L8, L10, L13). Leading teams whose followers work in different time zones is particularly difficult (L8, L13). Spreading across multiple time zones increases the need for coordination, especially when planning meetings. Often leaders must divide the team by time zone and have several meetings a day to allow all followers to actively participate (L2, L12, L19, L31): *"The team is effectively split in half between the people who are in the American time zone and those who are in the Asian time zone"* (L2). This multiple communication ties up valuable resources and makes effective leadership more difficult, as other leadership tasks could be neglected.

The **age structure of teams** presents a further challenge for leaders of VTs. Different generations often have different expectations and needs that leaders must address to create a productive work environment (L36): *"There are baby boomers, like me, and Generation Z [...]. You [as a leader] must make the work environment suitable for everyone"* (L36). As already mentioned in the micro-level challenges of follower traits, generational differences in technology skills pose a particular challenge, as older followers tend to require more guidance to use digital tools effectively, while younger followers often require less support and adapt more quickly to changes in the new work environment (L2, L3, L5, L20, L24, L28, L30, L32, L36): *"For example, I have a follower who is 62 and my youngest who is 23. And the 23-year-old finds it easy, she clicks and has no problem working with us digitally. Whereas the other one, he shows me that I must engage him in a completely different way and maybe he has other worries and fears"* (L28).

A particularly challenging feature of a global VT for leading VTs effectively is **multiculturalism**, as leaders must overcome (inter)cultural and language challenges (L2, L21).

3.2.2 Team Dynamics

The challenge of **interpersonal relations** is critical for leading VTs. A trusting relationship between team members and the leader enhances collaboration by establishing familiarity with and trust in the abilities and reliability of team members (L2, L3, L7, L9, L14, L15, L20, L25, L32, L33, L35): *"If you already know your people personally [...] it's easier to trust them"* (L20). This reduces the need for micromanagement and allows for more effective leadership. Effective team cohesion also requires trust and familiarity among peers. Pre- established relationships facilitate smoother communication and reduce the leader's effort to build trust within the team (L2, L3, L9, L33): *"The [Chinese] were already a team, they knew each other, and that's why they're much more relaxed [in meetings]"* (L2). Without such dynamics, the leadership burden increases as efforts to foster team cohesion and create a trusting work environment become more demanding. Conversely, the lack of interpersonal relationships between the leader and their followers is more challenging for leading VTs effectively. Explicitly, a lack of interpersonal relationships can hinder communication, as misunderstandings are more likely (L2, L15, L32).

3.2.3 Workplace Dynamics

Another challenge is **workspace design**. A well-defined and exclusive workspace promotes focused communication and supports the leadership process (L1-L3, L6-L8, L11, L16, L17, L20, L21, L28, L30, L31, L34): *"A single mother working at her kitchen table has different challenges than a leader with a twenty-square- meter home office"* (L16).

When a dedicated workspace is not possible, family responsibilities, such as childcare (L2, L3, L6, L7, L10, L12, L13, L15-L17, L20, L22, L27, L31, L32, L34) or pets (L7, L12, L22, L31), and disruptions from partners, especially when both work in the same space (L14, L20, L31, L32, L34), can negatively impact leadership effectiveness: *"If you have a partner who also works from home. If you then [...] have a one- or two-bedroom apartment, then both [...] must work in the same room. I think that would be very, very, very difficult. I think I would [go crazy]"* (L20). The challenge for leaders is considering these external factors and maintaining an adequate flow of communication.

3.3 Challenges of Leading VTs at the Macro Level

3.3.1 Organizational Structures

The **job profiles** of followers are a key challenge, as they determine the extent to which remote working is possible (L3, L9, L16, L19, L20, L25, L26, L29, L34-L36): *"There are job profiles that suffer greatly from 'I work from home'"* (L3). Leaders, therefore, need to tailor their strategies to the specific needs of different job roles. While knowledge workers can increasingly work from home, other roles, such as property management or laboratory work (L20, L29), limit the scope for virtual work: *"[Or], if you're a cook, you have to be in the kitchen, otherwise you can't cook"* (L35). This differentiation of job profiles requires a challenging and flexible leadership behavior from the leaders, which considers all job profiles in a VT to ensure the effectiveness of virtual collaboration (L19).

In addition to job profiles, **internal regulations** pose a further challenge for leaders of VTs. A key challenge is the decision-making authority of leaders. The extent and clarity of these authorities can impact the functioning of VTs and the effectiveness of leadership (L4, L35). Uncertainty about what decisions leaders can make independently, especially in the context of remote working arrangements, can lead to inefficiency and uncertainty: *"What am I actually allowed to decide as a leader when we [as an organization] say we are fully committed to remote work"* (L4).

Works councils can further limit these authorities. For example, works councils have a voice in the introduction of new tools and methods, which can limit the scope of leaders in designing the work environment (L13, L31): *"[...] You can imagine that the whole world is a bit more complex. We have nice institutions like works councils. So, it's not so easy for us to just say I'm going to introduce a new tool and use it with my team"* (L13).

A discrepancy between the strategic goals of top management and the actual reality of the work on the ground can make leadership even more challenging (L29, L35): *"[...] then they [the top management] come up with ideas that make you think, 'Hey, you don't get it at all, you don't understand what the problem is on the ground and now you want to implement this'"* (L29). For example, top management may demand that new tools be implemented without considering the team's time and technical resources.

Furthermore, a **low level of digitalization** in the company is a challenge for leaders of VTs. In companies with little experience in using digital platforms, implementing virtual working methods is often more complex and requires more adaptation and training (L3, L16, L24): *"So, if you work in a company like ours, which has always used collaboration platforms in the past due to its decentralized structure, [...] then the challenge is certainly a bit smaller than if you go to a medium-sized mechanical engineering company [...], for example, which has never had any digital communication except for the telephone in the past"* (L16).

In addition, the **lack of interoperability between digital tools** is a challenge for leaders when leading VTs. When technologies are not seamlessly integrated, unnecessary processes are created manually transferring data between tools (L1, L32): *"The main problem is that these tools need to be connected [...] otherwise highly skilled people waste time copying instead of doing value-adding work"* (L1). In addition, the need to integrate communication channels on mobile devices increases the pressure on leaders to be constantly available and able to act to remain agile and responsive (L2): *"Integration on mobile [...] everything has to be there so I can access it on my phone"* (L2). The ability to react in real-time is essential for leading VTs, but this requires continuous technological support, which is not always available.

3.3.2 National and International Conditions

Complying with national and international regulations and laws is a key challenge for leaders of VTs. In particular, the distinction between different types of remote work requires clarity, as different employment law requirements apply (L9, L31, L36): *"So, what we now understand by 'home office' is different from 'teleworking'. I belong to the generation when teleworking was introduced at IBM, and that means that the main workplace is at home. [...] And then, of course, the lawyers came on the scene: 'Wait a minute, of course the workplace regulation applies, it also applies at home, and then the working place has to be set up and data protection [...].'"* (L36). Leaders must ensure that workplace requirements are met at the office and home, which can lead to organizational and legal challenges, particularly regarding workplace regulations and data protection (L31).

Historical regulations based on traditional work environments, such as factory work, often no longer meet the needs of contemporary work models. Employment legislation must be modernized to reflect the reality of flexible working: *"Reality has almost overtaken legislation"* (L36). Leaders must balance legal compliance with the needs of followers to ensure a flexible but compliant working environment.

In addition to national regulations, leaders must comply with international regulations and laws when followers work across borders. Tax and social security regulations can create complications when followers work from.

different countries (L17). This requires leaders not only to have legal knowledge, but also to engage in strategic planning to comply with both national and international regulations while meeting the needs of followers.

Another challenge is the **quality of the technical infrastructure**. A stable, high-performance internet connection is essential for effective communication and collaboration. Bandwidth problems or disconnections can make leadership difficult, especially during large meetings or critical situations (L2, L3, L5, L6, L7, L8, L10, L12, L16, L19, L22, L24, L28, L30, L32, L36): *"If you [...] are in the wrong place, you will run into bandwidth problems if you want to transmit sound and images at the same time"* (L16). Leaders must be flexible and adaptable to quickly overcome technical difficulties and maintain the flow of communication (L32).

4 Discussion and Recommendations

Our study identifies challenges leaders face when leading VTs at micro, meso, and macro levels (Bommer et al., 1987) and enhances the understanding of e-leadership by subsequently comparing our results with the existing literature.

At the **micro level**, our findings align with some of the challenges described in the literature. Pulley & Sessa (2001) highlight the paradox between the need for rapid communication and the need for mindfulness in handling information. Our study confirms that in virtual environments, leaders struggle to perceive non-verbal cues and recognize followers' emotional states, increasing the risk of misunderstandings, as also noted by Van Wart et al. (2019). However, our detailed consideration of moderating virtual meetings is a unique contribution. While existing literature acknowledges communication challenges, our findings provide specific insights into difficulties ensuring balanced participation between introverted and extroverted followers, subtleties less addressed in prior research. The challenge of online meeting fatigue adds to discussions on leaders' digital health. Chamakiotis et al. (2021) mention the phenomenon of 'zoom fatigue'; our findings offer specific examples of how these stresses affect leadership and require strategies to mitigate them.

Another theme is the challenge of showing empathy and building trust. Chamakiotis et al. (2021) emphasize trust and relationship building in leading VTs, particularly in the context of Covid-19. Our findings confirm and extend this by addressing onboarding new team members. Our results show that the lack of informal interactions complicates integration and affects identification with the company, an issue marginally addressed in literature. 'Proximity bias' is another unique finding of our study. While Van Wart et al. (2019) discuss general challenges related to equal treatment in virtual environments, we highlight the challenge of 'proximity bias,' which means specifically that leaders unconsciously favor team members who are physically present over those who work entirely virtually.

In organization and control, our findings align with Pulley & Sessa (2001), who emphasize the need to balance flexibility and stability. The challenges we identify, such as time compression through tightly scheduled meetings and the difficulty of separating work and personal life, reflect the tensions described in the literature. However, we note that the flood of virtual communication channels and the lack of established communication rules create additional complexity. While Van Wart et al. (2019) mention underutilization of technologies, our findings highlight leaders feeling overwhelmed by too many tools, necessitating new clear communication strategies.

Our study also highlights specific traits and behaviors of followers as a challenge, including the technological skills of followers. While Van Wart et al. (2019) address insufficient understanding of technologies in general, our results show that age-related differences in technology affinity make collaboration difficult. Younger followers adapt quickly, while older followers often need more support – a generation gap less explored in e- leadership literature.

At the **meso level**, our results confirm the importance of team structure and dynamics. Chamakiotis et al. (2021) note leading VTs are characterized by a lack of face-to-face interaction, making trust building more challenging. Our study complements this by examining how team size affects active participation in meetings. We show that large virtual meetings reduce willingness to actively participate and challenge leaders to develop effective communication strategies.

Another difference is our analysis of geographical distance and time zone issues. While previous work focused on cultural differences, we provide new insights into practical difficulties of coordinating across time zones, broadening understanding of challenges in globally distributed teams.

Workplace dynamics, particularly the home workspace, are highlighted. While the existing literature addresses blurred work-life boundaries (Chamakiotis et al., 2021), we provide specific examples of how different home environments affect leadership effectiveness, as balancing family and work demands adds pressure on leaders.

At the **macro level**, our findings resonate with Chamakiotis et al. (2021), who highlight the need to consider legal and regulatory aspects in leading (global) VTs. Our study advances this understanding by discussing how intra- organizational regulations impact leaders' decision-making authority. While Van Wart et al. (2019) highlight security governance and data protection, we shed light on challenges posed by organizational structures limiting leaders' flexibility.

A unique contribution is the detailed consideration of technical infrastructure, particularly the issue of interoperability of digital tools. While literature emphasizes the need for effective technology use, our results show that the lack of tool integration creates additional burdens and impairs the efficiency of VTs.

By empirically analyzing the challenges e-leaders face at the micro, meso, and macro levels, the study contributes to advancing e-leadership theory (Avolio & Kahai, 2003). Understanding these challenges is critical for scholarship and practice. Scientifically, it enables adapting leadership theories to meet the complex demands of leading VTs. Practically, organizations can develop targeted strategies to address specific challenges, implementing effective training programs and leadership approaches supporting e-leaders in improving individual interactions (micro level), strengthening team dynamics (meso level), and adapting organizational structures (macro level), thus enhancing leadership effectiveness in VTs.

5 Conclusions, Limitations and Further Research

Our study confirms many challenges identified in existing literature on leading VTs and adds value by highlighting less studied aspects. Similarities include communication difficulties, trust building, and organizational challenges. Our unique contributions are in the detailed analysis of challenges in business context, such as moderating virtual meetings, onboarding new team members, the proximity bias phenomenon, team size, follower traits and behaviors, and technical infrastructure, structured by micro, meso and macro level.

Despite valuable findings, this study has limitations. First, data was collected only from leaders of German companies, potentially limiting generalizability due to cultural differences. Future studies should include leaders from different countries and cultural contexts to gain a more comprehensive understanding of e-leadership challenges. Second, the level of virtuality was not clearly defined. Fully virtual and hybrid teams were mixed. Since the challenges in full VTs may differ from those in hybrid teams, future research could distinguish between them to develop more specific challenges and strategies. Third, our study is based on qualitative data from 36 interviews, providing deep insights but lacking statistical representativeness. Quantitative studies could broaden the scope.

In summary, our study provides important insights into the complex demands of leading VTs. Addressing limitations in future research may help to yield more comprehensive findings. Through further research and the development of concrete action strategies, both research and practice can benefit from increasing the effectiveness of e-leadership and successfully meeting the challenges of an increasingly virtual work environment.

References

Avolio, B.J., Kahai, S.S.: Adding the "E" to e-leadership: hot it may impact your leadership. Organ. Dyn. **31**(4), 325–338 (2003). https://doi.org/10.1016/S0090-2616(02)00133-X

Avolio, B.J., Sosik, J., Kahai, S., Baker, B.: E-leadership: re-examining transformations in leadership source and transmission. Leadersh. Q. **25**(1), 105–131 (2014). https://doi.org/10.1016/j.leaqua.2013.11.003

Bommer, M., Gratto, C., Gravander, J., Tuttle, M.: A behavioral model of ethical and unethical decision making. J. Bus. Ethics **6**, 265–280 (1987)

Bonoma, T.V., Lawler, J.C.: Chutes and ladders: growing the general manager. MIT Sloan Manage. Rev. **30**(3), 27 (1989)

Braun, V., Clarke, V.: Using thematic analysis in psychology. Qual. Res. Psychol. **3**(2), 77–101 (2006). https://doi.org/10.1191/1478088706qp063oa

Braun, V., Clarke, V.: Reflecting on reflexive thematic analysis. Qual. Res. Sport, Exerc. Health **11**(4), 589–597 (2019). https://doi.org/10.1080/2159676X.2019.1628806

Braun, V., Clarke, V.: Can I use TA? Should I use TA? Should I not use TA? Comparing reflexive thematic analysis and other pattern-based qualitative analytic approaches. Couns. Psychother. Res. **21**(1), 37–47 (2021). https://doi.org/10.1002/capr.12360

Chamakiotis, P., Panteli, N., Davison, R.M.: Reimagining e-leadership for reconfigured virtual teams due to Covid-19. Int. J. Inf. Manage. **60**(June), 11 (2021). https://doi.org/10.1016/j.ijinfomgt.2021.102381

Contreras, F., Baykal, E., Abid, G.: E-Leadership and teleworking in times of COVID-19 and beyond: what we know and where do we go. Front. Psychol. **11**(December), 1–11 (2020). https://doi.org/10.3389/fpsyg.2020.590271

Daft, R. L., & Lane, P. G. (2015). Management (Eighth Edition). Thomson South-Western

DiCicco-Bloom, B., Crabtree, B.F.: The qualitative research interview. Med. Educ. **40**(4), 314–321 (2006). https://doi.org/10.1111/j.1365-2929.2006.02418.x

Elliott, V.: Thinking about the coding process in qualitative data analysis. Qual. Rep. **23**(11), 2850–2861 (2018). https://doi.org/10.46743/2160-3715/2018.3560

Flick, U.: Introducing Research Methodology: A beginner's Guide to Doing a Research Project. SAGE Publications Ltd. (2015)

Fusch, P.I., Ness, L.R.: Are We There Yet? Data Saturation in Qualitative Research. Walden Faculty and Staff Publications (2015). https://scholarworks.waldenu.edu/facpubs/455

Gilson, L.L., Maynard, M.T., Jones Young, N.C., Vartiainen, M., Hakonen, M.: Virtual teams research: 10 years, 10 themes, and 10 opportunities. J. Manag. **41**(5), 1313–1337 (2015). https://doi.org/10.1177/0149206314559946

Hafermalz, E., Riemer, K.: Interpersonal connectivity work: being there with and for geographically distant others. Organ. Stud. **41**(12), 1627–1648 (2020). https://doi.org/10.1177/0170840620973664

Kallio, H., Pietilä, A.M., Johnson, M., Kangasniemi, M.: Systematic methodological review: developing a framework for a qualitative semi-structured interview guide. J. Adv. Nurs. **72**(12), 2954–2965 (2016). https://doi.org/10.1111/jan.13031

Kuckartz, U.: Qualitative text analysis: a guide to methods, practice & using software. In: Landis, J.R., Koch, G.G. (eds.) (1977) The Measurement of Observer Agreement for Categorical Data. Sage publications (2014)

Landis, J.R., Koch, G.G.: The Measurement of Observer Agreement for Categorical Data. Sage publications (1977)

Larson, L., DeChurch, L.A.: Leading teams in the digital age: four perspectives on technology and what they mean for leading teams. Leadersh. Quart. **31**(1), 101377 (2020). https://doi.org/10.1016/j.leaqua.2019.101377

Nili, A., Tate, M., Barros, A., Johnstone, D.: An approach for selecting and using a method of inter- coder reliability in information management research. Int. J. Inf. Manage. **54**, 102154 (2020). https://doi.org/10.1016/j.ijinfomgt.2020.102154

Patton, M.Q.: Qualitative Research & Evaluation Methods: Integrating Theory and Practice. Sage Publications (2014)

Pulley, M.L., Sessa, V.I.: E-leadership: tackling complex challenges. Ind. Commer. Train. **33**, 225–229 (2001). https://doi.org/10.1108/00197850110405379

Richter, A.: Locked-down digital work. Int. J. Inf. Manage. **55**(May), 3 (2020). https://doi.org/10.1016/j.ijinfomgt.2020.102157

Sreejesh, S., Mohapatra, S., Anusree, M.R.: Business Research Methods. In: Business Research Methods (2014).https://doi.org/10.1007/978-3-319-00539-3

The Commission of the European Union. Commission Recommendation of 6 May 2003 concerning the definition of micro, small and medium-sized enterprises. In Official Journal of the European Union(2003). https://eur-lex.europa.eu/legal-content/EN/TXT/PDF/?uri=CELEX:32003H0361&from=EN

Van Wart, M., Roman, A., Wang, X.H., Liu, C.: Operationalizing the definition of e-leadership: identifying the elements of e-leadership. Int. Rev. Adm. Sci. **85**(1), 80–97 (2019). https://doi.org/10.1177/0020852316681446

Artificial Intelligence and Its Possible Advantages in Skin Cancer Diagnostics

Susanna Minder(✉) and Amelie Schweiger

IU International University, Munich, Germany
susanna.minder@iu.org, amelie.schweiger@iubh-dualesstudium.de

Abstract. The digitalization of various industries plays a significant role not only in Germany but also worldwide. It is not limited to sectors such as technology, industry, and education but increasingly impacts healthcare as well. In the healthcare sector, digitalization particularly influences communication, administration, data processing, and patient treatments (German Federal Ministry of Health, 2023). Through structured technical analysis of patient data, new therapies can be discovered, and better chances of recovery can be achieved. Artificial Intelligence (AI) contributes to these developments. AI, as a technical tool, can positively impact various processes. This includes accelerating medical research, introducing novel treatment methods, and optimizing and automating business and treatment processes (Pfannstiel, 2022, p. 1). This article examines the application of artificial intelligence in skin cancer diagnostics. The aim of the research is to identify the advantages of AI-based technologies in diagnostics and to show how this technology can be implemented. The insights and perspectives on the integration of AI in skin cancer diagnosis are captured in this article. The capabilities of precise image recognition and data processing as well as the competence for early detection of skin cancer lesions are included in the analysis. The results provide a comprehensive overview of the potential and positive developments resulting from AI applications in skin cancer diagnosis. These include early detection, reduction of misdiagnosis and increased efficiency.

Keywords: Artificial intelligence · skin cancer diagnostics · potential of AI · early detection

1 Introduction

The digital transformation across various industries plays a crucial role both in Germany and globally. It is no longer limited to sectors such as technology, industry, and education, but is increasingly influencing healthcare as well. Within healthcare, digitalization significantly affects communication, administration, data processing, and patient care (German Federal Ministry of Health, 2023). Through structured technical analysis of patient data, new therapies can be identified, leading to improved recovery outcomes. Artificial Intelligence (AI) is a key driver in these advancements, acting as a tool that can enhance various processes, including accelerating medical research, introducing innovative treatments, and optimizing and automating both administrative and clinical procedures (Pfannstiel, 2022, p. 1).

R. C. Geibel and S. Machavariani (Eds.): ISPC 2024, SPBE, pp. 557–568, 2025.
https://doi.org/10.1007/978-3-031-88052-0_44

In recent years, AI has seen remarkable progress in various medical fields. Particularly in diagnostics, AI holds the potential to complement or even surpass traditional methods. One of the most promising applications lies in skin cancer diagnostics, where AI-assisted systems have already shown impressive results in several studies (Haenssle et al., 2018; Esteva et al., 2017). These findings highlight the growing significance of using AI in skin cancer detection.

Skin cancer is one of the most commonly diagnosed cancers worldwide, posing a serious public health concern. In Germany alone, approximately 300,000 new cases are recorded annually, with the number steadily rising (Katalinic, 2023). Of these, over 250,000 cases are non-melanoma skin cancers, such as basal cell carcinoma and squamous cell carcinoma. In contrast, malignant melanoma, a more aggressive form of skin cancer, is relatively rare. The type of skin cancer plays a crucial role in determining treatment options and outcomes. Moreover, early detection is critical to the progression of the disease (AOK Federal Association GbR 2021).

In recent years, efforts in dermatology have increasingly focused on early diagnosis through public awareness campaigns, skin cancer screenings, and the use of dermatoscopy (Jutzi et al., 2022, p. 85). Despite these efforts, early detection remains a significant challenge for physicians. As a result, ongoing research aims to develop additional diagnostic tools and treatment methods. In this context, AI shows considerable promise. With its capability to process and analyze vast datasets, AI offers new avenues for the early identification and diagnosis of skin cancer. By acting as a support tool for physicians, AI provides a range of advantages that are worthy of further exploration (Jutzi et al., 2022, p. 85).

2 Skin Cancer

Skin cancer is one of the most common types of cancer in Germany. The Cancer Registry of Schleswig-Holstein projected around 309,000 new cases nationwide for 2023 (Katalinic, 2023). Generally, the term "skin cancer" refers to "semi-malignant and malignant neoplasms originating from the skin" (Schmitz 2024.a). In the medical field, the term "malignancy" denotes the severity and aggressiveness of the disease. Furthermore, there are various forms of skin cancer, with a distinction made between so-called "white" and "black" skin cancers (German Cancer Aid Foundation, 2021, p. 5). Types classified under "white" skin cancer, such as basal cell carcinoma and squamous cell carcinoma, are more prevalent compared to "black" skin cancer, such as malignant melanoma. Other types of skin cancer include Bowen's disease, Merkel cell carcinoma, dermatofibrosarcoma protuberans, and Kaposi's sarcoma. However, these occur much less frequently.

Basal cell carcinoma (BCC) is a "skin tumor originating from epidermal stem cells that grows locally, infiltratively and destructively, and metastasizes extremely rarely" (Haase, 2022). Synonyms include "basalioma" as well as "BCC" (the English term "basal cell carcinoma" and the abbreviation "BCC" derived from it). Typically, basal cell carcinomas are slow-growing tumors that usually do not cause pain in the affected individuals, often remaining unnoticed in the early stages (Aigner & Stephens, 2016, p. 115). The skin change often appears as a small, colorless nodule and is locally confined. Since there is no precursor to basalioma, even the smallest mutation constitutes a tumor that should be excised. Additionally, the carcinoma not only spreads across the surface, damaging adjacent tissues, but also invades deeper tissues over time (German Cancer Aid Foundation, 2021, p. 56).

Squamous cell carcinoma (SCC) is a "malignant skin tumor characterized by flat, exophytic-papillomatous, or ulcerative growth" (Schmitz, 2024.b). It is marked by metastasis to nearby lymph nodes, whereas spread to other organs, known as distant metastasis, is rare. In medicine, it is also referred to as "spinalioma", "squamous cell cancer" or "spinocellular carcinoma". Like basal cell carcinoma, squamous cell carcinoma is initially small and painless. However, unlike BCC, it grows significantly faster and has a precursor stage (Aigner & Stephens, 2016, p. 116). The precursor is actinic keratosis, a condition resulting from excessive UV radiation exposure and solar dermatitis (sunburns). It is characterized by recurrent redness of the skin, is not malignant, and the skin appears crusty and scaly. Without medical intervention, actinic keratosis can progress through continued growth into a full-blown squamous cell carcinoma (German Cancer Aid Foundation, 2021, p. 59). The emerging tumor exhibits crusts and a reddish discoloration of the ulcer. Squamous cell carcinoma is classified in medicine either by its location or according to the TNM classification system. The location-based classification distinguishes between occurrences on the head and neck and other skin areas, such as the upper and lower extremities. The TNM classification differentiates based on the size of the primary tumor (T), the metastasis to lymph nodes (N), and the presence of distant metastasis (M), indicating the extent and severity of the disease (Schmitz, 2024.b).

Malignant melanoma is defined as the "malignant transformation of melanin-producing cells" (Schöffel et al., 2016, p. 108). While these changes primarily occur in the skin's melanocytes, other areas such as mucous membranes, the meninges, the uveal tract (middle layer of the eye), and the conjunctiva can also be affected. Synonyms for this condition include "melanoblastoma," "cutaneous melanoma," "nevocarcinoma," and commonly, "black skin cancer." Malignant melanoma is an umbrella term for cancerous conditions affecting melanocytes, with various subtypes recognized in medical contexts. The three main forms are superficial spreading melanoma, nodular melanoma, and lentigo maligna melanoma.

Superficial spreading melanoma is the most common subtype, usually appearing on the back in men and on the legs in women. Initially, its growth is limited to the surface of the skin and the epidermis, but after two to four years, it progresses into the deeper dermis. Nodular melanoma, in contrast, grows into deeper layers from the outset, which leads to early metastasis. One key feature of nodular melanoma is its frequent lack of pigmentation, making it challenging to distinguish from normal skin (Schmitz, 2024.c). Unlike these two forms, lentigo maligna melanoma is characterized by its radial spread and does not exhibit thickening or nodule formation. It typically develops on the face, resembling freckles (Aigner & Stephens, 2016, p. 119).

Overall, malignant melanoma is much more aggressive and dangerous compared to non-melanoma skin cancers. This is mainly due to its tendency to metastasize to lymph nodes and other organs. When metastases spread to critical areas such as the brain or lungs, the disease reaches an advanced and life-threatening stage (Aigner & Stephens, 2016, p. 120).

3 Artificial Intelligence

"Artificial Intelligence describes the use of devices, computers, software programs, machines, and technologies that operate based on algorithms and analyze their environment" (Pfannstiel, 2022, p. 2). AI aims to support and ease the users' processes, meaning it can independently understand and solve questions or tasks. According to Pfannstiel (2022, p. 13), there are currently about twelve areas where AI can be applied.

One of the most widespread application fields is speech recognition. This operates in two directions: from analog to digital and from digital to analog. Two well-known examples are Amazon's "Alexa" and Apple's "Siri." Both systems can execute commands like playing music or answering questions about the weather. Beyond daily support, there are also systems used for transcribing interviews, recording meeting minutes, and assisting in research projects (Pfannstiel, 2022, p. 14). In addition to speech recognition, AI tools are also used for text recognition. These systems can read handwriting as well as recognize individual letters and fonts.

Another prominent application area of AI is process automation. Here, the tasks of employees are taken over by machines, robots, and software. This frees up human resources and increases productivity (Pfannstiel, 2022, p. 16).

In image recognition, AI is expected to identify specific features and properties of objects. This requires an algorithm that finds patterns in images and makes decisions based on these patterns. The algorithm must first be trained with a large dataset—in this case, images—to filter out differences and make comparisons. Classic examples of image recognition applications include facial and fingerprint recognition (Pfannstiel, 2022, p. 20).

In the field of neural networks, AI systems are designed to mimic the human brain through artificial neural networks. This means they can process and transmit information, functioning similarly to neurons in the human body. Deep learning, which also draws on human traits, aims for AI to emulate the human brain and develop a learning function. This occurs by creating an artificial neural network through algorithms that are continuously improved and expanded. As the network grows and considers more data, the system learns and achieves increasingly better results (Pfannstiel, 2022, p. 17).

The other six distinguishable areas are machine learning, expert systems, smart robots, evolutionary computation, big data, and natural language processing (Pfannstiel, 2022, p. 13).

In contrast to Pfannstiel, Prof. Dr. Claudia Bünte (2018, p. 5) believes that the term Artificial Intelligence cannot be uniformly and clearly defined due to the lack of a widely accepted definition of intelligence. She describes intelligence as "the human ability to think abstractly and rationally and derive purposeful action from it" (Bünte, 2018, p. 5). Based on this definition of intelligence, she defines Artificial Intelligence as "the field of computer science that deals with the acquisition of cognitive abilities typically associated with human intelligence, such as learning, problem-solving, and pattern recognition" (Bünte, 2018, p. 5).

The ways AI operates can be categorized into four groups: those in which humans are still involved in the work and those where human involvement is absent. Additionally, each of these groups is divided into whether the AI programs are capable of learning or not (Fig. 1).

	People Involved Operationally	People Not Involved Operationally
Pre-programmed Systems	Assistive Automata without Learning AI systems that support people in their work or decision-making. The programmed AI does not learn from these processes. *Example: Robot in manufacturing supports a human.*	Autonomous Automata without Learning Automata that take over work routines from people and can operate without human intervention. The programmed AI does not learn from these processes. *Example: Robot manufactures identical components autonomously.*
Adaptive Systems	Assistive Intelligence AI systems that mimic the work or decisions of humans and can learn from them. The AI is trained by people. *Example: X-ray diagnostics using AI; the doctor corrects and trains the AI.*	Autonomous Intelligence AI systems that adaptively respond to various situations and can operate autonomously without assistance. *Example: Image recognition AI works/learns autonomously.*

Fig. 1 .

Categorization of AI, source: own representation based on Bünte, 2018, S. 5

In the medical field, particularly in relation to AI, neural networks and deep learning are widely utilized. Neural networks are designed to replicate the function of the human brain, consisting of a network of artificial neurons. These systems process input through multiple interconnected layers, ultimately generating an output (Pfannstiel, 2022, pp. 184–185).

In medical applications, there are two primary types of neural networks: Deep Neural Networks (DNNs) and Convolutional Neural Networks (CNNs). DNNs are a broad category of algorithms capable of tackling a variety of tasks by analyzing features across multiple layers (Paaß & Hecker, 2020, pp. 26 & 40). CNNs, a specialized subset of DNNs, are optimized for image processing tasks. They employ convolutional filters to recognize spatial patterns such as edges, textures, and colors, making them particularly effective in analyzing medical images (Pfannstiel, 2022, p. 476; Paaß & Hecker, 2020, p. 105). For both types of networks, training with large datasets is essential to achieving high accuracy, requiring continuous adjustments and enhancements to the connections between artificial neurons (Paaß & Hecker, 2020, p. 88).

4 Artificial Intelligence in Healthcare

In the healthcare industry, artificial intelligence (AI) technologies are increasingly playing a central role, especially in the realms of diagnostics and clinical decision-making. According to Pfannstiel (2022, p. 89), AI's involvement is quite substantial, with approximately 21% of AI applications dedicated to diagnostics and around 18% focused on decision-making processes. These areas are crucial for the successful integration and application of AI technologies in healthcare settings.

The deployment of neural networks and their associated algorithms has become prevalent across various medical specialties, including radiology, pathology, and dermatology. In radiology, AI technologies are employed to enhance the interpretation of imaging results. By utilizing advanced pattern recognition capabilities, AI systems can assist radiologists in detecting and analyzing abnormalities within imaging data, thereby improving the accuracy and efficiency of radiological assessments.

In the field of pathology, AI is increasingly used for the automated analysis of tissue samples. This involves leveraging AI algorithms to process and evaluate histopathological data, which aids pathologists in diagnosing diseases more rapidly and with greater precision. The ability of AI to handle large volumes of data and identify subtle patterns contributes to more consistent and reliable diagnostic outcomes.

Dermatology is another area where AI has made significant strides, particularly in the diagnosis of skin conditions. AI systems are employed to analyze dermatological images, including those of skin lesions, to assist dermatologists in making accurate diagnoses. This is especially valuable in the detection of skin cancer, where timely and precise identification of malignant lesions is critical. AI programs are designed to support dermatologists by providing additional insights and recommendations based on the analysis of images, thereby enhancing the diagnostic process.

The following section will provide a more detailed exploration of how AI technologies are utilized in skin cancer diagnostics, outlining the specific applications and benefits of these systems in the context of dermatological evaluations (Samhammer et al., 2023, p. 2).

5 Brief Literature Review on AI-Assisted Diagnostic Methods in the Realm of Dermatology

Numerous studies underscore the efficiency and potential of AI-assisted diagnostic methods in various fields, particularly in dermatology. One of the pioneering and highly relevant studies in this area is the 2017 research conducted by Esteva et al., titled "Dermatologist-level classification of skin cancer with deep neural networks" (Esteva et al., 2017, p. 115). This study is notable for its innovative approach to utilizing artificial intelligence for medical diagnostics, specifically in evaluating skin lesions.

The primary aim of Esteva et al. (2017) was to investigate the effectiveness of a convolutional neural network (CNN) in analyzing skin lesions and to compare the diagnostic accuracy of the AI system with that of 21 experienced dermatologists. To achieve this, the researchers employed a CNN model developed by Stanford University. Initially, this model was trained on a vast dataset comprising approximately 1.28 million images. However, it is important to note that this dataset originally consisted of images depicting everyday objects, such as houses and animals, rather than images related to dermatological conditions.

Therefore, the CNN was first trained with about 130,000 clinical images of the skin (Paaß & Hecker, 2020, p. 17 and Winkler et al., 2020, p. 110). The training included normal and dermatoscopic photographs of healthy skin, benign skin lesions and malignant spots. The expanded dataset eventually comprised more than 2,000 diseases, classified into over 750 types. Using the modified CNN, the scientists tested the correct identification of squamous cell carcinomas versus benign keratoses and the correct distinction between malignant melanomas and nevi. The results of both tests show that AI-based diagnostics deliver similarly good results as those of specialists (Esteva et al., 2017, p. 115). This method in the study is considered a positive influence on the diagnosis of the corresponding skin diseases. It enables comparable diagnostics and meets the expertise of specialists in this regard. Moreover, it highlights the importance of the learning ability and the potential of AI programs in the context of deep learning (Young et al., 2020, p. 1504).

The second major scientific study on AI-assisted skin cancer diagnostics was conducted by Prof. Dr. Med. Haenssle and colleagues. In 2018, they published their findings under the research title "Man against machine: diagnostic performance of a deep learning convolutional neural network for dermoscopic melanoma recognition in comparison to 58 dermatologists" (Haenssle et al., 2018, p. 1836). As the title suggests, this study also involved a comparison of diagnostic results between AI and dermatologists. The researchers aimed to test and confirm the usefulness of a trained CNN for detecting melanocytic changes (Jutzi & Brinker, 2020, p. 15). Overall, Prof. Dr. Med. Haenssle's scientific research is very similar in fundamental aspects to the American study from 2017. Here too, a CNN that was previously trained with large datasets unrelated to medicine was used. In contrast to the other study, the AI system was then trained with about 100,000 purely dermatoscopic skin images and their corresponding diagnoses (Winkler et al., 2020, p. 111). For the test phase, two selected dermatologists chose 100 images from a previously compiled image repertoire. This included 300 images of malignant melanomas and nevi in various locations. Furthermore, the test phase was divided into two stages: In the first stage, the 58 participating dermatologists were given only the images based on which they had to make their diagnosis and a treatment proposal. In the second test, conducted four weeks later, the same doctors were given the same task with additional close-up images of the mutations and clinical information about the patients (Haenssle et al., 2018, p. 1837). The CNN analyzed only the dermatoscopic images and then made a diagnosis based on this. The study results show advantages for CNN-based diagnostics in both test stages. In both stage one and stage two, the CNN outperformed the overall performance of most dermatologists, confirming its usefulness. The superiority was particularly evident in specific locations such as the face (Sitaru & Zink, 2023, p. 21). In addition to the two studies discussed, other research has achieved similar results.

6 An AI Tool Example: FotoFinder Moleanalyzer Pro

Building on existing research into AI applications in healthcare, several advanced AI-based products have been developed for practical use in medical practices and clinics. One company at the forefront of this innovation is FotoFinder Systems GmbH. This company has invested extensively in creating AI-supported systems designed to enhance dermatological diagnostics. Some of their systems have already received partial approval as medical devices in Europe, signifying their integration into clinical settings and ongoing research projects (Sitaru & Zink, 2023, p. 21).

One of FotoFinder Systems GmbH's most well-known products is the FotoFinder Moleanalyzer Pro. This sophisticated system leverages artificial intelligence to analyze and evaluate skin lesions, providing a valuable tool for dermatologists. The Moleanalyzer Pro utilizes AI algorithms to assess various characteristics of skin lesions according to the ABCD criteria, which include Asymmetry, Border irregularity, Color variation, and Diameter (therefore the abbreviation ABCD). These criteria are essential for identifying potential malignancies and distinguishing between benign nevi and other types of skin abnormalities.

The FotoFinder Moleanalyzer Pro is designed to work in conjunction with dermatologists, supporting them in their diagnostic process rather than replacing human expertise. It offers detailed analyses of skin lesions and facilitates comparisons between different types of lesions. This collaboration ensures that dermatologists have access to comprehensive diagnostic information, which aids in making informed decisions regarding patient care.

According to FotoFinder Systems GmbH (n.d.), their AI systems provide several practical benefits. For instance, they help reduce the time required for examinations, particularly for patients with numerous nevi, which can be time-consuming to assess manually. Additionally, the use of AI reduces the dependency on epiluminescence microscopy images, which are traditionally used to examine skin lesions. By streamlining the diagnostic process and enhancing the efficiency of examinations, these AI tools contribute to improved patient outcomes and more effective management of dermatological conditions.

Overall, the integration of AI technologies like the FotoFinder Moleanalyzer Pro into dermatological practices represents a significant advancement in medical diagnostics, offering enhanced accuracy, efficiency, and support for healthcare professionals.

7 Diagnostic Using AI - Opportunities and Challenges

The use of AI-supported technologies in diagnostics offers several advantages to healthcare and its users, contributing to improved efficiency and treatment. However, it also comes with several challenges. One of the greatest potentials of AI in skin cancer diagnostics lies in aiding decision-making. The program assists doctors in the diagnostic process by providing comprehensive information about skin conditions and identifying characteristic disease features. Based on this data, it can recommend suitable therapy options, assess the need for excision, and predict healing prospects (Paaß & Hecker, 2020, p. 383; Sitaru & Zink, 2023, p. 23).

Another opportunity is enhancing diagnostics through AI-based data analysis, resulting in improved diagnostic accuracy. These tools have the capability to rapidly analyze and evaluate images and their contained data. They often recognize patterns and structures that may not be perceived by dermatologists, enabling quicker, more accurate diagnoses of potential skin cancers (Jörg, 2018, p. 86; Pfannstiel, 2022, p. 54). Compared to doctors, AI also tends to identify benign nevi and lesions less frequently as malignant diseases, thereby reducing misdiagnoses and unnecessary surgeries.

These aspects further translate into additional benefits of AI-driven skin cancer diagnostics. Patients benefit from improved prognosis due to early detection and correct therapy. In healthcare, resulting cost savings are of significant importance (Paaß & Hecker,

2020, pp. 17, 381). Detecting precursors or early stages of cancer often requires simpler, smaller, and hence less costly treatments. Moreover, more precise diagnoses reduce the need for follow-up examinations and treatments, further lowering costs.

An additional major benefit of AI-based skin cancer diagnostics is the potential for efficiency gains. Healthcare has long been affected by a shortage of skilled professionals. As an assistant system, AI can help alleviate these challenges for doctors, handling tasks such as data processing, analysis, and management that do not require human empathy. This allows doctors to use their time more efficiently, focusing on complex aspects and tasks that require empathy. Thus, AI enables optimal utilization of available resources (Paaß & Hecker, 2020, pp. 91–92).

While AI-based skin cancer diagnostics promise numerous benefits, they also pose several challenges that need careful consideration. Concerns about data privacy and compliance are critical. AI systems process highly sensitive patient data and clinical information, necessitating strict adherence to data protection regulations during processing and storage (Paaß & Hecker, 2020, p. 381).

The effectiveness of AI tools heavily relies on the quality and diversity of the training dataset, presenting additional challenges. Insufficiently diverse, erroneous, or non-representative data can lead to inaccurate or incorrect diagnoses by AI. Factors such as data quality, predominant training at specific locations, patient age, disease individuality, and imaging techniques can all affect AI accuracy (Jutzi et al., 2022, p. 89; Winkler et al., 2020, pp. 112–113).

Furthermore, there are challenges related to data availability in clinical settings. Many clinics and practices are not sufficiently digitized for AI applications. Moreover, medical facilities often collect large amounts of data that remain underutilized due to lacking technologies, interfaces, or data protection regulations, hindering effective use for training and improving AI-based diagnostic systems (Pfannstiel, 2022, p. 53; Samhammer et al., 2023, p. 2).

Issues such as societal acceptance of AI tools are also significant challenges. Broad acceptance from both patients and doctors is essential for AI to successfully support diagnostics. A study has shown that general acceptance of AI-based diagnostics exists on both sides but is contingent upon security, transparency, and understanding (Jutzi et al., 2022, pp. 89–90).

In literature, concerns about trust in technology and apprehensions that AI systems could replace doctors' roles are addressed. It is emphasized that doctors continue to serve as trusted individuals and mediators between AI and patients. Moreover, AI is not a substitute but rather a supportive measure in medical care (Paaß & Hecker, 2020, p. 412; Samhammer et al., 2023, pp. 4–6).

In summary, AI-based skin cancer diagnostics offer promising benefits, including improved decision-making, more precise diagnoses, and cost reductions. These systems enhance treatment outcomes for patients and increase efficiency in healthcare. Additionally, they present an opportunity to alleviate the current shortage of skilled professionals. However, these benefits must be balanced against significant challenges that require careful consideration during implementation to ensure compliance with legal requirements and efficient utilization.

8 Conclusion

This article examined the benefits of AI in skin cancer diagnostics through a literature analysis. The topic of the benefits and possibilities of AI applications in skin cancer diagnostics has been critically explored in numerous studies, particularly investigating improvements and diagnostic opportunities using AI. The results of this work aimed to highlight the advantages of AI in skin cancer diagnostics and the implementation possibilities for AI in medical settings.

With over 300,000 new cases per year, skin cancer is the most common form of cancer in Germany, distinguishing primarily between melanoma and non-melanoma types. Across all variants of the disease, high UV exposure has a significant impact on the development of malignant skin lesions. Furthermore, sources consistently emphasize the importance of early diagnosis and treatment for optimal chances of recovery. Therefore, researching the benefits of AI in skin cancer diagnostics is particularly significant.

In the past, diagnostics typically relied on clinical examination, dermatoscopy or biopsy. In recent years, methods have expanded to include AI-integrated systems utilizing convolutional neural networks (CNNs) and deep learning techniques for analyzing and assessing skin diseases. Literature analysis revealed that the use of AI technologies yields promising study results, indicating improved accuracy and reduced misdiagnoses.

Overall, numerous benefits of AI in skin cancer diagnostics have been identified. The most significant finding is the potential for early detection facilitated by AI-based diagnostics, which significantly influences disease progression and can positively impact it. The increased accuracy and diagnostic certainty have also been highlighted as positive developments. This opportunity arises from the functionality of AI programs, which can identify details that remain unnoticed by doctors, thereby reducing misdiagnoses. The enabled cost savings and efficiency improvements are further opportunities cited in the literature. Moreover, utilizing AI-based skin cancer diagnostics as a measure against healthcare workforce shortages is conceivable, offering promising solutions to this issue.

Despite these promising opportunities, several challenges and concerns must be considered. Challenges such as inadequate digitization, data privacy concerns, and societal acceptance have been identified. Nevertheless, the benefits of applying AI in skin cancer diagnostics outweigh these challenges.

Considering AI as a standalone diagnostic method is not advisable. AI can only be integrated as a supportive tool in the daily work of doctors, simplifying their tasks. It can handle activities that facilitate the work of doctors.

In summary, this work highlights the potential of AI-supported skin cancer diagnostics while emphasizing the need to balance opportunities and challenges. In the future, AI will continue to bring about further discoveries and advancements in medicine, significantly influencing healthcare with technologies and hopefully other positive developments.

References

Aigner, K.R., Stephens, F.O. (eds.): Onkologie Basiswissen. Springer, Berlin, Heidelberg (2016). https://doi.org/10.1007/978-3-662-48585-9

AOK Federal Association GbR: Neun Zahlen zum Thema Hautkrebs. Abgerufen von (2021). https://www.aok.de/pk/magazin/koerper-psyche/krebs/neun-zahlen-zum-thema-hautkrebs/

Bünte, C.: Künstliche Intelligenz – die Zukunft des Marketing: Ein praktischer Leitfaden für Marketing-Manager. Springer Gabler Verlag (2018). https://doi.org/10.1007/978-3-658-23319-8

Esteva, A., et al.: Dermato-logist-level classification of skin cancer with deep neural networks. Nature **542**(2), 115–118 (2017). https://doi.org/10.1038/nature21056

FotoFinder Systems GmbH (n.d.). Moleanalyzer Pro. Abgerufen von https://www.fotofinder.de/tech-nologie/kuenstliche-intelligenz/moleanalyzer-pro

German Cancer Aid Foundation: Hautkrebs-Screening und Hautkrebs-Früherkennung. Abgerufen von (2022). https://www.krebsinformationsdienst.de/tumorarten/hautkrebs/screening-frueh-erkennung.php

German Federal Ministry of Health: Digitalisierung im Gesundheitswesen. Abgerufen von (2023). https://www.bundesgesundheitsministerium.de/themen/digitalisierung/digitalisierung-im-ge-sundheitswesen.html

Haase, S.: Basalzellkarzinom. Pschyrembel Online. Abgerufen von (2022). https://www.pschyrem-bel.de/Basalzellkarzinom/K03FK/doc/

Haenssle, H.A., et al.: Man against machine: diagnostic perfor-mance of a deep learning convolutional neural network for dermoscopic melanoma recognition in comparison to 58 dermatologists. Ann. Oncol. **29**(8), 1836–1842 (2018). https://doi.org/10.1093/annonc/mdy166

Jutzi, T.B., Krieghoff-Henning, E.I., Brinker, T.J.: Künstliche Intelligenz auf dem Vormarsch – Hohe Vorhersage-Genauigkeit bei der Früherkennung pigmentierter Melanome. Aktuelle Dermatologie **48**(03), 84–91 (2022). https://doi.org/10.1055/a-1514-2013

Katalinic, A.: Update – Prognose und Zahlen zu Hautkrebs in Deutschland. Krebsregister Schleswig-Holstein. Abgerufen von (2023). https://www.krebsregister-sh.de/neue-prognose-zu-haut-krebs-in-deutschland-2023

Paaß, G., Hecker, D.: Künstliche Intelligenz: Was steckt hinter der Technologie der Zukunft? Springer-Verlag, Wiesbaden (2020). https://doi.org/10.1007/978-3-658-30211-5

Pfannstiel, M.A. (ed.): Künstliche Intelligenz im Gesundheitswesen: Entwicklungen, Beispiele und Perspektiven. Springer Fachmedien Wiesbaden, Wiesbaden (2022). https://doi.org/10.1007/978-3-658-33597-7

Samhammer, D., et al.: Klinische Entscheidungsfindung mit Künstlicher Intelligenz: Ein interdisziplinärer Governance-Ansatz. Springer-Verlag (2023). https://doi.org/10.1007/978-3-662-67008-8

Schmitz, K.J.: Hautkrebs. Pschyrembel Online. Abgerufen von (2024a). https://www.pschyrembel.de/Hautkrebs/K09J2/doc/

Schmitz, K.J.: Plattenepithelkarzinom der Haut. Pschyrembel Online. Abgerufen von (2024b). https://www.pschyrembel.de/Plattenepithelkarzinom%20der%20Haut/A0U2S/doc/

Schmitz, K.J.: Malignes Melanom. Pschyrembel Online. Abgerufen von (2024c). https://www.pschy-rembel.de/Malignes%20Melanom/K0DX1/doc/

Schöffel, N., Scholz, S.S., Bendels, M.H.K., Bundschuh, M., Groneberg, D.A.: Malignes Melanom: Aktuelle Aspekte zu Diagnostik und Therapie. Zentralblatt für Arbeitsmedizin, Arbeits-schutz und Ergonomie **66**(2), 108–111 (2016). https://doi.org/10.1007/s40664-016-0088-6

Sitaru, S., Zink, A.: Digitalisierung in der Dermatoonkologie: künstliche Intelligenz zur Diagnostik. best practice onkologie **18**(1–2), 20–26 (2023). https://doi.org/10.1007/s11654-022-00461-w

Winkler, J.K., Sies, K., Fink, C., Toberer, F., Enk, A., Haenssle, H.A.: Digitalisierte Bildverarbeitung: künstliche Intelligenz im diagnostischen Einsatz. Forum **35**(2), 109–116 (2020). https://doi.org/10.1007/s12312-019-00729-3

Young, A.T., Xiong, M., Pfau, J., Keiser, M.J., Wie, M.L.: Artificial intelligence in dermatology: a primer. J. Investig. Dermatol. **140**(8), 1504–1512 (2020). https://doi.org/10.1016/j.jid.2020.02.026

Cyber Security Data Science: Machine Learning Methods and Their Performance on Imbalanced Datasets

Mateo Lopez-Ledezma[1] (✉) and Gissel Velarde[2]

[1] Computational Systems Engineering, Universidad Privada Boliviana, Cochabamba, Bolivia
lopezmateo97@yahoo.com

[2] Extended Artificial Intelligence, IU International University of Applied Sciences, 99084 Erfurt, Germany
gissel.velarde@iu.or

Abstract. Cybersecurity has become essential worldwide and at all levels, concerning individuals, institutions, and governments. A basic principle in cybersecurity is to be always alert. Therefore, automation is imperative in processes where the volume of daily operations is large. Several cybersecurity applications can be addressed as binary classification problems, including anomaly detection, fraud detection, intrusion detection, spam detection, or malware detection. In many cases, the positive class samples, those that represent a problem, occur at a much lower frequency than negative samples, and this poses a challenge for machine learning algorithms since learning patterns out of under-represented samples is hard. This is known in machine learning as imbalance learning. In this study, we systematically evaluate various machine learning methods using two representative financial datasets containing numerical and categorical features. The Credit Card dataset contains 283726 samples, 31 features, and 0.2 percent of the transactions are fraudulent (imbalance ratio of 598.84:1). The PaySim dataset contains 6362620 samples, 11 features and 0.13 percent of the transactions are fraudulent (imbalance ratio of 773.70:1). We present three experiments. In the first experiment, we evaluate single classifiers including Random Forests, Light Gradient Boosting Machine, eXtreme Gradient Boosting, Logistic Regression, Decision Tree, and Gradient Boosting Decision Tree. In the second experiment, we test different sampling techniques including over-sampling, under-sampling, Synthetic Minority Over-sampling Techique, and Self-Paced Ensembling. In the last experiment, we evaluate Self-Paced Ensembling and its number of base classifiers. We found that imbalance learning techniques had positive and negative effects, as reported in related studies. Thus, these techniques should be applied with caution. Besides, we found different best performers for each dataset. Therefore, we recommend testing single classifiers and imbalance learning techniques for each new dataset and application involving imbalanced datasets as is the case in several cyber security applications. We provide the code with all experiments as open-source (Available at https://github.com/MateoLopez00/Imbalanced-Learning-Empirical-Evaluation.).

Keywords: Machine Learning · Cyber Security · Classification · Imbalance Learning · Data Science

R. C. Geibel and S. Machavariani (Eds.): ISPC 2024, SPBE, pp. 569–578, 2025.
https://doi.org/10.1007/978-3-031-88052-0_45

1 Introduction

Cyber security is gaining prominence worldwide as cybercrime increases. The cost of cybercrime to the global economy is estimated at 400 billion USD (Sarker et al., 2020). Cyber security data science aims at discovering patterns from data to detect anomalous, malicious, or fraudulent events that can harm a system. Applications in cyber security include anomaly detection, fraud detection, intrusion detection, spam detection, malware detection, and phishing detection (Sarker et al., 2020; Shaukat et al., 2020). Cyber security systems should detect possible attacks at any time, even if the number of operations increases suddenly. Availability and scalability pose a challenge to systems that depend on human monitoring, therefore, automation in cyber security is wanted. Artificial Intelligence (AI), and more specifically, machine learning allows intelligent automation based on the available data to detect cybercrime activities automatically.

Cyber security is now a trending topic just like data science and machine learning (Sarker et al., 2020). In some countries, the term data science is more popular than machine learning and vice versa. Some authors consider that data science would encompass machine learning (Sarker et al., 2020). Sculley et al. (2015) argue that the code devoted to purely machine learning algorithms in real- world systems represents a small percentage of the required infrastructure consisting of several tasks including configurations, data collection, feature extraction, data verification, analysis tools, process and machine resource management tools, serving infrastructure and monitoring. Still, the distinction between what is considered data science and machine learning is often not clear, and these terms may be used as synonyms in some fields or as complementary terms in other domains (Alpaydin, 2014). What is certain is that cyber security is a must for individuals, institutions, and governments, as cyber-attacks increase. Therefore, extracting patterns from data to automatically detect attacks can only be done computationally to stay alert 24 h a day, 7 days a week. However, in addition to availability and scalability, a fundamental component is the effectiveness of a system at detecting attacks. Therefore, detection quality depends on the performance of the machine learning methods in place.

In this paper, we present machine learning methods and their performance on two representative imbalanced datasets, as many cyber security applications will face the problem of learning from imbalanced distributions. Several cyber security machine learning applications can be addressed as binary classification problems, where the positive class samples represent a problem to a system. In many cases, the positive samples are under-represented in the datasets, and therefore, it is hard to learn statistics from the minority class (Lemaître, Nogueira, & Aridas, 2017; Kim & Hwang, 2022; Hajek et al. 2022; Li et al., 2023; Velarde et al., 2024; Yang et al., 2021).

We summarise the contributions of this study as follows:

- We systematically evaluate the performance of six machine learning algorithms in terms of recognition and speed in two representative cyber security datasets for fraud detection.
- We test the effects of imbalance learning techniques including sampling and ensembling.
- We show that imbalance classification depends strongly on the characteristics of each dataset, such that different classifiers should be evaluated for each dataset to select the best approach.

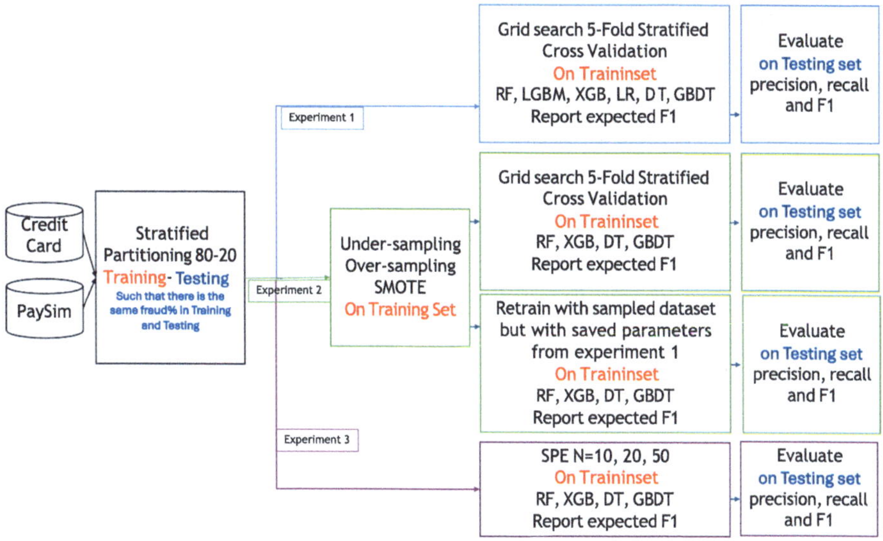

Fig. 1. A schematic representation of the method.

2 The Method

The proposed method can be seen in Fig. 1. Each dataset follows a stratified partition of 80–20 percent for training-testing sets, respectively. In the first experiment, we evaluate the performance of single classifiers: Random Forests (RF), Light Gradient Boosting Machine (LGBM), eXtreme Gradient Boosting (XGB), Logistic Regression (LR), Decision Tree (DT), and Gradient Boosting Decision Tree (GBT), see Sect. 2.2 for details. Each classifier goes under grid search on 5-Fold Stratified cross-validation on the training set, optimizing F1 score. In the second experiment, we evaluate the effect of sampling the training set to balance it, such that it has the same number of positive and negative samples, see Sect. 2.4. First, we use the parameters found in Experiment 1 on the resampled training set. Then, we retrain the classifiers with the resampled training set in 5-fold Stratified cross-validation. In the third experiment, we evaluate Self-Paced Ensembling (SPE) with N = 10, 20, and 50 base classifiers, see Sect. 2.4.

Both datasets were analyzed and cleaned before classifier initialization. We performed exploratory data analysis to understand the datasets' structure, number of features, types of features, and imbalance ratio. The Credit Card dataset presented in total 1081 duplicates but no missing (null) values. To address duplicated values, the first occurrences of each duplicated row have been kept and subsequent occurrences have been removed for each dataset. PaySim dataset did not present missing (null) values or duplicated rows.

2.1 The Datasets

We use two imbalanced datasets: **Credit Card** introduced in (Dal Pozzolo, Boracchi, Caelen, Alippi, & Bontempi, 2017), and **PaySim** introduced in (Lopez-Rojas, Elmir, & Axelsson, 2016), see Table 1.. Credit Card consists of 283726 credit card transactions of a European e-commerce, where daily fraud transactions vary over time, but roughly account for 0.2 percent of the transactions (Dal Pozzolo et al., 2017). PaySim consists of 6362620 simulated transactions from a real dataset of African mobile payments. Fraud transactions account for 0.13 percent of all transactions (Lopez-Rojas et al., 2016).

Table 1. Characteristics of Credit Card and PaySim Datasets.

Dataset	#Attributes	#Samples	Feature Format	Imbalance Ratio	Fraud %
Credit Card (Dal Pozzolo et al., 2017)	31	283726	Numerical	598.84:1	0.2
PaySim (Lopez-Rojas et al., 2016)	11	6362620	Numerical & categorical	773.70:1	0.13

2.2 Classifiers

We evaluated the following classifiers:

- **Random Forests (RF)** are combinations of trees that depend on an independently sampled vector with the same distribution of the trees in a forest (Breiman 2001).
- **Gradient Boosting Decision Tree (GBDT)** uses the principle of boosting to create a series of predictive models, each correcting the errors of its predecessors (Friedman, 2001).
- **Light Gradient Boosting Machine (LGBM)** aims at speeding up the training process of Gradient Boosting Decision Tree algorithms, delivering a scalable implementation by reducing the number of features (Ke et al., 2017).
- **eXtreme Gradient Boosting (XGB)** also belongs to the Gradient Boosting Decision Tree family, where successive models are added to correct the residuals or errors of previous models. This iterative approach minimizes the overall predictive error through a series of decision trees that progressively improve the model's accuracy (Chen & Guestrin, 2016).
- **Logistic Regression (LR)** is a statistical method for binary classification that estimates the probabilities of the outcomes based on a weight vector (Yu, Huang, & Lin, 2011).
- **Decision Tree (DT)** implements the divide-and-conquer strategy on a hierarchical data structure, and can be represented as a set of simple rules easy to interpret and visualize (Alpaydin, 2014; Quinlan, 1986).

2.3 Evaluation Criteria

In binary imbalance classification, the minority class has a substantially less number of samples than the majority class. Identifying the minority class is hard but essential (Velarde et al., 2024). Therefore, the minority class represents the positive class, and the majority class, the negative class.

Table 2. Confusion matrix for binary classification.

Actual	Predicted	
	Negative	Positive
Negative	*TN*	*FP*
Positive	*FN*	*TP*

Table 2. shows the confusion matrix for binary classification. The confusion matrix allows us to compute different evaluation metrics. We do not consider accuracy as an evaluation metric, since it does not reflect well the model performance and may be deceiving for imbalanced scenarios (Saito & Rehmsmeier, 2015; Liu et al., 2020; Velarde et al., 2024). The evaluation metrics considered in this study include

Recall =TP/TP+FN, Precision = TP/$TP + FP$, and F1 score=2 Recall × Precision/Recall + Precision

2.4 Imbalance Learning Techniques

We use four different imbalance learning techniques, including sampling and ensembling. Sampling techniques are used to change the training set original distribution.

- **Over-Sampling**: Aims at increasing the number of samples in the minority class by randomly resampling the minority class samples. This is a data augmentation technique. The size of the final training set after oversampling is two times the size of the original majority class, since we upsample the minority class until it is equal to the majority class. For example, for PaySim, the training set had 5083526 majority samples, and 6570 minority samples, we upsample the minority class so it also has 5083526 samples. The size of the final training set is two times the size of the original majority class.
- **Synthetic Minority Over-sampling Technique (SMOTE)**: Aims at balancing the class distribution by creating synthetic minority class examples and can under-sampling the majority class (Chawla, Bowyer, Hall, & Kegelmeyer, 2002). In our case, the minority class was increased to reach the size of the majority class.
- **Under-Sampling**: Randomly removes samples from the majority class. The size of the final training set after under-sampling is two times the size of the original minority class, since we under-sample the majority class until it is equal to the minority class. For example for PaySim, the training set had 5083526 majority samples, and 6570 minority samples, we under-sample the majority class so it also has 6570 samples. The size of the final training set is two times the size of the original minority class.

- **Self-Paced Ensemble (SPE)** is an ensemble learning technique designed to handle imbalanced datasets by iteratively re-weighting the training data to focus on "hard" examples, aiming to improve recognition of the minority class (Liu et al., 2020).

3 Results

The results of the three experiments are presented in this section. Both datasets, Credit Card and PaySim, are used independently in each experiment. See Appendix A for more information.

3.1 Experiment 1. Individual Classifiers.

Experiment 1 aims to evaluate individual classifiers without any sampling techniques. Figure 2 presents the experimental results of the six selected machine learning classifiers. XBG and RF are the best-performing classifiers, and their F1 score is similar in both datasets. However, XGB is much faster to train than RF, see Table **??**. GBDT and DT perform on a similar level on the Credit Card dataset, but DT outperforms all classifiers on PaySim. GDBT in contrast does a poor job on PaySim. LGBM is the weakest of all in both datasets. For the following experiments, we select four classifiers: XGB, RF, DT, and GBDT.

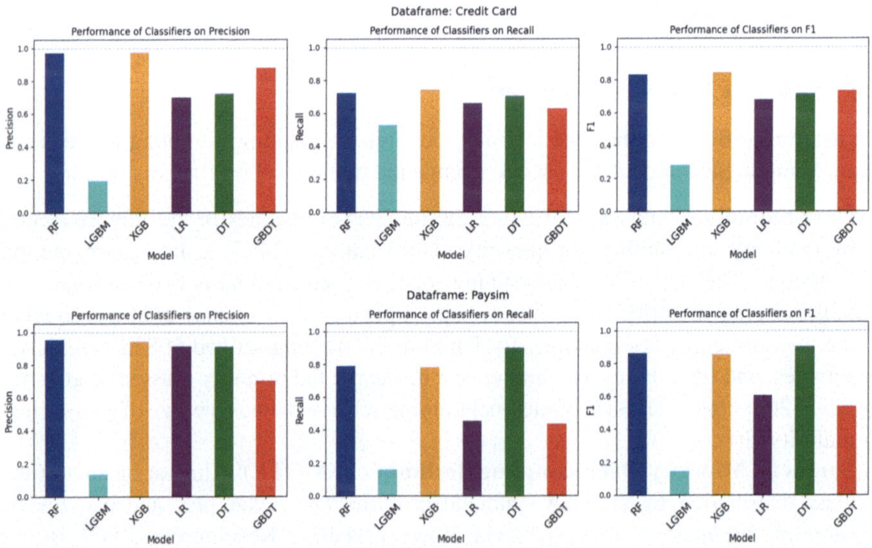

Fig. 2. Experiment 1. Performance of individual classifiers evaluated over Precision, Recall, and F1. The upper row of figures corresponds to the results on Credit Card. The lower row corresponds to the results on PaySim.

3.2 Experiment 2. Imbalance Learning Methods

Experiment 2 aims at evaluating the effect of sampling techniques, see Fig. 3. Compare the blue, orange, green, and red bars marked as (New) against the purple, brown, pink, and grey, marked as (Old) for No Sampling, Over-Sampling, SMOTE, and Under-Sampling, respectively. Sampling techniques have different effects. Over-Sampling has either no effect or helps improve recognition.

SMOTE most of the time worsens F1, except for GBDT, such that it improves recognition only when optimization is done on the resampled dataset. More generally, sampling techniques improve recall at the expense of lowering precision. However, RF, XGB, and DT prove robust to resampling the training set. In contrast, GBDT performs better when optimising over the resampled dataset, such that the orange, green, and red bars marked as (New) achieve higher F1 score than the brown, pink, and grey, marked as (Old).

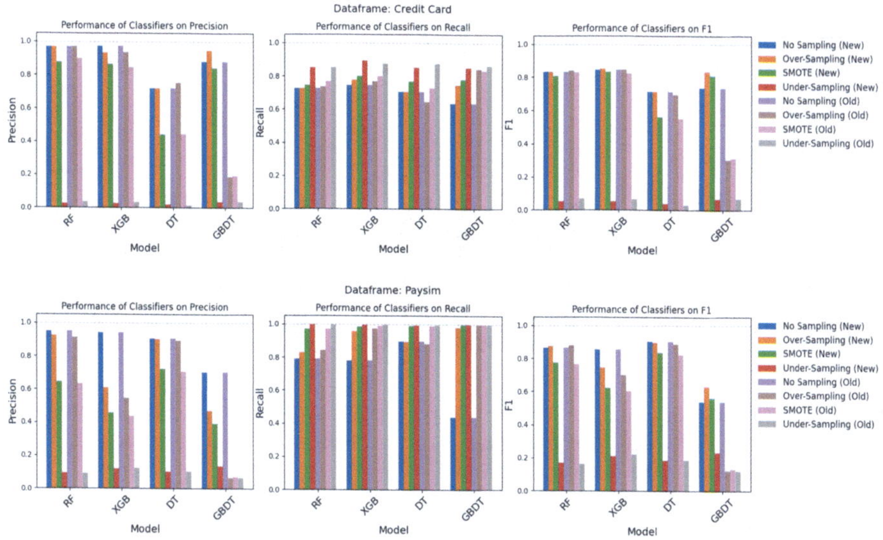

Fig. 3. Experiment 2. Effect of sampling techniques: No Sampling, Over-Sampling, Under- Sampling, and SMOTE. Evaluation over Precision, Recall, and F1. Blue, orange, green, and red, marked as (New), correspond to optimising classifiers using the resampled training set. Purple, brown, pink, and grey, marked as (Old), correspond to using the parameters found in Experiment 1 and re- training with the resampled dataset. The upper row of figures corresponds to the results on Credit Card. The lower row corresponds to the results on PaySim.

3.3 Experiment 3. SPE and the Number of Base Classifiers

Experiment 3 aims at evaluating SPE (ensembling), see Fig. 4. As in Experiment 2, we evaluate XGB, RF, DT, and GBDT as initial classifiers for SPE with N = 10, 20, and 50 classifiers. Interestingly, the more base classifiers, the higher the precision but the lower the recall. On Credit Card dataset, the optimal number of base classifiers is N = 20. On PaySim, there are different effects for each classifier. XGB performs best with no more than N = 10 base classifiers, while RF, DT, and GBDT do with N = 20 base classifiers. Increasing complexity seems unnecessary.

On Credit Card, XGB with Over-Sampling ($F1 = 0.851$, Experiment 2) performs similarly as in ensembling with SPE, N = 20 XGB base classifiers ($F1 = 0.854$, Experiment 3). On PaySim, the best F1 score was obtained by DT No-Sampling ($F1 = 0.902$, Experiment 1) just like in ensembling with SPE, N = 50 DT base classifiers ($F1 = 0.902$, Experiment 3). These results indicate that it is important.

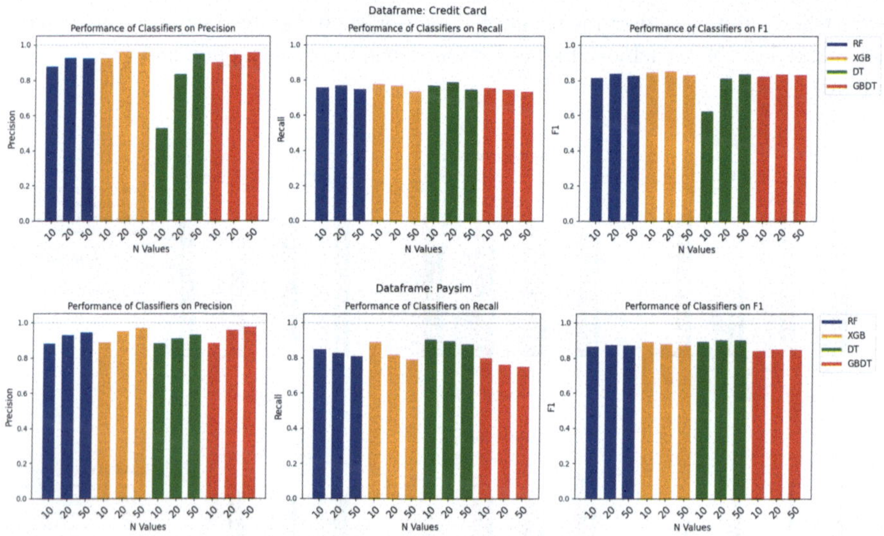

Fig. 4. Experiment 3. SPE and the number of base classifiers (N = 10, 20, 50) evaluated over Precision, Recall, and F1. The upper row of figures corresponds to the results on Credit Card. The lower row corresponds to the results on PaySim.

Figure 5 presents the execution times. Most of the time, XGB is the fastest, followed by DT, RF, and GBDT, which is the slowest algorithm. Given that under sampling removes samples, it makes execution times the fastest, followed by no sampling, over sampling, and SMOTE. The execution time of SPE increases with the number of base classifiers as expected.

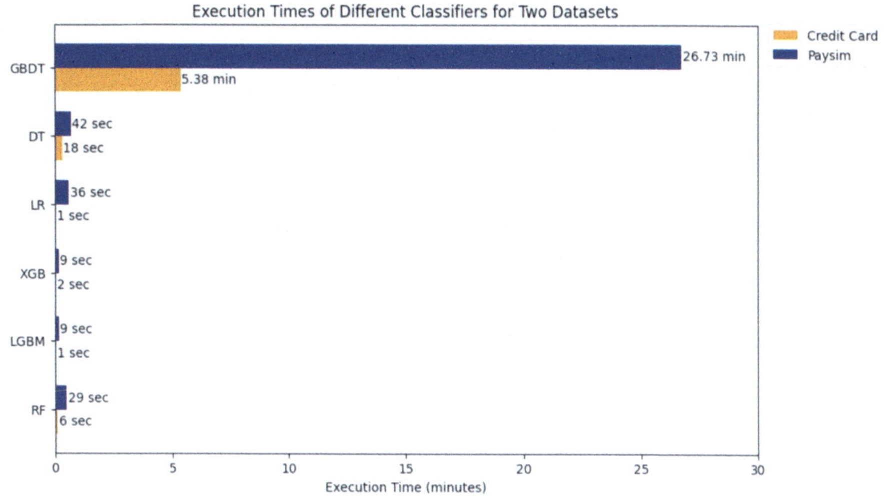

Fig. 5. Execution time (minutes:seconds) for a single run including no-sampling, sampling or ensembling when model training. Execution on Google Colab to evaluate different classifiers on each problem and dataset. These results align with the No Free Lunch Theorem (Wolpert & Macready, 1997).

4 Conclusion

This study extensively evaluated various machine learning strategies to address the challenge posed by imbalanced datasets, particularly in classification tasks where the minority class is crucial yet underrepresented. We presented three experiments executed on two highly imbalanced and representative datasets containing numerical and categorical features: Credit Card dataset (283726 samples, imbalance ratio: 598.84:1), and PaySim dataset (6362620 samples, imbalance ratio: 773.70:1). XGB and RF proved to be robust classifiers and performed well with or without sampling on both datasets in terms of classification accuracy, with XGB being faster than RF. Sampling techniques had positive and negative effects, similarly as reported by previous studies (Kim & Hwang, 2022; Hajek et al., 2022; Velarde et al., 2024). Sampling helped improve recall at the expense of deteriorating precision. While in many cases over-sampling the minority class helped improve recognition, under-sampling had a strong deteriorating effect, presumably due to loss of information. Except for GBDT, SMOTE had deteriorating effects, possibly because the generation of synthetic minority samples might intro- duce noise. Ensembling with SPE improved recognition in some cases. Therefore, we recommend evaluating different setups as these might perform differently depending on the dataset characteristics. The findings presented in this study contribute to better understanding and addressing several cyber- security applications formulated as binary classification problems with imbalanced data, including anomaly detection, fraud detection, intrusion detection, spam detection, or malware detection.

Author Contributions. M.L. experimental design, code, and preparation of tables and figures. G.V. supervision, experimental design, and writing.

References

Alpaydin, E.: Introduction to Machine Learning. MIT Press, Cambridge (2014)

Breiman, L.: Random forests. Mach. Learn. **45**, 5–32 (2001)

Chawla, N.V., Bowyer, K.W., Hall, L.O., Kegelmeyer, W.P.: Smote: synthetic minority over-sampling technique. J. Artif. Intell. Res. **16**, 321–357 (2002)

Chen, T., Guestrin, C.: XGBoost: a scalable tree boosting system. In: Proceedings of the 22nd ACM SIGKDD International Conference on Knowledge Discovery and Data Mining, pp. 785–794 (2016)

Dal Pozzolo, A., Boracchi, G., Caelen, O., Alippi, C., Bontempi, G.: Credit card fraud detection: a realistic modeling and a novel learning strategy. IEEE Trans. Neural Netw. Learn. Syst. **29**(8), 3784–3797 (2017)

Friedman, J.H.: Greedy function approximation: a gradient boosting machine. Ann. Statist. **29**, 1189–1232 (2001)

Hajek, P., Abedin, M.Z., Sivarajah, U.: Fraud detection in mobile payment systems using an XGBoost-based framework. Inf. Syst. Front. 1–19 (2022)

Ke, G., et al.: LightGBM: a highly efficient gradient boosting decision tree. In: Advances in Neural Information Processing Systems, vol. 30 (2017)

Kim, M., Hwang, K.-B.: An empirical evaluation of sampling methods for the classification of imbalanced data. PLoS ONE **17**(7), e0271230 (2022). https://doi.org/10.1371/journal.pone.0271260)

Lemaître, G., Nogueira, F., Aridas, C.K.: Imbalanced-learn: a python toolbox to tackle the curse of imbalanced datasets in machine learning. J. Mach. Learn. Res. **18**(17), 1–5 (2017). http://jmlr.org/papers/v18/16-365.html

Li, Y., et al.: Imbalanced least squares regression with adaptive weight learning. Inf. Sci. **648**, 119541 (2023)

Liu, Z., et al.: Self-paced ensemble for highly imbalanced massive data classification. In: 2020 IEEE 36th International Conference on Data Engineering (ICDE), pp. 841–852 (2020)

Lopez-Rojas, E., Elmir, A., Axelsson, S.: PaySim: a financial mobile money simulator for fraud detection. In: 28th European Modeling and Simulation Symposium, EMSS, Larnaca, pp. 249–255 (2013)

Quinlan, J.R.: Induction of decision trees. Mach. Learn. **1**, 81–106 (1986)

Saito, T., Rehmsmeier, M.: The precision-recall plot is more informative than the ROC plot when evaluating binary classifiers on imbalanced datasets. PLoS ONE **10**(3), e0118432 (2015)

Sarker, I.H., Kayes, A., Badsha, S., Alqahtani, H., Watters, P., Ng, A.: Cybersecurity data science: an overview from machine learning perspective. J. Big Data **7**, 1–29 (2020)

Sculley, D., et al.: Hidden technical debt in machine learning systems. In: Advances in Neural Information Processing Systems, vol. 28 (2015)

Shaukat, K., et al.: Performance comparison and current challenges of using machine learning techniques in cybersecurity. Energies **13**(10), 2509 (2020)

Velarde, G., et al.: Tree boosting methods for balanced and imbalanced classification and their robustness over time in risk assessment. Intell. Syst. App. **22**, 200354 (2024). https://doi.org/10.1016/j.iswa.2024.200354, https://www.sciencedirect.com/science/article/pii/S2667305324000309

Wolpert, D.H., Macready, W.G.: No free lunch theorems for optimization. IEEE Trans Evol. Comput. **1**(1), 67–82 (1997)

Yang, K., et al.: Progressive hybrid classifier ensemble for imbalanced data. IEEE Trans. Syst. Man Cybern. Syst. **52**(4), 2464–2478 (2021)

Yu, H.-F., Huang, F.-L., Lin, C.-J.: Dual coordinate descent methods for logistic regression and maximum entropy models. Mach. Learn. **85**, 41–75 (2011)

Strategies for Perfecting Delegation in the Digital Era

Mariam Burmistrova(✉)

East European University, Tbilis, Georgia
mariam.burmistrova@eeu.edu.ge

Abstract. In the rapidly evolving digital landscape, effective delegation is crucial for organizational efficiency and success. It has influence on fundamentally transforming traditional business processes. Among these, delegation is a critical component of effective management, which has undergone significant changes driven by technological advancements. The process of delegation is very important in terms of business relationships. In today's world, where companies are continually expanding and augmenting their human resources, effective task delegation is paramount amidst increased workloads. Developing digital competencies and implementing transparent workflows are crucial for managing tasks efficiently.

The paper underscores the significance of developing digital competencies and encouraging collaborative learning to enhance team members' ability to handle delegated tasks independently. By establishing robust communication channels and leveraging digital innovations, organizations can optimize their delegation processes, ensuring tasks are completed effectively and efficiently in a digitally-driven workplace.

Finding the right people, setting the right tasks, having relevant expectations, giving trust and freedom to subordinates, constant support, encouragement and feedback to employees is important for the right delegation process. This paper explores various strategies for perfecting delegation within the digital era, focusing on the integration of digital communication tools, workflow automation, and innovative management practices. The study will employee the quantitative and qualitative research methods, by using the questionnaire for a survey of managers and interviews with the strategic decision-makers.

By understanding and implementing these strategies, businesses can achieve greater operational agility, business leaders can streamline processes, improve productivity, foster a more collaborative culture, and work environment. Ultimately, this will lead to enhanced business performance, increased employee satisfaction, and a stronger competitive edge in the market. The practical implication would be that businesses will gain actionable insights and practical methods for leveraging digital tools to perfect delegation within their organizations, ensuring they stay ahead in the digital age.

Keywords: Delegation · Digital Competencies · Delegation Strategies · Digital Communication Tools

R. C. Geibel and S. Machavariani (Eds.): ISPC 2024, SPBE, pp. 579–597, 2025.
https://doi.org/10.1007/978-3-031-88052-0_46

1 Introduction

In today's business world, delegation has evolved beyond its conventional role and become a strategic approach enhanced by digital technologies. Advanced software and platforms have redefined how tasks are allocated and monitored, allowing leaders to better manage their teams and concentrate on key business areas. This shift is more than just passing on responsibilities; it's about integrating technology with human skills to create a collaborative environment that maximizes efficiency and drives innovation.

The delegation process is designed to enhance the significance of subordinates' roles, leading to greater job engagement and improved performance. Leaders and managers cannot handle every task on their own, making delegation essential for distributing responsibilities and empowering team members to contribute meaningfully. Delegation involves granting authority to subordinates to handle less critical tasks, allowing leaders to focus on more strategic responsibilities. Effective delegation is an essential management tool to achieve the best results (Ugoani, 2020).

For effectively delegate tasks very important to choose the right person for the job, explain why someone is chosen, provide the right instructions, provide right resources and training, delegate responsibility and authority, check the work and provide feedback, and always say thank you for some work. Delegate well "increase trust and commitment with your employees, improve productivity, and make sure the right people are performing the tasks that best suit them" (Genevieve 2024).

Delegation involves granting authority to others, making aptitude and competencies essential in the process. The focus should be on individuals, including their interests, while also considering the necessary skills, as these can be developed over time. Support structures are crucial for successful delegation and should include training, mentoring, coaching, and easy access to information (Benedict Mathebula, Brian Barnard, 2020).

This article explores the strategies for perfecting delegation in the digital era, emphasizing the integration of digital tools, the importance of trust and communication, and the need for continuous improvement in delegation practices. By leveraging these strategies, leaders can better navigate the challenges of modern work environments, allowing their teams to thrive and adapt to the demands of the digital world.

2 Theory

2.1 Delegation Process

The process of delegation is very important in terms of business relationships. In today's world, where companies are continually expanding and augmenting their human resources, effective task delegation is paramount amidst increased workloads. Delegation must be clearly structured from the top down, with the delegator having a thorough understanding of the tasks to be divided, along with the required quality and quantity for each.

Delegation involves assigning and transferring responsibilities to team members while the leader or manager retains oversight to provide guidance, mentorship, and support. It entails breaking down a larger workload into manageable tasks and entrusting these to individuals capable of handling them effectively. By entrusting others with portions of the work, a leader demonstrates confidence in the team's abilities to achieve, or even exceed, the quality of results that the leader could produce alone (Entrepreneurial Mindset, 2023).

Effective delegation fosters psychological empowerment by giving employees a sense of ownership and responsibility over their tasks. It also serves as a collaborative, well-coordinated, and comprehensive management approach, helping to motivate employees while assessing their performance and contribution to overall team success (Ugoani, 2020).

2.2 Understanding Delegation in the Digital Age

Delegation is the process of transferring responsibility for specific tasks from one person to another. Typically practiced by managers, supervisors, and other leaders, delegation helps improve efficiency, manage time more effectively, and provides opportunities for staff development and training. By delegating, leaders not only free up their own time for more strategic responsibilities but also empower their team members to grow and take on more responsibilities (Indeed, 2024).

In today's digital era, companies are confronted with both extraordinary challenges and opportunities. Rapid technological advancements, market fluctuations, and increasing complexity require organizations to be agile and responsive. In such a dynamic environment, leaders cannot afford to be bogged down by day-to-day operational tasks. Instead, they must rely on their teams to assume responsibilities and make well-informed decisions. With the fast pace of technological progress, businesses require leaders who can adeptly navigate the digital landscape. The intricacies of this era necessitate a broad range of skills and expertise that no single leader can possess entirely. As a result, leaders must leverage the collective knowledge and experience of their teams to capitalize on digital opportunities and address emerging challenges (Garro, 2023).

A crucial aspect of effective delegation is knowing when to delegate. For instance, a great leader recognizes when to assign tasks to an employee who could benefit from a confidence boost. Even better leaders delegate strategically for opportunity. Instead of relying on the same high performers for critical projects, they ensure everyone on the team has the chance to tackle more challenging tasks. Leaders carefully consider who receives these opportunities, taking into account each team member's capabilities, development needs, motivations, and availability. Additionally, leaders must ensure that tasks are never delegated when legal or business regulations prohibit it. This thoughtful approach not only enhances team growth but also fosters a more equitable and motivated work environment.

Task Prioritization it is important part of delegation:

- Identify which tasks should be delegated and which ones should be handled personally.
- Delegating tasks by setting SMART goals (Specific, Measurable, Achievable, Relevant, Time-bound) ensures clarity and accountability.
- Delegate tasks based on the principle that 70% of tasks should be those the employee knows how to do, 20% should be tasks they can learn with guidance, and 10% should stretch their abilities.

And after that Progress Reviews is important. Conduct regular check-ins and progress reviews to ensure the delegated task is on track and provide support where needed without micromanaging.

2.3 Key Strategies for Effective Delegation

Successful delegation demands a particular set of skills and strategies. Leaders must be adept at recognizing the strengths and areas for improvement within their teams, assigning tasks that align with each individual's capabilities, and setting clear expectations and limits. A deep understanding of team members' abilities, preferences, and developmental needs is essential for this process. By thoughtfully distributing tasks, leaders can optimize both team performance and overall efficiency.

Clear Communication and Expectations, Continuous Monitoring and Feedback, Empowering Teams Through Autonomy are key elements of delegation processes.

Based on Entrepreneurial Mindset, effective delegation strategies for coaches are following: 1. Identify core strengths and weakness; 2. Hire or collaborate with experts; 3. Set clear expectations; 4. Implement digital tools; 5. Regular check-ins and feedback; 6. Empower and trust; 7. Continuous learning and adaptation.

The fast-paced and constantly changing digital landscape presents distinct challenges for delegating tasks. To ensure that tasks are completed both efficiently and effectively, a more refined and strategic approach is essential. Based on Entrepreneurial Mindset, below are some key practices to follow when assigning tasks in the digital space.

1. Define Clear Objectives
2. Utilize Digital Collaboration Tools
3. Regularly Review Progress
4. Provide Access to Resources
5. Encourage Autonomy
6. Stay Updated on Trends
7. Document Processes

(Entrepreneurial Mindset, 2023).

Delegating responsibilities and tasks enables leaders to step back, gain a broader perspective, and clearly identify key priorities. However, to achieve optimal results for both their teams and the organization, leaders must refine this skill. Based on Rachelle Lee article, below are seven strategies leaders can adopt to delegate more effectively:

1. Have a clear vision - Establishing a clear vision is required for successful leadership.
2. Communicate effectively - While having a vision is important, communicating it is a separate challenge. Effective delegation hinges on clear and specific communication. In practice, poor communication skills can result in mismatched expectations and prevent team from achieving its objectives.
3. Use empathy - Empathy is the ability to understand and connect with another person's perspective and experiences. It plays a crucial role in effective delegation by offering insight into what motivates individuals to complete delegated tasks. Only motivated and engaged employees can perform at their best.

4. Give influence - To delegate successfully, managers must be able to influence how team members approach their tasks. Often, the person most familiar with improving a job is the one performing it, and they feel more invested in a shared goal when involved in solving problems that directly affect their work. Leaders can maximize this by allowing delegation to be guided by the team's suggestions and ideas. This approach enables team members to feel connected and empowered to influence their work.
5. Encourage accountability - Accountability is closely linked to trust. Leaders must hold themselves accountable just as much as their team members do. It's insufficient to emphasize accountability through words alone; it must be demonstrated through action. After establishing clear tasks and goals with team members, working collaboratively to create a concrete plan for assessing the delegated work throughout the assignment is crucial. The most effective leaders showcase accountability for resources, time, and project outcomes. When trust is higher, team members are more likely to commit to delegated tasks with enthusiasm, driving peak performance.
6. Provide motivation - Maintaining team's motivation to complete delegated tasks requires ongoing effort. Leaders link motivation to the goals of individual team members, the team as a whole, and the organization. Clear communication about the purpose of the work is essential for fostering motivation. Since motivation is personal and must be intrinsic, different individuals may be driven by various factors—some by recognition, others by autonomy, and some by incentives or status. Effective leaders take the time to understand what motivates each team member.
7. Negotiate with team - Negotiating tasks with team members can enhance effectiveness of a manager. Instead of merely issuing orders, engage team in the delegation process by allowing them to identify which tasks align best with their strengths and skills. This autonomy in task negotiation demonstrates a leader's trust in the team, leading to improved performance outcomes. Additionally, aligning tasks with individuals' strengths and skills helps prevent issues related to incomplete or incorrectly completed work, both of which can be costly in terms of time and resources (Rachelle Lee, 2021).

In the digital age, the rules of leadership are evolving. Many leaders struggle with delegation because they find it difficult to relinquish control over their own work. However, effective delegation brings significant benefits:

- Engagement improves – Team members feel more motivated and involved when they are assigned work that matters and aligns with their strengths.
- Productivity increases – Tasks are allocated to individuals best suited to handle them, leading to more efficient execution.
- Skills improve – Delegation provides opportunities for team members to develop and enhance their skills through hands-on experience.

By embracing delegation, leaders can drive better performance and foster a more empowered team (Management Best Practices, n.d.).

2.4 The Role of Digital Technologies in the Delegation Process

Digital technologies play a crucial role in enhancing the delegation process by improving communication, tracking progress, and facilitating collaboration across teams.

Task Management Platforms (like Jira, Trello, Asana) allow managers to delegate tasks with clear instructions, deadlines, and priorities. These platforms ensure everyone understands their responsibilities and how their work fits into the larger project. Tasks can be updated in real-time, reducing confusion and increasing accountability.

Collaboration Tools (like Slack, Microsoft Teams, or Zoom) make it easier for team members and leaders to communicate instantly, share updates, and clarify expectations. This helps ensure that any ambiguities in the delegation process are quickly addressed. Managers can also give feedback or offer guidance through these platforms, providing continuous support for delegated tasks.

Digital tools enable managers to monitor the progress of delegated tasks in real time. Tools like Jira and Trello offer visual boards, dashboards, and reports to track the status of tasks, deadlines, and project milestones:

- Trello is a very popular task management tool that uses boards, lists, and cards to help teams organize tasks. It allows managers to assign tasks, set deadlines, and track progress.
- Jira is an excellent tool for delegation, particularly in software development and project management contexts. It's widely used for tracking tasks, managing workflows, and ensuring effective collaboration among teams.

Digital technologies significantly enhance the delegation process by improving communication, providing real-time tracking, facilitating collaboration, ensuring accountability, and enabling flexibility. They allow leaders to manage tasks more effectively, monitor progress without micromanaging, and ensure team members are well-supported with clear instructions and feedback. These tools help make delegation more efficient and responsive to the complexities of modern, digitally-driven work environments.

3 Research Methods

The study employ both quantitative and qualitative research methods, by using the questionnaire for a survey of managers and interviews with the strategic decision-makers.

The theoretical framework has been developed by taking into account the methods and approaches found in scientific and practical literature. The material has been collected, analyzed, and interpreted. Additionally, a qualitative approach has been applied in the research.

The study utilized a survey with a structured questionnaire as its primary instrument for quantitative research. A comprehensive analysis and synthesis of data from all sources were conducted, leading to the formulation of conclusive findings.

A thorough analysis and synthesis of data from all sources were undertaken, resulting in the formulation of conclusive findings.

4 Results and Discussion

As part of the qualitative research, five middle or senior managers were interviewed. To maintain confidentiality and at the request of the experts, the names of specific individuals have not been disclosed to avoid identifying the company. The survey included 12 in-depth questions. During the qualitative research, several key insights emerged.

One respondent noted that digital transformation has streamlined the delegation process significantly. Tools like Microsoft Teams facilitate easier communication, enabling colleagues to assign tasks and receive updates quickly. This shift has necessitated adaptation to new technologies, fostering a more collaborative environment.

Digital transformation has fundamentally altered the approach to delegation, making it more efficient and transparent. Tools such as Microsoft Teams and Trello are particularly useful for tracking progress and assigning tasks. Microsoft Teams supports seamless communication, while Trello provides a clear overview of task statuses, deadlines, and responsibilities. These tools help ensure organized, timely completion of tasks.

Delegation practices have shifted from informal, in-person communication to a more structured, tech-driven approach. Digital tools like project management platforms (e.g., Trello or Microsoft Teams) enable efficient task delegation, real-time progress tracking, and improved accountability. A key lesson learned is the importance of clarity; while digital tools simplify task assignment, unclear instructions and deadlines can lead to confusion. Regular personal check-ins remain essential to ensure team members feel supported.

The main barriers to delegating tasks in a digital context are miscommunication and the overcomplication of simple tasks due to digital tools. Sometimes, team members misunderstand expectations conveyed through digital platforms, resulting in delays or errors. Additionally, certain digital tools can complicate straightforward tasks with excessive features or notifications. To address these challenges, it is crucial to provide clear instructions and regularly check in with team members to confirm their understanding.

To ensure team is well-equipped to handle delegated tasks, especially in terms of digital literacy and tools, first assess each team member's familiarity with the digital platforms use, based on their comfort level, provide targeted training sessions that cover both the basics and advanced features of these tools. Some respondents also have ongoing support mechanisms in place, like regular workshops on digital skills and one-on-one mentoring.

Regarding the evolution of the delegation process over the next five years, most respondents believe it will become more automated and data-driven, with AI and machine learning playing significant roles. Enhanced collaboration platforms will facilitate seamless communication and real-time updates. By embracing innovation now, individuals position themselves to transition smoothly as technology evolves.

Respondents identified the primary benefits of using digital tools for delegation as enhanced visibility and accountability. These tools enable visibility of task ownership, real-time progress tracking, and improved communication. However, challenges such as technical difficulties—connectivity issues or platform bugs—can disrupt workflow. Additionally, some team members may struggle with digital literacy or resist adopting new tools, leading to misunderstandings.

To improve the delegation process through feedback, one interviewee mentioned gathering input during weekly check-ins, encouraging discussions about challenges with the current delegation approach. For instance, feedback revealed that task instructions were often unclear, causing delays. As a result, the respondent began using project management tools to create more structured task assignments with clear deadlines and checkpoints, improving efficiency and reducing the need for constant follow-up.

Cultural factors significantly influence the approach to delegation. Interviewees noted that in a collaborative culture where open communication is encouraged, delegation tends to be more effective, as team members feel comfortable discussing their capabilities and seeking clarification. However, hierarchical structures can hinder initiative and discourage subordinates from voicing their opinions.

The study surveyed 53 individuals to provide a quantitative understanding of how delegation is managed and implemented within organizations .

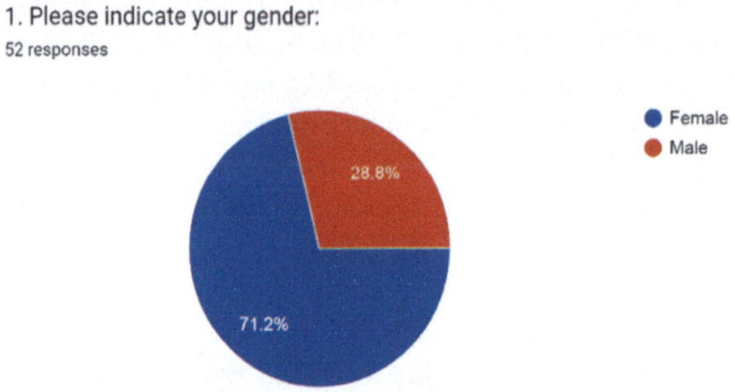

Fig. 1. Gender Distribution

As we can see from the graphic, 71.2% of the participants in this research were women, and 28.8% were men.

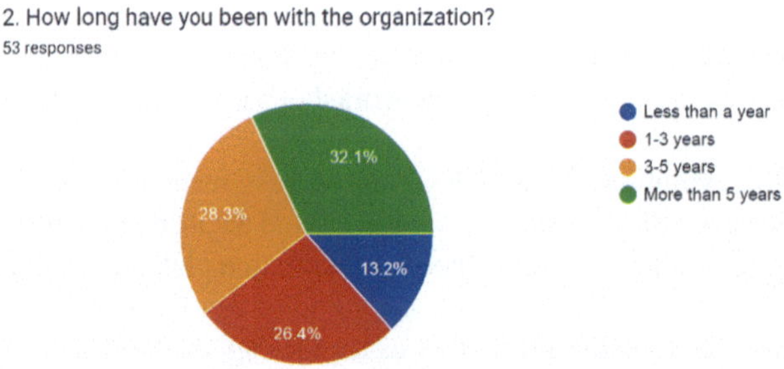

Fig. 2. Length of Tenure in the Organization

The answers to the second question were very interesting, as they indicate that most of the interviewees were responsible and trustworthy individuals, given their long-term employment with their respective companies. As we can see from Fig. 2, the largest group, 32.1%, consists of individuals who have been with their company for more than 5 years. Another 28.3% have worked for 3–5 years, 26.4% for 1–3 years, and only 13.2% have been with their company for less than a year. This suggests that most of the interviewees have significant experience, making them well-qualified to analyze delegation processes Fig.3.

For a clear understanding, it is crucial to clarify the frequency of task delegation. In our survey, participants indicated that 13.2% always delegate tasks to their subordinates,

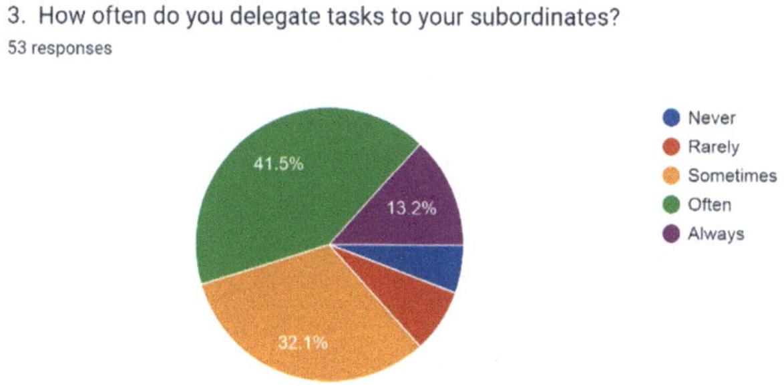

Fig. 3. Frequency of Task Delegation

41.5% often do, 32.1% sometimes, 7.5% rarely, and 5.7% never delegate tasks. It is particularly concerning when someone in a managerial position never delegates tasks to others. It is impossible to hold a significant position and do everything alone. This is, of course, not recommended, as subordinates seek opportunities for growth, and every task needs to be completed within a logical timeframe. For optimal results, it is crucial to delegate tasks effectively Fig 4.

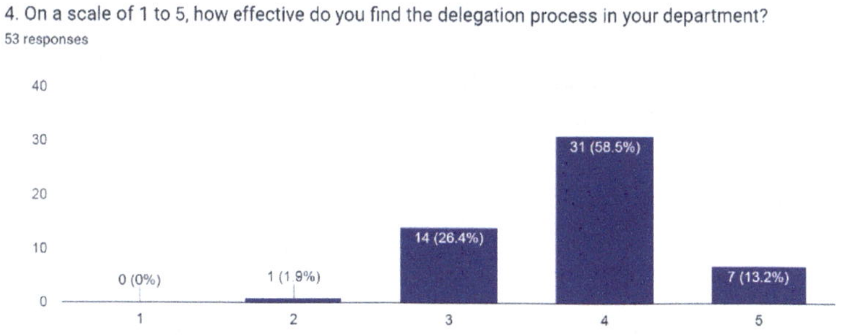

Fig. 4. Effectiveness of the delegation process

As we can see from the figure, 7 individuals (13.2%) believe that the delegation process is very effective, while 31 individuals (58.5%) consider it effective. Additionally, there are 14 individuals (26.4%) who hold intermediate views, and only 1 person believes that the process is not very effective Fig 5.

Most people, 41.5%, believe that the delegation process has a moderate impact on productivity, while 39.6% think it has a significant impact. Additionally, 15.1% believe it has a great impact, and only 3.8% think it has a slight impact. Notably, no respondents answered that delegation has no impact at all, which is an important aspect to consider Fig 6.

It is notable that delegation as a strategy during crisis situations is considered extremely effective by 11.3% of respondents, very effective by 34%, and moderately effective by 45.3%. 7.5% think it is slightly effective, and just 1.9% believe it is not effective at all Fig 7.

Among delegation methods, 'Define Roles,' 'Monitor Progress,' and 'Trust the Team' received the most responses, with over 50% of participants indicating these methods as

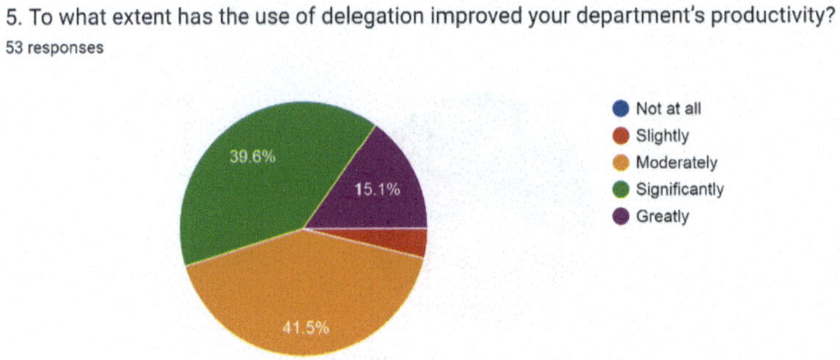

Fig. 5. Impact of Delegation on Departmental Productivity

Fig. 6. Effectiveness of Delegation as a Strategy in Crisis Situations

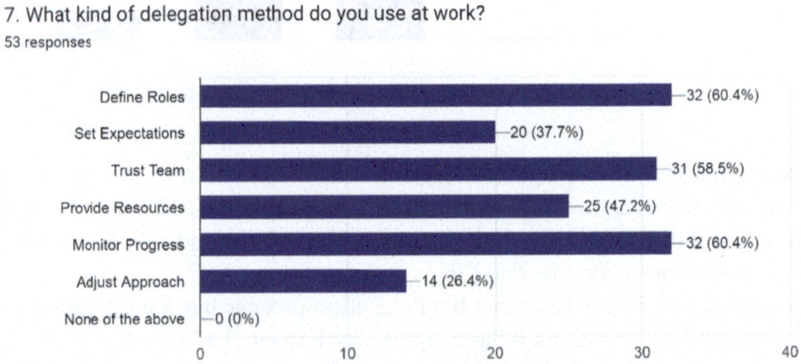

Fig. 7. Types of Delegation Methods Used at Work

the most useful at work. Other notable methods include ‘Provide Resources’ (47.2%), ‘Set Expectations’ (37.7%), and ’Adjust Approach’ (26.4%).

As we can see from Fig. 8, most of the interviewees - 47.2% - indicated that they allow moderate autonomy to their subordinates. Additionally, 32.1% grant high autonomy with minimal supervision, while 17% provide limited autonomy with regular check-ins.

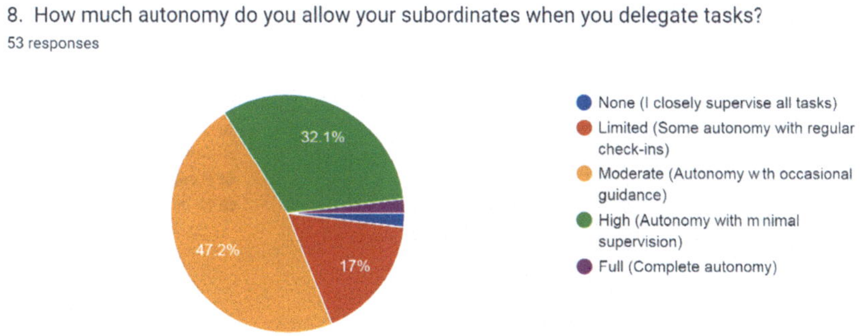

Fig. 8. Autonomy in Task Delegation

Only 1.9% offer full autonomy, and also 1.9% of the respondents reported allowing no autonomy at all Fig 9.

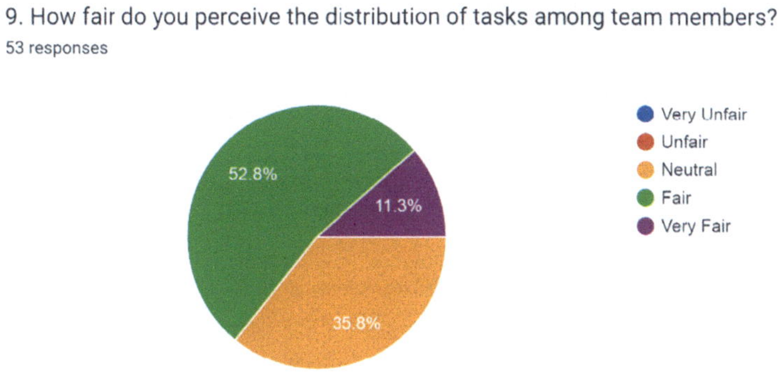

Fig. 9. Perceived Fairness of Task Distribution Among Team Members

Most of the interviewees, 52.8%, declared that they perceive the distribution of tasks as fair. Additionally, 11.3% stated that it is very fair, while 35.8% of interviewees held a neutral position Fig 10.

30.2% of respondents reported that they seek feedback from their team often. This indicates a proactive approach to improving the delegation process. 28.3% of respondents stated they seek feedback sometimes. 26.4% indicated that they seek feedback regularly. 15.1% of respondents reported that they seek feedback rarely. This indicates a potential gap in communication and may highlight a need for improvement in engaging with team members regarding the delegation process. Notably, no respondents selected "never," which is a positive sign, indicating that all participants recognize the importance of feedback, even if the frequency varies.

As we can see from Fig. 11, 49.1% of respondents agree that additional training on digital tools would enhance their ability to delegate tasks effectively, while 18.9% strongly agree with this statement. Additionally, 32.1% remain neutral on the issue Fig 12

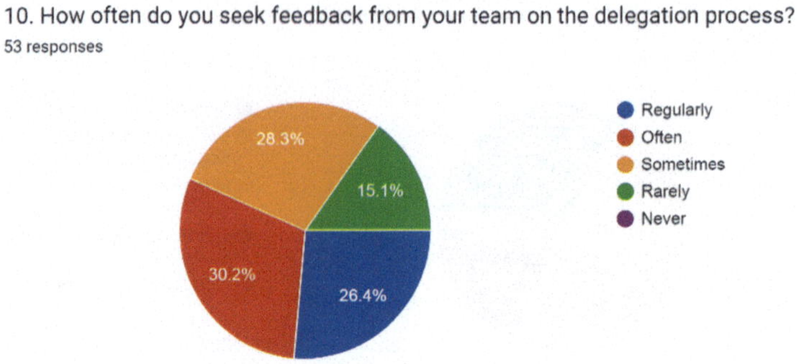

Fig. 10. Frequency of Feedback on the Delegation Process

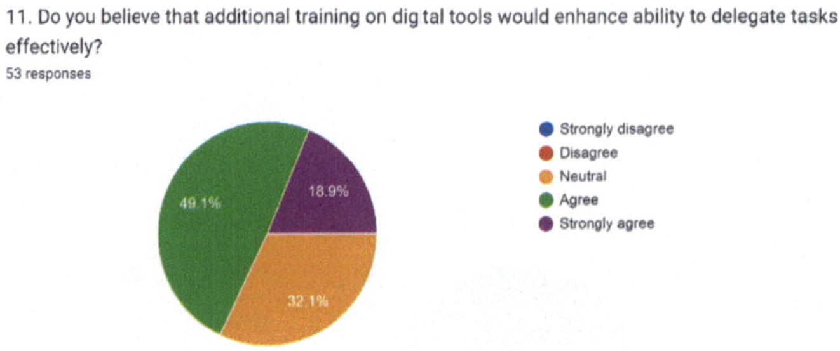

Fig. 11. Impact of Additional Training on Digital Tools for Task Delegation

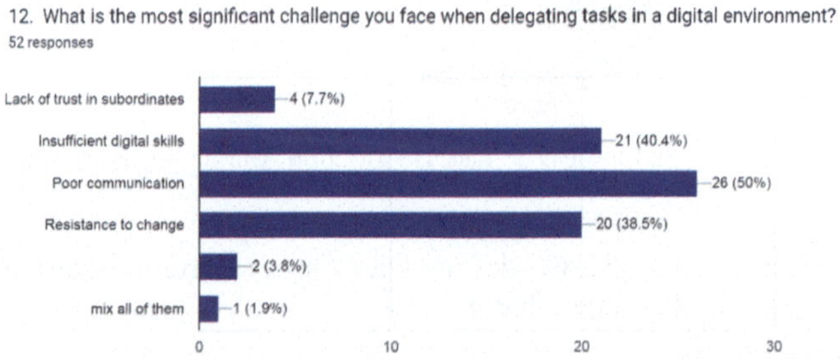

Fig. 12. Major Challenges in Task Delegation in a Digital Environment

The most significant challenge is poor communication, which accounts for 50%. Another important issue is insufficient digital skills, at 40.4%. The next challenges are resistance to change and a lack of trust in subordinates. Additionally, some respondents mentioned a mix of all these challenges Fig 13.

Among the respondents, 45.3% indicated that effective delegation has a moderate impact on work-life balance. Meanwhile, 34% reported that it has a significant impact, 13.2% stated it has a slight impact, 5.7% noted that it has a great impact, and 1.9% said it has no impact at all Fig 14.

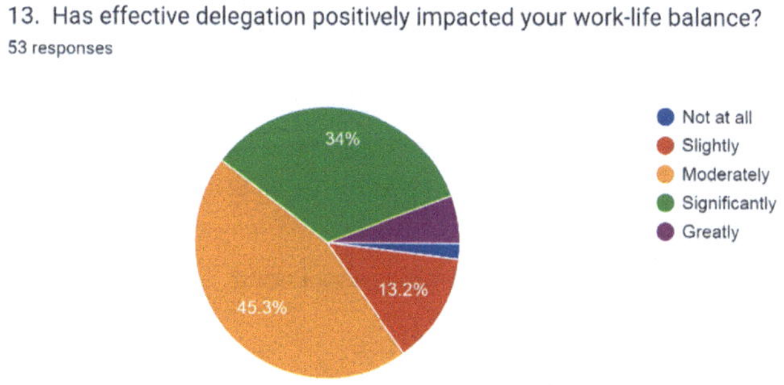

Fig. 13. Effective Delegation Impact on Work-Life Balance

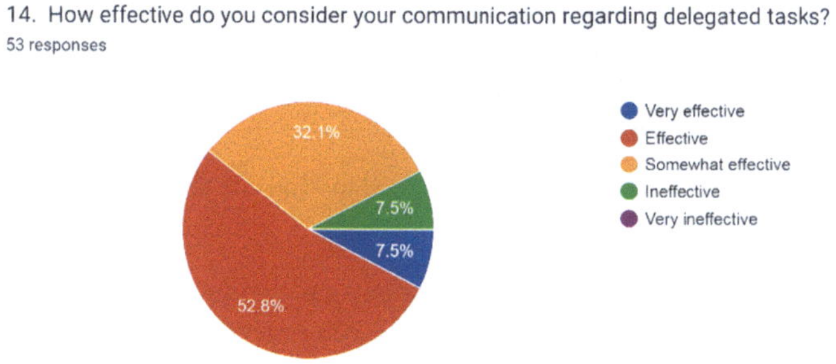

Fig. 14. Effectiveness of Communication Regarding Delegated Tasks

Most of the respondents believe that communication regarding delegated tasks is effective (52.8%). Meanwhile, 32.1% think it is somewhat effective, 7.5% believe it is ineffective, and another 7.5% said that it is very effective Fig 15.

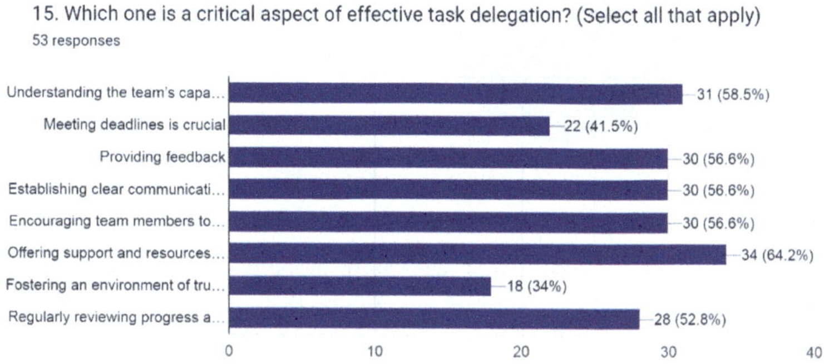

Fig. 15. Critical Aspects of Effective Task Delegation

The most critical aspects of effective task delegation include offering support and resources when needed, which 64.2% of respondents believe is important. Additionally, 58.5% think that understanding the team's capabilities and allocating tasks accordingly is crucial, while 56.6% emphasize the importance of providing feedback and establishing clear communication about expectations. Furthermore, 56.6% also agree that encouraging team members to take ownership of their tasks is vital. Among the respondents, 52.8% identify regularly reviewing progress and adjusting as necessary as a critical aspect, while 41.5% believe that meeting deadlines is essential. Only 34% think that fostering an environment of trust and accountability is critical.

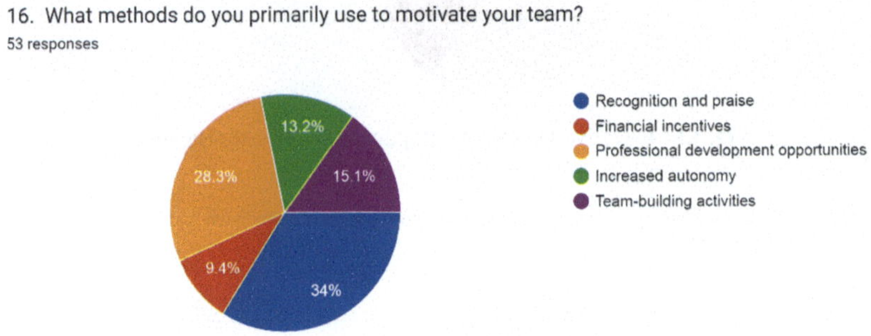

Fig. 16. Primary Methods Used to Motivate the Team

As we can see from Fig. 16, 34% of respondents use recognition and praise to motivate their teams, while 28.3% utilize professional development opportunities. Additionally, 15.1% implement team-building activities, and 9.4% offer financial incentives Fig 17.

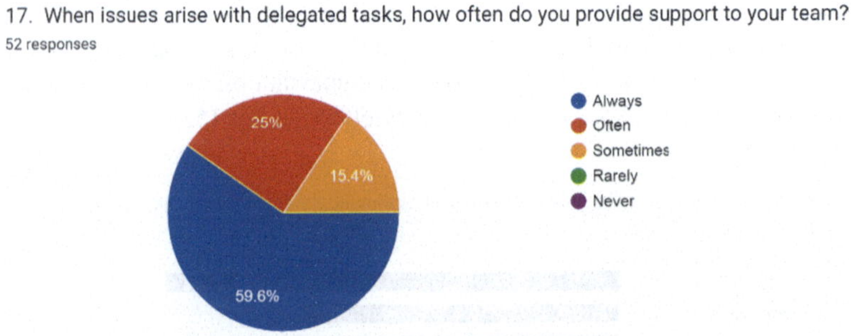

Fig. 17. Frequency of Support Provided for Delegated Task Issues

One question addressed issues that arise with delegated tasks. Most respondents, 59.6%, always provide support to their teams, while 25% often provide support. Additionally, 15.4% indicated that they only sometimes provide support when issues arise with delegated tasks Fig 18.

The question regarding which aspect of the delegation process is the most difficult revealed a difference of opinion. 25% percent of respondents believe that selecting the right person for the task is the most challenging, while 21.2% think that providing necessary resources and authority is difficult, along with defining clear objectives and expectations. Additionally, 15.4% consider monitoring progress and providing feedback to be the most challenging aspect. 9.6% feel that establishing clear communication

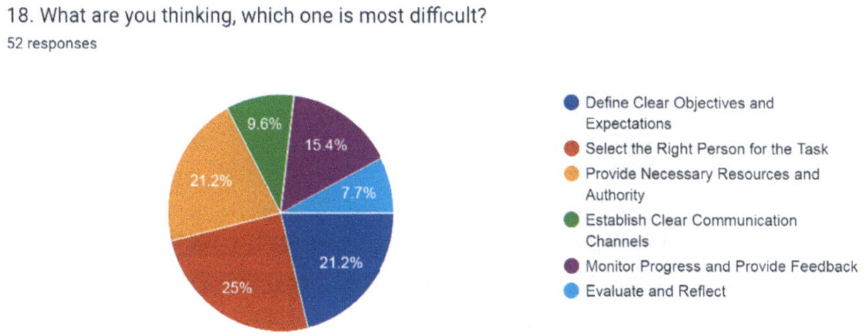

Fig. 18. Perceived Most Difficult Aspects of Task Delegation

channels is the most difficult issue, while 7.7% believe that evaluating and reflecting is the most challenging Fig 19

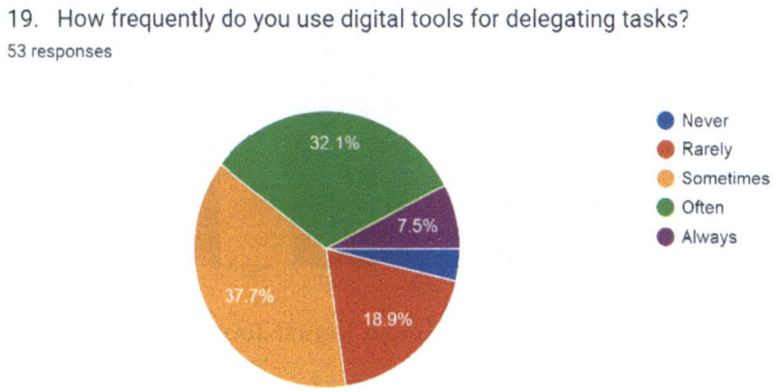

Fig. 19. Frequency of Digital Tool Usage for Task Delegation

Regarding the frequency of using digital tools for task delegation, 37.7% of respondents indicated that they sometimes use digital tools, while 32.1% said they often use them. Additionally, 18.9% reported using digital tools rarely, and 7.5% stated that they always use them. Only a small number of respondents, 3.8%, indicated that they never use digital tools for this purpose Fig 20

The most common digital tool for task delegation is Zoom, as 54.7% of respondents indicating. The next most utilized tools are Microsoft Teams and Jira. Other tools mentioned include Trello, Asana, and Slack. Notably, 22.6% of respondents declared that they do not use any of the tools listed above (Fig. 21).

The satisfaction level is not solely defined by the numbers; there are neutral positions as well as a positive feedback Fig 22

The most important benefit of using digital tools, according to 58.5% of respondents, is real-time progress tracking. The next most significant benefit, noted by 50.9% of interviewers, is easier feedback and communication. Other benefits include flexibility in managing remote teams, clear task assignment, increased accountability, and improved team collaboration (Fig. 23).

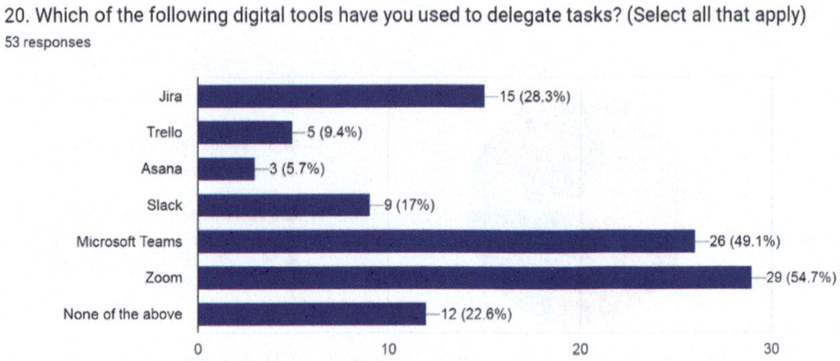

Fig. 20. Task Delegation Digital Tools

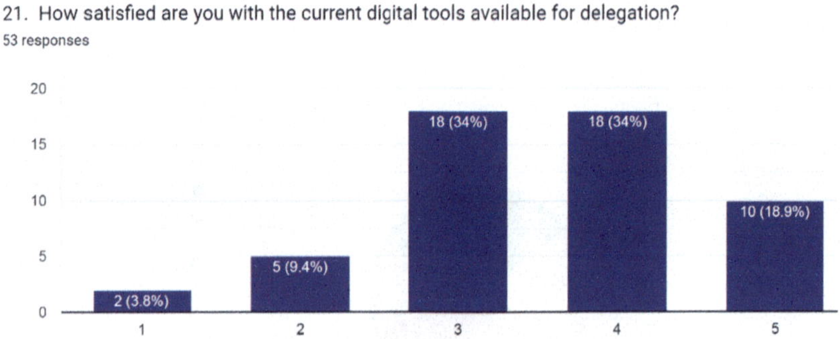

Fig. 21. Satisfaction with Current Digital Tools for Delegation

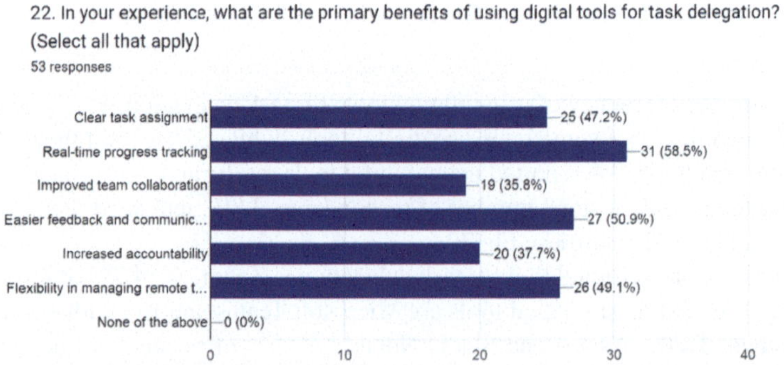

Fig. 22. Primary Benefits of Using Digital Tools for Task Delegation

Digital technologies have the ability to impact task progress tracking. According to 45.3% of respondents, these technologies somewhat improve tracking, while 35.8% believe they greatly enhance it. Conversely, 15.1% indicated that there is no impact on tracking, and unfortunately, 3.8% feel that digital technologies somewhat hinder tracking (Fig. 24).

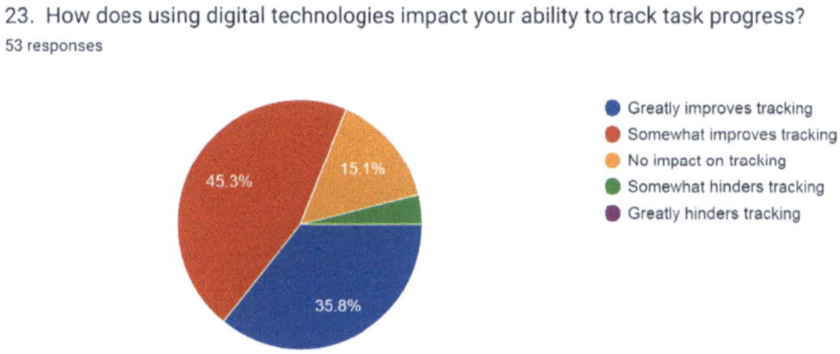

Fig. 23. Impact of Digital Technologies on Tracking Task Progress

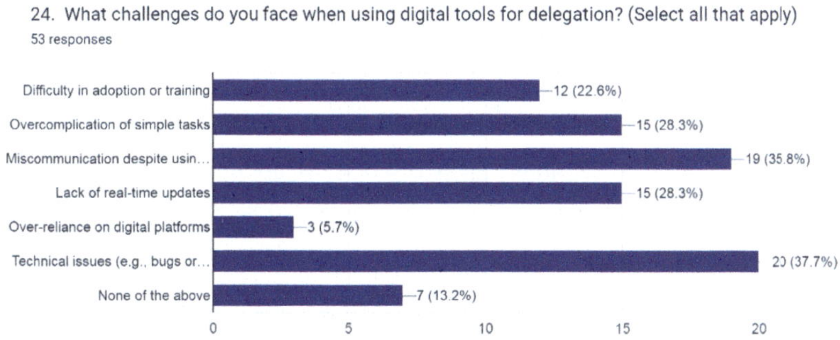

Fig. 24. Using Digital Tools for Delegation Challenges

Regarding the challenges faced, the most common response is technical issues, cited by 37.7% of respondents. Miscommunication, despite using tools, is a concern for 35.8% of respondents. Additionally, overcomplication of simple tasks and lack of real-time updates were also popular answers (Fig 25).

Fig. 25. Digital task management platforms valuable aspect

The aspect of task assignment and delegation is the most valued feature of digital task management platforms, with 52.8% of respondents highlighting its importance. Progress tracking and updates are also highly regarded, with 50.9% of respondents considering them very valuable.

5 Conclusions and Recommendations

The survey findings indicate that delegation practices have shifted from informal, face-to-face interactions to a structured, tech-driven approach, enhancing efficiency and accountability.

Organizations should provide training to improve team members' familiarity with digital tools. Tailoring sessions to individual comfort levels will ensure all employees can use these platforms effectively.

To mitigate miscommunication, emphasize clear and concise instructions in task assignments. Visual aids and checklists can help clarify expectations and reduce confusion.

Weekly check-ins can facilitate open discussions about the delegation process, helping identify areas for improvement and encouraging team members to voice concerns.

Organizations should promote open communication and collaboration. Encouraging team members to share ideas and feedback can enhance delegation practices and overall performance.

As technology evolves, organizations should consider automation and data-driven approaches to delegation. Integrating AI and machine learning can improve task management and provide valuable insights.

Despite the efficiencies of digital tools, regular personal check-ins are essential to ensure team members feel supported and engaged. These interactions reinforce relationships and clarify expectations.

In conclusion, embracing digital transformation and fostering a supportive culture are crucial for optimizing delegation practices in today's work environment. By addressing identified challenges and implementing these strategies, organizations can enhance efficiency, accountability, and overall team performance.

References

Mathebula, B., Barnard, B.: The factors of delegation success: accountability, compliance and work quality. **8**(1) (2020) https://www.researchgate.net/publication/339747499_The_factors_of_delegation_success_accountability_compliance_and_work_quality

Garro, E.M.: Delegate or Perish: Why Successful Leaders Trust Their Teams in the Digital Era. (2023) https://www.linkedin.com/pulse/delegate-perish-why-successful-leaders-trust-teams-era-mu%C3%B1oz-garro/

Entrepreneurial Mindset. Scaling in the Digital Era: The Power of Effective Delegation (2023). https://prashantchaudhari.com/2023/09/scaling-in-the-digital-era-the-power-of-effective-delegation/

Indeed Editorial Team.. 7 Effective Delegation Steps. (2024) https://www.indeed.com/career-advice/career-development/delegation-steps

Genevieve Conti. How to delegate tasks effectively *(and why it's important)* (2024) https://www.meistertask.com/blog/delegate-tasks-effectively
Management Best Practices (n.d.). *Leading in the Digital Age*: Delegation. https://www.pridestaff.com/blog/leading-in-the-digital-age-delegation/
Outsourcing or delegating tasks: delegating for growth: unlocking your business s potential (2024)
https://fastercapital.com/content/Outsourcing-or-delegating-tasks--Delegating-for-Growth--Unlocking-Your-Business-s-Potential.html#Streamlining-Delegation-in-the-Digital-Age
Delegating Strategically. https://f5webserv.wright.edu/~scott.williams/LeaderLetter/delegating.htm
Lee, R.: 7 Strategies for Leaders to Delegate Effectively. (2021) https://www.insightsforprofessionals.com/management/leadership/effective-delegation-strategies
Ugoani, J.: Effective delegation and its impact on employee performance (August 4, 2020). Int. J. Econ. Bus. Adm. **6**(3), 78–87 (2020). Available at SSRN: https://ssrn.com/abstract=3666808

Author Index

R. C. Geibel and S. Machavariani (Eds.): ISPC 2024, SPBE, pp. 599–600, 2025.
https://doi.org/10.1007/978-3-031-88052-0

The manufacturer's authorised representative in the EU is Springer Nature Customer Service Centre GmbH, Europaplatz 3, 69115 Heidelberg, Germany. If you have any concerns regarding our products, please contact ProductSafety@springernature.com

Printed and bound by CPI Group (UK) Ltd, Croydon, CR0 4YY
30/09/2026
02225568-0019